History of American Presidential Elections

HISTORY OF AMERICAN PRESIDENTIAL ELECTIONS 1789–2001

1928–1940
Volume VII

Arthur M. Schlesinger jr.

Editor

Albert Schweitzer Chair in the Humanities
City University of New York

Fred L. Israel

Associate Editor

Department of History
City College of New York

William P. Hansen

Managing Editor

Chelsea House Publishers

Philadelphia

CHELSEA HOUSE PUBLISHERS

The Chelsea House World Wide Web address is:
http://www.chelseahouse.com

Originally Published by Chelsea House Publishers in 1971.

Copyright © 2002 by Chelsea House Publishers,
a subsidiary of Haights Cross Communications.
All rights reserved.

First Printing

   1   3   5   7   9   8   6   4   2

Library of Congress Cataloging-in-Publication Data

History of American presidential elections, 1789–2001 / Arthur M.
Schlesinger, editor ; Fred L. Israel, associate editor ; managing
editor, William P. Hanson.
    p. cm.
  Includes bibliographical references and index.
  ISBN 0-7910-5713-5 (alk. paper)
  1. Presidents--United States--Election--History. 2.
Presidents--United States--Election--History--Sources. 3. United
States--Politics and government. 4. United States--Politics and
government--Sources. I. Schlesinger, Arthur Meier, 1917– . II.
Israel, Fred L. III. Hansen, William P.
  E183 .H58 2001
  324.973--dc21
                        2001047543

CONTENTS

Volume VII
1928–1940

Election of

1928

LAWRENCE H. FUCHS is Professor of American Civilization and Politics at Brandeis University and Founder of the American Studies Department there. He is the author of *The American Kaleidoscope: Race, Ethnicity and the Civic Culture*; *The Political Behavior of American Jews*; *Hawaii Pono: A Social History*; *Hawaii Pono: An Ethnic and Political History*; *John F. Kennedy and American Catholicism*; *Those Peculiar Americans: The Peace Corps and American National Character*; *American Ethnic Politics*; *Beyond Patriarchy: Jewish Fathers and Families*; and *When to Count by Race: Affirmative Action, Quotas and Equal Opportunity*.

Election of
1928

Lawrence H. Fuchs

Republican success in presidential elections since the Civil War had been virtually complete except for the two Cleveland victories, the plurality win of Woodrow Wilson in 1912, and his reelection in 1916. But by 1928, Cleveland and Wilson were no longer national heroes. For all his integrity and high ideals, Cleveland's name still was associated with economic depression. Wilson, despite his high-mindedness and progressive legislation, was remembered mainly as the President who led the United States into war and fruitless European entanglements.

Hard on the heels of disillusionment with the war, there followed that remarkable decade known as the twenties. It was a time of surface tranquility, and the Republicans seemed to symbolize the prevalent mood. Americans liked the 1924 slogan, "Keep Cool with Coolidge." The Republicans, having ostensibly defeated the plantocracy in the Civil War and, more significantly for the peace of mind of Main Street America, having buried the problems of racism by abandoning the cause of racial justice in 1876, in the 1920s also could claim chief responsibility for stemming the flood of immigration from southern and eastern Europe. For allegedly unruly, dirty, and anarchistic Jews and Italians had inundated the nation in unprecedented numbers. Unity was a precondition of tranquility, even if it was a false unity that served only to hide the divisiveness beneath the surface. Four years later, Herbert Hoover, brilliant engineer, humanitarian, industrial statesman, and energetic Secretary of Commerce, became the GOP's new candidate of prosperity and happiness.

Never more than a loose alliance of diverse forces, for seventy years after Appomattox the Democratic Party had been held in virtual receivership by two social groupings often seen as fundamentally threatening to American unity: the plantocracy of the South and the Irish-Catholics of the North. It seemed unlikely that such a party could gain much support.

To a considerable extent, during the twenties tranquility or happiness was measured in terms of material prosperity. Americans — a rootless, mobile, anti-traditional people — had long measured status by the consumption and display of material goods. Except for distress among groups of farmers, and unemployment among blacks, the new ethnics, and poor white mountain people, the ever-expanding American middle-class was prosperous. Happiness consisted of radios, washing machines, and automobiles.

Prosperity was indeed real. Between 1922 and 1927, the purchasing power of wages increased more than 10 percent. Rayon, refrigerators, telephones, cosmetics; and electrical appliances of all kinds were being cleared in large quantities from the shelves of Main Street's bustling stores. For every hundred dollars worth of business done in 1919, the five-and-ten-cent chain stores were doing $260 eight years later. More important, the grocery chains grossed $387 compared with $100 the year before Harding's election. In 1919, there were fewer than seven million passenger cars in the United States; by the time of Hoover's candidacy, there were more than twenty-three million. Coolidge prosperity was a fact to the people of Muncie, Indiana, a middle-sized city studied by a team of sociologists, who, interviewing 123 working class families, found that sixty of them had cars. Yet there were strange contradictions in Muncie's prosperity. Twenty-one of the twenty-six car owners who lived in shabby-looking houses actually had no bath tubs. Cars, garages, filling stations, restaurants, and tourist homes — not bath tubs — were what highly status-conscious, mobile Americans wanted.

Americans wanted to be entertained, and they wanted to show off. They did not want to be bothered with intellectual or moral issues. Annual radio sales between 1922 and 1928 increased more than 1000 percent from $60 million to $650 million. By the time of Hoover's nomination, it was possible for every third home in the nation to tune in the blare of the new jazz or the old barber shop quartet. Wherever electricity was, even in tenement houses, a flick of the dial could bring the Happiness Boys, Rudy Vallee, the Yale–Harvard football game, or a political convention itself. Motion pictures captivated Americans even more than radio. Clara Bow, Rudolph Valentino, Gloria Swanson, Douglas Fairbanks, Mary Pickford, and Charlie Chaplin became household names. In Muncie, everyone, rich and poor, men, women, and children, went to the movies an average of more than once a week.

Consumption was one way to show happiness. Ostentation was another. Party games, clubs, new kinds of associations and organizations, and travel at home and abroad expanded at a furious pace. In the year of Hoover's election, according to the Department of Commerce, over 430,000 people left the United States by ship for foreign ports and over three million cars crossed into Canada for at least one day. The service clubs boomed. Rotary, founded in 1905, had more than 150,000 members by 1928. The less prestigious Kiwanis Clubs rose from 250 in 1920 to eighteen hundred in 1929, and the Lions Clubs, formed as late as 1917, boasted more than twelve hundred clubs by the end of the decade. Boosterism, comradeship, noise-making, and keeping up with the latest gossip pervaded their weekly luncheons. But these were service clubs, after all, and this was America, where, if the business of the country was business, it still had to be justified by some higher purpose. For middle-class America could never quite forget that the United States was to be a new Zion, a city on a hill, whose air and people were more pure than those in foreign parts. It was not enough to sing songs, tell jokes, or even make money. Business especially had to be justified in terms of some noble goal. It had to have a redemptive and regenerative influence on human behavior. While showing off, the spokesmen for the service clubs proclaimed that the real justification for their organizations lay in the perfection of Christian ideals.

When the National Association of Credit Men held their annual convention in New York, they provided for the three thousand delegates a special devotional service at the Cathedral of St. John the Divine, where five prayer sessions were conducted by Protestant clergymen, a Roman Catholic priest, and a rabbi. The Credit Men listened to a sermon by Dr. S. Parkes Cadman on "Religion in Business." The Associated Advertising Clubs, meeting in Philadelphia, discussed "Spiritual Principles in Advertising" and "Advertising the Kingdom Through Press-Radio Service." Never mind that cabaret entertainment was provided for the delegates from 11:30 p.m. to 2:00 a.m. What really mattered was the earnestness with which American business believed it was a handmaiden of Christianity. Signal proof came in the popularity of a book by Bruce Barton, *The Man Nobody Knows*, which for two successive years (1925–26) was the best-selling nonfiction book in the United States. Barton's message was that Christianity bore a close resemblance to business. Jesus, he maintained, was not only "the most popular dinner guest in Jerusalem" and "an outdoor man" but a great executive who "picked up twelve men from the bottom rank of business and forged them into an organization that conquered the world." Jesus's parables were such magnificent advertisements that Barton confidently asserted that He, if alive in the 1920s, would be a national advertising genius.

Within the United States, a nation conceived by dissenting Protestants and forged in revolution against the banalities and corruptions of Europe, even advertising had to be pure. The Republican defense of business was ideologically insufficient without broader moral rationalizations; even the defense of prosperity was not enough. The very purity of American civilization was at stake in the election. For below the surface tranquility, the social habits of Americans were changing at a faster rate than ever before. Prosperity, born of the virtues of hard work, thrift, daring, and organizational acumen, had brought forth a plethora of goods and services that only the most rigorously self-denying Puritans could avoid.

Americans were caught in a double bind. Success at business meant more than just success at selling. Someone had to buy. But enjoyment for its own sake, if not sinful, was downright uncomfortable. Who could be a Puritan in Babylon except perhaps Calvin Coolidge? Surface insouciance could not hide entirely the deep tensions that always come with rapid change in individuals or societies. Americans felt that the foundations of an earlier innocence were being threatened.

The indices of real social change are not hard to find. The revolution in manners and morals so volubly discussed in the 1960s really began in the 1920s. Skirts went up, cigarettes came out, hip flasks went in, music and dance became sensuous, and the younger generation especially was in revolt against traditional standards of morality. A key to the revolution was the growing independence of American women. Their winning the vote in 1920 was certainly a sign of the times, but far more significant for understanding fundamental changes in American mores were the lifted hemlines. The president of the University of Florida was outraged and prophesied, "The lowcut gowns, the rolled hose and short skirts are born of the Devil and his angels, and are carrying the present future generations to chaos and destruction." But neither complaint nor prophesy could stop the trend. Only the sobering effect of massive economic depression would do that. After 1924, the hemline went up steadily until by 1927 the skirt had reached the knee, where it remained until late in 1929. With the short skirt and the boyishly slender figure the aim of young American women, petticoats almost vanished and the sales of corsets and brassieres fell sharply. Short hair, rouge, and lipstick went with short and skimpy clothes. In the year that Herbert Hoover took office, more than a pound of face powder and eight rouge compacts were sold for every adult woman in the United States; twenty-five hundred brands of perfume and fifteen hundred face creams were on the market. As for lipsticks, if all that sold in the United States that year were placed end-to-end, it was estimated that they would reach from New York to Reno, which, as Frederick Lewis Allen pointed out, "would seem an altogether logical destination." The flapper communicated youthful sophistication. She was willing to take her chances and brazenly advertised it.

One symbol of emancipation was cigarette smoking. During the Coolidge years cigarette smoking became commonplace among women of all ages. To forbid women cigarettes was a sign of oppression, and smoking became a declaration of freedom. In the ten years between 1918 and 1928, the total United States production of cigarettes more than doubled, largely because the barrier between the sexes in this, as in other matters, had been broken. Drinking was probably the other most important barrier to fall. Mixed parties, speakeasies, cocktail parties, and hotel room parties became commonplace for the middle classes. Women, who a few years before would have been scandalized at even the thought of going "blotto," downed cocktails as recklessly as men did.

If confession and sex magazines, movies, and plays stimulated fantasy, the auto-mobile helped to bring reality into the fantasy life of many young women. Enormous freedom was made possible by the increased use of closed automobiles. In 1919, a little more than 10 percent of the cars produced in the United States were closed; by 1927, the percentage had reached over 80 percent. Chaperons had long been frowned on in the United States, but young men and women of means could now move about in a protected living room on wheels far from the prying eyes or inquiries of fathers or younger siblings. The sexual revolution so prominent among younger women undoubtedly affected their mothers, too, as Kinsey was to show later. Evidence of a breakdown in family relations came with a sharp increase in the divorce rate, which doubled from 8.8 divorces per hundred marriages in 1910 to 18.5 divorces in the year of Hoover's election — almost one divorce for every six marriages.

Many Americans adopted the same schizophrenic attitude toward liquor as they held toward sex. America may have come to resemble Babylon more and more, but it preached purity as stridently as ever. The guardians of morality may have had difficulty with their wives and children on various counts, but they controlled the vote. The anomalous behavior of Americans with respect to Calvin Coolidge and liquor provided ample proof. Could anyone have been more conventional than Coolidge? Here was the embodiment of all the old American virtues. Yet the flapper could bob her hair and still vote for Coolidge. As for beer and rum, Americans enjoyed the luxury of being wet in their speakeasies and homes, while sticking with prohibition. What Hoover was to call an experiment "noble in purpose" represented the single most striking act of hypocrisy of the decade. Americans never drank so much; yet there was not a single major national political figure of old ethnic stock to go on record as clearly opposing prohibition.

This was America in 1928: buying and selling in a frenzy; engaged in a revolution in manners and morals; saturated with piety and moralism; and deeply anxious to regain a lost Eden — an Eden that, in fact, never existed.

What was that Eden, and who were its destroyers? The nation had historic answers to those questions, which even when not articulated in editorials, essays, serious nonfiction books, and patriotic speeches found expression in poetry and prose.

Nearly all the literature about the American Eden glorified the natural, pastoral character of American geography and the self-reliant, achieving character of American men and women. It was these characteristics that distinguished the United States from Europe. Here man lived closer to the alleged intrinsically beneficent and bountiful qualities of nature; and here, too, he lived in freedom to exercise choice and to achieve according to his ability and industry. Twentieth-century historians and essayists have written about "the pastoral ideal," "rural values," "the agrarian virtues," and of "the myth of the garden." From the earliest days of the Republic, nearly all prominent American writers have discussed the ideal of "self-sufficiency" or "independence" or "individual freedom." And many writers have assumed that these virtues — the agrarian ideal and independence — have been inextricably linked and mutually reinforcing. The historic enemies of the American dream have been clearly seen: large cities, factories, authoritarian rulers (whether kings or priests), and foreigners (particularly Catholics and Jews).

A republican nation, established on anti-Catholic predilections, found a vast, sparsely populated continent to explore and conquer, making it possible for many to translate the dream of self-reliant independent farmers into a reality. Long after commerce had become the dominant activity, and small towns the locale of most Americans, the agrarian myth and the self-reliant ideal prevailed. Even as the locomotive-linked cities grew and factories burgeoned, the agrarian myth was enlarged rather than diminished.

Of all the enemies of America's Eden, none had been attacked so bitterly or so persistently as the Catholic Church. To hundreds of thousands and even millions of Americans, the terms *subservience* and *corruption* were practically synonymous with the Church of Rome. Popular outbursts against Catholics in the United States frequently achieved massive proportions. Following the large-scale immigration of Irish-Catholics in the 1830s and 1840s, native American political parties were formed in New Orleans, Cincinnati, Charleston, Boston, and in every county of New York and New Jersey. The 1850s saw the rise of the Know Nothing Party, the only xenophobic nativist party in American history to win substantial power in national and state politics. The success of the Know Nothings was phenomenal. For almost twenty years, many American Protestants of the 1850s had been trained to believe that Roman Catholicism constituted a threat to vital American freedoms. It was hardly surprising that in 1854 the new party carried Massachusetts and Delaware, and, in alliance with the Whigs, captured Pennsylvania. In Massachusetts, the governor and all state officers were Know Nothings. In the fall congressional elections, about seventy-five members of the party were sent to Washington pledged to carry on the fight against popery. In the next year, Rhode Island, New Hampshire, and Connecticut were won by nativists, and in 1856 seven governors, eight senators, and 104 national representatives were elected after campaigning on anti-Catholic platforms; talk of a Know Nothing President became commonplace.

The national division over slavery and Reconstruction policies obscured the great tension between nativists and Catholics until the 1880s, when a widespread fear developed that Catholics might gain control over education. Once again, there arose the fear that the American Eden was being undermined from within by subtle, conspiratorial forces. A large number of secret, anti-Catholic societies sprang up throughout the country, the most important of which, the American Protective Association, was formed in 1887 in Clinton, Iowa, Herbert Hoover's home state. In 1893, the APA previously concentrated in the Middle West, surged eastward and westward, growing rapidly from a membership of approximately seventy thousand to perhaps half a million. With its elaborate rituals and paraphernalia, its uniforms, insignias, and its promise to save American civilization, it appealed to the American fear of cities, foreigners, and priests. Its leaders apparently believed that Americanism was locked in a life-and-death struggle with the Roman Catholic Church.

Following the frustrations of the First World War, nativism surged forth again. This time, fear of the ideology of the Catholic Church was accompanied by revived theories of racial superiority. Social Darwinism — belief in the moral superiority of technologically and organizationally complex societies — justified the growing conviction that the so-called Nordic race, having demonstrated its capacity for self-government, was best suited to govern others. Anxiety about the pollution of the race through contact with hordes of Poles, Italians, Irish, Jews, and Orientals, who were swarming into the United States in unprecedented numbers, was interlocked with anxiety about the loss of American Eden.

The widespread disillusionment and feeling of betrayal that followed the First World War was joined in the 1920s by the fear of internal changes in manners and morals. It was not enough to abandon the League of Nations. Old-stock Americans wanted to put distance between themselves and the newcomers already here. At least as important, they wanted to restrict the numbers and ethnic composition of future immigrants.

How quickly utopian idealism was replaced by xenophobia and racism! The familiar American pattern was reflected in Henry Ford's *Dearborn Independent*, which persisted throughout 1919 in advocating a League of Nations to make the world safe for democracy. When the promise of Wilson's idealism collapsed, the American mission to save the world turned inward. By 1920, Ford's newspaper reflected the deep sense of failure and postwar bitterness that swept America.

When bitterness followed disillusionment, the hunt for scapegoats began. "Americanism still has a mission to the world," maintained the *Independent*, but "we shall have to save ourselves before we can hope to save anyone else." How could America save itself? The answer: Purify the country. Restore the old virtues. Break up the cities. Keep out the foreigners, and, particularly, put down the Jews.

While Ford concentrated on anti-Semitism, others saw foreigners generally or southern and eastern Europeans, especially Catholics, as the main target. Foremost among the many organizations advocating 100 percent Americanism was the Ku Klux Klan. Where the nineteenth-century Klan championed white supremacy, admitting white men of every type and background to its membership, the new Klan accepted only native-born Protestant whites, narrowing its interpretation of racial purity and Americanism. The Klan grew rapidly with the failure of utopian war aims, the spread of crime, and the revolution in manners and morals associated with city life. It prospered in rural and small-town America, where millennial Americanism was associated with fundamentalist Protestantism. It was politically powerful in Oregon and Indiana and throughout the West as well as in the South, reaching a membership of between three and four million at the very time that a white Anglo-Saxon Protestant Harding Administration scandalized the western world with its dishonesty.

Militant Protestantism once again meant virulent anti-Catholicism. In the 1920s anti-Catholic books and pamphlets flooded the country, and anti-popery became the dominant prejudice. In 1920, Alabama set up a convent-inspecting commission to protect Protestant maidens (presumably vulnerable to kidnapping or seduction) against the alleged sexual aggression of priests. Tom Watson of Georgia, who campaigned successfully for a seat in the United States Senate, claimed that President Wilson had become a tool of the Pope. The governor of Florida warned that the Pope planned to invade that state to transfer the Vatican there.

America was changing, but its promise of a new Zion had not been fulfilled. It was clear that the promise of a new Jerusalem had been betrayed, and millions blamed the influence of Catholics in the cities.

Catholics had gained enormously in political power in recent decades. The Catholic population in the United States had soared from a little more than eight million to twenty million between 1891 and 1928. The largest increase was in New York, New Jersey, Pennsylvania, and New England, where non-Catholics were long accustomed to having Catholic mayors and even Catholic governors.

Foremost among Catholic political leaders in the 1920s was Alfred E. Smith, governor of New York. Born in 1873, an altar boy before he was ten, and a regular communicant at seven o'clock mass, Smith took up a newsboy's stand at the age of eleven to help support his family. After his father died in 1886, he left school to work in a variety of jobs — as a three-dollar-a-week helper to a truckman, as an eight-dollar-a-week laborer in an oil factory, and then as a twelve-dollar-a-week laborer in the Fulton Fish Market — as thousands of other New York lads had done before. Like many Irish boys, Al took an interest in politics. From his vantage point in the Fourth Ward of New York's Lower East Side, politics provided the zest, fun, and panache of life. It was clearly the route to status and prestige as well as power. Hard work in the Fourth Ward was rewarded in 1903, when Smith was picked to run for the state assembly in Albany. The remarkable political career of one of America's outstanding state governors had been launched.

Eight years later, Al Smith was designated majority leader of the assembly. While fiercely loyal to Tammany, Smith established a reputation as a knowledgeable, hard-working, progressive legislator. He had helped to pass laws to regulate private bankers, to protect the purchasers of coal against false weight, and to ratify the federal income tax amendment. Shaken by the Triangle Factory Fire of 1911, which pointed up the ugly conditions in which men and women worked, Smith pushed a number of bills to give the government the power to protect helpless laborers. A bureau of fire prevention was established. Other legislation forbade smoking near unprotected gas jets in factories. In 1912, Smith helped to enact rules for the ventilation of factories, for the examination of the physical fitness of working children, and for limiting the employment of women after childbirth. Later there came bills to improve cleanliness and to supply washing facilities and lunchrooms in factories, laws to license bakeries and to register all factories, legislation to compel employers to supply female employees with rest periods and with seats with backs. Smith fought for the creation of a bureau of employment in the Department of Labor and the limitation of working hours and for a workmen's compensation law. The faithful Tammany regular had become a leader in the fight for decent working conditions.

It was at the New York State constitutional convention in 1915 that Smith first came to national attention. Amidst an array of eminent lawyers and public servants from both parties, Smith appeared unsurpassed in his knowledge of government and politics. Members of both parties were impressed repeatedly by his extraordinary ability to get to the heart of things, to state issues in precise language, and to produce clear and promising ideas for reform.

Elected sheriff of New York County in 1916 and 1917, Smith, made big money — about fifty thousand dollars a year — through the anachronistic fee system that still prevailed. More important, he built a personal organization through the skillful use of patronage. Fast becoming one of the most popular men in Tammany and clearly one of the most able, he was chosen president of the Board of Aldermen in 1917. Now the governorship beckoned. In 1918, Smith made the first of five campaigns for governor, winning by a narrow margin. Two years later he lost because of the prevailing mood of isolationism, xenophobia, and conservatism that elected Harding. But he returned in 1922 with an overwhelming victory, and, moving against the national strength of the Republican Party in 1924, he defeated Colonel Theodore Roosevelt, son of the former President, by a large majority.

Smith's administrations were formidable. He surrounded himself with dedicated, competent advisers regardless of sex or religion. He continued to have remarkable success in effecting social legislation and improved his reputation for administrative efficiency. He opposed a book censorship bill that had wide Catholic backing and rejected a bill to establish a loyalty oath for teachers. He even pardoned Tim Larken, a radical agitator who had been imprisoned under the state's criminal anarchy law, insisting that the surest way to prove error was to give it free rein to compete with truth. One of the truths that Smith began to believe was that even a Catholic boy from New York's Lower East Side could become, through hard work and intelligence, President of the United States.

Al Smith's career as governor represented a triumph for the sons of immigrants and the political forces they represented, but it was precisely those forces that threatened the apostles of American purity. For all his brilliance as governor in regulating utilities, opening up a park system, reorganizing state government, establishing an executive budget, cutting taxes and advancing social legislation, the brown-derbied, cigar-chewing, East Side Catholic's aspirations for the Presidency brought fear to millions of Americans. As on most issues, Smith's position on prohibition was clear-cut. As governor in 1920, and thereafter, he consistently favored the repeal of the national amendment that prohibited the sale of intoxicating beverages. Rum, the defenders of the American Eden perceived, still went with Romanism, at least where Al Smith was concerned.

It was inevitable that Smith should be thought of as a presidential candidate. Ever since the Civil War, any popular and reasonably successful Democratic governor of New York became a potential candidate, particularly if the Democratic Party was out of national power. Samuel Tilden and Grover Cleveland, both popular and effective governors of New York, were nominated for the Presidency. Tilden was counted out in two southern states because of a deal made between Republicans and southern Democrats to end Reconstruction in 1876. Cleveland defeated Blaine in 1884 by carrying New York State with a large enough plurality in New York City to outweigh Republican gains in the rural areas. At the turn of the century, the southern wing of the party made its alliance with the Populists of the Middle West in nominating William Jennings Bryan, the fundamentalist, free-silver advocate from Nebraska, who was three times defeated for the Presidency. In many ways, Bryan was the antithesis of Smith. His Populism, sustained by the pastoral ideal, scornful of cities, Catholicism, and science, now ran deep in the Democratic grain.

The forces that Bryan and Smith represented clashed head-on in the Democratic convention of 1924. There the most divisive issue was the Ku Klux Klan. In general, the supporters of Smith wanted to condemn the Klan explicitly. Rural southerners and westerners preferred to remain silent, as had the Republican Party in its recently concluded convention. Meeting on the sultry evening of June 29, 1924, in Madison Square Garden in New York City, the convention delegates divided down the middle. The final vote: 546.15 for the Klan and 542.85 against. William Jennings Bryan, supporting leading candidate William G. McAdoo of California, former Secretary of the Treasury and Woodrow Wilson's son-in-law, sided with the Klan, though McAdoo remained silent. The vote on the issue showed that Smith had no chance of winning the two-thirds necessary for the nomination, but he stayed in the race to help stop McAdoo. Roll-call followed roll-call; bitterness and anger increased. When Bryan spoke, the New York City spectators burst into relentless hissing and booing. Stirring up the galleries, the sixty-four-year-old fundamentalist challenged, "You do not represent the future of our country." But Bryan, who one year later in Dalton, Tennessee, would help prosecute a teacher who exposed his students to theories of evolution, was rapidly being left behind by vast social changes. Never again would the Democratic Party nominate a candidate who represented the forces which Bryan symbolized.

In 1924, Smith, as a candidate for governor, ran 1,000,000 votes ahead of the presidential ticket led by compromise candidate John W. Davis. For the next four years, he and his supporters carefully planned to capture the 1928 convention. The road to the nomination in Houston in 1928 — a southern city was picked as a concession to southern predilections — was not completely smooth, though the Smith forces had been carefully organized. For a while it appeared there might even be a contest again with McAdoo, who remained dry and became increasingly bitter. But McAdoo declared in December 1927 that he would not be a candidate. The reasons remain obscure. Perhaps he realized that no one could beat the Republicans at a time of great national prosperity. Other party leaders were concerned that Smith represented precisely those elements of big-city Catholicism in the East who had not yet completely assimilated the American way of life. Those who had visions of Tammany, cigars, saloons, and New York's polyglot and alien population when they thought of Smith rallied around Senator Thomas Walsh of Montana, a Catholic but a dry who had played a major role in exposing the corrupt oil deals of the Harding Administration. Walsh, although a Catholic, could easily be identified with the American pastoral image; but his candidacy never won strong, widespread enthusiasm. He lacked an organizational apparatus and strong support in the Northeast. Most important, there was a growing feeling everywhere in the party that the Democrats could not possibly win without making a powerful appeal to the newer ethnics in the cities. The Democrats knew they could not win without carrying New York State, and Smith certainly had the best chance of doing that. Like McAdoo before him, Walsh withdrew; he also pledged his support to Smith. Undoubtedly, Walsh's decision was hastened by a convention of Democratic spokesmen representing eight Pacific and Rocky Mountain States at Ogden, Utah, who endorsed Smith's candidacy on September 23.

The convention itself was almost somnolent. Its keynoter was a distinguished scholar, Claude G. Bowers, an editor of the New York *Evening World*. He emphasized that corruption in America resulted from the failure to enforce prohibition. He also stressed the farm issue, demanding that "the hand of privilege be taken out of the farmer's pocket and off the farmer's throat!" Joseph T. Robinson of Arkansas, Minority Leader of the Democrats in the United States Senate, was picked to be permanent chairman of the convention. He had gained the approval of Smith's supporters and of the governor himself following his January 19 rebuke of Senator Tom Heflin of Alabama for his prejudice against Smith and Catholics.

For the third time in eight years, Governor Smith's name was placed in nomination by Franklin D. Roosevelt of New York. Several others were placed in nomination, but none of them were considered serious threats by convention time. Harmony prevailed in the adoption of the platform and in the nomination of Smith, who won on the first ballot. Senator Robinson, a dry from the South, was the overwhelming choice for the vice-presidential nomination. The ticket was balanced. Smith, the voice of the new city ethnics, embraced Robinson, dry and Protestant, a southerner, and promised to carry the banner of Democracy high. As one writer put it, "The Democratic donkey with a wet head and wagging a dry tail left Houston." The convention plank on prohibition did not accord with Smith's views, and he made it plain at once that his own convictions would prevail in his campaign. In his letter of acceptance, he shocked the drys with a strong statement of intention to work for modification of the Volstead Act. The prohibition issue would prove to be one that really helped the Republicans. For all that Smith maintained prohibition was a farce, which bred corruption in public service and disrespect for the law, prohibition gave the nation an opportunity to have its virtue and drink it too. The vast majority of Baptists, Methodists, and most other Protestant groups were in favor of prohibition, at least in the breach. While hundreds of Democratic leaders and Independents who had been thoroughly dry for many years remained with Smith, the New York governor could not hold in line convinced drys in the South and middle border states who might even have voted for a different kind of Catholic. Taking the strong stand that he did, Smith had greater difficulty making inroads among farmers in the Middle West and Rocky Mountain states who were dissatisfied with Republican agricultural policies; but he was a confirmed wet and never hedged on the question.

To millions, Smith's stand on prohibition was tantamount to support for saloons and alcoholism. It also fit the standard 100-percent American view of Irish-Catholic propensities for drink. Drink enslaved, and so did the Pope. Smith's nomination aroused anti-Catholic crusaders from a period of relative quiet. The Klan, reaching its peak in 1923 and 1924, had lost strength over the next several years. Now, with Smith in the race, the usual pathological appeals were rushed into circulation within a week through an estimated ten million handbills, leaflets, and posters with familiar titles such as "Popery in the Public Schools," "Convent Life Unveiled," "Convent Horrors," and "Crimes of the Pope." The alleged crimes of the Pope and Catholicism were more than a mix of xenophobic claptrap and projections of pathological sexuality. Underlying the most hysterical attacks was the widespread and sincere conviction that Americanism itself was threatened. Hundreds of thousands of non-Catholics — increasingly aware that America was no longer a nation of independent, ascetic, hard-working, Protestant farmers and villagers — believed that Smith's election would end the dream of an American Eden forever.

Of course, Al Smith had been as thrifty and hard-working as most frontiersmen, but the New York governor represented other qualities in the new America that were frightening to old-stock Americans. The renowned Kansas editor, William Allen White, saw in Smith's candidacy a threat to "the whole Puritan civilization, which has built a sturdy, orderly nation." To thousands of fundamentalist and prohibitionist farmers and small-town merchants, Smith was a stranger to the American dream. What they imagined to be his world — gambling, prostitution, saloons, and foreign accents — filled them with dread. The *Christian Century*, a nondenominational journal, summed up Protestant fears in more pretentious language than that used by White: "They [Protestants] cannot look with unconcern upon the seating of the representative of an alien culture, a Medieval Latin mentality, of an undemocratic hierarchy, and of a foreign potentate in the great office of the President of the United States." The Klan's Imperial Wizard wrote in the *North American Review* that a Catholic in the White House was unthinkable because "America was Protestant from birth" and "must remain Protestant if the Nordic stock is to finish its destiny." But the Klan's leader denied charges of bigotry, maintaining that he was fighting for the American values of "freedom and achievement" against the "theocratic autocracy" of Rome, which was "at odds with Americanism."

Hatred of Tammany Hall strengthened the opposition to Smith. For millions of Americans, Tammany Hall symbolized the evil corruption of the big city machine. No matter how great a statesman Smith could become, he could not shake loose his Tammany origins and affiliations in their eyes. No matter how often Democratic orators pointed to corruption in Republican-run cities such as Philadelphia and Chicago, Tammany stood above all as the metaphor for government by gift, bribe, and spoils. Tammany was not just any machine. It was the machine of New York City, home of foreigners, socialists, anarchists, free thinkers, and those in the vanguard of the revolution in manners and morals. Four years earlier, McAdoo had warned his supporters at the convention in Madison Square Garden "against the perilous and treacherous hospitality of this town." New York was, to millions of Americans, the home of sin. It was where Catholicism, Tammany, and liquor coalesced in the person of Al Smith. Smith was an acknowledged drinker, ring-kisser (he had kissed the ring of Cardinal Bonzano, the Papal Legate, when the Cardinal was publicly received in New York during Smith's governorship), and a proud and loyal son of Tammany.

Many Protestant prelates joined the crusade against Smith. Among them was the Methodist Bishop of Buffalo, who was at that time president of the New York State Anti-Saloon League. He warned, "No governor can kiss the papal ring and get within gunshot of the White House." The enthusiastically pro-Smith New York *World* deplored the attacks of the Bishop who claimed, "I am 100 percent Anglo-Saxon.... We are keepers of the Constitution, of the flag, and of American citizenship.... We will never surrender our priceless American heritage to the hands of foreigners who trample on our flag." Leaders from almost every Protestant denomination bewildered Smith with comparable attacks. The New York governor was baffled and hurt. True, he was Catholic, but he believed in personal liberty and the separation of Church and State just as much as the next fellow. Why hold him accountable for Papal bulls and encyclicals that he had never even read? He had been going to mass, saying his rosaries, and making confession all his life, and that never prevented him from living up to his oath of office or from being a superb governor in New York. He well knew that Cardinal Gibbons, the greatest of American Catholic leaders, had insisted that, "In our country, separation [of Church and State] is a necessity." Eighteen thousand people had heard President Roosevelt give honors to Cardinal Gibbons in 1911 and listened to the Rough Rider proclaim that "Presidents who are Catholic as well as Presidents who are Protestants, and, if we live long enough, Presidents who are Jewish as well as Presidents who are gentiles" will be elected in the future. Who spoke for America? Theodore Roosevelt? Or the self-appointed guardians of Americanism from the Ku Klux Klan?

Although Smith was convinced that most of the attacks on him came from bigots and lunatics, he could not ignore the issue forever. He was keenly aware that millions of rural Democrats were frightened by his Catholic, wet, and Tammany affiliations. He could not renounce Tammany, the organization that had nourished his success. His position as a wet was unequivocal. But on the Catholic question, surely he could allay the fears of many Americans who believed that the Church threatened American freedom. He believed in the good sense of the American people and in his own powers to persuade a large portion of them that his religion in no way threatened their security.

Pressure began to mount for Smith to deal with the issue head on. Even the Unitarians, through their publication The *Christian Register* of Boston, and its editor, Dr. Albert C. Dieffenbach, insisted that Smith answer charges against the Church. Wrote Dieffenbach, "They [fair-minded Protestants] will want to know whether an

American Catholic presidential candidate endorses the claim of the Papacy to temporal power ... its attitudes toward American public schools and its rejection of the claims of millions of American Christians to the right of self-government in religion, as well as in politics."

The most important challenge to Smith was presented by the editor and publisher of the *Atlantic Monthly*, Ellery Sedgwick, who published an open letter from a prominent New York attorney, Charles Marshall, which questioned the capacity of any Catholic in the Presidency to maintain the ideals of American freedom. Sedgwick long believed that the religious issue should come into the open on a high plane. When a leaflet by Marshall, who had a considerable knowledge of Canon Law, was brought to him by a friend, Sedgwick invited the New Yorker to write a piece for the *Atlantic*. Marshall, an Episcopalian, seemed genuinely uncertain as to whether Catholic dogma and the Constitution could be reconciled. Franklin Roosevelt, who acted as an intermediary between Smith and Sedgwick, found the business distasteful and deplored the need for any reply. If the article were to be answered at all, he wanted it done by a Protestant. He saw no point in discussing the fifty-year-old dicta of a Pope and preferred to have Smith continue to take the question of the Catholic issue lightly. But Smith disagreed, deciding that he could not ignore Marshall's letter and the questions it posed.

With the help of Father Francis P. Duffy, the famous chaplain of the 165th Regiment of the First World War, and Judge Joseph M. Proskauer, a personal and legal adviser to the governor, a reply was cleared by Patrick Cardinal Hayes of New York. Smith hoped that the exchange, which took place a full year and a half before the election, would bury the issue. Every word was scrutinized by his confidants. He showed that Catholic authorities had been quoted out of context, citing Archbishop Ireland and Cardinal Gibbons in praise of the public schools and the separation of church and state. Then, he gave his personal reply:

> I recognize no power in the institutions of my church to interfere with the operations of the Constitution of the United States or the enforcement of the law of the land. I believe in absolute freedom of conscience for all men and in the equality of all churches, all sects, and all beliefs before the law as a matter of right and not as a matter of favor. I believe in the absolute separation of church and state and in the strict enforcement of the provisions of the Constitution that Congress shall make no law respecting an establishment of religion or prohibiting the exercise thereof.... I believe in the support of the public schools as one of the cornerstones of American liberty.

The reply could not have been more clear-cut, and newspaper reaction was overwhelmingly favorable, although Republican papers such as the *New York Herald Tribune* sometimes seemed grudging in their acknowledgement of Smith's Americanism. Despite the favorable initial reaction, Smith's hopes of settling the issue were dashed. Despite the simplicity and clarity of his reply, anti-Catholic literature continued to inundate the country.

The attacks repeatedly underscored the fact that Smith's Catholicism was symbolic of many things that were changing in America. Few presidential nominations symbolize major changes in a society. Perhaps only Jackson's nomination was comparable to Smith's in this regard. To hundreds of thousands of old-stock Americans, Smith might just as well have been Jewish or black. New York City was still the Babylon of Babylons, a vast conglomeration of Orientals, Jews, eastern Europeans, and Catholics of every ethnic mixture. It was also the home of a growing number of Negroes who espoused the cause of Negritude. New York meant nightlife, short skirts, prostitution, Jewish intellectuals, and the Union Theological Seminary. One staunch Democrat, George Fort Milton, wrote to McAdoo that Smith's appeal was

> to the aliens who feel that the older America, the America of the Anglo-Saxon stock is a hateful thing which must be overturned and humiliated; to the northern Negroes, who lust for social equality and racial dominance; to the Catholics, who have been made to believe that they are entitled to the White House; and to the Jews who likewise are to be instilled with the feeling that this is the time for God's chosen people to chastise America.... If the dominance of such groups represent the newer American, which Smith is seeking to arouse, the Old America, the America of Jackson and of Lincoln and of Wilson, should rise up in wrath and defend it.

The whispering campaigns against Smith were scandalous. It often was rumored that he was a drunkard and encouraged prostitution. Even the high-minded William Allen White, in a speech before the Kansas Republican convention, argued that Smith was not only a friend of the saloon but had been politically allied with organized vice, including prostitution. Acknowledging that Smith was a man "of unusual intelligence, splendid courage, and rare political wisdom," he took it all back by accusing him of supporting immorality. After Walter Lippmann and others pointed out to White that Smith voted against bills to regulate gambling and prostitution only because he felt the laws were unconstitutional, unenforceable, and would encourage police corruption, the conscience-stricken Kansan modified his attacks against Smith. But most newspapers carried the charges in large print on the front page or close to it and buried the retraction in the inner pages.

Smith was attacked on his home ground, too, by Reverend John Roach Straton, a prominent New York City Baptist minister who enjoyed a wide radio audience over station WQAO. Straton saw the election of Smith as a boost for card playing, cocktail drinking, divorce, dancing, Clarence Darrow, nude art, prize fighting, and even greyhound racing. Smith was so angry at Straton's absurd charges that he wanted to answer them in the Calvary Baptist Church where they had been issued. Straton, obviously flattered by Smith's attention, agreed only to a full-fledged debate in Madison Square Garden. Smith thought the Church appropriate and asked for a straight yes or no answer. The fundamentalist leader dodged that challenge, but kept up his attacks. As might be expected, the strongest attacks came from the South. Immediately after Smith's nomination, Methodist Bishop James Cannon Jr.

and Baptist leader Dr. A. G. Barton issued a call for a conference of dry Southern Democrats to meet at Ashville, North Carolina. There, on July 18, the conferees launched a propaganda campaign to convince Democratic drys that the election of Hoover was morally necessary. An organization was established at Richmond, Virginia, with Bishop Cannon in command. Methodists, Baptists, Presbyterians, and Lutherans sent a steady fusillade of anti-Catholic, anti-Smith literature in the mails to their communicants. One zealous Methodist who worked tirelessly to defeat Smith was Deets Pickett, research secretary for *The Voice*, a monthly journal of the Methodist Board of Temperance, Prohibition, and Public Morals. Pickett admitted that there were some Catholics worthy of holding public office, but Smith was not one of these. "Personally," he wrote, "I want to say here and now that my people quit kissing hands in 1776 and I don't intend to resume that practice."

The anti-Catholic crusade even included a fairly high official of the Coolidge Administration, Mrs. Mabel Walker Willebrandt, an assistant attorney general for the United States, assigned to the enforcement of Prohibition. Mrs. Willebrandt talked frequently before church conferences and meetings. The fact that an Administration official was allowed to make such vitriolic attacks nettled Smith and eventually led to his strongest speech on the subject of religious prejudice.

In the meantime, newspapers favorable to the governor such as the New York *World* urged Hoover to repudiate the slanders against Smith. Papers supporting Hoover hinted that the *World* encouraged the whispering campaign by giving them prominence. The *New York Herald Tribune* correctly pointed out that the main fight over Catholicism was probably within the governor's own party. But with only one notable exception, Hoover did not publicly repudiate the vicious attacks against his opponent. In that one case, he objected to a letter written by Mrs. Willie W. Caldwell, a Virginia national committeewoman, who wrote to party workers that Hoover was trying to save the United States from being Romanized.

From the Iowan's point of view, there were slanders on both sides. He had tried in his acceptance speech to eliminate the religious issue by pointing out that he had come from Quaker stock. Since his ancestors had been persecuted for their religious beliefs, he hoped that all Americans would respect the right of every man to worship God according to his own conscience. In fact, the attacks on Hoover were weak compared with those on Smith. Never was the Republican nominee willing to acknowledge that the blatant vilification heaped on his opponent was un-American. To the end, he concluded that "the religious issue had *no* weight in the final results [italics mine]."

Senator Robinson traveled in the South and the West to plead for tolerance, but he could not stop the huge outpouring of anti-Catholic leaflets and cartoons. In Alabama, the chairman of the Republican state campaign committee, Oliver D. Street, made Smith's religion the major issue of the campaign. The party's official four-page circular declared, "The Catholic Church and Governor Smith's membership in it legitimately enter into this campaign as a very live and vital issue." Other Republican politicians saw a chance to capitalize on Smith's Catholicism and New

York background in connection with the racial issue. A picture of a prominent Harlem politician dictating to a white secretary was widely distributed in an effort to connect Smith's candidacy with the desire of black people for social equality and the end of racial segregation.

A particularly blatant speech by Mrs. Willebrandt to a group of Ohio Methodists provoked Smith to reply at Oklahoma City on September 20 in a nationally broadcast speech to an audience that included the Reverend John Roach Straton and others like him. (The meeting was not unlike that which John F. Kennedy faced in Houston nearly thirty-two years later.) The Klan was powerful in Oklahoma, and anti-Catholic feeling was strong. The governor read tributes to himself from outstanding Protestant leaders of both parties, including Charles Evans Hughes, Nicholas Murray Butler, Robert Lansing, and Virginia G. Gildersleeve. He answered the charges against him one by one. To those who maintained that he favored Catholics in his appointments, he answered that of his cabinet of fourteen, only three were Catholic, ten were Protestant, and one was Jewish. He challenged the Ku Klux Klan: "The Grand Dragon of the realm of Kansas, writing to the citizens of that state, urges my defeat because I am a Catholic and suggests ... that by voting against me he was upholding American ideals and institutions." Governor Smith continued, "Nothing could be so out of line with the spirit of America. Nothing could be so foreign to the teachings of Jefferson. Nothing could be so contradictory to our whole history." He urged the American people not to sit silently while vitriolic propaganda against his religion was injected into the political campaign. "I here and now drag them into the open," he said, "and denounce them as a treasonable attack upon the very foundations of American liberty." Governor Smith acknowledged that it might be more expedient for him to remain silent, but he was convinced that "Republicans high in the councils of the party have countenanced a large part of this form of campaign if they have not actually promoted it."

Like Kennedy in later years, he insisted that he did not want any member of his faith to vote for him on religious grounds. "I want them to vote for me only when in their hearts and consciences they become convinced that my election will promote the best interests of our country," but he also maintained, as Kennedy did in 1960, that any citizen who voted against him because of his religion was not a good citizen. Once again, he insisted that he believed as strongly in the separation of church and state as any American and urged the voters to decide the election on "the great and real issues of the campaign, and upon nothing else."

As was true following Smith's exchange with Marshall in the *Atlantic Monthly*, he was attacked by Protestant Republicans for giving greater circulation to the religious issue. Some of them acted as if Smith had invented the Anti-Saloon League, the Ku Klux Klan, and the Methodist Board of Temperance, Prohibition, and Public Morals. Nicholas Longworth, Speaker of the House of Representatives, told a Republican audience that it was not the Republicans' fault that the religious issue had been thrown into the campaign. Ex-Governor Henry J. Owen of Kansas echoed the same idea. The truth was that the Republican national committeemen of Alabama had already helped to distribute 250,000 copies of a circular attacking Smith for his religion; Mrs. Willebrandt's speeches urging people to vote for Hoover and against Smith were clearly based on an appeal to prejudice.

For ten days after the Oklahoma speech, the religious issue led all others in newspaper coverage according to the North American Newspaper Alliance. How deeply it cut, how pervasively, it is impossible to say. But there can be little question that Smith's religion accounted for large numbers of Democratic defectors, particularly in the South.

Almost every scholar who has looked at the 1928 election results has concluded that the religious issue made more noise than votes. Would Smith have won had he been a Protestant? The evidence strongly indicates a negative answer. The astounding thing about Smith's performance is that, despite his New York accent, Irish-Tammany upbringing, and unpopular, uncompromising stand against prohibition, he actually won 41 percent of the national two-party vote, more than any other Democratic candidate in the twentieth century with the exception of Wilson in 1916. That Smith won as many votes as he did was testimony to his extraordinary ability. His campaign probably was run as efficiently as any. He worked hard to develop a party organization and image that would win the confidence of America's businessmen, and, to an extent that surprised many, he succeeded. Undoubtedly, he never expected to win a majority of industrialists or even small businessmen, but he wanted to overcome the reputation that Democrats had acquired of being anti-business and to burst the Republican assertion that only Republican leadership was astute enough in business affairs to bring prosperity.

For this purpose, he chose to head his campaign John Jacob Raskob of Delaware, a Republican who had voted for Coolidge in 1924, and who had announced that he would vote for him in 1928 if the Vermonter chose to run again. Raskob was famous in business circles for having worked himself up from a stenographer to chairman of the finance committee of General Motors, a key position in the management of one of the most powerful corporations in the world. Smith asked for Raskob, even though the corporation executive was a wet and a Roman Catholic, because he wanted an efficient businessman in charge. Others from business, including James G. Gergard, a former United States ambassador to Germany under Wilson, Herbert H. Lehman, a Wall Street banker and importer, and Jessie H. Jones, a millionaire from Houston, were given critical roles in campaign strategy and finance. Because of this approach, the party (for the first time since Wilson) was almost able to match contributions and expenditures dollar for dollar with the GOP. A portion ($1,600,000) of total Democratic receipts constituted money borrowed from New York banks on the endorsements of Raskob, Lehman, and others.

The appeal to business included a promise in the platform and in Smith's speeches not to tamper with the tariff. The Democratic Party abandoned its traditional anti-tariff stand in obvious acquiescence to the nationwide conviction that Republican trade and financial policies promoted prosperity. When Smith's promise not to lower the tariff was challenged, he sent a questionnaire to all Democratic candidates for congressional office and subsequently exhibited the affirmative promise of 85 percent of them.

But the appeal to business by the Democrats could not possibly match that of the GOP. After all, the Republican Party was the party of business, and the vast majority of American voters knew it. Although Smith was convinced after the election that religious bigotry had beaten him, the evidence would seem to support Will Rogers's conclusion that no Democrat could have won in 1928. "You can't lick this prosperity thing," quipped the humorist.

The Republicans could hardly have picked a better candidate than Herbert Hoover to symbolize tranquility, prosperity, and purity. Born on a homestead in West Branch, Iowa, in 1874, Hoover grew up in a practically self-sufficient family. They produced their own vegetables, soap, and bread. Fuel was cut and brought from the woods ten miles away. In the fall, jars and barrels filled the cellar, which as Hoover put it in his memoirs, was "social security itself." In his memory, Hoover had lived the Jeffersonian idyll as a young boy. It is often forgotten that Hoover typified the Horatio Alger story at least as effectively as Smith and in a much more familiar format. Although his parents were poor and he was often hungry, he became a great mining engineer, a successful relief expediter to Belgium following the First World War, and a strong and able Secretary of Commerce. Generally thought to be above narrow partisan politics, he was acclaimed by Justice Louis D. Brandeis as one of the freshest faces in the Capitol. In 1919, Franklin D. Roosevelt felt him worthy of consideration for the Presidency.

Once Calvin Coolidge removed himself from consideration for reelection with his August 2, 1927, statement that "I do not choose to run for President in 1928," Hoover became the obvious choice as his successor. Charles Evans Hughes no doubt wanted to be nominated. His nomination and campaign in 1916 entitled him to further consideration, but Hoover rapidly emerged as the stronger candidate. Hughes had a reputation as a progressive when governor of New York in 1912, and in 1913, when appointed to the Supreme Court, he showed a friendly attitude toward labor. In his 1916 presidential campaign, he was able to pull the progressives and conservatives together, but not enough to overcome Wilson's lead. By 1928, he had been practically forgotten by the public, having been removed from politics by his service on the World Court. At no point did he represent a serious challenge to the Iowan.

Senator Charles Curtis from Kansas, Majority Floor Leader in the Senate, who eventually would be the vice-presidential nominee, was considered a presidential possibility by conservatives who did not like Hoover's record of independence in the Cabinet. Curtis was willing, but he was never really in the running. Though Hoover had been slightly irregular from the point of view of the stand-patters, he was safe enough compared to such progressives as Senator William Borah of Idaho and George Norris of Nebraska, both of whom had repeatedly opposed Coolidge's domestic policies.

Smith, wary of entering primaries against local favorite sons, allowed his name to be entered only in Nebraska, where he lost by a small margin; but Hoover entered many primaries despite the odds against challenging a favorite son. Presumably, he wanted to give his name greater circulation and to test the strength of his organization across the country. Because loyalty to the locality or to the state means so much more than the desire to support a national leader — and that was more true in 1929 than now — a national candidate was almost sure to lose against a gubernatorial or senatorial favorite son. Hoover won primaries only in those states where he was unopposed or ran against other than favorite son candidates. In Indiana, West Virginia, Illinois, and Nebraska, local patriotism and a strong sense of pride in the local organization and candidates led to his defeat. On April 10, he lost in Nebraska to George Norris by 90,000 votes and in Illinois to Governor Frank O. Lowden by over 1,000,000 votes. But Hoover's reputation remained largely untarnished. The favorite sons were expected to win, and Hoover did not speak out against them.

He did not have to. Even without victories in the primaries, the convention would be controlled by Hoover forces. Meeting on June 12 in Kansas City, Missouri, in the Great Hall built in 1900, Hoover swept to the nomination on the first ballot with 837 votes despite a minor effort to stop him by Lowden and Curtis. His nearest competitor, Senator Curtis, received only 72 votes and quickly accepted the vice-presidential nomination despite an earlier statement that he would refuse. For the first time in the history of national political parties, the candidates for President and Vice-President were chosen from states west of the Mississippi River. A favorite of the farmers of Kansas and of the corn belt, Curtis's nomination was intended to hold in line farmers suffering from economic depression attributed to Republican policies.

The convention was dominated by conservative Republicanism. Senator Simeon D. Fess of Ohio gave a keynote speech in which he failed even to mention the name of Theodore Roosevelt. Another Hoover supporter, Senator George H. Moses of New Hampshire, president *pro tem* of the Senate, was chosen as permanent chairman. Still another Hoover man, Senator Reed Smoot of Utah, chairman of the Senate Finance Committee and a strong defender of high tariffs, was selected as chairman of the Resolutions Committee, which produced a conservative and dull platform that essentially had been written by Smoot several days before the opening of the convention. The prohibition plank, was hammered out at the convention itself, pledged the Republican Party and its nominees to vigorous enforcement of the 18th Amendment.

On the issue where Republicans were most vulnerable — farm relief — they made it clear that the farmer and not the government had the job of lifting himself from "the serious condition of agriculture chiefly due to surplus crops." Here was the issue where the Democrats, if they had had a candidate who by virtue of temperament, background, personality, and religion was more sympathetic to the predilections of American farmers, could have made more headway. Champions of the farmers' cause at Kansas City dwelt on the loss of votes that would result from the failure to endorse an "equalization fee" that would have meant that the government itself would have marketed surplus crops abroad. The convention, in its political if not patriotic wisdom, proved right in the end. Farmers, going through hard times, a precursor of things to come for the nation, were not satisfied by the platform, but the threatened invasion of Kansas City by a convention of a thousand corn and wheat belt farmers never materialized, and the Republican Party was still safe in ignoring the pleas of farmers in economic distress.

In retrospect, it is easy to see that Hoover ran a near perfect campaign. He refused to debate controversial issues, including the religious affiliation of his Democratic opponent. The number of defections to the Democrats on the agricultural issue was small. Some farm leaders such as George N. Peek of Illinois, Frank W. Murphy of Minnesota, and Frank Lund of Iowa came out for Smith, as did Robert La Follette's organ the *Madison-Capitol Times* and, most important, Senator George Norris. But those breaks did not compare with defections from the Democrats, especially in the South, but also in the Middle West and Far West. So nervous were the Democrats about losses in the South, that the support of regular Democrats such as Carter Glass of Virginia and Josephus Daniels of North Carolina was received with a special enthusiasm that betrayed Democratic anxieties. Many farmers were of German and Scandinavian ancestry, and Hoover was especially popular with German voters because of his work for war relief in Germany following the war. The weight of the Administration's support was behind Hoover. Hoover-for-President clubs were formed among federal officeholders in the civil service with an initiation fee of ten dollars. Although such clubs never met, it was a practical method of assessing federal civil service employees in spite of laws against such practices. Whereas Coolidge had spent only $3.5 million in 1924, the men running the Hoover campaign — the best financed in history to that point — expended $10 million, $3 million more than Smith had at his disposal.

Hoover had already achieved an image of being above politics, and he tried to maintain it throughout the campaign. When his actions as relief administrator in Belgium had brought him to the attention of the American people, he was praised by leaders of both parties. In the formative period of the 1920 campaign, the Democratic New York *World* spoke favorably of his candidacy. Compared to most of his colleagues in the Harding and Coolidge Cabinets, Hoover seemed a giant of energy and intelligence. To many, he looked to be much stronger than the Presidents he served. He showed none of the weakness or intellectual vacuity of a Harding, or the timidity and inarticulateness of Coolidge. As the *Saturday Evening Post* put it after his nomination, "The Republican Party offers the voters a man, not a formula — a man of capacity, experience, and leadership conversant with large problems." Hoover calculated from the beginning of the campaign that he was ahead and could afford to remain aloof except for occasional appearances at dignified and almost nonpartisan affairs. Republican propaganda pictured him as a kindly, broad-minded statesman–engineer capable of assessing facts and making swift decisions on vast administrative problems. He refused to debate Smith, and not once did he publicly mention his name. The New York governor, frustrated repeatedly, bemoaned Hoover's unwillingness to debate, but it did no good. Hoover, without debating the issues, stood for tranquility, prosperity, and purity. Let Smith attack on those issues.

Al Smith tried. It had been characteristic of Smith as governor to "tell it like it is," and he continued to press that style as a presidential candidate. He had been warned to keep quiet in the Carolinas on the tariff and on immigration but made speeches there on both subjects. He had been told to ignore the attacks on his religion, but he faced the issue openly and specifically. On immigration, he could not possibly align his position with that of the vast majority of American voters who wanted to keep the doors closed to newer ethnic groups. Smith represented many of those people in New York and was sympathetic to the plight of their brethren overseas. Hoover waited, seemingly invulnerable and invincible. Smith struck, but appeared to be going nowhere. This was the pattern of the campaign from their acceptance speeches on. Hoover, speaking before seventy thousand in the great stadium of Stanford University, where he had paid for his studies by working at various jobs, gave an orthodox Republican presentation straight out of the platform on almost all the major issues of the day. Smith, who spoke in Albany on the steps of the State Capitol, presented his case in much greater detail and more provocatively.

But he did not have the issues, at least not as far as the vast majority of old-stock, middle-class Americans were concerned. Attempts to attack Republicans on the question of the scandals of the Harding Administration, beginning with Claude Bowers's convention keynote speech, and including a strong speech by Smith at Helena, Montana, on October 19 on the fraudulent oil leases granted in the early 1920s, made little impression. As far as most voters were concerned, the Teapot Dome issue had been buried in the Coolidge landslide of 1924.

Smith attempted to press other issues, too. The governor strongly believed in government ownership of power sites and plants. A speech on this subject in Nashville brought cries of socialism from the opposition. The farm issue might have converted more voters, but Democrats could hardly have picked a worse spokesman to exploit the disaffection of farmers with Republican policies. What did Smith, child of the Bowery and the Fish Market, know about corn and wheat?! It did little good to the farmers' psyches or pocketbooks when Raskob deputed R. A. Seligmann, the noted economist, to study the farm problem. Farm prices were falling, a precursor of the depression, but most farmers had not been hit hard yet, and the desire to maintain prohibition and the rural, Anglo-Saxon, Protestant virtues long believed to be the quintessence of American life, must have weighed more heavily in their feelings and thoughts than any discomfort they had with the failure of the Republican Administration to act more vigorously on farm relief.

Foreign policy was rarely discussed. The country was at peace, and most voters did not think twice about the forays of Marines into Central American republics. America was doing its job of improving the world through missionary activity, by spreading the virtues of plumbing and literacy in the Far East and in Latin America. The country was happy to forget the horrors of the First World War, which, after all, had been entered into by a Democratic Administration that had pledged not to go to war. For many German and Scandinavian farmers, Democrats lost whatever claim to their votes they might have had through Wilson's interventionist policies in Europe.

Apart from a minority of farmers, the nation's prosperity and that issue alone probably would have won for Hoover against anyone. American voters, as Louis Bean was to show later in a careful analysis of presidential elections, do not disturb the political status quo in times of high prosperity and domestic and foreign tranquility. The 1928 Republican platform attributed the great expansion in the wealth of the nation during the past fifty years, particularly during the past decade, to Republican policies. It was a theme of which Hoover was fond throughout the campaign. He pointed out that taxes had been reduced, the national income had been augmented by over 40 percent, and home ownership had grown by leaps and bounds under Republican Presidents. He spoke of nearly nine million more homes with electricity, six million more telephones, seven million more radio sets, and fourteen million additional automobiles under recent Republican rule. To what could the American people owe these benefits? The answer was clear to Hoover: the "hard working character of our people" and "the capacity for far sighted leadership and the industry, ingenuity and daring of the pioneers of new inventions ... the abolition of the saloon and the wisdom of our national policies."

Prosperity was the keynote. Thousands of small-town newspapers and metropolitan dailies were provided with boilerplate advertisements on the same theme. "Let's keep what we've got. Prosperity didn't just happen. Hoover and happiness or Smith and soup houses? Which shall it be? Hard times always come when the Democrats try to run the nation. Ask dad — he knows! Take no chances! Vote a straight Republican ticket!" Another campaign card went, "*Is your bread buttered*? Remember hard times when we had a Democratic president! You can't eat promises. Play safe! Vote a straight Republican ticket!" Perhaps the most famous of all slogans came from an advertisement sponsored by the Republican National Committee entitled "A Chicken For Every Pot."

In a few short years, those words would be turned against the Republicans, but in 1928 there were only four to five million unemployed, and these, mostly the unskilled, newer ethnics, Negroes in the rural South, and poor whites in mountain areas such as Appalachia, did not even vote for the most part. No matter how hard Smith might try to puncture the prosperity balloon ("Now just draw on your imagination for a moment and see if you can in your mind's eye see a man working at $17.30 going out to a chicken dinner in his own automobile with silk socks on."), he could not abolish the fact that real wages actually had gone up steadily under Republican rule.

One barely concealed and utterly irrelevant issue in the campaign that had an incalculable, although probably minor, effect in hurting the Democratic candidate was his alleged lack of social grace. Probably the vast majority of those who were affected by vulgar stories concerning Mr. and Mrs. Smith's lack of finesse would have voted Republican anyway. Smith made no bones about the fact that he lacked a college education and spoke unashamedly in an East Side accent. He refused to get rid of his brown derby, and he burned in anger at the slurs cast against his wife, a plain and simply educated daughter of Irish immigrants. Warren Harding, for all his personal and public laxity in morals, looked more like a President to the Babbitts of America than did Al Smith, an exemplar of efficiency and honesty in public service. Certainly, Herbert Hoover, a staunch representative of old-stock virtues, tall, urbane without being urban, ascetic and thrifty, and a self-made man from West Branch, Iowa, was to the conventionally minded more fit to be Chief of State.

With so many factors against him, the obvious query is not why Smith lost, but why he did so well. The turnout in 1928 was unprecedentedly high: 67.5 percent of the total eligible number of voters went to the polls, 10.9 percent more than in 1924. Hoover received over 21,000,000 votes and Smith slightly more than 15,000,000. The votes for minor party candidates were negligible. Norman Thomas, a sane, reasonable, Socialist candidate who campaigned actively, received a mere 267,835 votes, and more than 100,000 of these came from New York State alone. All together, the third parties received just under 400,000 votes (1.8 percent) in 1928 compared to Robert M. La Follette's vote of nearly 5,000,000 (17.13 percent) four years before.

This astounding turnout indicates that Smith's candidacy symbolized one of those rare watersheds in the history of American politics. The total vote for President was actually 7,750,000 more than for Coolidge, Davis, and La Follette in 1924. The vote in 1932, at the height of the depression, when many voters felt severe deprivation and desperately wanted change, was only 3,000,000 more than in 1928.

Hoover carried all but eight states, winning by an electoral vote of 444 to 87. On the surface, his victory was overwhelming. He cracked the Solid South, and his vote exceeded Coolidge's in total strength in over 95 percent of the counties in the nation (La Follette had won mostly progressive Republican votes and Smith could carry only forty-three of the 409 counties won by the candidate from Wisconsin). But the superficial observations of many following the election — that a Catholic could never be elected President, that prohibition had been sanctioned by popular mandate, and that the Republican Party was unbeatable — were shattered by events to come.

Probably the most significant result of the 1928 election was that for the first time in a century a Democratic candidate for President came close to winning a plurality in the fifty largest urban counties. Smith's candidacy produced defections from Jews, Italians, and other newer immigrant groups who had usually voted Republican in national elections. It would take the national catastrophe of an economic depression, the end of Prohibition, and the election of an aristocratic Protestant, Franklin Roosevelt, to bring about the coalition of farmers, old-stock laborers, Negroes, and newer ethnics that formed the Democratic majority in 1936. Smith began the work that Roosevelt was to complete. The *St. Paul Pioneer Press* rejoiced after Smith's defeat: "America is not yet dominated by its great cities. Control of its destiny still remains in the smaller communities and rural regions, with their traditional conservatism and solid virtues.... Main Street is still the principal thoroughfare of the nation." But not for long. Smith's victories in St. Louis, Cleveland, San Francisco, New York, Boston, San Antonio, and New Haven, and his strong race in Philadelphia, Pittsburgh, Chicago, Detroit, and Omaha indicated substantial inroads on the traditional Republican hegemony in America's great cities.

The usual Democratic pluralities in Atlanta, Birmingham, Dallas, Los Angeles, and Houston were lost, undoubtedly because of the religious and social issues that dominated the campaign in the South and Southwest. But Smith split the Republican North as well as the South, swinging 122 northern counties from the GOP column. Seventy-seven of those counties were predominantly Catholic, but it was not just religious sympathy that inspired support for Smith, as has been shown by the heavy Democratic vote in the same counties ever since. In the other twelve largest cities, Republican strength dropped precipitously from a plurality of 1,252,000 in 1924 to a Democratic plurality of 38,000.

Smith's candidacy and strength in the North and Northeast heralded the beginning of a new politics in America. In the long run, Democrats may have gained more than they lost by running a wet Catholic who lacked social graces. Before Smith, no other part of the country was more Republican than the industrial East. Since Smith, no other section has been so consistently Democratic. A huge proportion of the new voters of 1928 were the sons and daughters of immigrants in the cities who could never have followed the banner of William Jennings Bryan, defender of free silver and sometime apologist for the Ku Klux Klan. The "Great Commoner" had called the eastern part of the United States "the enemies' country." But in politics, there are no enemies. Only interests — and allies; and new interests were producing a new alliance — an alliance of ethnic and economic underdogs that the patrician Franklin Delano Roosevelt would lead for thirteen years. But to Smith must go the credit for breaking the traditional Republican hold on mining and industrial counties, many of which had not gone Democratic since at least 1896. It is doubtful if another candidate would have been able to win Massachusetts for the party of Jackson for the first time in a century. The voters in the cities with the largest proportion of foreign-born were already in political revolt. Four years later, farmers in severe distress and skilled and unskilled workers of older native American stock would join them. Hoover won the political battle of 1928, but the Republican Party, like the Federalists and Whigs before them, proved unable to read the true meanings of fundamental social changes and were already on their way toward becoming the minority party of the mid-twentieth century.

Appendix

Party Platforms of 1928

Democratic Platform

We, the Democratic Party in convention assembled, pause to pay our tribute of love and respect to the memory of him who in his life and in his official actions voiced the hopes and aspirations of all good men and women of every race and clime, the former President of the United States, Woodrow Wilson. His spirit moves on and his example and deeds will exalt those who come after us as they have inspired us.

We are grateful that we were privileged to work with him and again pay tribute to his high ideals and accomplishments.

We reaffirm our devotion to the principles of Democratic government formulated by Jefferson and enforced by a long and illustrious line of Democratic Presidents.

We hold that government must function not to centralize our wealth but to preserve equal opportunity so that all may share in our priceless resources; and not confine prosperity to a favored few. We, therefore, pledge the Democratic Party to encourage business, small and great alike; to conserve human happiness and liberty; to break the shackles of monopoly and free business of the nation; to respond to the popular will.

The function of a national platform is to declare general principles and party policies. We do not, therefore, assume to bind our party respecting local issues or details of legislation.

We, therefore, declare the policy of the Democratic Party with regard to the following dominant national issues:

THE RIGHTS OF THE STATES

We demand that the constitutional rights and powers of the states shall be preserved in their full vigor and virtue. These constitute a bulwark against centralization and the destructive tendencies of the Republican Party.

We oppose bureaucracy and the multiplication of offices and officeholders.

We demand a revival of the spirit of local self-government, without which free institutions cannot be preserved.

REPUBLICAN CORRUPTION

Unblushingly the Republican Party offers as its record agriculture prostrate, industry depressed, American shipping destroyed, workmen without employment; everywhere disgust and suspicion, and corruption unpunished and unafraid.

Never in the entire history of the country has there occurred in any given period of time or, indeed, in all time put together, such a spectacle of sordid corruption and unabashed rascality as that which has characterized the administration of federal affairs under eight blighting years of Republican rule. Not the revels of reconstruction, nor all the compounded frauds succeeding that evil era, have approached in sheer audacity the shocking thieveries and startling depravities of officials high and low in the public service at Washington. From cabinet ministers, with their treasonable crimes, to the cheap vendors of official patronage, from the purchasers of seats in the United States Senate to the vulgar grafters upon alien trust funds, and upon the hospital resources of the disabled veterans of the World War; from the givers and receivers of stolen funds for Republican campaign purposes to the public men who sat by silently consenting and never revealing a fact or uttering a word in condemnation, the whole official organization under Republican rule has become saturated with dishonesty defiant of public opinion and actuated only by a partisan desire to perpetuate its control of the government.

As in the time of Samuel J. Tilden, from whom the presidency was stolen, the watchword of the day should be: "Turn the rascals out." This is the appeal of the Democratic Party to the people of the country. To this fixed purpose should be devoted every effort and applied every resource of the party; to this end every minor difference on non-essential issues should be put aside and a determined and a united fight be made to rescue the government from those who have betrayed their trust by disgracing it.

ECONOMY AND REORGANIZATION

The Democratic Party stands for efficiency and economy in the administration of public affairs and we pledge:
> (a) Business-like reorganization of all the departments of the government.
> (b) Elimination of duplication, waste and overlapping.
> (c) Substitution of modern business-like methods for existing obsolete and antiquated conditions.

No economy resulted from the Republican Party rule. The savings they claim take no account of the elimination of expenditures following the end of the World War, the large sums realized from the sale of war materials, nor its failure to supply sufficient funds for the efficient conduct of many important governmental activities.

FINANCING AND TAXATION

> (a) The Federal Reserve system, created and inaugurated under Democratic auspices, is the greatest legislative contribution to constructive business ever adopted. The administration of the system for the advantage of stock market speculators should cease. It must be

administered for the benefit of farmers, wage earners, merchants, manufacturers and others engaged in constructive business.

(b) The taxing function of governments, free or despotic, has for centuries been regarded as the power above all others which requires vigilant scrutiny to the end that it be not exercised for purposes of favor or oppression.

Three times since the World War the Democrats in Congress have favored a reduction of the tax burdens of the people in face of stubborn opposition from a Republican administration; and each time these reductions have largely been made for the relief of those least able to endure the exactions of a Republican fiscal policy. The tax bill of the session recently ended was delayed by Republican tactics and juggled by partisan considerations so as to make impossible a full measure of relief to the greater body of taxpayers. The moderate reductions afforded were grudgingly conceded and the whole proceeding in Congress, dictated as far as possible from the White House and the treasury, denoted the proverbial desire of the Republican Party always to discriminate against the masses in favor of privileged classes.

The Democratic Party avows its belief in the fiscal policy inaugurated by the last Democratic Administration, which provided a sinking fund sufficient to extinguish the nation's indebtedness within a reasonable period of time, without harassing the present and next succeeding generations with tax burdens which, if not unendurable, do in fact check initiative in enterprise and progress in business. Taxes levied beyond the actual requirements of the legally established sinking fund are but an added burden upon the American people, and the surplus thus accumulated in the federal treasury, is an incentive to the increasingly extravagant expenditures which have characterized Republican administrations. We, therefore, favor a further reduction of the internal taxes of the people.

TARIFF

The Democratic tariff legislation will be based on the following policies:

(a) The maintenance of legitimate business and a high standard of wages for American labor.

(b) Increasing the purchasing power of wages and income by the reduction of those monopolistic and extortionate tariff rates bestowed in payment of political debts.

(c) Abolition of log-rolling and restoration of the Wilson conception of a fact-finding tariff commission, quasi-judicial and free from the executive domination which has destroyed the usefulness of the present commission.

(d) Duties that will permit effective competition, insure against monopoly and at the same time produce a fair revenue for the support of government. Actual difference between the cost of production at home and abroad, with adequate safeguard for the wage of the American laborer must be the extreme measure of every tariff rate.

    (e) Safeguarding the public against monopoly created by special tariff
        favors.
    (f) Equitable distribution of the benefits and burdens of the tariff among
        all.

Wage-earner, farmer, stockman, producer and legitimate business in general have
everything to gain from a Democratic tariff based on justice to all.

CIVIL SERVICE

Grover Cleveland made the extension of the merit system a tenet of our political
faith. We shall preserve and maintain the civil service.

AGRICULTURE

Deception upon the farmer and stock raiser has been practiced by the Republican
Party through false and delusive promises for more than fifty years. Specially favored
industries have been artificially aided by Republican legislation. Comparatively little
has been done for agriculture and stock raising, upon which national prosperity rests.
Unsympathetic inaction with regard to this problem must cease. Virulent hostility of
the Republican administration to the advocates of farm relief and denial of the right
of farm organizations to lead in the development of farm policy must yield to Democratic sympathy and friendliness.

Four years ago the Republican Party, forced to acknowledge the critical situation,
pledged itself to take all steps necessary to bring back a balanced condition between
agriculture and other industries and labor. Today it faces the country not only with
that pledge unredeemed but broken by the acts of a Republican President, who is
primarily responsible for the failure to offer a constructive program to restore equality
to agriculture.

While he has had no constructive and adequate program to offer in its stead,
he has twice vetoed farm relief legislation and has sought to justify his disapproval
of agricultural legislation partly on grounds wholly inconsistent with his acts, making
industrial monopolies the beneficiaries of government favor; and in endorsing the
agricultural policy of the present administration the Republican Party, in its recent
convention, served notice upon the farmer that the so-called protective system is not
meant for him; that while it offers protection to the privileged few, it promises continued world prices to the producers of the chief cash crops of agriculture.

We condemn the policy of the Republican Party which promises relief to agriculture only through a reduction of American farm production to the needs of the domestic
market. Such a program means the continued deflation of agriculture, the forcing of
additional millions from the farms, and the perpetuation of agricultural distress for years
to come, with continued bad effects on business and labor throughout the United States.

The Democratic Party recognizes that the problems of production differ as between agriculture and industry. Industrial production is largely under human control,
while agricultural production, because of lack of co-ordination among the 6,500,000

individual farm units, and because of the influence of weather, pests and other causes, is largely beyond human control. The result is that a large crop frequently is produced on a small acreage and a small crop on a large acreage; and, measured in money value, it frequently happens that a large crop brings less than a small crop.

Producers of crops whose total volume exceeds the needs of the domestic market must continue at a disadvantage until the government shall intervene as seriously and as effectively in behalf of the farmer as it has intervened in behalf of labor and industry. There is a need of supplemental legislation for the control and orderly handling of agricultural surpluses, in order that the price of the surplus may not determine the price of the whole crop. Labor has benefited by collective bargaining and some industries by tariff. Agriculture must be as effectively aided.

The Democratic Party in its 1924 platform pledged its support to such legislation. It now reaffirms that stand and pledges the united efforts of the legislative and executive branches of government, as far as may be controlled by the party, to the immediate enactment of such legislation, and to such other steps as are necessary to establish and maintain the purchasing power of farm products and the complete economic equality of agriculture.

The Democratic Party has always stood against special privilege and for common equality under the law. It is a fundamental principle of the party that such tariffs as are levied must not discriminate against any industry, class or section. Therefore, we pledge that in its tariff policy the Democratic Party will insist upon equality of treatment between agriculture and other industries.

Farm relief must rest on the basis of an economic equality of agriculture with other industries. To give this equality a remedy must be found which will include among other things:

(a) Credit aid by loans to co-operatives on at least as favorable a basis as the government aid to the merchant marine.

(b) Creation of a federal farm board to assist the farmer and stock raiser in the marketing of their products, as the Federal Reserve Board has done for the banker and business man. When our archaic banking and currency system was revised after its record of disaster and panic under Republican administrations, it was a Democratic Congress in the administration of a Democratic President that accomplished its stabilization through the Federal Reserve Act creating the Federal Reserve Board, with powers adequate to its purpose. Now, in the hour of agriculture's need, the Democratic Party pledges the establishment of a new agricultural policy fitted to present conditions, under the direction of a farm board vested with all the powers necessary to accomplish for agriculture what the Federal Reserve Board has been able to accomplish for finance, in full recognition of the fact that the banks of the country, through voluntary co-operation, were never able to stabilize the financial system of the country until the government powers were invoked to help them.

(c) Reduction through proper government agencies of the spread between what the farmer and stock raiser gets and the ultimate consumer pays, with consequent benefits to both.

(d) Consideration of the condition of agriculture in the formulation of government financial and tax measures.

We pledge the party to foster and develop co-operative marketing associations through appropriate governmental aid. We recognize that experience has demonstrated that members of such associations alone can not successfully assume the full responsibility for a program that benefits all producers alike. We pledge the party to an earnest endeavor to solve this problem of the distribution of the cost of dealing with crop surpluses over the marketed units of the crop whose producers are benefited by such assistance. The solution of this problem would avoid government subsidy, to which the Democratic Party has always been opposed. The solution of this problem will be a prime and immediate concern of a Democratic administration.

We direct attention to the fact that it was a Democratic Congress, in the administration of a Democratic President, which established the federal loan system and laid the foundation for the entire rural credits structure, which has aided agriculture to sustain in part the shock of the policies of two Republican administrations; and we promise thorough-going administration of our rural credits laws, so that the farmers in all sections may secure the maximum benefits intended under these acts.

MINING

Mining is one of the basic industries of this country. We produce more coal, iron and copper than any other country. The value of our mineral production is second only to agriculture. Mining has suffered like agriculture, and from similar causes. It is the duty of our government to foster this industry and to remove the restrictions that destroy its prosperity.

FOREIGN POLICY

The Republican administration has no foreign policy; it has drifted without plan. This great nation can not afford to play a minor role in world politics. It must have a sound and positive foreign policy, not a negative one. We declare for a constructive foreign policy based on these principles:

(a) Outlawry of war and an abhorrence of militarism, conquest and imperialism.

(b) Freedom from entangling political alliances with foreign nations.

(c) Protection of American lives and rights.

(d) Non-interference with the elections or other internal political affairs of any foreign nation. This principle of non-interference extends to Mexico, Nicaragua and all other Latin-American nations. Interference in the purely internal affairs of Latin-American countries must cease.

(e) Rescue of our country from its present impaired world standing and restoration to its former position as a leader in the movement for international arbitration, conciliation, conference and limitation of armament by international agreement.

(f) International agreements for reduction of all armaments and the end of competitive war preparations, and, in the meantime, the maintenance of an army and navy adequate for national defense.

(g) Full, free and open co-operation with all other nations for the promotion of peace and justice throughout the world.

(h) In our foreign relations this country should stand as a unit, and, to be successful, foreign policies must have the approval and the support of the American people.

(i) Abolition of the practice of the President of entering into and carrying out agreements with a foreign government, either de facto or de jure, for the protection of such government against revolution or foreign attack, or for the supervision of its internal affairs, when such agreements have not been advised and consented to by the Senate, as provided in the Constitution of the United States, and we condemn the administration for carrying out such an unratified agreement that requires us to use our armed forces in Nicaragua.

(j) Recognition that the Monroe Doctrine is a cardinal principle of this government promulgated for the protection of ourselves and our Latin-American neighbors. We shall seek their friendly cooperation in the maintenance of this doctrine.

(k) We condemn the Republican administration for lack of statesmanship and efficiency in negotiating the 1921 treaty for the limitation of armaments, which limited only the construction of battleships and ships of over ten thousand tons. Merely a gesture towards peace, it accomplished no limitation of armament, because it simply substituted one weapon of destruction for another. While it resulted in the destruction of our battleships and the blueprints of battleships of other nations, it placed no limitation upon construction of aircraft, submarines, cruisers, warships under ten thousand tons, poisonous gases or other weapons of destruction. No agreement was ratified with regard to submarines and poisonous gases. The attempt of the President to remedy the failure of 1921 by the Geneva Conference of 1928 was characterized by the same lack of statesmanship and efficiency and resulted in entire failure.

In consequence, the race between nations in the building of unlimited weapons of destruction still goes on and the peoples of the world are still threatened with war and burdened with taxation for additional armament.

WATERPOWER, WATERWAYS
AND FLOOD CONTROL

The federal government and state governments, respectively, now have absolute and exclusive sovereignty and control over enormous waterpowers, which constitute one of the greatest assets of the nation. This sovereign title and control must be preserved respectively in the state and federal governments, to the end that the people may be protected against exploitation of this great resource and that water powers may be expeditiously developed under such regulations as will insure to the people reasonable rates and equitable distribution.

We favor and will promote deep waterways from the Great Lakes to the Gulf and to the Atlantic Ocean.

We favor the fostering and building up of water transportation through improvement of inland waterways and removal of discrimination against water transportation. Flood control and the lowering of flood levels are essential to the safety of life and property, and the productivity of our lands, the navigability of our streams, the reclaiming of our wet and overflowed lands. We favor expeditious construction of flood relief works on the Mississippi and Colorado rivers and such reclamation and irrigation projects upon the Colorado River as may be found feasible.

We favor appropriations for prompt co-ordinated surveys by the United States to determine the possibilities of general navigation improvements and waterpower development on navigable streams and their tributaries and to secure reliable information as to the most economical navigation improvement, in combination with the most efficient and complete development of waterpower.

We favor the strict enforcement of the Federal Waterpower Act, a Democratic act, and insist that the public interest in waterpower sites, ignored by two Republican administrations, be protected.

Being deeply impressed by the terrible disasters from floods in the Mississippi Valley during 1927, we heartily endorse the Flood Control Act of last May, which recognizes that the flood waters of the Mississippi River and its tributaries constitute a national problem of the gravest character and makes provision for their speedy and effective control. This measure is a continuation and expansion of the policy established by a Democratic Congress in 1917 in the act of that year for controlling floods on the Mississippi and Sacramento rivers. It is a great piece of constructive legislation, and we pledge our party to its vigorous and early enforcement.

CONSERVATION AND RECLAMATION

We shall conserve the natural resources of our country for the benefit of the people and to protect them against waste and monopolization. Our disappearing resources of timber call for a national policy of reforestation. The federal government should improve and develop its public lands so that they may go into private ownership and become subjected to taxation for the support of the states wherein they exist. The Democratic administration will actively, efficiently and economically carry on reclamation projects and make equitable adjustments with the homestead entrymen for the mistakes the government has made, and extend all practical aid to refinance reclamation and drainage projects.

TRANSPORTATION

Efficient and economical transportation is essential to the prosperity of every industry. Cost of transportation controls the income of every human being and materially affects the cost of living. We must, therefore, promote every form of transportation to a state of highest efficiency. Recognizing the prime importance of air transportation, we shall encourage its development by every possible means. Improved roads are of vital importance not only to commerce and industry, but also to agriculture and rural life. The federal government should construct and maintain at its own expense roads upon its public lands. We reaffirm our approval of the Federal Roads Law, enacted by a Democratic administration. Common carriers, whether by land, water or rail, must be protected in an equal opportunity to compete, so that governmental regulations against exorbitant rates and inefficiency will be aided by competition.

LABOR

(a) We favor the principle of collective bargaining, and the Democratic principle that organized labor should choose its own representatives without coercion or interference.

(b) Labor is not a commodity. Human rights must be safeguarded. Labor should be exempt from the operation of anti-trust laws.

(c) We recognize that legislative and other investigations have shown the existence of grave abuse in the issuance of injunctions in labor disputes. No injunctions should be granted in labor disputes except upon proof of threatened irreparable injury and after notice and hearing and the injunction should be confined to those acts which do directly threaten irreparable injury. The expressed purpose of representatives of capital, labor and the bar to devise a plan for the elimination of the present evils with respect to injunctions must be supported and legislation designed to accomplish these ends formulated and passed.

(d) We favor legislation providing that products of convict labor shipped from one state to another shall be subject to laws of the latter state, as though they had been produced therein.

UNEMPLOYMENT

Unemployment is present, widespread and increasing. Unemployment is almost as destructive to the happiness, comfort, and well-being of human beings as war. We expend vast sums of money to protect our people against the evils of war, but no governmental program is anticipated to prevent the awful suffering and economic losses of unemployment. It threatens the well-being of millions of our people and endangers the prosperity of the nation. We favor the adoption by the government, after a study of this subject, of a scientific plan whereby during periods of unemployment appropriations shall be made available for the construction of necessary public works and the lessening, as far as consistent with public interests, of government construction work when labor is generally and satisfactorily employed in private enterprise.

Study should also be made of modern methods of industry and a constructive solution found to absorb and utilize the surplus human labor released by the increasing use of machinery.

ACCIDENT COMPENSATION TO GOVERNMENT EMPLOYEES

We favor legislation making fair and liberal compensation to government employees who are injured in accident or by occupational disease and to the dependents of such workers as may die as a result thereof.

FEDERAL EMPLOYEES

Federal employees should receive a living wage based upon American standards of decent living. Present wages are, in many instances, far below that standard. We favor a fair and liberal retirement law for government employees in the classified service.

VETERANS

Through Democratic votes, and in spite of two Republican Presidents' opposition, the Congress has maintained America's traditional policy to generously care for the veterans of the World War. In extending them free hospitalization, a statutory award for tuberculosis, a program of progressive hospital construction, and provisions for compensation for the disabled, the widows and orphans, America has surpassed the record of any nation in the history of the world. We pledge the veterans that none of the benefits heretofore accorded by the Wilson administration and the votes of Democrat members of Congress shall be withdrawn; that these will be added to more in accordance with the veterans' and their dependents' actual needs. Generous appropriations, honest management, the removal of vexatious administration delays, and sympathetic assistance for the veterans of all wars, is what the Democratic Party demands and promises.

WOMEN AND CHILDREN

We declare for equality of women with men in all political and governmental matters.

Children are the chief asset of the nation. Therefore their protection through infancy and childhood against exploitation is an important national duty.

The Democratic Party has always opposed the exploitation of women in industry and has stood for such conditions of work as will preserve their health and safety.

We favor an equal wage for equal service; and likewise favor adequate appropriations for the women's and children's bureau.

IMMIGRATION

Laws which limit immigration must be preserved in full force and effect, but the provisions contained in these laws that separate husbands from wives and parents from infant children are inhuman and not essential to the purpose or the efficacy of such laws.

RADIO

Government supervision must secure to all the people the advantage of radio communication and likewise guarantee the right of free speech. Official control in contravention of this guarantee should not be tolerated. Governmental control must prevent monopolistic use of radio communication and guarantee equitable distribution and enjoyment thereof.

COAL

Bituminous coal is not only the common base of manufacture, but it is a vital agency in our interstate transportation. The demoralization of this industry, its labor conflicts and distress, its waste of a national resource and disordered public service, demand constructive legislation that will allow capital and labor a fair share of prosperity, with adequate protection to the consuming public.

CONGRESSIONAL ELECTION REFORM

We favor legislation to prevent defeated members of both houses of Congress from participating in the sessions of Congress by fixing the date for convening the Congress immediately after the biennial national election.

LAW ENFORCEMENT

The Republican Party, for eight years in complete control of the government at Washington, presents the remarkable spectacle of feeling compelled in its national platform to promise obedience to a provision of the federal Constitution, which it has flagrantly disregarded and to apologize to the country for its failure to enforce laws enacted by the Congress of the United States. Speaking for the national Democracy, this convention pledges the party and its nominees to an honest effort to enforce the eighteenth amendment and all other provisions of the federal Constitution and all laws enacted pursuant thereto.

CAMPAIGN EXPENDITURES

We condemn the improper and excessive use of money in elections as a danger threatening the very existence of democratic institutions. Republican expenditures in senatorial primaries and elections have been so exorbitant as to constitute a national scandal. We favor publicity in all matters affecting campaign contributions and expenditures. We shall, beginning not later than August 1, 1928, and every thirty days thereafter, the last publication and filing being not later than five days before the election, publish in the press and file with the appropriate committees of the House and Senate a complete account of all contributions, the names of the contributors, the amounts expended and the purposes for which the expenditures are made, and will, at all times, hold open for public inspection the books and record relating to such matters. In the event that any financial obligations are contracted and not paid, our National Committee will similarly report and publish, at least five days before the election, all details respecting such obligations.

We agree to keep and maintain a permanent record of all campaign contributions and expenditures and to insist that contributions by the citizens of one state to the campaign committees of other states shall have immediate publicity.

MERCHANT MARINE

We reaffirm our support of an efficient, dependable American merchant marine for the carriage of the greater portion of our commerce and for the national defense.

The Democratic Party has consistently and vigorously supported the shipping services maintained by the regional United States Shipping Board in the interest of all ports and all sections of our country, and has successfully opposed the discontinuance of any of these lines. We favor the transfer of these lines gradually to the local private American companies, when such companies can show their ability to take over and permanently maintain the lines. Lines that can not now be transferred to private enterprise should continue to be operated as at present and should be kept in an efficient state by remodeling of some vessels and replacement of others.

We are unalterably opposed to a monopoly in American shipping and are opposed to the operation of any of our services in a manner that would retard the development of any ports or section of our country.

We oppose such sacrifices and favoritism as exhibited in the past in the matter of alleged sales, and insist that the primary purpose of legislation upon this subject be the establishment and maintenance of an adequate American merchant marine.

ARMENIA

We favor the most earnest efforts on the part of the United States to secure the fulfillment of the promises and engagements made during and following the World War by the United States and the allied powers to Armenia and her people.

EDUCATION

We believe with Jefferson and other founders of the Republic that ignorance is the enemy of freedom and that each state, being responsible for the intellectual and moral qualifications of its citizens and for the expenditure of the moneys collected by taxation for the support of its schools, shall use its sovereign right in all matters pertaining to education.

The federal government should offer to the states such counsel, advice, results of research and aid as may be made available through the federal agencies for the general improvement of our schools in view of our national needs.

MONOPOLIES AND ANTI-TRUST LAWS

During the last seven years, under Republican rule, the anti-trust laws have been thwarted, ignored and violated so that the country is rapidly becoming controlled by trusts and sinister monopolies formed for the purpose of wringing from the necessaries of life an unrighteous profit. These combinations are formed and conducted in violation of law, encouraged, aided and abetted in their activities by the Republican administration and are driving all small tradespeople and small industrialists out of business. Competition is one of the most sacred, cherished and economic rights of the American people. We demand the strict enforcement of the anti-trust laws and the enactment of other laws, if necessary, to control this great menace to trade and commerce, and thus to preserve the right of the small merchant and manufacturer to earn a legitimate profit from his business.

Dishonest business should be treated without influence at the national capitol. Honest business, no matter its size, need have no fears of a Democratic administration. The Democratic Party. will ever oppose illegitimate and dishonest business. It will foster, promote, and encourage all legitimate enterprises.

CANAL ZONE

We favor the employment of American citizens in the operation and maintenance of the Panama Canal in all positions above the grade of messenger and favor as liberal wages and conditions of employment as prevailed under previous Democratic administrations.

ALASKA–HAWAII

We favor the development of Alaska and Hawaii in the traditional American way, through self-government. We favor the appointment of only bona fide residents to office in the territories. We favor the extension and improvement of the mail, air mail, telegraph and radio, agricultural experimenting, highway construction, and other necessary federal activities in the territories.

PORTO RICO

We favor granting to Porto Rico such territorial form of government as would meet the present economic conditions of the island, and provide for the aspirations of her people, with the view to ultimate statehood accorded to all territories of the United States since the beginning of our government, and we believe any officials appointed to administer the government of such territories should be qualified by previous bona fide residence therein.

PHILIPPINES

The Filipino people have succeeded in maintaining a stable government and have thus fulfilled the only condition laid down by the Congress as a prerequisite to the granting of independence. We declare that it is now our duty to keep our promise to these people by granting them immediately the independence which they so honorably covet.

PUBLIC HEALTH

The Democratic Party recognizes that not only the productive wealth of the nation but its contentment and happiness depends upon the health of its citizens. It, therefore, pledges itself to enlarge the existing Bureau of Public Health and to do all things possible to stamp out communicable and contagious diseases, and to ascertain preventive means and remedies for these diseases, such as cancer, infantile paralysis and others which heretofore have largely defied the skill of physicians.

We pledge our party to spare no means to lift the apprehension of diseases from the minds of our people, and to appropriate all moneys necessary to carry out this pledge.

CONCLUSION

Affirming our faith in these principles, we submit our cause to the people.

Republican Platform

The Republican Party in national convention assembled presents to the people of the Nation this platform of its principles, based on a record of its accomplishments, and asks and awaits a new vote of confidence. We reaffirm our devotion to the Constitution of the United States and the principles and institution of the American system of representative government.

THE NATIONAL ADMINISTRATION

We endorse without qualification the record of the Coolidge administration.

The record of the Republican Party is a record of advancement of the nation. Nominees of Republican National conventions have for 52 of the 72 years since the creation of our party been the chief executives of the United States. Under Republican inspiration and largely under Republican executive direction the continent has been bound with steel rails, the oceans and great rivers have been joined by canals, waterways have been deepened and widened for ocean commerce, and with all a high American standard of wage and living has been established.

By unwavering adherence to sound principles, through the wisdom of Republican policies, and the capacity of Republican administrations, the foundations have been laid and the greatness and prosperity of the country firmly established.

Never has the soundness of Republican policies been more amply demonstrated and the Republican genius for administration been better exemplified than during the last five years under the leadership of President Coolidge.

No better guaranty of prosperity and contentment among all our people at home, no more reliable warranty of protection and promotion of American interests abroad can be given than the pledge to maintain and continue the Coolidge policies. This promise we give and will faithfully perform.

Under this Administration the country has been lifted from the depths of a great depression to a level of prosperity. Economy has been raised to the dignity of a principle of government. A standard of character in public service has been established under the chief Executive, which has given to the people of the country a feeling of stability and confidence so all have felt encouraged to proceed on new undertakings in trade and commerce. A foreign policy based on the traditional American position and carried on with wisdom and steadfastness has extended American influence throughout the world and everywhere promoted and protected American interests.

The mighty contribution to general well-being which can be made by a government controlled by men of character and courage, whose abilities are equal to their responsibilities, is self-evident, and should not blind us to the consequences which its loss would entail. Under this administration a high level of wages and living has been established and maintained. The door of opportunity has been opened wide to all. It has given to our people greater comfort and leisure, and the mutual profit has been evident in the increasingly harmonious relations between employers and employees, and the steady rise by promotion of the men in the shops to places at the council tables of the industries. It has also been made evident by the increasing enrollments of our youth in the technical schools and colleges, the increase in savings and life insurance accounts, and by our ability, as a people, to lend the hand of succor not only to those overcome by disasters in our own country but in foreign lands. With all there has been a steady decrease in the burden of Federal taxation, releasing to the people the greatest possible portion of the results of their labor from Government exactions.

For the Republican Party we are justified in claiming a major share of the credit for the position which the United States occupies today as the most favored nation on the globe, but it is well to remember that the confidence and prosperity which we enjoy can be shattered, if not destroyed, if this belief in the honesty and sincerity of our government is in any way affected. A continuation of this great public peace of mind now existing, which makes for our material well being, is only possible by holding fast to the plans and principles which have marked Republican control.

The record of the present Administration is a guaranty of what may be expected of the next. Our words have been made deeds. We offer not promises but accomplishments.

PUBLIC ECONOMY

The citizen and taxpayer has a natural right. to be protected from unnecessary and wasteful expenditures. This is a rich but also a growing nation with constantly increasing legitimate demands for public funds. If we are able to spend wisely and meet these requirements, it is first necessary that we save wisely. Spending extravagantly not only deprives men through taxation of the fruits of their labor, but oftentimes means the postponement of vitally important public works. We commend President Coolidge for his establishment of this fundamental principle of sound administration and pledge ourselves to live up to the high standard he has set.

FINANCE AND TAXATION

The record of the United States Treasury under Secretary Mellon stands unrivalled and unsurpassed. The finances of the nation have been managed with sound judgment. The financial policies have yielded immediate and substantial results.

In 1921 the credit of our government was at a low ebb. We were burdened with a huge public debt, a load of war taxes, which in variety and weight exceeded anything in our national life, while vast unfunded intergovernmental debts disorganized the economic life of the debtor nations and seriously affected our own by reason of the serious obstacles which they presented to commercial intercourse. This critical situation was evidenced by a serious disturbance in our own life which made for unemployment.

Today all these major financial problems have been solved.

THE PUBLIC DEBT

In seven years the public debt has been reduced by $6,411,000,000. From March 1921 to September 1928 over eleven billion dollars of securities, bearing high rates of interest, will have been retired or refunded into securities bearing a low rate of interest, while Liberty Bonds, which were selling below par, now command a premium. These operations have resulted in an annual saving in interest charges of not less than $275,000,000, without which the most recent tax reduction measure would not have been made possible. The Republican Party will continue to reduce our National debt as rapidly as possible and in accordance with the provision of existing laws and the present program.

TAX REDUCTION

Wise administrative management under Republican control and direction has made possible a reduction of over a billion eight hundred million dollars a year in the tax bill of the American people. Four separate tax reduction measures have been enacted, and millions of those least able to pay have been taken from the tax rolls.

Excessive and uneconomic rates have been radically modified, releasing for industrial and payroll expansion and development great sums of money which formerly were paid in taxes to the Federal government.

Practically all the war taxes have been eliminated and our tax system has been definitely restored to a peace time basis.

We pledge our party to a continuation of these sound policies and to such further reduction of the tax burden as the condition of the Treasury may from time to time permit.

TARIFF

We reaffirm our belief in the protective tariff as a fundamental and essential principle of the economic life of this nation. While certain provisions of the present law require revision in the light of changes in the world competitive situation since its enactment, the record of the United States since 1922 clearly shows that the fundamental protective principle of the law has been fully justified. It has stimulated the development of our natural resources, provided fuller employment at higher wages through the promotion of industrial activity, assured thereby the continuance of the farmer's major market, and further raised the standards of living and general comfort and well-being of our people. The great expansion in the wealth of our nation during the past fifty years, and particularly in the past decade, could not have been accomplished without a protective tariff system designed to promote the vital interests of all classes.

Nor have these manifest benefits been restricted to any particular section of the country. They are enjoyed throughout the land either directly or indirectly. Their stimulus has been felt in industries, farming sections, trade circles, and communities in every quarter. However, we realize that there are certain industries which cannot now successfully compete with foreign producers because of lower foreign wages and a lower cost of living abroad, and we pledge the next Republican Congress to an examination and where necessary a revision of these schedules to the end that American labor in these industries may again command the home market, may maintain its standard of living, and may count upon steady employment in its accustomed field.

Adherence to that policy is essential for the continued prosperity of the country. Under it the standard of living of the American people has been raised to the highest levels ever known. Its example has been eagerly followed by the rest of the world whose experts have repeatedly reported with approval the relationship of this policy to our prosperity, with the resultant emulation of that example by other nations.

A protective tariff is as vital to American agriculture as it is to American manufacturing. The Republican Party believes that the home market, built up under the protective policy, belongs to the American farmer, and it pledges its support of legislation which will give this market to him to the full extent of his ability to supply it. Agriculture derives large benefits not only directly from the protective duties levied on competitive farm products of foreign origin, but also, indirectly, from the increase in the purchasing power of American workmen employed in industries similarly protected. These benefits extend also to persons engaged in trade, transportation, and other activities.

The Tariff Act of 1922 has justified itself in the expansion of our foreign trade during the past five years. Our domestic exports have increased from 3.8 billions of dollars in 1922 to 4.8 billions in 1927. During the same period imports have increased from 3.1 billions to 4.4 billions. Contrary to the prophesies of its critics, the present tariff law has not hampered the natural growth in the exportation of the products of American agriculture, industry, and mining, nor has it restricted the importation of foreign commodities which this country can utilize without jeopardizing its economic structure.

The United States is the largest customer in the world today. If we were not prosperous and able to buy, the rest of the world also would suffer. It is inconceivable that American labor will ever consent to the abolition of protection which would bring the American standard of living down to the level of that in Europe, or that the American farmer could survive if the enormous consuming power of the people in this country were curtailed and its market at home, if not destroyed, at least seriously impaired.

FOREIGN DEBTS

In accordance with our settled policy and platform pledges, debt settlement agreements have been negotiated with all of our foreign debtors with the exception of Armenia and Russia. That with France remains as yet unratified. Those with Greece and Austria are before the Congress for necessary authority. If the French Debt Settlement be included, the total amount funded is eleven billion five hundred twenty-two million three hundred fifty-four thousand dollars. We have steadfastly opposed and will continue to oppose cancellation of foreign debts.

We have no desire to be oppressive or grasping, but we hold that obligations justly incurred should be honorably discharged. We know of no authority which would permit public officials, acting as trustees, to shift the burden of the War from the shoulders of foreign taxpayers to those of our own people. We believe that the settlements agreed to are fair to both the debtor nation and to the American taxpayer. Our Debt Commission took into full consideration the economic condition and resources of the debtor nations, and were ever mindful that they must be permitted to preserve and improve their economic position, to bring their budgets into balance, to place their currencies and finances on a sound basis, and to improve the standard of living of their people. Giving full weight to these considerations, we know of no fairer test than ability to pay, justly estimated.

The people can rely on the Republican Party to adhere to a foreign debt policy now definitely established and clearly understood both at home and abroad.

SETTLEMENT OF WAR CLAIMS

A satisfactory solution has been found for the question of War Claims. Under the Act, approved by the President on March 10, 1928, a provision was made for the settlement of War Claims of the United States and its citizens against the German, Austrian and Hungarian Governments, and of the claims of the nationals of these governments against the United States; and for the return to its owners of the property seized by the Alien Property Custodian during the War, in accordance with our traditional policy of respect for private property.

FOREIGN POLICIES

We approve the foreign policies of the Administration of President Coolidge. We believe they express the will of the American people in working actively to build up cordial international understanding that will make world peace a permanent reality. We endorse the proposal of the Secretary of State for a multilateral treaty proposed to the principal powers of the world and open to the signatures of all nations, to renounce war as an instrument of national policy and declaring in favor of pacific settlement of international disputes, the first step in outlawing war. The idea has stirred the conscience of mankind and gained widespread approval, both of governments and of the people, and the conclusion of the treaty will be acclaimed as the greatest single step in history toward the conservation of peace.

In the same endeavor to substitute for war the peaceful settlement of international disputes the administration has concluded arbitration treaties in a form more definite and more inclusive than ever before and plans to negotiate similar treaties with all countries willing in this manner to define their policy peacefully to settle justiciable disputes. In connection with these, we endorse the Resolution of the Sixth Pan American Conference held at Havana, Cuba, in 1928, which called a conference on arbitration and conciliation to meet in Washington during the year and express our earnest hope that such conference will greatly further the principles of international arbitration. We shall continue to demand the same respect and protection for the persons and property of American citizens in foreign countries that we cheerfully accord in this country to the persons and property of aliens.

The commercial treaties which we have negotiated and those still in the process of negotiation are based on strict justice among nations, equal opportunity for trade and commerce on the most-favored-nation principle and are simplified so as to eliminate the danger of misunderstanding. The object and the aim of the United States is to further the cause of peace, of strict justice between nations with due regard for the rights of others in all international dealings. Out of justice grows peace. Justice and consideration have been and will continue to be the inspiration of our nation.

The record of the Administration toward Mexico has been consistently friendly and with equal consistency have we upheld American rights. This firm and at the same time friendly policy has brought recognition of the inviolability of legally acquired rights. This condition has been reached without threat or without bluster, through a calm support of the recognized principles of international law with due regard to the rights of a sister sovereign state. The Republican Party will continue to support

American rights in Mexico, as elsewhere in the world, and at the same time to promote and strengthen friendship and confidence.

There has always been, as there always will be, a firm friendship with Canada. American and Canadian interests are in a large measure identical. Our relationship is one of fine mutual understanding and the recent exchange of diplomatic officers between the two countries is worthy of commendation.

The United States has an especial interest in the advancement and progress of all the Latin American countries. The policy of the Republican Party will always be a policy of thorough friendship and co-operation. In the case of Nicaragua, we are engaged in co-operation with the government of that country upon the task of assisting to restore and maintain peace, order and stability, and in no way to infringe upon her sovereign rights. The Marines, now in Nicaragua, are there to protect American lives and property and to aid in carrying out an agreement whereby we have undertaken to do what we can to restore and maintain order and to insure a fair and free election. Our policy absolutely repudiates any idea of conquest or exploitation, and is actuated solely by an earnest and sincere desire to assist a friendly and neighboring state which has appealed for aid in a great emergency. It is the same policy the United States has pursued in other cases in Central America.

The Administration has looked with keen sympathy on the tragic events in China. We have avoided interference in the internal affairs of that unhappy nation merely keeping sufficient naval and military forces in China to protect the lives of the Americans who are there on legitimate business and in still larger numbers for nobly humanitarian reasons. America has not been stampeded into making reprisals but, on the other hand, has consistently taken the position of leadership among the nations in a policy of wise moderation. We shall always be glad to be of assistance to China when our duty is clear.

The Republican Party maintains the traditional American policy of noninterference in the political affairs of other nations. This government has definitely refused membership in the League of Nations and to assume any obligations under the covenant of the League.

On this we stand.

In accordance, however, with the long established American practice of giving aid and assistance to other peoples, we have most usefully assisted by co-operation in the humanitarian and technical work undertaken by the League, without involving ourselves in European politics by accepting membership.

The Republican Party has always given and will continue to give its support to the development of American foreign trade, which makes for domestic prosperity. During this administration extraordinary strides have been made in opening up new markets for American produce and manufacture. Through these foreign contacts a mutually better international understanding has been reached which aids in the maintenance of world peace.

The Republican Party promises a firm and consistent support of American persons and legitimate American interests in all parts of the world. This support will never contravene the rights of other nations. it will always have in mind and support in every way the progressive development of international law, since it is through the operation of just laws, as well as through the growth of friendly understanding, that world peace will be made permanent. To that end the Republican Party pledges itself to aid and assist in the perfection of principles of international law and the settlement of international disputes.

CIVIL SERVICE

The merit system in government service originated with and has been developed by the Republican Party. The great majority of our public service employees are now secured through and maintained in the government service rules. Steps have already been taken by the Republican Congress to make the service more attractive as to wages and retirement privileges, and we commend what has been done, as a step in the right direction.

AGRICULTURE

The agricultural problem is national in scope and, as such, is recognized by the Republican Party which pledges its strength and energy to the solution of the same. Realizing that many farmers are facing problems more difficult than those which are the portion of many other basic industries, the party is anxious to aid in every way possible. Many of our farmers are still going through readjustments, a relic of the years directly following the great war. All the farmers are being called on to meet new and perplexing conditions created by foreign competition, the complexities of domestic marketing, labor problems, and a steady increase in local and state taxes.

The general depression in a great basic industry inevitably reacts upon the conditions in the country as a whole and cannot be ignored. It is a matter of satisfaction that the desire to help in the correction of agricultural wrongs and conditions is not confined to any one section of our country or any particular group.

The Republican Party and the Republican Administration, particularly during the last five years, have settled many of the most distressing problems as they have arisen, and the achievements in aid of agriculture are properly a part of this record. The Republican Congresses have been most responsive in the matter of agricultural appropriations, not only to meet crop emergencies, but for the extension and development of the activities of the Department of Agriculture.

The protection of the American farmer against foreign farm competition and foreign trade practices has been vigorously carried on by the Department of State. The right of the farmers to engage in collective buying and cooperative selling as provided for by the Capper–Volstead Act of 1922 has been promulgated through the Department of Agriculture and the Department of Justice, which have given most valuable aid and assistance to the heads of the farm organizations. The Treasury Department and the proper committees of Congress have lightened the tax burden on farming communities, and through the Federal Farm Loan System there has been made available to the farmers of the nation one billion eight hundred fifty millions of dollars for loaning purposes at a low rate of interest, and through the Intermediate Credit Banks six hundred fifty-five million dollars of short term credits have been made available to the farmers. The Post Office Department has systematically and generously extended the Rural Free Delivery routes into even the most sparsely settled communities.

When a shortage of transportation facilities threatened to deprive the farmers of their opportunity to reach waiting markets overseas, the President, appreciative and sensitive of the condition and the possible loss to the communities, ordered the reconditioning of Shipping board vessels, thus relieving a great emergency.

Last, but not least, the Federal Tariff Commission has at all times shown a willingness under the provisions of the Flexible Tariff Act to aid the farmers when foreign competition, made possible by low wage scales abroad, threatened to deprive our farmers of their domestic markets. Under this Act the President has increased duties on wheat, flour, mill feed, and dairy products. Numerous other farm products are now being investigated by the Tariff Commission.

We promise every assistance in the reorganization of the marketing system on sounder and more economical lines and, where diversification is needed, Government financial assistance during the period of transition.

The Republican Party pledges itself to the enactment of legislation creating a Federal Farm Board clothed with the necessary powers to promote the establishment of a farm marketing system of farmer-owned-and-controlled stabilization corporations or associations to prevent and control surpluses through orderly distribution.

We favor adequate tariff protection to such of our agricultural products as are affected by foreign competition.

We favor, without putting the Government into business, the establishment of a Federal system of organization for co-operative and orderly marketing of farm products.

The vigorous efforts of this Administration towards broadening our exports market will be continued.

The Republican Party pledges itself to the development and enactment of measures which will place the agricultural interests of America on a basis of economic equality with other industries to insure its prosperity and success.

MINING

The money value of the mineral products of the country is second only to agriculture. We lead the countries of the world in the production of coal, iron, copper and silver. The nation suffers as a whole from any disturbance in the securing of any one of these minerals, and particularly when the coal supply is affected.

The mining industry has always been self-sustaining, but we believe that the Government should make every effort to aid the industry by protection by removing any restrictions which may be hampering its development, and by increased technical and economic research investigations which are necessary for its welfare and normal development. The Party is anxious, hopeful, and willing to assist in any feasible plan for the stabilization of the coal mining industry, which will work with justice to the miners, consumers and producers.

HIGHWAYS

Under the Federal Aid Road Act, adopted by the Republican Congress in 192 1, and supplemented by generous appropriations each year, road construction has made greater advancement than for many decades previous. Improved highway conditions is a gauge of our rural developments and our commercial activity. We pledge our support to continued appropriations for this work commensurate with our needs and resources.

We favor the construction of roads and trails in our national forests necessary to their protection and utilization. In appropriations therefor the taxes which these lands would pay if taxable should be considered as a controlling factor.

LABOR

The Labor record of the Republican Party stands unchallenged. For 52 of the 72 years of our national existence Republican Administrations have prevailed. Today American labor enjoys the highest wage and the highest standard of living throughout the world. Through the saneness and soundness of Republican rule the American workman is paid a "real wage" which allows comfort for himself and his dependents, and an opportunity and leisure for advancement. It is not surprising that the foreign workman, whose greatest ambition still is to achieve a "living wage," should look with longing towards America as the goal of his desires.

The ability to pay such wages and maintain such a standard comes from the wisdom of the protective legislation which the Republican Party has placed upon the national statute books, the tariff which bars cheap foreign-made goods from the American market and provides continuity of employment for our workmen and fair profits for the manufacturers, the restriction of immigration which not only prevents the glutting of our labor market, but allows to our newer immigrants a greater opportunity to secure a footing in their upward struggle.

The Party favors freedom in wage contracts, the right of collective bargaining by free and responsible agents of their own choosing, which develops and maintains that purposeful co-operation which gains its chief incentive through voluntary agreement.

We believe that injunctions in labor disputes have in some instances been abused and have given rise to a serious question for legislation.

The Republican Party pledges itself to continue its efforts to maintain this present standard of living and high wage scale.

RAILROADS

Prompt and effective railroad service at the lowest rates which will provide for its maintenance and allow a reasonable return to the investor so they may be encouraged to advance new capital for acquired developments, has long been recognized by the Republican Party as a necessity of national existence.

We believe that the present laws under which our railroads are regulated are soundly based on correct principles, the spirit of which must always be preserved. Because, however, of changes in the public demands, trade conditions and of the character of the competition, which even the greatest railroads are now being called upon to meet, we feet that in the light of this new experience possible modifications or amendments, the need of which is proved, should be considered.

The Republican Party initiated and set in operation the Interstate Commerce Commission. This body has developed a system of railroad control and regulation which has given to the transportation public an opportunity not only to make suggestions for the improvement of railroad service, but to protest against discriminatory rates or schedules. We commend the work which that body is accomplishing under mandate of law in considering these matters and seeking to distribute equitably the burden of transportation between commodities based on their ability to bear the same.

MERCHANT MARINE

The Republican Party, stands for the American-built, American-owned, and American-operated merchant marine. The enactment of the White–Jones Bill is in line with a policy which the party has long advocated.

Under this measure, substantial aid and encouragement are offered for the building in American yards of new and modern ships which will carry the American flag.

The Republican Party does not believe in government ownership or operation, and stands specifically for the sale of the present government vessels to private owners when appropriate arrangements can be made. Pending such a sale, and because private owners are not ready as yet to operate on certain of the essential trade routes, the bill enacted allows the maintenance of these necessary lines under government control till such transfer can be made.

MISSISSIPPI FLOOD RELIEF AND CONTROL

The Mississippi Valley flood in which seven hundred thousand of our fellow citizens were placed in peril of life, and which destroyed hundreds of million of dollars' worth of property, was met with energetic action by the Republican Administration.

During this disaster the President mobilized every public and private agency under the direction of Secretary Hoover of the Department of Commerce and Dwight Davis, the Secretary of War. Thanks to their joint efforts, a great loss of life was prevented and everything possible was done to rehabilitate the people in their homes and to relieve suffering and distress.

Congress promptly passed legislation authorizing the expenditure of $325,000,000 for the construction of flood control works, which it is believed will prevent the recurrence of such a disaster.

RADIO

We stand for the administration of the radio facilities of the United States under wise and expert government supervision which will

(1) Secure to every home in the nation, whether city or country, the great educational and inspirational values of broadcast programs, adequate in number and varied in character, and

(2) Assign the radio communication channels, regional, continental, and transoceanic, — in the best interest of the American business man, the American farmer, and the American public generally.

WATERWAYS

Cheaper transportation for bulk goods from the midwest agricultural sections to the sea is recognized by the Republican Party as a vital factor for the relief of agriculture. To that end we favor the continued development in inland and in intra-coastal waterways as an essential part of our transportation system.

The Republican Administration during the last four years initiated the systematic development of the Mississippi system of inland transportation lanes, and it proposes to carry on this modernization of transportation to speedy completion. Great improvements have been made during this administration in our harbors, and the party pledges itself to continue these activities for the modernization of our national equipment.

VETERANS

Our country is honored whenever it bestows relief on those who have faithfully served its flag. The Republican Party, appreciative of this solemn obligation and honor, has made its sentiments evident in Congress. Our expenditures for the benefit of all our veterans now aggregate 750 million dollars annually. Increased hospital facilities have been provided, payments in compensation have more than doubled, and in the matter of rehabilitations, pensions, and insurance, generous provision has been made. The administration of laws dealing with the relief of veterans and their dependents has been a difficult task, but every effort has been made to carry service to the veteran and bring about not only a better and generous interpretation of the law, but a sympathetic consideration of the many problems of the veteran. Full and adequate relief for our disabled veterans is our aim, and we commend the action of Congress in further liberalizing the laws applicable to veterans' relief.

PUBLIC UTILITIES

Republican Congresses and Administrations have steadily strengthened the Interstate Commerce Commission. The protection of the public from exactions or burdens in rates for service by reason of monopoly control, and the protection of the smaller organizations from suppression in their own field, has been a fundamental idea in all regulatory enactments. While recognizing that at times Federal regulations might be more effective than State regulations in controlling intrastate utilities, the Party favors and has sustained State regulations, believing that such responsibility in the end will create a force of State public opinion which will be more effective in preventing discriminations and injustices.

CONSERVATION

We believe in the practical application of the conservation principle by the wise development of our natural resources. The measure of development is our national requirement, and avoidance of waste so that future generations may share in this natural wealth. The Republican policy is to prevent monopolies in the control and utilization of natural resources. Under the General Leasing Law, enacted by a Republican Congress, the ownership of the mineral estate remains in the Government, but development occurs through private capital and energy. Important for the operation of this law is the classification and appraisement of public lands according to their mineral content and value. Over five hundred million acres of public land have been thus classified.

To prevent wasteful exploitation of our oil products, President Coolidge appointed an Oil Conservation Board, which is now conducting an inquiry into all phases of petroleum production, in the effort to devise a national policy for the conservation and proper utilization of our oil resources.

The Republican Party has been forehanded in assuring the development of water power in accordance with public interest. A policy of permanent public retention of the power sites on public land and power privileges in domestic and international navigable streams, and one-third of the potential water power resources in the United States on public domain, has been assured by the Federal Water Powers Act, passed by a Republican Congress.

LAW ENFORCEMENT

We reaffirm the American Constitutional Doctrine as announced by George Washington in his "Farewell Address," to-wit:

"The Constitution which at any time exists until changed by the explicit and authentic act by the whole people is sacredly obligatory upon all."

We also reaffirm the attitude of the American people toward the Federal Constitution as declared by Abraham Lincoln:

"We are by both duty and inclination bound to stick by that Constitution in all its letter and spirit from beginning to end. I am for the honest enforcement of the Constitution. Our safety, our liberty, depends upon preserving the Constitution of the United States, as our forefathers made it inviolate."

The people through the method provided by the Constitution have written the Eighteenth Amendment into the Constitution. The Republican Party pledges itself and its nominees to the observance and vigorous enforcement of this provision of the Constitution.

HONESTY IN GOVERNMENT

We stand for honesty in government, for the appointment of officials whose integrity cannot be questioned. We deplore the fact that any official has ever fallen from this high standard and that certain American citizens of both parties have so far forgotten their duty as citizens as to traffic in national interests for private gain. We have prosecuted and shall always prosecute any official who subordinates his public duty to his personal interest.

The Government today is made up of thousands of conscientious, earnest, self-sacrificing men and women, whose single thought is service to the nation.

We pledge ourselves to maintain and, if possible, to improve the quality of this great company of Federal employees.

CAMPAIGN EXPENDITURES

Economy, honesty, and decency in the conduct of political campaigns are a necessity if representative government is to be preserved to the people and political parties are to hold the respect of the citizens at large.

The Campaign of 1924 complied with all these requirements. It was a campaign, the expenses of which were carefully budgeted in advance, and, which, at the close, presented a surplus and not a deficit.

There will not be any relaxing of resolute endeavor to keep our elections clean, honest and free from taint of any kind. The improper use of money in governmental and political affairs is a great national evil. One of the most effective remedies for this abuse is publicity in all matters touching campaign contributions and expenditures. The Republican Party, beginning not later than August 1, 1928, and every 30 days thereafter, — the last publication being not later than five days before the election — will file with the Committees of the House and Senate a complete account of all contributions, the names of the contributors, the amounts expended, and for what purposes, and will at all times hold its records and books touching such matters open for inspection.

The party further pledges that it will not create, or permit to be created, any deficit which shall exist at the close of the campaign.

RECLAMATION

Federal reclamation of arid lands is a Republican policy, adopted under President Roosevelt, carried forward by succeeding Republican Presidents, and put upon a still higher plane of efficiency and production by President Coolidge. It has increased the wealth of the nation and made the West more prosperous.

An intensive study of the methods and practices of reclamation has been going on for the past four years under the direction of the Department of the Interior in an endeavor to create broader human opportunities and their financial and economic success. The money value of the crops raised on reclamation projects is showing a steady and gratifying increase as well as the number of farms and people who have settled on the lands.

The continuation of a surplus of agricultural products in the selling markets of the world has influenced the Department to a revaluation of plans and projects. It has adopted a ten-year program for the completion of older projects and will hold other suggestions in abeyance until the surveys now under way as to the entire scope of the work are completed.

COMMERCIAL AVIATION

Without governmental grants or subsidies and entirely by private initiative, the nation has made extraordinary advances in the field of commercial aviation. Over 20,000 miles of air mail service privately operated are now being flown daily, and the broadening of this service is an almost weekly event. Because of our close relations with our sister republics on the south and our neighbor on the north, it is fitting our first efforts should be to establish an air communication with Latin-America and Canada.

The achievements of the aviation branches of the Army and Navy are all to the advantage of commercial aviation, and in the Mississippi flood disaster the work performed by civil and military aviators was of inestimable value.

The development of a system of aircraft registration, inspection and control is a credit to the Republican Administration, which, quick to appreciate the importance of this new transportation development, created machinery for its safeguarding.

IMMIGRATION

The Republican Party believes that in the interest of both native and foreign-born wage-earners, it is necessary to restrict immigration. Unrestricted immigration would result in widespread unemployment and in the breakdown of the American standard of living. Where, however, the law works undue hardships by depriving the immigrant of the comfort and society of those bound by close family ties, such modification should be adopted as will afford relief.

We commend Congress for correcting defects for humanitarian reasons and for providing an effective system of examining prospective immigrants in their home countries.

NATURALIZATION

The priceless heritage of American citizenship is our greatest gift to our friends of foreign birth. Only those who will be loyal to our institutions, who are here in conformity with our laws, and who are in sympathy with our national traditions, ideals, and principles, should be naturalized.

NAVY

We pledge ourselves to round out and maintain the Navy in all types of combatant ships to the full ratio provided for the United States by the Washington Treaty for the Limitation of Naval Armament and any amendment thereto.

HAWAII–ALASKA

We favor a continuance for the Territory of Hawaii of Federal assistance in harbor improvements, the appropriation of its share of federal funds and the systematic extension of the settlement of public lands by the Hawaiian race.

We indorse the policy of the present administration with reference to Alaska and favor a continuance of the constructive development of the territory.

WOMEN AND PUBLIC SERVICE

Four years ago at the Republican National Convention in Cleveland women members of the National Committee were welcomed into full association and responsibility in party management. During the four years which have passed they have carried with their men associates an equal share of all responsibilities and their contribution to the success of the 1924 campaign is well recognized.

The Republican Party, which from the first has sought to bring this development about, accepts wholeheartedly equality on the part of women, and in the public service it can present a record of appointments of women in the legal, diplomatic, judicial, treasury and other governmental departments. We earnestly urge on the women that they participate even more generally than now in party management and activity.

NATIONAL DEFENSE

We believe that in time of war the nation should draft for its defense not only its citizens but also every resource which may contribute to success. The country demands that should the United States ever again be called upon to defend itself by arms, the President be empowered to draft such material resources and such services as may be required, and to stabilize the prices of services and essential commodities, whether utilized in actual warfare or private activity.

OUR INDIAN CITIZENS

National citizenship was conferred upon all native born Indians in the United States by the General Indian Enfranchisement Act of 1924. We favor the creation of a Commission to be appointed by the President including one or more Indian citizens to investigate and report to Congress upon the existing system of the administration of Indian affairs and to report any inconsistencies that may be found to exist between the system and the rights of the Indian citizens of the United States. We also favor the repeal of any law and the termination of any administrative practice which may be inconsistent with Indian citizenship, to the end that the Federal guardianship existing over the persons and properties of Indian tribal communities may not work a prejudice to the personal and property rights of Indian citizens of the United States. The treaty and property rights of the Indians of the United States must be guaranteed to them.

THE NEGRO

We renew our recommendation that the Congress enact at the earliest possible date a Federal Anti-Lynching Law so that the full influence of the Federal Government may be wielded to exterminate this hideous crime.

HOME RULE

We believe in the essential unity of the American people. Sectionalism in any form is destructive of national life. The Federal Government should zealously protect the national and international rights of its citizens. It should be equally zealous to respect and maintain the rights of the States and territories and to uphold the vigor and balance of our dual system of government. The Republican party has always given its energies to supporting the Government in this direction when any question has arisen.

There are certain other well-defined Federal obligations such as interstate commerce, the development of rivers and harbors, and the guarding and conservation of national resources. The effort, which, however, is being continually made to have the Federal Government move into the field of state activities, has never had, and never will have the support of the Republican Party. In the majority of the cases state citizens and officers are most pressing in their desire to have the Federal Government take over these state functions. This is to be deplored for it weakens the sense of initiative and creates a feeling of dependence which is unhealthy and unfortunate for the whole body politic.

There is a real need of restoring the individual and local sense principles; there is a real need of restoring the individual and local sense of responsibility and self-reliance; there is a real need for the people once more to grasp the fundamental fact that under our system of government they are expected to solve many problems themselves through their municipal and State governments, and to combat the tendency that is all too common to turn to the Federal Government as the easiest and least burdensome method of lightening their own responsibilities.

Socialist Platform

PREAMBLE

We Americans are told that we live in the most prosperous country in the world. Certainly, our natural resources, our mechanical equipment, our physical power, the technical capacity of our engineers and the skill of our workers in farm and factory make it possible for us to attain a level of well-being of which our fathers never dared to dream.

Yet poverty abounds. The owners of our natural resources and industrial equipment and the government which they have made virtually their tool have not given us plenty, freedom or peace in any such degree as we have the right and duty to demand.

Men are hungry while farmers go bankrupt for lack of effective demand for food. Tenant farming has reached a proportion of almost 40 per cent; more than 40 per cent of the value of farm lands is covered by mortgages. Industrial workers are scarcely better off. In good years there are at least 1,000,000 unemployed. By a conservative estimate in these times of stock market prosperity the number has arisen to 4,000,000. About 1/3 of those of our population 65 years of age and upward are at least partially dependent upon some form of charity. While real wages have risen for certain groups they have risen scarcely more than half the increase of productive power of the workers. And what gains have been made are far from universal as the misery of textile workers and the tragedy of the coal fields — to cite only two examples — abundantly prove. In fact, at the present time a majority of workers obtain a wage insufficient to maintain themselves and families in health and decency. Furthermore the rapid increase in the use of machinery and the growing intensity of work are leading to quicker exhaustion and greater insecurity.

UNIONS BEREFT OF RIGHTS BY CLASS JUSTICE

Meanwhile the owning class has been using the government to curtail the power of the workers whose organized might, especially through their unions, has been chiefly responsible for whatever material gains they have made. To curb the workers, civil liberties are denied, injunctions are invoked against union activities and the courts are made the instruments of that class justice of which the Mooney case and the legalized murder of Sacco and Vanzetti were conspicuous examples.

Not only plenty and freedom but peace is endangered by this system under which the many are exploited for the profit of the few. Sons of the workers now die in President Coolidge's infamous little imperialist war in Nicaragua, as they died in President Wilson's similar wars in Haiti, Santo Domingo and Mexico, and above all in that great imperialistic war born of the trade and financial rivalries of the nations which cost our country forty billion dollars and hundreds of thousands of lives.

From the wars, waste and cruelty of a system where the rightful heritage of the workers is the private property of the few only the united efforts of farmers and workers of hand and brain, through their cooperatives, unions and political party, can save us. We must make government in cities, states and nation the servant of the people. That requires our own political party. We cannot place our trust in "good men" or political Messiahs. Bitter experience has proved that we cannot trust the alternate rule of the Republican and Democratic parties. They belong to the landlords, bankers, oil speculators, coal and power barons, in short to the capitalist class which finances them. Under their control the government by what it does and leaves undone, by its calculated inefficiency as well as its repression and corruption, makes our alleged democracy largely an illusion. Corruption is natural under parties which are the tools of the forces of privilege. It has become accepted even by the men who are victims of it.

LABOR'S WEAPON IN THE CLASS STRUGGLE

These things need not be. The Socialist Party offers itself as the political party of the producing classes, the workers in farm, factory, mine or office. It is our political weapon in the class struggle and in its triumph lies our hope of ending that struggle. Our record proves our good faith. As the only democratic labor party in the United States, we stand now as always, in America and in all lands, for the collective ownership of natural resources and basic industries and their democratic management for the use and benefit of all instead of the private profit of the privileged few.

With this ultimate aim in view, the Socialist Party enters the presidential campaign of 1928 with the following program:

PUBLIC OWNERSHIP AND CONSERVATION

To recover the rightful heritage of the people we propose:

1. Nationalization of our natural resources, beginning with the coal mines and water sites, particularly at Boulder Dam and Muscle Shoals.

2. A publicly owned giant power system under which the federal government shall cooperate with the states and municipalities in the distribution of electrical energy to the people at cost. Only when public agencies have full control over the generation, transmission and distribution of electrical power can the consumers be guaranteed against exploitation by the great electrical interests of the country. Public ownership of these and other industries must include employee representation in the management and the principle of collective bargaining must be recognized.

3. National ownership and democratic management of railroads and other means of transportation and communication.

4. An adequate national program for flood control, flood relief, reforestation, irrigation and reclamation.

UNEMPLOYMENT RELIEF

To relieve the tragic misery of millions of unemployed workers and their families we propose:

1. Immediate governmental relief of the unemployed by the extension of all public works and a program of long range planning of public works following the present depression. All persons thus employed to be engaged at hours and wages fixed by bona-fide labor unions.

2. Loans to states and municipalities without interest for the purpose of carrying on public works and the taking of such other measures as will lessen widespread misery.

3. A system of unemployment insurance.

4. The nation-wide extension of public employment agencies in cooperation with city federations of labor.

LABOR LEGISLATION

The lives and well-being of the producers and their families should be the first charge on society. We therefore urge:

1. A system of health and accident insurance and of old age pension as well as unemployment insurance. As long as workers are dependent primarily upon their employers rather than on the community for protection against the exigencies of old age, sickness, accident and unemployment, employers hostile or indifferent to the labor movement will be able to use their private insurance schemes as powerful weapons against organized labor.

2. Shortening the workday in keeping with the steadily increasing productivity of labor due to improvements in machinery and methods.

3. Securing to every worker a rest period of no less than two days in each week.

4. Enacting of an adequate federal anti-child labor amendment.

5. Abolition of the brutal exploitation of convicts under the contract system and substitution of a cooperative organization of industries in penitentiaries and workshops for the benefit of convicts and their dependents, the products to be used in public institutions, and the convict workers to be employed at wages current in the industry.

TAXATION

For the proper support of government and as a step toward social justice we propose:

1. Increase of taxation on high income levels, of corporation taxes and inheritance taxes, the proceeds to be used for old age pensions and other forms of social insurance.

2. Appropriation by taxation of the annual rental value of all land held for speculation.

CIVIL LIBERTIES

To secure to the people the civil rights without which democracy is impossible, we demand:

1. Federal legislation to enforce the first amendment to the constitution so as to guarantee effectually freedom of speech, press and assembly, and to penalize any official who interferes with the civil rights of any citizen.

2. Abolition of injunctions in labor disputes.

3. Repeal of the espionage law and of other repressive legislation and restoration of civil and political rights to those unjustly convicted under war time laws with reimbursement for time served.

4. Legislation protecting foreign born workers from deportation and refusal of citizenship on account of political opinions.

5. Modification of immigration laws to permit the reuniting of families and to offer a refuge for those fleeing from political or religious persecution.

6. Abolition of detective agencies engaged in interstate business.

ANTI-LYNCHING

As a measure of protection for the oppressed, especially for our Negro fellow citizens, we propose:

Enactment of the Berger anti-lynching bill making participation in lynching a felony.

POLITICAL DEMOCRACY

The constitution of the United States was drafted in 1787 and was designed to meet conditions utterly different from those prevailing today. In order to make our form of government better suited to exigencies of the times, we propose the immediate calling of a constitutional convention. A modernized constitution should provide, among other things, for the election of the President and Vice-President by direct popular vote of the people, for reduction of the representation in Congress of those states where large sections of the citizens are disfranchised by force or fraud, and proportional representation, and for the abolition of the usurped power of the Supreme Court to pass upon the constitutionality of legislation enacted by Congress.

CREDIT AND BANKING

For our emancipation from the money trust, we propose:

Nationalization of the banking and currency system, beginning with extension of the service of the postal savings banks to cover every department of the banking business.

FARM RELIEF

The Socialist Party believes that the farmer is entitled to special consideration because of the importance of agriculture, because of the farmers' present economic plight and because the farmer is unable to control the prices of what he buys and what he sells. Many of the party's demands, including public development of electrical energy, nationalization of coal and railroads, and reform of the credit system will be of distinct benefit to the farmer. As a further means of agricultural relief, we propose:

1. Acquisition by bona fide cooperative societies and by federal, state and municipal governments of grain elevators, stockyards, storage warehouses and other distributing agencies and the conduct of these services on a non-profit basis.

2. Encouragement of farmers' cooperative purchasing and marketing societies and of credit agencies.

3. Social insurance against losses due to adverse weather conditions, such as hail, drought, cyclone and flood.

INTERNATIONAL RELATIONS

We are unalterably opposed to imperialism and militarism. Therefore we propose:

1. Immediate withdrawal of American forces from Nicaragua and abandonment of the policy of military intervention in Central America and other countries.

2. That all private loans and investments of American citizens in foreign countries shall be made at the sole risk of the bondholders and investors. The United States government shall not resort to any military or other coercive intervention with foreign governments for the protection of such loans and investments.

3. Cancellation of all war debts due the United States from its former associated powers on condition of a simultaneous cancellation of all interallied debts and a corresponding remission of the reparation obligations of the Central Powers and on the further condition that our debtors reduce their military expenditures below pre-war level. The Socialist Party especially denounces the debt settling policy of our government in favoring the Fascist dictatorship of Italy and thereby helping to perpetuate the political enslavement of the Italian nation.

4. Recognizing both the services and the limitations of the League of Nations, the need of revision of its covenant and the Treaty of Versailles, we unite with the workers of Europe in demanding that the League be made all inclusive and democratic, and that the machinery for the revision of the peace treaty under article 19 of the covenant be elaborated and made effective. We favor the entry of the United States at the time and under conditions which will further these clauses and promote the peace of the world.

5. The recognition of the Russian government.

6. Aggressive activity against militarism, against the large navy and army program of our present administration, and in behalf of international disarmament.

7. Treaties outlawing war and the substitution of peaceful methods for the settlement of international disputes.

8. Independence of the Philippines on terms agreed upon in negotiations with the Filipinos; autonomy for Porto Rico and civil government for the Virgin Islands.

Biography of Secretary of Commerce Herbert C. Hoover
Who's Who In America, 1928

HOOVER, Herbert Clark, secretary of commerce; b. West Branch, Ia., Aug. 10, 1874; s. Jesse Clark and Hulda Randall (Minthron) H.; A.B. in Engring., Stanford, 1895; hon. degrees from Brown U., U. of Pa., Harvard, Yale, Columbia, Princeton, Johns Hopkins, George Washington, Dartmouth, Rutgers, University of Alabama, Oberlin, Liege, Brussels, Warsaw, Cracow, Oxford, Rensselaer, Tufts, Swarthmore, Williams, Manchester, Prague, Ghent, Lemberg, Cornell Coll.; *m.* Lou Henry, of Monterey, Calif., 1899; children — Herbert Clark, Allan Henry. Professional work in mines, rys., metall. works, in U.S., Mexico, Can., Australia, Italy, Great Britain, South Africa, India, China, Russia, etc., 1895–1913. Represented Panama-Pacific Internat. Expn. in Europe, 1913–14; chmn. Am. Relief Com., London, Eng., 1914–15; chmn. Commn. for Relief in Belgium, 1915–19; U.S. food administrator, June 1917–July 1, 1919; served as mem. War Trade Council; was chmn. U.S. Grain Corpn., U.S. Sugar Equalization Bd., Interallied Food Council, Food Sect. Supreme Economic Council, European Coal Council; dir. various economic measures in Europe during Armistice, including orgn. of food supplies to Poland, Serbia, Czechoslovakia, Germany, Austria, Roumania, Armenia, Baltic States, etc., 1919; chmn. Am. Relief Administration, engaged in Children's Relief in Europe, 1919–; v. chmn. Pres. Wilson's 2d Industrial Conf., 1920; chmn. European Relief Council, 1920–; apptd. sec. of commerce by President Harding, Mar. 5, 1921, reapptd. by President Coolidge. Chmn. President's Conf. on Unemployment, Sept. 20, 1921; mem. advisory com. Limitation of Armaments Conf., Nov. 1921; chmn. Colo. River Commn.; chmn. Spl. Mississippi Flood Relief Commn., 1927. Awarded gold medals, Civic Forum, Nat. Inst. Social Sciences, Nat. Acad. Sciences, Am. Inst. Mining and Metall. Engrs., Western Soc. Engrs. (all of U.S.), City of Lille, City of Warsaw; Audiffret prize, French Acad.; freeman, Belgian, Polish, Esthonian cities. Trustee Stanford U. since 1912. Mem. Am. Inst. Mining and Metal]. Engrs. (pres. 1920), Am. Engring. Council (pres. 1921), Am. Child Health Assn. (pres. 1922), World War Debt Com., etc. Author: American Individualism, 1922; also published addresses and tech. articles. Joint translator Agricola de Re Metallica. Home: Stanford University, Calif. Address: Dept. of Commerce, Washington, D.C.

Biography of Governor Alfred E. Smith
Who's Who In America, 1928

SMITH, Alfred Emanuel, governor; b. N.Y. City, Dec. 30, 1873; s. Alfred Emanuel and Catherine (Mulvehill) S.; ed. parochial sch.; *m.* Catherine A. Dunn, N.Y. City, 1900; children — Alfred E., Emily (Mrs. J. A. Warner), Catherine (Mrs. Francis Quillinan), Arthur, Walter. Clerk in office commr. of jurors, N.Y. City, 1895–1903; mem. N.Y. Assembly, 1903–15; became Dem. leader in Assembly, 1911, speaker of Assembly, 1913; del, State Consti. Conv., 1915; sheriff of New York Co., 1915–17; pres. Bd. of Aldermen of Greater New York, 1917; gov. of N.Y., 4 terms, 1919–1920, and 1923–1928 inclusive; nominated for pres. of U.S., 1928. Mem. Soc. of Tammany. Catholic. Clubs: Nat. Democratic, Press (New York); Ft. Orange (Albany); Wolferts Roost Country. Home: 25 Oliver St., New York, N.Y. Address: Albany, N.Y.

Open Letter from Charles C. Marshall to Governor Alfred E. Smith
The Atlantic Monthly
April 1927

New York lawyer Charles C. Marshall brought to the surface questions that were in the minds of many — reasonable men as well as bigots — concerning the alleged dual loyalties of American Roman Catholics to the Constitution and to the Holy See.

Sir: — The American people take pride in viewing the progress of an American citizen from the humble estate in which his life began toward the highest office within the gift of the nation. It is for this reason that your candidacy for the Presidential nomination has stirred the enthusiasm of a great body of your fellow citizens. They know and rejoice in the hardship and the struggle which have fashioned you as a leader of men. They know your fidelity to the morality you have advocated in public and private life and to the religion you have revered; your great record of public trusts successfully and honestly discharged; your spirit of fair play, and justice even to your political opponents. Partisanship bids fair to quail before the challenge of your personality, and men who vote habitually against your party are pondering your candidacy with sincere respect; and yet — through all this tribute there is a note of doubt, a sinister accent of interrogation, not as to intentional rectitude and moral purpose, but as to certain conceptions which your fellow citizens attribute to you as a loyal and conscientious Roman Catholic, which in their minds are irreconcilable with that Constitution which as President you must support and defend, and with the principles of civil and religious liberty on which American institutions are based.

To this consideration no word of yours, or on your behalf, has yet been addressed. Its discussion in the interests of the public weal is obviously necessary, and yet a strange reticence avoids it, often with the unjust and withering attribution of bigotry or prejudice as the unworthy motive of its introduction. Undoubtedly a large part of the public would gladly avoid a subject the discussion of which is so unhappily associated with rancor and malevolence, and yet to avoid the subject is to neglect the profoundest interests in our national welfare.

American life has developed into a variety of religious beliefs and ethical systems, religious and nonreligious, whose claims press more and more upon public attention. None of these presents a more definite philosophy or makes a more positive demand upon the attention and reason of mankind than your venerable Church, which recently at Chicago, in the greatest religious demonstration that the world has ever seen, declared her presence and her power in American life. Is not the time ripe and the occasion opportune for a declaration, if it can be made, that shall clear away all doubt as to the reconcilability of her status and her claims with American constitutional principles? With such a statement the only question as to your proud eligibility to the Presidential office would disappear, and the doubts of your fellow citizens not of the Roman Catholic Church would be instantly resolved in your favor.

The conceptions to which we refer are not superficial....

These conceptions have been recognized before by Roman Catholics as a potential obstacle to their participation in public office, Pope Leo XIII himself declaring, in one of his encyclical letters, that "it may in some places be true that for most urgent and just reasons it is by no means expedient for (Roman) Catholics to engage in public affairs or to take an active part in politics."

It is indeed true that a loyal and conscientious Roman Catholic could and would discharge his oath of office with absolute fidelity to his moral standards. As to that in general, and as to you in particular, your fellow citizens entertain no doubt. But those moral standards differ essentially from the moral standards of all men not Roman Catholics. They are derived from the basic political doctrine of the Roman Catholic Church, asserted against repeated challenges for fifteen hundred years, that God has divided all power over men between the secular State and that Church. Thus Pope Leo XIII, in 1885, in his encyclical letter on *The Christian Constitution of States*, says: "The Almighty has appointed the charge of the human race between two powers, the ecclesiastical and the civil, the one being set over divine, and the other over human things."

The deduction is inevitable that, as all power over human affairs, not given to the State by God, is given by God to the Roman Catholic Church, no other churches or religious or ethical societies have in theory any direct power from God and are without direct divine sanction, and therefore without natural right to function on the same basis as the Roman Catholic Church in the religious and moral affairs of the State. The result is that that Church, if true to her basic political doctrine is hopelessly committed to that intolerance that has disfigured so much of her history. This is frankly admitted by Roman Catholic authorities.

Pope Pius IX in the famous Syllabus (1864) said: "To hold that national churches, withdrawn from the authority of the Roman Pontiff and altogether separated, can be established, is error."

That great compendium of Roman Catholic teaching, the *Catholic Encyclopedia*, declares that the Roman Catholic Church "regards dogmatic intolerance, not alone as her incontestable right, but as her sacred duty." It is obvious that such convictions leave nothing in theory of the religious and moral rights of those who are not Roman Catholics....

Pope Leo XIII is explicit on this point: "The (Roman Catholic) Church, indeed, deems it unlawful to place the various forms of divine worship on the same footing as the true religion, but does not, on that account, condemn those rulers who, for the sake of securing some great good or of hindering some great evil, allow patiently custom or usage to be a kind of sanction for each kind of religion having its place in the State."

*   *   *

Furthermore, the doctrine of the Two Powers, in effect and theory, inevitably makes the Roman Catholic Church at times sovereign and paramount over the State. It is true that in theory the doctrine assigns to the secular State jurisdiction over secular matters and to the Roman Catholic Church jurisdiction over matters of faith and morals, each jurisdiction being exclusive of the other within undisputed lines. But the universal experience of mankind has demonstrated, and reason teaches, that many questions must arise between the State and the Roman Catholic Church in respect to which it is impossible to determine to the satisfaction of both in which jurisdiction the matter at issue lies.

Here arises the irrepressible conflict. Shall the State or the Roman Catholic Church determine? The Constitution of the United States clearly ordains that the State shall determine the question. The Roman Catholic Church demands for itself the sole right to determine it, and holds that within the limits of that claim it is superior to and supreme over the State....

The Roman Catholic Church, of course, makes no claim, and never has made any claim, to jurisdiction over matters that *in her opinion are solely secular and civil*. She makes the claim obviously only when the matter in question is not, *in her opinion*, solely secular and civil. But as determination of jurisdiction, in a conflict with the State, rests solely in her sovereign discretion, no argument is needed to show that she may in theory and effect annihilate the rights of all who are not Roman Catholics, sweeping into the jurisdiction of a single religious society the most important interests of human wellbeing. The education of youth, the institution of marriage, the international relations of the State, and its domestic peace, as we shall proceed to show, are, in certain exigencies, wrested from the jurisdiction of the State, in which all citizens share, and confided to the jurisdiction of a single religious society in which all citizens cannot share, great numbers being excluded by the barriers of religious belief. Do you, sir, regard such claims as tolerable in a Republic that calls itself free?

And, in addition to all this, the exclusive powers of the Roman Catholic Church are claimed by her to be vested in and exercised by a sovereignty that is not only created therefor by the special act of God, but is foreign and extraterritorial to these United States and to all secular states. This sovereignty, by the highest Roman Catholic authority, that of Pope Leo XIII, is not only superior in theory to the sovereignty of the secular State, but is substituted upon earth in place of the authority of God himself.

We quote Pope Leo in his encyclical letter on *The Christian Constitution of States*: "Over the mighty multitude of mankind, God has set rulers with power to govern, and He has willed that one of them (the Pope) should be the head of all." We quote Pope Leo in his encyclical letter on *The Reunion of Christendom*: "We who hold upon this earth the place of God Almighty."

It follows naturally on all this that there is a conflict between authoritative Roman Catholic claims on the one side and our constitutional law and principles on the other. Pope Leo XIII says: "It is not lawful for the State, any more than for the individual, either to disregard all religious duties or to hold in equal favor different kinds of religion." But the Constitution of the United States declares otherwise: "Congress shall make no law respecting an establishment of religion or prohibiting the free exercise thereof."

Thus the Constitution declares the United States shall hold in equal favor different kinds of religion or no religion and the Pope declares it is not lawful to hold them in equal favor. Is there not here a quandary for that man who is at once a loyal churchman and a loyal citizen?

Americans indulge themselves in the felicitation that they have achieved an ideal religious situation in the United States. But Pope Leo, in his encyclical letter on *Catholicity in the United States*, asserts: "It would be very erroneous to draw the conclusion that in America is to be sought the type of the most desirable status of the Church." The modern world reposes in the comfortable reflection that the severance of Church and State has ended a long and unhappy conflict, when the same Pope calls our attention to the error of supposing "that it would be universally lawful or expedient for State and Church to be, as in America, dissevered and divorced."

Is our law, then, in papal theory, no law? Is it contrary to natural right? Is it in conflict with the will and fiat of Almighty God? Clearly the Supreme Court and Pope Leo are profoundly at variance....

Citizens who waver in your support would ask whether, as a Roman Catholic, you accept as authoritative the teaching of the Roman Catholic Church that in case of contradiction, making it impossible for the jurisdiction of that Church and the jurisdiction of the State to agree, the jurisdiction of the Church shall prevail; whether, as statesman, you accept the teaching of the Supreme Court of the United States that, in matters of religious practices which in the opinion of the State are inconsistent with its peace and safety, the jurisdiction of the State shall prevail; and, if you accept both teachings, how you will reconcile them.

*   *   *

It is true that in the famous Oregon School cases the Supreme Court of the United States held a state law unconstitutional that forbade parents to educate their children at church schools of every denomination. But there was no assertion in the law that the church schools in question gave instruction inconsistent with the peace and safety of the State and there was no allegation of that tenor in the pleadings. On the record the church schools were void of offense. But, had that feature existed in the cases, it would necessarily have led to a reversal of the decision. There would have been a conflict between Church and State as to whether the instruction was inconsistent with the peace and safety of the State. The Roman Catholic Church, if true to her doctrine and dogma, would have had to assert exclusive jurisdiction over the determination of this point. Equally the State, in self-preservation, would have had to assert exclusive jurisdiction. The conflict would have been irreconcilable. What would have been the results and what the test of a sincere and conscientious Roman Catholic in executive office or on the bench?

*   *   *

A direct conflict between the Roman Catholic Church and the State arises on the institution of marriage, through the claim of that Church that in theory in the case of all baptized persons, quite irrespective of specific consent, Protestants and Roman Catholics alike, jurisdiction touching marriage is wrested from the State and appropriated to the Roman Catholic Church, its exercise reposing ultimately in the Pope....

... The Church proceeds in disregard of the law and sovereignty of the State, and claims, at its discretion, the right to annul and destroy the bond of the civil contract. The practical result of such claims in the conflict of Church and State appears in the light of the recent and notorious annulment of the Marlborough marriage.

*   *   *

In your opinion, sir, are such proceedings consistent with the peace and safety of States?

The Mexican situation has brought the claims of the Roman Catholic Church into great prominence in this country. It is inevitably linked with issues that will concern the Executive Office at Washington for the next term....

The claim here asserted for the Roman Catholic Church is exclusive of every other religious foundation as having any spiritual rights under the Saviour of Mankind; and it is bluntly asserted in a word that connotes a sovereign jurisdiction in theory over all men in spiritual affairs without regard to their assent. It is the last official promulgation of the ancient and dangerous theory of the Two Powers.

Americans, as well as other peoples, may deplore the Mexican standard of what is inconsistent with the peace and order of the State; but we submit that the application of the Mexican standard by the Mexican people in Mexican affairs, in the assertion of an undisputed national sovereignty within its own territory and over its own people, cannot be held contrary to reason, and null and void in law, however much it may impugn the sovereign claims of the Roman Catholic Church, afford a minority a reason for rebellion, or offend the sentiments of other nations.

*   *   *

"To this Society (the Roman Catholic Church)," wrote Pope Leo XIII in his encyclical letter on *The Christian Constitution of States*, "the only begotten Son of God entrusted all the truths which He had taught in order that it might keep and guard them and with lawful authority explain them, and at the same time He commanded all nations to hear the voice of the (Roman Catholic) Church as if it were His own, threatening those who would not hear it with everlasting perdition."

It is the voice of that Church that speaks to America by the American Hierarchy in the words of its distinguished counsel in the Mexican situation; and your fellow citizens are concerned to inquire what authority you ascribe to that voice.

We have no desire to impute to the Roman Catholic Church aught but high and sincere motives in the assertion of her claims as one of the Two Powers. Her members believe in those claims, and, so believing, it is their conscientious duty to stand for them. We are satisfied if they will but concede that those claims, unless modified and historically redressed, precipitate an inevitable conflict between the Roman

Catholic Church and the American State irreconcilable with domestic peace. With two illustrations — and those relating to English Christianity — we have done.

In the sixteenth century the decree of Pope Pius V in terms deposed Elizabeth, Queen of England, from the English throne and absolved her subjects from their allegiance. The result is well known. Much that pertained to the venerable forms of religion in the preceding centuries became associated in the popular mind of England with treason — even the Mass itself when celebrated in the Roman form. Roman Catholics were oppressed in their rights and privileges. Roman Catholic priests were forbidden within the realm. The mills of God turned slowly, but they turned. The Roman Catholics of England endured the penalties of hostile legislation with heroic fortitude and resignation. Public opinion slowly changed and gradually Roman Catholic disabilities were removed, and in 1850, under Cardinal Wiseman, the Roman Catholic Hierarchy was restored in England, with no other condition than that its sees should not use the ancient titles that the Hierarchy of the Church of England had retained. Peace and amity reigned within the realm, irrespective of different religions, and domestic repose marked a happy epoch. But the toleration and magnanimity of England bore strange fruit. Scarcely was the Roman Hierarchy restored to its ancient privileges when the astounding Apostolic Letter of Pope Leo XIII appeared (1896), declaring to the world that the orders of the Church of England were void, her priests not priests, her bishops not bishops, and her sacraments so many empty forms.

*   *   *

Is the record of the Roman Catholic Church in England consistent, sir, in your opinion, with the peace and safety of the State?

Nothing will be of greater satisfaction to those of your fellow citizens who hesitate in their endorsement of your candidacy because of the religious issues involved than such a disclaimer by you of the convictions here imputed, or such an exposition by others of the questions here presented, as may justly turn public opinion in your favor.

Yours with great respect,

Governor Alfred E. Smith's Reply
The Atlantic Monthly
May 1927

Smith's reply to Marshall emphasized his agreement with the position of important nineteenth-century American bishops in support of separation of church and state. The New York governor also stated for the first time in print his own strong convictions on the compatibility of Roman Catholicism with American patriotism.

Dear Sir: — In your open letter to me in the April *Atlantic Monthly* you "impute" to American Catholics views which, if held by them, would leave open to question the loyalty and devotion to this country and its Constitution of more than twenty million American Catholic citizens. I am grateful to you for defining this issue in the open and for your courteous expression of the satisfaction it will bring to my fellow citizens for me to give "a disclaimer of the convictions" thus imputed. Without mental reservation I can and do make that disclaimer. These convictions are held neither by me nor by any other American Catholic, as far as I know. Before answering the argument of your letter, however, I must dispose of one of its implications. You put your questions to me in connection with my candidacy for the office of President of the United States. My attitude with respect to that candidacy was fully stated in my last inaugural address as Governor when, on January 1, 1927, I said:

"I have no idea what the future has in store for me. Everyone else in the United States has some notion about it except myself. No man could stand before this intelligent gathering and say that he was not receptive to the greatest position the world has to give anyone. But I can say this, that I will do nothing to achieve it except to give to the people of the State the kind and character of service that will make me deserve it."

I should be a poor American and a poor Catholic alike if I injected religious discussion into a political campaign. Therefore I would ask you to accept this answer from me not as a candidate for any public office but as an American citizen, honored with high elective office, meeting a challenge to his patriotism and his intellectual integrity. Moreover, I call your attention to the fact that I am only a layman. The *Atlantic Monthly* describes you as "an experienced attorney" who "has made himself an authority upon canon law." I am neither a lawyer nor a theologian. What knowledge of law I have was gained in the course of my long experience in the Legislature, and as Chief Executive of New York State. I had no such opportunity to study theology.

∗   ∗   ∗

Taking your letter as a whole and reducing it to commonplace English, you imply that there is conflict between religious loyalty to the Catholic faith and patriotic loyalty to the United States. Everything that has actually happened to me during my long public career leads me to know that no such thing as that is true. I have taken an oath of office in this State nineteen times. Each time I swore to defend and maintain the Constitution of the United States. All of this represents a period of public service in elective office almost continuous since 1903. I have never known any conflict between my official duties and my religious belief. No such conflict could exist. Certainly the people of this State recognize no such conflict. They have testified to my devotion to public duty by electing me to the highest office within their gift four times. You yourself do me the honor, in addressing me, to refer to "your fidelity to the morality you have advocated in public and private life and to the religion you have revered; your great record of public trusts successfully and honestly discharged." During the years I have discharged these trusts I have been a communicant of the Roman Catholic Church. If there were conflict, I, of all men, could not have escaped it, because I have not been a silent man, but a battler for social and political reform. These battles would in their very nature disclose this conflict if there were any.

I regard public education as one of the foremost functions of government and I have supported to the last degree the State Department of Education in every effort to promote our public-school system. The largest single item of increased appropriations under my administration appears in the educational group for the support of common schools.... My aim — and I may say I have succeeded in achieving it — has been legislation for child welfare, the protection of working men, women, and children, the modernization of the State's institutions for the care of helpless or unfortunate wards, the preservation of freedom of speech and opinion against the attack of war-time hysteria, and the complete reorganization of the structure of the government of the State.

I did not struggle for these things for any single element, but in the interest of all of the eleven million people who make up the State. In all of this world I had the support of churches of all denominations. I probably know as many ecclesiastics of my Church as any other layman. During my long and active public career I never received from any of them anything except cooperation and encouragement in the full and complete discharge of my duty to the State. Moreover, I am unable to understand how anything that I was taught to believe as a Catholic could possibly be in conflict with what is good citizenship. The essence of my faith is built upon the Commandments of God. The law of the land is built upon the Commandments of God. There can be no conflict between them.

*   *   *

But, wishing to meet you on your own ground, I address myself to your definite questions, against which I have thus far made only general statements. I must first call attention to the fact that you often divorce sentences from their context in such a way as to give to them something other than their real meaning. I will specify. You refer to the Apostolic Letter of Pope Leo XIII as "declaring to the world that the orders of the Church of England were void, her priests not priests," and so forth. You say that this was the "strange fruit" of the toleration of England to the Catholics. You imply that the Pope gratuitously issued an affront to the Anglican Church. In fact, this Apostolic Letter was an answer to a request made at the instance of priests of the Anglican Church for recognition by the Roman Catholic Church of the validity of their priestly orders. The request was based on the ground that they had been ordained in succession from the Roman Catholic priests who became the first priests of the Anglican Church. The Apostolic Letter was a mere adverse answer to this request, ruling that Anglican priests were not Roman Catholic priests, and was in no sense the gratuitous insult which you suggest it to be. It was not directed against England or citizens of that Empire.

Again, you quote from the *Catholic Encyclopedia* that my Church "regards dogmatic intolerance, not alone as her incontestable right, but as her sacred duty." And you say that these words show that Catholics are taught to be politically, socially, and intellectually intolerant of all other people. If you had read the whole of that article in the *Catholic Encyclopedia*, you would know that the real meaning of these words is that for Catholics alone the Church recognizes no deviation from complete acceptance of its dogma. These words are used in a chapter dealing with that subject only. The very same article in another chapter dealing with toleration toward non-Catholics contains these words: "The intolerant man is avoided as much as possible by every highminded person.... The man who is tolerant in every emergency is alone lovable." The phrase "dogmatic intolerance" does not mean that Catholics are to be dogmatically intolerant of other people, but merely that inside the Catholic Church they are to be intolerant of any variance from the dogma of the Church.

Similar criticism can be made of many of your quotations. But, beyond this, by what right do you ask me to assume responsibility for every statement that may be made in any encyclical letter? As you will find in the *Catholic Encyclopedia* (Vol. V, p. 414), these encyclicals are not articles of our faith. The Syllabus of Pope Pius IX, which you quote on the possible conflict between Church and State, is declared by Cardinal Newman to have "no dogmatic force." You seem to think that Catholics must be all alike in mind and in heart, as though they had been poured into and taken out of the same mould. You have no more right to ask me to defend as part of my faith every statement coming from a prelate than I should have to ask you to accept as an article of your religious faith every statement of an Episcopal bishop, or of your political faith every statement of a President of the United States. So little are these matters of the essence of my faith that I, a devout Catholic since childhood, never heard of them until I read your letter....

Your first proposition is that Catholics believe that other religions should, in the United States, be tolerated only as a matter of favor and that there should be an established church. You may find some dream of an ideal of a Catholic State, having no relation whatever to actuality, somewhere described. But, voicing the best Catholic thought on this subject, Dr. John A. Ryan, Professor of Moral Theology at the Catholic University of America, writes in *The State and the Church* of the encyclical of Pope Leo XIII, quoted by you:

"In practice, however, the foregoing propositions have full application only to the completely Catholic State.... 'The propositions of Pope Pius IX condemning the toleration of non-Catholic sects do not now,' says Father Pohle, apply even to Spain or the South American republics, to say nothing of countries possessing a greatly mixed population.' He lays down the following general rule: 'When several religions have firmly established themselves and taken root in the same territory, nothing else remains for the State then to exercise tolerance towards them all, or, as conditions exist to-day, to make complete religious liberty for individual and religious bodies a principle of government.' "

That is good Americanism and good Catholicism....

The American prelates of our Church stoutly defend our constitutional declaration of equality of all religions before the law. Cardinal O'Connell has said: "Thus to every American citizen has come the blessed inheritance of civil, political, and religious liberty safe-guarded by the American Constitution ... the right to worship God according to the dictates of his conscience."

*　　*　　*

Archbishop Dowling, referring to any conceivable union of Church and State, says: "So many conditions for its accomplishment are lacking in every government of the world that the thesis may well be relegated to the limbo of defunct controversies."

I think you have taken your thesis from this limbo of defunct controversies.

*　　*　　*

Cardinal Gibbons has said: "American Catholics rejoice in our separation of Church and State, and I can conceive no combination of circumstances likely to arise which would make a union desirable to either Church or State.... For ourselves we thank God that we live in America, 'in this happy country of ours,' to quote Mr. Roosevelt, where 'religion and liberty are natural allies.' "

And referring particularly to your quotation from Pope Pius IX, Dr. Ryan, in *The State and the Church*, says: "Pope Pius IX did not intend to declare that separation is always unadvisable, for he had more than once expressed his satisfaction with the arrangement obtaining in the United States."

With these great Catholics I stand squarely in support of the provisions of the Constitution which guarantee religious freedom and equality.

I come now to the speculation with which theorists have played for generations as to the respective functions of Church and State. You claim that the Roman Catholic Church holds that, if conflict arises, the Church must prevail over the State....

*　　*　　*

What is the conflict about which you talk? It may exist in some lands which do not guarantee religious freedom. But in the wildest dreams of your imagination you cannot conjure up a possible conflict between religious principle and political duty in the United States, except on the unthinkable hypothesis that some law were to be passed which violated the common morality of all God-fearing men. And if you can conjure up such a conflict, how would a Protestant resolve it? Obviously by the dictates of his conscience. That is exactly what a Catholic would do. There is no ecclesiastical tribunal which would have the slightest claim upon the obedience of

Catholic communicants in the resolution of such a conflict. As Cardinal Gibbons said of the supposition that "the Pope were to issue commands in purely civil matters":

"He would be offending not only against civil society, but against God, and violating an authority as truly from God as his own. Any Catholic who clearly recognized this would not be bound to obey the Pope; or rather his conscience would bind him absolutely to disobey, because with Catholics conscience is the supreme law which under no circumstances can we ever lawfully disobey."

Archbishop Ireland said: "To priest, to Bishop, or to Pope (I am willing to consider the hypothesis) who should attempt to rule in matters civil and political, to influence the citizen beyond the range of their own orbit of jurisdiction that are the things of God the answer is quickly made: 'Back to your own sphere of rights and duties, back to the things of God.'"

Bishop England, referring to our Constitution, said: "Let the Pope and the Cardinals and all the powers of the Catholic world united make the least encroachment on that Constitution, we will protect it with our lives. Summon a General Council — let that Council interfere in the mode of our electing but an assistant to a turnkey of a prison — we deny the right, we reject the usurpation."

*   *   *

Under our system of government the electorate entrusts to its officers of every faith the solemn duty of action according to the dictates of conscience. I may fairly refer once more to my own record to support these truths. No man, cleric or lay, has ever directly or indirectly attempted to exercise Church influence on my administration of any office I have ever held, nor asked me to show special favor to Catholics or exercise discrimination against non-Catholics.

It is a well-known fact that I have made all of my appointments to public office on the basis of merit and have never asked any man about his religious belief....

I next come to education. You admit that the Supreme Court guaranteed to Catholics the right to maintain their parochial schools; and you ask me whether they would have so ruled if it had been shown that children in parochial schools were taught that the State should show discrimination between religions, that Protestants should be recognized only as a matter of favor, that they should be intolerant to non-Catholics, and that the laws of the State could be flouted on the ground of the imaginary conflict. My summary answer is: I and all my children went to a parochial school. I never heard of any such stuff being taught or of anybody who claimed that it was. That any group of Catholics would teach it is unthinkable.

*   *   *

Finally you come to Mexico. By inference from the brief of a distinguished lawyer you intimate that it is the purpose of organized Catholics to seek intervention by the United States....

My personal attitude, wholly consistent with that of my Church, is that I believe in peace on earth, good will to men, and that no country has a right to interfere in the internal affairs of any other country. I recognize the right of no church to ask armed intervention by this country in the affairs of another, merely for the defense of the rights of a church. But I do recognize the propriety of Church action to request the good offices of this country to help the oppressed of any land, as those good offices have been so often used for the protection of Protestant missionaries in the Orient and the persecuted Jews of eastern Europe.

I summarize my creed as an American Catholic. I believe in the worship of God according to the faith and practice of the Roman Catholic Pope and I recognize no power in the institutions of my Church to interfere with the operations of the Constitution of the United States or the enforcement of the law of the land. I believe in absolute freedom of conscience for all men and in equality of all churches, all sects, and all beliefs before the law as a matter of right and not as a matter of favor. I believe in the absolute separation of Church and State and in the strict enforcement of the provisions of the Constitution that Congress shall make no law respecting an establishment of religion or prohibiting the free exercise thereof. I believe that no tribunal of any church has any power to make any decree of any force in the law of the land, other than to establish the status of its own communicants within its own church. I believe in the support of the public school as one of the corner stones of American liberty. I believe in the right of every parent to choose whether his child shall be educated in the public school or in a religious school supported by those of his own faith. I believe in the principle of noninterference by this country in the internal affairs of other nations and that we should stand steadfastly against any such interference by whomsoever it may be urged. And I believe in the common brotherhood of man under the common fatherhood of God.

In this spirit I join with fellow Americans of all creeds in a fervent prayer that never again in this land will any public servant be challenged because of the faith in which he has tried to walk humbly with his God.

Address by Senator Simeon D. Fess
Kansas City, June 12, 1928

Emphasizing that the domestic life of Americans had been infused by "the longest period of sustained business prosperity in history" and that American foreign policy had been governed by "American genius" and "cosmopolitan philanthropy," Senator Fess's keynote speech epitomized Republican self-righteousness and self-congratulation in 1928.

*   *   *

The one commanding necessity at the close of the war was an administration with a policy to co-ordinate all these elements of material value in the production of wealth, a policy that would insure the maximum ability and responsibility in management, and the minimum loss of initiative and ambition in labor.

These problems were subjects of conferences soon after Republicans took full control. The best leadership in every branch of industry was enlisted to mobilize and co-ordinate all America in a campaign of "work and save": to lift the nation from the mire of economic prostration upon a plane of a standard of living never before experienced in the history of the world. This leadership sought to realize the maximum efficiency in both management and labor as applied to production, and to secure a more equitable distribution of the fruits of effort with the wholesome results of the most cordial relationship between labor and capital yet enjoyed in our country. Under that leadership we have reached the highest wage scale known in history, a principle which is maintained as sound economically, in that by increasing the output per unit, we decrease the cost without lowering wages, and thereby increase the buying power of the public. This principle in practice demonstrates the formula of modern industry, low cost of production of high grade goods made by well paid labor, and sold at a profit. Under this new law of production, ten per cent less labor produces twenty-five per cent more product.

Today we are in the longest period of sustained business prosperity in our history. To continue it free from the cycle of business depression is the prime concern of leadership in industry. In no field is there a better example of that prosperity than in house-building conducted under the leadership of the better homes movement in co-operation with the Commerce Department, which has enlisted the sympathetic efforts of dominant units in every community, resulting in a period of eight years in the construction of at least three million homes, entailing an annual investment of four billion dollars, or a total of over thirty billion dollars in resident building alone in city and country. These homes are generally equipped with modern conveniences unknown in the Old World, and only a few years ago would have been luxuries for the few Americans who could afford them. There are over three times the number of home owners among our laboring classes than can be found in all classes of citizens in the next greatest country of the world. In these homes live American citizens who consume fifty per cent more food, use ten times the number of telephones, twelve times as much electricity, thirty times as many automobiles, and in a similar ratio all modern conveniences of life, as can be found in the same number of homes in Great Britain. From these homes go one-third more children to school, and nearly ten times as many go to college as in the next greatest nation of the earth.

In addition to this scale of expenditure in maintaining the American standard of living, the savings deposits in savings banks and loan associations amount to seven times the total capital of all the national banks, all the state banks, and trust companies combined. It is this situation that has bewildered the peoples of other lands, as expressed in the reports of various foreign commissions. It is this situation which has caused the millions of the Old World to seek our shores, and made it necessary for us to adopt increasingly restrictive measures on immigration.

With the very best wishes for the welfare of all peoples of all other countries, the time is here when America must maintain rigid control as to who shall and who shall not come to our shores. The recent statutes on that subject will stand as a type of the most constructive legislation of this or any other administration.

The ambition of Republican leadership and policy is the open door to the maximum utilization of all our people of whatever class or race, profession or calling, to promote self-reliance and in the degree humanly possible to banish poverty from our midst.

*   *   *

The problem of Agriculture from the producer's standpoint is a more equitable distribution of what the consumer of food has to pay. The farmer's complaint is not that the consumer does not pay enough, but of what he pays the producer does not get his rightful share. The immediate problem is greater producer control over the products of his toil. His need is a seller's market to give him a voice in what he is to receive instead of subjecting him to the whims of an unregulated, and not infrequently a speculative, market where he is left to take whatever the buyer might be willing to give. To be substantial and effective, the machinery of this control must be farmer owned, farmer organized, and farmer operated, rather than operated by a bureau from Washington. Sound relief will avoid artificial stimulus such as government price fixing or government buying and selling. Such remedies will but defer the day of reckoning. All relief measures to be of permanent value must be constructive and grounded in economic principles underlying production and consumption. The solution is primarily economic, not political. It is more individual and collective than governmental. Whatever aid the government may give, the remedy lies most largely with the farmer himself, acting in unison with his associates to control his products. It is a matter of management rather than legal enactment, save in constructive legislation enabling the farmer to better handle his product, to better determine a market.

*   *   *

Next to raising his crop, the farmer is most interested in a market for his surplus, out of which he must obtain the needs of modern society. He is definitely interested in the sustained prosperity of non-agricultural industries, which make possible the buying power of the public. Far from these industries being an injury to him, his greatest hope lies in their continued prosperity. The nearer his market, the greater his savings, from the cost of transportation. While he appreciates the foreign market, it is negligible in contrast with his home market in which he sells 90 per cent of his product, hence his interest in the McKinley policy of protection to American industries. His highest interest demands that policy which enables American capital to invest in American industry at reasonable profit, in the employment of American labor, upon a wage scale that will maintain an American standard of living, which insures a buying power of the public necessary to supply a market for his product....

While the foregoing are largely governmental, there is no interference by the government with the independence of the farmer in conducting his business. His chief problem today is one of marketing, and is claiming the best talent of America in an effort to turn a buyers' market into a sellers' market, to give the producer the control of his product. To this end, this administration has enacted constructive and remedial legislation of no less than twenty-four separate pieces of legislation covering every phase of the agricultural problem. This program, recommended by the two agricultural commissions, representing the best agricultural talent in America, was pronounced by a non-partisan judgment as the most ambitious and important program of farm reha- bilitation ever presented to any nation at any time. The purpose of this program was to aid the farmer in his solution of his problem. The purpose of the administration in further aid is to avoid the government taking over from the farmer his own control of the great industry, but to assist him in that control....

*   *   *

The mobilization of productive energies of the American people in the advance- ment of progress is no better illustrated than in the new fields of radio and aviation. The sales in the radio industry in 1921 amounted to about $3,000,000.00. Today they are far in excess of $500,000,000.00. In 1922, when the first radio conference was held in Washington, it was made up of only a few enthusiasts. That conference of last year brought together the foremost experts of all the world....

The constructive policy of this administration is again seen in what has been done in the development of air navigation, first in the air mail and secondly, in civil aviation. The air mail progress has been outstanding both as to routes established, planes in use, miles covered, amount carried, at lowered costs and increased expedition and safety of delivery. This success induced capital to invest as soon as governmental cooperation was afforded, in securing good airports, powerful beacon lights, air mark- ings, emergency fields, and such facilities as would enable night flying with reasonable safety. Air mail is now an assured reality. The government is making contracts to carry mail at a much lower rate than was thought possible, and the time is near at hand when all our citizens will be served by this kind of mail service.

*   *   *

While material progress will ever be the primary concern of both legislation and administration, the perpetuity of the American system of government and her institutions calls for an aroused public opinion to support the respect for law, in the interest of the conservation and the development of our human resources.... It is not a question of tolerance or of liberty, but of life, both individual and national. The Republican Party is ready to call the roll on this false doctrine masquerading under the mask of liberty. It is ready to sound the moral tocsin against the present campaign of a noise-making minority whether in the interest of business profit or mere human indulgence. It stands for respect for law. It condemns the violation of law....

Disturbed foreign relations, both diplomatic and trade, were inevitable results of the great war. Adjustments, some of them difficult and complicated, have been made with all countries except Russia, through not less than seventy-five treaties entered into and ratified, through which understandings have been reached, and diplomatic and trade relations resumed.

The immediate task of the Republican Administration was peace, with honor, and without the loss of our independence and sovereignty as a nation. We had poured out our treasure of life and resources in the interest of maintaining national honor. We had experienced the horrors of war. We shared the world's desires to avoid future wars.

The League of Nations was proposed as the method to insure against future wars. This nation's decision had to be made whether it would pay the price of surrender of national sovereignty for what appeared then and realized now a fatuous promise of exemption from war. This stupendous issue and final decision are too fresh in all our minds to call for repetition. We still hold to the doctrine of our fathers to avoid alliances. We willingly cooperate with all nations on behalf of public welfare, but refuse to commit ourselves and our resources in advance to unknown controversies. We stand ready to assist, but the time and measure of that assistance is a matter of our own judgment and decision.

*   *   *

Our attention was next turned toward the problem of economic recovery of Europe. The war had left once prosperous countries in what seemed hopeless chaos. On all sides were observed the results and the victims of war; want and suffering everywhere, due to the ravages of war and the failure to get back to work. The uncertainty of reparations, the persistence of national bitterness, and the dislocations of all order, industrial, social, political, and the loss of needed capital, blocked recovery.

The tardiness of necessary steps to make peace adjustments clogged the channels of European credit, which otherwise would tap the reservoir of American credit awaiting safe investment.

After years of floundering of European statesmen in the bog of economic confusion in a vain effort to find relief, with no promise of success, the Republican leadership ventured to suggest a solution which in due time and after consideration was accepted, which placed the problem under the direction of American genius, and at once opened the way to economic recovery.

This effort having succeeded, our attention was next turned to insurance of permanent peace. It has ever been a fundamental principle with this country that complete and permanent prosperity is impossible with any nation that consumes through unproductive sources as much or more than it produces. No nation can permanently prosper if its military establishments consume more than the rest of the nation produces, hence our efforts to induce a limitation of European armies, following our example after the close of the war when we reduced from 4,000,000 to 137,000 men. This situation explains our anxiety to employ this method of comparative reduction of military forces as the surest plan for world peace, and prosperity of individual nations.

* * *

The attitude of the military countries of the Old World has been seriously disappointing to this country toward rational proposals for permanent peace. Declarations of Peace are ineffective when drowned out by the clatter of armament. Our good faith has been shown in our leadership in the Washington Limitation Conference, which was the boldest stroke for permanent peace in modern history; in the reduction of our armies to the small number of 137,000, a mere national police force, without waiting for agreements with European powers; in our loan adjustments, the terms of which provoked bitter criticism on the part of some of our citizens as unfair to our own people; in our willingness and our actual service to assist in the economic recovery of these nations; as well as in our cooperation in the work of rehabilitation. That leadership has been especially displayed in our consistent efforts to promote world peace, and never with more promise than today.

* * *

Our foreign policy rests upon two famous announcements, that of Washington in 1794, urging the country to remain neutral in Europe's disputes, and that of Monroe in 1823, urging Europe not to interfere in America.

This country under Republican leadership recently announced the following principles as fundamental in our conception of and our relation to other countries:

1. Every nation is entitled to existence and the right of self-defense.
2. Every nation is entitled to independence as an individual nation.
3. Every nation is in law equal to every other nation.
4. Every nation has the right to the control of its own territory.
5. Every nation can demand that its rights under international law be respected by every other nation.

Our history under Republican administration shows a new standard of cosmopolitan philanthropy never before aspired to by any nation of history. In Cuba we intervened partly on behalf of our peace of mind, and partly from humanitarian motives. We set up a government based upon popular will and supervised it until the Cuban people were able and ready to handle it alone. As a result, a people who had struggled for four-hundred years in a stage of continuous rebellion or revolution is today one of the most progressive, self-governing nations of the world, and a signal object lesson of the value of stable government to all peoples desiring self-government.

In Santo Domingo, after forty years of perennial insurrections, we answered the call of duty, reorganized the financial structure, and supervised its operations. We established her organization of safety and security, and in pursuance of treaty agreement continued to supervise them until stability of government was established, when we withdrew. The result is a well ordered administration of local self-government, and wonderful progress of a people which had formerly lived in constant turmoil.

In Haiti, we are pursuing the same course in the interest of the welfare of these people, and in pursuance of a treaty. When law and order become well established and assurance of a progressive government is promised, as in the case of Cuba and Santo Domingo, we will withdraw.

No chapter in the history of nation building has ever been written that will show a more unselfish service and greater humanitarian regard than that relating to what we have done for people like the Philippino and the peoples of the West India Islands.

On the American continent where we have exerted considerable influence if not authority, our main concern is and has been the welfare of the people of all the nations, big and little, with no selfish purpose beyond our interest in national peace. This welfare depends upon the maintenance of peaceful relations between the countries, and that stability in government which can and must avoid the habits of revolution so common in the countries of Central America. This is the basis of what we term our American policy toward all America.

The Republican Party has consistently stood for the principle of the Monroe Doctrine, as a sound policy for the western continent. It has confidence in the American principle of democratic government of the people, and has not hesitated to lend moral assistance and to extend her good offices to the countries struggling for that principle. To this end it has looked upon the Monroe Doctrine as sound in freeing these countries, our neighbors, from complications with foreign nations which might seize upon pretexts of protection of their nationals to violate the doctrine. Its violation is to be averted if possible. Its abandonment is unthinkable. Its maintenance on the other hand involves obligations to protect life and property, hence our concern in orderly government, free from insurrection, rebellion and revolution. To this end we gladly extend our good offices whenever we can render such service.

After years of unfortunate confusion in Mexico, which at times seriously strained our friendly relations over what appeared to be attempted confiscation, the situation has yielded to diplomacy, the rights of American citizens in that republic have been recognized and the way again opened for the two nations to cooperate in commercial growth and international good will....

... Since 19 10 our Marines have been in Nicaragua, save a short period after the last conference when they were withdrawn only to be sent back when insurrection, again threatened American lives and property. It is to be hoped that our influence in securing a fair election will be the step to real stability so that our Marines need not longer remain to protect American citizens doing business in that country. Another conference was recommended by the Havana conference to adopt further plans for adjustment of disputes arising in the new world.

The one undeviating principle for which America will continue to stand is protection of American citizens in their rights of life and property wherever they may be if they have a right to be there, whether on land or sea. As was recently said by the President on the memorable battlefield of Gettysburg: "A government that failed in its duty to protect the lives and property of its citizens would be justly condemned at home and covered with derision abroad."

We ask only our rights, we will ask nothing that is wrong. We demand from no one what we would not grant to everyone....

When the true history is written of our effort to promote stable government among the struggling people with which we have been closely connected, it will reveal aspiration upon our part and realizations upon theirs which will challenge the admiration of the world.

*   *   *

By the greatest majority ever given in the history of elections, the Republican Party under the leadership of Warren G. Harding, was called to the task of restoration, and at once grappled with the peace problems quite as dicerent [sic] as those of war. The manner in which the problems have been handled, first so well begun by the administration of our beloved and late lamented Warren G. Harding, and then by that of Coolidge, is too well known to call for further comment. All our people have some knowledge of the number, and most of them some idea of the complication, of these problems. Very few will deny the complete success in the effort of solution. Measured by those tests, the record of history is challenged to present a leadership with superior brilliancy and a higher rank in statesmanship than that of our present eminent leader. In a comparatively short period we are passed from war confusion to peace contentment; from economic disorders to sound principles of progress; from a period of general prostration to one of substantial prosperity in which all basic industries are on sound economic foundations. This remarkable record in administration reflects a type of political leadership at the head of the government rarely experienced in his or any other country.

Speech by John L. McNab
Kansas City, June 14, 1928

Stressing the wholesomeness and purity of Hoover's "Americanism," McNab, in nominating Hoover, described him as the perfect American hero, the self-made man, who, genius though he was, had not lost the common touch.

*   *   *

Our people are aroused to the need of a strong, courageous man to carry forward the constructive policies of a great administration.

This historic party of achievement has never been able to submit to the American People a greater record of constructive human action than the administration of Calvin Coolidge. And of the constructive part of that administration, from its inception, Herbert Hoover has been a vital and intimate part. History will not overlook the fact that the execution of the great emergency measures of the administration have been committed by the President to his Secretary of Commerce. He has been to his Chief and leader a loyal and devoted aide, a powerful and understanding friend, a never failing supporter in all his constructive designs.

*   *   *

There is something spiritual in this universal call of the people for this man. It is not based on political expediency. It is the result of the public will that the constructive policies of a Republican administration shall control this nation and the conviction that Herbert Hoover, of all living men, best represents the genius, pure and undefiled, of wholesome and forward-looking Americanism.

The story of his life is one of the great epics of modern achievement. Descended from seven generations of American ancestry, his career is a living example of the heights to which pure Americanism, by sustained effort and devotion, may reach.

At the age of four, death took his father from beside the forge in the State of Iowa. You loyal sons of Iowa have not forgotten that, have you?

That loss was compensated in the life which followed for he was reared in the sweet and tolerant atmosphere of an American Quaker home.

*   *   *

He emerged into public life in the first class of engineers to leave Stanford University. With pick in hand he mucked as a common laborer in the drifts of the old Mayflower mine in California. There were laid the foundations of that enduring sympathy he has always shown for the laboring man. But he has been no less the consistent and constructive friend of industry and commerce.

*   *   *

The world's greatest war broke suddenly over a startled world, He, with countless Americans, chanced to be in the City of London. The great war machine rolled over Belgium leaving starvation and ruin in its wake. Here indeed was a cause that called for all the spirituality and vision of man. He heard the old cry that for over a hundred years has rung out over the waters of an angry sea — "Women and children first." He heard the cry and answered. In the presence of gaunt and tottering children he knew neither friend nor foe. To him, hunger and innocence knew no nationality. Millions knocked at hunger's gate.

To organize relief; to secure the funds; to buy food-stuffs; to ship them across seas that swarmed with submarines; to negotiate with Governments, fierce and intolerant with the passions of war; to placate angry and imperious generals; to get food to the starving and starving to the food — here was a task such as never before confronted man. The feeding of those numberless millions of hungry children is the greatest practical romance in all history.

The call came overseas from his beloved homeland. The United States had cast her lot in the great struggle. He was named Food Administrator.... From the day he was appointed, he insisted that the one essential group in America that must have the protection of the American Government was the American farmer. To quicken production; to stimulate industry; to feed armies at a price that Governments could afford to pay; to resist the mercantile profiteer, and to see that the farmer received the just return for his product was a task that called for both statesmanship and courage. He imposed none of the crushing regulations which drove European peoples to despair. He enforced no drastic rationing upon the American people. He appealed to their cooperative patriotism. He brought farmers, business men and the women of the country into a unison of patriotic effort. — His measures trebled the surplus food in the United States. When the Armistice came he saw with the prophetic vision of a seer the peril that awaited the farmer and producer. Already food supplies were on hand for another year of gigantic combat. With the supplies of the southern hemisphere freed to European markets he saw American agriculture faced with the greatest peril in its history. Europe repudiated its contracts to buy the hogs and wheat of American farmers. Damming back that flood on the markets of the United States meant ruin from which our agriculturists would not have recovered in a quarter of a century.

It would require the gratitude of a generation of farm producers to repay Herbert Hoover for his efforts to save the whole industry from collapse. Only by an administrator with a spirit of prophecy to foresee the impending tragedy could the task have been accomplished. Only a man who possessed the respect of European powers could have exacted the agreements he demanded. He compelled the disposal in Europe of the huge surplus of farm products. To him is due the early opening of the blockade on Germany. Had it not been for his prestige and his genius of persuasion the doors of Europe would have been locked to the product of our fields and American agriculture would have crashed beyond all hope of recovery.

*   *   *

It would be an endless task to here review his widely diversified efforts while head of the Department of Commerce. He has quickened the industrial activities of the Nation. He has proved that Government business and morals go hand in hand. His every act has been touched by an impulse for better things. It was his initiative — that prevented the spread of unemployment which had brought stagnation and despair to the rest of the world. He fought to a triumphant conclusion a world wide monopoly which threatened the rubber purchasers of America.

He has made the Department of Commerce the most useful instrument for the advancement of the new economic world.

In the midst of crowding duties there came a call that stirred his soul. Human suffering once more was at the gate.

*   *   *

For the first time in history, torrential rains fell in thirty States at the same time. Seven hundred thousand were homeless; cities were flooded; the great and noble South saw its richest possessions go under the deluge.

To whom should the President turn in such an hour of crisis?

To whom but to the administrator whose public life had been a series of crowing triumphs in meeting human emergencies.

To whom but to the man whose name we present to you this day.

Within a week, in conjunction with the American Red Cross, the Secretaries of the Army and Navy, he had telegraph lines strung, food-stuffs moving, and the noble and splendid leaders of the South, most of whom were of a political faith not his own, from New Orleans to Memphis, organized for instant service. All the varied talents of a trained organizer and administrator were in full play. No more wonderful tribute was ever paid to a people than was uttered by Hoover in the City of Memphis when the flood was at its crest, of the gallant leaders of the South who watched with him beside the raging waters....

*   *   *

We are living in a swiftly changing era of American history. Since the great war the United States has become the center of the economic and industrial world. Vast forces fraught with evil if uncontrolled, freighted with blessings if understood, are in motion; no one is so fitted by years of training and experience; no one is so adapted by temperament and sympathy to direct these forces to the betterment of his country as this wholesome son of the sturdy forebears of the Middle West.

Listen, men and women of this Convention — all the world knows his public service, but only the few understand his graciousness and kindliness as an individual being. He is no super-man in private life. He loves his friends. He likes to laugh and play. He loves the world and craves its affection in return. Whether at home among his neighbors, with his companions on the fishing stream, or in the intimacy of his workshop, he is everywhere the considerate, refreshing human being.

*   *   *

I name him who rose from poverty to feed more hungry mouths than any other man in the history of the world.

I nominate him because he has labored with his hands and knows the problem of the toiler.

I name him as a great engineer who understands the problems of our inland waterways and the vast resources of river and lake and soil.

I name him as a great humanitarian, who in the midst of a woe of war gave his best that human beings might live and live abundantly.

I nominate him because as administrator of great projects he has never failed to leave a record of surpassing usefulness.

I name him as statesman and executive whose unfaltering courage, inflexible Americanism and understanding of nations and peoples have given him a grasp on national and international affairs that commands respect throughout the world.

I nominate him for his lofty character as a man and citizen; for his broad and kindly human sympathies; for his wholesome heart that rejoices above all things else that he has been useful to the people of his native land.

And now, engineer, practical scientist, minister of mercy to the hungry and the poor, administrator, executive, statesman, beneficent American, kindly neighbor, wholesome human being, I give you the name of Herbert Hoover.

Speech by Claude G. Bowers
Houston, June 26, 1928

This famous American historian saw the American people as having a clear choice between the people's party of Jefferson and the moneyed party of Hamilton. Bowers stressed what he saw as the corruption and heartlessness of the big businessmen who controlled the Republican party and urged Americans to take to their tents and "go forth to recover the government from the hands of those who pillage by law as well as those who steal by stealth."

The American Democracy has mobilized today to wage a war of extermination against privilege and pillage. We prime our guns against autocracy and bureaucracy. We march against that centralization which threatens the liberties of the people. We fight for the republic of the fathers, and for the recovery of the covenant from the keeping of a caste and class. We battle for the honor of the nation, besmirched and bedraggled by the most brazen and shameless carnival of corruption that ever blackened the reputation of a decent and self-respecting people.

*   *   *

We do not underestimate the enemy. The little gilded group that now owns and controls the government can pour a golden stream into the slush fund and make no impression on the fortunes they have legislated into their coffers. The enemy enters the campaign unembarrassed by a debt — Harry Sinclair has paid that off. It enters the campaign with his money in its pocket and his blessing on its head.

For forty years the party in power has conjured with the name of Lincoln while following the leadership of Hamilton; and now, after eight years of successful privilege and pillage, it throws off the Lincolnian mask. It could hardly keep the Lincoln mask on its face and Sinclair's money in its chest.

Thus at Kansas City, where they dramatized the issue, it was not Lincoln, but Hamilton, who rode at the head of the procession.

Thus they frankly base their policies on the political principles of Hamilton; and we go forth to battle for the principles of Thomas Jefferson. The issues are as fundamental as they were when Jefferson and Hamilton crossed swords more than a century ago. To understand the conflicting views of these two men on the functions of government is to grasp the deep significance of this campaign.

Now Hamilton believed in the rule of an aristocracy of money, and Jefferson in a democracy of men.

Hamilton believed that governments are created for the domination of the masses, and Jefferson that they are created for the service of the people.

Hamilton wrote to Morris that governments are strong in proportion as they are made profitable to the powerful; and Jefferson knew that no government is fit to live

2672

that does not conserve the interest of the average man.

Hamilton proposed a scheme for binding the wealthy to the government by making government a source of revenue to the wealthy; and Jefferson unfurled his banner of equal rights.

Hamilton wanted to wipe out the boundary lines of states, and Jefferson was the champion of their sovereign powers.

Hamilton would have concentrated authority remote from the people, and Jefferson would have diffused it among them.

*   *   *

Hamilton would have injected governmental activities into all the affairs of men; and Jefferson laid it down as an axiom of freedom that "that government is best which governs least."

You can not believe with Lincoln that "God loved the common people or he would not have made so many of them," and with Hamilton that the people are "a great beast."

You can not believe with Lincoln that the principles of Jefferson are "the definitions and the axioms of a free society," and with Hamilton that they are the definitions of anarchy.

You can not believe with Lincoln in a government "of the people, by the people and for the people," and with Hamilton in a government of the wealthy, by the influential and for the powerful.

*   *   *

We enter the campaign no strangers to the public. The brilliant record of our eight years of power is as a splotch of glorious sunshine against the smutty background of eight years of privilege and crime. In those eight years we wrote more progressive and constructive measures into law than had been written by the opposition in forty years of power.

One thing those eight years did — they buried beyond the reach of resurrection the ancient slander that the party of Wilson is incapable of constructive statesmanship.

*   *   *

And those eight years did one thing more — they gave another immortal to the skies.

What a majestic figure was he who led us in those fruitful years! The cold even light of his superb intellect played upon the most intricate problems of the times and they seemed to solve themselves. He lifted the people to such heights of moral grandeur as they had never known before and his name and purpose made hearts beat faster in lowly places where his praise was sung in every language in the world. And when, at length, his body broken, but his spirit soaring still, he fell stricken, while still battling for his faith, there passed to time and to eternity and to all mankind the everlasting keeping of the immortal memory of Woodrow Wilson.

*   *   *

Sixteen years ago the late Senator Beveridge warned us of the "invisible government." That invisible government now feels strong enough to take on visibility.

From the moment of the election of 1920 there was a mobilization of the Black Horse Cavalry of privilege and pillage, and it cantered down Pennsylvania Avenue, up and down from one end to the other. Strange creatures, unknown even to the capital, put in an appearance. Desk room was found for one of these in the Department of Justice. The Best Minds established a temple of the new patriotism in the Little Green House on K Street. Men who were the very symbols of privilege, whose fortunes had been built on the favors of government, were put in possession of the instrumentalities of the State. Acting on the Hamiltonian theory that governments are strong in proportion as they are made profitable to the powerful, the foremost of these was put in a strategic public position that he might personally supervise the delivery of the goods. The representatives of special interest hastened to the capital with their receipts for campaign contributions, to be given the key to the treasury and a guest card to the patriotic club on K Street where "there was a sound of revelry by night." Within five months the conditions in Washington had become a scandal and a stench. The reign of privilege and pillage had begun.

The moment the bell rang these men set themselves to the task of undoing the work of Woodrow Wilson and to the commercialization of the government. In the midst of the usual scandal they hurried a tariff law upon the statutes at a cost of from three to four billions a year to the consumers.

They found the tariff commission we created an embarrassment — they ignored it....

They found the Federal Trade Commission was mightily in the way — they packed it....

*   *   *

My friends, it is a tragic thing when a government of a mighty people can be mortgaged to a little group that could be crowded into the directors' rooms of the Aluminum Company of America. Under the rule of this regime, the average man has had no more stake in the government, for which he may be called upon to die, than if he had never touched our soil.

*   *   *

Thus while the little group represented by Mr. Mellon has found fine plucking in the vineyard of the state, there have been nothing but thorns and thistles for the tillers of the soil. And the result is a condition of ruination that is a disgrace to our civilization. More than a million farms have been abandoned. More than two million men have been driven from the paternal acres by economic necessity within the year. The hammer of the auctioneer knocking down farmlands sounds like the continuous bombardment of a major battle in the West. Does the ruling caste want figures? Then take this — in five years of the Coolidge prosperity there has been a depreciation in the value of farm lands and equipment of thirty billion dollars!

And what does the ruling caste say to this? They call it "temporary depression." And what does it propose? They propose that the farmers shall become better business men.

*   *   *

One day the head of the state by a scratch of the pen increased the tariff loot of the pig iron industry by fifty per cent; and the very next day he delivered a homily to the farmers on the wickedness of expecting profit from a governmental act.

One day Mr. Mellon offered an argument against a farm relief bill; and the next day a Republican senator, by substituting the words "tariff" for "farm relief," and "duties" for "equalization fee," converted the Mellon argument into a devastating denunciation of the very processes through which much of the Mellon fortune has been made.

One month ago the President of the United States bitterly denounced with contemptuous phrasing the revolving fund of a farm relief bill; and the very next day he heartily approved the revolving fund for the favored shipping interest.

And then, with millions of producers on the verge of bankruptcy and despair, they contemptuously kicked their case from court and adjourned the Congress with a cheer. Thus for eight long years they have stood in the midst of the wreckage of the farms and have done nothing — nothing to decrease the cost of transporting the farmer's produce to the marts; nothing toward rehabilitating his lost markets across the sea; but they have added a billion a year to the cost of the things the farmer has to buy.

*   *   *

We hold that the owner of a little shop, the proprietor of a store in an average town, is as much a business man as the barons of iron and steel. The man who owns and operates a ranch in Texas or Montana is as much a business man as the banker in New York. The men who till the soil and feed the nation are better business men to the Jeffersonian than the most successful speculator in stocks and bonds. We are unable to accept the language of the opposition, for we are interested in the Babbits, and they in the bulls and the bears.

We wage no war on big business if it be honest business; we find no fault with fortunes, however large, provided they are not accumulated through the misuse of governmental power. But we do protest against and war upon the commercialization of government that makes for corruption and crime.

*   *   *

We have seen the nation's oil reserves, set aside by the prescience of Roosevelt, and sacredly guarded by the honesty and wisdom of Wilson and Daniels, bartered away by a member of the cabinet for a bribe in a little black bag.

Shameful as these things are, more shameful far has been the cynical silence and indifference of the high functionaries of the state to whom the people had a right to look for the protection of the nation's property and the nation's honor. We submit in no spirit of political flub-dubbery that it is a shocking thing that we have waited vainly for seven years for one word, one syllable, one whisper of the mildest criticism of these criminals and crimes from a single representative of the administration.

They heard La Follette's denunciation of Teapot Dome — and were silent. They saw the various processes in the alienation of the nation's property — and were silent.

They heard the gossip of the capital that buzzed for weeks and months — and were silent. There was not a man among them with enough will power, or lung power, to blow a police whistle. Nay, more; when a warning of the impending crime was sent to a member of the cabinet, but recently knighted by the golden wand, he sent the letter to Albert B. Fall with this notation: "I should be glad to convey to this gentleman any reply you may suggest."

*   *   *

Imagine Andrew Jackson silent in the midst of such crimes; imagine Tilden; imagine Cleveland; imagine Wilson! Why, they would have thundered their denunciations from the loftiest station in the world and have scourged the rascals forth with scorpion whips tipped with consuming flame.

If the nation's oil reserves have been restored it is because the inquisitorial genius of Walsh of Montana exposed the crime and forced the proceedings that brought the restitution of the nation's stolen goods.

And why the silence in the watch-tower? Because the organization of the party of the men stationed there was a beneficiary of the crime. Not only did they know of the crime, and maintain silence — they knew of the division of the spoils and knew that a goodly part was being used to pay the party debt.

*   *   *

And thus the campaign deficits of the regime in power have been paid by Harry Sinclair, and now with pious platitudes that party enters another campaign free from debt — because there was a Teapot Dome.

And why this strange insensibility to the common instincts of honesty and honor? Now, bear in mind the Hamiltonian theory that governments are strong in proportion as they are made profitable to the powerful....

And so we go forth to recover the government from the hands of those who pillage by law as well as those who steal by stealth. Even as a minority we dragged these loathsome crimes to light. We exposed the stealing, the perjury, the silences of the sacrosanct. We forced the restitution of the nation's stolen goods. We compelled the dismissal of Daugherty and the prosecution of Fall. Put us in possession of the government and we will turn the light on every crack and crevice and cleanse the Augean stables from mow to manger.

We have no legislation to put upon the auction block. No Harry Sinclair has paid our party debt. We are free. We unfurl the Jeffersonian banner bearing Jefferson's device: "A good government is an honest government," and we invite all enemies of corruption to fight with us beneath its folds for the redemption of the violated honor of this republic.

Now they hope to drug the conscience of the nation with the doped soothing syrup of a fake prosperity; and we want to know what prosperity they mean. They point to a few powerful corporations enjoying the pap of paternalistic privilege, and our answer is that you can not judge the prosperity of a people by the earnings of a privileged monopoly.

*   *   *

Four million jobless men is not prosperity; a million abandoned farms is not prosperity; the utter ruin of the basic industry of America is not prosperity; the failure of 4,000 banks in the seven years of normalcy is not prosperity; 23,146 commercial failures in the year 1927 is not prosperity; and if this year's record is foreshadowed by the first four months there will be 28,000 commercial failures in 1928.

*　　*　　*

Thus through the stupidity of their dollar diplomacy we have stumbled into a petty war with Nicaragua that is taking its daily toll of American lives. Just why we have the war no one seems to know; just how we came to have the war no one cares to tell. Do they tell us that we are there to guarantee an honest election? Why, not long ago we were unable to guarantee an honest election in the city of Philadelphia. Do they say that we are there to prevent rioting in the election? Why, at the time we were sending the marines to Nicaragua we were campaigning with bombs in the city of Chicago.

Now we propose to end dollar diplomacy in Latin America in the interest of justice; but we propose it, too, in the interest of American business. We do not propose to sacrifice the future markets of our manufacturers and merchants to serve the interest of little groups of financiers and concessionaires. There, within a generation, loom our richest markets; and we are sowing the seed from which our rivals across the sea will reap the harvest in trade. We can not submit a bill of lading at the point of a bayonet and make the Latin-Americans take it. We can not write a bill of sale with a mailed fist. We can not match a marine with a musket against a British or German salesman with a smile. We can serve the ultimate ends of business better through the noble spirit of the Mobile speech of Woodrow Wilson than they have done with their dollar diplomacy, backed by the muskets of the marines who are dying needlessly today in the swamps of Nicaragua.

*　　*　　*

The predatory forces before us seek a triumph for the sake of the sacking. Their shock troops are the Black Horse Cavalry whose hoofbeats have made hideous music on Pennsylvania Avenue during the last eight years. They are led by money-mad cynics and scoffers — and we go forth to battle for the cause of man. In the presence of such a foe "he who dailies is a dastard and he who doubts is damned." In this convention we close debate and grasp the sword. The time has come. The battle hour has struck. Then to your tents, O Israel!

Speech by Governor Franklin D. Roosevelt
Houston, June 27, 1928

Nominating Al Smith for the third time in a rather lackluster speech, the future President urged the convention to accept the "Happy Warrior" for his demonstrated qualities of outstanding leadership and administrative abilities.

*   *   *

What sort of President do we need today?

A man, I take it, who has four great qualifications, every one of them an essential to the office: First of all, leadership, articulate, virile, willing to bear responsibility, needing no official spokesman to interpret the oracle; next, experience, not guessing, but knowledge, from long practice, of the science of governing, which is a very different thing from mere technical bureau organizing; then, honesty — the honesty that hates hypocrisy and can not live with concealment and deceit, and last, and in this time, most vital, that rare ability to make popular government function as it was intended to by the fathers, to reverse the present trend towards apathy and arouse in the citizenship an active interest — a willingness to reassume its share of responsibility for the nation's progress. So only can we have, once more, a government not just for the people, but by the people also.

*   *   *

Let us measure our present governor by those standards. Personal leadership is a fundamental of successful government. I do not mean the leadership of the band of good fellows and good schemers who followed President Harding, nor the purely perfunctory party loyalty which has part of the time in part of the country sustained the present chief executive. I mean that leadership which by sheer force of mind, by chain of unanswerable logic has brought friends and foes alike to enact vitally needed measures of government reform.

His staunchest political adversaries concede the governor's unique and unparalleled record of constructive achievement in the total reorganization of the machinery of government, in the business-like management of state finance, in the enactment of a legislative program for the protection of men, women and children engaged in industry, in the improvement of the public health, and in the attainment of the finest standard of public service in the interest of humanity. This he has accomplished by a personality of vibrant, many-sided appeal, which has swept along with it a legislature of a different political faith.

* * *

The second great need is experience. By this I refer not merely to length of time in office — I mean that practical understanding which comes from the long and thoughtful study of and daily dealings with the basic principles involved in the science of taxation, of social welfare, of industrial legislation, of governmental budgets and administration, of penology, of legislative procedure and practice, of constitutional law. In all these matters the governor of New York has developed himself into an expert, recognized and consulted by men and women of all parties. In any conference of scholars on these subjects he takes his place naturally as a trained and efficient specialist. He also possesses that most unusual quality of selecting appointees not only skilled in the theoretical side of their work, but able to give the highest administrative success to their task. The high standard of the appointees of the governor, their integrity, their ability, has made strong appeal to the citizens of his state, urban and rural, regardless of party. I add "rural" advisedly, for each succeeding gubernatorial election has shown for him even greater proportional gains in the agricultural sections than in the large communities of the state.

* * *

Now as to the requisite of honesty. I do not mean an honesty that merely keeps a man out of jail, or an honesty that, while avoiding personal smirch, hides the corruption of others. I speak of the honesty that lets a man sleep well of nights, fearing no senatorial investigation; that honesty that demands faithfulness to the public trust in every public servant; that honesty which takes immediate action to correct abuse.

The whole story of his constant and persistent efforts to insure the practice of the spirit as well as the letter of official and private probity in public places is so well understood by the voters of his state that more and more Republicans vote for him every time he is attacked. This, I think, is a subject which need not be enlarged upon. The voting public of the nation is fully wise enough to compare the ethical standards of official Albany with those of official Washington.

And now, last of all, and where the governor excels over all the political leaders of this day, comes the ability to interest the people in the mechanics of their governmental machinery, to take the engine apart and show the function of each wheel.

Power to impart knowledge of and create interest in government is the crying need of our time. The soul of our country, lulled by mere material prosperity, has passed through eight gray years.

* * *

The governor of the state of New York stands out today as having that purpose, as having proved during these same eight years not only his desire but his power to make the people as interested in their government as he is himself.

I have described so far qualities entirely of the mind — the mental and moral equipment without which no President can successfully meet the administrative and material problems of his office. It is possible with only these qualities for a man to be a reasonably efficient President, but there is one thing more needed to make him a great President. It is that quality of soul which makes a man loved by little children, by dumb animals, that quality of soul which makes him a strong help to all those in sorrow or in trouble, that quality which makes him not merely admired, but loved by all the people — the quality of sympathetic understanding of the human heart, of real interest in his fellowmen. Instinctively he senses the popular need because he himself has lived through the hardship, the labor and the sacrifice which must be endured by every man of heroic mould who struggles up to eminence from obscurity and low estate. Between him and the people is that subtle bond which makes him their champion and makes them enthusiastically trust him with loyalty and love.

*   *   *

Because of his power of leadership, because of his unequalled knowledge of the science of government, because of his uncompromising honesty, because of his ability to bring the government home to the people, there is no doubt that our governor will make an "efficient" President, but it is because he also possesses, to a superlative degree, this rare faculty of sympathetic understanding that I prophesy that he will also make a great President, and because of this I further prophesy that he will again place us among the nations of the world as a country which values its ideals as much as its material prosperity — a land that has no selfish designs on any weaker power, a land the ideal and inspiration of all those who dream of a kindlier, happier civilization in the days to come.

*   *   *

America needs not only an administrator, but a leader — a pathfinder, a blazer of the trail to the high road that will avoid the bottomless morass of crass materialism that has engulfed so many of the great civilizations of the past. It is the privilege of democracy not only to offer such a man but to offer him as the surest leader to victory. To stand upon the ramparts and die for our principles is heroic. To sally forth to battle and win for our principles is something more than heroic. We offer one who has the will to win — who not only deserves success but commands it. Victory is his habit — the happy warrior, Alfred E. Smith.

Acceptance Speech by Secretary of
Commerce Herbert C. Hoover
San Francisco, August 11, 1928

Hoover's acceptance speech tended to be vague compared to Smith's. It was a testimonial to the American business system and a statement of Hoover's philosophy of rugged individualism.

You bring, Mr. Chairman, formal notice of my nomination by the Republican Party to the Presidency of the United States. I accept. It is a great honor to be chosen for leadership in that party which has so largely made the history of our country in these last 10 years.

*　　*　　*

The points of contact between the Government and the people are constantly multiplying. Every year wise governmental policies become more vital in ordinary life. As our problems grow so do our temptations grow to venture away from those principles upon which our republic was founded and upon which it has grown to greatness. Moreover we must direct economic progress in support of moral and spiritual progress.

... Every man has a right to ask of us whether the United States is a better place for him, his wife and his children to live in, because the Republican Party has conducted the government for nearly eight years. Every woman has a right to ask whether her life, her home, her man's job, her hopes, her happiness, will be better assured by the continuance of the Republican Party in power. I propose to discuss the questions before me in that light.

*　　*　　*

No party ever accepted a more difficult task of reconstruction than did the Republican Party in 1921. The record of these seven and one-half years constitutes a period of rare courage in leadership and constructive action. Never has a political party been able to look back upon a similar period with more satisfaction. Never could it look forward with more confidence that its record would be approved by the electorate.

Peace has been made. The healing processes of good will have extinguished the fires of hate. Year by year in our relations with other nations we have advanced the ideals of law and of peace, in substitution for force. By rigorous economy federal expenses have been reduced by two billions per annum. The national debt has been reduced by six and a half billions. The foreign debts have been settled in large part and on terms which have regard for our debtors and for .our taxpayers. Taxes have been reduced four successive times. These reductions have been made in the particular interest of the smaller taxpayers.

For this purpose taxes upon articles of consumption and popular service have been removed. The income tax rolls today show a reduction of 80 per cent in the total revenue collected on income under $10,000 per year, while they show a reduction of only 25 per cent in revenues from incomes above that amount. Each successive reduction in taxes has brought a reduction in the cost of living to all our people.

Commerce and industry have revived. Although the agricultural, coal and textile industries still lag in their recovery and still require our solicitude and assistance, yet they have made substantial progress. While other countries engaged in the war are only now regaining their prewar level in foreign trade, our exports, even if we allow for the depreciated dollar, are 58 per cent greater than before the war....

But it is not through the recitation of wise policies in government alone that we demonstrate our progress under Republican guidance. To me the test is the security, comfort and opportunity that has been brought to the average American family. During this less than eight years our population has increased by 8 per cent. Yet our national income has increased by over thirty billions of dollars per year or more than 45 per cent. Our production — and therefore our consumption — of goods has increased by over 25 per cent. It is easily demonstrated that these increases have been widely spread among our whole people. Home ownership has grown. While during this period the number of families has increased by about 2,300,000 we have built more than 3,500,000 new and better homes. In this short time we have equipped nearly nine million more homes with electricity, and through it drudgery has been lifted from the lives of women. The barriers of time and distance have been swept away and life made freer and larger by the installation of six million more telephones, seven million radio sets, and the service of an additional 14 million automobiles. Our cities are growing magnificent with beautiful buildings, parks, and playgrounds. Our countryside has been knit together with splendid roads.

We have doubled the use of electrical power and with it we have taken sweat from the backs of men. The purchasing power of wages has steadily increased. The hours of labor have decreased. The 12-hour day has been abolished. Great progress has been made in stabilization of commerce and industry. The job of every man has thus been made more secure. Unemployment in the sense of distress is widely disappearing.

Most of all, I like to remember what this progress has meant to America's children. The portal of their opportunity has been ever widening. While our population has grown but 8 per cent we have increased by 11 per cent the number of children in our grade schools, by 66 per cent the number in our high schools, and by 75 per cent the number in our institutions of higher learning.

With all our spending we have doubled savings deposits in our banks and building and loan associations. We have nearly doubled our life insurance. Nor have our people been selfish. They have met with a full hand the most sacred obligation of man — charity. The gifts of America to churches, to hospitals, and institutions for the care of the afflicted, and to relief from great disasters, have surpassed by hundreds of millions any totals for any similar period in all human record.

One of the oldest and perhaps the noblest of human aspirations has been the abolition of poverty. By poverty I mean the grinding by under-nourishment, cold, and ignorance and fear of old age of those who have the will to work. We in America today are nearer to the final triumph over poverty than ever before in the history of any land. The poorhouse is vanishing from among us. We have not yet reached the goal but given a chance to go forward with the policies of the last eight years, and we shall soon with the help of God be in sight of the day when poverty will be banished from this nation. There is no guarantee against poverty equal to a job for every man. That is the primary purpose of the economic policies we advocate.

*   *   *

The most urgent economic problem in our nation today is in agriculture. It must be solved if we are to bring prosperity and contentment to one-third of our people directly and to all of our people indirectly. We have pledged ourselves to find a solution.

*   *   *

There are many causes for failure of agriculture to win its full share of national prosperity. The after-war deflation of prices not only brought great direct losses to the farmer but he was often left indebted in inflated dollars to be paid in deflated dollars. Prices are often demoralized through gluts in our markets during the harvest season. Local taxes have been increased to provide the improved roads and schools. The tariff on some products is proving inadequate to protect him from imports from abroad. The increases in transportation rates since the war has greatly affected the price which he receives for his products. Over six million farmers in times of surplus engage in destructive competition — with one another in the sale of their product, often depressing prices below those levels that could be maintained.

The whole tendency of our civilization during the last 50 years has been toward an increase in the size of the units of production in order to secure lower costs and a more orderly adjustment of the flow of commodities to the demand. But the organization of agriculture into larger units must not be by enlarged farms. The farmer has shown he can increase the skill of his industry without large operations. He is today producing 20 per cent more than eight years ago with about the same acreage and personnel. Farming is and must continue to be an individualistic business of small units and independent ownership. The farm is more than a business; it is a state of living. We do not wish it converted into a mass production machine. Therefore, if the farmers' position is to be improved by larger operations it must be done not on the farm but in the field of distribution. Agriculture has partially advanced in this direction through cooperatives and pools. But the traditional cooperative is often not a complete solution.

*   *   *

An adequate tariff is the foundation of farm relief. Our consumers increase faster than our producers. The domestic market must be protected. Foreign products raised under lower standards of living are today competing in our home markets. I would use my office and influence to give the farmer the full benefit of our historic tariff policy.

A large portion of the spread between what the farmer receives for his products and what the ultimate consumer pays is due to increased transportation charges. Increase in railway rates has been one of the penalties of the war. These increases have been added to the cost to the farmer of reaching seaboard and foreign markets and result therefore in reduction of his prices. The farmers of foreign countries have thus been indirectly aided in their competition with the American farmer. Nature has endowed us with a great system of inland waterways. Their modernization will comprise a most substantial contribution to midwest farm relief and to the development of twenty of our interior states. This modernization includes not only the great Mississippi system, with its joining of the Great Lakes and of the heart of midwest agriculture to the Gulf, but also a shipway from the Great Lakes to the Atlantic. These improvements would mean so large an increment in farmers' prices as to warrant their construction many times over. There is no more vital method of farm relief.

But we must not stop here.

An outstanding proposal of the Party program is the wholehearted pledge to undertake the reorganization of the marketing system upon sounder and more economical lines.... It pledges the creation of a Federal Farm Board of representative farmers to be clothed with authority and resources with which not only to still further aid farmers' cooperatives and pools and to assist generally in solution of farm problems but especially to build up with federal finance, farmer-owned and farmer-controlled stabilization corporations which will protect the farmer from the depressions and demoralization of seasonal gluts and periodical surpluses.

Objection has been made that this program, as laid down by the Party Platform, may require that several hundred millions of dollars of capital be advanced by the Federal Government without obligation upon the individual farmer. With that objection I have little patience. A nation which is spending ninety billions a year can well afford an expenditure of a few hundred millions for a workable program that will give to one-third of its population their fair share of the nation's prosperity. Nor does this proposal put the government into business except so far as it is called upon to furnish initial capital with which to build up the farmer to the control of his own destinies.

*   *   *

The working out of agricultural relief constitutes the most important obligation of the next Administration.... So far as my own abilities may be of service, I dedicate them to help secure prosperity and contentment in that industry where I and my forefathers were born and nearly all my family still obtain their livelihood.

*   *   *

The Republican principle of an effective control of imported goods and of immigration has contributed greatly to the prosperity of our country. There is no selfishness in this defense of our standards of living. Other countries gain nothing if the high standards of America are sunk and if we are prevented from building a civilization which sets the level of hope for the entire world. A general reduction in the tariff would admit a flood of goods from abroad. It would injure every home. It would fill our streets with idle workers. It would destroy the returns to our dairymen, our fruit, flax, and livestock growers, and our other farmers.

*   *   *

I am sure the American people would rather entrust the perfection of the tariff to the consistent friend of the tariff than to our opponents, who have always reduced our tariffs, who voted against our present protection to the worker and the farmer, and whose whole economic theory over generations has been the destruction of the protective principle.

Having earned my living with my own hands I cannot have other than the greatest sympathy with the aspirations of those who toil. It has been my good fortune during the past 12 years to have received the cooperation of labor in many directions, and in promotion of many public purposes.

The trade union movement in our country has maintained two departures of American individualism and American institutions. They have steadfastly opposed subversive doctrines from abroad. Our freedom from foreign social and economic diseases is in large degree due to this resistance by our own labor. Our trade unions, with few exceptions, have welcomed — all basic improvement in industrial methods. This largeness of mind has contributed to the advancing standards of living of the whole of our people. They properly have sought to participate — by additions to wages — in the result of improvements and savings which they have helped to make.

During these past years we have grown greatly in the mutual understanding between employer and employee. We have seen a growing realization by the employer that the highest practicable wage is the road to increased consumption and prosperity and we have seen a growing realization by labor that the maximum use of machines, of effort and of skill is the road to lower production costs and in the end to higher real wages. Under these impulses and the Republican protective system our industrial output has increased as never before and our wages have grown steadily in buying power. Our workers with their average weekly wages can today buy two and often three times more bread and butter than any wage earner of Europe. At one time we demanded for our workers a "full dinner pail." We have now gone far beyond that conception. Today we demand larger comfort and greater participation in life and leisure.

The Republican platform gives the pledge of the Party to the support of labor. It endorses the principle of collective bargaining and freedom in labor negotiations. We stand also pledged to the curtailment of excessive use of the injunction in labor disputes.

*   *   *

We cannot develop modernized water transportation by isolated projects. We must develop it as a definite and positive interconnected system of transportation. We must adjust reclamation and irrigation to our needs for more land. Where they lie together we must co-ordinate transportation with flood control, the development of hydroelectric power and of irrigation, else we shall as in the past commit errors that will take years and millions to remedy.

The Congress has authorized and has in process of legislation great programs of public works. In addition to the works in development of water resources, we have in progress large undertakings in public roads and the construction of public buildings.

All these projects will probably require an expenditure of upwards of one billion dollars within the next four years. It comprises the largest engineering construction ever undertaken by any government. It is justified by the growth, need and wealth of our country. The organization and administration of this construction is a responsibility of the first order. For it we must secure the utmost economy, honesty and skill. These works which will provide jobs for an army of men should so far as practicable be adjusted to take up the slack of unemployment elsewhere.

*　　*　　*

I recently stated my position upon the 18th Amendment which I again repeat:

"I do not favor the repeal of the 18th Amendment. I stand for the efficient enforcement of the laws enacted thereunder. Whoever is chosen President has under his oath the solemn duty to pursue this course.

"Our country has deliberately undertaken a great social and economic experiment, noble in motive and far-reaching in purpose. It must be worked out constructively."

Common sense compels us to realize that grave abuses have occurred — abuses which must be remedied. And organized searching investigation of facts and causes can alone determine the wise method of correcting them. Crime and disobedience of law cannot be permitted to break down the Constitution and laws of the United States.

Modification of the enforcement laws which would permit that which the Constitution forbids is nullification. This the American people will not countenance. Change in the Constitution can and must be brought about only by the straightforward methods provided in the Constitution itself. There are those who do not believe in the purposes of several provisions of the Constitution. No one denies their right to seek to amend it. They are not subject to criticism for asserting that right. But the Republican Party does deny the right of anyone to seek to destroy the purposes of the Constitution by indirection.

*　　*　　*

With the growth and increasing complexity of our economic life the relations of government and business are multiplying daily. They are yearly more dependent upon each other. Where it is helpful and necessary, this relation should be encouraged. Beyond this it should not go. It is the duty of government to avoid regulation as long as equal opportunity to all citizens is not invaded and public rights violated. Government should not engage in business in competition with its citizens. Such actions extinguish the enterprise and initiative which has been the glory of America and which has been the root of its pre-eminence among the nations of the earth. On the other hand, it is the duty of business to conduct itself so that government regulations or government competition is unnecessary.

Business is practical, but it is founded upon faith — faith among our people in the integrity of business men, and faith that it will receive fair play from the government. It is the duty of government to maintain that faith. Our whole business system would break down in a day if there was not a high sense of moral responsibility in our business world....

One of the greatest difficulties of business with government is the multitude of unnecessary contacts with government bureaus, the uncertainty and inconsistency of government policies, and the duplication of governmental activities. A large part of this is due to the scattering of functions and the great confusion of responsibility in our federal organization. We have, for instance, 14 different bureaus or agencies engaged in public works and construction, located in nine different departments of the government. It brings about competition between government agencies, inadequacy of control, and a total lack of co-ordinated policies in public works. We have eight different bureaus and agencies charged with conservation of our natural resources, located in five different departments of the government. These conditions exist in many other directions. Divided responsibility, with the absence of centralized authority, prevents constructive and consistent development of broad national policies.

* * *

The government can be of invaluable aid in the promotion of business. The ideal state of business is freedom from those fluctuations from boom to slump which bring on one hand the periods of unemployment and bankruptcy and on the other, speculation and waste. Both are destructive to progress and fraught with great hardship to every home. By economy in expenditures, wise taxation, and sound fiscal finance it can relieve the burdens upon sound business and promote financial stability. By sound tariff policies it can protect our workmen, our farmers, and our manufacturers from lower standards of living abroad. By scientific research it can promote invention and improvement in methods. By economic research and statistical service it can promote the elimination of waste and contribute to stability in production and distribution. By promotion of foreign trade it can expand the markets for our manufacturers and farmers and thereby contribute greatly to stability and employment.

Our people know that the production and distribution of goods on a large scale is not wrong. Many of the most important comforts of our people are only possible by mass production and distribution. Both small and big business have their full place. The test of business is not in its size — the test is whether there is honest competition, whether there is freedom from domination, whether there is integrity and usefulness of purpose. As Secretary of Commerce I have been greatly impressed by the fact that the foundation of American business is the independent business man. The Department by encouragement of his associations and by provision of special service has endeavored to place him in a position of equality in information and skill with larger operations. Alike with our farmers his is the stronghold of American individuality. It is here that our local communities receive their leadership. It is here that we refresh our leadership for larger enterprise. We must maintain his opportunity and his individual service. He and the public must be protected from any domination or from predatory business.

* * *

In this land, dedicated to tolerance, we still find outbreaks of intolerance. I come of Quaker stock. My ancestors were persecuted for their beliefs. Here they sought and found religious freedom. By blood and conviction I stand for religious tolerance both in act and in spirit. The glory of our American ideals is the right of every man to worship God according to the dictates of his own conscience.

*   *   *

For many years I have been associated with efforts to save life and health for our children. These experiences with millions of children both at home and abroad have left an indelible impression — that the greatness of any nation, its freedom from poverty and crime, its aspirations and ideals — are the direct quotient of the care of its children. Racial progress marches upon the feet of healthy and instructed children. There should be no child in America that is not born and does not live under sound conditions of health; that does not have full opportunity of education from the beginning to the end of our institutions; that is not free from injurious labor; that does not have every stimulation to accomplish the fullest of its capacities. Nothing in development of child life will ever replace the solicitude of parents and the surroundings of home, but in many aspects both parents and children are dependent upon the vigilance of government, national, state and local.

I especially value the contribution that the youth of the country can make to the success of our American experiment in democracy.... To interpret the spirit of the youth into the spirit of our government; to bring the warmth of their enthusiasm and the flame of their idealism into the affairs of the nation — is to make of American government as positive and living force, a factor for greatness and nobility in the life of the nation.

I think I may say that I have witnessed as much of the horror and suffering of war as any other American. From it I have derived a deep passion for peace. Our foreign policy has one primary object, and that is peace. We have no hates; we wish no further possessions; we harbor no military threats. The unspeakable experiences of the Great War, the narrow margins by which civilization survived from its exhaustion, is still vivid in men's minds. There is no nation in the world today that does not earnestly wish for peace — that is not striving for peace.

*   *   *

We have been and we are particularly desirous of furthering the limitation of armaments. But in the meantime we know that in an armed world there is only one certain guarantee of freedom — and that is preparedness for defense. It is solely to defend ourselves, for the protection of our citizens that we maintain armament. No clearer evidence of this can exist than the unique fact that we have fewer men in army uniform today than we have in police uniforms, and that we maintain a standing invitation to the world that we are always ready to limit our naval armament in proportion as the other naval nations will do likewise. We earnestly wish that the burdens and dangers of armament upon every home in the world might be lessened. But we must and shall maintain our naval defense and our merchant marine in the strength and efficiency which will yield to us at all times the primary assurance of liberty, that is, of national safety.

There is one of the ideals of America upon which I wish at this time to lay especial emphasis. For we should constantly test our economic, social and governmental system by certain ideals which must control them. The founders of our republic propounded the revolutionary doctrine that all men are created equal and all should have equality before the law. This was the emancipation of the individual. And since these beginnings, slowly, surely and almost imperceptibility, this nation has added a third ideal almost unique to America — the ideal of equal opportunity. This is the safeguard of the individual. The simple life of early days in our republic found but few limitations upon equal opportunity. By the crowding of our people and the intensity and complexity of their activities it takes today a new importance.

Equality of opportunity is the right of every American — rich or poor, foreign or native-born, irrespective of faith or color. It is the right of every individual to attain that position in life to which his ability and character entitle him. By its maintenance we will alone hold open the door of opportunity to every new generation, to every boy and girl. It tolerates no privileged classes or castes or groups who would hold opportunity as their prerogative. Only from confidence that this right will be upheld can flow that unbounded courage and hope which stimulates each individual man and woman to endeavor and to achievement. The sum of their achievement is the gigantic harvest of national progress.

This ideal of individualism based upon equal opportunity to every citizen is the negation of socialism. It is the negation of anarchy. It is the negation of despotism. It is as if we set a race. We, through free and universal education, provide the training of the runners; we give to the man equal start; we provide in the government the umpire of fairness in the race. The winner is he who shows the most conscientious training, the greatest ability, and the greatest character. Socialism bids all to end the race equally. It holds back the speedy to the pace of the slowest. Anarchy would provide neither training nor umpire. Despotism picks those who should run and those who should win.

*　　*　　*

Our purpose is to build in this nation a human society, not an economic system. We wish to increase the efficiency and productivity of our country but its final purpose is happier homes. We shall succeed through the faith, the loyalty, the self-sacrifice, the devotion to eternal ideals which live today in every American.

*　　*　　*

The Presidency is more than an administrative office. It must be the symbol of American ideals. The high and the lowly must be seen with the same eyes, met in the same spirit. It must be the instrument by which national conscience is livened and it must under the guidance of the Almighty interpret and follow that conscience.

Acceptance Speech by Governor Alfred E. Smith
Albany, August 22, 1928

In a long speech, the New York governor covered aspects of every major policy question facing the nation and attempted to give his own views in some detail on those questions, pointing up large differences between his positions and those held by his opponents. It was no surprise that he stressed farm relief, the tariff, or even American policies in Latin America; but many Democrats were astounded that he chose to face the divisive issues of Prohibition and immigration squarely.

Government should be constructive, not destructive; progressive, not reactionary. I am entirely unwilling to accept the old order of things as the best unless and until I become convinced that it can not be made better.

... A sharp line separates those who believe that an elect class should be the special object of the government's concern and those who believe that the government is the agent and servant of the people who create it. Dominant in the Republican Party today is the element which proclaims and executes the political theories against which the party liberals like Roosevelt and La Follette and their party insurgents have rebelled. This reactionary element seeks to vindicate the theory of benevolent oligarchy. It assumes that a material prosperity, the very existence of which is challenged, is an excuse for political inequality. It makes the concern of the government, not people, but material things.

I have fought this spirit in my own state. I have had to fight it and to beat it, in order to place upon the statute books every one of the progressive, humane laws for whose enactment I assumed responsibility in my legislative and executive career. I shall know how to fight it in the nation.

It is a fallacy that there is inconsistency between progressive measures protecting the rights of the people, including the poor and the weak, and a just regard for the rights of legitimate business, great or small....

Likewise, government policy should spring from the deliberate action of an informed electorate. Of all men, I have reason to believe that the people can and do grasp the problems of the government.... Great questions of finance, the issuance of millions of dollars of bonds for public projects, the complete reconstruction of the machinery of the state government, the institution of an executive budget, these are but a few of the complicated questions which I, myself, have taken to the electorate....

* * *

In the rugged honesty of Grover Cleveland there originated one of our party's greatest principles: "Public office is a public trust." That principle now takes on new meaning. Political parties are the vehicle for carrying out the popular will. We place

2690

responsibility upon the party. The Republican Party today stands responsible for the widespread dishonesty that has honeycombed its administration.

*   *   *

The Republican Party builds its case upon a myth. We are told that only under the benevolent administration of that party can the country enjoy prosperity. When four million men, desirous to work and support their families, are unable to secure employment there is very little in the picture of prosperity to attract them and the millions dependent upon them.

In the year 1926, the latest figures available show that one-twentieth of one per cent of the 430,000 corporations in this country earned forty per cent of their profits; forty per cent of the corporations actually lost money; one-fourth of one per cent of these corporations earned two-thirds of the profits of all of them. Specific industries are wholly prostrate and there is widespread business difficulty and discontent among the individual business men of the country.

*   *   *

When the Republican Party came into power in 1921 it definitely promised reorganization of the machinery of government, and abolition or consolidation of unnecessary and overlapping agencies. A committee was appointed. A representative of the President acted as chairman. It prepared a plan of reorganization. The plan was filed in the archives. It still remains there. After seven years of Republican control the structure of government is worse than it was in 1921. It is fully as bad as the system which existed in New York state before we secured by constitutional amendment the legislation which consolidated more than one hundred offices, commissions and boards into eighteen coordinated departments, each responsible to the governor. In contrast with this, the Republican Party in control at Washington, when faced with the alternative of loss of patronage for the faithful or more efficient and economical management of the government, permitted the old order to continue for the benefit of the patronage seekers.

*   *   *

With this has gone a governmental policy of refusal to make necessary expenditures for purposes which would have effected a real economy. The postmaster-general states that there was a large annual waste in the handling of mail, resulting from lack of modern facilities and equipment. Scarcely a large city in the country has adequate quarters for the transaction federal business. The government pays rent in the city of Washington alone of more than one million dollars annually. It is estimated that the government is paying rentals of twenty million dollars in the nation. True economy would be effected by the erection of federal buildings, especially in the numerous instances where sites acquired many years ago have been left vacant because the administration did not desire to have these expenditures appear in the budget. It is not economy to refuse to spend money and to have our soldiers living in barracks which the chief of staff of the army recently stated were indecent and below the standard for the meanest type of housing permitted anywhere. And the wise, properly-timed construction of needed public improvements would substantially tend to lessen the evils of unemployment.

If the people commission me to do it, I shall, with the aid of the Congress, effect a real reorganization and consolidation of governmental activities upon a business basis and institute the real economy which comes from prudent expenditure. I shall aid programs for the relief of unemployment, recognizing its deep, human and social significance, and shall strive to accomplish a national well-being resting upon the prosperity of the individual men and women who constitute the nation.

Acting upon the principle of "Equal opportunity for all, special privileges for none," I shall ask Congress to carry out the tariff declaration of our platform. To be sure, the Republican Party will attempt in the campaign to misrepresent Democratic attitude to the tariff. The Democratic Party does not, and under my leadership will not, advocate any sudden or drastic revolution in our economic system which would cause business upheaval and popular distress. This principle was recognized as far back as the passage of the Underwood Tariff Bill. Our platform restates it in unmistakable language. The Democratic Party stands squarely for the maintenance of legitimate business and a high standard of wages for American labor. Both can be maintained and at the same time the tariff can be taken out of the realm of politics and treated on a strictly business basis.

*   *   *

Against the practice of legislative log rolling, Woodrow Wilson pointed the way to a remedy. It provided for the creation and maintenance of a nonpolitical, quasi-judicial, fact-finding commission which could investigate and advise the President and Congress as to the tariff duties really required to protect American industry and safeguard the high standard of American wages.

I shall restore this commission to the high level upon which President Wilson placed it, in order that, properly manned, it may produce the facts that will enable us to ascertain how we may increase the purchasing power of everybody's income or wages by the adjustment of those schedules which are now the result of log-rolling and which upon their face are extortionate and unnecessary.

*   *   *

Through a long line of distinguished secretaries of state, Republican and Democratic alike, this country had assumed a position of world leadership in the endeavor to outlaw war and substitute reason for force. At the end of President Wilson's administration we enjoyed not only the friendship but the respectful admiration of the peoples of the world. Today we see unmistakable evidences of a widespread distrust of us and unfriendliness to us, particularly among our Latin-American neighbors.

I especially stress the necessity for the restoration of cordial relations with Latin-America and I take my text from a great Republican secretary of state, Elihu Root, who said: "We consider that the independence and equal rights of the smallest and weakest member of the family of nations deserve as much respect as those of the great empires. We pretend to no right, privilege or power that we do not freely concede to each one of the American republics."

The present administration has been false to that declaration of one of its greatest party leaders. The situation in Nicaragua fairly exemplifies our departure from this high standard. The administration has intervened in an election dispute between two conflicting factions, sent our troops into Nicaragua, maintained them there for years, and this without the consent of Congress. To settle this internal dispute, our marines have died and hundreds of Nicaraguans in turn have been killed by our marines. Without consultation with Congress, the administration entered on this long-continued occupation of the territory of a supposedly friendly nation by our armed troops.

To no declaration of our platform do I more heartily commit myself than the one for the abolition of the practice of the President of entering into agreements for the settlement of internal disputes in Latin-American countries, unless the agreements have been consented to by the Senate, as provided for in the Constitution of the United States. I personally declare what the platform declares: "Interference in the purely internal affairs of Latin-American countries must cease," and I specifically pledge myself to follow this declaration with regard to Mexico as well as the other Latin-American countries.

The Monroe Doctrine must be maintained, but not as a pretext for meddling with the purely local concerns of countries which, even though they be small, are sovereign and entitled to demand and receive respect for their sovereignty. And I shall certainly do all that lies in my power to bring about the fullest concerted action between this country and all the Latin-American countries with respect to any step which it may ever be necessary to take to discharge such responsibilities to civilization as may be placed upon us by the Monroe Doctrine.

... Our unwarranted intervention in internal affairs in Latin-America and this specious reason for it constitute the basis upon which other countries may seek to justify imperialistic policies which threaten world peace and materially lessen the effectiveness which might otherwise lie in the multilateral treaties.

*   *   *

In 1921 there was negotiated a treaty for the limitation of the construction of battleships and battle cruisers of over ten thousand tons. It was approved without party dispute as a start of the process of removing from the backs of the toiling masses of the world the staggering burden of the hundreds of millions of dollars that are wrung from them every year for wasteful transformation into engines of destruction. For seven years the Republican administration has followed it with nothing effective. No limitation has been placed upon land armaments, submarines, vessels of war of under ten thousand tons displacement, poisonous gases or any of the other machinery devised by man for the destruction of human life. In this respect our diplomacy has been futile.

I believe the American people desire to assume their fair share of responsibility for the administration of a world of which they are a part, without political alliance with any foreign nation. I pledge myself to a resumption of a real endeavor to make the outlawry of war effective by removing its causes and to substitute the methods of conciliation, conference, arbitration and judicial determination.

The President of the United States has two constitutional duties with respect to prohibition. The first is embodied in his oath of office. If, with one hand on the Bible and the other hand reaching up to heaven, I promise the people of this country that "I will faithfully execute the office of President of the United States and to the best of my ability preserve, protect and defend the Constitution of the United States," you may be sure that I shall live up to that oath to the last degree. I shall to the very limit execute the pledge of our platform "to make an honest endeavor to enforce the eighteenth amendment and all other provisions of the federal Constitution and all laws enacted pursuant thereto."

The President does not make the laws. He does his best to execute them whether he likes them or not. The corruption in enforcement activities which caused a former Republican prohibition administrator to state that three-fourths of the dry agents were political ward heelers named by politicians without regard to civil service laws and that prohibition is the "new political pork barrel," I will ruthlessly stamp out. Such conditions can not and will not exist under any administration presided over by me.

The second constitutional duty imposed upon the President is "To recommend to the Congress such measures as he shall judge necessary and expedient." Opinion upon prohibition cuts squarely across the two great political parties. There are thousands of so-called "wets and drys" in each. The platform of my party is silent upon any question of change in the law. I personally believe that there should be change and I shall advise the Congress in accordance with my constitutional duty of whatever changes I deem "necessary or expedient." It will then be for the people and the representatives in the national and state legislatures to determine whether these changes shall be made.

I will state the reasons for my belief. In a book, "Law and Its Origin," recently called to my notice, James C. Carter, one of the leaders of the bar of this country, wrote of the conditions which exist "when a law is made declaring conduct widely practiced and widely regarded as innocent to be a crime." He points out that in the enforcement of such a law "trials become scenes of perjury and subornation of perjury; juries find abundant excuses for rendering acquittal or persisting in disagreement contrary to their oaths," and he concludes, "Perhaps worst of all is that general regard and reverence for law are impaired, a consequence the mischief of which can scarcely be estimated." ...

I believe in temperance. We have not achieved temperance under the present system. The mothers and fathers of young men and women throughout this land know the anxiety and worry which has been brought to them by their children's use of liquor in a way which was unknown before prohibition. I believe in reverence for law. Today disregard of the prohibition laws is insidiously sapping respect for all law. I raise, therefore, what I profoundly believe to be a great moral issue involving the righteousness of our children's morals.

*　　*　　*

I believe, moreover, that there should be submitted to the people the question of some change in the provisions of the eighteenth amendment. Certainly no one foresaw when the amendment was ratified the conditions which exist today of bootlegging, corruption and open violation of the law in all parts of the country. The people themselves should, after this eight years of trial, be permitted to say whether existing conditions should be rectified. I personally believe in an amendment in the eighteenth amendment which would give to each individual state itself, only after approval by a referendum popular vote of its people, the right, wholly within its borders, to import, manufacture or cause to be manufactured and sell alcoholic beverages, the sale to be made only by the state itself and not for consumption in any public place. We may well learn from the experience of other nations. Our Canadian neighbors have gone far in this manner to solve this problem by the method of sale made by the state itself and not by private individuals.

There is no question here of the return of the saloon. When I stated that the saloon "is and ought to be a defunct institution in this country" I meant it. I mean it today. I will never advocate nor approve any law which directly or indirectly permits the return of the saloon.

*   *   *

Publicity agents of the Republican administration have written so many articles on our general prosperity, that they have prevented the average man from having a proper appreciation of the degree of distress existing today among farmers and stock-raisers. From 1910 to the present time the farm debt has increased by the striking sum of ten billions of dollars, or from four billion to fourteen billion dollars. The value of farm property between 1920 and 1925 decreased by twenty billions of dollars. This depression made itself felt in an enormous increase of bank failures in the agricultural districts. In 1927 there were 830 bank failures, with total liabilities of over 270 millions of dollars, almost entirely in the agricultural sections, as against 49 such failures during the last year of President Wilson's administration.

*   *   *

This country can not be a healthy, strong economic body if one of its members, so fundamentally important as agriculture, is sick almost to the point of economic death.

*   *   *

When, therefore, I say that I am in accord with our platform declaration that the solution of this problem must be a prime and immediate concern of the Democratic administration, I make no class appeal. I am stating a proposition as vital to the welfare of business as of agriculture.

*   *   *

It is bad logic, bad economics and an abandonment of government responsibility to say that as to agriculture alone, the government should not aid.

Twice a Republican Congress has passed legislation only to have it vetoed by a President of their own party, and whether the veto of that specific measure was right or wrong, it is undisputed that no adequate substitute was ever recommended to the Congress by the President and that no constructive plan of relief was ever formulated by any leader of the Republican Party in place of the plan which its Congress passed and its President vetoed....

Co-operative, co-ordinated marketing and warehousing of surplus farm products is essential just as co-ordinated, co-operative control of the flow of capital was found necessary to the regulation of our country's finances. To accomplish financial stability, the Federal Reserve System was called into being by a Democratic administration. The question for agriculture is complex. Any plan devised must also be co-ordinated with the other phases of our business institutions. Our platform declares for the development of cooperative marketing and an earnest endeavor to solve the problem of the distribution of the cost of dealing with crop surpluses over the marketed unit of the crop whose producers are benefited by such assistance.... I propose to substitute action for inaction and friendliness for hostility. In my administration of the government of my state, whenever I was confronted with a problem of this character, I called into conference those best equipped on the particular subject in hand. I shall follow that course with regard to agriculture. Farmers and farm leaders with such constructive aid as will come from sound economists and fair minded leaders of finance and business must work out the detail....

If I am elected, I shall immediately after election ask leaders of the type I have named irrespective of party to enter upon this task. I shall join with them in the discharge. of their duties during the coming winter and present to Congress immediately upon its convening, the solution recommended by the body of men best fitted to render this signal service to the nation....

Adequate distribution is necessary to bring a proper return to production. Increased efficiency of railroad transportation and terminal handling means lowering of cost which in turn reflects itself in the form of increased purchasing power through reduction in the cost of every-day necessities of life.

I believe in encouraging the construction and use of modern highways to carry the short haul of small bulk commodities and to aid in effective marketing of farm products.

*   *   *

With the development of inland waterways goes the control of floods thereon. The Mississippi flood of last year brought home to the nation the imperative need for a national policy of flood control. The last two administrations waited for this calamity and for universal demand that something be done instead of taking leadership in this important work....

*   *   *

Wide possibilities for public good are latent in what remains of our natural resources. I pledge myself to a progressive liberal conservation policy based upon the same principles to which I have given my support in the state of New York, and to fight against selfish aggression in this field wherever it appears and irrespective of whom it may involve. No nation in history has been more careless about the conservation of natural resources than has ours. We have denuded our forests. We have been slow to reclaim lands for development and have allowed to run to waste or have given to private exploitation our public waters with their great potential power for the development of electrical energy.

The value of this heritage can best be measured when we consider the recent disclosures of the methods employed by private monopolies to wrest our remaining water powers from public control.

No more dishonest or unpatriotic propaganda has ever been seen in this country than that disclosed by the investigation into the methods of certain utility corporations. Private corporations to gain control of public resources have procured the writing of textbooks for the public schools; have subsidized lecturers pretending to give to the country their own honest and unbiased advice; have employed as their agents former public officials and have endeavored to mislead public opinion by the retention of the services of leaders of the community in various parts of the country. Highly paid lobbyists penetrated into every state and into the legislative halls of the nation itself

As against propaganda, it is the duty of the Democratic Party to set up truth. The ownership of some of these great water powers is in the nation, of others in the several states. These sources of water power must remain forever under public ownership and control. Where they are owned by the federal government, they should remain under federal control. Where they are owned by an individual state, they should be under the control of that state, or where they are owned by states jointly, they should be under the control of those states.

... The government — federal, state or the authority representing joint states — must control the switch that turns on or off the power so greedily sought by certain private groups without the least regard for the public good.

I shall carry into federal administration the same policy which I have maintained against heavy odds in my own state. Under no circumstances should private monopoly be permitted to capitalize for rate-making purposes water power sites that are the property of the people themselves. It is to me unthinkable that the government of the United States or any state thereof will permit either direct or indirect alienation of water power sites.

*   *   *

It will be the policy of my administration while retaining government ownership and control, to develop a method of operation for Muscle Shoals which will reclaim for the government some fair revenue from the enormous expenditure already made for its development and which is now a complete waste. In this way the original peace-time purpose of the construction of this plant will be achieved. The nation will be reimbursed, agriculture will be benefited by the cheap production of nitrates for fertilizer and the surplus power will be distributed to the people.

*   *   *

The use of our national forests for recreation should be greatly extended. I also pledge myself to give the same continuing interest and support to a national park, reforestation and recreation program as have brought about the establishment of a great Conservation and State Park System in the state of New York.

*   *   *

Under the administration of Woodrow Wilson, a large body of progressive legislation for the protection of those laboring in industry, was enacted. Our, platform continues that tradition of the party. We declare for the principle of collective bargaining which alone can put the laborer upon a basis of fair equality with the employer;

for the human principle that labor is not a commodity; for fair treatment to government and federal employees; and for specific and immediate attention to the serious problems of unemployment.

From these premises it was inevitable that our platform should further recognize grave abuses in the issuance of injunctions in labor disputes which threaten the very principle of collective bargaining. Chief Justice Taft in 1919 stated that government of the relations between capital and labor by injunction was an absurdity. Justice Holmes and Justice Brandeis of the United States Supreme Court unite in an opinion which describes the restraints on labor imposed by a federal injunction as a reminder of involuntary servitude.

*   *   *

I shall continue my sympathetic interest in the advancement of progressive legislation for the protection and advancement of working men and women. Promotion of proper care of maternity, infancy and childhood and the encouragement of those scientific activities of the national government which advance the safeguards of public health, are so fundamental as to need no expression from me other than my record as legislator and as governor.

*   *   *

Every race has made its contribution to the betterment of America. While I stand squarely on our platform declaration that the laws which limit immigration must be preserved in full force and effect, I am heartily in favor of removing from the immigration law the harsh provision which separates families, and I am opposed to the principle of restriction based upon the figures of immigrant population contained in a census thirty-eight years old. I believe this is designed to discriminate against certain nationalities, and is an unwise policy. It is in no way essential to a continuance of the restriction advocated in our platform.

While this is a government of laws and not of men, laws do not execute themselves. We must have people of character and outstanding ability to serve the nation. To me one of the greatest elements of satisfaction in my nomination is the fact that I owe it to no one man. or set of men. I can with complete honesty make the statement that my nomination was brought about by no promise given or implied by me or any one in my behalf. I will not be influenced in appointments by the question of a person's wet or dry attitude, by whether he is rich or poor, whether he comes from the north, south, east or west, or by what church he attends in the worship of God. The sole standard of my appointments will be the same as they have been in my governorship — integrity of the man or woman and his or her ability to give me the greatest possible aid in devoted service to the people.

*   *   *

Address by Governor Alfred E. Smith
Oklahoma City, September 20, 1928

The religious issue would not die, so Smith, much angrier than in his reply to Marshall, chose Oklahoma City to denounce the Protestant fanatics and bigots who were terrified at the prospect of a Catholic in the White House.

A former Senator from your own State, a member of my own party, has deserted the party which honored him, upon the pretense, as he states it, that because I am a member of Tammany Hall I am not entitled to your support for the high office to which I have been nominated....

What Mr. Owen personally thinks is of no account in this campaign....

* * *

I know what lies behind all this and I shall tell you. I specifically refer to the question of my religion. Ordinarily, that word should never be used in a political campaign. The necessity for using it is forced on me by Senator Owen and his kind, and I feel that at least once in this campaign, I, as the candidate of the Democratic Party, owe it to the people of this country to discuss frankly and openly with them this attempt of Senator Owen and the forces behind him to inject bigotry, hatred, intolerance and un-American sectarian division into a campaign which should be an intelligent debate of the important issues which confront the American people.

In New York I would not have to discuss it. The people know me. But in view of the vast amount of literature anonymously circulated throughout this country, the cost of which must run into huge sums of money, I owe it to my country and my party to bring it out into the open. There is a well-founded belief that the major portion of this publication, at least, is being financed through political channels.

* * *

I can think of no greater disaster to this country than to have the voters of it divide upon religious lines. It is contrary to the spirit, not only of the Declaration of Independence, but of the Constitution itself. During all of our national life we have prided ourselves throughout the world on the declaration of the fundamental American truth that all men are created equal.

* * *

The Grand Dragon of the Realm of Arkansas, writing to a citizen of that State, urges my defeat because I am a Catholic, and in the letter suggests to the man, who happened to be a delegate to the Democratic convention, that by voting against me he was upholding American ideals and institutions as established by our forefathers.

2699

The Grand Dragon that thus advised a delegate to the national convention to vote against me because of my religion is a member of an order known as the Ku Klux Klan, who have the effrontery to refer to themselves as 100 per cent. Americans.

Yet totally ignorant of the history and tradition of this country and its institutions and, in the name of Americanism, they breathe into the hearts and souls of their members hatred of millions of their fellow countrymen because of their religious belief.

Nothing could be so out of line with the spirit of America. Nothing could be so foreign to the teachings of Jefferson. Nothing could be so contradictory of our whole history. Nothing could be so false to the teachings of our Divine Lord Himself. The world knows no greater mockery than the use of the blazing cross, the cross upon which Christ died, as a symbol to install into the hearts of men a hatred of their brethren, while Christ preached and died for the love and brotherhood of man.

I fully appreciate that here and there, in a great country like ours, there are to be found misguided people and, under ordinary circumstances, it might be well to be charitable and make full and due allowance for them. But this campaign, so far advanced, discloses such activity on their part as to constitute, in my opinion, a menace not alone to the party, but to the country itself.

*   *   *

One lie widely circulated, particularly through the southern part of the country, is that during my governorship I appointed practically nobody to office but members of my own church?

What are the facts? On investigation I find that in the cabinet of the Governor sit fourteen men. Three of the fourteen are Catholics, ten Protestants, and one of Jewish faith. In various bureaus and divisions of the Cabinet officers, the Governor appointed twenty-six people. Twelve of them are Catholics and fourteen of them are Protestants. Various other State officials, making up boards and commissions, and appointed by the Governor, make a total of 157 appointments, of which thirty-five were Catholics, 160 were Protestants, twelve were Jewish, and four I could not find out about.

I have appointed a large number of judges of all our courts, as well as a large number of county officers, for the purpose of filling vacancies. They total in number 177, of which sixty-four were Catholics, ninety were Protestants, eleven were Jewish, and twelve of the officials I was unable to find anything about so far as their religion was concerned.

This is a complete answer to the false, misleading and, if I may be permitted the use of the harsher word, lying statements that have found their way through a large part of this country in the form of printed matter.

If the American people are willing to sit silently by and see large amounts of money secretly pour into false and misleading propaganda for political purposes, I repeat that I see in this not only a danger to the party, but a danger to the country.

*   *   *

As contemptible as anything could possibly be is an article on the very front page of a publication devoted to the doings of a church wherein the gospel of Christ is preached. I refer to the Ashland Avenue Baptist, a publication coming from Lexington, Ky., in which a bitter and cruel attack is made upon me personally and is so ridiculous that ordinarily no attention should be paid to it. It speaks of my driving an automobile down Broadway at the rate of fifty miles an hour, and specially states I was driving the car myself while intoxicated.

Everybody who knows me knows full well I do not know how to drive an automobile, that I never tried it. As for the rest of the contemptible, lying statement, it is as false as this part.

*　　　*　　　*

I well know that I am not the first public man who has been made the object of such baseless slander. It was poured forth on Grover Cleveland and upon Theodore Roosevelt, as well as upon myself. But as to me, the wicked motive of religious intolerance has driven bigots to attempt to inject these slanders into a political campaign. I here and now drag them into the open and I denounce them as a treasonable attack upon the very foundations of American liberty.

I have been told that politically it might be expedient for me to remain silent upon this subject, but so far as I am concerned no political expediency will keep me from speaking out in an endeavor to destroy these evil attacks.

There is abundant reason for believing that Republicans high in the councils of the party have countenanced a large part of this form of campaign, if they have not actually promoted it. A sin of omission is some times as grievous as a sin of commission. They may, through official spokesmen, disclaim as much as they please responsibility for dragging into a national campaign the question of religion, something that according to our Constitution, our history and our traditions has no part in any campaign for elective public office.

Giving them the benefit of all reasonable doubt, they at least remain silent on the exhibition that Mrs. Willebrandt made of herself before the Ohio Conference of the Methodist Episcopal Church when she said:

"There are two thousand pastors here. You have in your church more than 600,000 members of the Methodist Church in Ohio alone. That is enough to swing the election. The 600,000 have friends in other states. Write to them."

This is an extract from a speech made by her in favor of a resolution offered to the effect that the conference go on record as being unalterably opposed to the election of Governor Smith and to endorse the candidacy of Herbert Hoover, the Republican candidate.

Mrs. Willebrandt holds a place of prominence in the Republican administration in Washington; she is an Assistant Attorney-General of the United States. By silence, after such a speech, the only inference one can draw is that the administration approves such political tactics. Mrs. Willebrandt is not an irresponsible person. She was Chairman of the Committee on Credentials in the Republican National Convention at Kansas City.

*　　　*　　　*

It needs no words of mine to impress that upon your minds. It is dishonest campaigning. It is un-American. It is out of line with the whole tradition and history of this government. And, to my way of thinking, is in itself sufficient to hold us up to the scorn of the thinking people of other nations.

One of the things, if not the meanest thing, in the campaign is a circular pretending to place someone of my faith in the position of seeking votes for me because of my Catholicism. Like everything of its kind, of course it is unsigned, and it would be impossible to trace its authorship. It reached me through a member of the Masonic order who, in turn, received it in the mail. It is false in its every line. It was designed on its very face to injure me with members of churches other than my own.

I here emphatically declare that I do not wish any member of my faith in any part of the United States to vote for me on any religious grounds. I want them to vote for me only when in their hearts and consciences they become convinced that my election will promote the best interests of our country.

By the same token, I cannot refrain from saying that any person who votes against me simply because of my religion is not, to my way of thinking, a good citizen.

Let me remind the Democrats of this country that we belong to the party of that Thomas Jefferson whose proudest boast was that he was the author of the Virginia statute for religious freedom. Let me remind the citizens of every political faith that that statute of religious freedom has become a part of the sacred heritage of our land.

The constitutional guaranty that there should be no religious test for public office is not a mere form of words. It represents the most vital principle that ever was given any people.

I attack those who seek to undermine it, not only because I am a good Christian, but because I am a good American and a product of America and American institutions. Everything I am, and everything I hope to be, I owe to those institutions.

The absolute separation of State and Church is part of the fundamental basis of our Constitution. I believe in that separation, and in all that it implies. That belief must be a part of the fundamental faith of every true American.

Let the people of this country decide this election upon the great and real issues of the campaign and upon nothing else.

For instance, you have all heard or read my Omaha speech on farm relief. Read the Democratic platform on farm relief, compare my speech and that platform plank with the platform plank of the Republican Party and the attitude of Mr. Hoover, so that you may decide for yourselves which of the two parties, or the two candidates, according to their spoken declarations, are best calculated to solve the problem that is pressing the people of this country for solution. By a study of that you will be conserving the interest of the cotton growers of this State and promoting its general prosperity.

Take my attitude on the development of our natural water power resources. Take the Democratic platform on that subject. Compare it with the Republican platform and with Mr. Hoover's attitude and record on the same subject, and find out from which of the two parties you can get and to which of the two candidates you can look forward with any degree of hope for the development of these resources under the control and ownership of the people themselves rather than their alienation for private profit and for private gain.

Compare the Democratic platform with the Republican platform and Mr. Hoover's attitude with mine on the all-important question of flood control and the conservation of our land and property in valley of the Mississippi. And then take the record and find out from which party you got the greatest comfort and hope for a determination of that question.

Take the subject of the reorganization of the government in the interest of economy and a greater efficiency. Compare the platforms. Compare the speeches of acceptance, and be sure to look into the record of the Republican failure to carry out its promises along these lines during the last seven and a half years.

I declare it to be in the interest of the government, for its betterment, for the betterment and welfare of the people, the duty of every citizen to study the platforms of the two parties, to study the records of the candidates and to make his choice for the Presidency of the United States solely on the ground of what best promotes interest and welfare of our great republic and all its citizens.

If the contest is fought on these lines, as I shall insist it must be, I am confident of the outcome in November.

THE VOTES IN THE 1928 ELECTION

States	Popular vote				Electoral vote	
	H. Hoover, Republican	A. Smith, Democrat	N. Thomas, Socialist	Foster, Workers	Hoover	Smith
Alabama	120,725	127,797	460	–	–	12
Arizona	52,533	38,537	–	184	3	–
Arkansas	77,751	119,196	429	317	–	9
California	1,162,323	614,365	19,595	216	13	–
Colorado	253,872	133,131	3,472	675	6	–
Connecticut	296,614	252,040	3,019	730	7	–
Delaware	68,860	36,643	329	59	3	–
Florida	144,168	101,764	4,036	3,704	6	–
Georgia	63,498	120,602	124	64	–	14
Idaho	99,848	53,074	1,308	–	4	–
Illinois	1,769,141	1,313,817	19,138	3,581	29	–
Indiana	848,290	562,691	3,871	321	15	–
Iowa	623,818	378,936	2,960	328	13	–
Kansas	513,672	193,003	6,205	320	10	–
Kentucky	558,064	381,070	837	293	13	–
Louisiana	51,160	164,655	–	–	–	10
Maine	179,923	81,179	1,068	–	6	–
Maryland	301,479	223,626	1,701	636	8	–
Massachusetts	775,566	792,758	6,262	2,464	–	18
Michigan	965,396	396,762	3,516	2,881	15	–
Minnesota	560,977	396,451	6,774	4,853	12	–
Mississippi	27,153	124,539	–	–	–	10
Missouri	834,080	662,562	3,739	–	18	–
Montana	113,300	78,578	1,667	563	4	–
Nebraska	345,745	197,959	3,434	–	8	–
Nevada	18,327	14,090	–	–	3	–
New Hampshire	115,404	80,715	455	173	4	–
New Jersey	926,050	616,517	4,897	1,257	14	–
New Mexico	69,645	48,211	–	158	3	–
New York	2,193,344	2,089,863	107,332	10,876	45	–
North Carolina	348,992	287,078	–	–	12	–
North Dakota	131,441	106,648	842	936	5	–
Ohio	1,627,546	864,210	8,683	2,836	24	–
Oklahoma	394,046	219,174	3,924	–	10	–
Oregon	205,341	109,223	2,720	1,094	5	–
Pennsylvania	2,055,382	1,067,586	18,647	4,726	38	–
Rhode Island	117,522	118,973	–	283	–	5
South Carolina	3,188	62,700	47	–	–	9
South Dakota	157,603	102,660	443	232	5	–
Tennessee	195,388	167,343	631	111	12	–
Texas	367,036	341,032	722	209	20	–
Utah	94,618	80,985	954	47	4	–
Vermont	90,404	44,440	–	–	4	–
Virginia	164,609	140,146	250	173	12	–
Washington	335,844	156,772	2,615	1,541	7	–
West Virginia	375,551	263,784	1,313	401	8	–
Wisconsin	544,205	450,259	18,213	1,528	13	–
Wyoming	52,748	29,299	788	–	3	–
	21,392,190	15,016,443	267,420	48,770	444	87

Reynolds, Socialist-Labor, 21,603; Varney, Prohibitionist, 20,106; Webb, Farm-Labor, 6,390. Total vote, 36,879,414.

Election of

1932

FRANK FREIDEL was Professor of History at Harvard University and was the most eminent scholar of 1930s American history, society, and culture. He authored *F.D.R. and the South* and *The Splendid Little War*, as well as a three-volume biography of Franklin D. Roosevelt.

Election of
1932

Frank Freidel

T he election of 1932, coming in the third year of the Great Depression, focused on the responsibility of the Government for the economic welfare of the American people. The debates of the campaign were less momentous than the aftermath of the election — the establishment by President Franklin D. Roosevelt of a new relationship between the Government and American society. Thereafter, the Federal Government took active, vigorous steps to promote and preserve prosperity, going far beyond the limited, tentative measures of President Herbert Hoover and his predecessors. The election also marked the beginning of a long period in which the Democratic Party, since 1892 the minority party, was the majority party among the electorate.

It would have taken a bold prophet indeed to have forecast in the afterglow of President Herbert Hoover's landslide victory in 1928 that only four years later he would be the victim of a comparable landslide victory for his Democratic opponent. The collapse of the boom of the 1920s, for which the Republicans had, understandably, taken credit, brought on Hoover the blame for the Depression. It was the prime factor in his defeat.

Even during its heyday in the New Era of the 1920s, the Republican Party was not so strong as the top-heavy victories in three successive presidential elections seemed to indicate. Democratic candidates had made impressive showings in the congressional elections of 1922 and 1926, and in 1930, before the Depression had become catastrophic, already had won control of the House of Representatives, and almost obtained a majority in the Senate. The appeal of Democrat Alfred E. Smith to urban voters was so great that in 1928 the results in several major cities had, for the first time, countered the Republican landslide and given Smith majorities. In New York, where Smith lost heavily despite his formidable margin in New York City, the Democratic candidate for governor, Franklin D. Roosevelt, won by a very narrow margin. Had prosperity continued, President Hoover could perhaps have looked to victory in 1932, but the Republican Party was far from invulnerable.

For its part, the Democratic Party had acute internal weaknesses that had to be overcome if it were to achieve victory even in a depression year like 1932. In both 1924 and 1928, it was seriously split over the issues of Catholicism and prohibition between its northern, urban wing — the ardent supporters of the Catholic, wet Smith — and its southern and western rural wings — predominantly Protestant and prohibitionist. The party had deadlocked between the two wings for three weeks in the 1924 convention before nominating a compromise candidate, John W. Davis, whose defeat was a foregone conclusion. In 1928, the party avoided deadlock, quickly nominating Smith, whose candidacy led to widespread defections in the South and West. The defeat of Smith in the 1928 election eliminated the urban wing from party control, as the defeat of William Gibbs McAdoo in the 1924 convention had ended southern and western domination. The defeats had prepared the way for the compromise essential to bridge over the gulf, and the Depression brought a new, transcendent issue that could relegate to the past the bitterness within the party over the wet–dry and religious controversies.

In the immediate aftermath of the 1928 election, when a vista of almost endless prosperity seemed to loom ahead, the newly elected governor of New York, Roosevelt, seemed the leading contender for the 1932 Democratic nomination. His had been the most significant Democratic victory in the year of the Hoover landslide. A country squire with urban connections and experience, he was the most influential party leader working through the 1920s among both urban and rural Democrats to restore party unity. As yet the prospect of winning the 1932 Democratic nomination seemed little more than an empty honor, scarcely worth a stubborn battle. Less than a year later, in October 1929, the great crash of the stock market triggered the Depression, and gave an entirely different appearance to the forthcoming presidential election. A Democratic Party moving toward unity and strength would have what was almost certainly a winning issue — unless, of course, a strong and obvious economic recovery were to take place before November 1932.

President Hoover's positive appeal to the electorate in the campaign of 1928 had been his identification with prosperity; he seemed to be taking responsibility for the continued economic well-being of the nation. "Given a chance to go forward with the policies of the last eight years," he had declared in his acceptance speech, "we shall soon with the help of God be in sight of the day when poverty will be banished from this nation." And in his Inaugural Address, he had asserted, "Our first object must be to provide security from poverty and want.... We want to see a nation built of home owners and farm owners. We want to see their savings protected. We want to see them in steady jobs. We want to see more and more of them insured against death and accident, unemployment and old age. We want them all secure."

When the privation and hardships of the Depression hit the American people they turned to the President, whose reiterated first concern had been their security, looking to him for succor. Nor did Hoover try to avoid his responsibilities as a deflationary sag after the Wall Street crash slowly carried the economy into ever-deepening depression. He took immediate steps of a minor nature and, as the crisis became serious, resorted to increasingly strong measures. Within most of these, there was a critical limitation — President Hoover's belief that the Federal Government should do no more than provide encouragement to business, which would voluntarily undertake the task of securing recovery. Through the prosperous years of the 1920s, he had emphasized, as he continued to insist during the Depression, that the only way to obtain national well-being was through private enterprise rather than federal legislation. That, he held, was the only proper means to attain the lofty end he had proposed in his acceptance speech and Inaugural Address. At one point during the Depression, in response to suggestions that the United States (like the Soviet Union) should issue a plan for its future, he sketched a glowing picture of abundance. It would be attained, he said, by the American people through their own efforts.

Even while Hoover continued to stress self-reliance, or what he had termed earlier "rugged individualism," the deepening Depression pushed him toward increasingly significant government intervention. Even before the stock market crash, several sectors of the American economy, such as bituminous coal mining in the Appalachians and textile manufacturing in New England, had been depressed. In the late 1920s, building construction had declined, and the sale of automobiles had started to sag. Above all, agriculture had suffered since the ending of government price supports on the great staples in 1920. By latter-day standards, the industrial worker had not fared well during the 1920s; his average pay of $1,500 in 1929 was only a third the real wages of workers forty years later, but the average cash income of farmers (with which to purchase manufactured goods and make payments on mortgages and taxes) was only $548 per year. Farm organizations throughout the 1920s sought some sort of government price-fixing scheme such as they had enjoyed during the First World War, but twice President Coolidge vetoed measures passed by the congressional farm bloc. Even before the Depression hit, President Hoover sought to redress the complaints of the farmers. He called Congress into special session in the spring of 1929 to pass the Agricultural Marketing Act, a device to try to raise farm prices. It created a Federal Farm Board with a half-billion-dollar revolving fund with which to buy surpluses. Congress in 1930 also passed the Hawley–Smoot Tariff, which placed prohibitively high barriers against farm imports as well as some manufactured goods (and provoked retaliation from other countries). It raised tariffs on farm products 30 percent, and on manufactured goods 12 percent. As late as the winter of 1930–31, the Farm Board was able to maintain the price of wheat within the United States at twenty-five to thirty cents per bushel above that in European markets, but by 1932 it had run out of funds, warehouses were overflowing, and prices within the United States had dropped to the world level. The funds of the Farm Board were too limited, and it possessed no power or enticement to persuade farmers to plant less.

At the time that Hoover took office, the great bull market of the 1920s had long since given him alarm. He blamed the Depression in part on the speculation during the Coolidge Administration. Twice he had tried to persuade President Coolidge to insist that the Federal Reserve Board raise interest rates, but Coolidge refused to interfere. Soon after he became President, Hoover did get the Federal Reserve Board to raise the rates, but this did little to quell speculation in the few remaining weeks before the crash.

At the beginning of September 1929, the stock market soared to a height that it would not again reach until the 1950s, then sagged for several weeks, and finally crashed spectacularly in late October. When it was temporarily stabilized in mid-November, stock prices were only half what they had been at the peak of the boom, yet far above the depths to which they intermittently declined during the next three years. *The New York Times* average for twenty-five industrial stocks was 452 at the peak in 1929, and only fifty-eight at the lowest point in 1932. The stock collapse led to a drop in real estate and other values, leading to deflation, and gradually declining employment.

In the first months after the stock market crash, the Depression developed slowly, seeming to require only limited government action. President Hoover obtained pledges from business and labor leaders that they would continue as before, without seeking changes in wages and hours. Significantly, Hoover also took mild steps to counter the deflationary cycle: a substantial tax cut, a lowering of Federal Reserve interest requirements, and a record-breaking appropriation for public works, $423 million. Together with the Farm Board's agricultural aid, these expedients counteracted to some extent the slow decline in production and employment through 1930. Businessmen became pessimistic, but thus far the Depression was not unusually severe.

European repercussions gave a sharp downturn to the American economy in the spring of 1931. The failure of the central bank in Austria threatened the financial systems of Germany and other nations. Desperate Europeans began to withdraw their gold holdings from American banks. President Hoover tried to stem the European crisis by agreeing to a moratorium for one year on German reparations payments and payment of war debts to the United States by former allies. The Federal Reserve Board raised interest rates to try to stop the withdrawal of gold. But the moratorium was of scant help to European countries, and the increase in interest rates speeded deflation within the United States.

By the summer of 1931, the Depression was becoming acute in the United States, and it continued to worsen for a year. President Hoover reluctantly turned toward more drastic government action. He proposed a comprehensive program, but the Democrats, in the ascendancy in Congress after the election of 1930, were slow to enact it. Hoover charged then and subsequently that they were hampering him in order to profit politically in the election of 1932. An examination of the views then and later of Democratic leaders in Congress would suggest rather that most of them did not approve of the Hoover program. The suggestions they made after Hoover was defeated and Roosevelt elected were for the most part more conservative, except on relief spending.

Congress did create in January 1932 a large-scale loan agency patterned somewhat after a First World War predecessor. This was the Reconstruction Finance Corporation, which in 1932 loaned $1.5 billion, a sum almost half the size of the previous national budget, but far from adequate to stop bank and business failures. Congress also debated the appropriation of large sums to provide relief for the millions of destitute being kept alive on pittances from private charity, and local and state governments. Since city and state governments were with few exceptions running out of funds and unable to borrow further, the pressure on the Federal Government became acute. Sympathetic congressmen tacked on amendments providing for direct relief onto a bill appropriating money to make seed loans to farmers in drought areas. Hoover, feeling that the Democratic congressmen were seeking to make him appear heartless, in February 1931 issued a public statement:

> This is not an issue as to whether people shall go hungry or cold in the United States. It is solely a question of the best method by which hunger and cold shall be prevented. It is a question as to whether the American people, on one hand, will maintain the spirit of charity and mutual self-help through voluntary giving and responsibility of local government as distinguished, on the other hand, from appropriations out of the Federal Treasury.... If we start appropriations of this character we have not only impaired something infinitely valuable in the life of the American people but have struck at the roots of self-government.... I am willing to pledge myself that if the time should ever come that the voluntary agencies of the country together with the local and state governments are unable to find resources with which to prevent hunger and suffering in my country, I will ask the aid of every resource of the Federal government because I would no more see starvation amongst our countrymen than would any Senator or Congressman.

By the summer of 1932, the point of desperation had clearly been reached. Hoover did recommend and sign a bill — but only after protesting against what he condemned as Democratic efforts to turn it into a pork-barrel measure with something for every congressional district. This bill appropriated what for the time seemed staggering sums for relief and recovery; it authorized the Reconstruction Finance Corporation to loan state and local governments $300 million for relief, and $1.5 billion for self-liquidating public works.

Although Hoover had gone much further than any preceding President in taking positive steps to combat the Depression, he had made little political headway for himself or his party. His measures, while significant innovations, were far below the scale economists would now consider minimal to counter the deflationary spiral. If he seemed cold and remote, it was in part because Democratic politicians maneuvered him into making statements that seemed to echo Grover Cleveland: "We cannot squander ourselves into prosperity." He became even more unpopular because the extent and degree of suffering in 1931–32 was far worse than the calm appraisals from the White House indicated. By the time the election came, according to the cautious estimates of Hoover himself, one worker out of five was unemployed. One out of three was unemployed in big cities such as Chicago. A large part of those still working were receiving such low wages or working so few hours that they barely survived. A quarter of the women employed in Chicago were earning less than ten cents an hour. Relief payments outside of a few relatively rich states like New York were usually a starvation level pittance; in Detroit payments were five cents a day per person. Hoover's Secretary of War, Patrick J. Hurley, proposed that restaurants help by saving the table leavings of their patrons for hungry people. It was an unnecessary suggestion. Few restaurant scraps went unsalvaged; few garbage piles were without scavengers. Edmund Wilson reported that in Chicago he saw a woman take off her glasses while hunting scraps for her son so that she would not see the maggots in the meat. Several hundred thousand unemployed, including many teenage boys and some girls, drifted about the country on freight cars, or camped in shantytowns along the tracks, under bridges, or in dumps — towns always known as "Hoovervilles."

Farmers fared little better, although most of them did have something to eat, as long as they could hold onto their farms. A quarter of them had lost their holdings before Hoover left office. In some areas cotton remained unpicked, farmers could pay so little to the pickers — not enough to keep the pickers fed. Mountains of produce went to waste. Corn held over from the previous year cost much less than the cheapest soft coal, so that many Iowa farmers kept themselves warm burning corn. Some sheep raisers found when they marketed their lambs that each brought no more than the cost of a pair of lamb chops in a railroad dining car. Evicted tenant farmers and migrant farm workers, traveling along the highways, shared the national hunger. They too made bitter jokes about the Hoover Administration. An Oklahoma editor, Oscar Ameringer, gave a ride to a family of these tenant farmers in Arkansas. The wife was clutching a chicken she had found killed on the highway, remarking, "They promised me a chicken in the pot, and now I got mine."

Amid the suffering and the fright, there was surprisingly little violence. There was not even much radicalism. One Republican senator created a flurry in the newspapers in May 1932, when he declared that the nation needed a Mussolini to rescue it from its difficulties. His was almost a lone voice, and his statement was not to be taken seriously. Rather, the electorate was waiting for the election of 1932 to bring a change. That was probably what was worrying the Republican senator.

The Republicans, despite the growing unpopularity of their party and the overwhelming unpopularity of their President, had no real choice in 1932 but to renominate him. Although Hoover had not been notable for his political skill, he did have firm enough control over the party machinery to prevent any serious challenge to his nomination. Nor was the nomination worth a serious fight had there been a strong contender. R. V. Peel and T. C. Donnelly, in their contemporary study of the 1932 campaign remarked, "After 1929 no stock depreciated in value more than that of the GOP."

There were only a few tentative efforts to obtain another candidate. The most serious, from the standpoint of the Democratic opposition, were the feelers among one-time Theodore Roosevelt Progressives, the Bull Moosers of 1912, on behalf of either Senator Hiram Johnson of California or Governor Gifford Pinchot of Pennsylvania. Johnson refused to become involved. Senator William E. Borah, another Republican progressive, declined even to allow the Idaho delegation to the convention to pledge itself to him as a favorite son. Indeed, Borah would not serve on the delegation. On the other hand, Pinchot did not stop Harold L. Ickes of Chicago from making a canvass upon his behalf. It showed so little support that Pinchot refused to be a candidate. But, had the Democrats not nominated Roosevelt or some like-minded figure, the progressives within the Republican Party might have formed a third party. Mrs. Pinchot reported to Borah after the Republican convention that she had been to Washington and seen Hiram Johnson, who felt as they did, and would "be delighted to come into a small group to talk things over next week — after we see what happens in the Democratic Convention."

A few Republicans seeking a more popular candidate tried to start a "draft Coolidge" movement in the fall of 1931. Coolidge, in such ill health that he could hardly participate in the 1932 campaign, firmly squelched proposals "that a former president should use his prestige to attempt to secure a nomination against a President of his own party." Senator Dwight Morrow of New Jersey, renowned for his skillful restoration of amicable relations with Mexico, and as the father-in-law of the aviator Charles Lindbergh, would have been a likely Republican choice had Hoover decided not to run a second time, but Morrow died in October 1931. As it was, the only open challenger to the President was a conservative former senator from Maryland, Dr. Joseph I. France. He entered presidential preferential primaries where, unopposed, he won empty victories; Republican conventions in these states chose Hoover delegates. At the national convention France received 4 votes.

The Republican convention, opening at Chicago on June 14, 1932, was a dull, dispirited gathering. There was little illusion among most of the delegates. Many of them were federal officeholders facing the loss of their positions in the almost inevitable overturn of the Republicans. Meanwhile, with the convention machinery being firmly run from the White House, the delegates had little to do but ratify its decisions. The only modification that the convention made in the platform draft that Secretary of the Treasury Ogden Mills brought from Washington was in the fabrication of the prohibition plank. Indeed, the delegates seemed to take little interest in the acute economic problems the depression had created, and preferred to focus on the question of whether or not the 18th (prohibition) Amendment to the Constitution should be retained. Mauritz Hallgren asserted in *The Nation*, "The sight of some hundreds of representatives, even of Republican officeholders, bawling for beer, while all about them is misery in the extreme, has virtually crushed what little faith I have left in

American society. The wet circus might at least have been partly excused had the convention in any substantial way recognized the need for action to meet the unemployment problem. But not a single voice was raised in behalf of the hungry millions."

On the second evening of the convention, when James R. Garfield of Ohio, chairman of the Resolutions Committee, read through the eighty-five-hundred-word platform, the delegates paid little attention to any of the thirty-seven planks except the one on prohibition. It was a compromise that Hoover's supporters had worked out at the convention. On the one hand, it defended prohibition, and, on the other, it asserted that, if the people of the states wished to modify it through a new amendment they should have the right to do so:

> We ... believe that the people should have an opportunity to pass upon a proposed amendment the provision of which, while retaining in the Federal Government power to preserve the gains already made in dealing with the evils inherent in the liquor traffic, shall allow states to deal with the problem as their citizens may determine, but subject always to the power of the Federal Government to protect those states where prohibition may exist and safeguard our citizens everywhere from the return of the saloon and attendant abuses.

The Republican platform was a comprehensive defense of the Hoover program, ranging from its economic policies to pledges to stamp out racketeering and illicit narcotic traffic. It promised "equal opportunity and rights for our Negro citizens" — a plank that was to have no counterpart in the Democratic platform. The fundamentally conservative nature of the platform was most evident in its conclusion, a damning of the Democratic record in Congress:

> In contrast with the Republican policies and record, we contrast those of the Democratic as evidenced by the action of the House of Representatives under Democratic leadership and control, which includes:
> "1. The issuance of flat currency;
> "2. Instructions to the Federal Reserve Board and the Secretary of the Treasury to attempt to manipulate commodity prices;
> "3. The guarantee of bank deposits;
> "4. The squandering of the public resources and the unbalancing of the budget through pork-barrel appropriations which bear little relation to distress and would tend through delayed business revival to decrease rather than increase employment.
> "Generally on economic matters we pledge the Republican Party —
> "1. To maintain unimpaired the national credit.
> "2. To defend and preserve a sound currency and an honest dollar.
> "3. To stand steadfastly by the principle of a balanced budget."

These economic matters led to no debate. Rather, the convention argued for hours whether to accept the prohibition plank or vote for outright repeal. Senator Hiram Bingham of Connecticut, who introduced a minority report of the Platform Committee, and President Nicholas Murray Butler of Columbia University denounced the prohibition plank as an insincere compromise. Ultimately, they were voted down, 681 to 472.

The Republican platform, the keynote address of Senator L. J. Dickinson of Iowa, and the address nominating Hoover by Representative Joseph L. Scott of California, all had much in common. They defended the Hoover Administration and spread out with pride the Republican record of the 1920s. With equal vigor they attacked the Democratic opposition. But the program they recommended for the future was nothing more than a continuation of the present policies of the Administration. In the preamble to the platform was the formula for overcoming the Depression, set forth in words that sounded as if they might be Hoover's own: "The people themselves, by their own courage, their own patient and resolute effort in the readjustments of their own affairs can and will work out the cure. It is our task as a party, by leadership and a wise determination of policy to assist that recovery." Senator Dickinson, excoriating the proposals of "zealots and demagogues, socialists and communists" for ending the Depression, suggested that the only sound solution was the reelection of the President. "Through all this shouting and turmoil, while our self-appointed saviors strutted in the lime-light of publicity," he declared, "the man in the White House continued patiently and persistently the great task of restoring our normal economic balance." Representative Scott, in his nominating speech, hinted that any more positive governmental program than Hoover's would mean dictatorship. "We deny the right of our political adversaries to arrogate to themselves the credit of placing human rights before property rights," he declaimed. Reminding the delegates that Lincoln had asserted (with reference to slavery), "God never made a man good enough to keep his fellow man in subjection," Scott addressed himself to Hoover and the Depression: "So, in these days of stark communism and ill-starred militarism, we had better renew our course.... [President Hoover] has taught us to strain our individual selves to the limit rather than cowardly to lie down under a paternal government because he knows that rewards come to those who bear the burden of the heat of the day."

There was scant indication in the convention oratory that any course other than that already fixed was essential to redress the acute national distress. The Administration leaders seemed to be confining the convention to a defense of the President's policies even though at that very time, June 1932, the country had slipped into the lowest depths of the Depression. There was no sign that these policies would suffice, and ample evidence throughout the country indicated that Hoover and the Republican Party were being held responsible for the national plight. Perhaps it made no difference that the convention did not put forth a strong set of proposals, since only an economic upswing far more positive than the meager improvement beginning soon after the convention could save the Hoover Administration in November.

In any event, the delegates reacted enthusiastically to Representative Scott's nominating speech, parading up and down the aisles for half an hour while the organ blared and balloons bearing Hoover's name drifted down upon them from nets hung under the rafters. The Republican managers were careful that there was no opportunity for the national radio audience to hear any dissent. When Senator France was being nominated, something went wrong with the public address system. When France tried to obtain the rostrum to withdraw and place the name of the popular Coolidge in nomination, police dragged him from the hall, ostensibly because his credentials were not in order. The convention managers were being overcautious; there was not the slightest likelihood of a stampede for Coolidge. The first ballot was:

Herbert Hoover	1,126.5
Senator John J. Blaine of Wisconsin	13
Calvin Coolidge	4.5
Joseph I. France	4
James J. Wadsworth Jr.	1
	1,149

Three delegates did not vote; one was absent.

Hoover's running mate, Vice-President Charles Curtis of Kansas, evoked little enthusiasm even among the delegates. He was notable only because he was partly of Indian ancestry and had spent much of his boyhood on a reservation. He was elderly, conservative, and dull. Republican publicists listing "Curtis epigrams" had to content themselves with words like these: "Expenses of Government should be reduced wherever and whenever it is possible to do so." The delegates would have liked to bolt to Coolidge's dynamic Vice-President, General Charles G. Dawes. When Dawes refused to permit his name to be placed in nomination, opposition to Curtis deteriorated. Five other candidates were nominated, but Curtis received the Republican nomination. When, at the end of the first ballot, he was only 19¼ ballots short of a majority, Pennsylvania switched its 75 votes to him. Curtis was a weak candidate, but that seemed to make little difference. The delegates left in the hands of the President, who had so successfully dominated the convention from its opening to its close, the task of rescuing himself and the party from impending disaster.

The Democrats for their part approached the campaign of 1932 with jubilant anticipation. The presidential nomination became a prize worth the most strenuous efforts, since almost any candidate they might choose seemed certain to be elected. Only a willful course of self-destruction such as the three-week deadlock at the 1924 convention could prevent victory in 1932. Yet the debacle of 1924 could conceivably be repeated, since the convention rules, inserted to protect the southern minority in the Jackson Administration, still required a two-thirds majority of the delegates to nominate a candidate. A repetition of the 1928 fiasco when the Solid South in the general election deserted the wet, Catholic candidate could also threaten defeat. These two recent disasters led to a certain wariness among most Democratic leaders, who by 1932 were ready to prefer national electoral victory to internecine triumph. Still, the prize was so desirable that the conflict, within bounds, was keen, and the result at the convention by no means certain until the last minute. The battle for the nomination was sharper and more dramatic than the national campaign that followed.

From the outset almost four years earlier, Governor Franklin D. Roosevelt was the front-runner. His task was to preserve his candidacy against all combinations among his opponents, and somehow to continue in front. Early candidacies often suffered political blight long before the presidential year. Roosevelt was aware of his peril and, having no choice but to be an early candidate, sought to put himself so far ahead of other contenders that they could not conceivably catch up with him.

Roosevelt was unusually well prepared to be a presidential contender. Unlike President Hoover, Roosevelt's absorbing interest, since he had left a New York law clerkship in 1910 to run for the state senate, had been political craftsmanship. In a number of campaigns and offices he had gradually perfected it.

Franklin D. Roosevelt was proud of his name, in itself a considerable asset during the Depression years. (He was also firm about how he wanted it pronounced, and sent word to the radio networks in 1931 that it was: "Ro-sevelt. With the accent on the first of the three syllables. And the *o* pronounced as if there were only one instead of two.") For some years he had followed in the footsteps of Theodore Roosevelt, his own remote cousin, and his wife's uncle. He too had served in the New York State legislature, had been Assistant Secretary of the Navy, and, after a considerable hiatus, became governor of New York. Much of the Roosevelt aura had rubbed off onto him, giving the impression that his election as President would bring a return to spectacular action. "There was never a more *true red blooded* fighting American than dear old Teddy Roosevelt," an admirer wrote in 1931. "To my mind I think that you would be a chip off the old block."

Within the Democratic Party, Roosevelt had sought as early as 1920 to establish himself as the young heir to Wilsonian progressivism. In that year, although only thirty-eight, he had received the Democratic nomination for Vice-President, perhaps in part because of his name, but even more because of his outstanding record as an effective Assistant Secretary of the Navy during the First World War. Although the Democratic cause was hopeless that year, he had campaigned energetically both as a progressive and an advocate of the League of Nations, obtaining a national network of friends among Democratic Party workers.

In 1921, a severe polio attack deprived Roosevelt of the use of his legs and seemed to remove him as a contender for high office. He continued actively in politics, even through months of acute pain as he convalesced. Since he was not an office-seeker, he was able to avoid much of the factionalism, and to seek throughout the 1920s to close the gap between the Democrats of the northeastern cities and those in the rest of the country. It was these qualifications that led Governor Alfred E. Smith of New York to choose Roosevelt in 1924 to lead his pre-convention campaign and place his name in nomination. Roosevelt was one of the few Democrats who came out of the 1924 convention with his reputation enhanced. In subsequent years, as Roosevelt developed Warm Springs, Georgia, as a treatment center for polio, he also strengthened his alliance with southern Democratic leaders. In 1928 he again nominated Smith, then was edged almost completely out of any voice in the Smith campaign. Yet Smith persuaded the reluctant Roosevelt a few weeks later to run for governor of New York in order to strengthen the ticket in that key state. (Roosevelt had reiterated that he did not want to seek office until he had regained the use of his legs. Moreover, he had not wanted to run in as bad a year as 1928.) After a slow start, his campaign gained momentum. Smith himself effectively squashed suggestions that Roosevelt was physically unable to hold office, saying, "A Governor does not have to be an acrobat."

Roosevelt quickly demonstrated his strength as governor of New York. In so doing, a coolness developed between him and Smith. As a renowned governor who had brilliantly reorganized the New York State administration, Smith had never taken Roosevelt very seriously, and may even have thought that he could continue behind the scenes to influence state affairs. He was stunned by both his national defeat and Roosevelt's failure to depend on him and his lieutenants for counsel. Roosevelt became very decidedly governor in his own right, which was vital if he was to be a serious contender for the presidential nomination. It also led to a bitter struggle in 1932 with Smith and his followers.

Roosevelt undertook the governorship of New York amidst unusual public attention, already the leading possibility for the 1932 presidential nomination. Even the sober *New York Times* pointed out editorially as early as November 1928 that Roosevelt was "within reach of the elements of party leadership." He continued his correspondence and occasional meeting with Democratic Party leaders from through-out the country, and undertook a mildly progressive course within the state of New York. He demonstrated himself to be a capable administrator and a brilliant political master over the Republican legislature from which he wrested considerable legis-lation. He won a substantial following among the upstate electorate by courting farmers and struggling to obtain cheaper electric power. He spoke to voters in person during frequent tours of the state and appealed to them effectively through informal radio talks, the forerunners of the presidential "fireside chats." James A. Farley, who became state chairman of the Democratic Party, began building an effective statewide organization. Louis McHenry Howe, who had been Roosevelt's alter ego since 1912, conducted from an office in New York City a swelling national correspondence — in effect a Roosevelt letter-writing factory. Both men were ready at the proper time to launch a carefully planned and coordinated national campaign.

By the late fall of 1929, in the aftermath of the stock market crash, Roosevelt's strategy was becoming apparent. He wrote the powerful Nevada senator, Key Pittman on November 18, 1929,

> Do you remember my telling you of my meeting with Jim Cox after the 1920 election? I told him that we Democrats would not elect a President until some fairly serious industrial or economic depression had occurred under a Republican administration. The great question now is whether we are headed for this period of depression or not.... I think that you people in the Senate are doing an excellent piece of work. The fact that we Democrats are not doing much talking and are letting the Republicans fight it out very publicly among themselves, is causing just the tight situation....

> Meanwhile, up here in Albany things are going along smoothly enough. I am preparing my program for the legislature and am stressing social welfare, judicial reform, reorganization and reform of town and county government, and, last but not least, electricity in the home through the development of the St. Lawrence water power.
> I hope much that I can see you some day soon.

The Republicans, determined to prevent Roosevelt from growing into a national challenger of President Hoover, had also worked out their basic strategy by the fall of 1929. They were attacking Governor Roosevelt for failing to intervene against corruption in Mayor Jimmy Walker's New York City, where two-thirds of the state's Democratic votes were to be found. Roosevelt sidestepped in 1929 and continued to dodge as pressure, directed by reform leaders like the Socialist Norman Thomas and a Democratic judge, Samuel Seabury, intensified in subsequent years. Roosevelt repeatedly protested that he would not act where to do so would exceed his legal power or deny a fair hearing to the accused. In February 1932, when he was under particularly strong pressure, Colonel E. M. House pointed out to him, "You could get the nomination and be elected by taking an unjust stand against Tammany, but you could not be nominated and elected if you were considered a wholehearted supporter of that organization." Roosevelt did not act, and in reply to a prominent Episcopalian clergyman who had also been a Harvard classmate he protested, "I wonder if you remember the action of a certain magistrate by the name of Pontius Pilate, who acted upon public clamor after first washing his hands?" Roosevelt may have been sincere, but his refusal to intervene in New York City caused many liberals to overlook his notable achievements as an administrator and to write him off as an amiable but ineffectual governor. Walter Lippmann, who preferred Newton D. Baker, felt that Roosevelt was straddling on all the important issues, and early in 1932 published the most widely quoted criticism against him: "Franklin D. Roosevelt is no crusader. He is no tribune of the people. He is no enemy of entrenched privilege. He is a pleasant man who, without any important qualifications for the office, would very much like to be President."

By the time these words appeared in 1932, Roosevelt was by far the most formidable contender for the Democratic presidential nomination. As the Depression had gradually become worse, he had become one of the most resourceful of the governors in dealing with it, although in a limited way. Not until 1931 did he become more daring than President Hoover was at the national level. He urged local communities to spend as much as they could for public works, and began to advocate state unemployment insurance and old-age benefits, to be financed by joint contributions from the employers, the employees, and the state.

Even before Roosevelt began his campaign for reelection as governor in 1930, he was all but an announced candidate for the 1932 Democratic nomination. In April, when he addressed the Jefferson Day dinner in New York City, he slipped out early so that the succeeding speaker, the influential progressive senator from Montana, Burton K. Wheeler, could propose Roosevelt as a presidential candidate who would stand for lower tariffs and public utility regulation. The first Democrat of national standing to come out for Roosevelt, Wheeler was trying to head off a new Smith movement. At the 1930 Governors' Conference in Salt Lake City, Roosevelt, despite his own protestations to the contrary, added to the impression that he was seeking the nomination. On the one hand, he aired his progressive proposals for ameliorating the Depression, and on the other he emphasized states' rights, and attacked Hoover and the Republicans for having accepted a "wholly new economic theory that high wages and high pressure selling could guarantee prosperity at all times regardless of supply and demand." Roosevelt was cutting both to the left and the right of the President.

On the troublesome prohibition issue, Roosevelt straddled successfully until the fall of 1930, when it became apparent that New York voters heavily favored repeal. At that time, he took a public stand similar to what the Republicans put in their 1932 platform, which favored repeal of the 18th Amendment, but protected state and local options where people felt otherwise. Already, Roosevelt was emphasizing that economic problems were far more important than prohibition. He entered the gubernatorial campaign of 1930 with the slogan "Bread Not Booze."

In the campaign of 1930, Roosevelt won reelection over a dull Republican candidate by an unprecedented plurality of 725,000 votes. He even carried the Republican upstate area by 167,000 votes, although only because a Prohibition Party candidate pulled 181,000 votes away from the "wringing-wet" Republican contender. Nevertheless, the campaign had demonstrated that Roosevelt was right in stressing depression issues, and that he was a phenomena] vote-getter.

From this point on, Roosevelt was the presidential aspirant that not only the Republicans but rival Democrats as well were determined to stop. Since, by encouraging "favorite son" candidates, the Democratic candidates might well muster the one-third of the delegates needed to block Roosevelt, the threat was serious. Roosevelt was far in front in the aftermath of the 1930 election, but it was essential for him to engage in the most adroit political maneuvering to stay ahead. He had no choice but to be the front-runner, so his managers made the most of it. On the day after the election, James Farley and Louis Howe drafted a statement that Farley, without consulting Roosevelt, gave to the press:

> I fully expect that the call will come to Governor Roosevelt when the first presidential primary is held, which will be late next year. The Democrats in the Nation naturally want as their candidate for President the man who has shown himself capable of carrying the most important state in the country by a record-breaking majority.

Out of respect for political conventionalities, Roosevelt for more than a year continued to pretend that he was not a candidate while Farley and others worked indefatigably to keep him in front of other contenders. What he said in response to Farley's initial statement was to come from him repeatedly, with variations. In November 1931, his words were,

I am giving no consideration or thought or time to anything except the duties of the Governorship. I repeat that now, and to be clearly understood, you can add that this applies to any candidacy national or otherwise, in 1932.

While Roosevelt pretended not to be a candidate, his close associate of many years, Louis McHenry Howe, in January 1931 opened "Friends of Roosevelt" headquarters in New York City to carry on an accelerated national correspondence and seek funds. Howe, asthmatic and unprepossessing, had all he could do to run this operation. Someone else was needed to solicit convention delegates in person throughout the nation. This task fell to Farley, who brought to it unusual qualifications. He was of Irish ancestry, and Catholic, which made him personally attractive to innumerable urban Democratic politicians, yet he was himself from a small town, and personally dry. He quickly established for himself a reputation for absolute reliability, loyalty to Roosevelt supporters whose names he knew by the thousands, together with a friendliness that made him an incomparable political organizer. Howe and Farley, together with the Bronx leader Edward J. Flynn, began to build support and to obtain substantial contributions from a handful of wealthy supporters. Their most difficult task was in trying to discourage, or at least avoid involvement with, unscrupulous organizers of Roosevelt clubs in several southern states, who, as in earlier organizing for the Ku Klux Klan, seemed interested primarily in collecting membership fees. In the end, these organizers proved more a nuisance than a serious embarrassment.

The first great challenge that Roosevelt faced was from the conservative Democrats, who, after Smith's 1928 candidacy, remained in control of the party machinery. John Raskob, chairman of the Democratic National Committee, earlier had been friendly toward Roosevelt, providing heavy loans and substantial donations for Roosevelt's Warm Springs Foundation. Politically his views were decidedly to the right of Roosevelt's, and a struggle for national leadership of the Democratic Party was inevitable. Raskob seemed to win the first skirmish after the 1930 election when he obtained the signatures of the three previous Democratic candidates for President and the two southern Democratic leaders respectively of the House and the Senate, John Nance Garner and Joseph Robinson, to an open letter pledging President Hoover their support in his recovery program. They omitted any mention of progressive issues, and to the dismay of most southerners, even accepted the highly protectionist Hawley–Smoot Tariff. Most southern and western Democrats disliked the letter.

Roosevelt had little difficulty in assuming leadership among the southern and western opposition to Raskob and among the eastern conservatives when they held a special meeting of the Democratic National Committee in the early spring of 1931. Raskob announced that the meeting would discuss plans for the 1932 campaign; his intention was to pass resolutions committing the party to a high tariff and prohibition repeal in 1932. He hoped through the repeal issue to separate Roosevelt, who had been reelected in New York on a repeal plank, from the dry South and West. It was an impossible strategy, since Roosevelt along with repeal had advocated states' rights-local option — the right of each state or area within a state to decide whether or not it wished to retain prohibition. At once, Roosevelt enlisted the support of a leading southerner, Representative Cordell Hull of Tennessee, who had just been elected to the Senate. The Roosevelt–Hull alliance (which Farley represented in Washington) so completely controlled the meeting of the National Committee that Raskob did not even submit resolutions to be brought to a vote. Not only had Roosevelt won the first important battle, but he had also convinced Hull and his southern associates that Roosevelt was a trustworthy ally, irrevocably at odds with Smith and Raskob. From this point on, the Roosevelt candidacy began to take on serious dimensions in the South and West. Hull noted in his memoirs that southern Democratic leaders began to look to Roosevelt as the only alternative to Smith–Raskob domination of the party.

In contrast to the Democratic conservatives, Roosevelt as governor of New York was increasingly demonstrating in 1931 and 1932 that he was dynamic and positive, ready to experiment vigorously in his search for programs to combat the Depression. In these programs he was not only establishing himself as a most resourceful governor, but was also directly challenging President Hoover. At first he was cautious in seeking stronger legislation to protect small depositors in weak banks; after the spectacular failure of the Bank of the United States, he sharply criticized the cautious banking community and firmly demanded reform. He was more impressive in his study of means to spread work to avoid seasonal unemployment and in his advocacy of unemployment insurance. While he did not obtain a law, at least he persuaded the legislature to establish a commission to study the problem. He was the first major political leader in the country to advocate unemployment insurance. At a conference with eastern governors, Roosevelt sought agreements to deal with unemployment problems through interstate compacts. These did not materialize. As private and local resources became exhausted in the summer of 1931, Roosevelt called the legislature into special session to establish a state relief agency (which became the model for the subsequent New Deal relief system), the Temporary Emergency Relief Administration. At the yearly governors' conferences, Roosevelt repeatedly took the lead in advocating immediate massive action against the depression. In June 1931 he told the governors,

> More and more, those who are the victims of dislocations and defects of our social and economic life are beginning to ask respectfully, but insistently of us who are in positions of public responsibility why government can not and should not act to protect its citizens from disaster. I believe the question demands an answer and that the ultimate answer is that government, both state and national, must accept the responsibility of doing what it can do — soundly with considered forethought, and along definitely constructive, not passive lines.

It was this viewpoint, politically unexceptionable as it would seem to later generations, that aroused increasing anger and antagonism among Democratic conservatives even as it kindled hope among the dispossessed. By the summer of

1931, economic conditions were so serious that Democratic politicians were ready to rally behind Roosevelt rather than the conservative alternatives. One of Roosevelt's supporters, Jesse I. Straus, president of the R. H. Macy and Company department stores, in the spring of 1931 quietly conducted a poll of the delegates and alternates to the 1928 convention, and announced that Roosevelt led in thirty-nine out of forty-four states. A poll of Democratic business and professional men (except in New York) showed Roosevelt leading Smith by a margin of 5 to 1, and the businessmen's favorite, Owen D. Young, chairman of the board of General Electric Company, by 2 to 1. When Farley in the summer of 1931 traveled through the Middle West and West, ostensibly to attend an Elks convention in Seattle, he sent exuberant reports from eighteen states. At this point, Roosevelt was far in front of any possible contender. The question was whether a combined conservative movement could stop him.

The conservatives, under the leadership of Smith, Raskob, and Jouett Shouse, secretary of the Democratic National Committee, spent the fall of 1931 not in promoting Smith, but in encouraging favorite sons. They also tried to develop a new national leader. When neither Owen Young nor Newton D. Baker, who had been Wilson's Secretary of War, gave them encouragement, they turned toward Melvin Traylor, the wealthy president of the First National Bank of Chicago, whose appeal lay in his poverty-stricken rural origins. They also tried to stir interest in the handsome, right-wing, wringing-wet governor of Maryland, Albert C. Ritchie, a titan in the eyes of H. L. Mencken. Since none of these men, all cautious on economic questions, had nearly the popular appeal of Smith, the pressure was increasingly on Smith to become the open challenger to Roosevelt.

It was Roosevelt who first formally announced his candidacy, on January 22, 1932, in order to meet legal requirements for entering the North Dakota primary. A few days later, Smith declared his availability for the nomination. The struggle was out in the open. A number of opinion polls, something of a novelty at the time, showed Roosevelt a clear favorite both for the nomination and for election over Hoover in November. Nevertheless, since Roosevelt had to obtain two-thirds of the votes in the convention, it was clear that the opposition had an excellent fighting chance to deadlock the convention and nominate a dark horse candidate.

Favorite sons and potential dark horses began to emerge. Some of these were like the lanky, entertaining governor of Oklahoma, William H. "Alfalfa Bill" Murry, who with his slogan, "Bread, Butter, Bacon, and Beans," captured innumerable headlines but few votes. Another potential challenger, Speaker of the House John Nance Garner of Texas, was quite a different matter. Garner, a West Texas banker who through long service and party regularity had risen to be Speaker, became the candidate of powerful newspaper publisher William Randolph Hearst. He chose Garner because of his opposition to American participation in the League of Nations, but it was Garner's western background that won him enthusiastic support throughout the Southwest. He became the leader of those who did not wish to join Roosevelt yet opposed Smith and the urban and conservative eastern Democratic leaders. Garner and his followers were far more opposed to Smith than they were to Roosevelt, who accordingly was careful not to antagonize them. Nor did Roosevelt dare risk the implacable opposition of Hearst, the foe of the internationalists. To the horror of devotees of Wilson and the League, Roosevelt in February 1932 declared in a speech that, because of the fashion in which the League had developed during the years since its founding, he did not favor American participation in it. He probably was expressing his genuine views at the time, but, in leaving the way open for nomination, he was also exposing himself to charges of opportunism.

During the fight for convention delegates during the spring of 1932, Roosevelt succeeded in amassing a substantial majority, but suffered sufficient setbacks to fall ominously below the required two-thirds. Through the Democratic organizations of southern and border states, he obtained the delegations of twelve of the sixteen states. One other delegation from the region was friendly. Initial victories in other parts of the country, combined with this southern sweep, made the Roosevelt organization overconfident. Stinging defeats followed. Tammany managed to grab for Smith a large block of delegates in Roosevelt's own New York; Smith won every delegate in Massachusetts, Rhode Island, and Connecticut. Whatever remaining chance there was for a first-ballot victory was shattered when Garner won the forty-four delegates of California. After all the contests for delegates were over, Roosevelt was still eighty short of the requisite two-thirds majority.

This was the pre-convention lineup of delegates: Garner claimed ninety delegates in California and Texas; Senator J. Hamilton Lewis, a favorite son personally favorable to Roosevelt, held the fifty-eight delegates of Illinois; Governor George White of Ohio held the state's delegation of fifty-two; Senator James M. Reed of Missouri was the state's favorite son, with thirty-six delegates; Murray had twenty-three delegates from Oklahoma and North Dakota; Governor Harry Byrd of Virginia held the state's twenty-four delegates, and Governor Ritchie the sixteen from Maryland. There were six uncertain delegates from Indiana. The claims of Smith to 209 delegates, and of Roosevelt to 690, were at a few points overlapping:

SMITH-INSTRUCTED OR FAVORABLE			
Connecticut	16	Pennsylvania	34 (claimed)
Massachusetts	36	Rhode Island	10
New Jersey	32	Canal Zone	6 (claimed)
New York	65 (claimed)	Philippines	6 (claimed)
	Puerto Rico	4 (claimed)	

ROOSEVELT-INSTRUCTED OR FAVORABLE			
Alabama	24	New Mexico	6
Arizona	6	New York	45 (claimed)
Arkansas	18	North Carolina	26
Colorado	12	North Dakota	9
Delaware	6	Oregon	10
Florida	14	Pennsylvania	60 (claimed)
Georgia	28	South Carolina	18
Idaho	8	South Dakota	10
Indiana	24 (claimed)	Tennessee	24
Iowa	26	Utah	8
Kansas	20	Vermont	8
Kentucky	26	Washington	16
Louisiana	20	West Virginia	16
Maine	12	Wisconsin	26
Michigan	38	Wyoming	6
Minnesota	24	Alaska	6
Mississippi	20	District of Columbia	6
Montana	8	Hawaii	6
Nebraska	16	Canal Zone	6
Nevada	6	Philippines	6 (claimed)
New Hampshire	8	Puerto Rico	6
		Virgin Islands	2

The strategy of Smith and the conservatives, the "Allies" as they came to call themselves at the convention, was, through the machinery of the Democratic National Committee, to maintain control over the chairing of the convention and then, through standing firm, to deadlock it. Out of the deadlock, the Allies hoped to nominate a compromise candidate.

The strategy of Roosevelt and his supporters was, through their strong membership on the Democratic National Committee, to wrest control over the chairing of the convention away from Raskob and Shouse. With the convention machinery in their control, they might then try to rescind the two-thirds rule (which would take only a simple majority of delegates' votes) and then proceed to nominate Roosevelt. Or, alternatively, they could stand firm and make sufficiently attractive offers to favorite sons to win them over after the first complimentary ballots. If that did not suffice, then it would be essential to obtain the Garner votes, which, as Roosevelt privately commented in advance "would clinch the matter." Operating for the Allies was the force of tradition — it would not be easy to wrest power from Raskob and Shouse, and even more difficult to persuade southerners to give up the two-thirds rule, which in effect gave them a veto over unpalatable nominations. On the other hand, Roosevelt could benefit from the southerners' dislike for Smith and most of his cohorts, and their fear that a deadlocked convention as in 1924 could lead to a donnybrook, ruining the party and guaranteeing Republican victory. Roosevelt made an asset of this fear. He wrote a Kentucky supporter, Robert W. Bingham of the Louisville *Courier-Journal*, "The drive against me seems to be on. All I can hope is that it will not develop into the kind of a row which will mean the re-election of Brother Hoover."

In the contest for convention machinery, Roosevelt had to accept a compromise that subjected him to later charges of deceitfulness. Some of Roosevelt's advocates, not realizing how disastrous it would be for Raskob to be temporary chairman, had pledged their support for what they thought a meaningless honor. They had forgotten that Raskob could hand down unfavorable rulings on vital matters. Consequently, when the Arrangements Committee met, Roosevelt had to agree that in exchange for obtaining Alben Barkley of Kentucky as temporary chairman, his men would "commend" (not recommend) Shouse for permanent chairman. Roosevelt regarded this as an empty gesture of goodwill, since he controlled a majority of the delegates at the convention and with them could then elect a friendly permanent chairman. The Roosevelt men later claimed that they had explained to Shouse what Roosevelt meant; Shouse ever afterwards interpreted "commend" as a binding promise to vote for him, and accused Roosevelt of bad faith.

As the delegates assembled at the Democratic national convention in Chicago late in June, both sides freely claimed victory. Farley was continuing his first-ballot predictions. Smith labeled these "Farley's Fairy Stories," and Shouse told reporters, "We have Roosevelt licked now." The Allies distributed to the delegates reprints of an attack columnist Heywood Broun made on Roosevelt, whom he labeled a "Feather Duster," the "cork-screw candidate." With the cooperation of the Chicago machine, they packed the galleries with raucous supporters of Smith who hissed Roosevelt and howled for prohibition repeal — tactics that would not help hold Garner supporters in the coalition. Meanwhile, as delegations arrived they were ushered into Roosevelt headquarters, where they were given the opportunity to talk by direct telephone wire with Roosevelt, who remained at the Governor's Mansion in Albany.

The first skirmish at the convention came before it opened — over the two-thirds rule. A gathering of Roosevelt leaders under the influence of Senator Huey Long of Louisiana, fearful of a Smith deadlock, voted to fight the rule. Other southern leaders supporting Roosevelt strongly objected. Southern objections to changing the rule had time to solidify, and it became apparent that the convention might vote down the change. Rather than risk defeat, Roosevelt announced that the rule would not be challenged. (Four years later he quietly had it abolished.)

On June 27, the Democratic convention began its sessions in the Chicago Stadium. After Senator Barkley had delivered a two-hour keynote address, the testing of strength could begin. When the Credentials Committee brought forth its recommendation that Roosevelt delegates be seated from Louisiana and Minnesota, the Roosevelt forces won by a margin of more than 100 votes. Then came a close fight over the seating of Roosevelt's choice as permanent chairman, Senator Thomas J. Walsh of Montana, rather than Shouse. Roosevelt won by 626 to 528 — a crucial victory, since Walsh, as an excellent parliamentarian, kept the convention from being turned at tight moments into an anti-Roosevelt machine.

The platform won easy acceptance. It had been drafted in previous months, under Roosevelt's supervision, primarily by the former Attorney General in Wilson's Cabinet, A. Mitchell Palmer. In it, Palmer had incorporated the consensus of several important senators favorable to Roosevelt. It emphasized economic problems rather than prohibition. The prohibition plank called for no more than the resubmitting of the question to the American people. Among many of the delegates there was strong sentiment for outright repeal. Farley did not care how the delegates voted, since, if they inserted the wringing-wet plank that Smith and Ritchie wished, they would eliminate a major reason for nominating one of them. With Roosevelt delegates free to vote as they wished, the repeal plank was inserted 934¾ to 213¾.

With both sides retaining their confidence, and in private seeking to make deals to switch delegates, nominating began on the afternoon of June 30. For hour after hour, the perspiring delegates were subjected to florid oratory and endless demonstrations that went on until dawn. Roosevelt sent word to Farley to proceed immediately to the balloting in spite of the exhaustion of the delegates; to do otherwise might seem an indication of weakness.

The first ballot began at 4:28 a.m. on the morning of July 1, and, since several of the delegations had to be polled man by man, it lasted an hour and a half. Roosevelt came out with almost as many votes as Farley had predicted in his more careful pre-convention estimates, 666¼ — only 104 short of two-thirds, and 464½ more than the nearest rival. But the hoped-for bandwagon switch did not materialize. A second ballot followed; Roosevelt received a few additional votes that Farley was keeping in reserve (since it was necessary that Roosevelt go a bit upward each time). But the Allies held their lines firm; Senator William Gibbs McAdoo kept California for Garner, and Mayor Anton Cermak of Chicago refused to switch the Illinois delegation. Roosevelt's floor leader, Arthur Mullen of Nebraska, tried to adjourn after the second ballot, but the Allies, striving for deadlock, insisted on a third ballot. It was nip and tuck, since several of the Mississippi delegates were eager to abandon Roosevelt. Mississippi was kept in line; Farley managed to muster a handful of additional votes, but brought the Roosevelt total up to only 682. Finally at 9:15 a.m. the convention adjourned until evening. The jubilant Allies were predicting that Roosevelt would crack on the fourth ballot, and there were whispers that Newton D. Baker would be the candidate.

This was the vote on the first 3 ballots:

	First	Second	Third
Roosevelt	666¼	677¾	682.79
Smith	201¾	194¼	190¼
Garner	90¼	90¼	101¼
Byrd	25	24	24.96
Traylor	42½	40¼	40¼
Ritchie	21	23½	23½
Reed	24	18	27½
White	52	50½	52½
Murray	23	–	–
Baker	8½	8½	8½
Will Rogers	–	22	–

The presidential nomination depended on whether or not the Roosevelt forces could quickly gain spectacular delegate strength. So it was that, despite their exhaustion, many of the delegates probed and negotiated in many directions. In subsequent years, there have been many accounts by those engaged in some of these negotiations, more than one of whom was convinced that he was responsible for the dramatic outcome. The probing turned out to be of consequence only in the negotiation for Garner delegates, where undoubtedly several efforts helped bring about the result for which Roosevelt was striving. At the heart was the work of Farley, who agreed with Howe that everything must be staked upon trying to win Texas. Farley conferred with Garner's manager, Representative Sam Rayburn, who promised to see what he could do. The Vice-Presidency was not mentioned.

Simultaneously, a number of people had been trying to persuade McAdoo to switch the California Garner delegates, but Hearst rather than McAdoo was the real controlling power over the delegation. Some people argued with Hearst, who became amenable — but in the final analysis only Garner could release the California delegates, or persuade the Texans to switch. In this respect, the final responsibility rested with Garner.

In Washington, Garner had no intention of being party to a potentially disastrous stalemate. He had not thought past compromise choices to be men likely to win. For that matter, on policies, Garner and his supporters were much closer to Roosevelt than to the Smith–Raskob forces. Garner had been ready to wait for three ballots. On the afternoon of July 1, he refused to accept a telephone message from Smith, but did receive Hearst's message recommending that the Garner delegates be released to Roosevelt. Garner called Rayburn telling him the nomination should come on the next ballot. Rayburn reported that the California delegation would switch to Roosevelt if released, but that the Texans would not do so unless Garner agreed to become candidate for Vice-President. Garner was reluctant to leave his powerful position as Speaker, but years later reminisced, "So I said to Sam, 'All right, release my delegates and see what you can do.' Hell, I'll do anything to see the Democrats win one more national election."

On the evening of July 1, when the convention reconvened, the morale of the Allies was still high since they had obtained Mississippi. McAdoo quickly exploded it when California was reached on the fourth ballot. He declared, "California came here to nominate a President; she did not come here to deadlock this convention or to engage in another disastrous contest like that of 1924." California's 44 votes thus went to Roosevelt. Illinois switched when it was reached on the roll-call, Indiana followed, and Governor Ritchie cast Maryland's votes for Roosevelt. With a total of 945 votes, Roosevelt was nominated on the fourth ballot. (Smith refused to release his delegates, and thus kept the nomination from being unanimous.)

Some opposition leaders remained bitter. Their failure had in some degree been caused by Smith's lack of resilience. He sought renomination as a vindication, and was not interested in maneuvering toward another candidate. As Mencken noted, "The failure of the opposition was the failure of Al Smith. From the moment he arrived on the ground it was apparent that he had no plan, and was animated only by his fierce hatred of Roosevelt, the cuckoo who had seized his nest. That hatred may have had logic in it, but it was impotent to organize allies." Shouse wrote Newton D. Baker a few days after the convention, "If McAdoo had not broken the pledges he made, Roosevelt would not have been nominated. On the fourth ballot there would have been serious defections from his ranks with the result that some other nominee would have been certain. That nominee would have been either you or Ritchie. I don't know which."

Nevertheless, there was no serious rift within the party. Unusually united, almost all of the delegates met the next day to nominate Garner for Vice-President, and to await the unprecedented arrival of Roosevelt to deliver his acceptance address before they adjourned. After a flight that was hours late because of buffeting headwinds, Roosevelt arrived at the Chicago Stadium. He brought with him an acceptance speech that had been fabricated in Albany, but Howe, meeting him at the airport, thrust into his hands a different one. He glanced through the new speech while en route to the convention. When Roosevelt rose to speak, he delivered the first page of Howe's draft but then switched to his familiar prepared text. It was a statement in generalities of what Roosevelt had earlier been advocating, and what the platform had spelled out: the domestic (i.e., Republican) causes of the Depression, and suggestions of the means to remedy it — rigid economy in the Government, a crop reduction program and rediscounting of mortgages for farmers, a lower tariff for businessmen, relief and mortgage refinancing for those in desperate straits, construction of self-sustaining public works, regulation of securities sales, and repeal of prohibition. All this was couched in the idealistic moral phraseology of the earlier progressive moment. "Today we shall have come through a period of loose thinking, descending morals, an era of selfishness, among individual men and women and among Nations," he declared. "To return to higher standards we must abandon false prophets and seek new leaders of our own choosing." In conclusion he declared,

> On the farms, in the large metropolitan areas, in the smaller cities and in the villages, millions of our citizens cherish the hope that their old standards of living and of thought have not gone forever. Those millions cannot and shall not hope in vain.
> I pledge you, I pledge myself, to a new deal for the American people. Let us all here assembled constitute ourselves prophets of a new order of competence and of courage. This is more than a political campaign; it is a call to arms. Give me your help, not to win votes alone, but to win in this crusade to restore America to its own people.

Out of the speech came the label "New Deal" for the Roosevelt program. The words were picked up by the political cartoonist Rollin Kirby, who drew a farmer gazing upward at an airplane with New Deal written on its wings. Within a few days the term was generally accepted.

The nomination of Roosevelt and the setting forth of a New Deal program established the lines of the Democratic contest against the incumbent President Hoover. On the ballots of various states there were nineteen other party names. The more significant of these were the Socialist, Communist, Prohibition, Farmer-Labor, Socialist-Labor, Liberty, and Jobless. All of these were insignificant sideshows attracting little attention and fewer votes. The very failure of third parties, even revolving around such crucial issues as the Depression and prohibition repeal, during this crisis period, warrants examination of the three most prominent ones.

Numerous intellectuals during the campaign, damning both Hoover and Roosevelt, insisted that the only candidate offering them an opportunity to vote honestly for significant change was Norman Thomas, the candidate of the Socialist Party. Some of these intellectuals, including Paul Douglas, at that time a University of Chicago economist, offered disillusioned Republican and Democratic voters the opportunity to pair their votes so they could cast their ballots for Thomas without hurting the chances of whichever major candidate they thought a lesser evil. Thomas in later years claimed that the New Deal swallowed up his party and enacted his platform of 1932. The Socialist platform called for much that did become part of the New Deal: heavy appropriations for relief and public works, free public employment agencies, unemployment insurance, old-age pensions, improved workmen's compensation programs, abolition of child labor, aid for homeowners and farmers facing difficulties with their mortgages, adequate minimum wages, heavier income taxes, and some aids to farmers. Some of these already were pledged in the Democratic platform. On the other hand, the greater part of the platform called for socialization of basic sectors of the American economy, including banks, several constitutional changes in the frame of Government (such as proportional representation), and strong planks supporting Negro rights and American entrance into the League. Altogether, the Socialist platform was far from a blueprint for the New Deal, although some of its proposals such as health insurance and civil rights did become parts of Democratic programs after the Second World War.

The Socialists hoped to poll a strong vote, as large as two million. Thomas campaigned in thirty-eight states, attracting polite attention wherever he went, but received only 885,000 votes.

The Communist Party, also hoping to profit from the crisis, met in Chicago in May 1932. It nominated for President William Z. Foster, best known for his leadership in the Steel Strike of 1919, and for Vice-President a thirty-nine-year-old Negro from Alabama, James W. Ford. They issued a forthrightly revolutionary platform: "Fight for the workers' way — for the revolutionary way out of the crisis — for the United States of Soviet America!" During the summer, Foster and Ford made a number of speeches, although they were several times put in jail. In mid-September, Foster became ill and canceled further speaking engagements. The Communists received little attention in newspapers or over the radio, though a number of writers and intellectuals endorsed the Foster–Ford ticket. They polled 103,000 votes.

The Prohibition Party, which since 1872 had offered candidates for the Presidency, hoped to benefit from the wet planks in both major party platforms. It had always urged other reform issues, and in its 1932 platform, as two contemporary observers, Roy V. Peel and Thomas C. Donnelly pointed out, proposed a nine-point recovery program "practically identical with that later urged by Governor Roosevelt." What made their platform distinctive was a plank proposing federal censorship of motion pictures. The Prohibition candidate for President was William D. Upshaw, who had long been a Democratic member of Congress from Georgia. He received 80,000 votes.

Both the Republicans and Democrats as they prepared for the campaign ignored the third parties; to most voters the only possible choice seemed to be between President Hoover and Roosevelt.

In the days immediately after the nomination of Roosevelt, President Hoover and most Republican leaders had few illusions that they had much chance to win. They were correct, and indeed in retrospect the most serious contest during the campaign was that between Roosevelt and his Democratic opponents over the Democratic nomination. The struggle between President Hoover and Roosevelt seemed reminiscent to some of the 1896 campaign between William McKinley and his agrarian challenger, William Jennings Bryan — but this time the agrarian revolt in the depressed West was being lead by a polished easterner. After visiting Hoover, Secretary of State Henry L. Stimson wrote in his diary on July 5,

> I found the President rather blue on the subject of Roosevelt. The people around him evidently had been rather overconfident ... and are now awake to the full power which Roosevelt will produce in the field to the radical elements of the West and the South. Roosevelt is not a strong character himself and our hope is that the four months' campaign will develop and prove that he has pretty well lost the confidence of the business elements in the East. But he is making his

appeal to the West, and in hard times it is very easy. An inflation campaign and soft money campaign make it look like some of the elements of 1896. But the difficulty is that then it was the Democrats who were in power during the hard times and now it is the Republicans who are in power. That gives us an uphill fight. Also there is no split yet in the Democratic Party as there was in 1896, and there is no Mark Hanna in the Republican Party to organize a very big educational campaign.

Only monumental folly on the part of the Democrats — of which there was no sign — or spectacular economic improvement — of which there were only slight signs — could rescue the Republicans. Between August 1932 and January 1933, *The New York Times* "Weekly Index of Business Activity" rose from two-thirds (66.2 percent) to nearly three-fourths (73.8 percent) of normal. Hoover and some of his followers asserted in later years that this marked the beginning of total recovery, destroyed, first, by lack of business confidence in Roosevelt, and second, after Roosevelt took office, by the New Deal policies. Whatever the sources of the moderate business upturn in the weeks before the election, it was not reflected in better living conditions for many Americans. Unemployment remained staggeringly high, and commodity prices remained so low that they were forcing farmers into bankruptcy. Poverty was visible everywhere in the United States, nowhere more so than in Washington, DC, where eleven thousand veterans of the First World War were encamped trying to persuade Congress to pay them immediately a bonus for their wartime services — a bonus not due them for several years. President Hoover had no intention of thus adding to the serious federal deficit (nor did his opponent Roosevelt). Congress voted them their rail fare home, but half the veterans lingered on. President Hoover ordered the army to drive the men from the Washington streets back to their camps. Chief of Staff Douglas MacArthur did more. Looking on the veterans as "a bad looking mob ... animated by the essence of revolution," he used soldiers wearing gas masks and carrying fixed bayonets to evict them from their hovels while newsreel cameras recorded the grim scenes. The eviction of the "bonus army" underscored the prevalent poverty, and added further to Hoover's unpopularity.

In theory at least, the Republicans had in operation the full party machinery with which to mount a massive effort to reelect Hoover. The President chose Everett Sanders to be the Republican chairman. Sanders had served three terms in the House of Representatives, and had served President Coolidge as a secretary and political adviser. Hoover also selected an executive committee for the party, which was to perform the duties of the Republican National Committee during the campaign. As these appointments indicated, Hoover was personally assuming responsibility for and direction of the campaign. He was bitter toward his many Republican critics in Congress who either deserted him or gave no more than token support, not wishing to associate themselves with an unpopular national candidate. State organizations were scarcely more useful. Even some of the members of Hoover's Cabinet seemed less than enthusiastic.

The Republicans had difficulty in raising money, but thanks to large contributions from a wealthy few faced defeat with a more substantial treasury than their opponents, about $2 million, which enabled them to buy more radio time than the Democrats — seventy hours at a cost of $437,000. As usual, they gave away or sold quantities of posters, pamphlets, buttons, and other souvenirs, including poster-type covers to place on the spare tire that customarily rode on the side or rear of automobiles.

Hoover may well have thought of himself during the campaign as the intrepid, high-principled captain, standing alone on the quarter-deck while the ship sank slowly beneath him. Scorning the new campaign techniques that were coming into use, Hoover himself wrote every single word of his speeches. There were nine of these major speeches, each of the "omnibus" variety touching on wide arrays of issues. Each sounded like a state paper, a manifesto warning of the greater disasters that would befall the American people if they discarded Hoover's wise and careful leadership for the radicalism of Roosevelt and his advisers. Hoover in addition to his own efforts assigned one or two Cabinet members to answer specific Democratic attacks. It was not a successful technique in the eyes of Stimson, who wrote in his diary, "Every time Roosevelt makes a speech, Mr. Hoover has [Secretary of the Treasury Ogden] Mills or [Secretary of War Pat] Hurley answer it, and the result is that it is rather wearing out the popularity of the two men."

In contrast, Roosevelt ran what in most respects was the first truly modern, well-organized presidential campaign. He took over the national party machinery immediately after his nomination, obtaining the election of James A. Farley as chairman of the Democratic National Committee. Throughout the campaign Farley was in charge of campaign tactics (but not ideology), working through the National Committee members and the regular Democratic organizations in all of the states (even though these organizations might have opposed Roosevelt before the election). There was some bitterness among Democrats at odds with these organizations who had fought for Roosevelt before the convention, but Farley felt his policy would bring the best results. Roosevelt was ready to reward these loyal early supporters after election day, but not before. The women's division was also carefully organized and vigorous. The letter writing from New York continued at a stepped-up pace. Numerous special committees came into existence, arranging speeches, turning out pamphlets, and obtaining pledges of support. All together, it was a large and energetic organization in which Farley did his best to make his influence felt down to the level of the precinct workers. "The fellow out in Kokomo, Indiana, who is pulling doorbells night after night," Farley once wrote, "gets a real thrill if he receives a letter on campaigning postmarked Washington or New York."

The exploration of campaign issues and the presentation of them in speech drafts was the work of Roosevelt's "brain trust," working under the general supervision of Professor Raymond Moley of Columbia University. For politicians to make use of academic specialists was nothing new, but Roosevelt recruited and utilized them on a larger scale and more systematically than ever before. His main speechwriter, beginning with the New York gubernatorial campaign of 1928, had been Samuel I. Rosenman, an expert on state issues. In the spring of 1932, as Roosevelt began to concern himself more completely with national problems, he added Moley (who had previously worked for him on crime prevention problems), and had Moley recruit a number of additional academic experts, mostly from Columbia University. The most conspicuous and important among these was Rexford G. Tugwell, an economist, whose thinking was well to the left of Roosevelt's and Moley's, and who in later years wrote in detail of his unsuccessful efforts to win Roosevelt over to his views. Roosevelt was receptive to ideas of almost any sort, as long as they were humane and democratic, but always weighed them in terms of their political feasibility. Neither Tugwell, nor Moley, nor Adolph A. Berle Jr., the other important academic brain-truster, was often completely satisfied with Roosevelt's decisions, but all did have an opportunity to expose him to fresh ideas, some of which in modified form became part of new programs. After the convention, Bernard Baruch (who had opposed Roosevelt's nomination) contributed a colorful conservative speechwriter to the group, General Hugh S. Johnson. Various politicians also came and went. It was, altogether, under the skillful management of Moley, an effective organization that could assemble speeches in keeping with Roosevelt's strategy.

From the beginning of the campaign to the end, Roosevelt kept the initiative, harrying and attacking President Hoover from both the right and the left. His speeches were relatively brief, interesting, and dramatic to millions of radio listeners. Ordinarily, each dealt with only a single subject. In addition to making speeches, Roosevelt engaged in innumerable meetings with politicians, winning over to at least nominal support from even the reluctant Smith. And there were countless motor cavalcades and whistle-stop gatherings where crowds roared their pleasure at seeing a smiling, confident Roosevelt.

Despite the warnings of political advisers that he might do himself more harm than good, Roosevelt decided to take his campaign directly to the people, first through a grand swing by train to the Pacific Coast and back. This displaying himself directly to the nation had a significant effect in those pre-television days. It demonstrated that Roosevelt's polio attack had not deprived him of the physical vigor essential to a President. Far from it, he appeared overflowing with good health and high spirits, and since he loved campaigning, the longer he campaigned the more buoyant he appeared. The contrast in personal appearance and in radio voice with the tired, dreary, depressed Hoover was an intangible difficult to measure, yet was an important factor in the campaign.

By October, all the public opinion polls then in operation, crude and uncertain though they were, indicated a sweeping Roosevelt victory. Consequently, in October, Roosevelt coasted at the very time when he might have been expected to make his greatest effort. He campaigned in the South even though he could not possibly lose a single southern state. There was no apparent reason. Perhaps he loved being in the South. Perhaps he was thinking ahead to his legislative program and wished to establish a strong rapport directly with the southern people so that he could later better pressure southern congressional leaders.

It was not until October that Hoover, except for his formal acceptance speech, focused his attention upon campaigning. It was too late to do anything but try to speak to a loyal minority for the historical record. Roosevelt could not be pressed hard enough to be forced to answer the contradictions that Hoover saw in some of his statements. Hoover was deadly serious in this campaigning, even though he had no illusions about the outcome. Years later he devoted a hundred pages in his *Memoirs* to an effort to set right for all time his campaign positions compared with those of his opponent.

President Hoover in his speeches again and again enumerated the many measures he had undertaken in order to combat the Depression. He pointed out what he deemed the errors of Roosevelt, and warned that, if the Democrats came in, the result would be far greater economic difficulties, if not indeed the breakdown of the Republic. On the one hand, he accused Roosevelt of equivocating on the issue of a high protective tariff, as indeed Roosevelt was. Roosevelt's statements, said Hoover, were like "the dreadful position of the chameleon on the Scotch plaid." Yet Hoover on another occasion charged that Roosevelt would so drastically lower the tariff that the "grass will grow in streets of a hundred cities, a thousand towns." But the tariff issue was minor. More important in Hoover's mind was his insistence that Roosevelt and the New Dealers represented an alien governmental philosophy that would destroy the traditional American system. He declared on November 5 concerning certain unspecified groups, "Indeed this is the same philosophy of government which has poisoned all Europe. They have been the fumes of the witch's cauldron which boiled in Russia and in its attenuated flavor spread over the whole of Europe, and would by many be introduced into the United States in an attempt to secure votes through protest of discontent against emergency conditions."

Nevertheless, Roosevelt, like Hoover, basically believed in laissez-faire economics. He was as orthodox as Hoover in his belief in a balanced budget. He was less orthodox in feeling that there could be beneficial modifications in monetary policy. Unlike Hoover, who believed that the Depression was of international origin, Roosevelt ascribed American roots to it. On foreign policy there was so little difference between the two men that Roosevelt did not mention it during the campaign. He remarked to Moley that Hoover was correct on the subject. Neither Hoover nor Roosevelt seemed to concern themselves particularly with the Negro votes, and did not direct remarks toward Negroes.

Professor Moley remarked after the campaign that in Roosevelt's speeches were to be found forecasts of almost all of the early New Deal policies. This was true. Yet the speeches so often veered either right or left and contained so many generalities that to contemporaries it would have been hard to have predicted from them what the New Deal might be. However, enough did grow out of them that affected the New Deal to make worthwhile a brief examination of some of the major themes.

Few Democrats, either to the right or left, failed to cheer when Roosevelt opened his campaign by lambasting the Republican economic policies of the 1920s. He did so in an address at Columbus, Ohio, on August 20. At the heart of the speech was an example of the way in which Roosevelt could make a dreary subject entertaining:

> A puzzled, somewhat skeptical Alice asked the Republican leadership some simple questions:
> "Will not the printing and selling of more stocks and bonds, the building of new plants and the increase of efficiency produce more goods than we buy?"
> "No," shouted Humpty Dumpty. "The more we produce the more we can buy."
> "What if we produce a surplus?"
> "Oh, we can sell it to foreign consumers."
> "How can the foreigners pay for it?"
> "Why, we will lend them the money."
> "I see," said little Alice, "they will buy our surplus with our money. Of course, these foreigners will pay us back by selling us their goods?"
> "Oh, not at all," said Humpty Dumpty. "We set up a high wall called the tariff."
> "And," said Alice at last, "how will the foreigners pay off these loans?"
> "That is easy," said Humpty Dumpty, "did you ever hear of moratorium?"

Politically more important was Roosevelt's major farm speech at Topeka, Kansas, in September. Weeks of work and the touches of at least twenty-five advisors had gone into it. At its heart, where the principal farm group, the Farm Bureau Federation, could see it, were specifications that would permit the domestic allotment system on which Roosevelt had already decided. But the specifications were drawn so broadly that those favoring inflation or other farm programs such as McNary–Haugenism were not specifically excluded. And all the possible farm legislation was talked about in such technical language that it would not frighten off easterners who did not wish the Federal Government to be generous to farmers. The speech would not completely satisfy many people; Henry A. Wallace had preferred Al Smith's more forthright McNary–Haugenite stand in 1928. On the other hand, the talk drove few people away, and Roosevelt's main task was to reap the anti-Hoover farm vote rather than to draw positive lists of specifics. The success of the speech, which drew a crowd of no less than eighteen thousand people, was to be found in its inoffensive ambiguities.

On the other hand, when Roosevelt spoke in Portland, Oregon, on September 21, he was crisply specific in outlining his power program. He insisted that regulatory commissions should be protectors of the peoples' interest and set rates on a prudent-investment basis. He advocated full regulation of utility securities and holding companies. While he did not wish complete public ownership, he proposed certain government-owned and -operated services to act as a yardstick to measure private rates. It was, in total, a firm statement of the views of Senator George Norris and the public power advocates. It was also, as Roosevelt pointed out, basically the power policy he had followed as governor of New York. The talk strengthened Roosevelt in the West and brought him additional support from Republican progressives.

Intellectuals at the time, and since, have been most interested in the speech that Roosevelt delivered at the Commonwealth Club in San Francisco several days later — a speech making a strong positive affirmation of political liberalism. It was based on a memorandum Berle had prepared for Roosevelt. In the speech, Roosevelt hypothesized a mature American economy in which it was the task of the Government to police irresponsible power in order to guarantee every citizen a comfortable living. Government should act as a guarantor of the common good within the existing economic system. This was to become the basic philosophy of the New Deal.

On the tariff, Roosevelt, as Hoover pointed out, fared not so well. He had learned that farmers would not favor a low tariff; yet it was an integral part of the southern Democratic tradition. Roosevelt ordered Moley to weave together in a single speech both low and high tariff ideas. The despairing Moley later commented, "One might as well weave glass fibers with cobwebs." The Republicans attacked delightedly, but Roosevelt was done no basic harm, and indeed may have saved himself from damage.

There were other inconsistencies. On October 13, speaking over the radio from Albany, Roosevelt answered queries of social workers and outlined an advanced program for social welfare and unemployment relief. On the other hand, at Pittsburgh only six days later, he delivered a diatribe Hugh Johnson had drafted, denouncing the reckless deficit financing of the Hoover Administration. How Roosevelt would reconcile the heavy expenditures his social welfare program would entail with a balanced federal budget was a question he had not yet faced. (As President he was to "balance" the regular federal budget and run a deficit far larger than Hoover's in an emergency budget.) Yet Roosevelt was sincere both in his humanitarianism and his fiscal conservatism. The only loophole he left at Pittsburgh was his pledge that, "If starvation and dire need on the part of any of our citizens make necessary the appropriation of additional funds which would keep the budget out of balance, I shall not hesitate to tell the American people the full truth and ask them to authorize the expenditure of that additional amount."

In the final weeks of the campaign, charges and countercharges between the two contending parties became more heated. President Hoover set his theme during the month in his address at Des Moines, October 4, when he declared, "Thousands of our people in their bitter distress and losses today are saying that 'things could not be worse.' No person who has any remote understanding of the forces which confronted this country during these last eighteen months ever utters that remark. Had it not been for the immediate and unprecedented actions of our government things would be infinitely worse today." When Roosevelt, speaking at Baltimore on October 25, ad libbed into an attack upon "the 'Four Horsemen' of the present Republican leadership: the Horsemen of Destruction, Delay, Deceit, Despair," his comment that the Republicans controlled the Congress, the Presidency, and the Supreme Court, aroused Hoover's indignation:

Aside from the fact that the charge that the Supreme Court has been controlled by any political party is an atrocious one, there is a deeper implication in that statement. Does it disclose the Democratic candidate's conception of the functions of the Supreme Court? Does he expect the Supreme Court to be subservient to him and his party? ...

My countrymen, I repeat to you, the fundamental issue in this campaign, the decision that will fix the national direction for a hundred years to come, is whether we shall go on in fidelity to the American traditions or whether we shall turn to innovations, the spirit of which is disclosed to us by many sinister revelations and veiled promises.

Roosevelt, listening on the radio, was furious and told his advisors he would not let anyone so impeach his patriotism. They persuaded him not to make any rebuttal, but rather to keep his own speeches above personal attacks. In his own final major appearance at Madison Square Garden on November 5, he declared,

From the time that my airplane touched ground at Chicago up to the present, I have consistently set forth the doctrine of the present-day democracy. It is the program of a party dedicated to the conviction that every one of our people is entitled to the opportunity to earn a living, and to develop himself to the fullest measure consistent with the rights of man.

It was up to the voters to choose, and to the surprise of few, Roosevelt was elected by a wide margin. He carried forty-two states compared with six for Hoover, with a total of 472 electoral votes to 59. The popular vote was equally decisive — 22,800,000 to 15,750,000 (57.4 to 39.7 percent). All the minor parties combined had received only 1,160,000 votes (2.9 percent). It had been a national victory, although Roosevelt was strongest in the South and the West. The percentage of the vote by sections was:

	Roosevelt	Hoover
New England	49.1%	48.4%
Middle Atlantic	50.5	45.4
East North Central	54.2	42.7
West North Central	60.6	37.2
South Atlantic	67.0	31.9
West South Central	83.4	16.2
Mountain	58.4	38.4
Pacific	58.2	36.7

While these are not the careful class analyses of the vote later made possible by scientific public opinion research, there are indications from some Chicago studies made at the time that the same groups that voted for Smith in 1928 voted for Roosevelt (but in 12 percent greater numbers) in 1932, and that the division in status between those who voted for and against Roosevelt was (with the exception of Negroes) approximately the same in 1932 as it was to be in 1936. Those of higher social and economic status consistently tended to vote more heavily Republican.

On the other hand, Roosevelt had campaigned more as a one-time progressive than as a future New Dealer, and as he planned the New Deal in the three months before he took office he thought of himself as the future President of all the American people. He had received a strong popular mandate and was to make vigorous use of it, but just what that use was to be, beyond the assumption by government of larger responsibilities for the economic welfare of the nation, only the future disclosed.

Appendix

Party Platforms of 1932

Democratic Platform

In this time of unprecedented economic and social distress the Democratic Party declares its conviction that the chief causes of this condition were the disastrous policies pursued by our government since the World War, of economic isolation, fostering the merger of competitive businesses into monopolies and encouraging the indefensible expansion and contraction of credit for private profit at the expense of the public.

Those who were responsible for these policies have abandoned the ideals on which the war was won and thrown away the fruits of victory, thus rejecting the greatest opportunity in history to bring peace, prosperity, and happiness to our people and to the world.

They have ruined our foreign trade; destroyed the values of our commodities and products, crippled our banking system, robbed millions of our people of their life savings, and thrown millions more out of work, produced widespread poverty and brought the government to a state of financial distress unprecedented in time of peace.

The only hope for improving present conditions, restoring employment, affording permanent relief to the people, and bringing the nation back to the proud position of domestic happiness and of financial, industrial, agricultural and commercial leadership in the world lies in a drastic change in economic governmental policies.

We believe that a party platform is a covenant with the people to have [*sic*] faithfully kept by the party when entrusted with power, and that the people are entitled to know in plain words the terms of the contract to which they are asked to subscribe. We hereby declare this to be the platform of the Democratic Party:

The Democratic Party solemnly promises by appropriate action to put into effect the principles, policies, and reforms herein advocated, and to eradicate the policies, methods, and practices herein condemned. We advocate an immediate and drastic reduction of governmental expenditures by abolishing useless commissions and offices, consolidating departments and bureaus, and eliminating extravagance to accomplish a saving of not less than twenty-five per cent in the cost of the Federal Government. And we call upon the Democratic Party in the states to make a zealous effort to achieve a proportionate result.

We favor maintenance of the national credit by a federal budget annually balanced on the basis of accurate executive estimates within revenues, raised by a system of taxation levied on the principle of ability to pay.

We advocate a sound currency to be preserved at all hazards and an international monetary conference called on the invitation of our government to consider the rehabilitation of silver and related questions.

We advocate a competitive tariff for revenue with a fact-finding tariff commission free from executive interference, reciprocal tariff agreements with other nations, and an international economic conference designed to restore international trade and facilitate exchange.

We advocate the extension of federal credit to the states to provide unemployment relief wherever the diminishing resources of the states makes it impossible for them to provide for the needy; expansion of the federal program of necessary and useful construction effected [sic] with a public interest, such as adequate flood control and waterways.

We advocate the spread of employment by a substantial reduction in the hours of labor, the encouragement of the shorter week by applying that principle in government service; we advocate advance planning of public works.

We advocate unemployment and old-age insurance under state laws.

We favor the restoration of agriculture, the nation's basic industry; better financing of farm mortgages through recognized farm bank agencies at low rates of interest on an amortization plan, giving preference to credits for the redemption of farms and homes sold under foreclosure.

Extension and development of the Farm Cooperative movement and effective control of crop surpluses so that our farmers may have the full benefit of the domestic market.

The enactment of every constitutional measure that will aid the farmers to receive for their basic farm commodities prices in excess of cost.

We advocate a Navy and an Army adequate for national defense, based on a survey of all facts affecting the existing establishments, that the people in time of peace may not be burdened by an expenditure fast approaching a billion dollars annually.

We advocate strengthening and impartial enforcement of the anti-trust laws, to prevent monopoly and unfair trade practices, and revision thereof for the better protection of labor and the small producer and distributor.

The conservation, development, and use of the nation's water power in the public interest.

The removal of government from all fields of private enterprise except where necessary to develop public works and natural resources in the common interest.

We advocate protection of the investing public by requiring to be filed with the government and carried in advertisements of all offerings of foreign and domestic stocks and bonds true information as to bonuses, commissions, principal invested, and interests of the sellers.

Regulation to the full extent of federal power, of

(a) Holding companies which sell securities in interstate commerce;

(b) Rates of utilities companies operating across State lines;

(c) Exchanges in securities and commodities.

We advocate quicker methods of realizing on assets for the relief of depositors of suspended banks, and a more rigid supervision of national banks for the protection of depositors and the prevention of the use of their moneys in speculation to the detriment of local credits.

The severance of affiliated security companies from, and the divorce of the investment banking business from, commercial banks, and further restriction of federal reserve banks in permitting the use of federal reserve facilities for speculative purposes.

We advocate the full measure of justice and generosity for all war veterans who have suffered disability or disease caused by or resulting from actual service in time of war and for their dependents.

We advocate a firm foreign policy, including peace with all the world and the settlement of international disputes by arbitration; no interference in the internal affairs of other nations; and sanctity of treaties and the maintenance of good faith and of good will in financial obligations; adherence to the World Court with appending reservations; the Pact of Paris abolishing war as an instrument of national policy, to be made effective by provisions for consultation and conference in case of threatened violations of treaties.

International agreements for reduction of armaments and cooperation with nations of the Western Hemisphere to maintain the spirit of the Monroe Doctrine.

We oppose cancellation of the debts owing to the United States by foreign nations.

Independence for the Philippines; ultimate statehood for Porto Rico.

The employment of American citizens in the operation of the Panama Canal.

Simplification of legal procedure and reorganization of the judicial system to make the attainment of justice speedy, certain, and at less cost.

Continuous publicity of political contributions and expenditures; strengthening of the Corrupt Practices Act and severe penalties for misappropriation of campaign funds.

We advocate the repeal of the Eighteenth Amendment. To effect such repeal we demand that the Congress immediately propose a Constitutional Amendment to truly represent the conventions in the states called to act solely on that proposal; we urge the enactment of such measures by the several states as will actually promote temperance, effectively prevent the return of the saloon, and bring the liquor traffic into the open under complete supervision and control by the states.

We demand that the Federal Government effectively exercise its power to enable the states to protect themselves against importation of intoxicating liquors in violation of their laws.

Pending repeal, we favor immediate modification of the Volstead Act; to legalize the manufacture and sale of beer and other beverages of such alcoholic content as is permissible under the Constitution and to provide therefrom a proper and needed revenue.

We condemn the improper and excessive use of money in political activities.

We condemn paid lobbies of special interests to influence members of Congress and other public servants by personal contact.

We condemn action and utterances of high public officials designed to influence stock exchange prices.

We condemn the open and covert resistance of administrative officials to every effort made by Congressional Committees to curtail the extravagant expenditures of the Government and to revoke improvident subsidies granted to favorite interests.

We condemn the extravagance of the Farm Board, its disastrous action which made the Government a speculator in farm products, and the unsound policy of restricting agricultural products to the demands of domestic markets.

We condemn the usurpation of power by the State Department in assuming to pass upon foreign securities offered by international bankers as a result of which billions of dollars in questionable bonds have been sold to the public upon the implied approval of the Federal Government.

And in conclusion, to accomplish these purposes and to recover economic liberty, we pledge the nominees of this convention the best efforts of a great Party whose founder announced the doctrine which guides us now in the hour of our country's need: equal rights to all; special privilege to none.

Republican Platform

We, the representatives of the Republican Party, in convention assembled, renew our pledge to the principles and traditions of our party and dedicate it anew to the service of the nation.

We meet in a period of widespread distress and of an economic depression that has swept the world. The emergency is second only to that of a great war. The human suffering occasioned may well exceed that of a period of actual conflict.

The supremely important problem that challenges our citizens and government alike is to break the back of the depression, to restore the economic life of the nation and to bring encouragement and relief to the thousands of American families that are sorely afflicted.

The people themselves, by their own courage, their own patient and resolute effort in the readjustments of their own affairs, can and will work out the cure. It is our task as a party, by leadership and a wise determination of policy, to assist that recovery.

To that task we pledge all that our party possesses in capacity, leadership, resourcefulness and ability. Republicans, collectively and individually, in nation and

State, hereby enlist in a war which will not end until the promise of American life is once more fulfilled.

LEADERSHIP

For nearly three years the world has endured an economic depression of unparalleled extent and severity. The patience and courage of our people have been severely tested, but their faith in themselves, in their institutions and in their future remains unshaken. When victory comes, as it will, this generation will hand on to the next a great heritage unimpaired.

This will be due in large measure to the quality of the leadership that this country has had during this crisis. We have had in the White House a leader-wise, courageous, patient, understanding, resourceful, ever present at his post of duty, tireless in his efforts and unswervingly faithful to American principles and ideals.

At the outset of the depression, when no man could foresee its depth and extent, the President succeeded in averting much distress by securing agreement between industry and labor to maintain wages and by stimulating programs of private and governmental construction. Throughout the depression unemployment has been limited by the systematic use of part-time employment as a substitute for the general discharge of employees. Wage scales have not been reduced except under compelling necessity. As a result there have been fewer strikes and less social disturbance than during any similar period of hard times.

The suffering and want occasioned by the great drought of 1930 were mitigated by the prompt mobilization of the resources of the Red Cross and of the government. During the trying winters of 1930–31 and 1931–32 a nation-wide organization to relieve distress was brought into being under the leadership of the President. By the Spring of 1931 the possibility of a business upturn in the United States was clearly discernible when, suddenly, a train of events was set in motion in Central Europe which moved forward with extraordinary rapidity and violence, threatening the credit structure of the world and eventually dealing a serious blow to this country.

The President foresaw the danger. He sought to avert it by proposing a suspension of intergovernmental debt payments for one year, with the purpose of relieving the pressure at the point of greatest intensity. But the credit machinery of the nations of Central Europe could not withstand the strain, and the forces of disintegration continued to gain momentum until in September Great Britain was forced to depart from the gold standard. This momentous event, followed by a tremendous raid on the dollar, resulted in a series of bank suspensions in this country, and the hoarding of currency on a large scale.

Again the President acted. Under his leadership the National Credit Association came into being. It mobilized our banking resources, saved scores of banks from failure, helped restore confidence and proved of inestimable value in strengthening the credit structure.

By the time the Congress met the character of our problems was clearer than ever. In his message to Congress the President outlined a constructive and definite program which in the main has been carried out; other portions may yet be carried out.

The Railroad Credit Corporation was created. The capital of the Federal Land Banks was increased. The Reconstruction Finance Corporation came into being and brought protection to millions of depositors, policy holders and others.

Legislation was enacted enlarging the discount facilities of the Federal Reserve System, and without reducing the legal reserves of the Federal Reserve Banks, releasing a billion dollars of gold, a formidable protection against raids on the dollar and a greatly enlarged basis for an expansion of credit.

An earlier distribution to depositors in closed banks has been brought about through the action of the Reconstruction Finance Corporation. Above all, the national credit has been placed in an impregnable position by provision for adequate revenue and a program of drastic curtailment of expenditures. All of these measures were designed to lay a foundation for the resumption of business and increased employment.

But delay and the constant introduction and consideration of new and unsound measures has kept the country in a state of uncertainty and fear, and offset much of the good otherwise accomplished.

The President has recently supplemented his original program to provide for distress, to stimulate the revival of business and employment, and to improve the agricultural situation, he recommended extending the authority of the Reconstruction Finance Corporation to enable it:

(a) To make loans to political subdivisions of public bodies or private corporations for the purpose of starting construction of income-producing or self-liquidating projects which will at once increase employment;

(b) To make loans upon security of agricultural commodities so as to insure the carrying of normal stocks of those commodities, and thus stabilize their loan value and price levels;

(c) To make loans to the Federal Farm Board to enable extension of loans to farm cooperatives and loans for export of agricultural commodities to quarters unable to purchase them;

(d) To loan up to $300,000,000 to such States as are unable to meet the calls made on them by their citizens for distress relief.

The President's program contemplates an attack on a broad front, with far-reaching objectives, but entailing no danger to the budget. The Democratic program, on the other hand, contemplates a heavy expenditure of public funds, a budget unbalanced on a large scale, with a doubtful attainment of at best a strictly limited objective.

We strongly endorse the President's program.

UNEMPLOYMENT AND RELIEF

True to American traditions and principles of government, the administration has regarded the relief problem as one of State and local responsibility.

The work of local agencies, public and private has been coordinated and enlarged on a nation-wide scale under the leadership of the President.

Sudden and unforeseen emergencies such as the drought have been met by the Red Cross and the Government. The United States Public Health Service has been of inestimable benefit to stricken areas.

There has been magnificent response and action to relieve distress by citizens, organizations and agencies, public and private throughout the country.

PUBLIC ECONOMY

Constructive plans for financial stabilization cannot be completely organized until our national, State and municipal governments not only balance their budgets but curtail their current expenses as well to a level which can be steadily and economically maintained for some years to come.

We urge prompt and drastic reduction of public expenditure and resistance to every appropriation not demonstrably necessary to the performance of government, national or local.

The Republican Party established and will continue to uphold the gold standard and will oppose any measure which will undermine the government's credit or impair the integrity of our national currency. Relief by currency inflation is unsound in principle and dishonest in results. The dollar is impregnable in the marts of the world today and must remain so. An ailing body cannot be cured by quack remedies. This is no time to experiment upon the body politic or financial.

BANKS AND THE BANKING SYSTEM

The efficient functioning of our economic machinery depends in no small measure on the aid rendered to trade and industry by our banking system. There is need of revising the banking laws so as to place our banking structure on a sounder basis generally for all concerned, and for the better protection of the depositing public there should be more stringent supervision and broader powers vested in the supervising authorities. We advocate such a revision.

One of the serious problems affecting our banking system has arisen from the practice of organizing separate corporations by the same interests as banks, but participating in operations which the banks themselves are not permitted legally to undertake. We favor requiring reports of and subjecting to thorough and periodic examination all such affiliates of member banks until adequate information has been acquired on the basis of which this problem may definitely be solved in a permanent manner.

INTERNATIONAL CONFERENCE

We favor the participation by the United States in an international conference to consider matters relating to monetary questions, including the position of silver, exchange problems, and commodity prices, and possible cooperative action concerning them.

HOME LOAN DISCOUNT BANK SYSTEM

The present Republican administration has initiated legislation for the creation of a system of Federally supervised home loan discount banks, designed to serve the home owners of all parts of the country and to encourage home ownership by making possible long term credits for homes on more stable and more favorable terms.

There has arisen in the last few years a disturbing trend away from home ownership. We believe that everything should be done by Governmental agencies, national State and local, to reverse this tendency; to aid home owners by encouraging better methods of home financing; and to relieve the present inequitable tax burden on the home. In the field of national legislation we pledge that the measures creating a home loan discount system will be pressed in Congress until adopted.

AGRICULTURE

Farm distress in America has its root in the enormous expansion of agricultural production during the war, the deflation of 1919, 1920 and the dislocation of markets after the war. There followed, under Republican Administrations, a long record of legislation in aid of the cooperative organization of farmers and in providing farm credit. The position of agriculture was gradually improved. In 1928 the Republican Party pledged further measures in aid of agriculture, principally tariff protection for agricultural products and the creation of a Federal Farm Board "clothed with the necessary power to promote the establishment of a farm marketing system of farmer-owned and controlled stabilization corporations."

Almost the first official act of President Hoover was the calling of a special session of Congress to redeem these party pledges. They have been redeemed.

The 1930 tariff act increased the rates on agricultural products by 30 per cent, upon industrial products only 12 per cent. That act equalized, so far as legislation can do so, the protection afforded the farmer with the protection afforded industry, and prevented a vast flood of cheap wool, grain, livestock, dairy and other products from entering the American market.

By the Agricultural Marketing Act, the Federal Farm Board was created and armed with broad powers and ample funds. The object of that act, as stated in its preamble, was:

"To promote the effective merchandising of agricultural commodities in interstate and foreign commerce so that ... agriculture will be placed on the basis of economic equality with other industries.... By encouraging the organization of producers into effective association for their own control ... and by promoting the establishment of a farm marketing system of producer-owned and producer-controlled cooperative associations."

The Federal Farm Board, created by the agricultural marketing act, has been compelled to conduct its operations during a period in which all commodity prices, industrial as well as agricultural, have fallen to disastrous levels.

A period of decreasing demand and of national calamities such as drought and flood has intensified the problem of agriculture.

Nevertheless, after only a little more than two years' efforts, the Federal Farm Board has many achievements of merit to its credit. It has increased the membership of the cooperative farms marketing associations to coordinate efforts of the local associations. By cooperation with other Federal agencies, it has made available to farm marketing associations a large value of credit, which, in the emergency, would not have otherwise been available. Larger quantities of farm products have been handled cooperatively than ever before in the history of the cooperative movement. Grain crops have been sold by the farmer through his association directly upon the world market.

Due to the 1930 tariff act and the agricultural marketing act, it can truthfully be stated that the prices received by the American farmer for his wheat, corn, rye, barley, oats, flaxseed, cattle, butter and many other products, cruelly low though they are, are higher than the prices received by the farmers of any competing nation for the same products.

The Republican Party has also aided the American farmer by relief of the sufferers in the drought-stricken areas, through loans for rehabilitation and through road building to provide employment, by the development of the inland waterway system, by the perishable product act, by the strengthening of the extension system, and by the appropriation of $125,000,000 to recapitalize the Federal land banks and enable them to extend time to worthy borrowers.

The Republican Party pledges itself to the principle of assistance to cooperative marketing associations, owned and controlled by the farmers themselves, through the provisions of the agricultural marketing act, which will be promptly amended or modified as experience shows to be necessary to accomplish the objects set forth in the preamble of that act.

TARIFF AND THE MARKETING ACT

The party pledges itself to make such revision of tariff schedules as economic changes require to maintain the parity of protection to agriculture with other industry.

The American farmer is entitled not only to tariff schedules on his products but to protection from substitutes therefor.

We will support any plan which will help to balance production against demand, and thereby raise agricultural prices, provided it is economically sound and administratively workable without burdensome bureaucracy.

The burden of taxation borne by the owners of farm land constitutes one of the major problems of agriculture.

President Hoover has aptly and truly said, "Taxes upon real property are easiest to enforce and are the least flexible of all taxes. The tendency under pressure of need is to continue these taxes unchanged in times of depression, despite the decrease in the owner's income. Decreasing price and decreasing income results in an increasing burden upon property owners ... which is now becoming almost unbearable. The tax burden upon real estate is wholly out of proportion to that upon other forms of property and income. There is no farm relief more needed today than tax relief."

The time has come for a reconsideration of our tax systems, Federal, State and local, with a view to developing a better coordination, reducing duplication and relieving unjust burdens. The Republican Party pledges itself to this end.

More than all else, we point to the fact that, in the administration of executive departments, and in every plan of the President for the coordination of national effort and for strengthening our financial structure, for expanding credit, for rebuilding the rural credit system and laying the foundations for better prices, the President has insisted upon the interest of the American farmer.

The fundamental problem of American agriculture is the control of production to such volume as will balance supply with demand. In the solution of this problem the cooperative organization of farmers to plan production, and the tariff, to hold the home market for American farmers, are vital elements. A third element equally as vital is the control of the acreage of land under cultivation, as an aid to the efforts of the farmer to balance production.

We favor a national policy of land utilization which looks to national needs, such as the administration has already begun to formulate. Such a policy must foster reorganization of taxing units in areas beset by tax delinquency and divert lands that are submarginal for crop production to other uses. The national welfare plainly can be served by the acquisition of submarginal lands for watershed protection, grazing, forestry, public parks and game preserves. We favor such acquisition.

THE TARIFF

The Republican Party has always been the staunch supporter of the American system of a protective tariff. It believes that the home market, built up under that policy, the greatest and richest market in the world, belongs first to American agriculture, industry and labor. No pretext can justify the surrender of that market to such competition as would destroy our farms, mines and factories, and lower the standard of living which we have established for our workers.

Because many foreign countries have recently abandoned the gold standard, as a result of which the costs of many commodities produced in such countries have, at least for the time being, fallen materially in terms of American currency, adequate tariff protection is today particularly essential to the welfare of the American people.

The Tariff Commission should promptly investigate individual commodities so affected by currency depreciation and report to the President any increase in duties found necessary to equalize domestic with foreign costs of production.

To fix the duties on some thousands of commodities, subject to highly complex conditions, is necessarily a difficult technical task. It is unavoidable that some of the rates established by legislation should, even at the time of their enactment, to be too low or too high. Moreover, a subsequent change in costs or other conditions may render obsolete a rate that was before appropriate. The Republican Party has, therefore, long supported the policy of a flexible tariff, giving power to the President, after investigation by an impartial commission and in accordance with prescribed principles, to modify the rates named by the Congress.

We commend the President's veto of the measure, sponsored by Democratic Congressmen, which would have transferred from the President to Congress the authority to put into effect the findings of the Tariff Commission. Approval of the measure would have returned tariff making to politics and destroyed the progress made during ten years of effort to lift it out of log-rolling methods. We pledge the Republican Party to a policy which will retain the gains made and enlarge the present scope of greater progress.

We favor the extension of the general Republican principle of tariff protection to our natural resource industries, including the products of our farms, forests, mines and oil wells, with compensatory duties on the manufactured and refined products thereof.

VETERANS

Our country is honored whenever it bestows relief on those who have faithfully served its flag. The Republican Party, appreciative of this solemn obligation and honor, has made its sentiments evident in Congress.

Increased hospital facilities have been provided, payments in compensation have more than doubled and in the matter of rehabilitations, pensions and insurance, generous provision has been made.

The administration of laws dealing with the relief of the veterans and their dependents has been a difficult task, but every effort has been made to carry service to the veterans and bring about not only a better and generous interpretation of the law but a sympathetic consideration of the many problems of the veteran.

We believe that every veteran incapacitated in any degree by reason of illness should be cared for and compensated, so far as compensation is possible, by a grateful nation, and that the dependents of those who lost their lives in war or whose death since the war in which service was rendered is traceable to service causes, should be provided for adequately. Legislation should be in accord with this principle.

Disability from causes subsequent and not attributable to war and the support of dependents of deceased veterans whose death is unconnected with war have been to some measure accepted obligations of the nation as a part of the debt due.

A careful study should be made of existing veterans' legislation with a view to elimination of inequalities and injustices and effecting all possible economies, but without departing from our purpose to provide on a sound basis full and adequate relief for our service disabled men, their widows and orphans.

FOREIGN AFFAIRS

Our relations with foreign nations have been carried on by President Hoover with consistency and firmness, but with mutual understanding and peace with all nations. The world has been overwhelmed with economic strain which has provoked extreme nationalism in every quarter, has overturned many governments, stirred the springs of suspicion and distrust and tried the spirit of international cooperation, but we have held to our own course steadily and successfully.

The party will continue to maintain its attitude of protecting our national interests and policies wherever threatened but at the same time promoting common understanding of the varying needs and aspirations of other nations and going forward in harmony with other peoples without alliances or foreign partnerships.

The facilitation of world intercourse, the freeing of commerce from unnecessary impediments, the settlement of international difficulties by conciliation and the methods of law and the elimination of war as a resort of national policy have been and will be our party program.

FRIENDSHIP AND COMMERCE

We believe in and look forward to the steady enlargement of the principles of equality of treatment between nations great and small, the concessions of sovereignty and self-administration to every nation which is capable of carrying on stable government and conducting sound orderly relationships with other peoples, and the cultivation of trade and intercourse on the basis of uniformity of opportunity of all nations.

In pursuance of these principles, which have steadily gained favor in the world, the administration has asked no special favors in commerce, has protested discriminations whenever they arose, and has steadily cemented this procedure by reciprocal treaties guaranteeing equality for trade and residence.

The historic American plan known as the most-favored-nation principle has been our guiding program, and we believe that policy to be the only one consistent with a full development of international trade, the only one suitable for a country having as wide and diverse a commerce as America, and the one most appropriate for us in view of the great variety of our industrial, agricultural and mineral products and the traditions of our people.

Any other plan involves bargains and partnerships with foreign nations, and as a permanent policy is unsuited to America's position.

CONDITIONS ON THE PACIFIC

Events in the Far East, involving the employment of arms on a large scale in a controversy between Japan and China, have caused worldwide concern in the past year and sorely tried the bulwarks erected to insure peace and pacific means for the settlement of international disputes.

The controversy has not only threatened the security of the nations bordering the Pacific but has challenged the maintenance of the policy of the open door in China and the administrative and political integrity of that people, programs which upon American initiation were adopted more than a generation ago and secured by international treaty.

The President and his Secretary of State have maintained throughout the controversy a just balance between Japan and China, taking always a firm position to avoid entanglements in the dispute, but consistently upholding the established international policies and the treaty rights and interests of the United States, and never condoning developments that endangered the obligation of treaties or the peace of the world.

Throughout the controversy our government has acted in harmony with the governments represented in the League of Nations, always making it clear that American policy would be determined at home, but always lending a hand in the common interest of peace and order.

In the application of the principles of the Kellogg pact the American Government has taken the lead, following the principle that a breach of the pact or a threat of infringement thereof was a matter of international concern wherever and however brought about.

As a further step the Secretary of State, upon the instruction of the President, adopted the principle later enlarged upon in his letter to the chairman of the Committee on Foreign Relations of the Senate that this government would not recognize any situation, treaty or agreement brought about between Japan and China by force and in defiance of the covenants of the Kellogg pact.

This principle, associated as it is with the name of President Hoover, was later adopted by the Assembly of the League of Nations at Geneva as a rule for the conduct of all those governments. The principle remains today as an important contribution to international law and a significant moral and material barrier to prevent a nation obtaining the fruits of aggressive warfare. It thus opens a new pathway to peace and order.

We favor enactment by Congress of a measure that will authorize our government to call or participate in an international conference in case of any threat of non-fulfillment of Article 2 of the Treaty of Paris (Kellogg–Briand pact).

LATIN-AMERICA

The policy of the administration has proved to our neighbors of Latin-America that we have no imperialistic ambitions, but that we wish only to promote the welfare and common interest of the independent nations in the western hemisphere.

We have aided Nicaragua in the solution of its troubles and our country, in greatly reduced numbers, at the request of the Nicaraguan Government only to supervise the coming election. After that they will all be returned to the United States.

In Haiti, in accord with the recommendations of the Forbes commission, appointed by the President, the various services of supervision are being rapidly withdrawn, and only those will be retained which are mandatory under the treaties.

Throughout Latin America the policy of the government of the United States has been and will, under Republican leadership, continue to be one of frank and friendly understanding.

WORLD COURT

The acceptance by America of membership in the World Court has been approved by three successive Republican Presidents and we commend this attitude of supporting in this form the settlement of international disputes by the rule of law. America should join its influence and gain a voice in this institution, which would offer us a safer, more judicial and expeditious instrument for the constantly recurring questions between us and other nations than is now available by arbitration.

REDUCTION OF ARMAMENT

Conscious that the limitation of armament will contribute to security against war, and that the financial burdens of military preparation have been shamefully increased throughout the world, the Administration under President Hoover has made steady efforts and marked progress in the direction of proportional reduction of arms by agreement with other nations.

Upon his initiative a treaty between the chief naval powers at London in 1930, following the path marked by the Washington Conference of 1922, established a limitation of all types of fighting ships on a proportionate basis as between the three great naval powers. For the first time, a general limitation of a most costly branch of armament was successfully accomplished.

In the Geneva disarmament conference, now in progress, America is an active participant and a representative delegation of our citizens is laboring for progress in a cause to which this country has been an earnest contributor. This policy will be pursued.

Meanwhile maintenance of our navy on the basis of parity with any nation is a fundamental policy to which the Republican Party is committed. While in the interest of necessary government retrenchment, humanity and relief of the taxpayer we shall continue to exert our full influence upon the nations of the world in the cause of reduction of arms, we do not propose to reduce our navy defenses below that if any other nation.

NATIONAL DEFENSE

Armaments are relative and, therefore, flexible and subject to changes as necessity demands. We believe that in time of war every material resource in the nation should bear its proportionate share of the burdens occasioned by the public need and that it is a duty of government to perfect plans in time of peace whereby this objective may be attained in war.

We support the essential principles of the National Defense Act as amended in 1920 and by the Air Corps Act of 1926, and believe that the army of the United States has, through successive reductions accomplished in the last twelve years, reached an irreducible minimum consistent with the self-reliance, self-respect and security of this country.

WAGES AND WORK

We believe in the principle of high wages.

We favor the principle of the shorter working week and shorter work day with its application to government as well as to private employment, as rapidly and as constructively as conditions will warrant.

We favor legislation designed to stimulate, encourage and assist in home building.

IMMIGRATION

The restriction of immigration is a Republican policy. Our party formulated and enacted into law the quota system, which for the first time has made possible an adequate control of foreign immigration.

Rigid examination of applicants in foreign countries prevented the coming of criminals and other undesirable classes, while other provisions of the law have enabled the President to suspend immigration of foreign wage-earners who otherwise, directly or indirectly, would have increased unemployment among native-born and legally resident foreign-born wage-earners in this country. As a result, immigration is now less than at any time during the past one hundred years.

We favor the continuance and strict enforcement of our present laws upon this subject.

DEPARTMENT OF LABOR

We commend the constructive work of the United States Department of Labor.

LABOR

Collective bargaining by responsible representatives of employers and employees of their own choice, without the interference of any one, is recognized and approved.

Legislation, such as laws, prohibiting alien contract labor, peonage labor and the shanghaiing of sailors; the eight-hour law on government contracts and in government employment; provision for railroad safety devices, of methods of conciliation, mediation and arbitration in industrial labor disputes, including the adjustment of railroad disputes; the providing of compensation for injury to government employees (the forerunner of Federal workers' compensation acts), and other laws to aid and protect labor are of Republican origin, and have had and will continue to have the unswerving support of the party.

EMPLOYMENT

We commend the constructive work of the United States Employment Service in the Department of Labor. This service was enlarged and its activities extended through an appropriation made possible by the President with the cooperation of the Congress. It has done high service for the unemployed in the ranks of civil life and in the ranks of the former soldiers of the World War.

FREEDOM OF SPEECH

Freedom of speech, press and assemblages are fundamental principles upon which our form of government rests. These vital principles should be preserved and protected.

PUBLIC UTILITIES

Supervision, regulation and control of interstate public utilities in the interest of the public is an established policy of the Republican Party, to the credit of which stands the creation of the Interstate Commerce Commission, with its authority to assure reasonable transportation rates, sound railway finance and adequate service.

As proof of the progress made by the Republican Party in government control of public utilities, we cite the reorganization under this administration of the Federal Power Commission, with authority to administer the Federal water power act. We urge legislation to authorize this commission to regulate the charges for electric current when transmitted across State lines.

TRANSPORTATION

The promotion of agriculture, commerce and industry requires coordination of transportation by rail, highway, air and water. All should be subjected to appropriate and constructive regulation.

The public will, of course, select the form of transportation best fitted to its particular service, but the terms of competition fixed by public authority should operate without discrimination, so that all common carriers by rail, highway, air and water shall operate under conditions of equality.

INLAND WATERWAYS

The Republican Party recognizes that low cost transportation for bulk commodities will enable industry to develop in the midst of agriculture in the Mississippi Valley, thereby creating a home market for farm products in that section. With a view to aiding agriculture in the middle west the present administration has pushed forward as rapidly as possible the improvement of the Mississippi waterway system, and we favor the continued vigorous prosecution of these works to the end that agriculture and industry in that great area may enjoy the benefits of these improvements at the earliest possible date.

The railroads constitute the backbone of our transportation system and perform an essential service for the country. The railroad industry is our largest employer of labor and the greatest consumer of goods. The restoration of their credit and the maintenance of their ability to render adequate service are of paramount importance to the public, to their many thousands of employees and to savings banks, insurance companies and other similar institutions, to which the savings of the people have been entrusted.

We should continue to encourage the further development of the merchant marine under American registry and ownership.

Under the present administration the American merchant fleet has been enlarged and strengthened until it now occupies second place among the merchant marines of the world.

By the gradual retirement of the government from the field of ship operations and marked economies in costs, the United States Shipping Board will require no appropriation for the fiscal year 1933 for ship operations.

ST. LAWRENCE SEAWAY

The Republican Party stands committed to the development of the Great Lakes–St. Lawrence seaway. Under the direction of President Hoover negotiation of a treaty with Canada for this development is now at a favorable point. Recognizing the inestimable benefits which will accrue to the nation from placing the ports of the Great Lakes on an ocean base, the party reaffirms allegiance to this great project and pledges it best efforts to secure its early completion.

HIGHWAYS

The Federal policy to cooperate with the States in the building of roads was thoroughly established when the Federal highway act of 1921 was adopted under a Republican Congress. Each year since that time appropriations have been made which have greatly increased the economic value of highway transportation and helped to raise the standards and opportunities of rural life.

We pledge our support to the continuation of this policy in accordance with our needs and resources.

CRIME

We favor the enactment of rigid penal laws that will aid the States in stamping out the activities of gangsters, racketeers and kidnappers. We commend the intensive and effective drive made upon these public enemies by President Hoover and pledge our party to further efforts to the same purpose.

NARCOTICS

The Republican Party pledges itself to continue the present relentless warfare against the illicit narcotic traffic and the spread of the curse of drug addiction among our people. This administration has by treaty greatly strengthened our power to deal with this traffic.

CIVIL SERVICE

The merit system has been amply justified since the organization of the Civil Service by the Republican Party. As a part of our governmental system it is now unassailable. We believe it should remain so.

THE EIGHTEENTH AMENDMENT

The Republican Party has always stood and stands today for obedience to and enforcement of the law as the very foundation of orderly government and civilization. There can be no national security otherwise. The duty of the President of the United States and the officers of the law is clear. The law, must be enforced as they find it enacted by the people. To these courses of action we pledge our nominees.

The Republican Party is and always has been the party of the Constitution. Nullification by non-observance by individuals or State action threatens the stability of government.

While the Constitution makers sought a high degree of permanence, they foresaw the need of changes and provided for them. Article V limits the proposals of amendments to two methods: (1) Two-thirds of both houses of Congress may propose amendments or (2) on application of the Legislatures of two-thirds of the States a national convention shall be called by Congress to propose amendments. Thereafter ratification must be had in one of two ways: (1) By the Legislatures of three-fourths of the several States or (2) by conventions held in three-fourths of the several States. Congress is given power to determine the mode of ratification.

Referendums without constitutional sanction cannot furnish a decisive answer. Those who propose them innocently are deluded by false hopes; those who propose them knowingly are deceiving the people.

A nation-wide controversy over the Eighteenth Amendment now distracts attention from the constructive solution of many pressing national problems. The principle of national prohibition as embodied in the amendment was supported and opposed by members of both great political parties. It was submitted to the States by members of Congress of different political faith and ratified by State Legislatures of different political majorities. It was not then and is not now a partisan political question.

Members of the Republican Party hold different opinions with respect to it and no public official or member of the party should be pledged or forced to choose between his party affiliations and his honest convictions upon this question.

We do not favor a submission limited to the issue of retention or repeal, for the American nation never in its history has gone backward, and in this case the progress which has been thus far made must be preserved, while the evils must be eliminated.

We therefore believe that the people should have an opportunity to pass upon a proposed amendment the provision of which, while retaining in the Federal Government power to preserve the gains already made in dealing with the evils inherent in the liquor traffic, shall allow the States to deal with the problem as their citizens may determine, but subject always to the power of the Federal Government to protect those States where prohibition may exist and safeguard our citizens everywhere from the return of the saloon and attendant abuses.

Such an amendment should be promptly submitted to the States by Congress, to be acted upon by State conventions called for that sole purpose in accordance with the provisions of Article V of the Constitution and adequately safeguarded so as to be truly representative.

CONSERVATION

The wise use of all natural resources freed from monopolistic control is a Republican policy, initiated by Theodore Roosevelt. The Roosevelt, Coolidge and Hoover reclamation projects bear witness to the continuation of that policy. Forestry and all other conservation activities have been supported and enlarged.

The conservation of oil is a major problem to the industry and the nation. The administration has sought to bring coordination of effort through the States, the producers and the Federal Government. Progress has been made and the effort will continue.

THE NEGRO

For seventy years the Republican Party has been the friend of the American Negro. Vindication of the rights of the Negro citizen to enjoy the full benefits of life, liberty and the pursuit of happiness is traditional in the Republican Party, and our party stands pledged to maintain equal opportunity and rights for Negro citizens. We do not propose to depart from that tradition nor to alter the spirit or letter of that pledge.

HAWAII

We believe that the existing status of self-government which for many years has been enjoyed by the citizens of the Territory of Hawaii should be maintained, and that officials appointed to administer the government should be bona-fide residents of the Territory.

PUERTO RICO

Puerto Rico being a part of the United States and its inhabitants American citizens, we believe that they are entitled to a good-faith recognition of the spirit and purposes of their organic act. We, therefore, favor the inclusion of the island in all legislative and administrative measures enacted or adopted by Congress or otherwise for the economic benefit of their fellow-citizens of the mainland.

We also believe that, in so far as possible, all officials appointed to administer the affairs of the island government should be qualified by at least five years of bona-fide residence therein.

ALASKA

We favor the policy of giving to the people of Alaska the widest possible territorial self-government and the selection so far as possible of bona-fide residents for positions in that Territory and the placing of its citizens on an equality with those in the several States.

WELFARE WORK AND CHILDREN

The children of our nation, our future citizens, have had the most solicitous thought of our President. Child welfare and protection has been a major effort of this administration. The organization of the White House Conference on Child Health and Protection is regarded as one of the outstanding accomplishments of this administration.

Welfare work in all its phases has had the support of the President and aid of the administration. The work of organized agencies — local, State and Federal — has been advanced and an increased impetus given by that recognition and help. We approve and pledge a continuation of that policy.

INDIANS

We favor the fullest protection of the property rights of the American Indians and the provision for them of adequate educational facilities.

REORGANIZATION OF GOVERNMENT BUREAUS

Efficiency and economy demand reorganization of government bureaus. The problem is nonpartisan and must be so treated if it is to be solved. As a result of years of study and personal contact with conflicting activities and wasteful duplication of effort, the President is particularly fitted to direct measures to correct the situation. We favor legislation by Congress which will give him the required authority.

DEMOCRATIC FAILURE

The vagaries of the present Democratic House of Representatives offer characteristic and appalling proof of the existing incapacity of that party for leadership in a national crisis. Individualism running amuck has displaced party discipline and has trampled underfoot party leadership. A bewildered electorate has viewed the spectacle with profound dismay and deep misgivings.

Goaded to desperation by their confessed failure, the party leaders have resorted to "pork barrel" legislation to obtain a unity of action which could not otherwise be achieved. A Republican President stands resolutely between the helpless citizen and the disaster threatened by such measures; and the people, regardless of party, will demand his continued service.

Many times during his useful life has Herbert Hoover responded to such a call, and his response has never disappointed. He will not disappoint us now.

PARTY GOVERNMENT

The delays and differences which recently hampered efforts to obtain legislation imperatively demanded by prevailing critical conditions strikingly illustrate the menace to self-government brought about by the weakening of party ties and party fealty.

Experience has demonstrated that coherent political parties are indispensable agencies for the prompt and effective operation of the functions of our government under the Constitution.

Only by united party action can consistent, well-planned and wholesome legislative programs be enacted. We believe that the majority of the Congressmen elected in the name of a party have the right and duty to determine the general policies of that party requiring Congressional action, and that Congressmen belonging to that party are, in general, bound to adhere to such policies. Any other course inevitably makes of Congress a body of detached delegates which, instead of representing the collective wisdom of our people, become the confused voices of a heterogeneous group of unrelated local prejudices.

We believe that the time has come when Senators and Representatives of the United States should be impressed with the inflexible truth that their first concern should be the welfare of the United States and the well-being of all of its people, and that stubborn pride of individual opinion is not a virtue, but an obstacle to the orderly and successful achievement of the objects of representative government.

Only by cooperation can self-government succeed. Without it election under a party aegis becomes a false pretense.

We earnestly request that Republicans throughout the Union demand that their representatives in the Congress pledge themselves to these principles, to the end that the insidious influences of party disintegration may not undermine the very foundations of the Republic.

CONCLUSION

In contrast with the Republican policies and record, we contrast those of the democratic as evidenced by the action of the House of Representatives under Democratic leadership and control, which includes:

1. The issuance of flat currency.

2. Instructions to the Federal Reserve Board and the Secretary of the Treasury to attempt to manipulate commodity prices.

3. The guarantee of bank deposits.

4. The squandering of the public resources and the unbalancing of the budget through pork-barrel appropriations which bear little relation

to distress and would tend through delayed business revival to decrease rather than increase employment.

Generally on economic matters we pledge the Republican Party:

1. To maintain unimpaired the national credit.

2. To defend and preserve a sound currency and an honest dollar.

3. To stand steadfastly by the principle of a balanced budget.

4. To devote ourselves fearlessly and unremittingly to the task of eliminating abuses and extravagance and of drastically cutting the cost of government so as to reduce the heavy burden of taxation.

5. To use all available means consistent with sound financial and economic principles to promote an expansion of credit to stimulate business and relieve unemployment.

6. To make a thorough study of the conditions which permitted the credit and the credit machinery of the country to be made available, without adequate check, for wholesale speculation in securities, resulting in ruinous consequences to millions of our citizens and to the national economy, and to correct those conditions at that they shall not recur.

Recognizing that real relief to unemployment must come through a revival of industrial activity and agriculture, to the promotion of which our every effort must be directed, our party in State and nation undertakes to do all in its power that is humanly possible to see that distress is fully relieved in accordance with American principles and traditions.

No successful solution of the problems before the country today can be expected from a Congress and a President separated by partisan lines or opposed in purposes and principles. Responsibility cannot be placed unless a clear mandate is given by returning to Washington a Congress and a Chief Executive united in principles and program.

The return to power of the Republican Party with that mandate is the duty of every voter who believes in the doctrines of the party and its program as herein stated. Nothing else, we believe, will insure the orderly recovery of the country and that return to prosperous days which every American so ardently desires.

The Republican Party faces the future unafraid!

With courage and confidence in ultimate success, we will strive against the forces that strike at our social and economic ideals, our political institutions.

Communist Platform

The Communist party is the political party of the oppressed masses of the people — the industrial workers, the persecuted Negroes, the toiling farmers.

The Communist party enters this election campaign explicitly to rally the toilers of city and country, Negro and white, in a united struggle for jobs and bread, for the fight against imperialist war.

The Communist party calls upon all workers to resist the attacks of the bosses and to fight to maintain and improve their living standards.

The Communist party calls upon the oppressed masses to rally under Communist leadership in the revolutionary struggle to overthrow capitalism and to establish a government in the United States of workers and farmers.

CAPITALISM CANNOT FEED THE PEOPLE

Capitalism has shown its inability to feed the people. The political parties of capitalism which rule the country — Republican and Democratic — have exposed their complete bankruptcy in this period of severe crisis.

Fifteen million workers, ready and anxious to work, and capable of producing the food, clothing and other goods so urgently needed by the people, are suffering enforced idleness.

Those workers who still desperately cling to their jobs have been forced to accept one drastic wage cut after another, until in some cases their wages are now 50 per cent below their former income.

Hoover's "stagger plan" has brought almost universal part-time work with great reductions in the weekly earnings of the workers. Only 15 per cent of the employed workers now have full time jobs. Eighty-five per cent of these workers are only working a few days per week.

The ruthless robbery of the farmers by the big banks, railroads and manufacturers, which has been going on for the past fifteen years, has during the crisis increased a hundredfold. Farmers, like the workers, are starving; they are being evicted from their homes; their farms are being grabbed by the parasite bankers.

Unemployment, part-time work and wage cuts have resulted in a lowering of the living standards of the entire working class by more than 50 per cent, bringing the American workers down to the level of the poorly-paid European workers.

PROMISES, BUT NO FOOD

The frequent promises of Hoover and his Republican and Democratic supporters about "returning prosperity" are being completely refuted by these undeniable facts. Instead of "returning prosperity," we find only that the suffering of the workers and farmers and of their wives and children becomes steadily worse.

What have the capitalist politicians — Republicans and Democrats — done about it? Warehouses are bursting with unused food and clothing. Hundreds of thousands of houses are standing empty. Idle factories are capable of producing all the goods the people need and more. Yet have these politicians taken any steps to start the factories going again, to open up the empty houses for the evicted workers, or to distribute the food and clothing now stacked up in the warehouses among the starving? Not a step!

Starvation in the midst of plenty. This is what is presented to the workers and toiling farmers of the United States by the ruling class, by the bankers, manufacturers, lawyers, publicists, politicians and their political parties.

THE CAPITALIST WAY OUT OF THE CRISIS

The capitalists and their political henchmen remain coldly unconcerned about the suffering of the masses. They think only about the profits of the rich. Their way out of the crisis is a way that will bring permanent poverty and misery to the workers and poor farmers, while the few rich bankers and manufacturers who control the country become still richer and still more powerful.

Their way out of the crisis — the capitalist way out — firstly, means direct help, not to the poor, but to the rich.

Under the guise of "economy" they categorically refuse unemployment insurance at the expense of the State and the employers. They refuse to appropriate money for a far-reaching public works program. They refuse to appropriate money for immediate relief for the starving workers and farmers. They refuse to pay the bonus to the ex-servicemen of the last war, most of whom are now unemployed or working only part-time.

In their opinion, the slop from the restaurants and hotels and the miserable charity system is good enough for the hungry masses. The employed workers, themselves suffering from part-time work and wage cuts, are being forced to pay for even the charity system. The abominable "block-aid," "community chest," and "family-help-family" systems, by means of forced collections in the factories and neighborhoods, are placing the burdens of charity also on the hungry masses and taking it off the rich who alone can afford to pay.

Yet the Republicans and Democrats, who control the National and State governments, despite their "economy" talk where the masses are concerned, have plenty of funds to aid the bankers and manufacturers and to provide huge amounts for graft and corruption.

The last session of Congress, the Democratic control of the House and with the approval of Hoover, appropriated billions of dollars for direct aid to the rich. Hoover's "Reconstruction Corporation" alone made $2,000,000,000 available for the big bankers. Changes in the banking, tariff and taxation laws, not only placed the burden of the huge government deficit on the middle class and chiefly on the broad masses, but paved the way for further trustification of industry, more firm control of industries and railroads by the Wall Street banks, and for still greater profits by the biggest and most powerful capitalists.

The capitalist way out of the crisis — secondly — embodies a further direct and brutal attack on the living standards of the toilers.

Workers' wages are being even more drastically slashed. The speed-up in the factories and mines is daily increased. More factories are being shut down; more workers are thrown into the streets to join the ranks of the unemployed. The miserable charity rations are being further reduced and the burdens of the charity system are being placed on the already breaking backs of the toilers. In this way the capitalists try to escape from the crisis — to maintain their bloated profits, while the workers are being forced nearer and nearer to the starvation level and even below.

MURDEROUS POLICE ATTACKS

When the workers, by strikes and demonstrations, fight to maintain their living standards and to resist these attacks of the bosses, they meet the sharpest terror. Their political rights guaranteed by the Constitution are denied them. Meetings, demonstrations and picket lines are ruthlessly smashed. Foreign-born workers are torn from their families and callously deported. The attack on the foreign-born is directed against the entire working class with the aim of dividing native and foreign-born workers. Workers are clubbed and gassed by the police on the instruction of the capitalists and their political hirelings. The Negro masses are Jim-Crowed and lynched. Workers are shot down and killed.

This terror is not the monopoly of one capitalist, one politician or one party. The Republican, Hoover, orders the gassing and brutal clubbing of the workers in Washington. The "liberal" Republican, Pinchot, orders the clubbing and murder of the Pennsylvania coal strikers. The Democratic Mayor Cermak orders the beating, gassing and killing of Negro workers on Chicago's South Side. Ford and his "progressive" henchman, Murphy, carries through the murder of four Detroit workers at Dearborn. The Socialist Mayor Hoan, backed by the progressive Republican La Follette, orders the same attacks on the Milwaukee workers.

All the capitalists and all their parties are determined to force through the lowering of the workers' living standard and the maintenance of their own profits by an unprecedented and growing terror.

The capitalist way out of the crisis — thirdly — provides for intense preparation for and the immediate launching of a new imperialist war in which the workers and farmers will be called upon to serve as cannon fodder.

In their greedy desire for greater profits the capitalists set out to wrest new markets from their imperialist rivals by armed force, and to further oppress the people of Latin America, of China, of the Philippines, etc., and rob them of their territory and natural resources.

In preparation for this war the terror against the workers is being carried through to crush all militancy among the workers' organizations; billions of dollars are spent for naval and military armaments, while the people starve.

Efforts are being made to herd the masses — workers, farmers, students — into military and auxiliary organizations in an effort to make them the cannon fodder to be ruthlessly slaughtered on the battlefields. All this is done behind the screen of fake peace talk and fake disarmament proposals.

WAR IN THE FAR EAST

The imperialist war has already started in the East, on the borders of the Soviet Union, with the robber attacks of Japanese imperialism on the Chinese people in Manchuria and Shanghai, with actual warfare against the Soviet Union daily threatened.

The Hoover–Stimson tools of Wall Street are openly preparing to throw the American workers into this war, and in the first place, into a war against the Soviet Union. The battle fleet has been concentrated in the Pacific Ocean where the most gigantic and demonstrative maneuvers are being carried out.

The call to war has already been sounded in the Far East. War in the interests of Wall Street and the imperialist master class threatens to engulf the workers of America and other countries. Increased hunger and misery for the masses, terror and war — this is the capitalist way out of the crisis. The election programs of Republicans, Democrats and Socialists, no matter how skillfully concealed, reflect only the differences between these parties on how to carry through this capitalist way out, how to get the masses to accept hunger, terror and war.

PERSECUTION OF NEGROES

The Negro people, always hounded, persecuted, disfranchised and discriminated against in capitalist America, are, during this period of crisis, oppressed as never before. They are the first to be fired when lay-offs take place. They are discriminated against when charity rations are handed out to the unemployed. They are cheated and robbed by the Southern white landlords and evicted from their land and homes when their miserable income does not enable them to pay rent. When they protest against this unbearable oppression and persecution they are singled out for police attacks in the North and for lynch victims in the South. Over 150 Negroes have been barbarously lynched at the instigation of the white ruling class since the crisis began. The Negro reformist misleaders are shamelessly aiding the white master class in these vicious attacks.

Every day of the crisis, every new effort of the bosses to find a capitalist way out of the crisis, brings new misery and new acts of terror to confront the oppressed Negro people.

WORKERS MUST MILITANTLY RESIST BOSSES' ATTACKS

Against these attacks of the employers, against these efforts of the capitalists to enrich themselves at the expense of the toilers, the workers, the farmers, Negro and white, must fight. They must rally all their forces for the most uncompromising class struggle against every effort of the capitalists to terrorize them into accepting worsened conditions, or to force them into another world imperialist slaughter.

The capitalists will never voluntarily yield an inch to the workers. They will continue ever more ruthlessly to maintain and increase their own profits and wealth by forcing the workers and farmers into greater misery. They will never voluntarily relax their pressure on the masses, nor will they cease for one moment their war preparations, particularly for a bloody war to crush the Soviet Union.

There is only one way out of the crisis for the workers. That is the way of mass struggles. A militant mass struggle can force concessions from the parasite ruling class. Such a struggle will lead to the final liberation from the horrors of capitalism.

In order to carry out this struggle, the workers and poor farmers, Negro and white, must organize. They must build powerful, fighting trade unions and unemployed councils and strong organizations of poor farmers. Under the leadership of the Communist party, the workers in such class organizations can defend their interests to-day, while fighting for the revolutionary way out of the crisis, for the overthrow of capitalism.

The most relentless struggle, now and through the election campaign, for the following demands — the demands of the Communist party — alone offers to the workers the means of defending their interests against the bosses' attack.

1. *Unemployment and social insurance at the expense of the state and employers.*

2. Against Hoover's wage-cutting policy.

3. Emergency relief for the impoverished farmers without restrictions by the government and banks; exemption of impoverished farmers from taxes, and no forced collection of rents or debts.

4. Equal rights for the Negroes and self-determination for the Black Belt.

5. Against capitalist terror; against all forms of suppression of the political rights of the workers.

6. Against imperialist war; for the defense of the Chinese people and of the Soviet Union.

WORKERS' AND FARMERS' GOVERNMENT WILL END MISERY

The Communist party calls upon the millions of workers and farmers, Negro and white, and particularly those rank and file workers who are now misled by the leaders of the Socialist party and the American Federation of Labor, to rally to fight for these demands. The mass fight for the demands can alone develop effective resistance to the starvation and war program of the capitalists.

The fight for these demands, as proposed by the Communist party, means even more. It is the starting point for the struggle for final victory of the toilers, for the establishment of the workers' and farmers' government in the United States. This is the workers' way out — the revolutionary way out of the crisis.

The Communist party proposes an organized mass struggle for the above immediate demands of the workers, as the first step toward the establishment of a *workers' and farmers' government.*

Such a *revolutionary government* alone can fully free the masses from misery and slavery, by talking over and operating the big industries, trusts, railroads and banks. Only such a government will open up every idle factory, mill and mine, and put the workers on their jobs again producing the goods which are needed for a hungry, starving population. Such a government will immediately seize and distribute to the hungry masses enormous stores of foodstuffs now kept locked up in the warehouses, thus caring for the masses and creating a demand for new production. It will open the millions of houses, now held empty by greedy private landlords, and provide comfortable housing for the million now living in the cellars, sewers, disgraceful public lodging houses and the terrible "Hoover cities" of the homeless unemployed. *It will immediately feed, clothe and house all the workers and put them busily at work reproducing all things necessary.*

There is plenty and to spare for all.

It is held away from the toilers by the capitalists and their private property and for their private profit. Only a revolutionary workers' and farmers' government can break through this paralysis of the capitalist crisis and start economic activity going full speed for the benefit of the masses of workers and farmers.

Moreover, such a revolutionary workers' and farmers' government alone can enforce full and complete equality for the oppressed Negro masses and grant unconditional independence to Hawaii, the Philippines and other colonial peoples now enslaved by Wall Street.

This is proven by the experiences of the Soviet Union. There the workers seized power in the revolution of 1917. With the government in their hands the last remnant of capitalism is being uprooted, Socialism is being built. The first Five-Year Plan is now being successfully completed; unemployment has been completely eliminated; wages are being steadily raised; the material and cultural level of the masses is being raised; no crisis such as in capitalist countries has affected their progress; the second Five-Year Plan is about to begin.

The Soviet Union stands out as proof that the workers can rule, not only in their own interests, but in the interests of all those who are oppressed by capitalism.

OLD PARTIES SERVE CAPITALISTS

The capitalist parties — Republican, Democratic and Socialist — together with their American Federation of Labor henchmen — will each appear in this election campaign in different garb; each will pretend to offer a way out of the crisis beneficial to the masses; each will freely promise jobs and plenty to workers when elected.

But behind all their false promises and all of their apparent differences, the workers must see their reactionary actions while in office, their brutal attacks on the workers and their protection of the rich. The workers must see that these parties have been and are now the defenders of the capitalists and the bitter enemies of the workers.

Leading the attack against the workers is the Hoover government, with its bi-partisan coalition of Republican–Democratic parties, composed of rapacious profit-seekers, loyal agents of Wall Street, corporation promoters, and the biggest capitalists themselves, as Mellon, Hoover, Smith, Raskob, and Young.

In order to trick those workers and farmers who are no longer fooled by two-party fakery — new demagogy and promises are being indulged in to make the masses choose "Progressives" and "Reactionaries" within the two old capitalist parties.

The difference between progressive and reactionary is merely on the surface, for the purpose of demagogy, to hide this same basic program of the capitalist way out of the crisis.

Openly supporting the Hoover program, is the officialdom of the American Federation of Labor. It fights against the workers and for the capitalists on every essential point. It fights against unemployment insurance, against the bonus for the ex-soldiers. It tries to stifle strikes and carries on strike-breaking where the workers take up the fight against the bosses' offensive. It fights for huge grants of money to the corporations and taxation of the masses; it supports new laws to help build greater monopolies, it helps prepare imperialist war, especially war against the Soviet Union. Through its deceitful "nonpartisan" policy of "reward friends and punish enemies," it delivers the workers gagged and bound to the Republicans and Democrats, "Progressives" and "Reactionaries," in order to further confuse and divide the working class. It decks itself out in "victories" like the so-called anti-injunction law which fastens injunctions and "yellow dog contracts" ever more firmly upon the workers than ever before.

The reactionary officialdom of the American Federation of Labor is an agency of capitalism among the workers for putting over the capitalist way out of the crisis.

THE SOCIALIST PARTY — THE AGENT OF THE BOSSES

The Socialist party, together with its self-styled "left-wing" — the Muste group — is the little brother of the American Federation of Labor. Its special task is to cover up the same program with the mask of Socialist phrases, and thus to prevent the awakening workers from organizing for a really effective struggle. It supports capitalistic monopoly and trustification under the hypocritical slogans of "nationalization of banks, railroads and mines" through the capitalist "nation." It covers the worst capitalist robberies as "steps toward socialism." It fights against the Workers' Unemployment Insurance Bill, and puts forth its own demagogical emasculated proposals to keep the workers from fighting for their own bill. Its leaders in trade unions help sign wage-cutting agreements, and break the strikes of workers who resist.

The Socialist party and the Farmer-Labor party of Minnesota carry through the same policies in America, as their brother party, the Labor party in England, which launched the wage-cutting campaign, cut down the unemployed insurance, raised high tariffs and taxes on the masses, and carried through inflation. They support and operate on the same principle as their brother party in Germany, the Social Democracy, which is in coalition with the monarchist Hindenburg and supports his emergency decrees which cut wages, destroyed social services, halved unemployment relief, and threw the burden of taxation upon the masses, carrying through the Fascist suppression of the working class and preparation for the open Fascist government.

The Socialist party in Milwaukee and in Reading, when it is in power, carries out the capitalist program of hunger and terror as their big brothers of the Republican and Democratic parties.

They support the pacifist swindle of the League of Nations and especially help prepare war on the Soviet Union, one of their principle occupations being daily slander against the workers' republic.

RALLY AGAINST STARVATION AND WAR

Against all these parties which openly or hiddenly attempt to force through the capitalist way out of the crisis, the Communist party calls upon the workers and farmers of America, white and Negro, to rally for the struggle against, starvation and war, for the immediate demands stated above, for the revolutionary way out of the crisis.

These measures represent what a large majority of workers and farmers *wish to have now*. These things can only be gotten by fighting for them. They cut across the capitalist way [*sic*] of the crisis, because they do not take into account capitalist profits, for which the capitalists and their lieutenants will fight to the death.

It was the Communist party alone which forewarned the workers of the approaching crisis long before the crisis began; it was the Communist party which alone raised the banner of mass struggle against unemployment, lynching, police terror, wage cuts and imperialist war.

The great hunger marches and demonstration of the unemployed in hundreds of cities; the strikes of the miners in Western Pennsylvania, Eastern Ohio, West Virginia and Kentucky; the textile strikes in Paterson, Lawrence and many other cities; the mass mobilization against terror in Chicago, Detroit, Harlan, etc.; the strong fight against lynching, for the defense of the Scottsboro boys; all these struggles of the masses, in which the Communist party played the leading role, are the best proof that the Communist party alone deserves the confidence of the workers.

The Socialist party and its "left" ally, the Muste group, especially has tried in the past and tries now to break up the workers' fight for the program put forward by the Communists, by bringing forward its own substitute of "something just as good," by making its fake program look as much as possible "like the Communists," by talking "revolutionary," by arguing for a choice of "the lesser evil," by putting themselves forth as "the same thing only more practical."

But all their demagogic claims are given the lie by the capitalist class itself, which takes the Socialist party and its leaders, especially its darlings, Norman Thomas, the respectable churchman, and Morris Hillquit, millionaire lawyer, to its heart.

The Socialist party is openly recognized by the capitalist press as the third capitalist party, which more and more becomes equally respectable in capitalist society with the other parties, as the capitalists more and more need it to fool and trick the awakening workers. Even to force concessions *now* from the three capitalist parties, there is no weapon so powerful as a militant daily struggle against the capitalist enemies and a strong vote for the Communist party.

FOR A UNITED STATES OF SOVIET AMERICA

In the election campaign of the Communist party, there is room for the organized participation and support of every worker in America, man and woman, white and Negro, without regard to whether he is a member of the Communist party or not.

Every worker and workers' organization which is ready to fight for the *immediate demands* is invited to be represented in the *Communist Campaign Committees* which will organize and conduct this campaign.

Support the Communist Election Campaign! Rally behind its platform and candidates! Make this the starting point of a gigantic mass movement against starvation, terror and war! Resist with all your energy and strength the brutal attacks of the capitalists! Fight for unemployment insurance against wage cuts, for relief for the farmers, for equality for the Negroes, against the murderous capitalist terror and against the plans for a new bloody imperialist war. Resist the carrying through of the capitalist way out of the crisis! Fight for the workers' way — for the revolutionary way out of the crisis — for the United States of Soviet America! Vote for the workers' candidates — the Communist candidates! Vote Communist!

Farmer-Labor Platform

BANKING, CURRENCY, GOLD STANDARD
AND ECONOMIC BALANCE

The fifth clause of Section 8 of Article I of the United States Constitution provides:

"The Congress shall have power to coin money, regulate the value thereof, and of foreign coin, and fix the standard of weights and measures."

"To coin money" means to print money for the use of the Nation, States, counties, townships, cities, towns, villages, school districts, and for the people, at cost of printing and service.

"Regulate the value thereof" means the Congress gives by an act, authority and debt-paying power to foreign coin (money) coming into the United States, the same as that which it authorizes to be coined or printed.

The United States Supreme Court decided:

"Congress is authorized to establish a national currency either in coin or in paper and to make that currency lawful money for all purposes as regards the National government of private individuals."

Organized Banking and Currency System

(a) We demand legislation to abolish the Federal Reserve Banking System (Fiscal Agent of the United States), private ownership of the United States Banking and Currency System, by repealing the present unconstitutional banking laws on that subject, and then placing them in the hands of the Communities, i.e., the Federal, State, and local governmental bodies, so that the profits, if any shall accrue to the people's governments, thereby preventing panics, depressions and crises, and private control of money.

Postal Savings Banks

(b) As a step to that goal, we demand a law to authorize Postal Savings Banks in each postoffice to accept deposits and permit checking accounts without limit in amount, make loans at uniform interest rate of 2 per cent per annum.

Currency and Free Coinage of Silver

(c) We demand laws providing for the issuance of sound money, full legal tender currency, by the Federal government. And we favor the opening of the mints to the free coinage of silver produced in the United States at its present weight and fineness, but only as coordinate money with that sound money currency, and not as redeemable money. All such money to be redeemable in service rendered by the government, and said money and credit based on same to be properly regulated as to volume in circulation.

Payment of International Debts

(d) Germany should print 11 1/2 billions of full legal tender currency, pay it to discharge the reparations due foreign nations that are indebted in like amount to the United States, each nation making it full legal tender and to tender such money in the United States in full payment of their debts; the United States Congress shall then make it full legal tender in the United States, and authorize the Secretary of the Treasury to accept it in full payment of such foreign nation's debts, place it in the Treasury and use it to pay, as they mature, bonds, compensation certificates in full, Treasury deficits and other indebtedness of the government. Additional issues of international currency can be created by international governmental agreement, free from control by or dictation from the international bankers.

Guarantee to Farmers

(e) (1) We favor a Federal and State government guarantee to the farmers of such prices for their products as will return to them the average cost of production plus a reasonable profit, which will give them a proper return upon their investment as well as a reasonable living. As a step to that goal, we favor the immediate enactment of a law based on the principles of the Bill H.R. 7797, now before Congress, the title of which reads: "*A Bill to abolish the Federal Farm Board. To secure to the farmer a price for agricultural products, at least equal to the cost of production thereof, and for other purposes.*"

Refinancing of Mortgages

(e) (2) For the benefit of farmers and other real estate owners, we favor the immediate enactment of a law based on the principles of the Bill S.F. 1197, now before Congress, the title of which reads: "*A bill to liquidate and refinance agricultural indebtedness,* and to encourage and promote agriculture, commerce, and industry, by establishing an efficient credit system, through which unjust and unequal burdens placed upon agriculture, during the period of price fixing and deflation, may be lightened by providing for the liquidating and refinancing of farm mortgages, and creating a Board of Agriculture to supervise same."

(f) We demand Federal and State government guarantees to the laborers of an opportunity to work at a living wage, or failing, which they shall be paid unemployment insurance benefits by a Federal and State Unemployment Insurance Plan.

Limit Speculation

(g) We favor effective legislation to prohibit gambling in securities or commodities.

Public Works Measures

(h) (1) We favor a three billion dollar annual appropriation by the Federal government for a period of five years if necessary, for the employment of labor on public works over the entire United States, the money to be issued by the government and paid for services rendered, but not to bear interest, namely modern homes for workers, bridge and highway construction, waterways, farm-to-market roads, abolition of toll gates, grade crossings, reforestation, rural school buildings, public grain elevators, water power development, public buildings, recreation facilities, including public parks, etc.

Local Improvements

(h) (2) That can be partially accomplished by the communities depositing with the Federal government their non-interest-bearing 25-year bonds as security for an equal amount of legal tender Federal government money which can be paid by such communities to employ millions of the unemployed on public works and improvements, to be redeemed through taxation, 4 per cent of the principal annually in accordance with H.R. 5857.

Redemption of Bonds

(i) Liberty bonds and all other Federal government bond issues to be redeemed by the Federal government legal tender currency within a period of five years in equal annual proportions and further Federal bond issues to be prohibited by law.

UNEMPLOYMENT, VETERAN'S BONUS,
DEBTORS AND OTHER RELIEF

We favor measures to accomplish the following:

(a) Temporary immediate aid to unemployed by Federal and State appropriations until —

Unemployment Insurance

(b) An intermediate system of the Unemployment Insurance is set in operation with funds to be provided by (1) Federal government, (2) State government,

(3) Employers, and (4) Employees, based on percentages of the pay rolls, which system will remain in operation for ten to twenty years or until permanent relief is attained by other means.

Cash Soldier Bonus

(c) The Federal government to issue two and one-half billion dollars full legal tender Treasury Notes, good for all debts, public and private, to pay the veterans their unpaid balance of compensation already voted to them.

Old-Age Pensions

(d) A Federal and State system of indigent, accident, sickness, maternity and old-age pensions for the needy.

Moratorium

(e) A five-year moratorium on the foreclosure of real estate mortgages, so worded that the debtor who claims inability to pay will have his property rights properly protected. Federal land banks to refinance such small interest-bearing debts as are required for the necessities of life of the creditor.

Flood Relief, Etc.

(f) A Federal commission to be created and funds appropriated by Congress in advance, to take care of sufferers from floods and other catastrophies, so that immediate relief can be given without calling Congress to meet in special session.

Exclusion of Immigrants

(g) Total exclusion of all immigrants until the period of unemployment has terminated.

PUBLIC AND PRIVATE OWNERSHIP

Government Ownership

We demand public ownership of all monopolies:

(a) The community to gradually assume ownership and operation of:

(I) Railroads and other means of transportation, telegraph, telephone and cable lines, all by the Federal government.

(II) Other public utilities, including power, light heat and water, by local or State authorities, or where necessary by the Federal government.

Provide Means to Distribute Profits and Surplus

(b) All other producing, distributing and retailing business to be privately owned and operated, but to pay all profits in excess of a certain percentage, to be fixed by Congress, on invested capital, to the government as taxes.

Patents

(c) The life of patents to be limited to ten years.

Compensation

(d) We favor the payment of a reasonable compensation for all property taken by the government bodies.

LABOR

We favor measures to accomplish the following:

Public Works and Six-Hour Day — Minimum Wage

(a) On public works establish a six-hour day, and a minimum wage of one dollar per hour for common labor, to be paid in full legal tender money issued by Congress.

Construct Mississippi River Waterway

(b) In order to control the overflow of the Mississippi River and to furnish work for unemployed, we favor the issuance of two billion dollars of full legal tender money to be issued to construct a one mile wide Mississippi channel from Cairo, Illinois, to the Gulf of Mexico, with concrete highways the full length of the 600-mile course on both sides of the waterway.

Reduce Working Hours

(c) Establish a reduced number of working hours per day in private industry in order to reduce unemployment.

Convict Labor

(d) Abolish exploitation of convict labor.

Stop Yellow-Dog Contracts

(e) No yellow-dog contract shall be enforceable in the courts, Federal or State.

(f) Prohibit by law injunctions in labor disputes.

TAXATION

We favor measures to accomplish the following: Higher Income Tax

(a) Increase income taxes on incomes over $10,000.

(b) Reduce all taxes. Balance the budget by paying all interest-bearing debts with full legal tender currency. This will abolish 50 per cent of our present burdensome taxation. Repeal the Garner–Hoover Sales Tax.

Higher Inheritance Tax

(c) Increase inheritance taxes in higher brackets.

Abolish Tax Exemptions

(d) Abolish all tax exemptions on property except homesteads up to the amount of $3,000.00, and personal property up to the amount of $1,000.00.

(e) Prohibit the tax on labor to pay debts and support war.

AMENDMENTS TO CONSTITUTION

We favor the calling of a Constitutional Convention to act on amendments as follows:

Lame Duck Congress

(a) Norris Act, abolishing lame duck sessions of Congress, and President to take office in January following election.

Election by Direct Vote

(b) Abolish the electoral college and decide presidential elections by popular vote.

Elect Federal Judges

(c) All Federal judges to be elected by popular vote for six years, on nonpartisan ballot, provide for recall.

Exclude Aliens

(d) The exclusion of all aliens in the determination of the representation in Congress.

Child Labor

(e) Complete abolition of labor by child wage earners.

Initiative, Referendum and Recall

(f) Provide for a National Initiative and Referendum and Recall, on any subject, including prohibition and the Eighteenth Amendment.

(g) The establishment of a one-house legislative body in order to fix responsibility of government.

THE TARIFF — FOREIGN AFFAIRS
AND NATIONAL DEFENSE

In view of the present improbability of getting International Agreement for several years to come, we favor the following principles until International Agreements are reached, or compelled by other circumstances, to abolish the tariffs and to adopt a sound economic system, and to preserve peace on earth.

The Tariff

(a) (1) The gradual reduction of all tariffs by International Agreement, except temporarily on those selected commodities the United States prices of which will be controlled and standardized as the result of the provisions of Plank No. 1(e).

(a) (2) Until such International Agreement is reached we favor the maintenance of the present tariff rates until January 1, 1937, except those which are now or may before that date be fostering exorbitant profits.

(a) (3) If no International Agreement is reached before January 1, 1937, we favor thereafter the reduction of the United States tariff rates then existing by 10 per cent per annum until January 1, 1944.

Tariff on Oil

(a) (4) We favor an immediate tariff duty on oil and such other products as may be necessary to protect our independent producers in the meantime.

Disarmament, Foreign Affairs and
National Defense

(b) (1) General disarmament by International Agreement.

League of Nations

(b) (2) United States shall not enter League of Nations or World Court, nor shall it voluntarily cancel the foreign inter-governmental debts.

Philippine Islands

(b) (3) Independence of the Philippine Islands, to be accomplished within a period of ten years.

Air, Army and Navy

(b) (4) A Department of National Defense under one head with three Assistant Secretaries: of Air, Army, and Navy.

(b) (5) Build up the Navy to the treaty limits immediately and provide an adequate Army.

PEOPLE'S RIGHTS

"We demand equality before the law, political and religious freedom, and restore the economic rights of labor."

Workmen's Compensation Act

(a) Repeal the Federal Employer's Liability Act provision which now disfranchises the rights of railroad men by compelling them to prove negligence where, under State Workmen's Acts, negligence is presumed.

Contempt of Court

(b) Permit trial by jury in all contempt cases with right to change of venue in all courts, State or Federal.

Free Speech

(c) The full observance by Courts, police and other government officers of the constitutional rights of free speech, in schools and other public places, free press, freedom of assembly, and impartial access to the use of movies and radio by minority groups.

Abolish Third Degree

(d) The Courts should be prohibited from receiving evidence unlawfully obtained whether by "third degree" or unlawful search and seizure, or otherwise, or by tapping of wires or other means of communication.

Outlaw Holding Companies

(e) Prohibit by law trust companies, holding companies, corporation farms and chain stores. Strict enforcement of the anti-trust law.

Abolish Bureaucracy

(f) The abolition of Government Bureaus, Commissions, Committees, exercising legislative or judicial powers of either Federal, State or local governments.

Prisoners' Compensation

(g) All prisoners should be compensated for their labor.

Treatment of Patients

(h) All United States hospitals shall permit the patients the kind of treatment and the practitioners the patients desire, whether they be allopathic, homeopathic, osteopathic, Christian Science, chiropractic, or any other practitioners.

Women's Equal Rights

We demand the repeal of all laws, that deny to women equal rights and liberty to earn a living, freedom of occupation, with the same opportunities for economic advancement as offered to men; that marriage or sex shall not exclude or discriminate against women in any occupation, profession or employment; or likewise in the rates of pay, hours of labor or working conditions, and that women shall enjoy equal protection of the law.

OATH TO SUPPORT PLATFORM

Candidates' Oaths

All candidates for National office, standing on this platform and party, shall be sworn to before a Notary Public in the presence of two members of the party, to support this platform in every respect.

Socialist Platform

"The Socialist party calls upon the nation's workers and all progressive citizens to unite with it in a mighty movement in behalf of justice, peace and freedom."

We are facing a breakdown of the capitalist system. This situation the Socialist Party has long predicted. In the last campaign it warned the people of the increasing insecurity in American life and urged a program of action which, if adopted, would have saved millions from their present tragic plight.

To-day in every city of the United States jobless men and women by the thousands are fighting the grim battle against want and starvation while factories stand idle and food rots on the ground. Millions of wage earners and salaried workers are hunting in vain for jobs while other millions are only partly employed.

Unemployment and poverty are inevitable products of the present system. Under capitalism the few own our industries. The many do the work. The wage earners and farmers are compelled to give a large part of the product of their labor to the few. The many in the factories, mines, shops, offices, and on the farms obtain but a scanty income and are able to buy back only a part of the goods that can be produced in such abundance by our mass industries.

Goods pile up. Factories close. Men and women are discharged. The Nation is thrown into a panic. In a country with natural resources, machinery, and trained labor sufficient to provide security and plenty for all, masses of people are destitute.

Capitalism spells not only widespread economic disaster but class strife. It likewise carries with it an ever-present threat of international war. The struggle of the capitalist class to find world markets and investment areas for their surplus goods and capital was a prime cause of the World War. It is to-day fostering those policies of militarism and imperialism which, if unchecked, will lead to another world conflict.

From the poverty, insecurity, unemployment, the economic collapse, the wastes, and the wars of our present capitalistic order, only the united efforts of workers and farmers, organized in unions and cooperatives, and above all in a political party of their own, can save the nation.

The Republican and Democratic Parties, both controlled by the great industrialists and financiers, have no plan or program to rescue us from the present collapse. In this crisis their chief purpose and desire has been to help the railroads, banks, insurance companies, and other capitalist interests.

The Socialist Party is to-day the one democratic party of the workers whose program would remove the causes of class struggles, class antagonisms, and social evils inherent in the capitalist system.

It proposes to transfer the principal industries of the country from private ownership and autocratic, cruelly inefficient management to social ownership and democratic control. Only by these means will it be possible to organize our industrial life on a basis of planned and steady operation, without periodic breakdowns and disastrous crises.

It proposes the following measures:

UNEMPLOYMENT AND LABOR LEGISLATION

1. A Federal appropriation of $5,000,000,000 for immediate relief for those in need to supplement State and local appropriations.

2. A Federal appropriation of $5,000,000,000 for public works and roads, reforestation, slum clearance, and decent homes for the workers, by Federal Government, States and cities.

3. Legislation providing for the acquisition of land, buildings, and equipment necessary to put the unemployed to work producing food, fuel, and clothing and for the erection of houses for their own use.

4. The 6-hour day and the 5-day week without reduction of wages.

5. A comprehensive and efficient system of free public employment agencies.

6. A compulsory system of unemployment compensation with adequate benefits, based on contributions by the Government and by employers.

7. Old-age pensions for men and women 60 years of age and over.

8. Health and maternity insurance.

9. Improved system of workmen's compensation and accident insurance.

10. The abolition of child labor.

11. Government aid to farmers and small home-owners to protect them against mortgage foreclosures and moratorium on sales for non-payment of taxes by destitute farmers and unemployed workers.

12. Adequate minimum wage laws.

SOCIAL OWNERSHIP

1. Public ownership and democratic control of mines, forests, oil, and power resources; public utilities dealing with light and power, transportation and communication, and of all other basic industries.

2. The operation of these publicly owned industries by boards of administration on which the wageworker, the consumer, and the technician are adequately represented; the recognition in each industry of the principles of collective bargaining and civil service.

BANKING

1. Socialization of our credit and currency system and the establishment of a unified banking system, beginning with the complete governmental acquisition of the Federal reserve banks and the extension of the services of postal savings banks to cover all departments of the banking business and the transference of this department of the post office to a Government-owned banking corporation.

TAXATION

1. Steeply increased inheritance taxes and income taxes on the higher incomes and estates of both corporations and individuals.

2. A constitutional amendment authorizing the taxation of all government securities.

AGRICULTURE

Many of the foregoing measures for socializing the power, banking, and other industries, for raising living standards among the city workers, etc., would greatly benefit the farming population.

As special measures for agricultural upbuilding, we propose:

1. The reduction of tax burdens, by a shift from taxes on farm property to taxes on incomes, inheritance, excess profits, and other similar forms of taxation.

2. Increased Federal and State subsidies to road building and education and social services for rural communities.

3. The creation of a Federal marketing agency for the purchase and marketing of agricultural products.

4. The acquisition by bona fide cooperative societies and by governmental agencies of grain elevators, stockyards, packing houses, and warehouses and the conduct of these services on a nonprofit basis. The encouragement of farmers' cooperative societies and of the consumers' cooperatives in the cities, with a view of eliminating the middleman.

5. The socialization of Federal land banks and the extension by these banks of long-term credit to farmers at low rates of interest.

6. Social insurance against losses due to adverse weather conditions.

7. The creation of national, regional, and State land utilization boards for the purpose of discovering the best uses of the farming land of the country, in view of the joint needs of agriculture, industry, recreation, water supply, reforestation, etc., and to prepare the way for agricultural planning on a national and, ultimately, on a world scale.

CONSTITUTIONAL CHANGES

1. Proportional representation.

2. Direct election of the President and Vice President.

3. The initiative and referendum.

4. An amendment to the Constitution to make constitutional amendments less cumbersome.

5. Abolition of the power of the Supreme Court to pass upon the constitutionality of legislation enacted by Congress.

6. The passage of the Socialist Party's proposed Worker's rights amendment to the Constitution empowering Congress to establish national systems of unemployment, health and accident insurance and old age pensions, to abolish child labor, establish and take over enterprises in manufacture, commerce, transportation, banking, public utilities, and other business and industries to be owned and operated by the Government, and generally, for the social and economic welfare of the workers of the United States.

7. Repeal the 18th amendment and take over the liquor industry under government ownership and control with the right of local option for each state to maintain prohibition within its borders.

CIVIL LIBERTIES

1. Federal legislation to enforce the first amendment to the Constitution so as to guarantee freedom of speech, press, and assembly, and to penalize officials who interfere with the civil rights of citizens.

2. The abolition of injunctions in labor disputes, the outlawing of "yellow-dog" contracts and the passing of laws enforcing the rights of workers to organize into unions.

3. The immediate repeal of the espionage law and other repressive legislation, and the restoration of civil and political rights to those unjustly convicted under wartime laws.

4. Legislation protecting aliens from being excluded from this country or from citizenship or from being deported on account of their political, social, or economic beliefs, or on account of activities engaged in by them which are not illegal for citizens.

5. Modification of the immigration laws to permit the reuniting of families and to offer a refuge to those fleeing from political or religious persecution.

THE NEGRO

The enforcement of constitutional guarantees of economic, political, and legal equality for the Negro.

The enactment and enforcement of drastic anti-lynching laws.

INTERNATIONAL RELATIONS

While the Socialist Party is opposed to all wars, it believes that there can be no permanent peace until Socialism is established internationally. In the meanwhile, we will support all measures that promise to promote good will and friendship among the nations of the world, including:

1. The reduction of armaments, leading to the goal of total disarmament by international agreement, if possible; but, if that is not possible, by setting an example ourselves. Soldiers, sailors, and workers unemployed by reason of disarmament to be absorbed, where desired, in a program of public works, to be financed in part by the savings due to disarmament. The abolition of conscription, of military training camps, and the Reserve Officers' Training Corps.

2. The recognition of the Soviet Union and the encouragement of trade and industrial relations with that country.

3. The cancellation of war debts due from the allied governments as part of a program for wiping out war debts and reparations, provided that such cancellation does not release money for armaments, but promotes disarmament.

4. The entrance of the United States into the World Court.

5. The entrance of the United States into the League of Nations under conditions which will make it an effective instrument for world peace and renewed cooperation with the working-class parties abroad to the end that the League may be transformed from a league of imperialist powers to a democratic assemblage representative of the aspirations of the common people of the world.

6. The creation of international economic organizations on which labor is adequately represented, to deal with problems of raw material, investments,

money, credit, tariffs, and living standards from the viewpoint of the welfare of the masses throughout the world.

7. The abandonment of every degree of military intervention by the United States in the affairs of other countries. The immediate withdrawal of military forces from Haiti and Nicaragua.

8. The withdrawal of United States military and naval forces from China and the relinquishment of American extraterritorial privileges.

9. The complete independence of the Philippines and the negotiation of treaties with other nations safeguarding the sovereignty of these islands.

10. Prohibition of the sales of munitions to foreign powers.

Committed to this constructive program, the Socialist Party calls upon the Nation's workers and upon all fair-minded and progressive citizens to unite with it in a mighty movement against the present drift into social disaster and in behalf of sanity, justice, peace, and freedom.

Acceptance Speech by Governor Franklin D. Roosevelt
Chicago, July 2, 1932

Governor Franklin D. Roosevelt's acceptance address was more striking at the time than it now appears. It was brief, optimistic, and all-encompassing in its generalities. The dramatic circumstances of its delivery before the Democratic national convention made it especially exciting to a national radio audience.

Chairman Walsh, my friends of the Democratic National Convention of 1932:

I appreciate your willingness after these six arduous days to remain here, for I know well the sleepless hours which you and I have had. I regret that I am late, but I have no control over the winds of Heaven and could only be thankful for my Navy training.

The appearance before a National Convention of its nominee for President, to be formally notified of his selection, is unprecedented and unusual, but these are unprecedented and unusual times. I have started out on the tasks that lie ahead by breaking the absurd traditions that the candidate should remain in professed ignorance of what has happened for weeks until he is formally notified of that event many weeks later.

My friends, may this be the symbol of my intention to be honest and to avoid all hypocrisy or sham, to avoid all silly shutting of the eyes to the truth in this campaign. You have nominated me and I know it, and I am here to thank you for the honor.

Let it also be symbolic that in so doing I broke traditions. Let it be from now on the task of our Party to break foolish traditions. We will break foolish traditions and leave it to the Republican leadership, far more skilled in that art, to break promises.

Let us now and here highly resolve to resume the country's interrupted march along the path of real progress, of real justice, of real equality for all of our citizens, great and small. Our indomitable leader in that interrupted march is no longer with us, but there still survives today his spirit. Many of his captains, thank God, are still with us, to give us wise counsel. Let us feel that in everything we do there still lives with us, if not the body, the great indomitable, unquenchable, progressive soul of our Commander-in-Chief, Woodrow Wilson.

I have many things on which I want to make my position clear at the earliest possible moment in this campaign. That admirable document, the platform which you have adopted, is clear. I accept it 100 percent.

And you can accept my pledge that I will leave no doubt or ambiguity on where I stand on any question of moment in this campaign.

As we enter this new battle, let us keep always present with us some of the ideals of the Party: The fact that the Democratic Party by tradition and by the continuing logic of history, past and present, is the bearer of liberalism and of progress and at the same time of safety to our institutions. And if this appeal fails, remember well, my friends, that a resentment against the failure of Republican leadership — and note well that in this campaign I shall not use the words "Republican Party," but I shall use, day in and day out, the words, "Republican leadership" — the failure of Republican leaders to solve our troubles may degenerate into unreasoning radicalism.

The great social phenomenon of this depression, unlike others before it, is that it has produced but a few of the disorderly manifestations that too often attend upon such times.

Wild radicalism has made few converts, and the greatest tribute that I can pay to my countrymen is that in these days of crushing want there persists an orderly and hopeful spirit on the part of the millions of our people who have suffered so much. To fail to offer them a new chance is not only to betray their hopes but to misunderstand their patience.

To meet by reaction that danger of radicalism is to invite disaster. Reaction is no barrier to the radical. It is a challenge, a provocation. The way to meet that danger is to offer a workable program of reconstruction, and the party to offer it is the party with clean hands.

This, and this only, is a proper protection against blind reaction on the one hand and an improvised, hit-or-miss, irresponsible opportunism on the other.

There are two ways of viewing the Government's duty in matters affecting economic and social life. The first sees to it that a favored few are helped and hopes that some of their prosperity will leak through, sift through, to labor, to the farmer, to the small business man. That theory belongs to the party of Toryism, and I had hoped that most of the Tories left this country in 1776.

But it is not and never will be the theory of the Democratic Party. This is no time for fear, for reaction or for timidity. Here and now I invite those nominal Republicans who find that their conscience cannot be squared with the groping and the failure of their party leaders to join hands with us; here and now, in equal measure, I warn those nominal Democrats who squint at the future with their faces turned toward the past, and who feel no responsibility to the demands of the new time, that they are out of step with their Party.

Yes, the people of this country want a genuine choice this year, not a choice between two names for the same reactionary doctrine. Ours must be a party of liberal thought, of planned action, of enlightened international outlook, and of the greatest good to the greatest number of our citizens.

Now it is inevitable — and the choice is that of the times — it is inevitable that the main issue of this campaign should revolve about the clear fact of our economic condition, a depression so deep that it is without precedent in modern history. It will not do merely to state, as do Republican leaders to explain their broken promises of continued inaction, that the depression is worldwide. That was not their explanation of the apparent prosperity of 1928. The people will not forget the claim made by them then that prosperity was only a domestic product manufactured by a Republican President and a Republican Congress. If they claim paternity for the one they cannot deny paternity for the other.

I cannot take up all the problems today. I want to touch on a few that are vital. Let us look a little at the recent history and the simple economics, the kind of economics that you and I and the average man and woman talk.

In the years before 1929 we know that this country had completed a vast cycle of building and inflation; for ten years we expanded on the theory of repairing the wastes of the War, but actually expanding far beyond that, and also beyond our natural and normal growth. Now it is worth remembering, and the cold figures of finance prove it, that during that time there was little or no drop in the prices that the consumer had to pay, although those same, figures proved that the cost of production fell very greatly; corporate profit resulting from this period was enormous; at the same time little of that profit was devoted to the reduction of prices. The consumer was forgotten. Very little of it went into increased wages; the worker was forgotten, and by no means an adequate proportion was, even paid out in dividends — the stockholder was forgotten.

And, incidentally, very little of it was taken by taxation to the beneficent Government of those years.

What was the result? Enormous corporate surpluses piled up — the most stupendous in history. Where, under the spell of delirious speculation, did those surpluses go? Let us talk economics that the figures prove and that we can understand. Why, they went chiefly in two directions: first, into new and unnecessary plants which now stand stark and idle; and second, into the call-money market of Wall Street, either directly by the corporations, or indirectly through the banks. Those are the facts. Why blink at them?

Then came the crash. You know the story. Surpluses invested in unnecessary plants became idle. Men lost their jobs; purchasing power dried up; banks became frightened and started calling loans. Those who had money were afraid to part with it. Credit contracted. Industry stopped. Commerce declined, and unemployment mounted.

And there we are today.

Translate that into human terms. See how the events of the past three years have come home to specific groups of people: first, the group dependent on industry; second, the group dependent on agriculture; third, and made up in large part of members of the first two groups, the people who are called "small investors and depositors." In fact, the strongest possible tie between the first two groups, agriculture and industry, is the fact that the savings and to a degree the security of both are tied together in that third group — the credit structure of the Nation.

Never in history have the interests of all the people been so united in a single economic problem. Picture to yourself, for instance, the great groups of property owned by millions of our citizens, represented by credits issued in the form of bonds and mortgages — Government bonds of all kinds, Federal, State, county, municipal; bonds of industrial companies, of utility companies; mortgages on real estate in farms and cities, and finally the vast investments of the Nation in the railroads. What is the measure of the security of each of those groups? We know well that in our complicated, interrelated credit structure if any one of these credit groups collapses they may all collapse. Danger to one is danger to all.

How, I ask, has the present Administration in Washington treated the interrelationship of these credit groups? The answer is clear: It has not recognized that interrelationship existed at all. Why, the Nation asks, has Washington failed to understand that all of these groups, each and everyone, the top of the pyramid and the bottom of the pyramid, must be considered together, that each and every one of them is dependent on every other; each and every one of them affecting the whole financial fabric?

Statesmanship and vision, my friends, require relief to all at the same time.

Just one word or two on taxes, the taxes that all of us pay toward the cost of Government of all kinds.

I know something of taxes. For three long years I have been going up and down this country preaching that Government — Federal and State and local — costs too much. I shall not stop that preaching. As an immediate program of action we must abolish useless offices. We must eliminate unnecessary functions of Government — functions, in fact, that are not definitely essential to the continuance of Government. We must merge, we must consolidate subdivisions of Government, and, like the private citizen, give up luxuries which we can no longer afford.

By our example at Washington itself, we shall have the opportunity of pointing the way of economy to local government, for let us remember well that out of every tax dollar in the average State in this Nation, 40 cents enter the treasury in Washington, D.C., 10 or 12 cents only go to the State capitals, and 48 cents are consumed by the costs of local government in counties and cities and towns.

I propose to you, my friends, and through you, that Government of all kinds, big and little, be made solvent and that the example be set by the President of the United States and his Cabinet.

And talking about setting a definite example, I congratulate this convention for having had the courage fearlessly to write into its declaration of principles what an overwhelming majority here assembled really thinks about the 18th Amendment. This convention wants repeal. Your candidate wants repeal. And I am confident that the United States of America wants repeal.

Two years ago the platform on which I ran for Governor the second time contained substantially the same provision. The overwhelming sentiment of the people of my State, as shown by the vote of that year, extends, I know, to the people of many of the other States. I say to you now that from this date on the 18th Amendment is doomed. When that happens, we as Democrats must and will, rightly and morally, enable the States to protect themselves against the importation of intoxicating liquor where such importation may violate their State laws. We must rightly and morally prevent the return of the saloon.

To go back to this dry subject of finance, because it all ties in together — the 18th Amendment has something to do with finance, too — in a comprehensive planning for the reconstruction of the great credit groups, including Government credit, I list an important place for that prize statement of principle in the platform here adopted calling for the letting in of the light of day on issues of securities, foreign and domestic, which are offered for sale to the investing public.

My friends, you and I as common-sense citizens know that it would help to protect the savings of the country from the dishonesty of crooks and from the lack of honor of some men in high financial places. Publicity is the enemy of crookedness.

And now one word about unemployment, and incidentally about agriculture. I have favored the use of certain types of public works as a further emergency means of stimulating employment and the issuance of bonds to pay for such public works, but I have pointed out that no economic end is served if we merely build without building for a necessary purpose. Such works, of course, should insofar as possible be self-sustaining if they are to be financed by the issuing of bonds. So as to spread the points of all kinds as widely as possible, we must take definite steps to shorten the working day and the working week.

Let us use common sense and business sense. Just as one example, we know that a very hopeful and immediate means of relief, both for the unemployed and for agriculture, will come from a wide plan of the converting of many millions of acres of marginal and unused land into timberland through reforestation. There are tens of millions of acres east of the Mississippi River alone in abandoned farms, in cut-over land, now growing up in worthless brush. Why, every European Nation has a definite land policy, and has had one for generations. We have none. Having none, we face a future of soil erosion and timber famine. It is clear that economic foresight and immediate employment march hand in hand in the call for the reforestation of these vast areas.

In so doing, employment can be given to a million men. That is the kind of public work that is self-sustaining, and therefore capable of being financed by the issuance of bonds which are made secure by the fact that the growth of tremendous crops will provide adequate security for the investment.

Yes, I have a very definite program for providing employment by that means. I have done it, and I am doing it today in the State of New York. I know that the Democratic Party can do it successfully in the Nation. That will put men to work, and that is an example of the action that we are going to have.

Now as a further aid to agriculture, we know perfectly well — but have we come out and said so clearly and distinctly? — we should repeal immediately those provisions of law that compel the Federal Government to go into the market to purchase, to sell, to speculate in farm products in a futile attempt to reduce farm surpluses. And they are the people who are talking of keeping Government out of business. The practical way to help the farmer is by an arrangement that will, in addition to lightening some of the impoverishing burdens from his back, do something toward the reduction of the surpluses of staple commodities that hang on the market. It should be our aim to add to the world prices of staples products the amount of a reasonable tariff protection, to give agriculture the same protection that industry has today.

And in exchange for this immediately increased return I am sure that the farmers of this Nation would agree ultimately to such planning of their production as would reduce the surpluses and make it unnecessary in later years to depend on dumping those surpluses abroad in order to support domestic prices. That result has been accomplished in other Nations; why not in America, too?

Farm leaders and farm economists, generally, agree that a plan based on that principle is a desirable first step in the reconstruction of agriculture. It does not in itself furnish a complete program, but it will serve in great measure in the long run to remove the pall of a surplus without the continued perpetual threat of world dumping. Final voluntary reduction of surplus is a part of our objective, but the long continuance and the present burden of existing surpluses make it necessary to repair great damage of the present by immediate emergency measures.

Such a plan as that, my friends, does not cost the Government any money, nor does it keep the Government in business or in speculation.

As to the actual wording of a bill, I believe that the Democratic Party stands ready to be guided by whatever the responsible farm groups themselves agree on. That is a principle that is sound; and again I ask for action.

One more word about the farmer, and I know that every delegate in this hall who lives in the city knows why I lay emphasis on the farmer. It is because one-half of our population, over 50,000,000 people, are dependent on agriculture; and, my friends, if those 50,000,000 people have no money, no cash, to buy what is produced in the city, the city suffers to an equal or greater extent.

That is why we are going to make the voters understand this year that this Nation is not merely a Nation of independence, but it is, if we are to survive, bound to be a Nation of interdependence — town and city, and North and South, East and West. That is our goal, and that goal will be understood by the people of this country no matter where they live.

Yes, the purchasing power of that half of our population dependent on agriculture is gone. Farm mortgages reach nearly ten billions of dollars today and interest charges on that alone are $560,000,000 a year. But that is not all. The tax burden caused by extravagant and inefficient local government is an additional factor. Our most immediate concern should be to reduce the interest burden on these mortgages.

Rediscounting of farm mortgages under salutary restrictions must be expanded and should, in the future, be conditioned on the reduction of interest rates. Amortization payments, maturities should likewise in this crisis be extended before rediscount is permitted where the mortgagor is sorely pressed. That, my friends, is another example of practical, immediate relief: Action.

I aim to do the same thing, and it can be done, for the small home-owner in our cities and villages. We can lighten his burden and develop his purchasing power. Take away, my friends, that spectre of too high an interest rate. Take away that spectre of the due date just a short time away. Save homes; save homes for thousands of self-respecting families, and drive out that spectre of insecurity from our midst.

Out of all the tons of printed paper, out of all the hours of oratory, the recriminations, the defenses, the happy-thought plans in Washington and in every State, there emerges one great, simple, crystal-pure fact that during the past ten years a Nation of 120,000,000 people has been led by the Republican leaders to erect an impregnable barbed wire entanglement around its borders through the instrumentality of tariffs which have isolated us from all the other human beings in all the rest of the round world. I accept that admirable tariff statement in the platform of this convention. It would protect American business and American labor. By our acts of the past we have invited and received the retaliation of other Nations. I propose an invitation to them to forget the past, to sit at the table with us, as friends, and to plan with us for the restoration of the trade of the world.

Go into the home of the business man. He knows what the tariff has done for him. Go into the home of the factory worker. He knows why goods do not move. Go into the home of the farmer. He knows how the tariff has helped to ruin him.

At last our eyes are open. At last the American people are ready to acknowledge that Republican leadership was wrong and that the Democracy is right.

My program, of which I can only touch on these points, is based upon this simple moral principle: the welfare and the soundness of a Nation depend first upon what the great mass of the people wish and need; and second, whether or not they are getting it.

What do the people of America want more than anything else? To my mind, they want two things: work, with all the moral and spiritual values that go with it; and with work, a reasonable measure of security — security for themselves and for their wives and children. Work and security — these are more than words. They are more than facts. They are the spiritual values, the true goal toward which our efforts of reconstruction should lead. These are the values that this program is intended to gain; these are the values we have failed to achieve by the leadership we now have.

Our Republican leaders tell us economic laws — sacred, inviolable, unchangeable — cause panics which no one could prevent. But while they prate of economic laws, men and women are starving. We must lay hold of the fact that economic laws are not made by nature. They are made by human beings.

Yes, when — not if — when we get the chance, the Federal Government will assume bold leadership in distress relief. For years Washington has alternated between putting its head in the sand and saying there is no large number of destitute people in our midst who need food and clothing, and then saying the States should take care of them, if they are. Instead of planning two and a half years ago to do what they are now trying to do, they kept putting it off from day to day, week to week, and month to month, until the conscience of America demanded action.

I say that while primary responsibility for relief rests with localities now, as ever, yet the Federal Government has always had and still has a continuing responsibility for the broader public welfare. It will soon fulfill that responsibility.

And now, just a few words about our plans for the next four months. By coming here instead of waiting for a formal notification, I have made it clear that I believe we should eliminate expensive ceremonies and that we should set in motion at once, tonight, my friends, the necessary machinery for an adequate presentation of the issues to the electorate of the Nation.

I myself have important duties as Governor of a great State, duties which in these times are more arduous and more grave than at any previous period. Yet I feel confident that I shall be able to make a number of short visits to several parts of the Nation. My trips will have as their first objective the study at first hand, from the lips of men and women of all parties and all occupations, of the actual conditions and needs of every part of an interdependent country.

One word more: Out of every crisis, every tribulation, every disaster, mankind rises with some share of greater knowledge, of higher decency, of purer purpose. Today we shall have come through a period of loose thinking, descending morals, an era of selfishness, among individual men and women and among Nations. Blame not Governments alone for this. Blame ourselves in equal share. Let us be frank in acknowledgment of the truth that many amongst us have made obeisance to Mammon, that the profits of speculation, the easy road without toil, have lured us from the old barricades. To return to higher standards we must abandon the false prophets and seek new leaders of our own choosing.

Never before in modern history have the essential differences between the two major American parties stood out in such striking contrast as they do today. Republican leaders not only have failed in material things, they have failed in national vision, because in disaster they have held out no hope, they have pointed out no path for the people below to climb back to places of security and of safety in our American life.

Throughout the Nation, men and women, forgotten in the political philosophy of the Government of the last years look to us here for guidance and for more equitable opportunity to share in the distribution of national wealth.

On the farms, in the large metropolitan areas, in the smaller cities and in the villages, millions of our citizens cherish the hope that their old standards of living and of thought have not gone forever. Those millions cannot and shall not hope in vain.

I pledge you, I pledge myself, to a new deal for the American people. Let us all here assembled constitute ourselves prophets of a new order of competence and of courage. This is more than a political campaign; it is a call to arms. Give me your help, not to win votes alone, but to win in this crusade to restore America to its own people.

Acceptance Speech by President Herbert C. Hoover
Washington, August 11, 1932

President Herbert C. Hoover's acceptance address, delivered weeks after his nomination, in keeping with political tradition of the time, was more a sober state paper than an effective piece of political oratory. It was typical of Hoover's campaign speeches.

Mr. Chairman and My Fellow Citizens:

In accepting the great honor you have brought me, I desire to speak so simply and so plainly that every man and woman in the United States who may hear or read my words cannot misunderstand.

The last three years have been a time of unparalleled economic calamity. They have been years of greater suffering and hardship than any which have come to the American people since the aftermath of the Civil War. As we look back over these troubled years we realize that we have passed through two stages of dislocation and stress.

Before the storm broke we were steadily gaining in prosperity. Our wounds from the war were rapidly healing. Advances in science and invention had opened vast vistas of new progress. Being prosperous, we became optimistic — all of us. From optimism some of us went to overexpansion in anticipation of the future, and from overexpansion to reckless speculation. In the soil poisoned by speculation grew those ugly weeds of waste, exploitation, and abuse of financial power. In this over-production and speculative mania we marched with the rest of the world. Then three years ago came retribution by the inevitable world-wide slump in consumption of goods, in prices, and employment. At that juncture it was the normal penalty for a reckless boom such as we have witnessed a score of times in our history. Through such depressions we have always passed safely after a relatively short period of losses, of hardship and adjustment. We adopted policies in the Government which were fitting to the situation. Gradually the country began to right itself. Eighteen months ago there was a solid basis for hope that recovery was in sight.

Then there came to us a new calamity, a blow from abroad of such dangerous character as to strike at the very safety of the Republic. The countries of Europe proved unable to withstand the stress of the depression. The memories of the world had ignored the fact that the insidious diseases left by the Great War had not been cured. The skill and intelligence of millions in Europe had been blotted out by battle, disease, and starvation. Stupendous burdens of national debts had been built up. Poisoned springs of political instability lay in the treaties which closed the war. Fears and hates held armaments to double those before the war. Governments were

2792

fallaciously seeking to build back by enlarged borrowing, by subsidizing industry and employment with taxes that slowly sapped the savings upon which industry must be rejuvenated and commerce solidly built. Under these strains the financial systems of many foreign countries crashed one by one.

New blows from decreasing world consumption of goods and from failing financial systems rained upon us. We are part of a world the disturbance of whose remotest populations affects our financial system, our employment, our markets, and prices of our farm products. Thus beginning eighteen months ago, the world-wide storm rapidly grew to hurricane force and the greatest economic emergency in all history. Unexpected, unforeseen, and violent shocks with every month brought new dangers and new emergencies. Fear and apprehension gripped the heart of our people in every village and city.

If we look back over the disasters of these three years, we find that three quarters of the population of the globe has suffered from the flames of revolution. Many nations have been subject to constant change and vacillation of government. Others have resorted to dictatorship or tyranny in desperate attempts to preserve some sort of social order.

I may pause for one short illustration of the character of one single destructive force arising from these causes which we have been compelled to meet. That was its effect upon our financial structure. Foreign countries, in the face of their own failures not believing that we had the courage or ability to meet this crisis, withdrew from the United States over $2,400,000,000, including a billion in gold. Our own alarmed citizens withdrew over $1,600,000,000 of currency from our banks into hoarding. These actions, combined with the fears they generated, caused a shrinkage of credit available for conduct of industry and commerce by several times even these vast sums. Its visible expression was bank and business failures, demoralization of security and real property values, commodity prices, and employment. This was but one of the invading forces of destruction.

Two courses were open. We might have done nothing. That would have been utter ruin. Instead, we met the situation with proposals to private business and the Congress of the most gigantic program of economic defense and counter attack ever evolved in the history of the Republic. We put it into action.

Our measures have repelled these attacks of fear and panic. We have maintained the financial integrity of our Government. We have coöperated to restore and stabilize the situation abroad. As a nation we have paid every dollar demanded of us. We have used the credit of the Government to aid and protect our institutions, public and private. We have provided methods and assurances that there shall be none to suffer from hunger and cold. We have instituted measures to assist farmers and home owners. We have created vast agencies for employment. Above all, we have maintained the sanctity of the principles upon which this Republic has grown great.

In a large sense the test of success of our program is simple. Our people, while suffering great hardships, have been and will be cared for. In the long view our institutions have been sustained intact and are now functioning with increasing confidence of the future. As a nation we are undefeated and unafraid. Government by the people has not been defiled.

With the humility of one who by necessity has stood in the midst of this storm I can say with pride that the distinction for these accomplishments belongs not to the Government or to any individual. It is due to the intrepid soul of our people. It is to their character, their fortitude, their initiative, and their courage that we owe these results. We of this generation did not build the great Ship of State. But the policies I have inaugurated have protected and aided its navigation in this storm. These policies and programs have not been partisan. I gladly give tribute to those members of the Democratic Party in Congress whose patriotic coöperation against factional and demagogic opposition has assisted in a score of great undertakings. I likewise give credit to Democratic as well as Republican leaders among our citizens for their coöperation and help.

A record of these dangers and these policies in the last three years will be set down in books. Much of it is of interest only to history. Our interest now is the future. I dwell upon these policies and problems only where they illustrate the questions of the day and our course in the future. As a government and as a people we still have much to do. We must continue the building of our measures of restoration. We must profit by the lessons of this experience.

Before I enter upon a discussion of these policies I wish to say something of my conception of the relation of our Government to the people and of the responsibilities of both, particularly as applied to these times. The spirit and devising of this Government by the people was to sustain a dual purpose — on the one hand to protect our people among nations and in domestic emergencies by great national power, and on the other to preserve individual liberty and freedom through local government.

The function of the Federal Government in these times is to use its reserve powers and its strength for the protection of citizens and local governments by supporting our institutions against forces beyond their control. It is not the function of the Government to relieve individuals of their responsibilities to their neighbors, or to relieve private institutions of their responsibilities to the public, or of local government to the States, or of State governments to the Federal Government. In giving that protection and that aid the Federal Government must insist that all of them exert their responsibilities in full. It is vital that the programs of the Government shall not compete with or replace any of them but shall add to their initiative and their strength. It is vital that by the use of public revenues and public credit in emergency the Nation shall be strengthened and not weakened.

And in all these emergencies and crises, and in all our future policies, we must also preserve the fundamental principles of our social and economic system. That system is founded upon a conception of ordered freedom. The test of that freedom is that there should be maintained equality of opportunity to every individual so that he may achieve for himself the best to which his character, ability, and ambition entitle him. It is only by this release of initiative, this insistence upon individual responsibility, that we accrue the great sums of individual accomplishment which carry this Nation forward. This is not an individualism which permits men to run riot in selfishness or to override equality of opportunity for others. It permits no violation of ordered liberty. In the race after the false gods of materialism men and groups have forgotten their country. Equality of opportunity contains no conception of exploitation by any selfish, ruthless, class-minded men or groups. They have no place in the American system. As against these stand the guiding ideals and concepts of our Nation. I propose to maintain them.

The solution of our many problems which arise from the shifting scene of national life is not to be found in haphazard experimentation or by revolution. It must be through organic development of our national life under these ideals. It must secure that coöperative action which builds initiative and strength outside of government. It does not follow, because our difficulties are stupendous, because there are some souls timorous enough to doubt the validity and effectiveness of our ideals and our system, that we must turn to a State-controlled or State-directed social or economic system in order to cure our troubles. That is not liberalism; it is tyranny. It is the regimentation of men under autocratic bureaucracy with all its extinction of liberty, of hope, and opportunity. Of course, no man of understanding says that our system works perfectly. It does not. The human race is not perfect. Nevertheless, the movement of a true civilization is toward freedom rather than regimentation. This is our ideal.

Ofttimes the tendency of democracy in presence of national danger is to strike blindly, to listen to demagogues and slogans, all of which would destroy and would not save. We have refused to be stampeded into such courses. Ofttimes democracy elsewhere in the world has been unable to move fast enough to save itself in emergency. There have been disheartening delays and failures in legislation and private action which have added to the losses of our people, yet this democracy of ours has proved its ability to act.

Our emergency measures of the last three years form a definite strategy dominated in the background by these American principles and ideals, forming a continuous campaign waged against the forces of destruction on an ever widening or constantly shifting front.

Thus we have held that the Federal Government should in the presence of great national danger use its powers to give leadership to the initiative, the courage, and the fortitude of the people themselves; but it must insist upon individual, community, and state responsibility. That it should furnish leadership to assure the coördination and unity of all existing agencies, governmental and private, for economic and humanitarian action. That where it becomes necessary to meet emergencies beyond the power of these agencies by the creation of new government instrumentalities, they should be of such character as not to supplant or weaken, but rather to supplement and strengthen, the initiative and enterprise of the people. That they must, directly, or indirectly, serve all the people. Above all, that they should be set up in such form that once the emergency is passed they can and must be demobilized and withdrawn, leaving our governmental, economic, and social structure strong and whole.

We have not feared boldly to adopt unprecedented measures to meet the unprecedented violence of the storm. But, because we have kept ever before us these eternal principles of our nation, the American Government in its ideals is the same as it was when the people gave the Presidency into my trust. We shall keep it so. We have resolutely rejected the temptation, under pressure of immediate events, to resort to those panaceas and short cuts which, even if temporarily successful, would ultimately undermine and weaken what has slowly been built and molded by experience and effort throughout these hundred and fifty years.

It was in accordance with these principles that in the first stage of the depression I called the leaders of business and of labor and agriculture to meet with me and induced them, by their own initiative, to organize against panic with all its devastating destruction; to uphold wages until the cost of living was adjusted; to spread existing employment through shortened hours; and to advance construction work, public and private, against future need.

In pursuance of that same policy, I each winter thereafter assumed the leadership in mobilizing all the voluntary and official organizations throughout the country to prevent suffering from hunger and cold, and to protect the million families stricken by drought. When it became advisable to strengthen the States that could not longer carry the full burden of relief to distress, I held that the Federal Government should do so through loans to the States and thus maintain the fundamental responsibility of the States. We stopped the attempt to turn this effort to the politics of selfish sectional demands. We kept it based upon human need.

It is in accordance with these principles that, in aid to unemployment, we are expending some six hundred millions in Federal construction of such public works as can be justified as bringing early and definite returns. We have opposed the distortion of these needed works into pork-barrel nonproductive works which impoverish the Nation.

It is in accord with these principles and purposes that we have made provision for one billion five hundred millions of loans to self-supporting works so that we may increase employment in productive labor. We rejected projects of wasteful nonproductive works allocated for the purpose of attracting votes instead of affording relief. Thereby, instead of wasteful drain upon the taxpayer, we secure the return of their cost to Government agencies and at the same time we increase the wealth of the Nation.

It was in accordance with these principles that we have strengthened the capital of the Federal land banks — that, on the one hand, confidence in their securities should not be impaired, and on the other, that farmers indebted to them should not be unduly deprived of their homes. The Farm Board by emergency loans to the farmers' coöperatives served to stem panics in agricultural prices and saved hundreds of thousands of farmers and their creditors from bankruptcy. We have created agencies to prevent bankruptcy and failure of their coöperative organizations, and we are erecting new instrumentalities to give credit facilities for live-stock growers and the orderly marketing of farm products.

It was in accordance with these principles that in the face of the looming European crises we sought to change the trend of European economic degeneration by my proposal of the German moratorium and the standstill agreements as to

German private debts. We stemmed the tide of collapse in Germany and the consequent ruin of its people, with its repercussion on all other nations of the world. In furtherance of world stability we have made proposals to reduce the cost of world armaments by a billion dollars a year.

It was in accordance with these principles that I first secured the creation by private initiative of the National Credit Association, whose efforts prevented the failure of hundreds of banks, and loss to countless thousands of depositors who had loaned all their savings to them.

As the storm grew in intensity we created the Reconstruction Finance Corporation with a capital of two billions to uphold the credit structure of the Nation, and by thus raising the shield of Government credit we prevented the wholesale failure of banks, of insurance companies, of building and loan associations, of farm-mortgage associations, of livestock-loan associations, and of railroads in all of which the public interest is paramount. This disaster has been averted through the saving of more than 5,000 institutions and the knowledge that adequate assistance was available to tide others over the stress. This was done not to save a few stockholders, but to save twenty-five millions of American families, every one of whose very savings and employment might have been wiped out and whose whole future would have been blighted had those institutions gone down.

It was in accordance with these principles that we expanded the functions and powers of the Federal Reserve banks that they might counteract the stupendous shrinkage of credit due to fear, to hoarding, and to foreign withdrawals.

It is in accordance with these principles that we are now in process of establishing a new system of home loan banks so that through added strength by coöperation in the building and loan associations, the savings banks, and the insurance companies we may relax the pressure of forfeiture upon home owners and procure the release of new resources for the construction of more homes and the employment of more men.

It was in accordance with these principles that we have insisted upon a reduction of governmental expenses, for no country can squander itself to prosperity on the ruins of its taxpayers, and it was in accordance with these purposes that we have sought new revenues to equalize the diminishing income of the Government in order that the power of the Federal Government to meet the emergency should be impregnable.

It is in accordance with these principles that we have joined in the development of a world economic conference to bulwark the whole international fabric of finance, monetary values, and the expansion of world commerce.

It is in accordance with these principles that I am today organizing the private industrial and financial resources of the country to coöperate effectively with the vast governmental instrumentalities which we have in motion, so that through their united and coördinated efforts we may move from defense to powerful attack upon the depression along the whole national front.

These programs, unparalleled in the history of depressions in any country and in any time, to care for distress, to provide employment, to aid agriculture, to maintain the financial stability of the country, to safeguard the savings of the people, to protect their homes, are not in the past tense — they are in action. I shall propose such other measures, public and private, as may, be necessary from time to time to meet the changing situations and to further speed economic recovery. That recovery may be slow, but we will succeed.

And come what may, I shall maintain through all these measures the sanctity of the great principles under which the Republic over a period of one hundred and fifty years has grown to be the greatest nation on earth.

I should like to digress for one instant for an observation on the last three years which should exhilarate the faith of all Americans — that is the profound growth of the sense of social responsibility which this depression has demonstrated.

No government in Washington has hitherto considered that it held so broad a responsibility for leadership in such times. Despite hardships, the devotion of our men and women to those in distress is demonstrated by the national averages of infant mortality, general mortality, and sickness, which are less today than in times of prosperity. For the first time in the history of depressions, dividends, profits, and cost of living have been reduced before wages have suffered. We have been more free from industrial conflict through strikes and lockouts and all forms of social disorder than even in normal times. The Nation is building the initiative of men toward new fields of social coöperation and endeavor.

So much for the great national emergency and the principles of government for which we stand and their application to the measures we have taken.

There are national policies wider than the emergency, wider than the economic horizon. They are set forth in our platform. Having the responsibility of this office, my views upon them are clearly and often set out in the public record. I may, however, summarize some of them.

1. I am squarely for a protective tariff. I am against the proposal of "a competitive tariff for revenue" as advocated by our opponents. That would place our farmers and our workers in competition with peasant and sweated labor products.

2. I am against their proposals to destroy the usefulness of the bipartisan Tariff Commission, the establishment of whose effective powers we secured during this administration twenty-five years after it was first advocated by President Theodore Roosevelt. That instrumentality enables us to correct any injustice and to readjust the rates of duty to shifting economic change, without constant tinkering and orgies of log-rolling in Congress. If our opponents will descend from vague generalizations to any particular schedule, if it be higher than necessary to protect our people or insufficient for their protection, it can be remedied by this bipartisan commission.

3. My views in opposition to cancellation of war debts are a matter of detailed record in many public statements and a recent message to the Congress. They mark a continuity of that policy maintained by my predecessors. I am hopeful of such drastic reduction of world armament as will save the taxpayers in debtor countries a large part of the cost of their payments to us. If for any particular annual payment we were offered some other tangible form of compensation, such as the expansion

of markets for American agriculture and labor, and the restoration and maintenance of our prosperity, then I am sure our citizens would consider such a proposal. But it is a certainty that these debts must not be canceled or the burdens transferred to our people.

4. I insist upon an army and navy of a strength which guarantees that no foreign soldier will land on American soil. That strength is relative to other nations. I favor every arms reduction which preserves that relationship.

5. I favor rigidly restricted immigration. I have by executive direction, in order to relieve us of added unemployment, already reduced the inward movement to less than the outward movement. I shall adhere to that policy.

6. I have repeatedly recommended to the Congress a revision of the railway transportation laws, in order that we may create greater stability and greater assurance of vital service in all our transportation. I shall persist in it.

7. I have repeatedly recommended the Federal regulation of interstate power. I shall persist in that. I have opposed the Federal Government undertaking the operation of the power business. I shall continue that opposition.

8. I have for years supported the conservation of national resources. I have made frequent recommendations to the Congress in respect thereto, including legislation to correct the waste and destruction of these resources through the present interpretations of the antitrust laws. I shall continue to urge such action.

9. This depression has exposed many weaknesses in our economic system. There have been exploitation and abuse of financial power. We will fearlessly and unremittingly reform such abuses. I have recommended to the Congress the reform of our banking laws. Unfortunately this legislation has not yet been enacted. The American people must have protection from insecure banking through a stronger system. They must be relieved from conditions which permit the credit machinery of the country to be made available without adequate check for wholesale speculation in securities with ruinous consequences to millions of our citizens and to national economy. I recommended to the Congress emergency relief for depositors in closed banks. For seven years I have repeatedly warned against private loans abroad for nonproductive purposes. I shall persist in those matters.

10. I have insisted upon a balanced Budget as the foundation of all public and private financial stability and of all public confidence. I shall insist on the maintenance of that policy. Recent increases in revenues, while temporary, should be again examined, and if they tend to sap the vitality of industry, and thus retard employment, they must be revised.

11. The first necessity of the Nation, the wealth and income of whose citizens has been reduced, is to reduce expenditures on government, national, state, and local. It is the relief of taxes from the backs of men which liberates their powers. It is through lower expenditures that we get lower taxes. This must be done. Considerable reduction in Federal expenditures has been attained. If we except those extraordinary expenditures imposed upon us by the depression, it will be found that the Federal Government is operating for $200,000,000 less annually today than four years ago. The Congress rejected recommendations from the administration which would have

saved an additional $150,000,000 this fiscal year. The opposition leadership insisted, as the price of vital reconstruction legislation and over my protest, upon adding $300,000,000 of costs to the taxpayer through public works inadvisable at this time. I shall repeat my proposals for economy. The opposition leadership in the House of Representatives in the last four months secured passage by the House of $3,000,000,000 in such raids. They have been stopped. I shall continue to oppose raids upon the Federal Treasury.

12. I have repeatedly for seven years urged the Congress either themselves to abolish obsolete bureaus and commissions and to reorganize the whole Government structure in the interest of economy, or to give someone the authority to do so. I have succeeded partially in securing authority, but I regret that no substantial act under it is to be effective until approved by the next Congress.

13. With the collapse in world prices and depreciated currencies the farmer was never so dependent upon his tariff protection for recovery as he is at the present time. We shall hold to that. We have enacted many measures of emergency relief to agriculture. They are having effect. I shall keep them functioning until the strain is past. The original purpose of the Farm Board was to strengthen the efforts of the farmer to establish his own farmer-owned, farmer-controlled marketing agencies. It has greatly succeeded in this purpose, even in these times of adversity. The departure of the Farm Board from its original purpose by making loans to farmers' coöperatives to preserve prices from panic served the emergency, but such action in normal times is absolutely destructive to the farmers' interests.

We still have vast problems to solve in agriculture. No power on earth can restore prices except by restoration of general recovery and markets. Every measure we have taken looking to general recovery is of benefit to the farmer. There is no relief to the farmer by extending government bureaucracy to control his production and thus curtail his liberties, nor by subsidies that bring only more bureaucracy and ultimate collapse. I shall oppose them.

The most practicable relief to the farmer today aside from the general economic recovery is a definite program of readjustment and coördination of national, state, and local taxation which will relieve real property, especially the farms, from unfair burdens of taxation which the current readjustment in values has brought about. To that purpose I propose to devote myself.

14. I have always favored the development of rivers and harbors and highways. These improvements have been greatly expedited. We shall continue that work to completion. After twenty years of discussion between the United States and the great nation to the north, I have signed a treaty for the construction of the Great Lakes–St. Lawrence seaway. That treaty does not injure the Chicago to the Gulf waterway, the work upon which, together with the whole Mississippi system, I have expedited, and in which I am equally interested. We shall undertake this great seaway, the greatest public improvement upon our continent, with its consequent employment of many men as quickly as the treaty is ratified.

15. Our views upon sound currency require no elucidation. They are indelibly a part of Republican history and policies. We have affirmed them by preventing the

Democratic majority in the House from effecting wild schemes of uncontrolled inflation.

16. I have furnished to the Congress and to the States authoritative information upon the urgent need of reorganization of law enforcement agencies, the courts and their procedure, that we may reduce the lawlessness and crime in the country. I have recommended specific reforms to the Congress. I shall again press this necessity.

17. Upon my recommendations the Congress has enacted the most extensive measures of prison reform of two generations. As a result, and despite the doubling of the number of persons under Federal restraint in three years, we are today returning them to society far better fitted for citizenship.

18. There are many other important subjects fully set forth in the platform and in my public statements in the past.

19. The leadership of the Federal Government is not to be confined to economic and international questions. There are problems of the home, of education of children, of citizenship, the most vital of all to the future of the Nation. Except in the case of aid to States which I have recommended for stimulation of the protection and health of children, they are not matters of legislation. We have given leadership to the initiative of our people for social advancement through organization against illiteracy, through the White House conferences on protection and health of children, through the National Conference on Home Ownership, through stimulation to social and recreational agencies. There are the visible evidences of spiritual leadership by government. They will be continued and constantly invigorated.

20. My foreign policies have been devoted to strengthening the foundations of world peace. We inaugurated the London naval treaty which reduced arms and limited the ratios between the fleets of the three powers. We have made concrete proposals at Geneva to reduce armaments of the world by one third. It would save the taxpayers of the world a billion a year. It would save us over $200,000,000 a year. It would reduce fear and danger of war. We have expanded the arbitration of disputes. I have recommended joining the World Court under proper reservations preserving our freedom of action. We have given leadership in transforming the Kellogg–Briand pact from an inspiring outlawry of war to an organized instrument for peaceful settlements backed by definite mobilization of world public opinion against aggression. We shall, under the spirit of that pact, consult with other nations in times of emergency to promote world peace. We shall enter no agreements committing us to any future course of action or which call for use of force to preserve peace.

Above all, I have projected a new doctrine into international affairs, the doctrine that we do not and never will recognize title to possession of territory gained in violation of the peace pacts. That doctrine has been accepted by all the nations of the world on a recent critical occasion, and within the last few days has been accepted again by all the nations of the Western Hemisphere. That is public opinion made tangible and effective.

This world needs peace. It must have peace with justice. I shall continue to strive unceasingly, with every power of mind and spirit, to explore every possible path that leads toward a world in which right triumphs over force, in which reason rules over passion, in which men and women may rear their children not to be devoured by war but to pursue in safety the nobler arts of peace.

I shall continue to build on that design.

Across the path of the Nation's consideration of these vast problems of economic and social order there has arisen a bitter controversy over the control of the liquor traffic. I have always sympathized with the high purpose of the Eighteenth Amendment, and I have used every power at my command to make it effective over the entire country. I have hoped it was the final solution of the evils of the liquor traffic against which our people have striven for generations. It has succeeded in great measure in those many communities where the majority sentiment is favorable to it. But in other and increasing number of communities there is a majority sentiment unfavorable to it. Laws opposed by majority sentiment create resentment which undermines enforcement and in the end produces degeneration and crime.

Our opponents pledge the members of their party to destroy every vestige of constitutional and effective Federal control of the traffic. That means over large areas the return of the saloon system with its corruption, its moral and social abuse which debauched the home, its deliberate interference with those States endeavoring to find honest solution, its permeation of political parties, and its pervasion of legislatures, which even touched at the capital of the Nation. The Eighteenth Amendment smashed that regime as by a stroke of lightning. I cannot consent to the return of that system.

At the same time we must recognize the difficulties which have developed in making the Eighteenth Amendment effective and that grave abuses have grown up. In order to secure the enforcement of the amendment under our dual form of government, the constitutional provision called for concurrent action on one hand by the State and local authorities and on the other by the Federal Government. Its enforcement requires independent but coincident action of both agencies. An increasing number of States and municipalities are proving themselves unwilling to engage in such enforcement. Owing to these forces there is in large sections an increasing illegal traffic in liquor. But worse than this there has been in those areas a spread of disrespect not only for this law but for all laws, grave dangers of practical nullification of the Constitution, a degeneration in municipal government, and an increase in subsidized crime and violence. I cannot consent to the continuation of this regime.

I refuse to accept either of these destinies, on the one hand to return to the old saloon with its political and social corruption, or on the other to endure the bootlegger and the speakeasy with their abuses and crime. Either is intolerable. These are not the ways out.

Our objective must be a sane solution, not a blind leap back to old evils. Moreover, such a step backward would result in a chaos of new evils never yet experienced, because the local systems of prohibitions and controls which were developed over generations have been in large degree abandoned under the amendment.

The Republican platform recommends submission of the question to the States, that the people themselves may determine whether they desire a change, but insists that this submission shall propose a constructive and not a destructive change. It does not dictate to the conscience of any member of the party.

The first duty of the President of the United States is to enforce the laws as they exist. That I shall continue to do to the utmost of my ability. Any other course would be the abrogation of the very guaranties of liberty itself.

The Constitution gives the President no power or authority with respect to changes in the Constitution itself; nevertheless, my countrymen have a right to know my conclusions upon this matter. They are clear and need not be misunderstood. They are based upon the broad facts I have stated, upon my experience in this high office, and upon the deep conviction that our purpose must be the elimination of the evils of this traffic from this civilization by practical measures.

It is my belief that in order to remedy present evils a change is necessary by which we resummon a proper share of initiative and responsibility which the very essence of our Government demands shall rest upon the States and local authorities. That change must avoid the return of the saloon.

It is my conviction that the nature of this change, and one upon which all reasonable people can find common ground, is that each State shall be given the right to deal with the problem as it may determine, but subject to absolute guarantees in the Constitution of the United States to protect each State from interference and invasion by its neighbors, and that in no part of the United States shall there be a return of the saloon system with its inevitable political and social corruption and its organized interference with other States.

American statesmanship is capable of working out such a solution and making it effective.

My fellow citizens, the discussion of great problems of economic life and of government often seems abstract and cold. But within their right solution lie the happiness and hope of a great people. Without such solution all else is mere verbal sympathy.

Today millions of our fellow countrymen are out of work. Prices of the farmers' products are below a living standard. Many millions more who are in business or hold employment are haunted by fears for the future. No man with a spark of humanity can sit in my place without suffering from the picture of their anxieties and hardships before him day and night. They would be more than human if they were not led to blame their condition upon the government in power. I have understood their sufferings and have worked to the limits of my strength to produce action that would really help them.

Much remains to be done to attain recovery. The emergency measures now in action represent an unparalleled use of national power to relieve distress, to provide employment, to serve agriculture, to preserve the stability of the Government, to maintain the integrity of our institutions. Our policies prevent unemployment caused by floods of imported goods and laborers. Our policies preserve peace. They embrace coöperation with other nations in those fields in which we can serve. With patience and perseverance these measures will succeed.

Despite the dislocation of economic life our great tools of production and distribution are more efficient than ever before; our fabulous natural resources, our farms, our homes, our skill are unimpaired. From the hard-won experience of this depression we shall build stronger methods of prevention and stronger methods of protection to our people from the abuses which have become evident. We shall march to far greater accomplishment.

With united effort we can and will turn the tide toward the restoration of business, employment, and agriculture. It will call for the utmost devotion and wisdom. Every reserve of American courage and vision must be called upon to sustain us and to plan wisely for the future.

Through it all our first duty is to preserve unfettered that dominant American spirit which has produced our enterprise and individual character. That is the bedrock of the past, and that is the guaranty of the future. Not regimented mechanisms but free men is our goal. Herein is the fundamental issue. A representative democracy, progressive and unafraid to meet its problems, but meeting them upon the foundations of experience and not upon the wave of emotion or the insensate demands of a radicalism which grasps at every opportunity to exploit the sufferings of a people.

With these courses we shall emerge from this great national strain with our American system of life and government strengthened. Our people will be free to reassert their energy and enterprise in a society eager to reward in full measure those whose industry serves its well-being. Our youth will find the doors of equal opportunity still open.

The problems of the next few years are not only economic. They are also moral and spiritual. The present check to our material success must deeply stir our national conscience upon the purposes of life itself. It must cause us to revalue and reshape our drift from materialism to a higher note of individual and national ideals.

Underlying every purpose is the spiritual application of moral ideals which are the fundamental basis of happiness in a people. This is a land of homes, churches, schoolhouses dedicated to the sober and enduring satisfactions of family life and the rearing of children in an atmosphere of ideals and religious faith. Only with these high standards can we hold society together, and only from them can government survive or business prosper. They are the sole insurance to the safety of our children and the continuity of the Nation.

If it shall appear that while I have had the honor of the Presidency I have contributed the part required from this high office to bringing the Republic through this dark night, and if in my administration we shall see the break of dawn to a better day, I shall have done my part in the world. No man can have a greater honor than that.

I have but one desire: that is, to see my country again on the road to prosperity which shall be more sane and lasting through the lesson of experience, to see the principles and ideals of the American people perpetuated.

I rest the case of the Republican Party on the intelligence and the just discernment of the American people. Should my countrymen again place upon me the responsibilities of this high office, I shall carry forward the work of reconstruction. I shall hope long before another four years have passed to see the world prosperous and at peace and every American home again in the sunshine of genuine progress and genuine prosperity. I shall seek to maintain untarnished and unweakened those fundamental traditions and principles upon which our Nation was founded and upon which it has grown. I shall invite and welcome the help of every man and woman in the preservation of the United States for the happiness of its people. This is my pledge to the Nation and to Almighty God.

THE VOTES IN THE 1932 ELECTION

States	Popular vote — F. D. Roosevelt, Democrat	Popular vote — Herbert Hoover, Republican	Popular vote — Norman Thomas, Socialist	Electoral vote — Hoover-Curtis	Electoral vote — Roosevelt-Garner
Alabama	207,910	34,675	2,030	–	11
Arizona	79,264	36,104	2,618	–	3
Arkansas	189,602	28,467	1,269	–	9
California	1,324,157	847,902	63,299	–	22
Colorado	250,877	189,617	13,591	–	6
Connecticut	281,632	288,420	20,480	8	–
Delaware	54,319	57,073	1,376	3	–
Florida	206,307	69,170	775	–	7
Georgia	234,118	19,863	461	–	12
Idaho	109,479	71,312	526	–	4
Illinois	1,882,304	1,432,756	67,258	–	29
Indiana	862,054	677,184	21,338	–	14
Iowa	598,019	414,433	20,467	–	11
Kansas	424,204	349,498	18,276	–	9
Kentucky	580,574	394,716	3,853	–	11
Louisiana	249,418	18,853	–	–	10
Maine	128,907	166,631	2,489	5	–
Maryland	314,314	184,184	10,489	–	8
Massachusetts	800,148	736,959	34,305	–	17
Michigan	871,700	739,894	39,205	–	19
Minnesota	600,806	363,959	25,476	–	11
Mississippi	140,168	5,180	686	–	9
Missouri	1,025,406	564,713	16,374	–	15
Montana	127,286	78,078	7,891	–	4
Nebraska	359,082	201,177	9,876	–	7
Nevada	28,756	12,674	–	–	3
New Hampshire	100,680	103,629	947	4	–
New Jersey	806,630	775,684	42,998	–	16
New Mexico	95,089	54,217	1,776	–	3
New York	2,534,959	1,937,963	177,397	–	47
North Carolina	497,566	208,344	5,591	–	13
North Dakota	178,350	71,772	3,521	–	4
Ohio	1,301,695	1,227,679	64,094	–	26
Oklahoma	516,468	188,165	–	–	11
Oregon	213,871	136,019	15,450	–	5
Pennsylvania	1,295,948	1,453,540	91,119	36	–
Rhode Island	146,604	115,266	3,138	–	4
South Carolina	102,347	1,978	82	–	8
South Dakota	183,515	99,212	1,551	–	4
Tennessee	259,817	126,806	1,786	–	11
Texas	760,348	97,959	4,450	–	23
Utah	116,750	84,795	4,087	–	4
Vermont	56,266	78,984	1,533	3	–
Virginia	203,979	89,637	2,382	–	11
Washington	353,260	208,645	17,080	–	8
West Virginia	405,124	330,731	5,133	–	8
Wisconsin	707,410	347,741	53,379	–	12
Wyoming	54,370	39,583	2,829	–	3
	22,821,857	15,761,841	884,781	59	472

Reynolds, Socialist-Labor, 33,275; Foster, Communist, 102,991; Upshaw, Prohibitionist, 81,869; Harvey, Liberty, 53,425; Coxey, Farm-Labor, 7,309. Total vote, 39,816,522.

Election of

1936

WILLIAM E. LEUCHTENBURG is William Rand Kenan Professor of History at the University of North Carolina at Chapel Hill. Winner of both the Bancroft and Parkman prizes, he is past president of the American Historical Association and the Organization of American Historians. Among his books are *Franklin D. Roosevelt and the New Deal, 1932–1940*; *The Perils of Prosperity*; and *In the Shadow of FDR: From Harry Truman to Bill Clinton*.

Election of
1936

William E. Leuchtenburg

The historian who writes about the campaign of 1936 has one big advantage over the people who lived at the time — he knows how it all turned out. So decisive were the election results that it seems, in retrospect, that everyone must always have recognized that the campaign would end in a landslide victory. But at the beginning of 1936, the outcome seemed very much in doubt. The January poll of the American Institute of Public Opinion declared that, if Roosevelt held five states listed as borderline Democrat, he would win, but by the small majority of 25 electoral votes. Even more alarming to the Democrats were the findings of the prestigious *Literary Digest* poll, that "*Great* and *Sure* Barometer" that had come within 1 percent of calling FDR's popular majority in 1932. When in the fall of 1935 the *Digest* asked what people thought of the New Deal, 63 percent of the straw ballots were disapproving; Roosevelt's policies found favor in only twelve states, almost all in the South. The Democratic National Committee's statisticians virtually wrote off New York and Illinois, and saw only an outside chance for victory in Ohio, Indiana, and Minnesota. When the *Literary Digest* launched its presidential poll that summer, it stated, "Not since Hughes battled Wilson in 1916 have the lines been so sharply drawn, the outcome so in doubt."

To be sure, the Democrats had won resounding victories in 1932 and in the 1934 midterm elections, but they had enjoyed short-lived intervals of success before, under

Cleveland and Wilson, only to have the country return to Republicanism. The nationally syndicated columnist Paul Mallon wrote in July 1935 that for three-quarters of a century it had been understood "that this is a Republican country; that the Republicans alone can bring prosperity; that the voters merely chastise them occasionally, but always restore them to favor after a brief, unsatisfactory experience with the Democrats." The 1936 election would demonstrate whether Roosevelt's first term in office was only another such interregnum or whether his election in 1932 had marked the beginning of a significant realignment in American politics.

The 1936 election would also give the country its first opportunity in a national contest to indicate whether Big Government was to be a permanent feature of American society. In little more than two years, the New Deal had established such novel agencies as the Agricultural Adjustment Administration (AAA), which dispensed bounties to farmers; the Works Progress Administration (WPA), which operated a multi-billion-dollar relief operation for the unemployed; and the Public Works Administration (PWA), which constructed highways, schools, and bridges. Conservatives deplored this proliferation of alphabet agencies and expressed their displeasure at such episodes as the devaluation of the dollar and the slaughter of pigs to raise farm prices. But Democratic campaigners found that they made the greatest headway by emphasizing "the politics of the deed" — the many ways that the National Government was distributing direct benefits to the people. Mayor Daniel Shields of Johnstown, Pennsylvania, a Republican for thirty years, pointed out that the WPA had saved his city and added, "Johnstown should vote solid for President Roosevelt."

Because of the New Deal, the parties divided on issues in 1936 as they had at no previous time in this century. As late as 1931, one congressman had remarked, "The aisles don't mean anything except a good place to walk in and walk out." By 1936, the aisles that demarcated the two parties in Congress separated two different theories of the role of government, even though neither party was an ideological monolith. The Democratic Party, the historic defender of states' rights, had become the instrument of the Welfare State, while the Republican Party, the traditional advocate of a strong national union, now championed a weak central government. When in the spring of 1936 the Gallup Poll asked respondents whether they favored an amendment to ban child labor, Democrats answered "yes" almost 3 to 1, while a majority of Republicans replied "no." The ensuing campaign centered on a range of issues markedly different from those that had seemed significant as recently as 1932. A Little Rock newspaper commented, "Such matters as tax and tariff laws have given way to universally human things, the living problems and opportunities of the average man and the average family."

The President believed that he would win the greatest response by exploiting the class antagonisms of the Great Depression. When he took office in March 1933, he had attempted to forge an all-class alliance in which business would have a central role. Well before the 1936 campaign, however, he had come to question the feasibility of government cooperation with business since so many corporation leaders opposed his policies. In the spring and summer of 1935, a new circle of advisers, some of whom were proteges of Justice Louis Brandeis, encouraged him to declare war on Big Business. Thomas G. Corcoran was quoted as saying, "Fighting with a businessman is like fighting with a Polack. You can give no quarter." In early May 1936, aboard the yacht *Potomac*, Roosevelt told Raymond Moley, the leader of the 1932 "Brain Trust," that businessmen as a class were stupid and that they had no sense of moral indignation about the sins of other businessmen. Newspaper publishers were just as bad. The President thought that nothing would help him more than to have newspapers, bankers, and business aligned against him, for their attacks would only win him more votes.

To take advantage of the class cleavages in 1936, Roosevelt directed the Democratic National Committee to concentrate its fire not on the Republicans, but on such symbols of wealth as the American Liberty League, associated by the public with the du Ponts of Delaware and J. Howard Pew Jr. of the Sun Oil Company. The President, for his part, missed few opportunities to point out that the rich and well-born detested him, and he seemed to take a puckish pleasure in the fact. At Harvard's tercentenary celebration in 1936, where undergraduates booed him, Roosevelt noted that at the 200th anniversary celebration a century before "many of the alumni of Harvard were sorely troubled by the state of the Nation. Andrew Jackson was President. On the 250th anniversary of the founding of Harvard College, alumni were again sorely troubled. Grover Cleveland was President." He paused. "Now, on the 300th anniversary, I am President."

The 1936 campaign would range over a wide variety of issues, but the significance of the election would lie in these questions: whether the Democrats could make good their claim to be the nation's new majority party; whether the country would put its stamp of approval on Big Government; and whether class would prove the most important determinant of how the electorate made its choices on November 3.

The devastating outcome of the 1934 elections left the Republicans with almost no men of national stature as potential presidential nominees in 1936. So closely was Herbert Hoover linked to the disaster of the Depression that few party leaders seriously considered renominating him again, although he retained the support of a number of his old associates. Nor did it seem wise to choose a man from the East, if the party hoped to win the allegiance of the midwestern farmer. Even the Old Guard agreed that the Republican nominee must come from west of the Alleghenies, a vast region that had gone solidly to the Democrats in 1932. Eastern industrialists looked for a candidate who combined the ancient Republican virtues with a mild reputation for liberalism. Some thought they had such a man in Frank Lowden, the former Illinois governor who had been a front-runner in 1920. However, the septuagenarian "Sage of Sinnissippi" made clear he did not wish to run and privately deplored the dearth of outstanding candidates, a situation he blamed on the direct primary. Others admired the bombast of Arthur Vandenberg, but the Michigan senator was shrewd enough to prefer to wait until 1940 when Roosevelt, because of the two-term tradition, would not be a candidate.

A poll of party leaders by the former executive director of the Republican National Committee in September 1935 showed Senator William E. Borah of Idaho the leading contender with 367 votes, over one hundred more than his nearest rival. The "Lion of Idaho" had been a national figure for three decades; in Europe no senator was so well known. He had a reputation, rather inflated, for progressivism, and many farmers admired his stand on currency issues. But Borah, at seventy, was too old, and his views on inflation and social legislation made him unacceptable to the Old Guard. Few took his showing in the poll seriously, for he had displayed strength in other election years without winning the nomination. Even when he captured the Wisconsin primary and ran strongly in downstate Illinois, he failed to impress. James A. Farley, the Democratic national chairman, remarked to Roosevelt, "I have always felt personally that Borah was a quarter-mile runner. He generally broke well at the barrier with those who always ran, but by the time they reached the head of the stretch, he was well back in the field, and never heard from after that."

The same poll reported Borah's closest rival to be Chicago publisher Frank Knox. Chairman of the Credentials Committee at the Bull Moose convention in 1912, and Leonard Wood's floor manager in 1920, he could claim to speak for the Theodore Roosevelt tradition. He had in fact been a Rough Rider in the Spanish-American War and was fond of aping Colonel Roosevelt's mannerisms. Knox, too, was a colonel, a commission he had won in World War I, in which he had enlisted as a private and saw service overseas. He had once worked with Vandenberg on the Grand Rapids *Herald*, had published newspapers in three states, had managed the Hearst chain for three years, and as publisher of the Chicago *Daily News* operated a journal known for its distinguished staff of foreign correspondents. He had the advantage, too, of coming from a big state, but Knox had never held public office, and he was opposed in his own state by the most powerful Republican newspaper, the *Chicago Tribune*. Moreover, he offended many by his spread-eagle nationalism, and, for all his claims to the T.R. legacy, he was an ardent conservative. Knox, said one writer, "stands for everything that Mencken and Lewis kidded the country about in the last decade."

Since neither Borah nor Knox met with approval, party leaders began to turn their attention to the forty-eight-year-old governor of Kansas, Alfred Mossman Landon, better known as Alf, a nickname he had acquired in the Kansas oil fields. Landon had once said that the party was not "so hard up as to name a man from Kansas," a state with few electoral votes and usually safely Republican, but he had exceptional qualifications. One of only seven GOP governors in the country, Landon was the sole Republican chief executive elected in 1932 who gained reelection in spite of the Democratic tide of 1934. Expected to run well in the farm belt, Landon had the kind of personality that Main Street would find attractive: the pleasant manners and easy charm of a man who spent his summer evenings on the front porch swing of a white frame house in a small town. James MacGregor Burns has written, "Middle class by every test and in every dimension, he had the shrewd, guileless face, the rimless glasses, and the slightly graying hair that made him indistinguishable from a million other middle-aged Americans."

Landon stood at the central crossroads of the party. As a successful independent oil operator, he would appeal to businessmen. An advocate of retrenchment, a balanced budget, and the gold standard, he was more orthodox on fiscal and monetary matters than many eastern conservatives. On the other hand, he had been allied with the progressive wing of the Republican Party in Kansas since the Teddy Roosevelt era. A Bull Moose county chairman in 1912, he had served as private secretary to progressive governor Henry Allen in 1922; had voted for Robert M. La Follette in 1924; and had backed the campaign of William Allen White, the nationally known Emporia editor, against the Ku Klux Klan. As governor, Landon had chaired a meeting in Topeka at which Socialist leader Norman Thomas spoke, and he had refused to sanction a proposed investigation of alleged "Red" activities in the university. Under his leadership, Kansas had abolished the poll tax, strengthened utility regulation, and injected new life into the "blue sky" laws. Governor Landon had pledged help to Roosevelt in the war against the Depression and had endorsed New Deal projects in words that were to be quoted against him during the campaign. But he was wary of strong central government and sought "the middle of the road between a government by plutocracy and a government by bureaucracy." He summed up his position in November 1935 when he wrote, "I think four more years of the same policies that we have had will wreck our parliamentary government, and four years of the old policies will do the job also."

Governor Landon's campaign received its greatest impetus from newspaper editors and publishers. The Kansas City *Star* and other regional publications got Landon off to a good start in his contest with Knox, whose own bid rested on the fact that he was a midwestern publisher. But Landon did not capture national attention until the Hearst chain took up his cause, much as the Luce empire would promote Wendell Willkie's bid in 1940. In July 1935, William Randolph Hearst assigned Damon Runyon and Adela Rogers St. John to write articles on Landon for two Hearst magazines, *Cosmopolitan* and *Good Housekeeping*; Runyon's "Horse and Buggy Governor" created a national stir. In December, Hearst, accompanied by his longtime friend, the actress Marion Davies, led an entourage that included Paul Block, head of another newspaper chain, and Cissy Patterson, publisher of the Washington *Herald*, to Topeka to look Landon over. "I think he is marvelous!" Hearst said on leaving the governor's office. "I thought of Lincoln," confided Mrs. Patterson.

The publicists promoted Landon as a "liberal Coolidge," a wonder-worker who had proven in Kansas that one could be humane without being a spendthrift. New Dealers might scoff that Landon's reputation rested in good part on the achievements of his Democratic predecessor and on the millions the Federal Government had poured into Kansas. But Landon's campaign manager, John D. M. Hamilton, a forty-four-year-old Topeka lawyer who had risen through the ranks in Republican politics, found that eastern financiers placed a high value on the governor's role as budget-balancer. On the other hand, William Allen White, who stumped the country for his fellow Kansan, fretted that the governor was being oversold as a conservative. Landon, White told the New York Republican Club, was "about as much like Coolidge as the Wild Man of Borneo is like Billy Sunday."

With the help that newspaper publicity men like Hearst could offer, Landon moved rapidly into first position among the contenders, a vantage point he was careful to protect. He decided to stay out of the primary contests in the thirteen states that chose delegates in that fashion. Confident of victory, Landon did not want to jeopardize his chances by antagonizing party leaders who were favorite sons. Nor did he have the money for expensive primary campaigns. If he raised funds from men of wealth, the Democrats would claim he was the rich man's candidate. However, in more than one state Landon was entered in primaries against his wishes. In California his slate was defeated by an uninstructed ticket that some thought represented a stop-Landon maneuver, but in New Jersey he won a smashing 4–1 victory over Borah.

By the time the Republican national convention opened on June 9 in Cleveland's civic auditorium, Landon had the nomination all but cinched. The only threat came on the second day, when Hoover received a thunderous ovation in response to his call for a "crusade for liberty." For a moment it seemed that the delegates might be so carried away as to nominate him for a third time. But Borah refused to join Knox and Vandenberg in a stop-Landon movement, and Hoover hesitated to announce himself as a candidate. By the next morning, all of Landon's opponents had withdrawn. In seconding Landon's nomination, Vandenberg announced, "I belong to but one bloc and it has but one slogan — 'stop Roosevelt.'" That night the delegates chose Landon on the first ballot, 984 to 19 for Borah (18 from Wisconsin, 1 from West Virginia), although the Idaho senator had pulled out of the race. Subsequently, the convention made the nomination unanimous.

As early as the summer of 1935, Hearst had said that "Landon and Knox would make a very appealing ticket," but it took the Republicans a while to reach the same conclusion. The Landon circle, curiously, had not settled on a vice-presidential nominee. Some, including Hamilton, favored a coalition ticket with an anti-New Deal Democrat like Lewis Douglas, who had resigned as Roosevelt's budget director, but this proposal encountered too many objections. Governor Styles Bridges of New Hampshire was eliminated because "Landon–Bridges falling down" would offer irresistible possibilities to Democratic sloganeers. Even on the night Landon was nominated, he and his aides remained undecided. Not until dawn did they agree on Vandenberg, only to have the Michigan Senator turn down the invitation. They then resolved to get "off the rocks with Landon and Knox." Knox consented, and the delegates approved.

In a year in which the GOP was burdened by the accusation that it was the tool of Big Business, the Republican ticket, as Donald McCoy has noted, "was headed by two old Bull Moosers, and its national committee was loaded with Main

Street rather than Wall Street figures." Landon and Knox, who knew one another only slightly, tried to make up for their distance by affecting T.R. lingo like "bully" in their correspondence. "WE ARE AT ARMAGEDDON," Knox wired Landon after he had been nominated. He added in an odd phrase, "CONDITIONS CALL FOR A DISPLAY OF THE SAME GREAT QUALITIES WHICH ENDEARED US BOTH TO THEODORE ROOSEVELT."

Governor Landon found platform-making unexpectedly difficult. In anticipation of his nomination, he had designated the Cincinnati civic reformer, Charles P. Taft, to coordinate the drafting of planks to be submitted to the convention. But to the dismay of the Landon forces, the Resolutions Committee turned out to be controlled by party conservatives. William Allen White, the governor's representative on the committee, had to fight for days to restore Landon's ideas to the platform draft. Borah exploited the plight of the Landon group by inserting his own notions on isolationism, anti-monopoly, and currency. White got most of the Landon proposals reinstated, but, wearied by the struggle, did not see to it that the governor's convictions on labor, monetary matters, and civil service were included.

Landon decided to shun a floor fight in favor of a more effective way of winning his points. After the Resolutions Committee had completed its work (and all his rivals had withdrawn), Landon sent a telegram that he asked Hamilton to read to the convention. On the night of June 11, Hamilton read the wire in which Landon explained that he wanted the delegates to have his interpretation of several planks before they voted on the nomination of a presidential candidate. He announced he favored "a Constitutional amendment permitting the states to adopt such legislation as may be necessary to adequately protect women and children in the matter of maximum hours, minimum wages, and working conditions." He interpreted the plank demanding "a sound currency to be preserved at all hazards" to mean "a currency expressed in terms of gold and convertible into gold," but stipulated that it should not "be made effective until and unless it can be done without penalizing our domestic economy and without injury to our producers of agricultural products and other raw materials." He also advocated the application of the civil service merit system to "the entire post office department," as well as to all other administrative posts below the rank of assistant secretary. The delegates responded without enthusiasm to Hamilton's reading, but since they went on to nominate Landon the telegram gained quasi-official status as a gloss on the platform.

From its opening sentence warning that America was in peril, the platform left the impression that the country was on the verge of collapse. The substance, however, was somewhat more moderate than the tone, and some were surprised by how much of the New Deal the party was willing to accept. It approved national regulation of utilities and of the marketing of securities, supplementary payments to the aged, soil conservation, "a national land-use program," and, "as an emergency measure," federal subsidies to farmers. Although it did not go nearly as far as the Democratic platform and still generally viewed government as a menace, the Republican platform marked an advance over the party's position four years earlier.

When the GOP was accused of stealing the 1932 Democratic platform, Republicans replied, "Why not? The Democrats have no more use for it. Moreover it is in perfectly good condition — it was never used."

In winning the Republican nomination, Landon became the first of a series of GOP candidates who would confront a fundamental question of strategy: whether to take sharp issue with a popular Democratic incumbent or become a "me too" candidate. If Landon veered in a conservative direction, he risked the displeasure of an electorate that appeared to approve much of the New Deal. But if he endorsed most of the Administration's actions, he would blur his own identity and leave voters with no reason to prefer him to Roosevelt. If he combined the two approaches, he would appear vacillating and unsure of himself.

At the beginning of his campaign, Landon emphasized his progressive pro-clivities. At Chautauqua he braved the wrath of Hearst by saying, "In Kansas we insist that no teacher should be required to take any oath not required of all citizens," and before a convention of the American Legion in Kansas he denounced racial and religious bigotry. Landon also deliberately sought to dissociate himself from the Old Guard and from ostentatious wealth. Hoover was treated so coolly that he took little part in the campaign, and Paul Block was told he could not attach his private railroad car to the campaign train. Since Landon believed he could win only by carrying the Midwest, he tried to out-promise the New Dealers in order to attract farm votes. In Des Moines in late September, he pledged drought relief, seed loans, conservation, aid to the tenant farmer, and perhaps even crop insurance, a program that appeared to be more costly and far-reaching than the AAA. For a budget-balancer this was strange doctrine. Moreover, his concern for the midwestern farm vote led him to take unexpected stands. At Minneapolis he compromised his belief in the low tariff by charging that reciprocal trade had "sold the American farmer down the river."

Democrats seized the opportunity to point to the inconsistency between Landon's image as a Kansas Coolidge and his pledges of Government largesse. "You cannot be an old-guard Republican in the east and a New Deal Republican in the west," Roosevelt said. "You cannot repeal taxes before one audience and promise to spend more of the taxpayers' money before another audience." Secretary of the Interior Harold Ickes charged that Landon was a "changeling candidate," a foe of Government power who had once been a state socialist in favor of publicly owned telephone and natural gas distribution systems. When Landon countered that he had consistently supported Government ownership "as a gun behind the door" to secure fair utility rates, Ickes rejoined, "I wonder how many other concealed weapons he carries about. The utility interests had better frisk him before they go any further."

The Republicans left an impression of floundering and divided counsels, mostly because of the split between Landon and his running mate. While Landon, at least in the opening days of his campaign, was trying to distinguish his position from that of the Old Guard, Colonel Knox was making extravagant charges. "The

New Deal candidate," Knox insisted, "has been leading us toward Moscow." The contrast between such speeches and Landon's early remarks led *Time* to write: "The Republican gospel of salvation being preached by Alf Landon on one hand and that being preached by John Hamilton and Frank Knox on the other seemed about as dissonant and confusing to voters as the competing Christianities of a Boston Unitarian and a hard-shell Southern Baptist would be to Hottentot bushmen."

Knox's speeches probably did less damage to the Republican cause than the activities of John Hamilton, who, in a year when class feeling ran high, left the unfortunate impression that he preferred the milieu of Long Island estates to Main Street. "If John Hamilton is a progressive," wrote William Allen White, "Wally Simpson is a nun." To Landon's dismay, Hamilton surrounded him with conservative advisers. "Why don't you ever bring workingmen to see me?" Landon asked his manager. "All I ever see are stuffed-shirt businessmen and bankers." A month after the election White wrote a Kansas progressive, "You are dead right that the great damage was done to Landon when he selected his ultra-conservative advisors. Hamilton was awful.... He loved the rich and was proud to associate with them, and his association with them advertised their control of the party. The stink of money was over the whole campaign." More startling was the judgment Hoover offered in a letter to White: "When the Republican Party starts out to mix populism, oil, Hearst, munitions and the Liberty League, it is bound to come to grief. You used the exact phrase that I did to some of the gentlemen in charge — that is, that if the money was taken from Du Pont, Pew and Company they would 'sell the Party down the river.' And I am not sure that it has not been sold."

Hamilton may not have "sold" the Republican Party, but he did see to it that the campaign did not suffer from lack of funds. He tapped the bank accounts not only of Republican industrialists but of the Liberty League's "angels." Huge sums were funneled into the party. The Republicans and their allies subsequently reported $14,198,203 in expenditures to the Democratic forces' $9,228,407.

Nevertheless, Hamilton and his associates dissipated much of this advantage in allocating funds. Too often the Republicans left the impression that the campaign was a struggle of the few against the many. The Republican national committee employed twenty-four workers in its industrial division, headed by the salt tycoon, Sterling Morton, but only three on its labor staff. The GOP distributed literature estimated at from 125 million to 170 million pieces, but some of the flyers expressed open contempt for the poor. Handbills accused the Administration of providing "Free lunch to hoboes, Relief Clients, Underprivileged Transients, and others who won't work, and those who have missed the Social Values of the More Abundant Life," and of having supplied a "Large quantity of PWA picks, spades, shovels, rakes, etc. etc., which have been used only to lean on."

The Republicans broke new ground in using "spot announcements" on radio for the first time, but here too Hamilton erred by identifying the party too closely with New York City business interests. To sell Landon to the American public, the GOP hired Hill Blackett, senior partner of the leading agency in radio advertising with such choice accounts as General Mills and Proctor and Gamble. *Variety* commented, "Political parties are being reduced to merchandise which can be exchanged for votes in accordance with a well-conceived marketing plan, taking stock of income levels, race, local problems, exactly as does a commercial sponsor. This differs no whit from the tactics employed by Lifebuoy, Chase and Sanborn, or any other of a thousand consumer commodities."

Even when the Republicans did make a strong bid for the vote of the disadvantaged, it did not turn out well. To appeal to Negro voters, the party financed a national tour by Jesse Owens, the hero of the 1936 Olympics, and distributed three-minute movies to Negro theaters (Mamie Smith and the Beale Street Boys sang "Oh, Susannah"). Landon, who had a good record on civil rights issues, came out in favor of an anti-lynching law and denounced "the attempt of the New Deal to use relief rolls as modern reservations on which the great colored race is to be confined forever as a ward of the federal government." But this effort to hold the Negro in the Republican column made little headway. The NAACP protested that the governor's proposal to shift relief administration to the states would increase discrimination against Negroes, and the Baltimore *Afro-American* reminded black voters, "ABRAHAM LINCOLN IS NOT A CANDIDATE IN THE PRESENT CAMPAIGN."

Much of the responsibility for turning the campaign in a conservative direction lay not with Hamilton but with Landon. As early as September, it had become clear that there were sharp limits to the governor's progressivism, and, in particular, that he advocated a diminished role for the National Government. On September 26 in Milwaukee, he denounced the Social Security Act as "unjust, unworkable, stupidly drafted and wastefully financed." In Detroit in mid-October, Landon began to drum home a new question: whether Roosevelt "intends to change the form of our government — whether labor, agriculture, and business are to be directed and managed by government." Thereafter, his addresses became increasingly shrill. The policies of the New Deal, he argued in Baltimore, would lead to the guillotine.

At a rally in Madison Square Garden, Landon raised a series of questions about Roosevelt's intentions. To each, he gave the same answer, and soon the crowd was joining him in the refrain, "The answer is: no one can be sure." The most important question, Landon asserted, was "whether our American form of government is to be preserved." He charged that Roosevelt had carried out nine unconstitutional acts, had urged Congress to pass laws of doubtful validity, and had belittled both the Supreme Court and the Constitution. "What are the intentions of the President with respect to the Constitution?" Landon asked. "Does he believe changes are required? If so, will an amendment be submitted to the people, or will he attempt to get around the Constitution by tampering with the Supreme Court? The answer is: no one can be sure." He pointed out that forty-eight hours later Roosevelt would be standing at the same spot in Madison Square Garden, just two days before Election Day. Landon flung a challenge: "Tell us where you stand, Mr. President. Tell us not in generalities, but clearly so that no one can mistake your meaning. And tell us why you have evaded the issue until the eve of the election." (Years later Landon said that he had heard from Paul Block that Roosevelt might attempt to pack the Court, and he had raised this challenge in the anticipation that the President would evade it and hence could not say he had a mandate to reform the judiciary.)

Landon's criticism of Big Government, however inadvisable at a time when millions depended on bounty from Washington, had the advantage of coinciding with the views of the older America that gave the Kansas governor his strongest backing. The Republicans, with "Oh, Susannah" as their theme song, appealed to nostalgia for a simpler day, and in distributing forty-two million sunflower buttons, emphasized their candidate's rural background. At a time when the Irish Catholic Jim Farley was rounding up polyglot ethnic support for Roosevelt, the Yankee Protestant John Hamilton's organization was making the most headway with old-stock, rural Americans. "There is one thing quite noticeable of all our crowds," observed one of Landon's lieutenants. "They have that clean upstanding appearance." Landon himself said that he felt during the campaign "like the country boy going to take a job in Toronto for the first time."

The GOP hoped that the country would find Landon's unpretentious small-town manner a pleasant relief from the cosmopolitan Roosevelt with his public-relations smile, his Groton accent, and his polished style. A Republican inserted in the *Congressional Record* in 1936 a bit of doggerel that had already become a staple of business throwaways. It read in part,

> I'm tired, oh, so tired, of the whole New Deal,
> Of the juggler's smile and the barker's spiel,
> Of the mushy speech and the loud bassoon,
> And tiredest of all of our leader's croon.

A Republican congressman from Missouri, who criticized Roosevelt for fishing from cruisers and yachts, noted approvingly that, "being so plain and simple," Alf got "a cane pole and a can of worms." Landon, too, believed the contrast to FDR would prove advantageous, for "the American people have always been fearful, in the end, of a great man."

The Republicans did not apologize for the fact that Landon was a poor speaker — they boasted of it. In Minneapolis he was introduced as a man who was not a "radio crooner." "Do urge Governor Landon not to try to improve his delivery," the ex-Bull Mooser Amos Pinchot advised a Republican official. When a New York financier wrote Landon that he was worried about the candidate's performance on the radio, the governor replied, "But we agreed a long time ago, I think, that Mr. Roosevelt would be defeated by his direct antithesis. In other words, I don't want to get too much out of character."

Yet Landon's personality and his attributes as a speaker could hardly be expected to attract the kind of national following that the magnetic Roosevelt was winning. H. L. Mencken wrote that the governor "is an honest fellow, and would make an excellent President, but he simply lacks the power to inflame the boobs." Moreover, the Republican candidate never learned how to impress metropolitan audiences with his capacity for leadership or how to turn a phrase that would capture headlines. In fact, his most memorable statement was a sentence that has become hallowed in the annals of campaign trivia: "Wherever I have gone in this country, I have found Americans."

Landon seemed to many only a fair-to-middling hinterland governor who lacked FDR's preparation for dealing with the problems of Washington, London, and Vienna. According to one tale, when Hearst visited Landon in 1935, he asked the governor what he thought of the international situation. Landon stared at the floor, and after pondering the question for a full five minutes, answered, "Well, Mr. Hearst, I'll tell you. I don't think International ought to be getting all of that business. I think it ought to be divided up with Deering, the Moline people and some of the independents in the plow business."

As Landon's campaign floundered, the Republicans resorted to desperate devices. They eagerly embraced a scheme advanced by Detroit businessmen to exploit the fact that on January 1, 1937, the payroll tax provision of the Social Security Act would take effect. By concealing the requirement that employers also had to contribute to the pension fund and by raising doubts about what would happen to the money, they hoped to arouse indignation at the Administration over deductions from the worker's wages. In the final two weeks of the campaign, factory placards announced, "YOU'RE SENTENCED TO A WEEKLY PAY REDUCTION FOR ALL YOUR WORKING LIFE. YOU'LL HAVE TO SERVE THE SENTENCE UNLESS YOU HELP RE-VERSE IT NOVEMBER 3." A message inserted in pay envelopes read:

> Effective January, 1937, we are compelled by a Roosevelt 'New Deal' law to make a 1 percent deduction from your wages and turn it over to the government. Finally, this may go as high as 4 percent. You might get this money back ... but only if Congress decides to make the appropriation for this purpose. There is NO guarantee. Decide before November 3 — election day — whether or not you wish to take these chances.

On the final weekend of the campaign the Republicans carried this roorback to excessive lengths. Landon said, "Imagine the field opened for federal snooping. Are these twenty-six million going to be fingerprinted? Are their photographs going to be kept on file in a Washington office? Or are they going to have identification tags put around their necks?" John Hamilton had no doubt that every worker in the Social Security system would be required to wear a metal dog tag, "such as the one I hold in my hand." The Hearst press made its customary contribution to the clarification of public issues by showing a picture of a man wearing such a tag above the caption "YOU." Since the Social Security Act was probably the most popular New Deal measure, the scheme, although momentarily effective, appears to have backfired by Election Day. It had the enormous disadvantage for the Republicans of once again identifying their cause with that of the factory owners. After the election, Representative Hamilton Fish told party workers that this last-minute operation probably "drove millions of the wage earners out of our party in the big industrial centers." In a campaign in which the Welfare State and class alignments were crucial, the Republicans had stumbled on an issue that put them on the wrong side of both questions.

Landon's best hope of victory lay in the possibility that a sizeable number of votes would be diverted from Roosevelt by the emergence of a powerful third party. In 1935, Democrats feared most of all an alliance of the flamboyant Louisiana Senator, Huey Pierce Long, with the demagogic "Radio Priest," the Reverend Charles E. Coughlin of Royal Oak, Michigan, and Dr. Francis Townsend, the head of an old-age pension organization. When Long was murdered in September 1935, the Reverend Gerald L. K. Smith, a Shreveport minister who was described as a combination of Savonarola and Elmer Gantry, laid claim to the leadership of Long's Share-Our-Wealth Society. Each of these movements, as David Bennett has noted, offered panaceas based on "the manipulation of money," and each promised to heal psychic wounds that New Deal medicine did not reach. While Share-Our-Wealth had its greatest following in the Deep South, Coughlin's National Union for Social Justice mustered most of its adherents from Irish and German Catholics in the working class districts of northeastern and midwestern cities, and Townsend's Old Age Revolving Pensions Limited found its most ardent support in the Far West. The potential strength of this combination appeared to be enormous.

By the fall of 1935, Townsendism had become the strongest of the three movements. One magazine called it "easily the outstanding political sensation of the year." In December, Edwin Witte, one of the authors of the Social Security Act, wrote, "The battle against the Townsend Plan has been lost, I think, in pretty nearly every state west of the Mississippi, and the entire Middle-Western area is likewise badly infected." A poll of editors taken by the Portland *Oregonian* indicated that the Townsendites had the power to decide the outcome of congressional races almost everywhere in Washington, California, Oregon, Idaho, Nevada, and Colorado. "Fear of the Townsend opposition," observed the columnist Frank Kent, "smears the whole Western political picture."

Even before the 1936 campaign began, the Democrats took steps to blunt each of these three threats, with mixed success. The Roosevelt Administration patched up differences with Long's heirs in an accommodation that was criticized as a "second Louisiana purchase." The governor of Louisiana made it clear that Gerald L. K. Smith was *persona non grata* in his state, and Louisiana politicians liquidated the Share-Our-Wealth organization. In June 1936, the Louisiana legislature made an unusual move. It recessed to travel to Texas, where the President was visiting, and there adopted a resolution "praising divine providence for providing a great leader, Franklin D. Roosevelt, who saved the nation from ruin and chaos." In Congress Democrats joined with Republicans to investigate Dr. Townsend's organization and block the Frazier–Lemke bill to refinance farm mortgages with issues of paper money, a measure which Father Coughlin supported. They succeeded in airing internal dissension in the Townsend group and in defeating the Frazier–Lemke proposal, but at a cost. The congressional probe threw Dr. Townsend into the arms of Gerald L. K. Smith, and the rejection of the Frazier–Lemke measure precipitated the creation of the third party Democrats had hoped could be forestalled.

The details of the founding of the new party remain obscure, but in the five weeks that followed the defeat of the Frazier–Lemke bill, Father Coughlin appears to have been the prime mover. In the first two weeks of June, Coughlin's lieutenants negotiated with the Gerald Smith and Townsend forces, for by early June Smith had won a reluctant Townsend to an uneasy pledge of alliance. "Dr. Townsend and I," he declared, "stood under the historic arch at Valley Forge and vowed to take over the government." In the June 12 issue of his organ, *Social Justice*, Coughlin wrote, "The activities of the National Union will increase tremendously immediately following June 16th or 17th. Approximately at that time I shall lay down a plan for action which will thrill you and inspire you beyond anything that I have ever said or accomplished in the past." But on June 16, Smith beat Coughlin to a headline by publicizing the new coalition.

On June 19, Representative William Lemke of North Dakota announced he was running for President on a "Union Party" ticket. Thomas O'Brien, a Boston Irish Catholic lawyer who had worked his way through Harvard University and Harvard Law School as a railway brakeman and had served as counsel to unions and as district attorney, would be his running mate. That night, Coughlin, who had probably handpicked both men, stated that Lemke was "eligible for indorsation" by the National Union for Social Justice. The ticket, Coughlin cried, was "Lemke and Yale, Agriculture and Republican! O'Brien and Harvard, Labor and Democrat! East and West! Protestant and Catholic!" In this informal manner, without the benefit of a national nominating convention but with the benefit of clergy, the new party was born.

Despite the Union Party's origins, its platform did not specifically endorse either the Townsend Plan or sharing the wealth, and it omitted half the principles of the National Union for Social Justice, including labor's right to organize, the nationalization of key resources, and the control of private property for the public good. The platform did reflect Coughlin's cheap money, anti-banker outlook in recommending a central bank under congressional control, limits on net income and inheritance, and conscription of wealth as well as men in the event of war. A strange amalgam of progressive and conservative elements, it embraced old-age security, anti-monopoly, and public works planks, but also called for the protection of private property from confiscation by unnecessary taxation.

So little did most Americans know about "Liberty Bill" Lemke, that even some of his rural followers thought his first name was Frazier. To eastern city-dwellers, he seemed an odd sort. Nearly completely bald, his head was dotted with yellow freckles, and his face was pitted by smallpox scars. One eye was glass, the other "always screwed up a little as if he were on the verge of imparting secret information." His baggy suit looked as though it had just been handed to him by the warden and his blue work shirt, bright-colored galluses, and farmer's cap all revealed his rural origins. H. L. Mencken wrote a friend, "Lemke is not a human being at all, but a werewolf. I had several long gabbles with him in Cleveland. Get him on his favorite project — to dig 250,000 lakes out in the cow country — and you will howl. With his glass eye, his bald head, and his large yellow freckles, he is the most astonishing looking candidate that I have ever seen."

Yet Lemke had a more cosmopolitan background and more modern ideas than his appearance suggested. He had attended the University of North Dakota, Georgetown University, and Yale Law School. Westbrook Pegler pointed out that he had not only gone to Yale but "went around more colleges than an old-time tramp tackle and ... is positively no hick." The first presidential candidate to use an airplane extensively, he traveled thirty thousand miles by air.

However, Lemke's ideas revealed his Populist and Nonpartisan League background. He derived his money notions from his hero, Charles Lindbergh (father of the aviator) and from W. H. "Coin" Harvey, with whom he corresponded regularly. Representative of a district in which two-thirds of the farms had been foreclosed during the Depression, Lemke wanted a "just" price for the farmer and a "just" wage for the worker, but he was as critical as any Tory of the eastern New Dealers with their social-service emphases. He denounced Secretary of Agriculture Henry A. Wallace as "the greatest vandal in history" and Roosevelt as "the bewildered Kerensky of a provisional government."

The Union Party ticket worried the Democrats because Lemke would draw chiefly from former Roosevelt supporters. An American Institute of Public Opinion poll reported that, of those who favored Lemke, 70 percent had voted for Roosevelt in 1932, only 9 percent for Hoover. (Of course, many of these FDR voters who defected to Lemke might have backed Landon, or stayed away from the polls, if there had not been a Union Party candidate.) Lemke did not conceive of himself as merely a gadfly but thought he could capture enough states to throw the election into the House, where he and his allies would have enhanced bargaining power. In a close election, even his own state of North Dakota could spell the difference. Coughlin told reporters that Lemke needed only 6 percent of the electoral vote to transfer the final decision to the House of Representatives.

Some thought Lemke would have little trouble polling well over 6 percent, because of the enthusiasm his sponsors elicited. Townsend claimed to have ten million followers; Smith put his Share-Our-Wealth legions at six million; and on the eve of the National Union for Social Justice convention in August, Coughlin told reporters that if he did not deliver nine million votes to Lemke he would stop broadcasting. The convention at Cleveland's Municipal Stadium left no doubt that the Radio Priest's supporters gave him unquestioning fealty. Throughout the proceedings Coughlin was called simply "Father": "Father says," "Father thinks," "Father told us." In her speech nominating him as president of the National Union, Helen Elizabeth Martin of the Bronx told delegates that "for those of us who haven't a material father — whose father is in the Great Beyond — he can be our father, and we won't need to feel lonesome." A Maryland delegate proposed, "Resolved, that we give thanks to the mother of the Reverend Charles E. Coughlin for bearing him." The devotion of Dr. Townsend's admirers at the national convention of his organization in Cleveland a month earlier seemed no less impressive. *The New York Times* observed that they "would follow him anywhere — into Old Guard Republicanism, socialism or a movement to set up a Stuart monarchy in Kansas."

Ostensibly, the Union Party repudiated both major parties, but in fact it aimed almost all its fire at Roosevelt. Coughlin based his campaign not on praise for Lemke but on abuse of the President. In one speech, he devoted two minutes to endorsing Lemke, five minutes to criticizing Landon, and an hour to denouncing the Roosevelt Administration. He asserted at one and the same time that the New Deal was "bent on communistic revolution" and that it had surrendered to "international bankers." He ridiculed one of the AAA's officials, Mordecai Ezekiel, as "the modern Margaret Sanger of the pigs." Gerald L. K. Smith, who seemed to share little of the redistributionist outlook of Huey Long despite his claim to leadership of Share-Our-Wealth, said the choice between Roosevelt and Lemke was one between "the Russian primer or the Holy Bible," and insisted, "We are going to keep and re-establish the old Holy Bible, Red-White-and Blue, Honest-to-God, Go-to-Meetin', bread-and-butter, wood splittin' America." Townsend called the President a "political savage." By mid-October he was asking his supporters to vote for Landon in any state where Lemke was not on the ballot.

In part because they sensed the conservative predisposition of the Union Party, despite its anti-banker ideology, most progressives and radicals rejected the Lemke ticket. Norman Thomas, the Socialist leader, dismissed the new party as a union of "two and a half rival messiahs ... plus some neopopulists." Neither farm nor labor groups gave Coughlin the support he had counted on. The National Farm Holiday Association dropped Lemke, while *Labor*, the organ of the railway unions, dismissed O'Brien as a "Boston attorney." Many liberals abhorred Coughlin's increasingly pronounced anti-Semitism, as well as Smith's anti-democratic ambitions and his promise "to drive that cripple out of the White House."

As support for the Union Party dwindled, Coughlin became progressively more violent in his rhetoric. At the Townsendite convention in mid-July, he ripped off his coat and clerical collar and denounced the President as a "great betrayer and liar." In August he cried, "As I was instrumental in removing Herbert Hoover from the White House, so help me God, I will be instrumental in taking a Communist from the chair once occupied by Washington." On September 25, he called Roosevelt "anti-God" and proposed using bullets "when an upstart dictator in the United States succeeds in making this a one-party form of government and when the ballot is useless." If they were to achieve their aims, Coughlin told his followers, they would have to "ride roughshod over the press of this country." When in the last week in October Coughlin called Roosevelt a "scab President," even his indulgent bishop felt he had gone too far and required him to apologize. By then Coughlin had been reprimanded by the Vatican publication, *L'Osservatore Romano*. The Pope was rumored to have taken various steps to silence him, and Catholic clergymen in the United States had made common cause against the obstreperous priest.

In the summer of 1936, the Reverend Maurice Sheehy, Assistant to the Rector of the Catholic University of America, informed the President that a meeting of four bishops, three monsignori, and two priests in New York had agreed on a plan to answer Coughlin's attacks. Roosevelt, he said, should ignore the Michigan priest and let the President's friends within the Church deal with him, advice that the White House readily accepted. Two of the bishops worked with Father Sheehy to secure statements from other prelates denying that Roosevelt was a Communist, and Sheehy also supplied Democratic propaganda to the Catholic press. In September 1936, the extremely influential Cardinal Mundelein of Chicago announced his support of the Administration. On October 8, the Reverend John A. Ryan, the best-known clerical advocate of social reform, delivered an important address over a national radio network on "Roosevelt Safeguards America." He denounced Coughlin's "ugly, cowardly, and flagrant calumnies" and said those who made such allegations were breaking the eighth commandment. "The charge of communism directed at President Roosevelt," Monsignor Ryan declared, "is the silliest, falsest, most cruel and most unjust accusation ever made against a President in all the years of American history."

Coughlin's and Smith's performances not only provoked such censure from party critics and cost Lemke popular support but deepened the divisions within the Union Party. When Smith declared he planned to "seize the government of the United States," Townsend and Lemke rebuked him. At best, the leaders of the movement had not been mutual admirers. Coughlin had once called the Townsend Plan "economic insanity," and Townsend said that Coughlin's sixteen-point program had "fourteen points too many." Moreover, as *The Nation* pointed out, "The grand conclave of Messrs. Townsend, Smith, Coughlin, and Lemke at Cleveland violated every tradition of demagoguery. Obviously, there is nothing so damaging to a panacea as another panacea on the same platform. For a demagogue to admit even in a whisper that another demagogue has any of the truth is to demoralize the whole Utopian market." Well before Election Day, the inherent disharmony of the leaders and of their followings had become manifest, and it was clear that Lemke was going to fall far short of the millions of votes he had been promised.

The New Deal reforms antagonized so many of the country's leading Democrats that Republicans anticipated a large-scale defection from Roosevelt in 1936. As early as September 1933, Newton D. Baker, who had been Wilson's Secretary of War and a leading contender for the presidential nomination in 1932, had written John W. Davis, the Democratic presidential nominee in 1924, "In domestic matters just how much opportunity for personal initiative is to be left seems hard to guess. I never felt so regimented and disciplined in my life." In June 1935, William Pattangall, Maine's chief justice, resigned from the bench to join with Bainbridge Colby, who had been Secretary of State under Wilson, and other Democrats in a "Hartford Convention" to form an alliance against FDR. At Macon, Georgia, in January 1936, a convention of dissident Democrats coalesced behind Eugene Talmadge, the governor of Georgia. On every seat lay a copy of the Georgia Woman's World featuring a photograph of Mrs. Roosevelt escorted by two Negroes and including a denunciation of the President for allowing "negroes to come to the White House banquets and sleep in the White House beds" and of the anti-lynching bill for encouraging "permissive ravishment."

However, none of Roosevelt's critics captured so much attention as Alfred E. Smith, who had run unsuccessfully for the presidency in 1928 on the same Democratic ticket on which FDR won election as governor of New York. Long before 1936, Smith and Roosevelt had come to a parting of the ways, but it was not clear whether Smith would carry his disapproval of the New Deal to the point of bolting his party. On January 25, 1936, clad in white tie and tails that seemed a far cry from the brown derby that had once been his trademark, Smith told a banquet of two thousand, including a dozen du Ponts, that Roosevelt and his lieutenants were headed in a socialist direction. "It is all right with me if they want to disguise themselves as Norman Thomas or Karl Marx, or Lenin, or any of the rest of that bunch," he cried, "but what I won't stand for is allowing them to march under the banner of Jefferson, Jackson and Cleveland." In November Smith warned that he and other disaffected Democrats would probably "take a walk."

Smith made his address under the auspices of the American Liberty League, an organization that had been founded in 1934 by a group of industrialists and anti-Administration Democrats like John J. Raskob, a high du Pont official who had been displaced as the Democratic Party's national chairman. The Liberty League claimed to be an association of liberty-loving Americans of all classes, but it was patently an organization of the well-to-do. It never succeeded in setting up a labor or farm division, and most of its support came from men of wealth who found it difficult to dissemble their class bias. A Chicago attorney who headed the Illinois division of the Liberty League stated, "The New Deal is nothing more or less than an effort sponsored by inexperienced sentimentalists and demagogues to take away from the thrifty what the thrifty or their ancestors have accumulated, or may accumulate, and give it to others who have not earned it."

When the Liberty League was set up, Frank Knox hoped that it would "eventuate in the formation of an independent democratic group like the Palmer–Buckner ticket in 1896 of Gold Democrats." Instead of running an independent slate, the "Jeffersonian Democrats" campaigned for Landon and Knox. In addition to Colby, their leaders included Joseph T. Ely, former governor of

Massachusetts, James Reed, who had been the United States senator from Missouri, Henry Breckinridge, onetime Assistant Secretary of War, and Richard Cleveland, Grover's son. In October at Carnegie Hall, Al Smith accused the New Dealers of having stolen the party from its rightful owners. The Administration would accept support from anybody, he protested: "even a communist with wire whiskers and a torch in his hands is welcome so long as he signs on the dotted line." He wound up his address by saying, "I am an American before I am a Democrat. I firmly believe that the remedy for all the ills that we are suffering from today is the election of Alfred M. Landon."

This endorsement may have hurt Landon more than it helped him, for it was charged that Smith had betrayed his party and deserted his class. In November, the *New Republic* published Slater Brown's "Empedocles on the Empire State":

> But enough of talk.
> Hand me a stovepipe hat, I'll take a walk.
> I'll step off this here parapet and fall
> Not back into Oliver Street but into Wall
> Where du Pont's acolytes from ten to three
> Do homage to the Goddess Liberty.
> Where members of his League in suppliance kneel
> Before the post of motors, oil or steel,
> Telling their beads and wondering if 'twas wrong
> To play Steel short or Studebaker long.

By dividing the country on class lines in the midst of the Depression, the right-wing Democrats gave Roosevelt an added advantage. The Liberty League, in particular, proved an embarrassment to the Republicans, because it was transparently an upper-class front. Jim Farley said that it "ought to be called the American Cellophane League" because "first, it's a du Pont product and second, you can see right through it." Another critic jeered that the Liberty Leaguers apparently thought the American Revolution "was fought to make Long Island safe for polo players." Their political efforts failed miserably. In primaries in New Jersey, Pennsylvania, Maryland, and Massachusetts, Roosevelt overwhelmed Breckinridge and Talmadge by margins that ran as high as 18–1. Nor did they succeed in rallying most of the conservative Democrats to Landon. Anti-Roosevelt senators like Carter Glass, Harry Byrd, and Millard Tydings refused to bolt, and in the end even the regimented Newton Baker stayed with his party.

Since Roosevelt had no serious opposition for renomination to a second term, he could concentrate his pre-convention activities on the party platform. Although he did not plan to go to Philadelphia until the main business of the convention had been completed, he gave close attention to drafting the platform, a task in which he was assisted by his trusted associate from Albany days, Samuel Rosenman. The President instructed Rosenman to keep the platform short and to base it on the sentence of the Declaration of Independence stating self-evident truths.

"It is no secret," Rosenman has written, "that the first draft of a platform on which a President is to run for reelection is generally prepared at the White House and not at the convention." At the White House on the Sunday evening before the opening of the Democratic convention gathered Roosevelt, Senator Robert F. Wagner, who would be chairman of the Resolutions Committee, and several aides including Rosenman, Assistant Attorney General John Dickinson, Ambassador William C. Bullitt, and Stanley High, a former Republican who had been recruited by the President as a speechwriter and had proven to be a gifted phrase-maker. A little after midnight, the group broke up after assigning Rosenman the task of piecing together a draft. "I must say that I considered myself wholly inadequate to the task," Rosenman recalls. "I had hardly made a practice of reading party platforms, let alone writing them." Rosenman and High worked through the night, and a typed draft was on his tray when the President had breakfast the next morning.

In the President's bedroom the Administration put the final touches on the document. Donald Richberg, former NRA Administrator, added a plank on the Supreme Court, Bullitt a foreign affairs section, and Harry Hopkins, who headed the WPA, a peroration. A freshly typed draft was prepared for Wagner to take to Philadelphia, when Robert M. La Follette Jr. phoned. "I think you ought to know that the peroration which Harry gave you and which I understand the President is using was given to Harry by me, and it is practically the same peroration which my father used back in 1924 when he ran for President on the Progressive ticket," the Wisconsin senator said. Roosevelt ordered a new peroration written while Wagner waited. When that assignment had been completed, Wagner departed for the convention, the manuscript in hand.

At Philadelphia Senator Wagner steered the platform draft through his committee and won the approval of the delegates. Although some changes were made, the document closely followed the lines laid down at the White House, especially in approving New Deal doctrines of Government responsibility. The platform stated, "We hold this truth to be self-evident — that government in a modern civilization has certain inescapable obligations to its citizens, among which are: (1) Protection of the family and the home; (2) Establishment of a democracy of opportunity for all the people; (3) Aid to those overtaken by disaster." The platform also reflected Roosevelt's determination to exploit class antagonisms. The original draft promised to "rid our land of kidnappers, bandits, and malefactors of great wealth," and even after being modified at Philadelphia the plank grouped criminals and financiers in the same paragraph.

When the President came to Philadelphia on June 27 to accept the nomination, he found more than one hundred thousand people gathered at rain-soaked Franklin Field. His speech wove together, not altogether successfully, two separate threads, a conciliatory approach offered by Moley and Corcoran and a militant emphasis suggested by Rosenman and High. The President plucked from each such phrases as "rendezvous with destiny" contributed by Corcoran and "economic royalist" coined by High. As a hundred spotlights played on him, Roosevelt told the cheering throng,

> Governments can err, Presidents do make mistakes, but the immortal Dante tells us that divine justice weighs the sins of the cold-blooded and the sins of the warm-hearted in different scales.
>
> Better the occasional faults of a Government that lives in a spirit of charity than the consistent omissions of a Government frozen in the ice of its own indifference.
>
> There is a mysterious cycle in human events. To some generations much is given. Of other generations much is expected. This generation of Americans has a rendezvous with destiny.

But the most controversial passages of his speech came when he sounded the class theme by hitting out at "economic royalists" who took "other people's money" to impose a "new industrial dictatorship." "These economic royalists complain that we seek to overthrow the institutions of America," he said. "What they really complain of is that we seek to take away their power." The stadium crowd, noted the newspaperman, Marquis Childs, cheered ecstatically "as though the roar out of the warm, sticky night came from a single throat."

The President took advantage of his enormous popularity and the strength of urban elements in the New Deal to put through a reform that had once been denied him. Backed by northern delegations dominated by their big-city components, the Administration assaulted the century-old rule requiring a two-thirds vote to nominate a Democratic presidential candidate. The Roosevelt forces chose the chairman of the convention's Rules Committee, Senator Bennett Champ Clark of Missouri, to lead the fight, because they knew he would carry out his assignment with a special ardor. Clark had seen the Baltimore convention of 1912 deny his father, who had a majority of the votes for several ballots, the Democratic nomination and hence, in a year when the Republicans were divided, the Presidency. Advocates of repeal claimed that the change would make the Democrats a more national party and would facilitate their ability to expand in the North. Southern opponents insisted that abolition of the rule would punish the South, which had been loyal to the party, by turning over control to populous northern states that often went Republican. Conservatives chimed in that abrogation would make it easier for a President to dictate his own nomination or that of someone acceptable to him, because he would now require only a simple majority of the delegates.

In 1932, Roosevelt had been balked in a premature attempt to wipe out the two-thirds rule, but in 1936 the advocates of change overwhelmed the opposition. The convention tried to mollify the South by giving increased representation at future conventions to states that the Democrats carried. But astute southerners soon recognized that the change in the convention rules symbolized a significant loss in their section's power in the party. Less than two years later, Senator Josiah Bailey of North Carolina would write of his party, "Since the abolition of the Two-Thirds Rule, there is grave danger that it will fall into the hands of very objectionable men whose politics are entirely distasteful to the Southern Democracy. They get elected by the negro vote in New York, Pennsylvania, Boston, Chicago, and the cities of the Middle West. They are common fellows of the baser sort."

Roosevelt had not been content to rest on the organization that had put him in office in 1932 but instead had created a broadly based coalition centered on the support of the masses in the great cities. FDR's leadership of this urban coalition was a new role for him, since he had long felt more comfortable with rural and small town audiences. As late as 1932 he had confided, "Al Smith knows these city people better. He can move them. I can't." Moreover, in 1932 many of the urban machine leaders had opposed his nomination. Frank Hague, the Jersey City boss, had called him "the weakest candidate before the people." But in 1936 Hague backed him enthusiastically, and Roosevelt, who had little of the patrician reformer's distaste for machines, praised Hague and cooperated with bosses like Ed Kelly in Chicago. In other cities, the Great Depression had encouraged the rise of a different kind of urban leader, typified by Pittsburgh's David Lawrence and Detroit's Frank Murphy, who worked closely with union leaders and established "Little New Deals" in their states. As a consequence of the Democratic success in 1932 and 1934, Farley could count on the assistance not only of these municipal organizations but of thirty-seven state administrations with their armies of officeholders and beneficiaries.

The Democratic Party's urban coalition drew strength from the gratitude of ethnic groups for New Deal welfare measures and for "recognition" in the dispensing of patronage. The President's many Catholic and Jewish advisers made him an attractive figure to ethnic minorities, and Catholic ward politicians felt they had a friend at court in Jim Farley. While Harding, Coolidge, and Hoover named eight Catholics to federal judgeships, Roosevelt in his years in the White House appointed fifty-one, including the first Italo-American ever to attain this honor. Catholic theologians praised New Deal measures for fulfilling the social teaching of papal encyclicals. At the Democratic convention in Philadelphia a scarlet-robed Roman Catholic bishop gave the convocation. To win the backing of various nationality and religious groups, the President suggested calling home ambassadors to send them on campaign tours of cities with large populations from the countries to which they were assigned abroad. In the 1936 campaign, Roosevelt received the support of such groups as the Lithuanian Roman Catholic Alliance of America, the Slovak Catholic Sokol of New Jersey, the Croatian Catholic Union of America, and the National Alliance of Bohemian Czech Catholics of America.

At the same time that he wooed Catholics and Jews, the President, an Episcopalian, did not neglect his fellow Protestants, who were thought to be predominantly Republican. Jim Farley recalls a conversation with Roosevelt about setting up one of the auxiliary committees of the campaign:

"In the Committee of Twelve," he continued, "I would like to have five clergymen. I think we should have a Catholic priest, a Baptist minister, a Presbyterian minister, an Episcopalian minister, and a rabbi."

"What about the Methodists?" I asked.

"Well, we could leave out the Jews," he laughed. "No, there are more of them than there are Episcopalians. Take the Jews and leave out the Episcopalians."

Before his death, Louis Howe, FDR's closest political associate, had suggested the creation of an organization to win the allegiance of clergymen, social workers, and men of good will to the President. Roosevelt and Farley approved the idea and set up the Good Neighbor League with the social worker, Lillian Wald, and philanthropist George Foster Peabody, as co-chairmen. Although the League included a labor leader and a rabbi, it directed its main appeal to middle class Protestants who were attracted by the social ideals of the New Deal but had an ancestral distrust of the party of Rum, Romanism, and Rebellion. Many who admired Roosevelt were uneasy about a range of Democratic policies from the repeal of the prohibition amendment to expansion of the Government payroll attributed to Farley. To reassure Protestants, the Democratic national committee named Stanley High, who had once served as editor of the *Christian Herald*, as organizer of the League, an appointment that served to counter allegations that the President relied exclusively on Jewish and Catholic advisers. Directors of the Good Neighbor League included suffragist Mrs. Carrie Chapman Catt and Methodist bishop Reverend Edgar Blake. Endorsement by such prominent spokesmen for moral causes helped persuade voters who might otherwise have spurned the Democrats.

The Democratic Party appeared to face an even more formidable task in trying to gain the support of Negro voters. Ever since the Civil War era, the Negro had been wedded to the Republicans, the party of Lincoln. Despite the impact of the Great Depression and the lily-white policies pursued by the Hoover Administration, Negroes had voted solidly for Hoover in 1932. In Cincinnati's predominantly black Ward Sixteen, Hoover had received almost three-quarters of the ballots, and in Chicago he had run more strongly in Negro wards than he had in 1928. After Roosevelt took office, many Negro leaders, already suspicious of the Democrats as the party of the white ruling class in the South, expressed their displeasure at the acquiescence by the New Deal in the pattern of racial segregation. The young political scientist Ralph Bunche protested that "the New Deal only serves to crystallize those abuses and oppressions which the exploited Negro citizenry of America have long suffered under laissez-faire capitalism."

But many Negroes found the Roosevelt Administration exceptionally responsive to their needs. Although the Negro was discriminated against in many New Deal projects, he also received relief substantially greater than his proportion of the population. Furthermore, Roosevelt named an unusually large number of Negroes to important Government posts. By 1936, thirty or forty advisers, including Robert C. Weaver and William H. Hastie in the Department of the Interior, held places in the President's "Black Cabinet." Mrs. Roosevelt and Secretary of the Interior Ickes, a former president of the Chicago NAACP, played an especially conspicuous role in the battle against racial discrimination. As early as 1934 in states like Pennsylvania, Negro voters began a massive swing to the Democratic Party. That same year, Chicago sent to Congress Arthur W. Mitchell, the first Negro ever to be nominated for a congressional seat by the Democrats.

In 1936, the Roosevelt Administration made a bold bid for the Negro vote, even at the risk of alienating southern whites. Twelve states, including the border states of Kentucky and West Virginia, sent ten black delegates and twenty-two alternates to the Philadelphia convention, an unprecedented showing in a party that had permitted no Negro to attend in any formal capacity before 1924. The convention was the first to seat a Negro woman as a regular delegate and the first to provide for a Negro press conference and to seat Negroes in the regular press box. As a Negro minister gave the invocation at one session, another "first," Senator "Cotton Ed" Smith stormed out crying, "My God, he's black as melted midnight." (Carter Glass refused to join the walkout. "God knows I stand in need of prayer," the Virginia senator said. "I wish every Negro in the country would pray for me.") When Congressman Mitchell became the first Negro ever to address a Democratic convention, Smith stalked out for good and went home to South Carolina. "I cannot and will not be a party to the recognition of the Fourteenth and Fifteenth Amendments," he explained. Throughout the ensuing campaign, northern Democrats courted the Negro voter, with growing evidence of success. Negroes who once would not have turned out to see any Democrat lined the streets of New York for Roosevelt.

Since much of Roosevelt's following among urban ethnic groups came from factory workers, labor unions in 1936 had a unique opportunity to contribute to the President's reelection. Four years earlier, organized labor had been of little help to Roosevelt, because in the big industries few employees were unionized. But Labor had a new political significance in 1936, chiefly as a result of the emergence in the intervening years of the Committee for Industrial Organization (subsequently to be known as the Congress of Industrial Organizations) under the militant leadership of John L. Lewis of the United Mine Workers. A lifelong Republican, Lewis had voted for Hoover in 1932, while his CIO collaborators, Sidney Hillman of the Amalgamated Clothing Workers and David Dubinsky of the International Ladies' Garment Workers Union, had backed the Socialists that year. They had come to value the benefits of a Democratic Administration for industrial labor, and they were dismayed that Roosevelt planned to entrust the Labor campaign once again to the conservative foe of the CIO, Daniel Tobin of the AFL Teamsters. Lewis and Hillman moved swiftly to take matters in their own hands.

With the cooperation of Major George Berry of the AFL International Printing Pressmen's Union, the CIO leaders set up Labor's Non-Partisan League. "Non-Partisan" suggested to some that unions, while seeking to reelect Roosevelt, did not identify with the Democratic Party, to others that the organization bridged the AFL and CIO without taking sides in their dispute. The League carried out an ambitious operation to mobilize the Labor vote in the large industrial states. It held 109 rallies in the city of Chicago, sent seventy speakers through Ohio to talk to union meetings, and beamed a national radio broadcast to workers daily in the final month of the campaign. In Pennsylvania, thirty-five thousand union officials engaged in the drive to get the workingman to the polls.

The League also provided a big chunk of the bankroll for Roosevelt's campaign. When Lewis, who aimed to buy his way into national decision-making, decided to make a huge contribution, he arrived at the White House with a photographer prepared to record the event for maximum publicity effect. But after the United Mine Workers' chief magnanimously offered Roosevelt a draft for $250,000, the President answered, "No, John, I don't want your check, much as I appreciate the thought. Just keep it and I'll call on you, if and when any small need arises." As Andre Maurois later wrote, "Lewis then grasped that the campaign was going to be very much more expensive." During the following weeks, nearly half a million dollars left the union treasury, without attracting much notice in the newspapers. In all, Labor made available $770,218, including loans of $85,000; $469,000 came from the Mine Workers. These figures contrasted markedly with the $7,500, which represented the total union contribution to La Follette in 1924, and with the $95,000 that was the grand sum given by the national AFL to presidential campaigns in the preceding thirty years. While Labor advanced these munificent amounts, the proportion of donations from businessmen tailed off sharply. In 1932, bankers and brokers gave 24 percent of all contributions of $1,000 or more to the Democrats; in 1936, less than 4 percent. As one political scientist observed, it was a "new chapter" in the history of the labor movement "when an organization of miners is the largest contributor to a major political party."

Labor's Non-Partisan League proved especially effective in New York City, where Dubinsky, as well as Emil Rieve of the Hosiery Workers, resigned from the Socialist Party to take part in the campaign to reelect Roosevelt. Hillman told the Executive Board of the Amalgamated Clothing Workers,

> In my judgment, up to a few years ago we had no labor movement in this country. Even in our so-called radical organizations we paid lip service to the need for organization, but what did we actually do toward making a real labor movement? That, I am sure, would have been impossible without the NRA....
>
> "Now ... are we supposed to let the chance go by and wait until the Socialist Party comes into power? There is no labor party — let us not fool ourselves about that. And since there is no labor party, are we just to sit down and admit that we cannot do anything? ... You talk labor party. But can you have a labor party without an economic labor movement? I do not mean to criticize the Socialist movement, but it is composed of intellectuals.... I say to you that the defeat of Roosevelt and the introduction of a real Fascist administration such as we will have is going to make the work of building a labor movement impossible.

As veteran socialists in the garment unions followed Hillman and Dubinsky into the Roosevelt coalition, Norman Thomas protested, "This is to repeat the mistake of the German Social Democrats who voted for Hindenburg because they did not want Hitler."

In New York, Labor's Non-Partisan League took advantage of defections from the socialists to create a new statewide third party, the American Labor Party. It was organized around three needles trades unions: the men's clothing workers headed by Hillman, the ladies' garment union under Dubinsky, and the millinery workers led by Max Zaritsky. The ALP also found a home for right-wing socialists, mobilized by labor lawyer Louis Waldman. New York's right-wing socialists had been purged from the Socialist Party in May but had taken with them such important publications as the *New Leader* and Abe Cahan's *Jewish Daily Forward*, as well as institutions like the Rand School of Social Science and Camp Tamiment. In August, organized as the Social Democratic Federation, they voted to affiliate with the ALP. "Ironically," David Shannon has pointed out, the anti-Stalinist socialists, who "had thought the majority Socialists too close to communism, now had avowed Communist comrades in their new American Labor Party." The ALP not only enlisted Social Democrats in support of Roosevelt but made it possible for independents who disapproved of Tammany Hall to vote for FDR without pulling down the Democratic levers.

Although in previous campaigns union labor had divided its support, in 1936 Roosevelt achieved a near-monopoly of backing from union leaders. While William Green, the AFL president, did not give Roosevelt an outright endorsement, he did say, "I estimate that 90 percent of labor, organized and unorganized, is for Mr. Roosevelt's re-election.... Such unanimous action by labor has never been taken in any campaign heretofore so far as I know." "Big Bill" Hutcheson of the Carpenters, who had traded punches with Lewis in a symbolic fight between the craft unionists and the industrial unionists, headed the labor division of the Republican National Committee, but large segments of his own union deserted him to back Roosevelt. "The labor leaders are all tied up with this administration," Landon wrote glumly.

Labor's Non-Partisan League put a stress on New Deal ideology and "the politics of the deed" that was matched by only one branch of the Democratic National Committee: the Women's Division. In 1934 the energetic head of the division, Mary W. Dewson, had urged Democratic women to appoint twenty-two of their number in each county to serve as an information corps on the work of New Deal agencies. By 1936, there were fifteen thousand of these "reporters" prepared to tout the virtues of the New Deal in a campaign year. At Miss Dewson's request, Farley agreed to expand the news bulletin of the National Democratic Women's Club in Washington into a monthly magazine, the *Democratic Digest*, which included in each issue a syllabus of the activities of a New Deal agency. The Women's Division also sponsored regional conferences and institutes that featured explorations of significant Government policies.

In the 1936 campaign, Molly Dewson's indefatigable work between elections made a big contribution to energizing the Democratic bid for votes. At the Philadelphia convention, the Democrats accredited 219 women delegates (compared to sixty at the Republican convention) and 302 female alternates. Democratic women shared the limelight when eight of them made seconding speeches for the President's nomination, and each state was empowered to name a woman alternate to the Resolutions Committee. At the convention, Miss Dewson unveiled one of her creations, the "rainbow fliers," a set of brightly colored leaflets each devoted to a particular field of the New Deal. They proved so popular that during the campaign the Democrats distributed eighty-three million, more than four-fifths of all the party's literature.

The record of the New Deal enabled the President to seek votes less as the Democratic nominee than as the leader of a liberal movement that cut across party lines. The Roosevelt Administration worked with Progressives in Wisconsin and Farmer-Laborites in Minnesota, as well as with the American Labor Party in New York, and the President snubbed the Democratic senatorial nominee in Nebraska to endorse George Norris, who ran as an Independent. After Roosevelt's nomination, Bob La Follette and veteran labor attorney Frank Walsh put together a coalition of independent progressives to form yet another of FDR's auxiliary organizations. On September 11, 1936, a Progressive Conference of liberals of all parties, including such luminaries as Mayor Fiorello La Guardia of New York, endorsed the President, and many of the independent progressives played an active role in persuading non-Democrats to vote for Roosevelt.

The President recognized the importance of having the campaign revolve around him rather than his Republican rival, and he did not deign to mention Landon by name. He was annoyed when in late May in a speech to Michigan Democrats at Grand Rapids Farley referred to Landon as "the governor of a typical prairie state." The President sent a memo scolding him:

> I thought we had decided any reference to Landon or any other Republican candidate was inadvisable.
>
> Now that the water is over the dam, a somewhat facetious reference to Frank Knox by you might soften the effect of the Landon reference. Another good rule which should be passed down the line to all who are concerned with speech material is that no section of the country should be spoken of as "typical" but only with some laudatory adjective. If the sentence had read "One of those splendid prairie States," no one could have picked us up on it, but the word "typical" coming from any New Yorker is meat for the opposition.

Republicans made the most of Farley's blunder. When Landon came to Los Angeles, the California national committeeman, Earl Warren, introduced him by saying, "We glory in this opportunity to welcome to California this Governor of a typical prairie state."

Throughout the year, Roosevelt made a special effort to court Republicans, especially those of a progressive persuasion. He made a point of never suggesting that Republican voters were his opponents, and he featured in his campaign such former GOP leaders as Secretary Ickes. For their part, Republican Senators James Couzens of Michigan and Peter Norbeck of South Dakota backed FDR, while other GOP senators — William E. Borah, Hiram W. Johnson, Gerald P. Nye, and Minority Leader Charles L. McNary — took no part in the presidential campaign. Senator Arthur Capper, a Republican from Landon's home state, pointedly advised Kansas voters that they could split their tickets. As a consequence of these defections,

Landon was stripped of the support of much of the liberal wing of his party. In sum, Landon faced a virtually impossible task in overcoming the formidable coalition arrayed against him — urban machines, nationality groups, the Good Neighbor League, socialist defectors, the Women's Division, independent progressives, progressive Republicans, and assorted New Deal beneficiaries, as well as such predetermined blocs of votes as the Solid South.

A master of timing, Roosevelt refused to launch his campaign until the attention centered on the Republican national convention and the new GOP nominee began to wane. In July, while Democratic politicians chafed, he went cruising. The President did not go on the stump until August, and even then he confined himself to a "nonpolitical" inspection of flooded regions, although on August 14 at Chautauqua he gave an important address in which he committed himself to peace. Yet, everyone understood the tour had partisan implications. When Roosevelt told Farley that "of course, there won't be anything political about the inspection trips," he gave him a broad wink, threw back his head, and laughed.

Roosevelt snapped up a suggestion that he meet with governors of the Dust Bowl states, and in late August and early September the presidential train carried him through the Dakotas, Wisconsin, and Iowa. Wherever he went, the rains came. (But they also fell on Alf Landon during his tour. In this election, the Lord was nonpartisan.) At Des Moines the President conferred with midwestern governors, including his rival, the governor of Kansas. Not since 1912, when Woodrow Wilson encountered William Howard Taft at Boston's Copley Plaza Hotel, had two major party presidential candidates come together during a campaign. Their exchange was cordial. In fact, Senator Capper remarked, "Harmony dripped so steadily from every rafter that I fully expected one of the candidates to withdraw."

The President did not open his formal campaign until September 29, when he spoke to the New York State Democratic convention in Syracuse. Roosevelt began by dealing directly with the charge that he had succumbed to communist influence, an allegation that particularly disturbed many Catholics. Republicans had voiced this accusation frequently, and on September 19 in a front-page editorial the Hearst chain claimed that Moscow had ordered American communists to back Roosevelt. "Naturally the Communists flock to him," Hearst said. " 'Every bird knows its own nest.' " To the President's discomfiture, the communists, who once had denounced him as a "social fascist," were now in a United Front phase. While they sought to poll the largest possible vote for Earl Browder and his running mate James Ford, a Negro, they focused their criticism on Landon rather than Roosevelt. At Syracuse the President told his fellow Democrats, "I have not sought, I do not seek, I repudiate the support of any advocate of Communism or any other alien 'ism' which would by fair means or foul change our American democracy."

Not content with this defensive stance, Roosevelt brandished the main weapon in his arsenal: identifying his opponents with the privileged few. He gibed, "In the summer of 1933, a nice old gentleman wearing a silk hat fell off the end of a pier. He was unable to swim. A friend ran down the pier, dived overboard and pulled him out; but the silk hat floated off with the tide. After the old gentleman had been revived he was effusive in his thanks. He praised his friend for saving his life. Today, three years later, the old gentleman is berating his friend because the silk hat was lost." Hoover later commented, "I have some inside information about that incident. The old gentleman was surreptitiously pushed off the dock in order that the hero could gain the plaudits of the crowd as a life saver."

Roosevelt varied this appeal to class differences with boasts of the gains his Administration had secured, but he was sometimes hard put to square the actions he had taken with his campaign pledges in 1932. Especially embarrassing was his Pittsburgh address in which he had denounced Hoover as a profligate spender and promised to slash the federal budget. Rosenman recalls,

> Just before the start of the campaign of 1936, he said to me: "I'm going to make the first major campaign speech in Pittsburgh at the ball park in exactly the same spot I made that 1932 Pittsburgh speech; and in the speech I want to explain my 1932 statement. See whether you can prepare a draft giving a good and convincing explanation of it."
>
> That evening I went in to see the President in his study and said that as long as he insisted on referring to the speech, I had found the only kind of explanation that could be made. He turned to me rather hopefully and, I think, with a little surprise, and said, "Fine, what sort of an explanation would you make?"
>
> I replied, "Mr. President, the only thing you can say about that 1932 speech is to deny categorically that you ever made it."

Instead, Roosevelt decided to make no direct mention of his 1932 speech but to expound on why the budget had not been balanced. When he came to Forbes Field on October 1, he said, "The only way to keep the Government out of the red is to keep the people out of the red. And so we had to balance the budget of the American people before we could balance the budget of the national Government." Some people in 1933 had urged him to let nature take its course, but the President recalled, "I rejected that advice because Nature was in an angry mood." He declared, "To balance our budget in 1933 or 1934 or 1935 would have been a crime against the American people. To do so we should either have had to make a capital levy that would have been confiscatory, or we would have had to set our face against human suffering with callous indifference. When Americans suffered, we refused to pass by on the other side. Humanity came first."

Having gotten past the impediment presented by his 1932 speech, Roosevelt offered himself in his more congenial role of prosperity-maker. In so doing he employed an analogy appropriate to a ballpark speech:

> Compare the scoreboard which you have in Pittsburgh now with the scoreboard which you had when I stood here at second base in this field four years ago. At that time, as I drove through these great valleys, I could see mile after mile of this greatest mill and factory area in the world, a dead panorama of silent

black structures and smokeless stacks. I saw idleness and hunger instead of the whirl of machinery. Today as I came north from West Virginia, I saw mines operating, I found bustle and life, and hiss of steam, the ring of steel on steel — the roaring song of industry.

A week later in Chicago, Landon replied, "If the administration wants a baseball analogy — if they want the score — it is easy to give. It is written across this country: Twenty-five billion dollars spent. Thirteen billion dollars added to the public debt. Eleven million unemployed left on base."

The President's critics had claimed that his failure to balance the budget would have disastrous consequences, and Roosevelt himself was uneasy about the mounting deficits, but an economic upsurge in 1936 came at a propitious time. Since March 1935, a "Roosevelt boom" had sent prices soaring on the stock market. In 1936, Allied Chemical climbed almost 69 points, Paramount Pictures preferred 94½. The gross national product was half again as high as it had been in 1933, and the farmers' net income had risen some $3.5 billion since Roosevelt had taken office. With eight million jobless, the country still had a long way to go to achieve full employment. But as one report noted, "Even to the casual observer the signs of returning prosperity were unmistakable: crowded resorts, highways congested with week-end trippers, fewer empty theater seats, the rising popularity of night clubs, and record crowds at baseball and football games."

Roosevelt perceived that, for all the good will New Deal legislation had won, his strongest card in bidding for reelection would be hard evidence that the country was "in the money" again. He instructed Secretary of Agriculture Wallace, "Henry, through July, August, September, October and up to the fifth of November, I want cotton to sell at twelve cents. I do not care how you do it. That is your problem. It can't go below twelve cents. Is that clear?" When the WPA planned to dismiss relief workers on October 1, Roosevelt scolded Secretary of the Treasury Henry Morgenthau Jr., "You tell Corrington Gill that I don't give a goddamn where he gets the money from but not one person is to be laid off on the first of October."

The President made the most of the contrast between America in 1936 and in 1932. From a rear platform in Colorado Springs on October 12, he said, "You know, there has been a good deal of difference in tourists. In 1932, when I came out through here, there were a lot of tourists — but they were riding in box cars. This year there are more of them — and they are riding in Pullmans." As the economic indices continued to climb, Roosevelt moved farther ahead of his Republican rival. "I knew the case was hopeless as early as June," Landon told a reporter twenty years later. "Shortly after I was nominated in June, I sent for Mr. Benjamin Anderson of the Chase National Bank and Colonel Ayres of the Cleveland Trust Co. I asked them what business conditions would be like from June to November. They advised me each month would be better than the succeeding month. I realized then the campaign was pretty hopeless."

However often he dwelt on his success as prosperity-maker, Roosevelt never abandoned his role as champion of the forgotten man. At Madison Square Garden on the eve of the election, the President, angered by the Republican charge that workers might not receive their Social Security benefits, let out all the stops in an unrestrained attack on his opponents as the minions of avaricious interests. He told an explosively cheering, chanting crowd:

> Tonight I call the roll — the roll of honor of those who stood with us in 1932 and still stand with us today.
>
> Written on it are the names of millions who never had a chance — men at starvation wages, women in sweatshops, children at looms.

Having identified himself with the cause of the sweatshop laborer, he pinned the blame for the worker's misfortunes on the capture of the Republican Party and the National Government by wealth and greed. As the crowd roared its approval, the President said,

> For twelve years this Nation was afflicted with hear-nothing, see-nothing, do-nothing Government. The Nation looked to Government but the Government looked away. Nine mocking years with the golden calf and three long years of the scourge! Nine crazy years at the ticker and three long years in the breadlines! Nine mad years of mirage and three long years of despair! Powerful influences strive today to restore that kind of government with its doctrine that that Government is best which is most indifferent....
>
> They had begun to consider the Government of the United States as a mere appendage to their own affairs. We know now that Government by organized money is just as dangerous as Government by organized *mob.*
>
> Never before in all our history have these forces been so united against one candidate as they stand today. They are unanimous in their *hate* for *me — and I welcome their hatred.*
>
> I should like to have it said of my first Administration that in it the forces of selfishness and of lust for power met their match. I should like to have it said of my second Administration that *in it these forces met their master.*

Roosevelt wound up his speech by responding to Landon's challenge:

> This is our answer to those who, silent about their own plans, ask us to state our objectives.
>
> *Of course* we will continue to seek to improve working conditions for the workers of America.... *Of course* we will continue to work for cheaper electricity in the homes and on the farms of America.... *Of course* we will continue our efforts for young men and women ... for the crippled, for the blind, for the mothers, our insurance for the unemployed, our security for the aged....
>
> For these things, too, and for a multitude of things like them, we have only just begun to fight.

As Roosevelt toured the country in 1936, the response of crowds startled veterans of previous campaigns. In 1932 the country had voted less for Roosevelt than against Hoover. "Mr. Roosevelt was no great popular idol during the presidential campaign of 1932," wrote Ernest K. Lindley. "Vast crowds came out to look at him eagerly, hopefully. They liked him but went away still skeptical." But in the intervening years many Americans had come to view the President as one who was intimately concerned with their welfare. In the 1936 campaign he heard people cry out, "He saved my home," "He gave me a job." At Bridgeport, Connecticut, he rode past signs saying, "Thank God for Roosevelt," and in the Denver freight yards a message scrawled in chalk on the side of a boxcar read, "Roosevelt Is My Friend."

Ambassador Breckinridge Long, who had ridden on the campaign train in 1932, found an "astonishing" contrast when he accompanied the President four years later. He noted in his diary:

> Four years ago ... the people were quiet and undemonstrative. There was a glumness and semblance of sullenness about their faces and their demeanor. They were awe-struck and in a terrible quandary....
>
> This year the crowds were larger than they were then and they were very enthusiastic. They passed any bounds for enthusiasm — really wild enthusiasm — that I have ever seen in any political gathering....
>
> [In] Detroit ... the President spoke from the steps of the city hall, which opens onto a sort of circular space into which streets lead from five or six different directions. The whole space was a seething mass of people, standing packed closely together, and up each street as far as one could see in the dim electric light ... the crowd was just as thick. It was boisterous in its enthusiasm, and it was almost impossible for the cars following the President to keep in line with him because of the seething people [who] swarmed around his car as it started away. In addition, the streets were lined all the way from Hamtramck through the city to the railroad station....
>
> Even at small stops, where there was no possibility of the train to stop and where it would go whizzing by at forty, fifty, and sixty miles an hour, and all the way from seven o'clock in the morning till midnight, there would be assembled anywhere from ten to two or three hundred people. Every crossroad would have its collection.

Newspapermen observed the same phenomenon. Marquis Childs wrote of the President's reception in Jersey City, "From the moment that the procession of cars rolled out of the Holland Tunnel the thunder of bombs assaulted the ear, and the whole city under a cloudless blue sky seemed one mass of flag-waving humanity." Chicago, he reported, gave Roosevelt an even more impressive welcome:

> In the early evening the President rode for five miles in an open car through streets so crowded that only a narrow lane was left. In spite of protests of the Secret Service people had been allowed to swarm off the curbs and it was all that the motorcycle police could do to force a way through for the presidential cavalcade.
>
> This was King Crowd. They were out to have a large time and they had it. Every kind of band — bagpipers, piano accordions, jazz, fife-and-drum, bugle corps — lined the narrow lane of humanity through which the presidential party passed. As the parade turned off Michigan Boulevard into West Madison Street, the mass of people became denser and noisier. They shrieked from rooftops; they sang and danced; they leaned from tenement windows and left windows to wave and shout. And all the time a rain of torn paper fluttered down, like gray snow in the half-lighted streets.

Despite the evidence of Roosevelt's popularity, a surprising number of political experts anticipated a close election and even a Landon victory. On September 18,

Arthur Krock wrote in *The New York Times* that "the Republican Party will poll a far larger popular and electoral vote than in 1932.... Roosevelt's big majorities are over." Two weeks before the election Archibald Crossley, head of the Crossley Political Poll, lunched in New York's financial district with thirteen other pollsters or political writers. Their consensus: a narrow Landon victory. The Cleveland *News* calculated that a consensus of more than three thousand separate straw votes taken by newspapers and magazines showed a Landon triumph with 307 electoral votes. But the biggest splash was made by the final reckoning of the *Literary Digest* poll, which had called every election correctly since 1920. The *Digest* forecast an electoral margin of 370–161 for Landon. Roosevelt led in no states outside the South and border regions save New Mexico and Utah; he trailed in Rhode Island by almost 3 to 1, in Massachusetts by 3½ to 1.

However, the Gallup and Crossley polls, the *Fortune* survey, a group of more than twelve thousand editors canvassed by *Liberty*, a confidential survey of Washington correspondents, and the professional odds-makers all predicted a Roosevelt victory by a substantial margin. As early as March, Bernard Baruch had complained he could not find Republicans willing to wager even in Palm Beach. The private polls prepared by the Nielsen Corporation for the Republicans showed the President with so substantial a lead that many GOP leaders were skeptical of the *Literary Digest*'s findings. But it was left for Jim Farley to make the prediction that would become the most famous in the history of political prognostication. On November 2, the Democratic chairman wrote Roosevelt that he had studied the memoranda he had received on the election prospects. "After looking them all over carefully and discounting everything that has been given in these reports," Farley said, "I am still definitely of the opinion that you will carry every state but two — Maine and Vermont."

Landon had few illusions about his chances. The economic indicators were running against him, and the crowds were too cool. Railroad workers in Shopton, Iowa, the location of the Santa Fe railroad shops, had to be all but dragged from a porch railing to be photographed with him. In Maine he was told that a meeting he addressed was one of the warmest ever held in that state. "Senator, it may have been warm for Maine," Landon responded, "but it was damn cold for Kansas." When, despite his chilly reception in that state, the Republicans carried Maine in its traditional early election in September, Landon voiced the old cry, "As Maine goes, so goes the nation," and for a moment hope flickered. But before the campaign had ended, Landon knew he had no chance. At lunch on October 28, two former Republican senators, after telling Landon he would not win New Jersey, asked him if he thought he would carry the country. "No chance," the governor replied. On election night when a photographer asked the Republican candidate to pose beside a large "Landon Victory Cake," he said to his wife, "Come on, Mother, and get your picture took. It will be the last chance."

When the first election returns reached the President's home at Hyde Park, he leaned back, blew a smoke ring, and said, "Wow!" New Haven, Connecticut had gone to FDR by 15,000 votes — the earliest indication of the power of

Roosevelt's urban coalition. Through the night, to the accompaniment of Tommy Corcoran's accordion, the wire services chattered the glad tidings of a landslide victory. The President's 27,751,841 votes (to Landon's 16,679,491) set a new mark. His percentage of the popular vote (60.8 percent) was the greatest in recorded history (adequate records do not exist before 1824). In fourteen states, at least as late as 1960, no Democratic presidential candidate had ever matched Roosevelt's 1936 percentage. Nor had anyone ever equalled FDR's more than eleven million plurality. Even more impressive was the tally in electoral votes, 523 to 8, the greatest electoral triumph since James Monroe had won in 1820 at a time of party breakdown. Every state but Maine and Vermont fell into the Democratic column. "I knew I should have gone to Maine and Vermont," the President said, "but Jim wouldn't let me."

Except for Maine and Vermont, Roosevelt's victory combination bracketed the country. The Democrats made their traditionally strong showing in the South, which after a deviation in 1928 had become "solid" again in 1932. Roosevelt received 76 percent of the two-party vote in that section, and in South Carolina, long the banner Democratic state, he rolled up a stunning 98.57 percent. The President did next best in the Far West with 68 percent of the two-party vote; he carried California and Washington by 2 to 1. He polled roughly his national average in the West Central states with 61 percent, the Middle Atlantic states with 60 percent, and the East Central states with 59 percent. Only in New England, with 54 percent, did Roosevelt run several points below his national average. Farley should never have made his prediction about Maine and Vermont, Molly Dewson said. With enough work, they could have carried Vermont.

Yet in no election in the history of the two-party system had section made so little difference. Even in the Northeast, a Democratic presidential candidate carried Delaware and Connecticut for the first time since 1912 and Pennsylvania for the first time since 1856. "As Maine goes," it was now said, "so goes Vermont." The main sectional impact of the election was to reduce the influence of the South in the Democratic Party. While the South contributed twenty-six of the thirty-seven seats held by the Democrats in 1918, they had twenty-six of seventy-five in 1936. In 1920 almost every Democratic congressman came from the South (107 of 131); by 1936 southerners were a minority with 116 of 333. The most influential voices in Democratic Party councils now came from the northern cities, which commanded big blocs of electoral votes. In 1936, the Democrats recognized for the first time that there were greater rewards from appeals to northern Negroes than to southern whites. The South, irritated by this turn of events, would remain "solid" for only two more elections.

Landon had suffered the most crushing electoral defeat of any major party candidate in history, and his popular percentage (36.5) percent was the smallest for any Republican nominee since Taft's in 1912 when the party divided. In only four states did Landon get as much as 45 percent of the vote. The GOP was left with only eighty-eight seats in the House of Representatives (compared to 333 for the

Democrats — who gained eleven — thirteen to minor parties, one vacant) and just sixteen in the Senate (compared to seventy-five for the Democrats — who picked up six — four to minor parties, one vacant). The Republican Portland (Maine) *Press-Herald* called the 1936 election "a death blow perhaps to the Republican Party," and other periodicals speculated about whether the GOP would not, like its predecessor the Whig Party, disappear from the political scene. "If the outcome of this election hasn't taught you Republicans not to meddle in politics," jeered one writer, "I don't know what will."

Yet Landon did not do quite so badly as first impressions suggested. Roosevelt's enormous margin in the Electoral College exaggerated the dimensions of his victory, for Landon's 36.5 percent of the popular vote earned him only 1.5 percent of the electoral vote. Since Landon's defeat in 1936 seems much more overwhelming than Hoover's in 1932, it is often overlooked, too, that Landon polled nearly a million more votes than Hoover had. Even FDR's percentage of the popular vote was not so exceptional as many thought; it roughly approximated Harding's in 1920. If Landon polled the smallest percentage ever received by a Republican presidential candidate in a predominantly two-party race, he gained a higher proportion than either Cox or Davis had on the Democratic line in the 1920s. Although Landon carried only 459 counties to Roosevelt's 2,636, this was still eighty-seven more than Hoover had won.

Landon also gained back some of the GOP's following in the countryside. While Roosevelt received 59 percent of the two-party vote of farmers, only slightly under his overall national average, Landon did reasonably well with corn and wheat growers and even better with dairymen. However, the governor found his greatest support in the traditional Republican stronghold, the market town. FDR received 61 percent of the farm vote in Iowa but only 48 percent of the town vote. In a tier of states from South Dakota to Oklahoma, and including contiguous Iowa, Missouri, and New Mexico, Landon improved on Hoover's performance in 1932, as he also did in five southern and border states.

Lemke received 892,390 votes (2 percent) and no electoral votes. He polled his largest state total in Ohio (132,212), but recorded the best percentage (13.4) in his own state of North Dakota. He held the balance of power in no state save New Hampshire, where a shift of the whole bloc of 4,819 Lemke voters would have put the state in Landon's column. It was a disappointing showing, far below Coughlin's expectation. On the other hand, Lemke would have done appreciably better if he had not failed to qualify for a line on the ballot in fourteen states, including New York, where Coughlin had a large following, California, the seat of Townsend strength, and Louisiana, the stronghold of Share-Our-Wealth. In some other states he could not use the name "Union Party"; in Ohio and Pennsylvania, he ran as the candidate of the Royal Oak party. Lemke drew some comfort from the fact that he won reelection to Congress on the Republican ticket. In Massachusetts, O'Brien, as a candidate for the U.S. Senate, drew enough votes from James Michael Curley to permit Henry Cabot Lodge Jr. to win a narrow victory.

Samuel Lubell has contended that Lemke's vote was the product not of economic protest but of foreign policy concerns, especially Irish-American Anglophobia and German-American fear that Roosevelt would lead the country into another war against the Reich. He pointed out that, of the thirty-nine counties outside of North Dakota where Lemke got more than 10 percent of the vote, twenty-eight were predominantly German, and that in the four cities where Lemke polled over 5 percent — St. Paul, Dubuque, Boston, and Cincinnati — his support appears to have come from German and Irish voters. Lubell does not explain why this minority was so disposed when the vast majority of German and Irish voters backed the major parties. Moreover, there may be more compelling explanations of even this limited ethnic pattern. Lemke was of German descent, O'Brien a Catholic Irish-American, and Coughlin had a considerable following in both groups. Most important, foreign policy issues did not figure prominently in the campaign, and the image of Roosevelt as an interventionist had not crystallized by 1936.

When international concerns did become paramount in Roosevelt's second term, the Union Party remnant, which lasted only until the spring of 1939, failed to capitalize on them. In its declining years, the party was captured in some areas by anti-Semites, to the dismay of Lemke who agreed to serve as sponsor of the American Jewish Congress — an ironic denouement to Coughlin's efforts. The National Union for Social Justice also failed to survive Lemke's defeat. On the day after the election, Father Coughlin said, "The National Union may be compared to Joe Louis in his recent fight against Max Schmeling. Our aim now is a trip to the showers, and a new training camp for our comeback, if and when it is required." But three days later he conceded his Union was "thoroughly discredited," and he disbanded it.

The two major parties dominated the election with 97.3 percent of the popular returns and all the electoral votes. (The minor parties' 2.7 percent does not include the American Labor Party totals that were recorded for Roosevelt.) The biggest portion of the minor party tally was accounted for by the Union Party, which made its appearance in only this one presidential election. Each of the minor parties that had taken part in previous contests — the Socialist, Communist, Prohibitionist, and the Socialist Labor parties — suffered a decline in 1936 from its total four years earlier. One unwelcome newcomer, the Christian Party, headed by William Dudley Pelley, founder of the quasi-fascist Silver Shirt Legion of America, got less than 1,600 votes.

Norman Thomas and his running mate George Nelson of the Farmers Union polled 188,497 votes (0.4 percent), a precipitous drop from the 884,781 (2.2 percent) Thomas had won on the Socialist line in 1932. The party had not received so few votes since 1900, when their percentage was much higher. In some states the drop-off all but wiped out the party as an effective force; Thomas's total in Iowa plunged from 20,467 to 1,373, in Illinois from 67,258 to 7,530. Thomas had been unable to hold his ranks against the appeal of the New Deal. Although he retained the support of John Dewey and Reinhold Niebuhr, most intellectuals backed FDR. A. Philip Randolph, the able leader of the Brotherhood of Sleeping Car Porters, directed the Labor League for Thomas and Nelson, but no large unions backed the ticket. Two Socialists, Jerry Voorhis of California and Andrew J. Biemiller of Wisconsin, who left the Socialist Party for the Democrats, would subsequently represent that party in Congress. Thomas had no doubt of the cause of his grief. From 1931 to 1934, he later said, "it looked as if we were going to go places.... What cut the ground out pretty completely from under us was ... Roosevelt in a word. You don't need anything more."

The 1936 election confirmed the status of the Democrats as the country's new majority party. It established that Roosevelt's election in 1932 had not been an erratic event of history but signaled the beginning of a new era in party warfare. As the divisions over slavery had precipitated the long era of Republican predominance, the Great Depression realigned the electorate in favor of the Democrats. Henceforth, the Republicans, long known as the party of good times, were fated to be thought of as the party of economic breakdown. On the other hand, the Democrats, who had been in power during the panics of 1837, 1857, and 1893, and the recession of 1913, came to be regarded as, if not the party of good times, at least the shield of "one third of a nation." From the Wall Street crash through 1968, the Republicans were to win only two congressional elections, in large part because of the legacy of the Depression and the New Deal. In the 1950s, a Chicago Democrat said, "Franklin Roosevelt was the greatest precinct captain we ever had. He elected everybody — governors, senators, sheriffs, aldermen."

While the 1936 contest bears many of the marks of V. O. Key's definition of a "critical election" — intense involvement, profound readjustments of power, the formation of new and durable electoral groups — it should be categorized rather as the capstone of a "critical period," another Key conception. The big reshuffling had come four years earlier when Franklin D. Roosevelt became the first Democratic candidate to win election with a majority of the vote since Franklin Pierce's triumph in 1852. Yet it was by no means clear during FDR's first term that this transformation would endure. The Survey Research Center analysts have commented,

> The nationwide shift toward the Democratic Party during the 1930s was not fully accomplished in a single election. Although Mr. Roosevelt's margin of victory in 1932 was large..., it was not until 1936 that the Democratic wave reached its peak. The long-entrenched Republican sympathies of the electorate may not have given way easily in the early years of the Depression. Had not Mr. Roosevelt and his New Deal won the confidence of many of these people during his first administration — or even his second — there might have been a return to earlier party lines similar to that which occurred in 1920. From this point of view we may do well to speak of a realigning electoral era rather than a realigning election.

The Democratic vote in 1936 contrasted vividly with the returns in the 1920s, the apogee of the age of Republican supremacy. Roosevelt tripled the Democratic presidential total in 1920, while Landon received roughly the same figure that the Republicans had polled sixteen years earlier. Some states showed a staggering change; Michigan, which gave the Democratic presidential candidate only 152,000 votes in 1924, chalked up 1,017,000 for FDR in 1936. In one article, Key, drawing on the New England experience, suggested that this realignment took place in 1928. But in the nation as a whole the salient change did not occur until the onset of the depression. Pennsylvania, the "Verdun of Toryism," returned Democratic majorities in no more than four of its sixty-seven counties in the 1920s; in 1936, Roosevelt captured forty-one. In California, the Republicans boasted 78 percent of the registered voters as late as 1930. However, in the next six years, the totals for Democratic registrants rose 313 percent, while GOP adherents dropped off 24 percent. By 1936, the Democrats had 60 percent of California's registration, a ratio that persisted into the 1960s.

The realignment in 1936 appears to have resulted in part from a movement of voters across party lines but to a much larger extent from the emergence of "new identifiers." Some conservative Democrats crossed over to the GOP, like the Minneapolis man who wrote, "I was born and raised a Democrat, but if this President is a Democrat, I do not know a speckled cow from a grasshopper." On the other hand, probably an even larger number of Republicans — for example, urban Negroes — migrated to the party of the New Deal. Most of the Democratic gains very likely came less from "conversion" of Republicans than from first voters and others who had not previously voted but now participated in an enlarged electorate. Of the increased turnout of nearly six million over 1932, the Democrats secured almost five million. That first voters made a disproportionate contribution to the Democratic margin is indicated by the fact that FDR's share of the two-party vote fluctuated with age, from 68 percent of the twenty-one to twenty-four year old bracket to 55 percent of those fifty-five and over.

If section was the hallmark of the era of Republican supremacy, social stratification distinguished partisan disposition in 1936. Gallup found that in 1936 Roosevelt, who got 62.5 percent of the two-party vote nationally, received 42 percent of the upper income share of the two-party vote, 60 percent of middle income, and 76 percent of lower income. His proportion of the labor vote varied inversely with skill — 61 percent from white collar employees, 67 percent from skilled artisans, 74 percent from semi-skilled workers, and 81 percent from unskilled laborers. He won 84 percent of the ballots cast for the major parties by relief recipients and 80 percent of the labor union vote. (In New York, the President polled 275,000 votes on the ALP line.) As one workingman put it, "Mr. Roosevelt is the only man we ever had in the White House who would understand that my boss is a son-of-a-bitch."

When the *Literary Digest* folded shortly after the 1936 election, most commentators pointed to the impact of class politics. The *Digest* had been right in every election up until 1936, and woefully mistaken that year, it was argued, because the *Digest*'s sample failed to allow for the influence of class, which was pivotal in 1936, but had not been as recently as 1932. This analysis may be correct, but certain demurrers should be noted. Although data are inadequate, there were discernible class influences on partisan alignment well before the Depression. Moreover, some studies have revealed a sharp class cleavage in the 1932 election. Furthermore, class differences in 1936 were obscured by the fact that Roosevelt received so large a share of the vote that he ran quite well among the more prosperous. Yet there can be little doubt that a sizeable number of lower-income voters — reliefers, Negroes, industrial unionists, New Deal beneficiaries, erstwhile socialists — switched over to the Democrats in 1936, while still others cast their first votes for FDR.

The 1936 outcome led many people to dismiss editorials as reflecting the class bias of publishers and to discount the influence of the press on public opinion. Although in 1932 Roosevelt had enjoyed the support of both Hearst and Colonel Robert R. McCormick of the *Chicago Tribune*, each of whom soon became bitter foes of the New Deal, in 1936 even such normally Democratic newspapers as the St. Louis *Post-Dispatch* endorsed Landon. Many publishers shared the hostility of other businessmen toward the President, and they had been especially aggrieved when the National Recovery Administration insisted that they meet wages and hours standards. Although FDR held his own among small circulation newspapers, he had the backing of only one-fifth of the large dailies in 1936, and the behavior of some journals toward Roosevelt, that "traitor to his class," lost all sense of proportion. When immoral practices were exposed in Wisconsin, the *Chicago Tribune* headlined,

"ROOSEVELT AREA IN WISCONSIN IS HOTBED OF VICE"

As the majorities for the President mounted on Election Night, a crowd in Chicago burned a truckload of the *Tribune*. Subsequently, when a Chicagoan was asked what he thought of the campaign that his city's three largest dailies were waging against syphilis, he replied, "I hate to see it." His questioner, startled, asked, "Why?" "Because I hate to see syphilis win," the man answered.

The transit of lower-income groups to the Democrats took place largely in the great cities. The President rolled up margins of better than 2–1 in Detroit, 3–1 in San Francisco and New York City (which gave him a lavish 1,367,000 plurality), and 4–1 in Milwaukee. In many metropolises, the change in urban allegiance had come with the "Al Smith Revolution" in 1928. Roosevelt actually got fewer votes in Boston and Lowell in 1936 than Smith had in 1928. However, in Los Angeles Smith polled only 28.7 percent in 1928 while Roosevelt received 57.3 percent in 1932 and 67.0 in 1936. In Philadelphia, Roosevelt in 1932 had built Smith's 39.5 percent up only to 42.9 percent; the big leap came in 1936, when FDR amassed 60.5 percent. Flint, which had given Smith a mere 19 percent in 1928, voted 72 percent Roosevelt in 1936; San Diego jumped from 32 to 65 percent in the same period. Democratic registration in Pittsburgh, which had been an incredibly low 3 percent in 1929, had reached 18.5 percent by September 1933, but this was still less than one-fifth of registered voters. In April 1936, however, Dave Lawrence announced that for the first time since the Civil War Pittsburgh had more Democrats registered than Republicans, and in November Roosevelt carried every ward in the city.

The President's impressive showing in metropolitan areas concealed a divergence between core city and suburb. In 1936, Landon polled only 24 percent of the New York City vote but 54 percent of the nearby suburbs, 30 percent of the Cleveland vote but 54 percent of the suburbs, 33 percent of Chicago's vote but 50 percent of the suburbs. These differences reflected the influence less of locality than of socioeconomic status.

Roosevelt's success in the cities derived in large part from his attention to ethnic groups, especially the newer immigrants. Congressman John Dingell told the President that in Hamtramck, Michigan, "where the population is almost one hundred percent Polish, you received almost one hundred percent of the vote." Jews, who admired FDR's liberal programs and his association with "Brain Trust" intellectuals, gave the President enthusiastic support, although not to the degree that they would when he became an outspoken foe of Hitler's. In Paterson, New Jersey's predominantly Jewish Fourth Ward, Landon barely eked out 30 percent of the vote. Estimates of Roosevelt's share of Catholic ballots varied from better than 70 percent to 81 percent. As early as August, Monsignor Ryan found that "everybody in California is for Roosevelt, especially the nuns." Another cleric reckoned that 103 of the 106 American bishops had voted for the President. Immediately after the election, Monsignor R. F. Keegan, Secretary to Cardinal Hayes, wrote Roosevelt, "You are an answer to prayer — the prayer of all of us close to the man in the street, the factory, on the farm, and for whom any other result would have been the worst calamity that could have befallen America."

While Roosevelt scored heavily with non-Protestant nationality groups, he received only a bare majority of the Protestant vote. John H. Fenton has noted, "the fears of some native white Hoosiers that the party of Franklin Roosevelt was an advance agent for a plundering horde of foreigners led by the pope." In much of the nation, Landon ran particularly well among native-born rural voters of Anglo-Saxon descent. Perhaps more noteworthy, however, may have been the degree to which the President cut into the native-born vote, long regarded as the Republicans' special domain. In winning so large a share of working-class ballots, Roosevelt united groups that had hitherto been divided by race and nationality. The 1936 election, Norman Graebner has written, marked the first time since the Civil War that native laborers voted Democratic.

Of all the changes in 1936, none demonstrated so historic a shift of allegiance as that of the Negro voter. Negroes in northern states, Gallup reported, gave Roosevelt 76 percent of their major party ballots. The Democrats made deep inroads into the Republican hold on black districts in the northern cities. Roosevelt, who had received only 23 percent of the Negro vote in Chicago in 1932, won 49 percent in 1936, almost breaking even. In Cincinnati's Ward Sixteen, FDR, who had polled less than 29 percent in 1932, improved to better than 65 percent in 1936, a higher proportion than he received in the city as a whole. Even in the South, Negro ballots helped to swell Roosevelt's totals. "Every Negro I have registered so far has said he would vote for President Roosevelt," reported a registrar in Columbia, South

Carolina. "They say Roosevelt saved them from starvation, gave them aid when they were in distress."

Roosevelt's reelection in 1936 represented not only a personal triumph but a victory for his ideas. William Allen White observed, "The water of liberalism has been dammed up for forty years by the two major parties. The dam is out. Landon went down the creek in the torrent." To be sure, many ballots must have been cast for FDR by voters who admired his personality and cared not a hoot about his principles, especially since the President, had given so few specifics about his plans for his second term. Henry Breckinridge wrote sourly, "The people have spoken and in the fullness of time Roosevelt will tell us what they have said." It is true, too, that the President profited from improving economic conditions. But no such considerations should cloud the fact that the election was widely interpreted as a ratification of the Welfare State. The voters had been offered an opportunity to reject the party that had identified itself with the growth of the central government and had instead given that party a thumping endorsement. In authenticating the position of the Democrats as the nation's majority party and acknowledging the decisive influence of class in American politics, the voters on November 3, 1936 made unmistakably clear that Big Government was here to stay.

Appendix

Party Platforms of 1936

Democratic Platform

We hold this truth to be self-evident — that the test of a representative government is its ability to promote the safety and happiness of the people.

We hold this truth to be self-evident — that 12 years of Republican leadership left our Nation sorely stricken in body, mind, and spirit; and that three years of Democratic leadership have put it back on the road to restored health and prosperity.

We hold this truth to be self-evident — that 12 years of Republican surrender to the dictatorship of a privileged few have been supplanted by a Democratic leadership which has returned the people themselves to the places of authority, and has revived in them new faith and restored the hope which they had almost lost.

We hold this truth to be self-evident — that this three-year recovery in all the basic values of life and the reestablishment of the American way of living has been brought about by humanizing policies of the Federal Government as they affect the personal, financial, industrial, and agricultural well-being of the American people.

We hold this truth to be self-evident — that government in a modern civilization has certain inescapable obligations to its citizens, among which are:

(1) Protection of the family and the home.

(2) Establishment of a democracy of opportunity for all the people.

(3) Aid to those overtaken by disaster.

These obligations, neglected through 12 years of the old leadership, have once more been recognized by American Government. Under the new leadership they will never be neglected.

FOR THE PROTECTION OF THE FAMILY AND THE HOME

(1) We have begun and shall continue the successful drive to rid our land of kidnappers and bandits. We shall continue to use the powers of government to end the activities of the malefactors of great wealth who defraud and exploit the people.

Savings and Investment

(2) We have safeguarded the thrift of our citizens by restraining those who would gamble with other peoples savings, by requiring truth in the sale of securities;

by putting the brakes upon the use of credit for speculation; by outlawing the manipulation of prices in stock and commodity markets; by curbing the overweening power and unholy practices of utility holding companies; by insuring fifty million bank accounts.

Old Age and Social Security

(3) We have built foundations for the security of those who are faced with the hazards of unemployment and old age; for the orphaned, the crippled, and the blind. On the foundation of the Social Security Act we are determined to erect a structure of economic security for all our people, making sure that this benefit shall keep step with the ever-increasing capacity of America to provide a high standard of living for all its citizens.

Consumer

(4) We will act to secure to the consumer fair value, honest sales and a decreased spread between the price he pays and the price the producer receives.

Rural Electrification

(5) This administration has fostered power rate yardsticks in the Tennessee Valley and in several other parts of the Nation. As a result, electricity has been made available to the people at a lower rate. We will continue to promote plans for rural electrification and for cheap power by means of the yardstick method.

Housing

(6) We maintain that our people are entitled to decent, adequate housing at a price which they can afford. In the last three years, the Federal Government, having saved more than two million homes from foreclosure, has taken the first steps in our history to provide decent housing for people of meagre incomes. We believe every encouragement should be given to the building of new homes by private enterprise; and that the Government should steadily extend its housing program toward the goal of adequate housing for those forced through economic necessities to live in unhealthy and slum conditions.

Veterans

(7) We shall continue just treatment of our war veterans and their dependents.

FOR THE ESTABLISHMENT OF A DEMOCRACY OF OPPORTUNITY

Agriculture

We have taken the farmers off the road to ruin.

We have kept our pledge to agriculture to use all available means to raise farm income toward its pre-war purchasing power. The farmer is no longer suffering from 15-cent corn, 3-cent hogs, 2 1/2-cent beef at the farm, 5-cent wool, 30-cent wheat, 5-cent cotton, and 3-cent sugar.

By Federal legislation, we have reduced the farmer's indebtedness and doubled his net income. In cooperation with the States and through the farmers' own committees, we are restoring the fertility of his land and checking the erosion of his soil. We are bringing electricity and good roads to his home.

We will continue to improve the soil conservation and domestic allotment program with payments to farmers.

We will continue a fair-minded administration of agricultural laws, quick to recognize and meet new problems and conditions. We recognize the gravity of the evils of farm tenancy, and we pledge the full cooperation of the Government in the refinancing of farm indebtedness at the lowest possible rates of interest and over a long term of years.

We favor the production of all the market will absorb, both at home and abroad, plus a reserve supply sufficient to insure fair prices to consumers; we favor judicious commodity loans on seasonal surpluses; and we favor assistance within Federal authority to enable farmers to adjust and balance production with demand, at a fair profit to the farmers.

We favor encouragement of sound, practical farm cooperatives.

By the purchase and retirement of ten million acres of sub-marginal land, and assistance to those attempting to eke out an existence upon it, we have made a good beginning toward proper land use and rural rehabilitation.

The farmer has been returned to the road to freedom and prosperity. We will keep him on that road.

Labor

We have given the army of America's industrial workers something more substantial than the Republicans' dinner pail full of promises. We have increased the worker's pay and shortened his hours; we have undertaken to put an end to the sweated labor of his wife and children; we have written into the law of the land his right to collective bargaining and self-organization free from the interference of employers; we have provided Federal machinery for the peaceful settlement of labor disputes.

We will continue to protect the worker and we will guard his rights, both as wage-earner and consumer, in the production and consumption of all commodities, including coal and water power and other natural resource products.

The worker has been returned to the road to freedom and prosperity. We will keep him on that road.

Business

We have taken the American business man out of the red. We have saved his bank and given it a sounder foundation; we have extended credit; we have lowered interest rates; we have undertaken to free him from the ravages of cutthroat competition.

The American business man has been returned to the road to freedom and prosperity. We will keep him on that road.

Youth

We have aided youth to stay in school; given them constructive occupation; opened the door to opportunity which 12 years of Republican neglect had closed.

Our youth have been returned to the road to freedom and prosperity. We will keep them on that road.

Monopoly and Concentration of Economic Power

Monopolies and the concentration of economic power, the creation of Republican rule and privilege, continue to be the master of the producer, the exploiter of the consumer, and the enemy of the independent operator. This is a problem challenging the unceasing effort of untrammeled public officials in every branch of the Government. We pledge vigorously and fearlessly to enforce the criminal and civil provisions of the existing anti-trust laws, and to the extent that their effectiveness has been weakened by new corporate devices or judicial construction, we propose by law to restore their efficacy in stamping out monopolistic practices and the concentration of economic power.

Aid to Those Overtaken by Disaster

We have aided and will continue to aid those who have been visited by widespread drought and floods, and have adopted a Nation-wide flood-control policy.

Unemployment

We believe that unemployment is a national problem, and that it is an inescapable obligation of our Government to meet it in a national way. Due to our stimulation of private business, more than five million people have been reemployed; and we shall continue to maintain that the first objective of a program of economic security is maximum employment in private industry at adequate wages. Where business fails to supply such employment, we believe that work at prevailing wages should be provided in cooperation with State and local governments on useful public projects, to the end that the national wealth may be increased, the skill and energy of the worker may be utilized, his morale maintained, and the unemployed assured the opportunity to earn the necessities of life.

The Constitution

The Republican platform proposes to meet many pressing national problems solely by action of the separate States. We know that drought, dust storms, floods, minimum wages, maximum hours, child labor, and working conditions in industry, monopolistic and unfair business practices cannot be adequately handled exclusively by 48 separate State legislatures, 48 separate State administrations, and 48 separate State courts. Transactions and activities which inevitably overflow State boundaries call for both State and Federal treatment.

We have sought and will continue to seek to meet these problems through legislation within the Constitution.

If these problems cannot be effectively solved by legislation within the Constitution, we shall seek such clarifying amendment as will assure to the legislatures of the several States and to the Congress of the United States, each within its proper jurisdiction, the power to enact those laws which the State and Federal legislatures, within their respective spheres, shall find necessary, in order adequately to regulate commerce, protect public health and safety and safeguard economic security. Thus we propose to maintain the letter and spirit of the Constitution.

THE MERIT SYSTEM IN GOVERNMENT

For the protection of government itself and promotion of its efficiency, we pledge the immediate extension of the merit system through the classified civil service — which was first established and fostered under Democratic auspices — to all non-policy-making positions in the Federal service.

We shall subject to the civil service law all continuing positions which, because of the emergency, have been exempt from its operation.

CIVIL LIBERTIES

We shall continue to guard the freedom of speech, press, radio, religion and assembly which our Constitution guarantees; with equal rights to all and special privileges to none.

GOVERNMENT FINANCE

The Administration has stopped deflation, restored values and enabled business to go ahead with confidence.

When national income shrinks, government income is imperilled. In reviving national income, we have fortified government finance. We have raised the public credit to a position of unsurpassed security. The interest rate on Government bonds has been reduced to the lowest point in twenty-eight years. The same Government bonds which in 1932 sold under 83 are now selling over 104.

We approve the objective of a permanently sound currency so stabilized as to prevent the former wide fluctuations in value which injured in turn producers, debtors, and property owners on the one hand, and wage-earners and creditors on the other, a currency which will permit full utilization of the country's resources. We assert that today we have the soundest currency in the world.

We are determined to reduce the expenses of government. We are being aided therein by the recession in unemployment. As the requirements of relief decline and national income advances, an increasing percentage of Federal expenditures can and will be met from current revenues, secured from taxes levied in accordance with ability to pay. Our retrenchment, tax and recovery programs thus reflect our firm determination to achieve a balanced budget and the reduction of the national debt at the earliest possible moment.

FOREIGN POLICY

In our relationship with other nations, this Government will continue to extend the policy of the Good Neighbor. We reaffirm our opposition to war as an instrument of national policy, and declare that disputes between nations should be settled by peaceful means. We shall continue to observe a true neutrality in the disputes of others; to be prepared, resolutely to resist aggression against ourselves; to work for peace and to take the profits out of war; to guard against being drawn, by political commitments, international banking or private trading, into any war which may develop anywhere.

We shall continue to foster the increase in our foreign trade which has been achieved by this administration; to seek by mutual agreement the lowering of those tariff barriers, quotas and embargoes which have been raised against our exports of agricultural and industrial products; but continue as in the past to give adequate protection to our farmers and manufacturers against unfair competition or the dumping on our shores of commodities and goods produced abroad by cheap labor or subsidized by foreign governments.

THE ISSUE

The issue in this election is plain. The American people are called upon to choose between a Republican administration that has and would again regiment them in the service of privileged groups and a Democratic administration dedicated to the establishment of equal economic opportunity for all our people.

We have faith in the destiny of our nation. We are sufficiently endowed with natural resources and with productive capacity to provide for all a quality of life that meets the standards of real Americanism.

Dedicated to a government of liberal American principles, we are determined to oppose equally, the despotism of Communism and the menace of concealed Fascism.

We hold this final truth to be self-evident — that the interests, the security and the happiness of the people of the United States of America can be perpetuated only under democratic government as conceived by the founders of our nation.

Republican Platform

America is in peril. The welfare of American men and women and the future of our youth are at stake. We dedicate ourselves to the preservation of their political liberty, their individual opportunity and their character as free citizens, which today for the first time are threatened by Government itself.

For three long years the New Deal Administration has dishonored American traditions and flagrantly betrayed the pledges upon which the Democratic Party sought and received public support.

The powers of Congress have been usurped by the President.

The integrity and authority of the Supreme Court have been flouted.

The rights and liberties of American citizens have been violated.

Regulated monopoly has displaced free enterprise.

The New Deal Administration constantly seeks to usurp the rights reserved to the States and to the people.

It has insisted on the passage of laws contrary to the Constitution.

It has intimidated witnesses and interfered with the right of petition.

It has dishonored our country by repudiating its most sacred obligations.

It has been guilty of frightful waste and extravagance, using public funds for partisan political purposes.

It has promoted investigations to harass and intimidate American citizens, at the same time denying investigations into its own improper expenditures.

It has created a vast multitude of new offices, filled them with its favorites, set up a centralized bureaucracy, and sent out swarms of inspectors to harass our people.

It has bred fear and hesitation in commerce and industry, thus discouraging new enterprises, preventing employment and prolonging the depression.

It secretly has made tariff agreements with our foreign competitors, flooding our markets with foreign commodities.

It has coerced and intimidated voters by withholding relief to those opposing its tyrannical policies.

It has destroyed the morale of our people and made them dependent upon government.

Appeals to passion and class prejudice have replaced reason and tolerance.

To a free people, these actions are insufferable. This campaign cannot be waged on the traditional differences between the Republican and Democratic parties. The responsibility of this election transcends all previous political divisions. We invite all Americans, irrespective of party, to join us in defense of American institutions.

CONSTITUTIONAL GOVERNMENT AND FREE ENTERPRISE

We pledge ourselves:

1. To maintain the American system of Constitutional and local self government, and to resist all attempts to impair the authority of the Supreme Court of the United States, the final protector of the rights of our citizens against the arbitrary encroachments of the legislative and executive branches of government. There can be no individual liberty without an independent judiciary.

2. To preserve the American system of free enterprise, private competition, and equality of opportunity, and to seek its constant betterment in the interests of all.

REEMPLOYMENT

The only permanent solution of the unemployment problem is the absorption of the unemployed by industry and agriculture. To that end, we advocate:

Removal of restrictions on production. Abandonment of all New Deal policies that raise production costs, increase the cost of living, and thereby restrict buying, reduce volume and prevent reemployment. Encouragement instead of hindrance to legitimate business.

Withdrawal of government from competition with private payrolls. Elimination of unnecessary and hampering regulations.

Adoption of such other policies as will furnish a chance for individual enterprise, industrial expansion, and the restoration of jobs.

RELIEF

The necessities of life must be provided for the needy, and hope must be restored pending recovery. The administration of relief is a major failing of the New Deal. It has been faithless to those who must deserve our sympathy. To end confusion, partisanship, waste and incompetence, we pledge:

1. The return of responsibility for relief administration to nonpolitical local agencies familiar with community problems.

2. Federal grants-in-aid to the States and territories while the need exists, upon compliance with these conditions: (a) a fair proportion of the total relief burden to be provided from the revenues of States and local governments; (b) all engaged in relief administration to be selected on the basis of merit and fitness; (c) adequate provision to be made for the encouragement of those persons who are trying to become self-supporting.

3. Undertaking of Federal public works only on their merits and separate from the administration of relief.

4. A prompt determination of the facts concerning relief and unemployment.

SECURITY

Real security will be possible only when our productive capacity is sufficient to furnish a decent standard of living for all American families and to provide a surplus for future needs and contingencies. For the attainment of that ultimate objective, we look to the energy, self-reliance and character of our people, and to our system of free enterprise.

Society has an obligation to promote the security of the people, by affording some measure of protection against involuntary unemployment and dependency in old age. The New Deal policies, while purporting to provide social security, have, in fact, endangered it.

We propose a system of old age security, based upon the following principles:

1. We approve a pay-as-you-go policy, which requires of each generation the support of the aged and the determination of what is just and adequate.

2. Every American citizen over sixty-five should receive the supplementary payment necessary to provide a minimum income sufficient to protect him or her from want.

3. Each state and territory, upon complying with simple and general minimum standards, should receive from the federal government a graduated contribution in proportion to its own, up to a fixed maximum.

4. To make this program consistent with sound fiscal policy the Federal revenues for this purpose must be provided from the proceeds of a direct tax widely distributed. All will be benefited and all should contribute.

We propose to encourage adoption by the states and territories of honest and practical measures for meeting the problems of unemployment insurance.

The unemployment insurance and old age annuity sections of the present Social Security Act are unworkable and deny benefits to about two-thirds of our adult population, including professional men and women and all those engaged in agriculture and domestic service, and the self employed while imposing heavy tax burdens upon all. The so-called reserve fund estimated at forty-seven billion dollars for old age insurance is no reserve at all, because the fund will contain nothing but the Government's promise to pay, while the taxes collected in the guise of premiums will be wasted by the Government in reckless and extravagant political schemes.

LABOR

The welfare of labor rests upon increased production and the prevention of exploitation. We pledge ourselves to:

Protect the right of labor to organize and to bargain collectively through representatives of its own choosing without interference from any source.

Prevent governmental job holders from exercising autocratic powers over labor.

Support the adoption of state laws and interstate compacts to abolish sweatshops and child labor, and to protect women and children with respect to maximum hours, minimum wages and working conditions. We believe that this can be done within the Constitution as it now stands.

AGRICULTURE

The farm problem is an economic and social, not a partisan problem, and we propose to treat it accordingly. Following the wreck of the restrictive and coercive A.A.A., the New Deal Administration has taken to itself the principles of the Republican Policy of soil conservation and land retirement. This action opens the way for a non-political and permanent solution. Such a solution cannot be had under a New Deal Administration which misuses the program to serve partisan ends, to promote scarcity and to limit by coercive methods the farmer's control over his own farm.

Our paramount object is to protect and foster the family type of farm, traditional in American life, and to promote policies which will bring about an adjustment of agriculture to meet the needs of domestic and foreign markets. As an emergency measure, during the agricultural depression, federal benefits payments or grants-in-aid when administered within the means of the Federal government are consistent with a balanced budget.

We propose:

1. To facilitate economical production and increased consumption on a basis of abundance instead of scarcity.

2. A national land-use program, including the acquisition of abandoned and non-productive farm lands by voluntary sale or lease, subject to approval of the legislative and executive branches of the States concerned, and the devotion of such land to appropriate public use, such as watershed protection and flood prevention, reforestation, recreation, and conservation of wild life.

3. That an agricultural policy be pursued for the protection and restoration of the land resources, designed to bring about such a balance between soil-building and soil-depleting crops as will permanently insure productivity, with reasonable benefits to cooperating farmers on family-type farms, but so regulated as to eliminate the New Deal's destructive policy towards the dairy and live-stock industries.

4. To extend experimental aid to farmers developing new crops suited to our soil and climate.

5. To promote the industrial use of farm products by applied science.

6. To protect the American farmer against the importation of all live stock, dairy, and agricultural products, substitutes thereof, and derivatives therefrom, which will depress American farm prices.

7. To provide effective quarantine against imported live-stock, dairy and other farm products from countries which do not impose health and sanitary regulations fully equal to those required of our own producers.

8. To provide for ample farm credit at rates as low as those enjoyed by other industries, including commodity and live-stock loans, and preference in land loans to the farmer acquiring or refinancing a farm as a home.

9. To provide for decentralized, non-partisan control of the Farm Credit Administration and the election by National Farm Loan Associations of at least one-half of each Board of Directors of the Federal Land Banks, and thereby remove these institutions from politics.

10. To provide in the case of agricultural products of which there are exportable surpluses, the payment of reasonable benefits upon the domestically consumed portion of such crops in order to make the tariff effective. These payments are to be limited to the production level of the family type farm.

11. To encourage and further develop cooperative marketing.

12. To furnish Government assistance in disposing of surpluses in foreign trade by bargaining for foreign markets selectively by countries both as to exports and imports. We strenuously oppose so-called reciprocal treaties which trade off the American farmer.

13. To give every reasonable assistance to producers in areas suffering from temporary disaster, so that they may regain and maintain a self-supporting status.

TARIFF

Nearly sixty percent of all imports into the United States are now free of duty. The other forty percent of imports compete directly with the product of our industry. We would keep on the free list all products not grown or produced in the United States in commercial quantities. As to all commodities that commercially compete with our farms, our forests, our mines, our fisheries, our oil wells, our labor and our industries, sufficient protection should be maintained at all times to defend the American farmer and the American wage earner from the destructive competition emanating from the subsidies of foreign governments and the imports from low-wage and depreciated-currency countries.

We will repeal the present Reciprocal Trade Agreement Law. It is futile and dangerous. Its effect on agriculture and industry has been destructive. Its continuation would work to the detriment of the wage earner and the farmer.

We will restore the principle of the flexible tariff in order to meet changing economic conditions here and abroad and broaden by careful definition the powers of the Tariff Commission in order to extend this policy along nonpartisan line s.

We will adjust tariffs with a view to promoting international trade, the stabilization of currencies, and the attainment of a proper balance between agriculture and industry.

We condemn the secret negotiations of reciprocal trade treaties without public hearing or legislative approval.

MONOPOLIES

A private monopoly is indefensible and intolerable. It menaces and, if continued, will utterly destroy constitutional government and the liberty of the citizen.

We favor the vigorous enforcement of the criminal laws, as well as the civil laws, against monopolies and trusts and their officials, and we demand the enactment of such additional legislation as is necessary to make it impossible for private monopoly to exist in the United States.

We will employ the full powers of the government to the end that monopoly shall be eliminated and that free enterprise shall be fully restored and maintained.

REGULATION OF BUSINESS

We recognize the existence of a field within which governmental regulation is desirable and salutary. The authority to regulate should be vested in an independent tribunal acting under clear and specific laws establishing definite standards. Their determinations on law and facts should be subject to review by the Courts. We favor Federal regulation, within the Constitution, of the marketing of securities to protect investors. We favor also Federal regulation of the interstate activities of public utilities.

CIVIL SERVICE

Under the New Deal, official authority has been given to inexperienced and incompetent persons. The Civil Service has been sacrificed to create a national political machine. As a result the Federal Government has never presented such a picture of confusion and inefficiency.

We pledge ourselves to the merit system, virtually destroyed by New Deal spoilsmen. It should be restored, improved and extended.

We will provide such conditions as offer an attractive permanent career in government service to young men and women of ability, irrespective of party affiliations.

GOVERNMENT FINANCE

The New Deal Administration has been characterized by shameful waste, and general financial irresponsibility. It has piled deficit upon deficit. It threatens national bankruptcy and the destruction through inflation of insurance policies and savings bank deposits.

We pledge ourselves to:

Stop the folly of uncontrolled spending.

Balance the budget — not by increasing taxes but by cutting expenditures, drastically and immediately.

Revise the federal tax system and coordinate it with state and local tax systems.

Use the taxing power for raising revenue and not for punitive or political purposes.

MONEY AND BANKING

We advocate a sound currency to be preserved at all hazards.

The first requisite to a sound and stable currency is a balanced budget.

We oppose further devaluation of the dollar.

We will restore to the Congress the authority lodged with it by the Constitution to coin money and regulate the value thereof by repealing all the laws delegating this authority to the Executive.

We will cooperate with other countries toward stabilization of currencies as soon as we can do so with due regard for our National interests and as soon as other nations have sufficient stability to justify such action.

FOREIGN AFFAIRS

We pledge ourselves to promote and maintain peace by all honorable means not leading to foreign alliances or political commitments.

Obedient to the traditional foreign policy of America and to the repeatedly expressed will of the American people, we pledge that America shall not become a member of the League of Nations nor of the World Court nor shall America take on any entangling alliances in foreign affairs.

We shall promote, as best means of securing and maintaining peace by the pacific settlement of disputes, the great cause of international arbitration through the establishment of free, independent tribunals, which shall determine such disputes in accordance with law, equity and justice.

NATIONAL DEFENSE

We favor an army and navy, including air forces, adequate for our National Defense.

We will cooperate with other nations in the limitation of armaments and control of traffic in arms.

BILL OF RIGHTS

We pledge ourselves to preserve, protect and defend, against all intimidation and threat, freedom of religion, speech, press and radio; and the right of assembly and petition and immunity from unreasonable searches and seizures.

We offer the abiding security of a government of laws as against the autocratic perils of a government of men.

FURTHERMORE

1. We favor the construction by the Federal Government of head-water storage basins to prevent floods, subject to the approval of the legislative and executive branches of the government of the States whose lands are concerned.

2. We favor equal opportunity for our colored citizens. We pledge our protection of their economic status and personal safety. We will do our best to further their employment in the gainfully occupied life of America, particularly in private industry, agriculture, emergency agencies and the Civil Service.

We condemn the present New Deal policies which would regiment and ultimately eliminate the colored citizen from the country's productive life, and make him solely a ward of the federal government.

3. To our Indian population we pledge every effort on the part of the national government to ameliorate living conditions for them.

4. We pledge continuation of the Republican policy of adequate compensation and care for veterans disabled in the service of our country and for their widows, orphans and dependents.

5. We shall use every effort to collect the war debt due us from foreign countries, amounting to $12,000,000 — one-third of our national debt. No effort has been made

by the present administration even to reopen negotiations.

6. We are opposed to legislation which discriminates against women in Federal and State employment.

CONCLUSION

We assume the obligations and duties imposed upon Government by modern conditions. We affirm our unalterable conviction that, in the future as in the past, the fate of the nation will depend, not so much on the wisdom and power of government, as on the character and virtue, self-reliance, industry and thrift of the people and on their willingness to meet the responsibilities essential to the preservation of a free society.

Finally, as our party affirmed in its first Platform in 1856: "Believing that the spirit of our institutions as well as the Constitution of our country guarantees liberty of conscience and equality of rights among our citizens we oppose all legislation tending to impair them," and "we invite the affiliation and cooperation of the men of all parties, however differing from us in other respects, in support of the principles herein declared."

The acceptance of the nomination tendered by the Convention carries with it, as a matter of private honor and public faith, an undertaking by each candidate to be true to the principles and program herein set forth.

Union Party Platform

1. America shall be self-contained and self-sustained — no foreign entanglements, be they political, economic, financial or military.

2. Congress and Congress alone shall coin and issue the currency and regulate the value of all money and credit in the United States through a central bank of issue.

3. Immediately following the establishment of the central bank of issue Congress shall provide for the retirement of all tax-exempt, interest-bearing bonds and certificates of indebtedness of the Federal Government and shall refinance all the present agricultural mortgage indebtedness for the farmer and all the home mortgage indebtedness for the farmer and all the home mortgage indebtedness for the city owner by the use of its money and credit which it now gives to the private bankers.

4. Congress shall legislate that there will be an assurance of a living annual wage for all laborers capable of working and willing to work.

5. Congress shall legislate that there will be an assurance of production at a profit for the farmer.

6. Congress shall legislate that there will be assurance of reasonable and decent security for the aged, who, through no fault of their own, have been victimized and exploited by an unjust economic system which has so concentrated wealth in the hands of a few that it has impoverished great masses of our people.

7. Congress shall legislate that American agricultural, industrial, and commercial markets will be protected from manipulation of foreign moneys and from all raw material and processed goods produced abroad at less than a living wage.

8. Congress shall establish an adequate and perfect defense for our country from foreign aggression either by air, by land, or by sea, but with the understanding that our naval, air, and military forces must not be used under any consideration in foreign fields or in foreign waters either alone or in conjunction with any foreign power. If there must be conscription, there shall be a conscription of wealth as well as a conscription of men.

9. Congress shall so legislate that all Federal offices and positions of every nature shall be distributed through civil-service qualifications and not through a system of party spoils and corrupt patronage.

10. Congress shall restore representative government to the people of the United States to preserve the sovereignty of the individual States of the United States by the ruthless eradication of bureaucracies.

11. Congress shall organize and institute Federal works for the conservation of public lands, waters, and forests, thereby creating billions of dollars of wealth, millions of jobs at the prevailing wage, and thousands of homes.

12. Congress shall protect small industry and private enterprise by controlling and decentralizing the economic domination of monopolies to the end that these small industries and enterprises may not only survive and prosper but that they may be multiplied.

13. Congress shall protect private property from confiscation through unnecessary taxation with the understanding that the human rights of the masses take precedence over the financial rights of the classes.

14. Congress shall set a limitation upon the net income of any individual in any one year and a limitation of the amount that such an individual may receive as a gift or as an inheritance, which limitation shall be executed through taxation.

15. Congress shall reestablish conditions so that the youths of the Nation, as they emerge from schools and colleges, will have the opportunity to earn a decent living while in the process of perfecting and establishing themselves in a trade or profession.

Radio Address by Reverend Charles E. Coughlin
New York, June 19, 1936

Father Coughlin, the politically minded priest from Royal Oak, Michigan who num-
bered his radio audience in the millions, chose the airwaves as the vehicle for an-
nouncing the formation of the Union Party. Since he often criticized the influence of
intellectuals in the New Deal, some thought it odd that he would stress his candidate's
Ivy League background in this speech.

Ladies and gentlemen, may I gratefully acknowledge that these broadcasting facilities have been extended to me by the Columbia Broadcasting System?

It is my purpose to engage your attention as I discuss, first, why I do not find it morally possible to support either the Republicans and their platform or the Democrats and their promises. Second, I shall make plain where the National Union for Social Justice, including myself, will stand in relation to the forthcoming elections in November of this year.

To clarify both of these answers permit me to preface my remarks which necessitated the establishment of a change in our progressive civilization.

In the Autumn of 1932 it was my privilege to address the American people on the causes of the so-called depression and upon the obvious remedies required to bring about a permanent recovery.

Those were days which witnessed a complete break down of the financial system under which our Western civilization had been developed. It was also evident that under this financial system there resulted a concentration of wealth and a multiplication of impoverished families. Unjust wages and unreasonable idleness were universally recognized as contradictions in an age of plenty. To my mind it was inconceivable that irrational and needless want should exist in an age of plenty.

Were there not plenty of raw materials in America? Were not our citizens and our countrysides inhabited by plenty of skilled inventors, engineers, executives, workmen and farmers? At no time in the history of civilization was it possible for man to produce such an abundant supply, thanks to the benedictions of mass production machinery. At no time within the last two centuries was there such a demand on the part of our population for the thousands of good things capable of being produced in our fields and in our factories.

What was the basic cause which closed factories, which created idleness, which permitted weeds to overrun our golden fields and plowshares to rust? There was and is but one answer. Some call it lack of purchasing power. Others, viewing the problem in a more philosophic light, recognize that the financial system which was able to function in an age of scarcity was totally inadequate to operate successfully in an age of plenty.

Let me explain this statement briefly: Before the nineteenth century the ox-cart, the spade and the crude instruments of production were handicaps to the rapid creation of real wealth.

By 1932 a new era of production had come into full bloom. It was represented by the motor car, the tractor and the power lathe, which enabled the laborer to produce wealth ten times more rapidly than was possible for his ancestors. Within the short expanse of 150 years the problem of production had been solved, due to the ingenuity of men like Arkwright and his loom, Fulton and his steam engine, and Edison and his dynamo. These and a thousand other benefactors of mankind made it possible for the teeming millions of people throughout the world to transfer speedily the raw materials into the thousand necessities and conveniences which fall under the common name of wealth.

Thus, with the advent of our scientific era, with its far-flung fields, its spacious factories, its humming motors, its thundering locomotives, its highly trained mechanics, it is inconceivable how such a thing as a so-called depression should blight the lives of an entire nation when there was a plenitude of everything surrounding us, only to be withheld from us because the so-called leaders of high finance persisted in clinging to an outworn theory of privately issued money, the medium through which wealth is distributed.

I challenged this private control and creation of money because it was alien to our Constitution, which says "Congress shall have the right to coin and regulate the value of money." I challenged this system of permitting a small group of private citizens to create money and credit out of nothing, to issue it into circulation through loans and to demand that borrowers repay them with money which represented real goods, real labor and real service. I advocated that it be replaced by the American system — namely, that the creation and control of money and credit are the rights of the people through their democratic government.

Has this American system of money creation and control been our practice?

Unfortunately, no. Our governments, through a policy of perversion and sub-terfuge, established, step by step, the Federal Reserve Banking System. Power was given to a handful of our fellow-citizens to create and control more than 90 per cent of all our money, mostly by a mere stroke of the fountain pen; to issue it into circulation as real legal tender; and to exact of the hundred and twenty-five million citizens the obligation of paying it back with interest, not through a stroke of the fountain pen but through arduous hours of toil, of sweat and of heartaches. Before the year 1932 very few persons fully realized the existence of this financial bondage.

Millions of citizens began asking the obvious questions: "Why should the farmer be forced to follow his plow at a loss?" "Why should the citizens — at least 90 per cent of them — be imprisoned behind the cruel bars of want when, within their grasp, there are plenty of shoes, of clothing, of motor cars, of refrigerators, to which they are entitled?"

As a result of these and similar questions, my friends, an intellectual revolution was generated in America. The moral problems of foods, of clothing, of shelter demanded a solution. The solution in democratic America must come from democratic legislation under the leadership of a sympathetic President who will initiate, in part, legislation and append his signature to just laws.

At last, when the most brilliant minds amongst the industrialists, bankers and their kept politicians had failed to solve the cause of the needless depression, there appeared upon the scene of our national life a new champion of the people, Franklin Delano Roosevelt! He spoke golden words of hope. He intimated to the American people that the system of permitting a group of private citizens to create money, then to issue it to the government as if it were real money, then to exact payment from the entire nation through a system of taxation earned by real labor and service, was immoral. With the whip of his scorn he castigated these usurers who exploited the poor. With his eloquent tongue he lashed their financial system which devoured the homes of widows and orphans.

No man in modern times received such plaudits from poor as did Franklin Roosevelt when he promised to drive the money changers from the temple — the money changers who had clipped the coins of wages, who had manufactured spurious money and who had brought proud America to her knees.

March 4, 1933! I shall never forget the inaugural address, which seemed to re-echo the very words employed by Christ Himself as He actually drove the money changers from the temple.

The thrill that was mine was yours. Through dim clouds of depression this man Roosevelt was, as it were, a new savior of his people!

Oh, just a little longer shall there be needless poverty! Just another year shall there be naked backs! Just another moment shall there be dark thoughts of revolution! Never again will the chains of economic poverty bite into the hearts of simple folks, as they did in the past days of the Old Deal!

Such were our hopes in the springtime of 1933.

My friends, what have we witnessed as the finger of time turned the pages of the calendar? Nineteen hundred and thirty-three and the National Recovery Act which multiplied profits for the monopolists; 1934 and the AAA which raised the price of foodstuffs by throwing back God's best gifts into His face; 1935 and the Banking Act which rewarded the exploiters of the poor, the Federal Reserve bankers and their associates, by handing over to them the temple from which they were to have been cast!

In 1936, when our disillusionment is complete, we pause to take inventory of our predicament. You citizens have shackled about your limbs a tax bill of $35,000,000,000, most of which, I repeat, was created by a flourish of a fountain pen. Your erstwhile savior, whose golden promises ring upon the counter of performance with the cheapness of tin, bargained with the money changers that, with seventy billion laboring hours in the ditch, or in the factory, or behind the plow, you and your children shall repay the debt which was created with a drop of ink in less than ten seconds.

Is that driving the money changers out of the temple?

Every crumb you eat, every stitch of clothing you wear, every menial purchase which you make is weighted down with an unseen tax as you work and slave for the debt merchants of America. But the $55,000,000,000 of debt bonds, held mostly by

the debt merchants and the well circumstanced of this country, have been ably safeguarded from taxation by this peerless leader who sham battles his way along the
avenue of popularity with his smile for the poor and his blindness for their plight.

Is that driving the money changers from the temple?

You laborers of America who work no more than an average of 200 days a
year at $5 a day are forced to contribute at least fifty days of your labor — to steal
it from your wives and your children, to deprive them of the conveniences and the
luxuries advertised in every paper and magazine — as tribute for the benefit of the
sacrosanct bondholders.

Is that driving the money changers from the temple?

You farmers of America, of whom 3,000 every week are driven over the hill
to the poorhouse through the ruthless confiscation which is still protected under the
guise of friendship, are forced to bear the burden of $8,000,000,000 of mortgage debt
on farms at 6 per cent — farms which have depreciated 50 per cent during these last
five years, farms which cannot be operated at a profit except temporarily through the
immoral Tugwellism of destruction.

Is that driving the money changers from the temple, or is it driving Americans
from their homes?

For God's command of "increase and multiply," spoken to our first parents, the
satanic principle of "decrease and devastate" has been substituted.

It is not pleasant for me who coined the phrase, "Roosevelt or ruin" — a phrase
fashioned upon promises — to voice such passionate words. But I am constrained to
admit that "Roosevelt and ruin" is the order of the day because the money changers
have not been driven from the temple.

My friends, I come before you tonight not to ask you to return to the Landons,
to the Hoovers, to the Old Deal exploiters who honestly defended the dishonest system
of gold standardism and rugged individualism. Their sun has set, never to rise again.

America has turned its back definitely upon the platitudinous platforms of
"ragged individualism." Who at Cleveland dared call into question the plutocratic
privilege enjoyed by the Federal Reserve bankers? Who among these moribund New
Deal critics dared campaign for an annual, decent wage for the laborer and production
at a profit for the farmer? Alas! These Punch and Judy Republicans, whose actions
and words were dominated by the ventriloquists of Wall Street, are so blind that they
do not recognize, even in this perilous hour, that their gold basis and their private
coinage of money have bred more radicals than did Karl Marx or Lenin. To their
system of ox-cart financialism we must never return!

Review the Landon platform with its proposal to revive the gold standard which succeeded in prostrating civilization. Hypocritically, it proposes the restoration to Congress of the right to coin and regulate money now held by the
President.

Pause to consider the colossal fraud that this insincere wording attempts to
perpetrate upon people of this country: "Restore to Congress the power of coining
and regulating money by repealing the laws relative to such now held by the
President!"

Why, every intelligent person must recognize that our objective is to restore to Congress its constitutional power to coin and regulate money, now held not by the President, not by the Secretary of the Treasury, but by the Federal Reserve Bank, a privately owned corporation.

On the other hand, the Democratic platform is discredited before it is published. Was there not a 1932 platform? By Mr. Roosevelt and its colleagues was it not regarded as a solemn pledge to the people? Certainly it was! And where is it today? Under the direction of Rexford Tugwell, the power and the brains behind the White House throne, it was plowed under like the cotton, slaughtered like the pigs.

What credence, therefore, can prudent citizens place in the poetic pledges to be pronounced at Philadelphia by the Democrats?

In the history of American literature it will take its place alongside Eugene O'Neill's "Strange Interlude." Its offstage remarks in 1936 are supposed to remain unheard by the American public. But, judging by the previous platform, we know that while security for the aged will be advocated aloud, prosperity for the poorhouse will be the whispered order.

Therefore, the veracity of the future upstage pledges must be judged by the echoings of the golden voice of a lost leader.

Said he, when the flag of hope was proudly unfurled on March 4, 1933: "Plenty is at our doorsteps, but the generous use of it languished in the very sight of the supply.... Primarily, this is because the rulers of the exchange of mankind's goods have failed through their own stubbornness and their own incompetence — have admitted their failure and abdicated. Practices of the unscrupulous, money changers stand indicted in the court of public opinion, rejected by the hearts and minds of men.

"True, they have tried, but their efforts have been cast in the pattern of an outworn tradition, Faced by failure of credit, they have proposed only the lending of more money."

These words, my friends, are not mine. These are the caustic, devastating words uttered by Franklin Delano Roosevelt on March 4, 1933, condemning Franklin Delano Roosevelt in November of 1936.

Alas! The temple still remains the private property of the money changers. The golden key has been handed over to them for safekeeping — the key which now is fashioned in the shape of a double cross.

Oh, would that another Milton could write the story of "Paradise Lost" to the people! Would that the blind bard could reconstruct the theme of "Paradise Regained" by the bankers!

Neither Old Dealer nor New Dealer, it appears, has courage to assail the international bankers, the Federal Reserve bankers. In common, both the leaders of the Republicans and the Democrats uphold the old money philosophy. Today in America there is only one political party — the banker's party. In common, both old parties are determined to sham battle their way through this November election with hope that millions of American citizens will be driven into the no-man's land of financial bondage.

My friend, there is a way out, a way to freedom! There is an escape from the dole standard of Roosevelt, the gold standard of Landon. No longer need you be targets in "no-man's land" for the financial crossfire of the sham-battlers!

Six hours ago the birth of "the Union party" was officially announced to the newspapers of the nation, thereby confirming information which hitherto was mine unofficially The new candidate for President, together with his sponsors, formally requested my support as they handed to me his platform. I have studied it carefully. I find that it is in harmony substantially with the principles of social justice.

As presented to me, this platform reads as if it were born in the hearts of a group of rebels.

If you think so, you are right in thinking so, because this group rebels against the bankers' bonds, their tax-exempt bonds, their radicalism and their financial slavery.

Who is the candidate for President of the Union party? He is one who has left his mark for erudition in the halls of Yale University and who already has carved for himself a niche of fame in the industrial and agricultural temple of America. He is a man who has made promises in the past and has kept them. He is a battler who has entered into fights and has fought them. He is an American and not an internationalist, a liberty lover and not a slave trader, who will fight for financial freedom as did his prototype, Lincoln, who waged war for physical freedom.

I refer to Congressman William Lemke of North Dakota, who has thrown his "cap" into the Presidential ring at the request of thousands of independent friends. Now that he has taken the step and has officially asked the National Union for its support, we declare him, on the strength of his platform and of his splendid record, eligible for indorsation.

He has chosen as a running mate for the Vice Presidency Thomas Charles O'Brien, eminent former District Attorney of Boston, counsel for the Brotherhood of Railroad Trainmen and firm exponent of social justice. For ten years before graduating from Harvard University Mr. O'Brien labored as a baggageman.

Lemke and Yale, Agriculture and Republican! O'Brien and Harvard, Labor and Democrat!

Protestant and Catholic, possessing one program of driving the money changers from the temple, of permitting the wealth of America to flow freely into every home!

The National Union still adheres firmly to its policy of endorsing and supporting candidates for Congress in any political party who have pledged allegiance to our principles.

Tonight it does not depart from its policy in endorsing the Union party candidate for President of the United States — a poor man who has worked with his hands against the hostile forces of nature and with his soul against the destructive forces of private money control.

God speed William Lemke and his friends as they proceed to file in each State!

This is a new day for America with its new "Union Party." Lemke has raised a banner of liberty for you to follow as you carry it unsullied into the ranks of the money changers' servants now occupying the White House and the halls of Congress.

Behind it will rally agriculture, labor, the disappointed Republicans and the outraged Democrats, the independent merchant and industrialist and every lover of liberty who desires to eradicate the cancerous growths from decadent capitalism and avoid the treacherous pitfalls of red communism.

"Why Labor Should Support the Socialist Party" by Norman Thomas in the *American Socialist Monthly* July, 1936

Norman Thomas, the presidential candidate of the Socialist Party, responded in this article to an earlier essay by John L. Lewis in which the head of the United Mine Workers and leader of the CIO had endorsed FDR. Thomas also refers to Sidney Hillman of the Amalgamated Clothing Workers. Hillman had supported Thomas in 1932 but was now allied with Lewis in Labor's Non-Partisan League behind Roosevelt.

This article is written with special reference to the brief and positive statement by John L. Lewis telling why labor should support Roosevelt. The case I want to present is much bigger than the support, or failure to support, any individual. I am arguing *for* something and not *against* someone. Least of all am I trying to raise the issue of the personal merits of myself or any other candidate as against Mr. Roosevelt.

Another word of preliminary explanation may be in order. I deeply appreciate the fact that Mr. Lewis has contributed a statement to the American Socialist Monthly. It is a good omen for the future, an evidence of a new point of view on his part, that he is willing to argue the case. I, in common with socialists generally, am a hundred per cent behind the efforts of the Committee for Industrial Organization to organize the unorganized on industrial lines. We are very hopeful for the success of that movement. Some time we expect to work with the leaders of that movement and the rank and file on the political front even as now we want to work with them on the economic front. I am not taking a Socialist-Labor Party position as against a Farmer-Labor Party. I share the hope of my comrades for the development of a Farmer-Labor Party that may be a genuine instrument in the emancipation of the workers.

The Party has declared itself officially on what the conditions are for a successful and genuine Farmer-Labor Party. I suspect that Mr. Lewis himself would admit that those conditions were not met by anything done at that recent conference at the Hotel Morrison or by the program which it laid down. There is therefore nothing except for those who are convinced socialists to make their own campaign. Anything else would be a kind of suicide, a confession that our socialist diagnosis and our socialist program were wrong. Mr. Lewis, I am sure, will not argue that Mr. Roosevelt has been a socialist or that he has offered the equivalent of Socialism to the workers, and I suspect that he is logical enough to agree that convinced socialists can scarcely support with good conscience a man who is trying to prolong capitalism by reforming it somewhat.

Mr. Lewis' position is that of an ardent labor man who is not a socialist; who takes stock of the reforms of advantage to labor which Roosevelt has brought about; who hopes for others that he may bring about, and then declares for the vital importance of reelecting Roosevelt. It will be observed that he has not declared for the Democratic Party but only for Mr. Roosevelt. However, he and his associates will have to vote for Roosevelt *and Garner*, and then, I suppose, pray whatever gods there are that they may spare the President's life so that we shall not get Garner! Loose as political affiliation is in the United States it is impossible to vote for Roosevelt without voting for the Democratic Party, and the Democratic Party is no vehicle for effective reform.

Even from a standpoint of mere immediate demands of a very moderate sort the position of Mr. Lewis and his friends is open to question at two points: first, as to the value of the things done or proposed by Mr. Roosevelt; second, as to the danger which threatens the country if Mr. Roosevelt should not be reelected.

Under the first head let me briefly call attention to some indisputable facts. Profits under the New Deal Administration have increased far faster than wages or employment. There are still, according to labor's own figures, around twelve million unemployed. The percentage of recovery of employment is lower in America than in many other capitalist countries without the blessings of Mr. Roosevelt. Average wages for average workers in terms of purchasing power stood still last year. Employment increased 2 1/2 per cent and, according to one set of figures, the profits of some 800 large corporations increased 47 per cent. Another set of figures using a different list of corporations gives the average increase as 36 per cent.

Before NRA was killed by the Supreme Court it left a great deal to be desired. Has Mr. Lewis forgotten that the Administration's settlements of disputes in the steel, the automobile and the rubber industries were in the main very favorable to the employers. Has he forgotten that the Administration did nothing to help the strikers in the Colt Arms plant in Hartford except to continue War Department orders to the firm whose workers struck after the Labor Board had declared that NRA had been violated?

Mr. Lewis, to his great credit, sent an investigator of his own into Arkansas. That investigator brought back a report of the desperate plight of sharecroppers and agricultural workers. In many ways they are worse, not better off, under this New Deal Administration. The beneficiaries of the agricultural program of the New Deal have been the landowners, the great planters. Thousands of the workers have simply been driven completely out of a job because of the reduction of acreage. Right now there is a desperate strike going on in Arkansas. That state is represented in the Senate by the Floor Leader of the Democratic Party, Mr. Roosevelt's personal friend for whose re-election he is about to make an appeal at a centenary celebration in Arkansas. But the record of the state in dealing with the strike is a record of brutality and injustice, some of it administered by mobs and some by courts. Whatever little benevolence the Administration may have intended in Arkansas and other cotton producing states has been frustrated by local committees of

Democrats and not a single promise made by the Administration for bettering conditions has been carried out. Evidently the President's friendship for labor does not extend to those who are not yet powerful enough to give him payment with interest for anything that he may do.

This judgment is confirmed when one considers that the President has repeatedly made Florida the base of his winter vacation without commenting on flogging and murder as a weapon of the dominant class in a Democratic state.

Mr. Lewis is familiar with the situation in Indiana. In Sullivan County, a coal mining county, for more than two years Governor McNutt maintained a bastard but very dangerous form of military law. Roosevelt never protested. As a matter of fact Governor McNutt is now the designated spokesman for Roosevelt at the great Convention of National Education Association in Portland, Oregon, in July.

When we turn from civil liberties to the world peace situation, the case against Mr. Roosevelt is even more complete. He has no real program of peace; no real program to take profit out of war or preparation for war; no adequate program for neutrality. He is giving us the greatest Army and Navy in our peacetime history. Under him we are spending about a billion dollars a year on military and naval establishments, and there are men who have avowed quite frankly that one purpose of the larger army is to keep labor in its place.

One of the chief indictments against Mr. Roosevelt is that his view of politics makes him less than candid in dealing with issues. He has denounced the Supreme Court without giving us the slightest hint of the kind of procedure he would use to curb the Court of the kind of amendment he wants to insert in the Constitution. It is by no means clear that his appointees to the Supreme Court bench will be a great improvement on what we now have. One of the likeliest first appointments will be that of Senator Robinson of Arkansas, representative of the cotton planting and public utility interests of that state, and a man as fundamentally illiberal as anyone now on the bench.

By contrast, bad as I think the Republican Party is, I doubt its power to end Federal relief or Federal aid to relief or the reverse some of the useful New Deal legislation which has not yet been upset by the Supreme Court. The Republican Party which wins will not be equivalent to the Liberty League. It will not present a solid front. It will still be necessary and possible to organize across party lines in Congress for the support of more or less liberal legislation. Moreover, Mr. Lewis may find that it will be easier in the face of Republican reaction to organize a militant Farmer-Labor Party than to do it in the face of Roosevelt's smile. Yet such a party is absolutely necessary because the Democratic Party without Roosevelt is at least as bad as the Republican. At best it will only be four more years that the Democratic Party will have Roosevelt. In anticipation of the fact that this is his last term some of his party may be pretty recalcitrant so that his own good intentions, whatever they may be, may not be very well carried out. Speaking of good intentions, of course I am writing before the Democratic Convention. Possibly the Platform may reveal the President's hand. But so far all we know is that he wants us to vote that he has done a good job and to trust him for the rest. That is not sound or satisfactory procedure in a democracy.

But, the alternative, Mr. Lewis may say, as Sidney Hillman did tell the Amalgamated Convention, is the Liberty League, and the Liberty League equals American fascism. That is not the case. The Liberty League represents reaction, the type of reaction that may help prepare the way for fascism, or which if it is successful enough will make fascism unnecessary. One of the worst things that Hillman, if not Lewis, is doing is to confuse the minds of the workers on the subject of fascism. The danger of fascism does not arise chiefly from sheer stark reaction such as the Liberty League magnates want. It arises from the demagogue who appeals to a dissatisfied middle-class and wears the garments of liberalism or radicalism. The Republican Party is not in any realistic sense as yet fascist. It still hopes to go back more or less to the times of Coolidge. The struggle against fascism is not a struggle against one or another type of capitalism primarily. It is a struggle for a cooperative commonwealth. It is a struggle which requires a fundamental education of workers and their organization in their own behalf. This is denied or delayed by the "trust Roosevelt" doctrine. When that "trust Roosevelt" doctrine is preached as intolerantly as Sidney Hillman preached it to the Amalgamated Convention; when such bitter abuse is showered on Joseph Schlossberg for not silently going along with the majority, the men responsible for such tactics in a labor union are helping to stir up the very mob mindedness to which the real fascist demagogue appeals.

Fascism in America will not call itself fascism. It will doubtless denounce European fascism along with communism and socialism. It will not talk the language of the Liberty League. It will not get the support of great business until a new economic catastrophe toward which we drift in spite of anything that Roosevelt has done or will do is upon us. Then some of the magnates will support fascism as a second choice or as an alternative to a cooperative commonwealth.

Against this danger of an American fascism arising out of economic catastrophe or out of new war — for a new war would mean fascism at home — the election of Roosevelt will be little protection. Indeed, it may even weaken our defenses by lulling the workers to a false security. The vital protection is the organization and education of the workers themselves, and that cannot be done by whooping it up for a good man in a bad party, a good man, moreover, who at best is doing nothing except to try to reform capitalism a little. The workers must achieve their own salvation. That requires them not to rally around a benefactor or support a Messiah but to organize in their own behalf economically and politically. Mr. Lewis knows that well enough in the economic field. He would never for an instant say that it was enough on the coal fields to support the good employer. Unless labor learns that there is a reasonably close analogy on the political field, labor will always be selling itself for a cheap price. And it will not always get even that low price.

We are justified by an appeal to history. In 1916 there seemed to be a very strong case for voting for Wilson because he kept us out of war. We got into war, into the same war into which Hughes would have led us. Repeatedly during the period before, Hitler finally took power the German workers felt that it was necessary to take less than they desired and to vote for a Hindenburg to keep out Hitler. They elected Hindenburg but they did not keep out Hitler. First they got Hindenburg, then Hindenburg helped give them Hitler, then Hindenburg died and they had Hitler alone. By the same token, the election of Roosevelt will neither prevent reaction nor fascism. The one hope of that lies in a clear-cut socialist program. It is not the Old Deal, not the New Deal which has failed. It is the capitalism of which both are the expression. There are immediate reforms worth while to labor, some of which have been imperfectly advocated by Mr. Roosevelt. But Germany which had all reforms possible within capitalism, Germany where the workers had won more rights, in so far as they can have rights under capitalism, than they have yet demanded in America, found that these reforms were not an adequate barrier to fascism. It is considerations like these which lead me to believe that this year more than ever before it is imperative to have a vigorous socialist campaign, to get the maximum of labor interest, labor understanding, labor support, labor votes for the Socialist Party. Only so is there reasonable hope that after the 1936 election there will emerge a Farmer-Labor Party of the right sort. These are the reasons why those of us who are enthusiastic supporters of the Committee for Industrial Organization cannot be supporters of Mr. Lewis' other committee, the Non-Partisan Committee for Roosevelt. Instead we have to declare our positive faith in Socialism, the hope of the world. To declare this faith is perfectly consistent with the advocacy of measures to strengthen labor on the march and to make war less likely. In this spirit we enter our great campaign.

Campaign Memorandum of Eleanor Roosevelt
from *The Roosevelt Letters,* July 16, 1936

Eleanor Roosevelt performed in 1936 the role that Louis Howe had played in previous campaigns. This memorandum reveals the First Lady's close attention to political detail.

To the President
 Mr. Farley
 Mr. Michelson
 Mr. High
 Mr. Early
 Miss Dewson:

I spent part of Tuesday afternoon and the morning of Wednesday at Democratic Headquarters. I had a conference with Miss Dewson and Mr. Farley; a conference with Mrs. Owen and Miss Dewson; and a conference with Mr. Michelson.

My impression is that the women are further along in their organization and more ready to go than any other unit as yet. I hear from outside sources that the Landon headquarters are set up and ready to work full time. They have continuity people writing for the radio, they have employed advertising people to do their copy, and the whole spirit is the spirit of a crusade.

My feeling is that we have to get going and going quickly, as I stated yesterday. I sat down and analyzed things which I thought necessary to organization. Some of the things I had in mind Mr. Michelson answered, a few things Mr. Farley answered for me at the time of the conference. I am putting them down again simply as a matter of record to get the answers in black and white.

I hope the answers will be mailed to reach us at Eastport, Maine, on the 27th or 28th of July, when the President expects to be there.

1. At the meeting in Washington, the President said that Mr. Michelson, Steve Early, Stanley High and Henry Suydam would constitute the publicity steering committee, and I take it this must include radio, speeches, movies, pamphlets, fliers, news releases and trucks or whatever news goes out to the public. This committee is extremely important.

Because of the importance of this committee, I hope a meeting will be held immediately for organizing and defining the duties of the members and that you will have the minutes kept at every meeting in order that a copy may go to the President and if the committee is willing, one to me as well so that I may know just what is done each time also.

2. Who is responsible for studying news reports and suggesting answers to charges, etc.?

3. Who is responsible, not for the mechanics of radio contracts for I understand you have a good man, but for the planning of a radio campaign, getting the speakers through the speakers' bureau, making the arrangements in the states for people to listen and getting in touch with Chester Davis, for instance on agriculture or any other people appointed as particular advisors on special subjects? In other words, who is making decisions under your committee on the above questions?

4. Who is in charge of research? Have we a department with complete information concerning all activities of the New Deal, and also concerning Landon and his supporters? If Miss Blackburn is in charge of this department as she was in the last campaign, have the heads of all campaign departments, men, women and young Democrats, been notified as to where to apply for information? This information should go out to the state committees also.

I gather if the President o.k.'s it, the aggressive campaign against Landon's record will begin before Landon's acceptance speech. Who is to collect and maintain the complete data up to date and to check on all inconsistencies in Landon's pronouncements or those of his campaign managers as they relate to his former statements or record? Is there adequate material on this now at hand?

5. What definite plans have we made for tying in the other publicity organizations, both of men and women with the national publicity organization? I feel that anything of importance should go directly from a member of your committee and from the women in charge of national publicity to every publicity person in charge in the states.

6. Have you mapped out continuous publicity steps which will be taken between now and November? Is there any way at least of charting a tentative plan of strategy for the whole campaign, changing of course, as new things occur?

7. In the doubtful and Republican states what special attention do you plan to give and have you collected any data as yet on these states?

8. Who is handling news reels and will it be a committee or just one person and will your committee direct the activities?

9. Has your committee assigned as yet to each member definite fields for supervision?

10. How many people are now working on campaign speeches, both for men, women and young Democrats? Who is going over them for criticism so they cover all the necessary subjects?

11. Who is your man making contacts with newspapers all over the country?

12. Who is responsible for sending regular news to friendly newspapers? By this I mean features stories, pictures, mats, boiler plate, etc.

I feel Mr. Rayburn should come at once to plan the policy and mechanics of the speakers' bureau. Then he could leave for a time.

I think it would be well to start some Negro speakers, like Mrs. Bethune to speak at church meetings and that type of Negro organization.

More and more my reports indicate that this is a close election and that we need very excellent organization. That is why I am trying to clarify in my own mind the functions at headquarters and have the President see a picture of the organization as clearly as possible in order that he may make any suggestions that he thinks necessary.

Address by Governor Alfred M. Landon
Chicago, October 9, 1936

Landon spoke at Chicago Stadium to twenty-five thousand of his followers, who cheered and whistled when he promised to balance the budget. The "British economist" to whom Landon refers is John Maynard Keynes, whose influence on the Administration was often exaggerated by critics of the New Deal.

Tonight I am going to talk about the Federal budget. And incidentally, I, too, am going to talk about it in billions.

First, let me make my position absolutely clear. If I am elected, the budget is going to be balanced. It is going to be balanced not be depriving our needy of relief, not by refusing necessary aid to our farmers, not by swamping the country with taxes.

The budget is going to be balanced by cutting out waste and extravagance; by putting an end to the use of public funds for political purposes; by restoring hard-working, painstaking, common-sense administration.

This question of balancing the budget is of vital importance to every man, woman and child in this country.

Let me give you three reasons why this is true.

It is true because "upon the financial stability of the United States Government depends the stability of trade and employment and of the entire banking, saving and insurance system of the country."

These words are not mine. They were spoken by Candidate Roosevelt at Pittsburgh four years ago.

It is true because "if the nation, like a spendthrift, throws discretion to the winds, is willing to make no sacrifice at all in spending, extends its taxing to the limit of the people's power to pay and continues to pile up deficits, it is on the road to bankruptcy."

Those words are not mine. They were also spoken by Candidate Roosevelt at Pittsburgh four years ago.

It is true because "taxes are paid in the sweat of every man who labors, because they are a burden on production.... If excessive, they are reflected in idle factories, tax-sold farms and in hordes of the hungry tramping the streets and seeking jobs in vain."

And those prophetic words are not mine. They were spoken by Candidate Roosevelt at Pittsburgh four years ago.

Those are three reasons why "I regard reduction in Federal spending as one of the most important issues of this campaign." Even those words are not mine. They were spoken by Candidate Roosevelt at Pittsburgh four years ago.

Now let us turn to the record. Let us see if Federal spending was reduced; if taxes were lowered; if deficits were stopped. Every one knows the answer, but it cannot be emphasized too much.

Four years ago the federal Government spent just over five billion dollars. Last year it spent just under nine billion dollars.

Four years ago the gross Federal debt was $21,000,000,000. Today it is $34,000,000,000.

Those are the facts. Instead of a decrease, we have had an enormous increase all along the line — an increase in spending, an increase in taxes, an increase in debt — all of which, as every housewife knows only too well, have increased the cost of living.

That is only a summary of what has happened to the financial pledges of Candidate Roosevelt. Now consider what has happened to the financial pledges of President Roosevelt.

Time after time we have been assured by the President and his spokesmen that no more taxes would be imposed. But under this administration fourteen bills increasing the tax burden have been jammed through Congress.

And as for his assurances that the budget would be balanced — well, these political hush-darlings have become annual fixtures. The first one was shortly after he took office in 1933. The next was in January, 1934. The next in January, 1935. The next in January, 1936. And the last at Pittsburgh two weeks ago. And this last, as usual, was accompanied by the promise that no more taxes would be necessary.

In other words, as usual, the President expressed the hope that some time, somehow, revenues will overtake expenditures. The way expenditures are running today, Jesse Owens himself could not overtake them.

That is the record. Instead of a balanced budget, we have a confession of incompetence — a confession by those in charge of our government that they have set loose a flood of spending that they are unable to stop.

Let us examine this policy of spending. Let us look at the theory used to justify it, the amounts involved, and the threat to the country if it is continued.

The simple and amazing theory behind this spending was sold to the administration by a British economist. He said that if only the United States Government would spend four hundred million dollars a month it would prime the pump and all would be well.

Of course, as a foreigner, he found ardent followers in this administration, although he had none in his own government. His formula was eagerly adopted, with one important change. The administration concluded that if four hundred million dollars a month for useful projects would be good medicine, six hundred million a month thrown around at random would be even better. So we started spending, not for the multitude of things we really needed, but for every conceivable thing. The lid was off. It is still off. We have been spending at the rate of six hundred million a month and more ever since.

Just consider what this meant. It meant making a special virtue of spending for spending's sake.

It meant saying to some eight hundred thousand government employees:

"Don't watch out for the resources of the government. Get rid of them as fast as possible."

What has been the result of this policy? In the three and one-third years ending June 30 last, the Federal Government spent more than twenty-five billion dollars. This was more than all of the Presidents of the United States from George Washington to Woodrow Wilson spent in one hundred and twenty-four years.

And what excuse does the President give for spending more than all the Presidents from Washington to Wilson? For ignoring his promises made at Pittsburgh four years ago — or perhaps we should say twenty-five billion dollars ago?

Speaking last week at Pittsburgh he said:

"We had to balance the budget of the American people before we could balance the budget of the national government." And then he added: "That makes common sense, doesn't it?"

This is a mighty melodious phrase, but, with 11,000,000 unemployed, with almost 20,000,000 people on the relief rolls, with the banks stuffed with government bonds, with the government spending double its income — this does not make common sense.

In his last speech, the President overlooked this record. That is not surprising. At least it is no more surprising than the method of bookkeeping adopted by this administration. For the first time in history — in war or in peace — in prosperity or in depression — the Treasury of the United States is keeping two sets of books.

This is the kind of bookkeeping we find when countries are faced with inflation or bankruptcy — when governments can stay in power only by deceiving the public. It is the kind of bookkeeping, for instance, from which the French people suffered during the serious inflation ten years ago.

Under such a system, items are transferred and retransferred, as they are by this administration, without rhyme or reason, from one set of books to the other. No definite line is drawn between ordinary expenditures and so-called emergency expenditures. No one, unless he is in the confidence of those who juggle the figures, can determine accurately what is going on. Of course, you can rely on the daily Treasury statement to present accurate figures. But, with the present mystery of the two sets of books, the secrecy surrounding the two-billion-dollar stabilization fund, and the juggling of revenue and expenditure items, not even an expert can obtain a clear picture of the exact condition of the United States Treasury.

But in spite of this system of bookkeeping, in spite of all this juggling of figures, there are certain facts that it has been impossible for this administration to hide. One of these facts is the vast increase in the ordinary routine cost of our government.

In 1934, the first full year of the present administration, the ordinary activities of the Federal Government, exclusive of debt retirement, cost $2,505,000,000. For the present year the estimated cost is $3,407,000,000 — an increase of $902,000,000.

In order to place these figures on a comparable basis, I have put the cost of the Veterans' Administration in 1934 at the 1937 figure, and I have eliminated all such new items as the bonus, Triple A, Civilian Conservation Corps and Social Security.

In other words, this nine hundred and two million dollar increase was purely and simply an increase in the ordinary routine expenses of the Federal Government — an increase of 36 per cent in the expenses which the Democratic platform, and the Democratic candidate of 1932, pledged to cut not less than 25 per cent. An administration that boasts of that record does not deserve another chance.

Now consider the so-called emergency expenditures.

In the name of emergency, this administration has created no less than seventy-five new bureaus, agencies and what-nots.

Certainly no one can seriously maintain that all of these conflicting bureaus are necessary. Neither can anyone seriously maintain that it is necessary for our government to have hundreds upon hundreds of press and publicity agents — hundreds upon hundreds of just plain barkers carrying on party propaganda at the expense of the taxpayer.

There is still another set of figures connected with emergency expenses that deserve attention. There are the expenditures classified as relief.

Now the fact of the matter is that since the NRA was kicked out there has been a substantial recovery in this country. Yet in spite of this, relief expenses keep right on increasing.

At the present time we are spending for so-called relief at the rate of $3,500,000,000 a year, or $1,500,000,000 more than in the fiscal year ending June 30, 1934. And still, in spite of all this spending, the administration has not redeemed its pledge to give every man on relief a job.

Now obviously there is something wrong here. Everybody knows what it is. A lot of the money spent in the name of relief had nothing to do with relief. And a lot of the money has been wasted.

If I am elected there will be an end to this spending of relief funds for other purposes,. There will be no more wholesale waste and extravagance. And there will be efficient administration of our public affairs. That is how the budget can be balanced — how it can be balanced without reducing by a single dollar the necessary payments to those actually in need.

The Federal Government has become a vast sieve through which taxpayers' money is being poured in constantly increasing volume.

Never in the history of government has there been such profligate spending. Anyone at all familiar with what has been going on could almost count on the fingers of one hand foolish experiments the government could cut out and save at least a billion dollars any time it wanted to.

What can ultimately be accomplished in the way of reduction it is impossible to determine, since detailed figures are not available, and future commitments are unrevealed.

But I mean to balance the budget. And I am not going to take four years to do it. With a reduction in government expenditures, I am convinced there will be such a rebirth of confidence that we will have a real recovery — the kind of recovery that means re-employment. That in turn, will not only reduce expenditures further, but will expand government income.

If the family incomes of this country are to be relieved from this intolerable burden — if the specter of inflation and bankruptcy is to be set at rest — a change of administration is absolutely imperative.

Election-eve repentance will not do. The give-me-another chance plea will not serve. No matter how sincere the good intentions of the present administration may be, they can never be translated into an effective program of economy.

The reasons for this are obvious: An administration which starts a policy of spending for spending's sake dares not stop it. An administration which creates a multitude of new offices, which embarks on all manner of new ventures, which spends money to keep itself in power, dares not risk the angry votes that would result from economy.

Today, our various governments, Federal, State and local, are taking, through taxation, almost 20 per cent of the national income. One-fifth of the average income of every man, woman and child in this country goes to the cost of government — one dollar out of every five.

This is altogether too much. But even this is not the whole story. In addition, they are spending enormous sums obtained by borrowing. When this borrowing is added to what government takes from us in taxes, we find it is spending 30 per cent of the national income, or a dollar and a half out of every five.

In the matter of borrowing the Federal Government is the outstanding offender. For every dollar the Federal Government has received since March, 1933, it has spent two dollars.

This is an appalling situation. It cannot be casually tossed aside — as the President attempted to do at Pittsburgh last week — with the explanation that the debts will be paid out of an increasing national income. When the government finances its costs by borrowing, it mortgages the future income of every family. And if our government is to remain honest its debts have to be paid. And they have to be paid, not out of some impersonal fund known as "national income," but "In the sweat of every man that labors."

We cannot — we must not — place this burden upon our children. We must remember that they too, may have emergencies. We must make it possible for them to live their lives without having to pay for the financial follies of their parents.

Every generation the necessary activities of government increase. This is inevitable because of the increasing complexity of civilization. Unless we watch carefully every penny we spend, unless we cut out every trace of waste and extravagance, these necessary activities are going to suffer. Every dollar that is spent foolishly means a dollar less for the things that are necessary and wise.

Let me quote once more the words of the President. In March, 1933, he said:

"Too often in recent history liberal governments have been wrecked on the rocks of loose fiscal policy."

He spoke truly. A loose fiscal policy — and that is certainly a polite term for what we have today — will wreck any government. It will wreck the government of the United States unless we stop it. We must put the spenders out. For remember: those who preach spending, practice spending and brag about spending, cannot stop spending. This is the lesson of history. That is the record of this administration. They are proud of their spending. They talk of it as though preserving the financial integrity of the United States were only a game.

The American people know that it is more than a game — that our very existence depends upon keeping our financial house in order. But if the administration wants a baseball analogy — if they want the score — it is easy to give. It is written clear across this country:

Twenty-five billion dollars spent.

Thirteen billion dollars added to the public debt.

Eleven million unemployed left on base.

Extemporaneous Remarks by President Franklin D. Roosevelt
The *Emporia* (Kansas) *Gazette*, October 13, 1936

When his campaign train reached Emporia, Kansas, the President directed these genial remarks to William Allen White, the country's best-known small-town editor. White supported much of the New Deal but was a loyal Republican partisan who, in this campaign, served as one of Landon's aides.

My friends, I am very glad to come to Emporia. But I do not see Bill White. (*Laughter, applause.*)

I wish he were here because I have known him for a great many years, and he is a very old friend of mine. He is a very good friend of mine for three and a half years out of every four years.

(*Somebody in the audience said that Mr. White was in the audience and coming up. The President said, "Where is he?" Mr. White then came toward the rear platform.*)

Hello, Bill, glad to see you. Come on over here. How are you?

Now that I see him, I shall not say anything about the other six months. (*Laughter, applause.*)

You get so much politics in Emporia both ways that you do not need any political speech, but I do want to say this: I have been tremendously impressed all through this summer and autumn with the great interest that is being taken by the voters of the United States in national problems. It has been demonstrated in the last week or two by an increased registration and by increased enrollments. I am quite confident that we shall have several million more voters go to the polls this election day. That is entirely as it should be. I believe also that the people, more and more, are making up their own minds. They are not believing everything that is said to them; and I am quite certain that they are not believing everything they read.

(Audience: "No.")

In other words, they are winnowing out the chaff from the grain; and it is a fine thing that the public in this country is taking such an interest in its own Government.

Yes, the people are not being swayed this year by some of the things that have swayed them in the past because, taking them by and large, our economic problems are in far better shape than they were four years ago. I think they are sounder than they have been for a great many years.

Certainly everything I have seen on this trip makes me know down in the bottom of my heart that the people appreciate that things are better and are sounder. We have a little more time than we had in those days to make up our minds about things. Thank the Lord, we are going into this election with a smile on our faces.

The bitterness that comes up every four years in our American system of government does not last and that is good too.

And so, my friends, I am very glad to have had the chance to stop here. I always wish on these trips that I could go through by motor instead of by train; that I could talk to more people; that I could see more of the problems of industry and agriculture at first hand.

I think I must have been preordained for the career of the commercial traveler because I like to travel so much. It is one of the great privileges of the Presidency that I have the opportunity to go around this country so that I may get a first-hand picture of conditions.

Some day I hope I shall be able to come back to Emporia and spend a little more time with you and, when I get back, it may be in one of those three-and-a-half-year periods when Bill White is with me.

(The President then turned to Mr. White and said, "How are you? All right?" to which Mr. White replied, "Fine." There was a great deal of applause when the President shook hands with Mr. White.)

Address by President Franklin D. Roosevelt
Chicago, October 14, 1936

An estimated 150,000 people marched from Chicago's Union Station, where the President arrived, to the Chicago Stadium to hear him speak. In his address, the President boasted of the economic gains his Administration had secured, a theme that he alternated with appeals to class differences during the campaign.

Mr. Chairman, Governor Horner, Mayor Kelly, my friends
of the great State of Illinois:

I seem to have been here before. Four years ago I dropped into this city from the airways — an old friend come in a new way — to accept in this hall the nomination for the Presidency of the United States. I came to a Chicago fighting with its back to the wall — factories closed, markets silent, banks shaky, ships and trains empty. Today those factories sing the song of industry; markets hum with bustling movement; banks are secure; ships and trains are running full. Once again it is Chicago as Carl Sandburg saw it — "The City of the big shoulders" — the city that smiles. And with Chicago a whole Nation that had not been cheerful for years is full of cheer once more.

On this trip through the Nation I have talked to farmers, I have talked to miners, I have talked to industrial workers; and in all that I have seen and heard one fact has been clear as crystal — that they are part and parcel of a rounded whole, and that none of them can succeed in his chosen occupation if those in the other occupations fail in their prosperity. I have driven home that point.

Tonight, in this center of business, I give the same message to the business men of America — to those who make and sell the processed goods the Nation uses and to the men and women who work for them.

To them I say:

Do you have a deposit in the bank? It is safer today than it has ever been in our history. It is guaranteed. Last October 1st marked the end of the first full year in fifty-five years without a single failure of a national bank in the United States. Is that not on the credit side of the Government's account with you?

Are you an investor? Your stocks and bonds are up to five- and six-year high levels.

Are you a merchant? Your markets have the precious life-blood of purchasing power. Your customers on the farms have better incomes and smaller debts. Your customers in the cities have more jobs, surer jobs, better jobs. Did not your Government have something to do with that?

Are you in industry? Industrial earnings, industrial profits are the highest in four, six, or even seven years! Bankruptcies are at a new low. Your Government takes some credit for that.

Are you in railroads? Freight loadings are steadily going up. Passenger receipts are steadily going up — have in some cases doubled — because your Government made the railroads cut rates and make money.

Are you a middleman in the great stream of farm products? The meat and grain that move through your yards and elevators have a steadier supply, a steadier demand and steadier prices than you have known for years. And your Government is trying to keep it that way.

Some people say that all this recovery has just happened. But in a complicated modern world recoveries from depressions do not just happen. The years from 1929 to 1933, when we waited for recovery just to happen, prove the point.

But in 1933 we did not wait. We acted. Behind the growing recovery of today is a story of deliberate Government acceptance of responsibility to save business, to save the American system of private enterprise and economic democracy — a record unequaled by any modern Government in history.

What had the previous Administration in Washington done for four years? Nothing. Why? For a very fundamental reason. That Administration was not industrially-minded or agriculturally-minded or business-minded. It was high-finance-minded — manned and controlled by a handful of men who in turn controlled and by one financial device or another took their toll from the greater part of all other business and industry.

Let me make one simple statement. When I refer to high finance I am not talking about all great bankers, or all great corporation executives, or all multimillionaires — any more than Theodore Roosevelt, in using the term "malefactors of great wealth," implied that all men of great wealth were "malefactors." I do not even imply that the majority of them are bad citizens. The opposite is true.

Just in the same way, the overwhelming majority of business men in this country are good citizens and the proportion of those who are not is probably about the same proportion as in the other occupations and professions of life.

When I speak of high finance as a harmful factor in recent years, I am speaking about a minority which includes the type of individual who speculates with other people's money — and you in Chicago know the kind I refer to — and also the type of individual who says that popular government cannot be trusted and, therefore, that the control of business of all kinds and, indeed, of Government itself should be vested in the hands of one hundred or two hundred all-wise individuals controlling the purse strings of the Nation.

High finance of this type refused to permit Government credit to go directly to the industrialist, to the business man, to the homeowner, to the farmer. They wanted it to trickle down from the top, through the intricate arrangements which they controlled and by which they were able to levy tribute on every business in the land.

They did not want interest rates to be reduced by the use of Government funds, for that would affect the rate of interest which they themselves wanted to charge. They did not want Government supervision over financial markets through which they manipulated their monopolies with other people's money.

And in the face of their demands that Government do nothing that they called "unsound," the Government, hypnotized by its indebtedness to them, stood by and let the depression drive industry and business toward bankruptcy.

America is an economic unit. New means and methods of transportation and communications have made us economically as well as politically a single Nation.

Because kidnappers and bank robbers could in high-powered cars speed across state lines it became necessary, in order to protect our people, to invoke the power of the Federal Government. In the same way speculators and manipulators from across State lines, and regardless of State laws, have lured the unsuspecting and the unwary to financial destruction. In the same way across State lines, there have been built up intricate corporate structures, piling bond upon stock and stock upon bond — huge monopolies which were stifling independent business and private enterprise.

There was no power under Heaven that could protect the people against that sort of thing except a people's Government at Washington. All that this Administration has done, all that it proposes to do — and this it does propose to do — is to use every power and authority of the Federal Government to protect the commerce of America from the selfish forces which ruined it.

Always, month in and month out, during these three and a half years, your Government has had but one sign on its desk — "Seek only the greater good of the greater number of Americans." And in appraising the record, remember two things. First, this Administration was called upon to act after a previous Administration and all the combined forces of private enterprise had failed. Secondly, in spite of all the demand for speed, the complexity of the problem and all the vast sums of money involved, we have had no Teapot Dome.

We found when we came to Washington in 1933, that the business and industry of the Nation were like a train which had gone off the rails into a ditch. Our first job was to get it out of the ditch and start it up the track again as far as the repair shops. Our next job was to make repairs — on the broken axles which had gotten it off the road, on the engine which had been worn down by gross misuse.

What was it that the average business man wanted Government to do for him — to do immediately in 1933?

1. Stop deflation and falling prices — and we did it.

2. Increase the purchasing power of his customers who were industrial workers in the cities — and we did it.

3. Increase the purchasing power of his customers on the farms — and we did it.

4. Decrease interest rates, power rates and transportation rates — and we did it.

5. Protect him from the losses due to crime, bank robbers, kidnappers, blackmailers — and we did it.

How did we do it? By a sound monetary policy which raised prices. By reorganizing the banks of the Nation and insuring their deposits. By bringing the business men of the Nation together and encouraging them to pay higher wages, to shorten working hours, and to discourage that minority among their own members who were engaging in unfair competition and unethical business practices.

Through the A.A.A., through our cattle-buying program, through our program of drought relief and flood relief, through the Farm Credit Administration, we raised the income of the customers of business who lived on the farms. By our program to provide work for the unemployed, by our C.C.C. camps, and other measures, greater purchasing power was given to those who lived in our cities.

Money began going round again. The dollars paid out by Government were spent in the stores and shops of the Nation; and spent again to the wholesaler; and spent again to the factory; and spent again to the wage earner; and then spent again in another store and shop. The wheels of business began to turn again; the train was back on the rails.

Mind you, it did not get out of the ditch itself, it was hauled out by your Government.

And we hauled it along the road. P.W.A., W.P.A., both provided normal and useful employment for hundreds of thousands of workers. Hundreds of millions of dollars got into circulation when we liquidated the assets of closed banks through the Reconstruction Finance Corporation; millions more when we loaned money for home building and home financing through the Federal Housing program; hundreds of millions more in loans and grants to enable municipalities to build needed improvements; hundreds of millions more through the C.C.C. camps.

I am not going to talk tonight about how much our program to provide work for the unemployed meant to the Nation as a whole. That cannot be measured in dollars and cents. It can be measured only in terms of the preservation of the families of America.

But so far as business goes, it can be measured in terms of sales made and goods moving.

The train of American business is moving ahead.

But you people know what I mean when I say it is clear that if the train is to run smoothly again the cars will have to be loaded more evenly. We have made a definite start in getting the train loaded more evenly, in order that axles may not break again.

For example, we have provided a sounder and cheaper money market and a sound banking and securities system. You business men know how much legitimate business you lost in the old days because your customers were robbed by fake securities or impoverished by shaky banks.

By our monetary policy we have kept prices up and lightened the burden of debt. It is easier to get credit. It is easier to repay.

We have encouraged cheaper power for the small factory owner to lower his cost of production.

We have given the business man cheaper transportation rates.

But above all, we have fought to break the deadly grip which monopoly has in the past been able to fasten on the business of the Nation.

Because we cherished our system of private property and free enterprise and were determined to preserve it as the foundation of our traditional American system, we recalled the warning of Thomas Jefferson that "widespread poverty and concentrated wealth cannot long endure side by side in a democracy."

Our job was to preserve the American ideal of economic as well as political democracy, against the abuse of concentration of economic power that had been insidiously growing up among us in the past fifty years, particularly during the twelve years of preceding Administrations. Free economic enterprise was being weeded out at an alarming pace.

During those years of false prosperity and during the more recent years of exhausting depression, one business after another, one small corporation after another, their resources depleted, had failed or had fallen into the lap of a bigger competitor.

A dangerous thing was happening. Half of the industrial corporate wealth of the country had come under the control of less than two hundred huge corporations. That is not all. These huge corporations in some cases did not even try to compete with each other. They themselves were tied together by interlocking directors, interlocking bankers, interlocking lawyers.

This concentration of wealth and power has been built upon other people's money, other people's business, other people's labor. Under this concentration independent business was allowed to exist only by sufferance. It has been a menace to the social system as well as to the economic system which we call American democracy.

There is no excuse for it in the cold terms of industrial efficiency.

There is no excuse for it from the point of view of the average investor.

There is no excuse for it from the point of view of the independent business man.

I believe, I have always believed, and I will always believe in private enterprise as the backbone of economic well-being in the United States.

But I know, and you know, and every independent business man knows, that this concentration of economic power in all-embracing corporations does not represent private enterprise as we Americans cherish it and propose to foster it. On the contrary, it represents private enterprise which has become a kind of private government, a power unto itself — a regimentation of other people's money and other people's lives.

Back in Kansas I spoke about bogey-men and fairy tales which the real Republican leaders, many of whom are part of this concentrated power, are using to spread fear among the American people.

You good people have heard about these fairy tales and bogey-men too. You have heard about how antagonistic to business this Administration is supposed to be. You have heard all about the dangers which the business of America is supposed to be facing if the Administration continues.

The answer to that is the record of what we have done. It was this Administration which saved the system of private profit and free enterprise after it had been dragged to the brink of ruin by these same leaders who now try to scare you.

Look at the advance in private business in the last three and a half years; and read there what we think about private business.

Today for the first time in seven years the banker, the storekeeper, the small factory owner, the industrialist, can all sit back and enjoy the company of their own ledgers. They are in the black. That is where we want them to be; that is where our policies aim them to be; that is where we intend them to be in the future.

Some of these people really forget how sick they were. But I know how sick they were. I have their fever charts. I know how the knees of all of our rugged individualists were trembling four years ago and how their hearts fluttered. They came to Washington in great numbers. Washington did not look like a dangerous bureaucracy to them then. Oh, no! It looked like an emergency hospital. All of the distinguished patients wanted two things — a quick hypodermic to end the pain and a course of treatment to cure the disease. They wanted them in a hurry; we gave them both. And now most of the patients seem to be doing very nicely. Some of them are even well enough to throw their crutches at the doctor.

The struggle against private monopoly is a struggle for, and not against, American business. It is a struggle to preserve individual enterprise and economic freedom.

I believe in individualism. I believe in it in the arts, the sciences and professions. I believe in it in business. I believe in individualism in all of these things — up to the point where the individualist starts to operate at the expense of society. The overwhelming majority of American business men do not believe in it beyond that point. We have all suffered in the past from individualism run wild. Society has suffered and business has suffered.

Believing in the solvency of business, the solvency of farmers and the solvency of workers, I believe also in the solvency of Government. Your Government is solvent.

The net Federal debt today is lower in proportion to the income of the Nation and in proportion to the wealth of the Nation than it was on March 4, 1933.

In the future it will become lower still because with the rising tide of national income and national wealth, the very causes of our emergency spending are starting to disappear. Government expenditures are coming down and Government income is going up. The opportunities for private enterprise will continue to expand.

The people of America have no quarrel with business. They insist only that the power of concentrated wealth shall not be abused.

We have come through a hard struggle to preserve democracy in America. Where other Nations in other parts of the world have lost that fight, we have won.

The business men of America and all other citizens have joined in a firm resolve to hold the fruits of that victory, to cling to the old ideals and old fundamentals upon which America has grown great.

Address by Governor Alfred M. Landon
New York, October 29, 1936

In the final week of the campaign, Landon delivered his most effective political speech to an enthusiastic throng at Madison Square Garden. His references to the Supreme Court anticipated the President's "Court-packing" proposal the following year.

We are drawing to the end of a great campaign — a campaign that transcends all party lines. Tonight I am here, not alone as the representative of a great party; I am here as the representative of a great cause — a cause in which millions of my fellow-citizens are joined — a cause in which Democrats, independents and Republicans are fighting shoulder to shoulder.

Let me begin by restating the basic principles of my political creed.

I believe in our constitutional form of government — a government established by the people, responsible to the people and alterable only in accordance with the will of the people.

I believe in our indivisible union of indestructible States.

I believe in the American system of free enterprise, regulated by law.

I believe in the liberty of the individual as guaranteed by the Constitution.

I believe in the rights of minorities as protected by the Constitution.

I believe in the liberties secured by the Bill of Rights and in their maintenance as the best protection against bigotry and all intolerance, whether of race, color or creed.

I believe in an independent Supreme Court and judiciary, secure from executive or legislative invasion.

I believe that in the future, as in the past, the hopes of our people can best be realized by following the American way of life under the American Constitution.

I believe in the principles of civic righteousness exemplified by Theodore Roosevelt and I pledge myself to go forward along the trail he blazed.

In the light of this creed I have already outlined my stand on the chief issues of the campaign. Tonight I am going to review my position and contrast it with that of my opponent.

It is fitting that I should start with the problem of agriculture. Your City of New York is the greatest market for farm products in the country. As consumers you want an ample supply of food at fair prices. As wage-earners you need the buying power of a prosperous farm population.

The welfare of agriculture is also the welfare of industry. A fair adjustment between the two is not a matter of politics, it is a matter of national necessity.

Now let us look at the record.

In direct defiance of the 1932 Democratic platform, which condemned the unsound policy of crop restriction, the Triple A was enacted. The Triple A restricted agricultural production by 36,000,000 acres.

This administration has rewarded scarcity and penalized plenty. Not only has it failed to correct the basic ills of agriculture, it has added to them. I am from a great agricultural State and I know.

I know how this program dislocated our agricultural system. I know, for instance, that almost overnight it forced the Southern farmer out of cotton into crops competing with the North and West. It led him into dairy farming and the raising of livestock. This affected not only the farmer of the North and West. It also affected the farmer of the South, who lost a large part of his cotton export market.

Luckily for this administration, the full damage of its program has been hidden by the droughts.

Government has a moral obligation to help repair the damage caused to the farmer by this administration's destructive experiments. Farming, by its very nature, cannot readjust itself as rapidly as industry to the aftereffects of economic planning. During the period of readjustment, and until foreign markets are reopened, the government must help the farmer.

We can do this without violating the Constitution. We can do this without imposing such burdens as the processing tax upon the consumer. We can do this within the limits of a balanced budget. And don't forget I am going to balance the budget.

The Republican party also proposes a sound long-term program of conservation and land use. This is the only permanent solution of the farm problem and is essential to the preservation of the nation's land resources. We propose to stop muddling and meddling and to begin mending.

And what does the President mean to do for agriculture? Is he going to continue the policy of scarcity?

The answer is: No one can be sure.

Now let us turn to industry. What was the basic declaration of the Democratic platform of 1932? It was that the anti-trust laws — the laws protecting the little fellow from monopoly — should be strengthened and enforced.

And what did the administration do? It created the NRA. This law gave the sanction of government to private monopoly. It endorsed the vicious policy of price-fixing. It disregarded the interest of 130,000,000 Americans as consumers. It attempted to tell every business man, large and small, how to run his business.

The NRA was the direct opposite of the American system of free competition. It was an attempt to supplant American initiative with Washington dictation. And what happened? Monopolies prospered and a little New Jersey pants-presser went to jail.

I am against private monopoly. I am against monopolistic practices. I am against the monopoly of an all-powerful central government. And while I am President I intend to see that the anti-trust laws are strengthened and enforced without fear or favor.

I intend to see that government bureaucracy never again starts choking business. I intend to see that American initiative has a chance to give jobs to American workers. And I intend to broaden the market for American products by encouraging freer interchange of goods in world trade.

And what does the President propose for industry? He pays tribute to free in-itiative at Chicago on a Wednesday and to planned economy at Detroit on a Thursday. One day the President's son says the NRA will be revived. The next day the President's son says it will not. When the President was asked about NRA last Tuesday in a press conference, he said: "You pay your money and you take your choice." What does he mean?

The answer is: No one can be sure.

Growing out of the troubles of agriculture and industry is the intensely human problem of unemployment. What is the record on this?

In 1932 the President said that 11,000,000 Americans were looking for work. Today, according to the American Federation of Labor, there are still 11,000,000 Americans looking for work. Yet the President boasts of recovery — in one city in terms of a baseball game and in another city in terms of a patient he has cured.

These fellow-citizens of ours can and will be re-employed. There is no need for one-fifth of our working population to be condemned to live in an economic world apart. There is work to be done in this country — more than enough to give jobs to all the unemployed. This work will start just as soon as uncertainty in gov-ernment policies is replaced by confidence.

There can be no confidence when the government is proud of spending more than it takes in.

There can be no confidence when the government creates uncertainty about the value of money.

There can be no confidence when the government threatens to control every detail of our economic life.

There can be no confidence when the government proclaims that the way to have more is to produce less.

In short, there can be no confidence while this administration remains in power.

As Chief Executive I intend to follow a course that will restore confidence.

I intend to be open and aboveboard on the policies of my administration.

I intend in the task of reconstruction to make use of the best talent available irrespective of party.

I intend to throw out all plans based on scarcity.

I intend to put an end to this administration's policy of 'try anything once.' The time has come for a steady hand at the wheel.

And what does the President propose to restore confidence? Another 'breath-ing-spell'?

The answer is: No one can be sure.

Of course re-employment cannot come overnight. In the meantime those in need must have relief. Consider the administration's record here.

The Democratic platform in 1932 condemned the 'improper and excessive use of money in political activities.'

In defiance of this pledge we have had an outrageous use of public money for political purposes. Public funds appropriated for relief have been used in an attempt to buy the votes of our less fortunate citizens. But it will not do them any good. The votes of the American people are not for sale.

As Chief Executive I intend to see that relief is purged of politics. There is ample money in this country to take care of those in need. When I am President they will be taken care of. This is the plain will of the American people.

And what does the President propose to do about relief? How does he propose to free the victims of the depression from political exploitation?

The answer is: No one can be sure.

In a highly industrialized society we must provide for the protection of the aged.

The present administration claims it has done this through its Social Security Act. But the act does not give security. It is based upon a conception that is fundamentally wrong. It assumes that the American people are so improvident that they must be compelled to save by a paternal government.

Beginning next Jan. 1, workers, no matter how small their wages, will have their pay docked — they will have their pay docked for the purpose of building up a phantom reserve fund — a fund that any future Congress can spend any time it sees fit and for any purpose it sees fit.

I cannot understand how any administration would dare to perpetrate such a fraud upon our workers.

The Republican party proposes to replace this unworkable hodgepodge by a plan that is honest, fair and financially sound. We propose that the funds for security payments shall be provided as we go along. We propose that they shall be obtained from a direct and specific tax widely distributed. We propose that all American citizens over 65 shall receive whatever additional income is necessary to keep them from need.

I repeat: The workers will start to pay for the present plan next Jan. 1. They will pay as wage-earners through a direct deduction from their pay. They will pay both as wage-earners and consumers through the tax levied on their employers' payrolls. And don't let any one tell you otherwise. Even the Democratic Attorney General of New York admits this. Last March, before the New York Court of Appeals, he said that a tax on employers' payrolls, although levied on the employer, will be — and I quote — "shifted either to wage-earners or consumers or both."

And what does the President propose to do about these taxes? Is he going to continue a plan that takes money from workers without any assurance that they will get back what they put in?

The answer is: No one can be sure.

Since the NRA was declared unconstitutional — and largely because it was declared unconstitutional — there has been some improvement in business.

But there has been no reduction in the total of government spending. In the year ended last June the Federal Government spent nearly $9,000,000,000. This is an all-time peace-time high.

We will spend this year over $900,000,000 more for the ordinary routine expenditures of government than in 1934. And we will spend $1,500,000,000 more for relief than in 1934.

Under this administration seventy-five new agencies have been created. Two hundred and fifty thousand additional employees have been foisted on the taxpayers. The Federal payroll has reached the staggering sum of $1,500,000,000 a year.

As I said at Chicago, any one at all familiar with what has been going on could almost count on the fingers of one hand foolish experiments the government could cut out and save at least $1,000,000,000 any time it wanted to.

I pledge myself to put an end to extravagance and waste. I pledge myself to stop the policy that glorifies spending. I pledge myself to balance the budget.

And what is the President going to do? Is he going to stop his policy of spending for spending's sake?

The answer is: No one can be sure.

I come finally to the underlying and fundamental issue of this campaign. This is the question of whether our American form of government is to be preserved.

Let us turn once more to the record.

The President has been responsible for nine acts declared unconstitutional by the Supreme Court.

He has publicly urged Congress to pass a law, even though it had reasonable doubts as to its constitutionality.

He has publicly belittled the Supreme Court of the United States.

He has publicly suggested that the Constitution is an outworn document.

He has retained in high office men outspoken in their contempt for the American form of government.

He has sponsored laws which have deprived States of their Constitutional rights.

Every one of these actions — and the list is by no means complete — strikes at the heart of the American form of government.

Our Constitution is not a lifeless piece of paper. It is the underlying law of the land and the charter of the liberties of our people. The people, and they alone, have the right to amend or destroy it. Until the people in their combined wisdom decide to make the change, it is the plain duty of the people's servants to keep within the Constitution. It is the plain meaning of the oath of office that they shall keep within the Constitution.

Our Federal system allows great leeway. But if changes in our civilization make amendment to the Constitution desirable it should be amended. It has been amended in the past. It can be in the future.

I have already made my position clear on this question. I am on record that, if proper working conditions cannot be regulated by the States, I shall favor a constitutional amendment giving the States the necessary powers.

And what are the intentions of the President with respect to the Constitution? Does he believe changes are required? If so, will an amendment be submitted to the people, or will he attempt to get around the Constitution by tampering with the Supreme Court?

The answer is: No one can be sure.

We want more than a material recovery in this country. We want a moral and spiritual recovery as well. We have been allowing material things to obscure the great religious and spiritual values. But life is more than bread. Character is the supreme thing. We have been weakening those very qualities upon which character is built. It would be tragedy if in our attempt to win prosperity we should lose our own souls. It would be an overwhelming disaster if we should forget that it is righteousness that exalteth a nation.

Forty-eight hours from tonight, standing where I am standing, there will be a President of the United States. He will be seeking re-election.

A little more than forty-eight hours after he has spoken, the American people will be streaming to the polls.

Here once again I ask him to speak what is in his mind. It is his duty, not only as President, but also as an American, to tell what his purposes and intentions really are. It is his duty, as it is my duty, to trust the "combined wisdom of the people." For the Constitution, which he swore to uphold, stands squarely on the "combined wisdom of the people." When the ballot speaks, it speaks the "combined wisdom of the people."

The people of this country will not trust a man who does not trust them. If he trusts them he will answer the questions being asked from one end of the country to the other.

Does he favor reviving the principles of the National Recovery Act? Or does he favor the American system of free initiative?

Does he favor reviving the principles of the Agricultural Adjustment Act? Or does he favor allowing the farmer to be a lord on his own farm?

Does he favor concentrating more and more power in the hands of the Chief Executive? Or does he favor a return to the American form of government?

These three things are inseparable. If he wants the AAA, he must have the NRA. If he wants the NRA, he must have the AAA. And both are impossible without increased powers for the Chief Executive.

And so, in closing this meeting, I leave a challenge with the President. I say to him: Mr. President, I am willing to trust the people. I am willing to stand up and say openly that I am against economic planning by the government. I am against the concentration of power in the hands of the Chief Executive.

Tell us where you stand, Mr. President. Tell us not in generalities, but clearly, so that no one can mistake your meaning. And tell us why you have evaded the issue until the eve of the election.

I leave my gage at your feet.

My gage is the gauge of your confidence, Mr. President, your confidence in the American people.

My gage is the gauge of your duty, Mr. President, your duty to the American people.

My gage is the gauge of your faith, Mr. President, your faith in the American people.

By the words that you speak in forty-eight hours the American people will know the measure of your confidence and your duty and your faith in their wisdom.

Speech by President Franklin D. Roosevelt
New York, October 31, 1936

President Roosevelt delivered this address two nights after Governor Landon had taunted him to clarify his aims. In this speech the President carried to a new pitch of intensity the class theme of his campaign.

Senator Wagner, Governor Lehman, ladies and gentlemen:

On the eve of a national election, it is well for us to stop for a moment and analyze calmly and without prejudice the effect on our Nation of a victory by either of the major political parities.

The problem of the electorate is far deeper, far more vital than the continuance in the Presidency of any individual. For the greater issue goes beyond units of humanity — it goes to humanity itself.

In 1932 the issue was the restoration of American democracy; and the American people were in a mood to win. They did win. In 1936 the issue is the preservation of their victory. Again they are in a mood to win. Again they will win.

More than four years ago in accepting the Democratic nomination in Chicago, I said: "Give me your help not to win votes alone, but to win in this crusade to restore America to its own people."

The banners of that crusade still fly in the van of a Nation that is on the march.

It is needless to repeat the details of the program which this Administration has been hammering out on the anvils of experience. No amount of misrepresentation or statistical contortion can conceal or blur or smear that record. Neither the attacks of unscrupulous enemies nor the exaggerations of overzealous friends will serve to mislead the American people.

What was our hope in 1932? Above all other things the American people wanted peace. They wanted peace of mind instead of gnawing fear.

First, they sought escape from the personal terror which had stalked them for three years. They wanted the peace that comes from security in their homes: safety for their savings, permanence in their jobs, a fair profit from their enterprise.

Next, they wanted peace in the community, the peace that springs from the ability to meet the needs of community life: schools, playgrounds, parks, sanitation, highways — those things which are expected of solvent local government. They sought escape from disintegration and bankruptcy in local and state affairs.

They also sought peace within the Nation: protection of their currency, fairer wages, the ending of long hours of toil, the abolition of child labor, the elimination of wild-cat speculation, the safety of their children from kidnappers.

And, finally, they sought peace with other Nations — peace in a world of unrest. The Nation knows that I hate war, and I know that the Nation hates war.

I submit to you a record of peace; and on that record a well-founded expectation for future peace — peace for the individual, peace for the community, peace for the Nation, and peace with the world.

Tonight I call the roll — the roll of honor of those who stood with us in 1932 and still stand with us today.

Written on it are the names of millions who never had a chance — men at starvation wages, women in sweatshops, children at looms.

Written on it are the names of those who despaired, young men and young women for whom opportunity had become a will-o'-the-wisp.

Written on it are the names of farmers whose acres yielded only bitterness, business men whose books were portents of disaster, home owners who were faced with eviction, frugal citizens whose savings were insecure.

Written there in large letters are the names of countless other Americans of all parties and all faiths, Americans who had eyes to see and hearts to understand, whose consciences were burdened because too many of their fellows were burdened, who looked on these things four years ago and said, "This can be changed. We will change it."

We still lead that army in 1936. They stood with us then because in 1932 they believed. They stand with us today because in 1936 they know. And with them stand millions of new recruits who have come to know.

Their hopes have become our record.

We have not come this far without a struggle and I assure you we cannot go further without a struggle.

For twelve years this Nation was afflicted with hear-nothing, see-nothing, do-nothing Government. The Nation looked to Government but the Government looked away. Nine mocking years with the golden calf and three long years of the scourge! Nine crazy years at the ticker and three long years in the breadlines! Nine mad years of mirage and three long years of despair! Powerful influences strive today to restore that kind of government with its doctrine that that Government is best which is most indifferent.

For nearly four years you have had an Administration which instead of twirling its thumbs has rolled up its sleeves. We will keep our sleeves rolled up.

We had to struggle with the old enemies of peace-business and financial monopoly, speculation, reckless banking, class antagonism, sectionalism, war profiteering.

They had begun to consider the Government of the United States as a mere appendage to their own affairs. We know now that Government by organized money is just as dangerous as Government by organized mob.

Never before in all our history have these forces been so united against one candidate as they stand today. They are unanimous in their hate for me — and I welcome their hatred.

I should like to have it said of my first Administration that in it the forces of selfishness and of lust for power met their match. I should like to have it said of my second Administration that in it these forces met their master.

The American people know from a four-year record that today there is only one entrance to the White House — by the front door. Since March 4, 1933, there has been only one pass-key to the White House. I have carried that key in my pocket. It is there tonight. So long as I am President, it will remain in my pocket.

Those who used to have pass-keys are not happy. Some of them are desperate. Only desperate men with their backs to the wall would descend so far below the level of decent citizenship as to foster the current pay-envelope campaign against America's working people. Only reckless men, heedless of consequences, would risk the disruption of the hope for a new peace between worker and employer by returning to the tactics of the labor spy.

Here is an amazing paradox! The very employers and politicians and publishers who talk most loudly of class antagonism and the destruction of the American system now undermine that system by this attempt to coerce the votes of the wage earners of this country. It is the 1936 version of the old threat to close down the factory or the office if a particular candidate does not win. It is an old strategy of tyrants to delude their victims into fighting their battles for them.

Every message in a pay envelope, even if it is the truth, is a command to vote according to the will of the employer. But this propaganda is worse — it is deceit.

They tell the worker his wage will be reduced by a contribution to some vague form of old-age insurance. They carefully conceal from him the fact that for every dollar of premium he pays for that insurance, the employer pays another dollar. That omission is deceit.

They carefully conceal from him the fact that under the federal law, he receives another insurance policy to help him if he loses his job, and that the premium of that policy is paid 100 percent by the employer and not one cent by the worker. They do not tell him that the insurance policy that is bought for him is far more favorable to him than any policy that any private insurance company could afford to issue. That omission is deceit.

They imply to him that he pays all the cost of both forms of insurance. They carefully conceal from him the fact that for every dollar put up by him his employer puts up three dollars — three for one. And that omission is deceit.

But they are guilty of more than deceit. When they imply that the reserves thus created against both these policies will be stolen by some future Congress, diverted to some wholly foreign purpose, they attack the integrity and honor of American Government itself. Those who suggest that, are already aliens to the spirit of American democracy. Let them emigrate and try their lot under some foreign flag in which they have more confidence.

The fraudulent nature of this attempt is well shown by the record of votes on the passage of the Social Security Act. In addition to an overwhelming majority of Democrats in both Houses, seventy-seven Republican Representatives voted for it and only eighteen against it and fifteen Republican Senators voted for it and only five against it. Where does this last-minute drive of the Republican leadership leave these Republican Representatives and Senators who helped enact this law?

I am sure the vast majority of law-abiding businessmen who are not parties to this propaganda fully appreciate the extent of the threat to honest business contained in this coercion.

I have expressed indignation at this form of campaigning and I am confident that the overwhelming majority of employers, workers and the general public share that indignation and will show it at the polls on Tuesday next.

Aside from this phase of it, I prefer to remember this campaign not as bitter but only as hard-fought. There should be no bitterness or hate where the sole thought is the welfare of the United States of America. No man can occupy the office of President without realizing that he is President of all the people.

It is because I have sought to think in terms of the whole Nation that I am confident that today, just as four years ago, the people want more than promises.

Our vision for the future contains more than promises.

This is our answer to those who, silent about their own plans, ask us to state our objectives.

Of course we will continue to seek to improve working conditions for the workers of America — to reduce hours over-long, to increase wages that spell starvation, to end the labor of children, to wipe out sweatshops. Of course we will continue every effort to end monopoly in business, to support collective bargaining, to stop unfair competition, to abolish dishonorable trade practices. For all these we have only just begun to fight.

Of course we will continue to work for cheaper electricity in the homes and on the farms of America, for better and cheaper transportation, for low interest rates, for sounder home financing, for better banking, for the regulation of security issues, for reciprocal trade among nations, for the wiping out of slums. For all these we have only just begun to fight.

Of course we will continue our efforts in behalf of the farmers of America. With their continued cooperation we will do all in our power to end the piling up of huge surpluses which spelled ruinous prices for their crops. We will persist in successful action for better land use, for reforestation, for the conservation of water all the way from its source to the sea, for drought and flood control, for better marketing facilities for farm commodities, for a definite reduction of farm tenancy, for encouragement of farmer cooperatives, for crop insurance and a stable food supply. For all these we have only just begun to fight.

Of course we will provide useful work for the needy unemployed; we prefer useful work to the pauperism of a dole.

Here and now I want to make myself clear about those who disparage their fellow citizens on the relief rolls. They say that those on relief are not merely jobless — that they are worthless. Their solution for the relief problem is to end relief — to purge the rolls by starvation. To use the language of the stock broker, our needy unemployed would be cared for when, as, and if some fairy godmother should happen on the scene.

You and I will continue to refuse to accept that estimate of our unemployed fellow Americans. Your Government is still on the same side of the street with the Good Samaritan and not with those who pass by on the other side.

Again — what of our objectives?

Of course we will continue our efforts for young men and women so that they may obtain an education and an opportunity to put it to use. Of course we will continue our help for the crippled, for the blind, for the mothers, our insurance for the unemployed, our security for the aged. Of course we will continue to protect the consumer against unnecessary price spreads, against the costs that are added by monopoly and speculation. We will continue our successful efforts to increase his purchasing power and to keep it constant.

For these things, too, and for a multitude of others like them, we have only just begun to fight.

All this — all these objectives — spell peace at home. All our actions, all our ideals, spell also peace with other nations.

Today there is war and rumor of war. We want none of it. But while we guard our shores against threats of war, we will continue to remove the causes of unrest and antagonism at home which might make our people easier victims to those for whom foreign war is profitable. You know well that those who stand to profit by war are not on our side in this campaign.

"Peace on earth, good will toward men" — democracy must cling to that message. For it is my deep conviction that democracy cannot live without that true religion which gives a nation a sense of justice and of moral purpose. Above our political forums, above our market places stand the altars of our faith — altars on which burn the fires of devotion that maintain all that is best in us and all that is best in our Nation.

We have need of that devotion today. It is that which makes it possible for government to persuade those who are mentally prepared to fight each other to go on instead, to work for and to sacrifice for each other. That is why we need to say with the Prophet: "What doth the Lord require of thee — but to do justly, to love mercy and to walk humbly with thy God." That is why the recovery we seek, the recovery we are winning, is more than economic. In it are included justice and love and humility, not for ourselves as individuals alone, but for our Nation.

That is the road to peace.

Editorial from *The Literary Digest*
November 14, 1936

Until 1936 The Literary Digest *had achieved consistent success in picking presidential winners. Many viewed its failure in 1936 as evidence of the new importance of class voting. In this article the* Digest *puzzles over its experience.*

In 1920, 1924, 1928, and 1932, *The Literary Digest* polls were right. Not only right in the sense that they showed the winner; they forecast the *actual popular vote* with such a small percentage of error (less than 1 per cent in 1932) that newspapers and individuals everywhere heaped such phrases as "uncannily accurate" and "amazingly right" upon us.

Four years ago, when the Poll was running his way, our very good friend Jim Farley was saying that "no sane person could escape the implication" of a sampling "so fairly and correctly conducted."

Well, this year we used precisely the same method that had scored four bull's-eyes in four previous tries. And we were far from correct. Why? We ask that question in all sincerity, because *we want to know.*

Oh, we've been flooded with "reasons." Hosts of people who feel they have learned more about polling in a few months than we have learned in more than a score of years have told us just where we were off. Hundreds of astute "second-guessers" have assured us, by telephone, by letter, in the newspapers, that the reasons for our error were "obvious." Were they?

Suppose we review a few of these "obvious reasons."

The one most often heard runs something like this: "This election was different. Party lines were obliterated. For the first time in more than a century, *all* the havenots' were on one side. THE DIGEST, polling names from telephone books and lists of automobile owners, simply did not reach the lower strata." And so on....

— Well, in the first place, the "have-nots" did not reelect Mr. Roosevelt. That they contributed to his astonishing plurality, no one can doubt. But the fact remains that a majority of farmers, doctors, grocers and candlestickmakers *also* voted for the President. As Dorothy Thompson remarked in the New York *Herald Tribune*, you could eliminate the straight labor vote, the relief vote and the Negro vote, and *still* Mr. Roosevelt would have a majority.

So that "reason" does not appear to hold much water. Besides —

We *did* reach these so-called "have-not" strata. In the city of Chicago, for example, we polled *every third registered voter*. In the city of Scranton, Pennsylvania, we polled every *other* registered voter. And in Allentown, Pennsylvania, likewise other cities, we polled *every* registered voter.

Is that so? chorus the critics, a little abashed, no doubt. Well, they come back, you must have got the right answer in *those* towns, anyway.

Well, we didn't. The fact is that we were as badly off there as we were on the national total.

— In Allentown, for example, 10,753 out of the 30,811 who voted returned ballots to us showing a division of 53.32 per cent. to 44.67 per cent. in favor of Mr. Landon. What was the actual result? It was 56.93 per cent. for Mr. Roosevelt, 41.17 per cent. for the Kansan.

In Chicago, the 100,929 voters who returned ballots to us showed a division of 48.63 per cent. to 47.56 per cent. in favor of Mr. Landon. The 1,672,175 who voted in the actual election gave the President 65.24 per cent., to 32.26 per cent. for the Republican candidate.

What happened? Why did only one in five voters in Chicago to whom THE DIGEST sent ballots take the trouble to reply? And why was there a preponderance of Republicans in the one-fifth that did reply? Your guess is as good as ours. We'll go into it a little more later. The important thing in all the above is that all this conjecture about our "not reaching certain strata" simply will not hold water.

— Now for another "explanation" dinned into our ears: "You got too many Hoover voters in your sample."

Well, the fact is that we've *always* got too big a sampling of Republican voters. That was true in 1920, in 1924, in 1928, and even in 1932, when we *over*estimated the Roosevelt popular vote by three-quarters of 1 per cent.

In 1928 in Chicago, we underestimated the Democratic vote by a little more than 5 per cent., overestimated the Republican vote by the same margin.

We wondered then, as we had wondered before and have wondered since, why we were getting better cooperation in what we have always regarded as a public service from Republicans than we were getting from Democrats. Do Republicans live nearer mail-boxes? Do Democrats generally disapprove of straw polls?

We don't know that answer. All we know is that in 1932, when the tide seemed to be running away from Hoover, we were perturbed about the disproportion of Republican voters in our sampling. Republican and Democratic chieftains from all points in the country were at the telephones day after day for reports of what the Democrats called our "correctly conducted" system. And then the result came along, and it was so right, we were inclined to agree that we had been concerned without reason, and this year, when it seemed logical to suppose that the President's vote would be lighter, even if he won (hadn't that been the rule on reelections for more than a hundred years?) we decided not to worry.

— So the statisticians did our worrying for us on that score, applying what they called the "compensating-ratio" in some cases, and the "switch-factor" in others. Either way for some of the figure experts, it didn't matter; interpret our figures for 2,376,523 voters as they would, the answer was still Landon. Then other statisticians took our figures and so weighted, compensated, balanced, adjusted and interpreted them that they showed Roosevelt.

We did not attempt to interpret the figures, because we had no stake in the result other than the wish to preserve our well-earned reputation for scrupulous book-keeping. So we sent out more than ten million ballots, exactly as we had sent them out before. We don't know what proportion went to persons who had voted for Roosevelt in 1932 or what proportion went to persons who had voted for Hoover, because our polls are secret always, and the ballots come back with no signatures, no identifying characteristics of any sort except the post-marks.

— However, since the basis of the 1936 mailing-list was the 1932 mailing-list, and since the overwhelming majority of those who responded to our Poll in 1932 voted for Mr. Roosevelt, it seems altogether reasonable to assume that the majority of our ballots this year went to people who had voted for Mr. Roosevelt in 1932. There simply was no way by which THE DIGEST could assure itself or the public that the marked ballots would come back in the same proportion. We couldn't very well send duplicate ballots to indifferent Democrats, or personal letters prodding them into action, because we didn't know which were Democrats and which were Republicans, let alone which would vote for Roosevelt and which for Landon.

If any of the hundreds who have so kindly offered their suggestions and criticism can tell us how we could get voters to respond proportionately, and still keep the poll secret, as we believe it ought always to be, then we wish these critics would step up and do so. And with arguments more convincing than the familiar ones about our not reaching the "lower strata" and "sampling too many Republicans." Because those two theories explain nothing; they only add to the multiplicity and confusion of words — words — words.

— And there's another "explanation" that doesn't seem to hold much water, when you examine it closely. That's the one that argues that we polled too many voters, that cites the experience of another poll that sent out less than a fourth as many ballots and came closer to being right. The answer here is that the Baltimore *Sunpapers* polled more persons per square mile in Maryland than we did anywhere except in the cities — and the *Sunpapers* were a lot nearer right than this "model poll" for Maryland. Also, the man who came nearer the right answer than all the polls put together was Jim Farley, and Jim based his prediction on reports from tens of thousands of precinct leaders in every city, town and hamlet in the country.

So-what?

So we were wrong, altho we did everything we knew to assure ourselves of being right.

We conducted our Poll as we had always done, reported what we found, and have no alibis. We drew no special satisfaction from our figures, and we drew no conclusions from them. The result was disappointing only in the sense that it threw our figures out the window, and left us — without even the satisfaction of knowing why.

— As for the immediate future, THE DIGEST feels that in truth "the Nation has spoken." THE DIGEST hails a magnificent President against whom it never uttered one word of partisan criticism. THE DIGEST can not support him, in the sense that newspapers support a President editorially, because THE DIGEST does not editorialize. But it can obtain genuine satisfaction from the knowledge that its several Editors, as

American citizens, and its millions of readers, as American citizens, will stand behind the First Citizen.

Speaking of the President, there is a spot of comfort for us in the knowledge that he himself was pretty badly off on his Electoral total, and that he "laughed it off" in his genial way. His last guess was 360 votes to Mr. Landon's 171. (On June 5 he had estimated his margin at 315 to 216.)

As for the more distant future, the questions have been asked: Will THE DIGEST conduct another Poll? Will it change its methods?

The answer to the first question we phrase in others: Should the Democratic Party have quit in 1924, when it reached modern low-ebb in power and confidence, instead of going on to the greatest triumph in its history? Should the Republican Party have quit in 1912, when it carried only two States? Should the University of Minnesota, with the greatest record in modern football, give up the sport because it finally lost one game, after a string of twenty-one victories?

The answer to the second question is: We'll cross that bridge when we come to it.

"How the Negro Voted in the Presidential Election"
by Earl Brown in *Opportunity*
December, 1936

One of the crucial developments in 1936 was the switch of the Negro vote from the Republican party, to which it had been committed since the era of Abraham Lincoln, to the Democrats. In this article in the Negro magazine Opportunity the change is analyzed by Earl Brown, a political reporter for The New York Herald Tribune.

No group, class, race, sect or section reelected President Roosevelt. He won because a majority of American citizens of all classes voted for him. This statement ought to be convincing enough; nevertheless, the most sanguine political victory invariably hides certain facts and trends; and I know of no political event with more currents and cross-currents than a Presidential election. Years to come a few historians and many politicians will be analyzing the Roosevelt triumph of '36, and the further they get away from it the more they will have to say about it.

It was predicted that the Negroes would vote more than ever before in the recent election. They did. It is estimated that approximately 2,000,000 of them went to the polls on Election Day; and if you don't believe 2,000,000 are a lot of votes, spend an evening with a precinct captain, when he is out trying to "bag" two.

Equally as important as the size of the Negro vote is the fact that for the first time since the passage of the Fifteenth Amendment the majority of the colored people voted for a Democratic Presidential candidate. By so doing, the race has finally become an integral part of both major parties, and thereby it has gained in political stature and importance. As long as the so-called Negro vote was part and parcel of one party, the race was politically frozen; it was impossible for it to be accepted on an equal basis with the rest of the electorate.

The increased political activity of the Negro in the South during the last three years and particularly during the campaign, is probably the most important political movement among the Negroes since the Reconstruction period. Many people believe that the race cannot become properly balanced politically until the southern suffrage problem is solved; for it not only prohibits the Negroes in that section from becoming an integral part of the body politic, but it also prevents any semblance of real Democracy there. Because the Negroes are disfranchised in Dixie, the poor whites are too; and comparatively only a handful of voters exercise their suffrage privilege there in any election.

The present trends among the Negroes in the South are, however, most significant. More Negroes voted in that section this year than since Reconstruction.

In Memphis, nearly fifty per cent of the Negro voters voted for Roosevelt; in Durham and Raleigh, over four thousand colored voters went to the polls and most of them supported Roosevelt. In South Carolina, it is alleged that a few liberal white people urged some Negroes to vote. In Virginia, three Negroes, two Communists and one Republican, ran for the State legislature and received a few scattered votes. Throughout the South, but particularly in North Carolina and Tennessee, the colored people have depicted a political awakening, which, judged by the size and momentum it has attained in the last few years, will break the traditionally Solid South wide open in the near future.

Meantime, there has been little or no opposition to the Negro's political activities in Dixie by the whites. After the election the press releases carried no stories about the whites intimidating the blacks because some of them went to the polls and voted. Although the Negroes did not swarm to the polls there in large numbers, there was, nevertheless, a decided change in attitude by the whites toward those who did.

The main cause, no doubt, for the increased political activity of the race below the Mason–Dixon line, as well as a more intelligent attitude on the part of the whites toward it, is the New Deal. It has done more to abolish sectionalism than any other force in the history of the nation. The New Deal, through its relief measures and social-economic legislation, has partly welded the American Empire into one nation; and by so doing it has taught the people in all sections that the success of each part depends on the efficient functioning of the Federal or Central Government.

Meanwhile, however, it is well to state here that the political future of the race in the South will be no bed of roses. Intrenched economic and racial groups there are bound to fight to the last ditch against what they call the encroachment of the Negroes on the inalienable preserve of the white man — political equality. However, the outcome of the southern political enigma depends in part on how liberal and determined Mr. Roosevelt is in his second term. If he truckles to the white politicians from Dixie the Negro can expect nothing. On the other hand, if he heeds the advice of the liberal white and colored citizens, who do not necessarily have any axes to grind, he can help to create a wholesome political condition there instead of the present unjust one. In the last analysis, however, the political future of the race in the South rests primarily upon the determination and courage of the Negroes themselves to take an active part in it, for after all politics is a game in which the *quid pro quo* is certainly the *sine qua non*. If the Negro has nothing to offer and if he won't fight intelligently for what he wants, he may expect nothing in return.

If certain good political portents are discernible in the South, they are even more so in the North, for it is in this section that the race definitely broke away from the shackles of, single-partyism on Election Day. Seventeen Negroes were elected to State legislatures in nine states, out of which number twelve were Democrats and five Republicans. Five Negro Democrats were elected to the Pennsylvania State legislature, four Republicans were elected in

Illinois, one Republican in Nebraska, two Democrats in New York, one in New Jersey, West Virginia, Kansas, Indiana and Michigan. In addition, Arthur W. Mitchell was re-elected to the House of Representatives from the First Congressional District of Illinois, which is situated in Chicago.

The election of John Adams Jr., a Negro lawyer of Omaha, Nebraska, to the new unicameral legislature of that state was, in many respects, more important than the re-election of Mitchell to Congress. Although many white people voted for Congressman Mitchell, his opponent was another Negro. On the other hand, Adams was opposed by a white man and elected by white voters. Besides, he received more votes in his district, the Fifth, than any of the other forty-two successful candidates, all of whom were white.

It is true that Negroes have opposed white candidates for office before and that they have been elected to minor offices mainly because of the support given them by white voters. But the election of a Negro to the one-chamber legislature in Nebraska this year under those circumstances indicates a better feeling toward the Negroes in their attempt to win important political positions. It also demonstrates the ability of Mr. Adams; and his success is all the more remarkable because of the comparatively few Negroes in his state, and because he won on the Republican ticket, while the state went Democratic.

The election of five Negroes to the Pennsylvania legislature on the Democratic ticket was nothing short of a revolution among the voters of that state. Four of them won in Philadelphia and one in Pittsburgh, where large Negro populations are located. Less than five years ago there were fewer than five thousand Negro Democrats in the Keystone State; on Election Day, over 100,000 of the state's 200,000 colored voters supported the Democratic ticket. Approximately the same relative gains were made by the Democratic party among the Negro voters in New York, New Jersey, West Virginia, Ohio, Michigan, Missouri and Indiana. Because of the battle put up by Oscar DePriest against Congressman Mitchell for the right to represent the First Congressional District of Illinois in the House, the national and local Democratic parties failed to corral a large majority of the Negro vote in that State.

The Negro voters in New York went Democratic by four to one. Never before in the history of Harlem and other Negro belts in the city did so many Negroes go to the polls. At noon on Election Day, nine hundred Negroes were in the line at one polling place anxious to cast their ballots; and nowhere else in the city did so many people stand in line at one time in order to exercise their suffrage privilege.

In addition to relief and the liberal program of the Roosevelt administration, the genius-like organizing ability of James A. Farley, chairman of the Democratic National Committee, was responsible for thousands of colored voters going to the polls. Farley made no difference between white and black in his successful attempt to capture the nation. In most of the northern states the Negro political leaders were accepted in the inner councils of the party. This not only encouraged the politicians but it convinced the voters that the Democratic party was playing square with the race. Mr. Farley is really a national district or ward leader; and like all successful leaders he was out to win regardless of class or color. Unlike the average local politician, however, he kept his battle on a high plane.

The contest between Congressman Mitchell and Oscar DePriest for a seat in Congress was one of the most interesting fights in the entire campaign. This was so not because of Mr. Mitchell but because of his opponent, who is evidently one of the best politicians in the country. DePriest actually carried the Negro wards in Chicago for himself and Governor Landon, but was defeated because of the huge vote piled up for Mitchell in the white wards in the First Congressional District. In face of the landslide for Roosevelt and other Democratic candidates in the State, the moral victory of DePriest on the South Side of Chicago was a tribute to his political sagacity and popularity. On the other hand, the ability of Mitchell to hold together the support of the local Democratic machine headed by Mayor Edward J. Kelly, Patrick Nash and "Hinky Dink" Kenna, boss of the white wards in the district, proves his political wisdom. The pay-off in politics is always on the winner, and Mitchell won. By virtue of his office, he is the foremost Negro politician in the country.

Before the election, both parties went after the so-called Negro vote hammer and tong. It was said to be the balance of power in at least nine states; and in a close election it was expected that the Negro vote in these states would decide the election. These nine states are New York, Pennsylvania, New Jersey, Ohio, Michigan, Indiana, Illinois, Missouri and West Virginia. Because, however, Roosevelt's victory was a landslide, the so-called Negro vote was only a "widow's mite." It did not decide the issue in any state; but it did contribute to the swell of ballots, which were cast for President Roosevelt. It should be obvious by now that the so-called Negro vote is similar to any other kind of vote in the country, for as American citizens the Negroes react the same as other citizens in an election. Although the colored voters occasionally vote this way or that because of some real or imaginary race issue, they have more often voted the way the majority of the electorate votes than for some special purpose. Numerous times Negro voters have supported white candidates instead of those of their own color.

The Negro vote is now important not because of any balance of power it may have in the doubtful states, but because it has become partly integrated into the fabrics of both parties. If the Negro belongs to neither party, but, like many white voters, shifts his support, not as a Negro, but as an American voter from one party to the other, he will have achieved real political equality.

Probably the weakest phase of the campaign in so far as the colored people were concerned were the Negro national political leaders in both parties. In the first place, the electorate reacted spontaneously to Roosevelt; they made their minds up to vote for him solely because they considered him to be a Messiah. Not since the time of Lincoln has a President risen so high in the estimation of the people; he transcended both politics and party; he was indeed the People's choice.

Nevertheless, the Negro leaders had a remarkable opportunity to gain for the race a more secure position in both parties if they had not insisted on conducting the same old "Uncle Tom" campaigns. The Negro Republican leaders are more to blame for this than the Democrats, for they knew the colored voters were leaving the Republican party and yet they would not tell John D. M. Hamilton, chairman of the Republican National Committee, and other leaders of the party, the truth about the demands and new political ideology of the race. Instead, they continued to preach the outmoded doctrine of "Lincoln freed the slaves," when they knew it would not win a vote. If some Negro Republican leader had had courage enough to tell his party leaders the truth, the race would have risen in the minds of the leaders. Francis E. Rivers, who led the Republican campaign in the East among the Negroes, did attempt to infuse a new philosophy in the minds of the white leaders, but he was ignored for the older heads, who must be criticized for their show of political ineptitude.

While positions in the Democratic national set-up are comparatively new to colored politicians, this is no excuse for the unnecessary wrangling and jockeying for top positions by those who were interested solely in furthering their own ends. This policy did not benefit the politicians and certainly not the race, which, in the minds of the Democratic leaders, still is minus first class Negro political leaders. The point is the Negro politicians must learn that they have to discount immediate personal gain for the welfare of the race. If they ever get wisdom enough to do this they are bound to come in for a much bigger "cut" in the future than they can ever hope to get by "chiseling" as they go along.

The Negro, however, is now in a better political position than he has ever been before. This is true because the people in this country, regardless of race, have taken a brand new interest in the Federal Government. Washington, D.C., has been brought to the poor man's door step as well as the rich man's. He feels, in addition, a definite responsibility for the government; and at the same time he is grateful for the good Roosevelt has done for him personally. The spread of Democracy included the black man this time and he showed his appreciation for the good it has done by supporting its continuation. It is now up to the President to prove that he really means business. All Negro citizens are waiting to see him "go to town."

THE VOTES IN THE 1936 ELECTION

States	Popular vote				Electoral vote	
	F. D. Roosevelt, Democrat	Alf Landon, Republican	William Lemke, Union	Norman Thomas, Socialist	Landon and Knox	Roosevelt and Garner
Alabama	238,196	35,358	551	242	–	11
Arizona	86,722	33,433	3,307	317	–	3
Arkansas	146,765	32,039	4	446	–	9
California	1,766,836	836,431	–	11,331	–	22
Colorado	295,021	181,267	9,962	1,593	–	6
Connecticut	382,189	278,685	21,805	5,683	–	8
Delaware	69,702	54,014	442	172	–	3
Florida	249,117	78,248	–	–	–	7
Georgia	255,364	36,942	141	68	–	12
Idaho	125,683	66,256	7,684	–	–	4
Illinois	2,282,999	1,570,393	89,439	7,530	–	29
Indiana	934,974	691,570	19,407	3,856	–	14
Iowa	621,756	487,977	29,687	1,373	–	11
Kansas	464,520	397,727	–	2,766	–	9
Kentucky	541,944	369,702	12,501	632	–	11
Louisiana	292,894	36,791	–	–	–	10
Maine	126,333	168,823	7,581	783	5	–
Maryland	389,612	231,435	–	1,629	–	8
Massachusetts	942,716	768,613	118,639	5,111	–	17
Michigan	1,016,794	699,733	75,795	8,208	–	19
Minnesota	698,811	350,461	74,296	2,872	–	11
Mississippi	157,318	4,443	–	329	–	9
Missouri	1,111,043	697,891	14,630	3,454	–	15
Montana	159,690	63,598	5,549	1,066	–	4
Nebraska	347,454	247,731	12,847	–	–	7
Nevada	31,925	11,923	–	–	–	3
New Hampshire	108,460	104,642	4,819	–	–	4
New Jersey	1,083,850	720,322	–	3,931	–	16
New Mexico	105,838	61,710	924	343	–	3
New York	3,293,222	2,180,670	–	86,897	–	47
North Carolina	616,141	223,283	–	21	–	13
North Dakota	163,148	72,751	36,708	552	–	4
Ohio	1,747,122	1,127,709	132,212	117	–	26
Oklahoma	501,069	245,122	–	2,221	–	11
Oregon	266,733	122,706	21,831	2,143	–	5
Pennsylvania	2,353,788	1,690,300	67,467	14,375	–	36
Rhode Island	165,233	125,012	19,569	–	–	4
South Carolina	113,791	1,646	–	–	–	8
South Dakota	160,137	125,977	10,338	–	–	4
Tennessee	327,083	146,516	296	685	–	11
Texas	734,485	103,874	3,281	1,075	–	23
Utah	150,246	64,555	1,121	432	–	4
Vermont	62,124	81,023	–	–	3	–
Virginia	234,980	98,336	233	313	–	11
Washington	459,579	206,892	17,463	3,496	–	8
West Virginia	502,582	325,486	–	832	–	8
Wisconsin	802,984	380,828	60,297	10,626	–	12
Wyoming	62,624	38,739	1,653	200	–	3
	27,751,597	16,679,583	882,479	187,720	8	523

Browder, Communist, 80,150; Colvin, Prohibitionist, 37,847; Aiken, Socialist-Labor, 12,777. The Roosevelt vote in N.Y. State includes 274,924 cast by the American Labor Party. Total vote: 45,646,817.

Election of

1940

ROBERT E. BURKE was Professor of History at the University of Washington and managing editor of *Pacific Northwest Quarterly*. He authored *New Deal for California* and coauthored *The Federal Union*; *The American Nation*; and *A History of American Democracy*.

Election of
1940

Robert E. Burke

F ranklin Roosevelt's second Administration was chiefly a troubled time. Ironi-cally, his political prestige had never been higher than in November 1936, when he won all but two states in his reelection campaign against the liberal but hapless Republican candidate, Governor Alfred M. Landon of Kansas. In this same election, the Democrats increased their already swollen majorities in Congress and improved their commanding positions in state capitals throughout the country. Yet less than a month after his second Inaugural Address Roosevelt was in serious political difficulty. He proposed an enlargement of the United States Supreme Court, which had declared key parts of his program to be unconstitutional, and his "bombshell message" to Congress was received by all but the most devoted New Dealers with a distinct chilliness. Enemies of the New Deal, frustrated through much of his first term, at last had a popular issue with which to belabor FDR. By the summer of 1937, thanks to a startling series of pro-New Deal Supreme Court decisions and to exceedingly astute leadership on the part of his opponents (headed in public by members of his own party), Roosevelt was humiliated by the Senate's open burial of his "court packing" scheme.

His legislative accomplishments in 1937–38 were by no means insignificant — a public housing law, the second Agricultural Adjustment Administration Act, and the Fair Labor Standards (or "wages and hours") Act. When seen in perspective, these major attainments appear to constitute a rounding out of the New Deal program and are even more impressive because they were achieved in the President's second (and presumably last) term, when political analysts contend that little can be accomplished.

While it is uncertain if President Roosevelt's prestige with the American people at large suffered appreciably from his defeat on the Court Plan, there can be no doubt that he lost much popular confidence because of the "Roosevelt Recession." This brief but jolting depression began in the fall of 1937 with a sharp drop-off in the New York Stock Exchange. Within weeks many businesses were in trouble and unemployment grew rapidly. While several New Deal economists had foreseen this recession and attributed it to the Administration's newly instituted and essentially conservative budget-balancing policies, they were unable at first to affect decision-making. For months the President stuck by his policies, abetted by such economically conservative advisors as Secretary of the Treasury Henry Morgenthau Jr. and Secretary of Agriculture Henry A. Wallace. By the early spring of 1938, when the recession showed no signs of letting up, Roosevelt suddenly decided to take the advice of the more committed New Deal spenders such as Secretary of the Interior Harold L. Ickes and Relief Administrator Harry Hopkins. The President asked Congress for a huge relief and public works appropriation, and both houses obliged by quickly passing the Administration's bill. This sudden resumption of "pump-priming" had a distinctly favorable effect on the economy. While the experience probably cured FDR of the last vestiges of his economic orthodoxy, it gave his enemies a new weapon — evidence that Roosevelt's much-touted recovery was exceedingly insecure.

The legislative battles over the Court and reorganization proposals and the wages-and-hours law, added to the loss of face suffered by the President over the "Roosevelt Recession," resulted in a division in the Democratic Party leadership both in the Congress and in the states. The conservative coalition of Republicans and disaffected Democrats in Congress seemed a very formidable block in the way of any further reforms Roosevelt and his New Deal stalwarts may have had in mind. Indeed, it was not certain by the spring of 1938 that liberal elements would be able to retain control of the party and nominate a 1940 ticket that would uphold the accomplishments of the Administration and pledge to carry them further.

It was in this atmosphere that President Roosevelt embarked on his celebrated "purge" campaign with one of his radio "fireside chats" on June 24, 1938. In his speech he identified himself as leader of the Democratic Party, charged with the responsibility of seeing that its candidates remained faithful to their liberal platform pledges. This pronouncement put Democratic candidates, the incumbent members of Congress, and aspirants for the presidential nomination in 1940 on notice that Roosevelt would not support them if their overall record was not in accord with the principles of the New Deal. The highly publicized purge campaign that followed was hastily thrown together and severely limited in its scope, but it had great symbolic importance. Roosevelt's endorsement of several faithful New Deal senators may have helped them win renomination. His opposition, in their own home states, was too little and too late to bring about the defeat of anti-Administration conservative Democratic senators in Georgia, South Carolina, and Maryland, but it did warn Democratic officeholders that the President was unwilling to support those party members he felt had betrayed their trust. The purge had one major success, the defeat for renomination of the conservative obstructionist chairman of the House Rules Committee, Representative John J. O'Connor of New York City. In this race, unlike the senatorial contests in the South, careful preparation and professional management of the Administration's campaign led to success.

The November 1938 "off-year" elections were held in the ominous atmosphere of the tense weeks that followed the Munich crisis. Roosevelt played no open role in these elections, except for a single radio broadcast in which he endorsed the Democratic ticket in his home state and spoke fondly of a few embattled liberals in other states. Significantly, he did not refer to himself as the leader of the Democratic Party, nor did he ask the voters to return a Democratic Congress to power. The elections resulted in the first important Republican gains in a decade, with very strong showings for the GOP in the Northeast and Midwest. Republicans won eight new Senate seats (for a total of twenty-three in the new Congress), eighty-one new House posts (where their total would now be 169), and a net gain of thirteen governorships (making eighteen in all).

While the Democratic Party was still dominant, predictions of a Republican demise after the disastrous 1936 election were clearly premature. Republican success in winning control of state governments in Connecticut, Michigan, Ohio, and Pennsylvania (from the Democrats), Wisconsin (from the Progressives), and Minnesota (from the Farmer-Labor Party) was particularly significant. Furthermore, the GOP had some badly needed new faces: Robert A. Taft and John W. Bricker, newly elected Ohio senator and governor; Governor Harold E. Stassen of Minnesota; and Thomas E. Dewey, the "racket-busting" district attorney who almost won the governorship of New York from the popular incumbent, Herbert H. Lehman.

President Roosevelt, even though he was increasingly preoccupied with urgent problems of defense and foreign policy, gave no sign that he was going to abandon either his domestic program or his control over the Democratic Party. In his annual message of January 4, 1939, he warned of international dangers and stressed his Administration's foresight: "Never have there been six years of such far-flung internal preparedness in our history." In a much-quoted passage, he seemed to herald the end of experimentation: "We have now passed the period of internal conflict in the launching of our program of social reform. Our full energies may now be released to invigorate the processes of recovery in order to preserve our reforms, and to give every man and woman who wants to work a real job at a living wage." Three nights later FDR warned his fellow Democrats at the annual Jackson Day dinner that they could expect to retain power for their party "only so long as it can, as a party, get those things done which non-Democrats, as well as Democrats, put it in power to do." The President professed to be pleased at the prospect that the Republicans would now have some strength of their own. "The first effect of the gains made by the Republican Party in the recent election should be to restore it to the open allegiance of those who entered our primaries and party councils with deliberate intent to destroy our party's unity and effectiveness." His message was a simple one: the Democratic Party deserved power only if it remained liberal and (as he saw it) responsive to the needs of the people. The implications of FDR's Jackson Day address were clear enough for anyone to see.

The year 1939 brought the Roosevelt Administration a series of domestic setbacks at the hands of a Congress now dominated by a southern Democratic–Republican coalition, especially powerful in the House. The new Republican minority leader of the House, Representative Joseph W. Martin Jr. of Massachusetts, proved to be highly adept at marshaling his forces behind proposals of anti-New Deal Democrats, often led by his friend Representative Eugene Cox of Georgia. Relief spending was cut drastically, and certain programs, notably the Federal Theater Project, were eliminated. The Administration resisted a series of efforts to modify its pro-organized labor policies. The only major piece of domestic legislation passed in 1939 was the Administrative Reorganization Act, a modified version of the rejected 1937–38 bill, important chiefly for its provision permitting the establishment of the Executive Office of the President. Even this measure was not passed without heroic efforts by Administration leaders, indicating how far Congress had gone in its willingness to stifle every proposal coming from the White House.

It was to be foreign policy that would be Franklin Roosevelt's principal concern in 1939. In his January 4 State of the Union Message he warned, "There are many methods short of war, but stronger and more effective than mere words, of bringing home to aggressor governments the aggregate sentiments of our own people." He hinted broadly that he would ask Congress to alter the Neutrality Act of 1937, with its mandatory arms embargo: "At the very least, we can and should avoid any action, or any lack of action, which will encourage, assist, or build up an aggressor. We have learned that when we deliberately try to legislate neutrality, our neutrality laws may operate unevenly and unfairly — may actually give aid to an aggressor and deny it to the victim. The instinct of self-preservation should warn us that we ought not to let that happen any more." Unfortunately for his cause, Roosevelt decided to leave the initiative up to the Democratic leadership of Congress, perhaps sensing that his own growing unpopularity in both houses might imperil his program. The seniority rule, however, was unkind to the Administration. Neither the chairman of the Senate Committee on Foreign Relations, the erratic and bibulous Key Pittman of Nevada, nor the clownish chairman of the House Committee on Foreign Affairs, Sol Bloom of New York, was a competent leader. Leaders of the Senate "peace bloc," such as Arthur H. Vandenberg of Michigan and William E. Borah of Idaho, both Republicans, were more than a match for Pittman. Faced by divided counsels and inadequate aid from the State Department and White House, Pittman allowed matters to drift through the early months of 1939, even after the Nazi takeover of the remains of Czechoslovakia in March made the coming of war to Europe seem closer than ever before. Late in May, at the belated request of Secretary of State Cordell Hull, Sol Bloom introduced an Administration measure for the modification of the Neutrality Act. Bloom's bill would have repealed the arms embargo and given the President extensive discretionary powers, including the right to designate combat zones off-limits to American vessels. His measure also provided that title to goods exported to belligerents would pass to them before the materials left the United States ("cash-and-carry," as it was dubbed). The committee, by a strict party line vote of twelve Democrats in favor and eight Republicans against, reported the Bloom bill on June 13. With the House Democratic leadership expecting early passage, and trouble in the Senate, the House instead adopted an amendment by John M. Vorys (Republican, Ohio) that retained the embargo on arms and ammunition while lifting it on "implements of war" (things that might be used for peaceful purposes). It was Hamilton Fish Jr. of New York, who forced the vote on the Vorys amendment; the roll-call on April 30 found the Republicans solidly opposed, 150 in favor to 7 against, while the Democrats were badly divided.

With the adoption of the Vorys amendment, which destroyed the heart of the Administration's bill, attention turned back to the Senate, where Pittman was still dragging his feet. The showdown came in a meeting of the Foreign Relations Committee on July 12, when a motion was carried by one vote to postpone any further consideration of neutrality legislation until the next session of Congress (January 1940, unless summoned earlier by the President). The deciding vote against the Administration was cast by Walter F. George, an old Wilsonian internationalist known to favor repeal of the embargo, but also one of the would-be victims of Roosevelt's 1938 purge. The President tried for one more week to get his bill passed. Finally, he summoned a small bipartisan meeting of Senate leaders to see if something could be done. Borah told the gathering that war was not about to break out, regardless of what the President contended: "I have my own sources of information which I have provided for myself, and on several occasions I've found them more reliable than the State Department." Although Borah's words were to attain a sort of immortality of their own, it was what Vice-President John Nance Garner told Roosevelt that mattered: "You haven't got the votes, and that's all there is to it."

When the Nazis invaded Poland on September 1, 1939, and declarations of war by Britain and France followed, President Roosevelt told his people by radio, "This nation must remain a neutral nation, but I cannot ask that every American remain neutral in thought as well." His own dislike of the Nazis and his determination to aid the western Allies was, of course, very widely known. On September 5 he, issued two neutrality proclamations, one of the traditional sort, warning Americans against committing non-neutral acts, the other in conformity with the Neutrality Act of 1937. This second placed an embargo on the sale of arms, ammunition, and implements of war to belligerents. Roosevelt now had to face the nightmare he had so long worried about, a situation in which Allied control of the seas would be rendered meaningless. Neutrality would favor the aggressor, Germany, since it would deny American war materials to those resisting the Nazis.

Roosevelt decided to call Congress into special session to secure repeal (or at least modification) of the embargo act. This time he prepared his campaign with care, knowing that the matter was far too serious to be left up to people like Pittman and Bloom. First, he cultivated dissident southern Democrats, either directly or through neutral politicians. Second, he sought and found support among the leaders of the business community, long since disaffected as a consequence of the New Deal. Finally, he decided to stress bipartisanship, inviting the defeated 1936 Republican candidates, Landon and Colonel Frank Knox, to attend a White House conference with leaders of both parties in Congress. On September 21, the day after the conference, a grim-faced President made a powerful address to a joint session of Congress. He called for "a greater consistency through the repeal of the embargo provisions, and a return to international law," for the protection of the Western Hemisphere. He insisted, however, that the Government had the obligation to keep American ships and citizens out of combat zones, and he flatly opposed the extension of loans and credits to belligerents. An international lawyer might have had trouble locating precedents for such things, but Franklin Roosevelt was selling a policy and not practicing law, and he knew well that he would have to win votes away from the powerful "peace bloc." Furthermore, the President favored "requiring the foreign buyer to take transfer of title in this country to commodities purchased by belligerents." This requirement and the ban on credits ensured that purchases would "be made in cash, and all cargoes ... be carried in the purchasers' own ships, at the purchasers' own risk."

The isolationists — or "peace bloc," as they liked to call themselves — went into action at once. A group of twenty-four gathered in Senator Hiram Johnson's office and vowed to fight the Administration's efforts. Both Johnson and Borah were now long past their prime, but they had strong supporters among the younger men, including Vandenberg, Gerald P. Nye (Republican, North Dakota), Robert M. La Follette Jr. (Progressive, Wisconsin), Burton K. Wheeler (Democrat, Montana), and Bennett C. Clark (Democrat, Missouri). It was a skilled, formidable group, but the Administration did not lack able supporters of its own. These included Landon and Knox, former Secretary of State Henry L. Stimson, publisher Henry Luce, and editor William Allen White. The Pittman Bill passed the Senate after prolonged and bitter debate on October 27, by a vote of 63 to 30. Only twelve Democrats voted no, while fifteen Republicans were opposed. The crucial vote in the House came on November 2 over a measure that would have required the House members of the Conference Committee to insist on the retention of the arms embargo. This resolution went down to defeat, supported by only thirty-seven Democrats and opposed by 217; Republicans, however, favored the measure, 142–24. On the final roll-call on the conference committee report, only six Republican senators and nineteen Republican congressmen favored the Pittman embargo repeal bill. The Republican Party in both houses of Congress had an almost completely isolationist voting record as 1940 opened. Would this have an effect on the party's chances at winning the election?

Early in 1940, Republican prospects for the presidential campaign were clouded by two puzzling phenomena — the Second World War and Franklin D.

Roosevelt. The war was then in what was popularly if inelegantly called its "phony" stage in western Europe; it was not yet certain whether it would develop into major, bloody strife. Poland had been conquered and Russia was in the process of overwhelming Finland, but Germany and its major western opponents, Britain and France, were holding back. Would a kind of stalemate continue indefinitely and the war never really materialize? Military experts disputed among themselves on this point and many others. Meanwhile, the American Administration pursued its policy of neutrality-in-favor-of-the-Allies and continued to build up its own military strength.

The Roosevelt phenomenon puzzled Democrats and independents as well as Republicans. Indeed, the President kept his intentions about a possible third term a secret from his own intimates; his remarks were either cryptic or evasive, both in public and (apparently) in private. Surviving friends continue to argue about Roosevelt's intentions thirty years later, and historians have no really firm evidence about when he decided to do what. All that is certain is that, until well into the spring, no one knew for sure what FDR would do in 1940. By that time, the phenomenon of the war had also been clarified. Whether there was a cause-and-effect relationship here is not entirely clear, but in the practical politics of the time this scarcely made any difference.

In the early months of 1940, there appeared to be three serious candidates for the Republican presidential nomination: District Attorney Thomas E. Dewey, and Senators Robert A. Taft and Arthur H. Vandenberg. A Gallup Poll of Republicans published on March 25 indicated that Dewey was the choice of 43 percent, Vandenberg of 22 percent, and Taft of 17 percent; no other potential candidate secured as much as 10 percent of the sample. Another poll published the same day indicated the Republican nomination prediction of a segment of the voting public at large. A majority (51 percent) expected Dewey to be the candidate, with 24 percent picking Vandenberg and 17 percent Taft. While these and other polls seemed conclusive enough, there existed a certain amount of doubt about the strength of each of the three. This doubt would be intensified if the international situation deteriorated — and if President Roosevelt decided to be a candidate again. An assessment of the attributes of the Republican contenders shows clearly enough that the party, resurrected though it was, was still far from robust.

Dewey had two serious shortcomings — his youth and his lack of an important political office. At thirty-seven, he was only two years over the constitutional minimum age for the Presidency. When he announced his candidacy in December 1939, the terrible-tempered Secretary of the Interior, Harold L. Ickes, chortled that Dewey had "thrown his diaper into the ring." This rather nasty jibe, destined to go into the annals of political wisecracks, was quoted frequently and served to remind people of Dewey's youth in a time of crisis. While he was one of the country's most important prosecutors, with a long list of important criminal convictions to his credit, he had lost his bid for the governorship of New York in 1938. Apparently recognizing that he would have to demonstrate his energy and competence before the public if he were to have any chance at the nomination, he entered the presidential preference primaries, and won most of them. With the bulk of his own New York delegation pledged to him plus the convention votes he picked up in the primaries and the popular strength he was shown to have by the opinion polls, Dewey was a formidable candidate by early spring. His brand of Republicanism was a moderate one, as befitted the former running-mate of Mayor Fiorello La Guardia, and his foreign policy was one well suited to the holder of the office of District Attorney of New York County. In essence, Dewey was a personality in search of policy as well as power.

Taft, the son of former President William Howard Taft, was a conservative fifty-year-old freshman U.S. Senator from Ohio. Joining the small and not very hardy band of Republicans in the Senate, he had soon drawn attention to himself as a relentless, articulate opponent of the New Deal domestic policies and Roosevelt's foreign program. He worked closely with the southern Democrats to become one of the leaders of the Senate's conservative coalition. While it is true that he became a rather tardy convert to the arms embargo repeat in the fall of 1939, this was almost the only blotch on his otherwise-perfect isolationist voting record. Taft's strength lay with the Old-Guard Republican organization men and women, the people who still remembered his father with affection and who saw in the son a hope for a restoration of the "good old days" before the First World War. These people may have been naive, but they were devoted and hard working; their strength was concentrated in the Midwest and South. By arrangement with his fellow leader, Governor John W. Bricker, Taft had the powerful Ohio delegation as the core of his convention support. Taft's recent entry into national politics was not the liability it might have been in other times simply because of the previous weakness of his party. He did, however, have one serious shortcoming as a politician, an aloof, almost icy, public personality (quite unlike his affable father's). Taft seemed quite unhappy in the role of political campaigner and indulged in it as little as he could manage. Thus, he avoided the primaries and cultivated his fellow professional politicians.

Vandenberg was a veteran senator, a member of the upper house since 1928. Although he was only in his mid-fifties, he somehow appeared to be older. A journalist before he entered Congress, Vandenberg seemed to be almost a caricature of the pompous, old-fashioned, spread-eagle orator in manner and appearance; he was a cartoonist's delight. His voting record was slightly more liberal than Taft's, as well as a decade longer, but in foreign policy matters his isolationism was perfectly consistent. It is not clear that Vandenberg was really serious about his candidacy in 1940, although it is possible that he thought that he would win out on the basis of his political experience. It is certain that he did not campaign widely, either out of inertia or overconfidence. When Dewey went to Wisconsin for a whirlwind campaign and displayed his stamina as well as a new-found fondness for isolationism, Vandenberg stayed in Washington. On April 2, Dewey swept the Wisconsin primary, seriously damaging Vandenberg's hopes. When Dewey repeated the feat in Nebraska a week later, Vandenberg was typed as a loser even in his own Midwest. Vandenberg's Michigan delegation was his power base. but he seemed to be the hero only of the stern, unbending isolationists of the West, still mourning the recent demise of their ancient hero, Borah of Idaho.

In retrospect, it can be seen that Dewey, Taft, and Vandenberg were essentially fairweather candidates. It is quite possible that any one of them might have been nominated and elected President of the United States if the war in western Europe had remained "phony" and if Roosevelt had decided not to seek reelection. But on April 9, the day of the Nebraska primary, Nazi forces invaded Denmark and Norway; Denmark fell at once, Norway was occupied after three weeks of resistance. On May 10, the Germans launched their *blitzkrieg* against the Low Countries and France. By June 22, the Battle of France was over and an armistice had been signed. German power seemed to many to be invincible; some expected Britain to be bombed into submission or conquered by invasion. Thus, by the time the Republican national convention met at Philadelphia on June 24, the world crisis had increased the probability that Roosevelt would run again. It had also emphasized the weaknesses of the three major Republican aspirants.

Fortunately for the Republican Party, in 1940 there was an alternative (albeit an unlikely one) to the three major candidates for the nomination. Wendell L. Willkie, head of the great Commonwealth and Southern utilities corporation, had been brought to the attention of the American public and especially to the convention delegates by an energetic and well-financed publicity campaign. His emergence as a serious contender for the nomination coincided with the very world crisis that brought trouble to the three apparent front-runners and can only be explained in terms of that crisis. The current edition of *Who's Who in America* listed him as a Democrat. When Willkie arrived in Philadelphia seeking the Republican nomination for President, he was told semi-publicly by Old-Guard former Senator Jim Watson, "Well, Wendell, you know that back home in Indiana it's all right if the town whore joins the church, but they don't let her lead the choir the first night."

Had the times been "normal," Willkie's nomination by the Republican national convention would have been inconceivable. Forty-eight years old, Indiana-born and educated, Willkie was the son of two active attorneys, themselves the children of German immigrants. He was both a Wall Street lawyer and the head of a privately owned utility, and thus he simultaneously held two of the least popular positions a candidate for the Presidency could have had. Furthermore, he had never once run for office and had never even held an appointive post in government at any level.

Wendell Willkie began his own law practice in Akron, Ohio, in 1919 and remained there until 1929, when he moved to New York City to join a law firm that represented Commonwealth and Southern. Less than four years later, Willkie had risen to the presidency of the corporation at a difficult time, the worst of the Great Depression. Between 1933 and 1939, he became the very symbol of beleaguered private enterprise as he sought to defend his private utility in the losing struggle against the Tennessee Valley Authority. Willkie was both a hard fighter and a highly attractive personality, a tousled, rumpled figure, informal and folksy with his Hoosier twang, enthusiastic and very nearly indefatigable. Not until he had been convinced by Supreme Court decisions that his was a losing cause — and until he got the Roosevelt Administration and Congress to agree to limit the area of TVA operations — did he finally quit. He drove a hard bargain when he finally sold his company's properties in its region to the TVA in 1939.

In spite of the Wall Street–utilities connection that made many western progressives permanently suspicious of him, Willkie was no reactionary. Indeed, he was far more of a liberal than a conservative. He was openly sympathetic with much New Deal social legislation and with the labor movement. Unlike most Republicans, he strongly supported the reciprocal trade agreements program. Finally, he was quite convinced that healthy economic growth was attainable with an enlightened policy on the part of the Federal Government. He loved to debate with those who considered the economy "mature" and the unemployment problem permanent.

Nor was Willkie an isolationist. In Ohio he had been an associate and strong partisan of Newton D. Baker, Woodrow Wilson's second Secretary of War and the recognized upholder of the Wilsonian faith. In 1924, Willkie had been a delegate from Ohio to the Democratic national convention at Madison Square Garden, where he had voted (in vain) for an explicit endorsement of American membership in the League of Nations. After this time, Willkie's interest in world affairs seems to have diminished for a while, especially after he moved to New York and became deeply involved in the intricate affairs of Commonwealth and Southern. But by the late 1930s, Willkie was again identifying himself with his old Wilsonian persuasion in a form now commonly known as "collective security against aggression." He condemned Hitler's Third Reich as the Nazis expanded into central Europe and as they continued their persecution of the Jewish people. Moreover, he advocated the lifting of the arms embargo and other measures to assist Britain and France. By the time the Republican convention met in late June 1940, Willkie alone among the possible nominees for President had a clear, consistent anti-isolationist position on foreign policy.

It is not at all surprising that among Willkie's ever-widening circle of friends and admirers he should have won growing respect as the epitome of the businessman–statesman — and a potentially superb, if highly unorthodox, candidate for the Republican nomination. Contrary to widespread popular belief at the time and to political folklore in the years since 1940, the "Draft Willkie" movement was not an overnight affair that suddenly swept the convention off its feet. Arthur Krock, in his influential *New York Times* column, named him as the "darkest horse" but the one to watch, as early as August 1939 (when Willkie had at last made his well-publicized peace with the TVA).

By this time a secret Willkie campaign force was already in existence. The prime mover was the youthful and energetic Russell Davenport, managing editor of Henry R. Luce's business magazine, *Fortune*. Davenport's chief early associates were Charlton MacVeagh, a young Wall Street financier with experience in publishing and extensive Republican Party contacts, and Frank Altschul, wealthy New York banker, a masterful fund-raiser with impeccable Republican credentials. These three complemented one another; Davenport was expert at publicity; MacVeagh was adept at getting along with party politicians, and Altschul was a near-genius at raising money from the business community. Other important members of the original Willkie team were his close friend and advisor Irita Van Doren, editor of the *New York Herald Tribune* book review section, and Congressmen Bruce Barton of New York, who had entered politics after one of the most brilliant careers in the history of the advertising business.

The Willkie publicity mounted rapidly in the early spring of 1940. But even before then his name had been kept before the public by a widely noticed series of personal and radio appearances and by the publication of a large number of articles by and about him in newspapers and magazines. The mass-circulation *Reader's Digest* ran a piece by him in December 1939. The liberal weekly *The New Republic* ran another article by Willkie in its March 18, 1940 issue.

But the Willkie campaign really broke into the open with the publication of a piece entitled "We the People" in the April issue of *Fortune*. This article appeared under Willkie's name, although it was largely the work of Russell Davenport, who also contributed an editorial underlining its importance. The main article was a vigorous liberal critique of the New Deal, which it said had "acquired a vested interest in depression." Willkie–Davenport charged that the Administration was defeatist and had retarded economic recovery because of its anti-business bias. Although there were conservative overtones in "We the People," Willkie's essential liberalism came through clearly:

> Some of the recent reforms must be modified in order to protect our power; other, new reforms may have to be introduced. For instance, there has grown up a new concept of public welfare. Our new outlook must include this. Government, either state or federal, must be responsible not only for the destitute and the unemployed, but for elementary guarantees of public health, the rehabilitation of farmers, rebuilding of the soil, preservation of the national forests, clearance and elimination of city slums and so forth.

He particularly stressed the need for increased productivity and left no doubt that he sincerely believed that it could be attained if the Federal Government would only adopt policies "*primarily* for the sake of generating opportunities for private enterprise." Willkie attacked the New Deal for its inability to conquer the Depression; these points appealed strongly to conservatives who might otherwise have been put off by his approval of the Administration's social welfare program. "We the People" took a firm anti-isolationist position in foreign policy, condemning "aggressive countries" and calling for freer world trade and improved standards of living in other parts of the world. Willkie–Davenport concluded, "We do not want a New Deal any more. We want a New World."

One of the many interested readers of the Fortune piece was Oren Root Jr., twenty-eight year old New York lawyer and grandnephew of former Secretary of

State Elihu Root. Oren Root had not yet met Willkie, but he had been attracted to him while watching him deliver one of his vigorous speeches. Root was especially impressed with the "petition" accompanying the Willkie article, a brief hard-hitting summary of the people's alleged grievances against Franklin D. Roosevelt. Root decided to have copies of the petition printed for wide circulation and he placed an advertisement in the *Herald Tribune* asking for aid in the distribution of the document. Davenport and his associates had already secured the establishment of about two thousand Willkie "mailing clubs," with the assistance of private utility companies throughout the country. These clubs were alerted by telegram to Root's appeal, and Root and his friends were almost inundated by responses. Davenport was apparently alarmed at what he felt was a premature campaign, but after all it was Davenport who had brought Willkie's candidacy into the open and he could scarcely deny Root the chance to do his own part. This episode indicates that the Willkie campaign was still an amateurish affair, in spite of its strong financial support and of the really talented people involved.

Between April 9, when Root began to mail out his petitions, and June 24, when the Republican national convention met, the Willkie bandwagon picked up speed as well as eminent passengers. The Luce magazines — *Time*, *Life*, and *Fortune* — the Scripps-Howard newspapers (ardent supporters of Roosevelt in 1932 and 1936), the Cowles newspapers in Minneapolis and Des Moines (as well as the Cowles magazine *Look*), and the *New York Herald Tribune* were all enlisted in the cause, although the latter held back its front-page endorsement until June 27. Important supporters were gathered in the business-financial world by Altschul and his associates: Lammont DuPont, Ernest T. Weir, Thomas W. Lamont, Edgar Monsato Queeny, and Joseph N. Pew Jr. This group was bitterly anti-New Deal and (with the possible exception of Lamont) basically conservative, but they felt drawn to Willkie as one of their own — and as a possible winner. Even the conservative Republican national chairman John D. M. Hamilton was a secret member of the Willkie camp, as was Governor Harold E. Stassen of Minnesota, the convention keynoter. Joseph W. Martin of Massachusetts, Republican minority leader of the House and permanent chairman of the convention, was also a secret Willkie man. Indeed, the convention machinery was completely, if surreptitiously, controlled by the Willkie forces.

Willkie arrived in Philadelphia two days before the convention opened to take charge of his own campaign, a most unorthodox step. Willkie clubs deluged the delegates with thousands of telegrams and uncounted numbers of letters and phone calls. Hundreds of "Willkie amateurs" showed up in person to buttonhole delegates, circulate petitions, and in various other ways throw their energies into the fight. The Willkie crusade had an almost religious fervor about it at this stage; it drew its strength from middle-class business and professional people who did not normally engage in political activity and who were generally suspicious of those who did so. The forces of the regular candidates — Dewey, Taft and Vandenberg, as well as the usual favorite sons — hardly knew how to cope with the Willkie drive; one delegate said that his campaign was "unfair to organized politics."

The convention began on Monday, June 24, just four days after President Roosevelt had dramatically appointed important Republicans to the chief defense positions in his cabinet. The new Secretary of War was Henry L. Stimson of New York, who had held the same position under President William Howard Taft and had been Hoover's Secretary of State. The publisher of the *Chicago Daily News*, Colonel Frank Knox, 1936 vice-presidential candidate with Landon, was named Secretary of the Navy. These appointments were intended to give a bipartisan flavor to the Administration, to bring able men into leadership of the defense effort, and (no doubt) to take some of the sting out of the anticipated criticism by Republican orators of alleged negligence in the defense build-up. Needless to say, many Republicans were infuriated by what they considered the apostasy of Stimson and Knox; National Chairman John D. M. Hamilton sought to banish them from the party.

The keynote speaker, Harold Stassen, liberal "boy governor" of Minnesota, did not mention Stimson and Knox, however; his remarks were mostly on domestic matters, and his criticisms of Democratic foreign and defense policies were exceedingly general. Congressman Martin, the permanent chairman, a secret Willkie supporter with a consistent isolationist voting record, avoided the war issue in his address to the convention on its second day; he confined his remarks to patriotic pronouncements designed to appeal to his audience. Former President Hoover spoke to the convention that night, blistering the New Deal's record, foreign as well as domestic; if he was trying to stampede the convention into nominating himself he failed, for he roused little enthusiasm among the delegates. The platform plank on foreign policy, finally revised and polished for acceptance on Wednesday, was in line with Hoover's position. It favored "the extension to all peoples fighting for liberty, or whose liberty is threatened, of such aid as shall not be in violation of international law or inconsistent with the requirements of our own defense." This was eminently satisfactory even to such last-ditch isolationists as Congressman Hamilton Fish. At the same time, the vagueness of the plank made it seem flexible to the Willkie people, who decided not to contest it while they were still seeking to win the nomination for their candidate.

A simple majority of the one thousand delegates was necessary. Dewey, the apparent leader, decided that his best chance lay in getting the largest possible vote on the first ballot; if he could get four hundred or so he might be able to count on the bandwagon spirit to bring him the rest. Taft, with his fifty-two Ohio delegates, one hundred more from the South and about one hundred from scattered areas, decided to move cautiously, building up his count from ballot to ballot. Vandenberg had the 38 votes of Michigan and about the same number from various places; his only hope was to win after the leaders became deadlocked. While there were several favorite-son candidates, it was evident by the second day that only Willkie was a serious rival for the leaders. That night a secret meeting of emissaries from Dewey and Taft was held, in an effort to settle things on the first ballot. But the Taft people would not step aside for Dewey, and the Dewey people would not step aside for Taft. And thus passed the only real opportunity to stop Willkie on the first ballot.

The Willkie strategy was similar to Taft's: begin with a small but respectable vote and add to it from ballot to ballot, as the delegates were freed of their obligations to favorite sons and other faltering candidates. The Willkie managers hoped that this would have the added benefit of not arousing a "stop-Willkie" coalition until it was too late. It was well known that many of the delegates in the Dewey camp were tied to their man by only the most fragile of threads. In view of his youth and his rather minor position as a county prosecutor, Dewey did not inspire confidence among those who wanted a man who could win in November. On Wednesday, before the roll-call for nominations began, Governor Stassen officially assumed the role of Willkie's floor manager. Willkie's name was placed in the running as Indiana's favorite son by Congressman Charles Halleck. He replied to those who had stressed their own candidate's long records as party workers by asking, "Is the Republican Party a closed corporation? Do you have to be born in it?" After Halleck's speech, Martin recessed the convention until the following morning, allowing time for Halleck's remarks to be widely publicized and for the delegates to ponder the implications of his questions.

The balloting began late Thursday afternoon. Two votes were taken before a dinner recess was called. The totals for the chief candidates were:

	First ballot	Second ballot
Dewey	360	338
Taft	189	203
Willkie	105	171
Vandenberg	76	73

These ballots clearly illustrated Dewey's vulnerability and Vandenberg's continued weakness. They also showed that both Taft and Willkie had reserve strength and that the contest would be between them. After the recess, Dewey went steadily downhill: 315 on the third ballot; 250 on the fourth; a mere 57 on the fifth. The corresponding figures for Vandenberg were 72, 61, and 42; he, too, was fading fast. On the third ballot Willkie took the lead over Taft and never lost it. Their vote was 259 to 212 on the third; 306 to 254 on the fourth; and 429 to 377 on the fifth. The sixth ballot was the last. As the galleries kept up their chant of "We Want Willkie," delegates began to abandon their favorite sons (including Vandenberg). By the time Virginia cast its vote, Willkie had his majority. As others began to switch, a motion by Governor Bricker of Ohio to make the vote unanimous was carried with a roar.

Wendell Willkie won the Republican nomination for President in the early hours of Friday June 28. There remained only the problem of choosing a running-mate. Congressman Martin, well aware of the way in which the Democrats would put the "Power Trust" label on Willkie, strongly recommended Senator Charles L. NcNary of Oregon, a strong advocate of public power and reclamation projects.

McNary's high tariff views and his consistent isolationism were in striking contrast with Willkie's positions, but the veteran western senator would give what the professionals call "balance" to the ticket. McNary agreed to run with great reluctance and only out of loyalty to the party whose Senate Leader he had long been. When the choice of McNary had been ratified, Willkie appeared briefly before the convention to state that he had made no pledges except to advance "your cause" and to preserve democracy; he promised them a "crusading, vigorous, fighting campaign." With characteristic tactlessness he concluded, "And so, you Republicans, I call upon you to join me." It was a proper climax for a most untypical presidential candidate.

By the time of Willkie's victory at Philadelphia the Democratic Party appeared to be destined to nominate Franklin D. Roosevelt for a third term. The President had not yet spoken out about his intentions, but he had not eliminated himself from the race. Nor had he disavowed the endorsements he had received from such New Deal stalwarts as Senator Joseph Guffey of Pennsylvania and Governor Culbert L. Olson of California and from certain members of the Cabinet (Ickes, Wallace, Hopkins, and Attorney General Frank Murphy). He flatly refused to discuss his political future at press conferences.

It is noteworthy that those who endorsed FDR for a third term frequently contended that he was the only Democrat who could win in 1940. And, especially after the outbreak of the Second World War, his supporters began to stress his experience in foreign affairs and to do variations on that old political adage, "Don't change horses in the middle of the stream." Roosevelt's own attitude (something always difficult to pin down) was perhaps best expressed in a letter he sent to Colonel Frank Knox at the end of 1939, when he was already trying to get Knox to take a seat in the Cabinet:

> If things continue as they are today and there is a stalemate or what might be called a normal course of war in Europe, I take it that we shall have an old fashioned hot and bitter campaign this Summer and Autumn. Such campaigns — viewing with alarm and pointing with pride — are a little stupid and a little out of date, and their appeal to prejudice does little to encourage a more intelligent electorate....
>
> On the other hand, if there should develop a real crisis such as you suggest — a German–Russian victory — it would be necessary to put aside in large part strictly old fashioned party government, and the people would understand such a situation. If this develops, I want you to know that I would still want you as a part of such an Administration.

While Roosevelt was being cautious, his implication seemed to be that he had little taste for running again unless "a real crisis" developed in Europe; if this were to happen he clearly expected to run and to win. It is notable, however, that FDR did not flatly declare himself out of the race if the European war continued to run "a normal course," even in this private letter to one of the most eminent Republican supporters of his foreign policy.

Meanwhile, several other Democratic candidacies had been at least tentatively considered by the White House. Indeed, the list of people who had been led to believe that they were under consideration, or had convinced themselves that they had been so led, was a very long one. Roosevelt himself certainly encouraged Harry Hopkins, well before the second term was half over. Hopkins was made Secretary of Commerce early in 1939, as part of an obvious build-up, but drastic surgery and continued illness put an end to his presidential aspirations.

Others who were encouraged by the White House were Paul V. McNutt and Cordell Hull. McNutt, former governor of Indiana and High Commissioner to the Philippines, was named as the first head of the new Federal Security Agency in the summer of 1939. McNutt clubs began to appear about the country, but his candidacy flickered and died when his campaign failed to win any significant support outside Hoosier circles. On various occasions, Roosevelt told Secretary of State Hull that he hoped Hull would be the next President. It is doubtful that Roosevelt was being more than polite to his sixty-eight-year-old Cabinet officer, and it is certain that the presidential candidacy of Hull failed to excite many Democratic politicians outside the South.

More important than any of these possibilities for the presidential nomination were two "self-starters," Vice-President John Nance Garner of Texas and Postmaster-General (and Democratic national chairman) James A. Farley of New York. Relations between Roosevelt and his running-mate of 1932 and 1936 had deteriorated since the beginning of the Great Court Fight in February 1937; by now they scarcely existed. Garner openly opposed much of the later New Deal program, and he made no secret of his long-lived isolationism. He was not willing to run again with FDR even if Roosevelt had wanted him to do so. In December 1939, "Cactus Jack" Garner announced that he was willing to accept the presidential nomination. He was not, however, willing to campaign for it since he seemed to find public speaking a great bore. New Dealers, as well as most "regulars" were determined to stop the seventy-one-year-old Garner, and they did so in one primary after another, culminating in his utter humiliation in the California election in May. Even in Texas, Garner was reduced to the status of a mere favorite son, since Congressmen Sam Rayburn and Lyndon B. Johnson were able to arrange for the delegation to switch to Roosevelt after casting a complimentary vote for Garner.

The candidacy of Farley was a far more difficult matter for the President. FDR had asked his veteran campaign manager to run for governor of New York in 1938, impressing on Farley that this would be part of a build-up for higher office. But Farley refused to run, preferring to seek the Presidency (or perhaps the Vice-Presidency) in 1940. Early that year, he announced that a slate pledged to him had been entered in the Massachusetts primary. The Roosevelt forces, still attempting to placate the valuable Farley, did not oppose his delegation in this primary, the only one Farley contested. In New York, the President vainly sought to secure a favorite-son vote for Governor Herbert H. Lehman; in time a compromise was worked out, giving Farley a sizeable minority of the delegation. The Postmaster-

General was embittered when he read frequent press reports that he was considered ineligible for the Presidency by many people (including FDR) because of his Roman Catholic faith. Farley was further disappointed by the great party bosses who ran the city and state machines and who had often proclaimed their complete loyalty to him (in exchange, of course, for his many favors to them). They were now quite unwilling to support him because they were convinced that only Roosevelt could carry many of the Democratic state tickets to victory.

Roosevelt summoned Farley to Hyde Park early in July, a week before the Democratic National Convention was scheduled to meet in Chicago. The President informed a not-too-surprised Farley what he intended to tell the convention: that he did not seek renomination but was willing to run again if drafted. Farley replied that he would not stand aside, since he disapproved of the third-term candidacy; he also announced that he would soon resign from the Cabinet and from the national chairmanship. Thus, the 1940 campaign would have to be managed by someone else. This meeting, which must have been highly unpleasant for both men, terminated a long and mutually profitable friendship.

The Democratic national convention met in Chicago on Monday July 15 under the watchful eye of Mayor Edward J. Kelly. The mayor, one of the most powerful city bosses of his time, had visited with the President and a group of intimate White House advisors just a week before and was fully aware of FDR's political plans. Kelly, as host to the convention, violated political etiquette when, in his opening greetings, he came out with an endorsement of Roosevelt:

> The salvation of the nation rests in one man, because of his experience and great humanitarian thinking. I think I know that the President has no wish to labor longer under the burden of this office. He has discouraged every advance I have made toward his becoming a candidate. He is not a candidate.
>
> But this convention faces a world condition that surmounts any man's convenience. We must overrule his comfort and convenience and draft Roosevelt.

That night, Farley, as national chairman, addressed the delegates in what many knew would probably be his swan song. He warmly endorsed the record of the Democratic Administration (without mentioning Roosevelt's name) and asserted, "The choice still lies between a party unable to cope with the conditions and problems of the 20th Century and a party which has made this nation the last stronghold of genuine democracy in a world of violence and ruthless force." He pledged his support to the nominees of the convention and to "our successors" in the party organization. Speaker of the House William B. Bankhead of Alabama came next, delivering a lengthy keynote address in which he lauded the Administration's domestic accomplishments in great detail and praised its foreign policy and defense achievements. Like Farley, Bankhead was careful not to mention the President by name.

Even before the convention opened, Secretary of Commerce Harry L. Hopkins, fresh from nearly continuous conferences with FDR and his trusted political associates, had moved into a suite in the Blackstone Hotel to act as the President's personal emissary. A direct telephone line to the White House symbolized his authority. The rumpled, restless, rough-spoken Hopkins, never before involved in any way with a national party convention, had the task of coordinating the communications between Roosevelt and his convention forces. One of his goals was to make the President's renomination as painless and as much like a draft as possible. The other was to see to it that the convention ratified FDR's own choice for his running-mate.

Before Hopkins left Washington, he knew that Roosevelt was leaning toward Henry A. Wallace for the vice-presidential nomination; this did not please Hopkins, who had never been one of Wallace's admirers, but he was utterly loyal to the President. Roosevelt's reasons for preferring Wallace are not entirely clear. The Secretary of Agriculture had recently overcome his worries about deficit spending and become a thoroughgoing New Dealer. Furthermore, he was an ardent, outspoken supporter of Roosevelt's foreign policy. Finally, the President seemed to believe that Wallace, although he had never run for elective office and was only a recent convert to the Democratic Party, would have considerable strength in the midwestern farm states, where disillusionment with the Roosevelt regime had long been evident.

FDR apparently gave serious consideration to only two other possible running-mates, Secretary Hull and Senator James F. Byrnes of South Carolina. Hull was probably passed over because of his age and his lack of enthusiasm for certain New Deal domestic programs. Byrnes, a powerful supporter of the Administration as well as a personal friend of the President, had two serious liabilities: he was an ex-Catholic and he was a southerner. His presence on the ticket with Roosevelt would not have strengthened it, and might have brought danger in the North and West, where many voters disliked the racial attitudes of the white South.

Hopkins carried with him to Chicago a longhand letter from the President for delivery to Speaker Bankhead, in which Roosevelt said that he had no wish to remain in office after January 1941, and asked Bankhead to tell the convention this fact in the course of his keynote address. Roosevelt also toyed with the idea of sending a similar letter to Senator George W. Norris (Independent, Nebraska), long a symbol of nonpartisanship in American public life. But neither letter was delivered, since FDR and his associates concluded that they might not produce the desired effect — a "draft" of Roosevelt by the convention. Bankhead was not very friendly, and Norris was not even a Democrat. Instead, on the second day of the convention the President told his press conference that he had sent a message to the delegates. This message was delivered that night at the conclusion of his characteristically rambling speech by the convention's permanent chairman, Alben Barkley of Kentucky, Senate majority leader and faithful New Dealer. Barkley read what Roosevelt had written out for him:

> I and other close friends of the President have long known that he has no wish to be a candidate again. We know, too, that in no way whatsoever has he exerted any influence in the selection of delegates or upon the opinions of delegates.
>
> Tonight, at the specific request and authorization of the President, I am making this simple fact clear to the Convention.

The President has never had, and has not today, any desire or purpose to continue in the office of President, to be a candidate for that office, or to be nominated by the Convention for that office.

He wishes in all earnestness and sincerity to make it clear that all the delegates to this Convention are free to vote for any candidate.

At the conclusion of Barkley's speech, the giant amplifying system of the Coliseum blared forth with shouts of "Illinois wants Roosevelt," "America wants Roosevelt," and even "The world wants Roosevelt." These shouts, which stirred up some floor demonstrations, went on for over an hour. Meanwhile, all the microphones in the hall had been cut off, except that reserved for the chairman. Warren Moscow, an enterprising reporter for *The New York Times*, traced the voice to the electrician's office in the basement and found that it belonged to Chicago's Superintendent of Sewers. Moscow discovered that city officer, on special assignment by Mayor Kelly, hard at work on the job of stirring up a demonstration via the loud speaker system. Barkley finally restored order and recessed the convention after midnight. Moscow's discovery was reported in the *Times* and elsewhere, and "the voice from the sewer" has ever since been accorded a somewhat inglorious place in the annals of American politics.

On the following afternoon (July 17), the platform, a draft of which Hopkins had brought with him from Washington, was adopted. The President himself had resolved the committee's knottiest problem by advising it to add the words "except in case of attack" to the plank disavowing any intention to "participate in foreign wars" or to send Americans "to fight in lands across the sea." The only excitement over the platform on the convention floor came when a Minnesota congressman sought to amend in an anti-third term pledge; the delegates shouted down his motion.

Roosevelt's renomination was accomplished swiftly that night, but not without some bitterness. Senator Lister Hill, Alabama New Dealer, placed the President's name before the convention in a short but rousing speech; most states, as the roll-call proceeded, seconded the nomination. Three other candidates were formally placed in nomination: Garner, Farley, and Senator Millard Tydings, Maryland conservative and enemy of FDR, and one of the targets of the 1938 purge. Farley's nominating speech was made by an aged and bitter anti-New Dealer, Senator Carter Glass of Virginia. But only one ballot was needed. The vote (omitting fractions) was:

Roosevelt	946
Farley	72
Garner	61
Tydings	9
Hull	5

Roosevelt's nomination was made unanimous on the motion of Farley.

There still remained the problem of a running-mate for the President, since Vice-President Garner was both unwilling and unwanted. Soon after the convention recessed for the night, Mayor Kelly phoned FDR and learned to his dismay that

Wallace was still the President's choice. Hopkins phoned Sam Rosenman in the White House to check with FDR's chief speech drafter on the matter. When Rosenman confirmed that Wallace was the one, Hopkins replied, "There's going to be a hell of a lot of opposition. So far there must be at least ten candidates who have more votes than Wallace. It'll be a cat-and-dog fight, but I think that the Boss has enough friends here to put it over." Hopkins was right in every respect.

Delegates who had gone along with the third-term nomination because they felt it was necessary were appalled at the prospect of Wallace as Vice-President. If Roosevelt had not been adamant, it is certain that the convention would not have agreed to the Wallace nomination. Wallace was scarcely a Democrat, and he had the general reputation of being an aloof, mystical, and impractical person (although his detractors had to admit that he was both an able agricultural scientist and an effective administrator). Few delegates knew Wallace or saw any advantage in his nomination. Eight names were placed in nomination for Vice-President and in the course of the convention deliberations many harsh words were said, both about Wallace and about the dictatorial methods that were allegedly being employed to nominate him. The galleries frequently booed and hissed Wallace's name. Although half of those named withdrew from the contest, some did so with ill-concealed bitterness.

Before the actual balloting began, Eleanor Roosevelt spoke to the convention to appeal for unity behind her husband. She had come to Chicago to try to heal the party's wounds and hopefully to secure the acceptance of Wallace by acclamation. Her calm, dignified address — plus the hard practical work done on the floor of the convention by the loyal if somewhat disappointed Senator Byrnes — aided the Agriculture Secretary's cause in the time of crisis. It took only a single ballot, in which Wallace received 626 votes and Speaker Bankhead (his only serious rival) got 329, chiefly from southern and border states. Roosevelt, in the meanwhile, had been angered by the convention's attitude toward Wallace and had Rosenman prepare drafts of a withdrawal message in case the delegates had refused to ratify his choice of running-mate.

With the nomination of Wallace by the convention, however, Roosevelt was ready to accept renomination. He did so by means of a radio address beginning at 12:25 a.m. on Friday, July 19. In this message, he spoke of his "mixed feelings," his "desire for retirement on the one hand, and that quiet, invisible thing called 'conscience' on the other." He said that he had fully intended to retire after his second term but that a public statement to that effect would have tied his hands in the world crisis. He thanked the convention for its endorsement and made it clear that he would not run as a mere Democrat: "But I know you will understand the spirit in which I say that no call of Party alone would prevail upon me to accept reelection to the Presidency." He referred to the many people he had summoned to serve in the country's defense and questioned whether he had the right to "decline to serve my country in my own personal capacity, if I am called upon to do so by the people of my country." He promised to serve if drafted in the election, thanked the convention for the nomination of Wallace ("his practical idealism will be of great service to me individually and to the nation as a whole"), and paid a graceful tribute to Jim Farley.

Roosevelt, in his acceptance broadcast, emphasized that he would be almost completely absorbed by foreign policy and defense matters. He warned, however, that he would campaign under certain circumstances: "I shall not have the time or the inclination to engage in purely political debate. But I shall never be loath to call the attention of the nation to deliberate or unwitting falsifications of fact, which are sometimes made by political candidates." Toward the end of his speech he gave, in a single sentence, a clue to his basic strategy: "If our Government should pass to other hands next January — untried hands, inexperienced hands — we can merely hope and pray that they will not substitute appeasement and compromise with those who seek to destroy all democracies everywhere, including here." It was a somber message, one in which he reiterated his determination to aid victims of aggression and to preserve democracy and freedom. After the unpleasantries and tensions of the convention, the clear, dignified address must have been reassuring to many previously disgruntled delegates.

Wendell Willkie, meanwhile, was preparing his campaign against the man he liked to call "the Champ." He resigned his position at Commonwealth and Southern and began to busy himself with the problems of putting together his political team. He had won the nomination with the aid of certain professional politicians, but the impetus behind his drive had come from important parts of the business community and from an intensive propaganda campaign. His personal magnetism was probably his greatest single asset, but how could he make it widely felt, in the course of his indictment of the New Deal and his promise of an even newer one? And how could he run as the true liberal he felt himself to be (and to a very considerable extent surely was), while running as the candidate of an essentially conservative party? How could he overcome the suspicions of the professional Republican leaders in many parts of the country who viewed him as an interloper, in order to win their energetic support in the campaign? Finally, how could he compete for attention with the Commander-in-Chief at a time when the Administration's defense program was moving swiftly ahead?

These were among the more difficult problems Willkie had to face, and they proved to be ones that he never could resolve satisfactorily. While the "Willkie amateurs," symbolized by the almost ever-present Russell Davenport, continued to play a vigorous part in the campaign, the candidate felt that he had to have the fullest assistance of the "pros," who were in close touch with the faithful party workers. Early in July, just before he departed for a three-week vacation in Colorado, Willkie appointed Governor Stassen as the head of an advisory campaign committee of professionals of widely varying ideological persuasions. He also replaced Republican national chairman John D. M. Hamilton with the somewhat reluctant House minority leader, Congressman Martin. Hamilton, a man with more than his share of enemies and with the reputation of having been the 1936 "architect of defeat," remained as the well-paid executive director. The affable Martin seemed to Willkie to be the very epitome of the best type of professional politician, in spite of the fact that Martin's conservative-isolationist record was a striking contrast with Willkie's own policy professions. It is very doubtful if Martin had much real influence outside the House of Representatives Republican membership, a group with a record like his own. His political acquaintanceship outside the state of Massachusetts was limited. Willkie's own lack of political experience was shown by the approach he made to campaign management. Some analysts believed that he relied too much on his "amateurs," often offending the established leadership by so doing. Others felt that he tried too hard to appease the professionals, of whom he was still in some awe. In retrospect, it seems clear enough that Willkie did both of these things simultaneously, thus compounding the already-existing confusion in his campaign.

Willkie publicly asserted that he would be his own speechwriter with the wisecrack, "I roll my own." This was the remark of a supremely confident orator, well aware that his articulateness was a large part of his charm but thoroughly oblivious to the demands of actual, sustained campaigning. He obviously had no intention of following the fatherly advice of his running-mate, Senator McNary, who told him at their first encounter, "Don't forget, young fellow, in politics you'll never be in trouble by not saying too much." Willkie was inexperienced at reading set speeches in front of the fixed microphones employed in 1940; he had trouble with his emphases and did not always remember to speak directly into the mike. Furthermore, he had an almost irresistible tendency to ad lib, varying his speeches until newspapermen found that their advance texts were often of little use. Finally, Willkie never learned the art of pacing himself — his voice was often rasping and hoarse from overuse as well as from unnecessary shouting, and he himself was often haggard with fatigue as the campaign wore on.

Willkie began his campaign against FDR with his acceptance speech, delivered to a huge throng at his old hometown of Elwood, Indiana, on August 17. It was carefully written but far too long; Willkie doggedly read it through in the intense heat. The speech was a disappointment to those looking forward to old-fashioned political oratory. While there was a good bit of fire in the speech, its line of reasoning was scarcely one that would appeal to a mob of about two hundred thousand crammed into a town of eleven thousand normal population in the middle of summer. Willkie's shortcomings as an orator speaking before a crowd were evident to all who listened over the radio.

The main argument in the acceptance speech came early, when Willkie frankly identified himself as "a liberal Democrat who changed his party affiliation because he found democracy in the Republican Party rather than the New Deal party." He was making an appeal to Democrats as well as independents for support in a crusade to preserve "American liberty." He contended that the Republican leadership, in and out of Congress, had already joined this crusade. His chief attack on the New Deal was aimed at its alleged defeatism: "What we need in

America is a new leadership that believes in America. I represent here today the forces that will bring that leadership to you." Willkie insisted that the country was quite unable to live in isolation and expressed his sympathy with the countries that had recently lost their freedom. "In the foreign policy of the United States ... I would do everything to defend American democracy and I would refrain from doing anything that injured it." He endorsed the Administration's defense program, generally, and specifically pledged his support to "some form of selective service," as well as to the fullest possible aid to beleaguered Britain. While offering his overall approval to the Administration's expressed aims in foreign policy, he expressed serious doubts about Roosevelt's management of that policy: "There have been occasions when many of us have wondered if he is deliberately inciting us to war." He said that he considered that "it is the first duty of a President to try to maintain peace." He moved on to an endorsement of a long list of New Deal reform measures but argued that these were not enough: "I say that we must substitute for the philosophy of distributed scarcity the philosophy of unlimited productivity." Toward that end, he challenged the President to meet him in a series of debates in different parts of the country, to thrash out the "fundamental issues." The Elwood speech put forward the most advanced independent positions Willkie was to put forth during the campaign. Significantly, it was the only campaign speech not composed under stress of time and the only one that Willkie was to read verbatim.

President Roosevelt did not rise to Willkie's challenge to debate. He preferred, as always, to ignore his challengers in public, to choose his own weapons and to follow his own timetable. In his own radio acceptance speech to the Democratic convention a month before, he had announced the circumstances under which he would be willing to speak out on political matters. Roosevelt, although preoccupied with defense and foreign affairs, did not neglect to attend to his political fences. With the resignation of James A. Farley it was necessary to choose a new national chairman. Roosevelt picked his old friend Edward J. Flynn of New York, "Boss of The Bronx," an expert political technician. Flynn, who preferred to keep out of the limelight and did not want to live in Washington, did not succeed to Farley's other job, Postmaster-General; another close political associate of the President, Frank C. Walker, was named to this position. Harry Hopkins also withdrew from the Cabinet, partly on health grounds and partly because, after the Chicago convention, he had become a political liability. He was kept out of the subsequent campaign by Boss Flynn, who had a completely free hand in political management and who silenced or exiled several other New Dealers. Secretary Ickes, however, with his marvelous gift for invective and his widespread popularity as "Honest Harold," was highly welcome. Ickes made the Administration's informal reply to the Elwood address with his usual vitriol. His description of the Republican nominee, who had taken such pains in his acceptance address to identify himself as a Hoosier, as "a simple barefoot Wall Street lawyer," was to become another of the 1940 campaign's contributions to the permanent annals of American politics.

Most of the President's time in the summer of 1940 was consumed by matters of defense and foreign policy. He sought and secured from Congress huge defense appropriations; he signed a $4 billion bill on July 20 and another for $5.25 billion on September 6. On August 18, while the Battle of Britain raged on into its tenth consecutive day, he conferred on mutual defense matters with the Canadian Prime Minister, W. L. Mackenzie King, at Ogdensburg, New York. Roosevelt toured defense installations, as he was to continue to do throughout the campaign; while he made no political utterances on these occasions, he did command public attention as Commander-in-Chief. For one of his most important defense measures, selective service (or "the draft," as it was commonly called), the President sought advance support from Willkie. He did not get it, and he had to content himself with Willkie's endorsement of the principle of selective service in the Elwood address. Passage of the draft act was bitterly opposed by isolationists of both parties, as well as by some who felt that the measure was a dangerous thing to pass in a "peacetime" election year. Significantly, Senator McNary voted in favor of the bill, while Taft, Vandenberg, and most other Senate Republicans voted "no." National Chairman Martin was one of fifty-two House Republicans to vote for selective service; 112 voted against it. With strong Democratic majorities in both houses, and Willkie's moral support, the Administration won passage of the Selective Service Act, which FDR signed on September 16.

In the meanwhile, Roosevelt had sought his opponent's aid on another vital matter, a plan to provide fifty American destroyers of World War I vintage to the British, in exchange for the transfer of a chain of British bases in the Western Hemisphere. The "destroyer–bases deal" had been under negotiation between the President and Prime Minister Winston Churchill for some time, but it became highly urgent as the British found their position more and more precarious. Early in August, FDR phoned the liberal Kansas editor-publisher, William Allen White, to seek his aid in winning the advance endorsement of their mutual friend, Willkie, as well as Willkie's assistance in lining up Republican congressional support. Willkie, finding himself in a very difficult position with his fellow Republicans, declined to commit himself. When Roosevelt secured an opinion from his Attorney General that he could transfer the ships and accept the bases without the authority of Congress, the President again sought Willkie's public support. Once more Willkie declined to join forces with his opponent. The President then went ahead on his own, making a public announcement on September 3. Willkie at once announced that, while he approved of the scheme, he regretted that FDR "did not deem it necessary in connection with this proposal to secure the approval of Congress or permit public discussion prior to adoption." Three days later, after conferring with Senator Vandenberg, Willkie shifted his position. He called the deal "the most arbitrary and dictatorial action ever taken by any President in the history of the United States." Clearly, bipartisan foreign policy was going to be out of the question during the two months remaining in the 1940 campaign.

Ten days after the destroyer–bases deal was announced, Willkie began his long campaign train trips. His journeys took him to Chicago, the Southwest, and the Pacific Coast and back, up to New England and the Middle Atlantic states, back to the Midwest, and finally to Madison Square Garden, where he gave his wind-up speech on November 2. The August Gallup Polls looked very promising for Willkie, but by the middle of September they indicated that he was running behind in New York, New Jersey, and Pennsylvania and was headed for almost certain defeat. But by mid-October, Gallup's interviewers found that the decline in his popularity had been arrested. Illinois, Indiana, and Michigan were reported as switched to Willkie, and the campaign now looked like "a horse race." Soon after this, President Franklin Roosevelt announced that he would make a series of five frankly political addresses to reply to those he considered guilty of "systematic and deliberate falsification of the facts." The Roosevelt forces, having felt at the outset that Willkie was a very strong candidate, had been heartened by his popularity slump. Now the President's managers were alarmed at the sudden rise in Willkie's political fortunes.

How was it that Willkie's prestige varied so greatly during the campaign? At the time of his nomination, he seemed to be a fresh, attractive personality who might be capable of providing the country with vigorous new leadership — the very kind of leadership which most of the country had felt Franklin Roosevelt had given during his first term. However, during August and September (critical months in the Battle of Britain), the President took some decisive steps in his role as Commander-in-Chief. His huge defense program and his firm commitment to aid Britain were never more prominently displayed — and the polls showed that they were welcomed by most Americans. Two of Willkie's basic arguments — that FDR was not rearming the country quickly enough and that he was holding back prosperity — were seriously weakened, for many people who could see the achievements of the rapidly developing defense boom. While Willkie had long professed his concern for the safety of the British, he had declined to associate himself with the destroyer–bases deal and, after it was announced, had criticized the President's handling of it. Fortunately for Roosevelt, the general public reaction to the ships–bases arrangement was highly favorable; even the bitterly anti-New Deal *Chicago Tribune* approved, although for curious reasons.

Willkie, as he set out on his first campaign swing, was thus already in a difficult position. His weaknesses as a campaigner were soon evident. His first two days were so jammed with speeches, many of them both casual and unprepared, that he badly strained his voice. He showed signs of resentment over the attacks which labeled him an "appeaser" and as the candidate of pro-Nazi elements. At Joliet, Illinois, on September 14, the second day of his trip, he made the flat charge that Roosevelt "telephoned Mussolini and Hitler and urged them to sell Czechoslovakia down the river at Munich." His press secretary had to admit that Willkie had "misspoken." At Peoria, the candidate modified his position, although he continued to identify FDR with the Munich appeasement. Willkie frequently coupled this charge with the more tenable contention that Roosevelt's policies had often been isolationist during his first term. Unfortunately for the Willkie cause, the American people seemed much less interested in his rather strained historical interpretations than in the here-and-now problems of national defense and security.

On his western swing, Willkie developed his several campaign themes, sometimes in impromptu remarks. At Coffeyville, Kansas, where Willkie had once taught school, he indicted the Administration for being power-grasping and incompetent in its economic programs. In a much-noticed passage, he proclaimed that if "you return this Administration to office, you will be serving under an American totalitarian government before the long third term is up." At San Diego, the Republican nominee endorsed the aged one-time progressive Senator Hiram Johnson, the very symbol of rigid isolationism, as a "true liberal." At Hollywood Bowl, Willkie reminded a crowd of seventy-five thousand of Roosevelt's 1932 promise to cut government costs by a quarter and of the 1940 Democratic platform pledge that the United States would not participate in a European war. "I hope and pray," said Willkie, "that he remembers the pledge of the 1940 platform better than he did the one of 1932. If he does not, you better get ready to get on the transports." This note was to be repeated again and again, more and more stridently as Willkie began to treat Roosevelt as a warmonger.

At Portland, in the home state of his rather unenergetic running-mate Senator McNary, Willkie sought to remove his "power trust" onus. He denied that he was opposed to federal hydroelectric development projects, although he did say that he was in favor of allowing the people of a region to decide whether the distribution of power should be over publicly or privately owned facilities. At Seattle on September 23, he delivered his last major speech before turning back toward the East. In it he made a vigorous plea for labor support, saying, "Some time back the New Dealers gave up talking about jobs and just talked about unemployment." He reiterated his endorsement of "every one of the social gains that labor has made," including the right of collective bargaining and social security, even promising to expand the latter program. He asserted, in another of his attacks on the Administration's spirit, "The New Deal candidate does not believe there are any more jobs, whereas I know there are." While these remarks must have seemed incongruous when delivered in a city beginning to show all the signs of a defense boomtown, they unquestionably represented Willkie's most fundamental thinking on domestic economic policy.

As his campaign train moved east from Seattle, it was already evident that it was Willkie's increasingly bitter attacks on Roosevelt's management of foreign policy that were making the strongest impression on the public. He soon discovered, as he toured Michigan industrial cities at the end of September, that he had not won over the workingmen. He found himself booed and jeered, bombarded with fruit and eggs, in scenes of tumult and near-violence. Even his pledge at Pittsburgh to appoint his Secretary of Labor from the leadership of the labor movement — a statement that he must have thought would be helpful to his cause — was marred by his *faux pas*, "And it won't be a woman, either." This was, of course, a slap at Secretary Frances Perkins, but it was also a slap at the whole feminine sex, and the Democrats were able to make the most of it.

During the first half of October, Willkie's speeches were increasingly critical of Roosevelt's defense program and of FDR's conduct of foreign relations. At Philadelphia he charged that the Administration "lacked the ability to get things done." In a radio speech he contended, "We are being edged toward war by an administration that is alike careless in speech and action." At Boston on October 11, he promised a huge crowd in a ballpark: "We shall not undertake to fight anybody else's war. Our boys shall stay out of European wars." Willkie's campaign seemed to be moving ahead at last — the polls were suddenly more favorable and the Republican leaders began to show confidence in their candidate. It is ironic that it took Willkie's strident charges that the New Deal had totalitarian leanings, that it was mismanaging national defense, and that it was blundering into war, to put real life into his campaign. It had been a long time since Elwood.

The Democratic campaign had been underway all the while the President was being non-political in public. Under the general direction of Chairman Flynn, pro-Roosevelt speakers blistered the Republican congressional voting record on both domestic and foreign issues and repeatedly reminded the public of the desperate straits in which FDR had found the country in 1933 and of what the New Deal had accomplished. They tagged the Republican Party as the vehicle of isolationism and appeasement; many insisted that the aggressor nations hoped for the defeat of Franklin Roosevelt. Among the major spokesman for the Democratic cause were Governor Herbert H. Lehman of New York, Secretary Ickes, Mayor Fiorello La Guardia of New York City (who said that he favored "Roosevelt with his known faults to Willkie with his unknown virtues"), Senator Norris of Nebraska (who was perhaps the foremost spokesman for public power and who did yeoman work in parts of the country where federal reclamation and power projects were popular), and the vice-presidential nominee, Henry A. Wallace. Wallace proved to be a more effective campaigner than most had expected, especially in the areas of foreign and agricultural policies. One of Wallace's tours lasted from September 22 to October 7; he delivered ten or more speeches a day in twenty-three states from coast to coast. Indeed, Wallace's energy added much to the Democratic effort to keep up the attack on Willkie.

Roosevelt delivered a rousing defense of his labor record to the Teamsters Union convention in Washington on September 11, but he began it by saying that he wasn't able to tell whether he was delivering a political speech or not. On several other occasions in the next few weeks he gave ostensibly "non-political" speeches, but they contained political overtones that could scarcely be missed. At Philadelphia on October 23, he openly entered the campaign, with the first of a brilliant series of five addresses. These speeches were drafted by Samuel Rosenman and the playwright Robert E. Sherwood, with some suggestions from the newspaper columnist Dorothy Thompson (a former enemy of FDR) and the vigorous criticism of Harry Hopkins. As usual, the President retouched them in his own highly effective style. As set political speeches, the five were among the most devastating Roosevelt ever made. As a group, they managed both to reply to Willkie's many charges and simultaneously to put the Republicans on the defensive.

In the Philadelphia address, while referring to many "falsifications," Roosevelt replied in detail to two of them. The first was the charge that he had made secret treaties or agreements to involve the nation in war: "I give to you and to the people of this country this most solemn assurance: There is no secret treaty, no secret obligation, no secret commitment, no secret understanding in any shape or form, direct or indirect, with any other Government, or any other nation in any part of the world, to involve this nation in any war or for any other purpose." Most of the rest of the speech contained Roosevelt's refutation, in great detail, of Willkie's charge that the New Deal had failed to bring about economic recovery. He pointed out that a story in the financial section of *The New York Times* (which was supporting Willkie) said that, "Dreams of business 'flat on its back' must come from smoking campaign cigars or else the speakers are talking about some other country." The President jibed, "Wouldn't it be nice if the editorial writers of *The New York Times* could get acquainted with their own business experts?" He concluded with a brief statement that the Administration was not arming for a foreign war, but for self-protection. His last sentence was, "It is for peace that I have labored; and it is for peace that I shall labor all the days of my life."

At Madison Square Garden on October 28, FDR gave the second of his five admittedly political speeches, a blistering attack on the Republican Party record in defense and foreign policies. He quoted Representative Fish, former President Herbert Hoover, and Senators Vandenberg and Taft, with savage effect. For example, Taft in February 1940 had asserted that the "increase of the Army and Navy over the tremendous appropriations of the current year seems to be unnecessary if we are concerned solely with defense." FDR was not going to let the people forget in October what Taft had said in February. He charged that the Republican leadership had been "playing politics with defense" and that they were "playing politics with the national security of America today." He called the roll of the opponents of the repeal of the arms embargo, ending with "a perfectly beautiful rhythm — Congress-men Martin, Barton and Fish." This refrain, which he soon repeated, was received with howls of laughter; it, too, went into the permanent annals of politics.

Two nights later, in Boston, President Roosevelt delivered the third in his series of political speeches. He expanded on his Administration's defense accomplishments, and, contending that he was refuting rumors, assured "the mothers and fathers of America that each and every one of their boys in training will be well housed and well fed." In what was destined to be the most frequently quoted of his campaign remarks of 1940, Roosevelt said flatly, "I have said this before, but I shall say it again and again and again: Your boys are not going to be sent into any foreign wars." Rosenman recalled later that he had suggested that Roosevelt qualify this statement with the phrase, "except in case of attack," as he had done in the past and would do again, but Roosevelt refused with the remark, "If we're attacked it's no longer a foreign war." In the Boston speech, Roosevelt dwelt at length on the conservative-isolationist record of the Republican national chairman, Congressman Martin of Massachusetts. And he did not neglect to point out that he was one of "that great historic trio. Martin, Barton and Fish." The Boston audience, many of whom must have heard the last speech, joined in the refrain.

Two more Roosevelt political addresses remained, one in Brooklyn on November 1, and the wind-up speech in Cleveland the next night. At Brooklyn, Roosevelt referred to "the very strange assortment of political bedfellows who have been brought together in the Republican political dormitory." Although he did not say so, FDR was replying to John L. Lewis, head of the Congress of Industrial Organizations and of the United Mine Workers, whose increasing bitterness toward the President had culminated in his endorsement of Willkie. Roosevelt noted that there had grown up an alliance "forming within the Republican Party between the extreme reactionary and the extreme radical elements of this country." He noted a recent pro-Republican paid advertisement in the Communist organ, the *Daily Worker*. He spoke fondly of his Administration's economic and social accomplishments, achieved in spite of the opposition of Republican leaders, and charged these leaders with hypocrisy in their present professions of support for New Deal reforms.

In the Cleveland speech, which Rosenman considered to be the greatest of all Roosevelt's addresses, the President stuck a positive, idealistic note, giving to his campaign an unusually vigorous and effective conclusion. He spoke of his vision of an America without poverty or monopoly, with economic, cultural, and educational opportunities for all, and a beneficent government guaranteeing to those who work "a fair share in the national income." He spoke of "a great storm raging now, a storm which makes things harder for the world," saying that it was "the true reason that I would like to stick by these people of ours until we reach the clear, sure footing ahead." He concluded, "The spirit of the common man is the spirit of peace and good will. It is the spirit of God. And in His faith is the strength of all America." Although Willkie continued to campaign during the last two weeks before the election, Roosevelt managed to capture public attention. Willkie's speeches, now beginning to show signs of his growing fatigue, were no match for the superlative ones delivered by FDR in what one historian has aptly termed "The Two-Weeks Blitz." Willkie's wind-up address at Madison Square Garden on November 2, delivered after he had listened over the radio to FDR's Cleveland address, was essentially a rather tired summary of his oft-repeated charges against the New Deal and "the third-term candidate."

Suddenly, the bitter, sometimes vicious, frequently confused campaign of 1940 was over. The final Gallup Poll gave Roosevelt 52 percent of the popular vote and Willkie 48 percent, but indicated a "strong trend" toward Willkie, with nineteen states and 274 electoral votes in doubt. For a while, early on election night, the returns from the East looked dangerous for Roosevelt; the President grimly shut himself up with his radio at Hyde Park. But in the end Roosevelt was reelected quite decisively. He won 449 electoral votes to Willkie's 82, with a popular vote margin of nearly five million. Still, Willkie made a considerably better showing against Roosevelt than either Hoover in 1932 or Landon in 1936. He carried a total of 1,147 counties throughout the country; Landon had won only 459. Significantly, Roosevelt was victorious in every city with a population of more than four hundred thousand, except Cincinnati. Republicans made a net gain of five national senators and two governors, although they lost ground slightly in the House.

It is important to note where Willkie's voting strength lay. He carried ten states — the ever-faithful Maine and Vermont (although by unimpressive margins); politically important Michigan and Indiana (by very close votes); and a tier of six western farm states — North Dakota, South Dakota, Nebraska, Kansas, Colorado, and (alas, for Henry Wallace) Iowa. Farm belt disaffection was a certainty of life in 1940. Close observers noted that Roosevelt had done poorly, as might have been expected, in areas where there were significant numbers of voters of Italian, German, or Irish birth or extraction. New York gave Roosevelt an uncomfortably close margin, approximately 225,000 votes. Indeed, the New York Democratic vote for the President (45 percent) was less than that cast for Willkie (48 percent); the 417,418 votes FDR secured as the candidate of the American Labor Party, however, more than made up the difference.

The bitterness between Roosevelt and Willkie was short-lived. They had been rather friendly enemies during Willkie's Commonwealth and Southern days. They became political allies soon after the election, when Willkie conceded his defeat with extraordinary graciousness and took to the radio to plead for an end to internal differences. "We must constitute ourselves a vigorous, loyal and public-spirited opposition," he proclaimed. Soon Willkie was giving full support to the Administration's foreign policy, including the vital Lend-Lease Act of 1941, and was even acting as a wartime emissary for his recent political enemy. In time, Roosevelt came to have the highest regard for Willkie, even to the extent of suggesting that they constitute a coalition ticket in 1944. Truly, the 1940 election has no parallel in American history.

Appendix

Party Platforms of 1940

Democratic Platform

PREAMBLE

The world is undergoing violent change. Humanity, uneasy in this machine age, is demanding a sense of security and dignity based on human values.

No democratic government which fails to recognize this trend — and take appropriate action — can survive.

That is why the Government of this nation has moved to keep ahead of this trend; has moved with speed incomprehensible to those who do not see this trend.

Outside the Americas, established institutions are being overthrown and democratic philosophies are being repudiated by those whose creed recognizes no power higher than military force, no values other than a false efficiency.

What the founding fathers realized upon this continent was a daring dream, that men could have not only physical security, not only efficiency, but something else in addition that men had never had before — the security of the heart that comes with freedom, the peace of mind that comes from a sense of justice.

To this generation of Americans it is given to defend this democratic faith as it is challenged by social maladjustment within and totalitarian greed without. The world revolution against which we prepare our defense is so threatening that not until it has burned itself out in the last corner of the earth will our democracy be able to relax its guard.

In this world crisis, the purpose of the Democratic Party is to defend against external attack and justify by internal progress the system of government and way of life from which the Democratic Party takes its name.

FULFILLING AMERICAN IDEAL

Toward the modern fulfillment of the American ideal, the Democratic Party, during the last seven years, has labored successfully:

1. *To strengthen democracy, by defensive preparedness against aggression, whether by open attack or secret infiltration*;
2. *To strengthen democracy by increasing our economic efficiency*; and
3. *To strengthen democracy by improving the welfare of the people.*

These three objectives are one and inseparable. No nation can be strong by armaments alone. It must possess and use all the necessary resources for producing goods plentifully and distributing them effectively. It must add to these factors of material strength the unconquerable spirit and energy of a contented people, convinced that there are no boundaries to human progress and happiness in a land of liberty.

Our faith that these objectives can be attained is made unshakable by what has already been done by the present Administration — in stopping the waste and exploitation of our human and natural resources, in restoring to the average man and woman a stake in the preservation of our democracy, in enlarging our national armaments, and in achieving national unity.

We shall hold fast to these gains. We are proud of our record. Therefore the Party in convention assembled endorses wholeheartedly the brilliant and courageous leadership of President Franklin D. Roosevelt and his statesmanship and that of the Congress for the past seven trying years. And to our President and great leader we send our cordial greetings.

WE MUST STRENGTHEN DEMOCRACY
AGAINST AGGRESSION

The American people are determined that war, raging in Europe, Asia and Africa, shall not come to America.

We will not participate in foreign wars, and we will not send our army, naval or air forces to fight in foreign lands outside of the Americas, except in case of attack. We favor and shall rigorously enforce and defend the Monroe Doctrine.

The direction and aim of our foreign policy has been, and will continue to be, the security and defense of our own land and the maintenance of its peace.

For years our President has warned the nation that organized assaults against religion, democracy and international good faith threatened our own peace and security. Men blinded by partisanship brushed aside these warnings as war-mongering and officious intermeddling. The fall of twelve nations was necessary to bring their belated approval of legislative and executive action that the President had urged and undertaken with the full support of the people. It is a tribute to the President's foresight and action that our defense forces are today at the peak of their peacetime effectiveness.

Weakness and unpreparedness invite aggression. We must be so strong that no possible combination of powers would dare to attack us. We propose to provide America with an invincible air force, a navy strong enough to protect all our seacoasts and our national interests, and a fully-equipped and mechanized army. We shall continue to coordinate these implements of defense with the necessary expansion of industrial productive capacity and with the training of appropriate personnel. Outstanding leaders of industry and labor have already been enlisted by the Government to harness our mighty economic forces for national defense.

Experience of other nations gives warning that total defense is necessary to repel attack, and that partial defense is no defense.

We have seen the downfall of nations accomplished through internal dissension provoked from without. We denounce and will do all in our power to destroy the treasonable activities of disguised anti-democratic and un-American agencies which would sap our strength, paralyze our will to defend ourselves, and destroy our unity by inciting race against race, class against class, religion against religion and the people against their free institutions.

To make America strong, and to keep America free, every American must give of his talents and treasure in accordance with his ability and his country's needs. We must have democracy of sacrifice as well as democracy of opportunity.

To insure that our armaments shall be implements of peace rather than war, we shall continue our traditional policies of the good neighbor; observe and advocate international respect for the rights of others and for treaty obligations; cultivate foreign trade through desirable trade agreements; and foster economic collaboration with the Republics of the Western Hemisphere.

In self-defense and in good conscience, the world's greatest democracy cannot afford heartlessly or in a spirit of appeasement to ignore the peace-loving and liberty-loving peoples wantonly attacked by ruthless aggressors. We pledge to extend to these peoples all the material aid at our command, consistent with law and not inconsistent with the interests of our own national self-defense — all to the end that peace and international good faith may yet emerge triumphant.

We do not regard the need for preparedness a warrant for infringement upon our civil liberties, but on the contrary we shall continue to protect them, in the keen realization that the vivid contrast between the freedom we enjoy and the dark repression which prevails in the lands where liberty is dead, affords warning and example to our people to confirm their faith in democracy.

WE MUST STRENGTHEN DEMOCRACY BY INCREASING OUR ECONOMIC EFFICIENCY

The well-being of the land and those who work upon it is basic to the real defense and security of America.

The Republican Party gives its promises to the farmer and its allegiance to those who exploit him.

Since 1932 farm income has been doubled; six million farmers, representing more than 80 per cent of all farm families, have participated in an effective soil conservation program; the farm debt and the interest rate on farm debt have been reduced, and farm foreclosures have been drastically curtailed; rural highways and farm-to-market roads have been vastly improved and extended; the surpluses on the farms have been used to feed the needy; low cost electricity has been brought to five million farm people as a result of the rural electrification program; thousands of impoverished farm families have been rehabilitated; and steps have been taken to stop the alarming growth of farm tenancy, to increase land ownership, and to mitigate the hardships of migratory farm labor.

The Land and the Farmer

We pledge ourselves:

To make parity as well as soil conservation payments until such time as the goal of parity income for agriculture is realized.

To extend and enlarge the tenant-purchase program until every deserving tenant farmer has a real opportunity to have a farm of his own.

To refinance existing farm debts at lower interest rates and on longer and more flexible terms.

To continue to provide for adjustment of production through democratic processes to the extent that excess surpluses are capable of control.

To continue the program of rehabilitation of farmers who need and merit aid.

To preserve and strengthen the ever-normal granary on behalf of the national defense, the consumer at home and abroad, and the American farmer.

To continue to make commodity loans to maintain the ever-normal granary and to prevent destructively low prices.

To expand the domestic consumption of our surpluses by the food and cotton stamp plan, the free school lunch, low-cost milk and other plans for bringing surplus farm commodities to needy consumers.

To continue our substantially increased appropriations for research and extension work through the land-grant colleges, and for research laboratories established to develop new outlets for farm products.

To conserve the soil and water resources for the benefit of farmers and the nation. In such conservation programs we shall, so far as practicable, bring about that development in forests and other permanent crops as will not unduly expand livestock and dairy production.

To safeguard the farmer's foreign markets and expand his domestic market for all domestic crops.

To enlarge the rural electrification [*sic*].

To encourage farmer-owned and controlled cooperatives.

To continue the broad program launched by this Administration for the coordinated development of our river basins through reclamation and irrigation, flood control, reforestation and soil conservation, stream purification, recreation, fish and game protection, low-cost power, and rural industry.

To encourage marketing agreements in aid of producers of dairy products, vegetables, fruits and specialty crops for the purpose of orderly marketing and the avoidance of unfair and wasteful practices.

To extend crop insurance from wheat to other crops as rapidly as experience justifies such extension.

To safeguard the family-sized farm in all our programs.

To finance these programs adequately in order that they may be effective.

In settling new lands reclaimed from desert by projects like Grand Coulee, we shall give priority to homeless families who have lost their farms. As these new lands are brought into use, we shall continue by Federal purchase to retire from the plow submarginal lands so that an increased percentage of our farmers may be able to live and work on good land.

These programs will continue to be in the hands of locally-elected farmer committees to the largest extent possible. In this truly democratic way, we will continue to bring economic security to the farmer and his family, while recognizing the dignity and freedom of American farm life.

Industry and the Worker

Under Democratic auspices, more has been done in the last seven years to foster the essential freedom, dignity and opportunity of the American worker than in any other administration in the nation's history. In consequence, labor is today taking its rightful place as a partner of management in the common cause of higher earnings, industrial efficiency, national unity and national defense.

A far-flung system of employment exchanges has brought together millions of idle workers and available jobs. The workers' right to organize and bargain collectively through representatives of their own choosing is being enforced. We have enlarged the Federal machinery for the mediation of labor disputes. We have enacted an effective wage and hour law. Child labor in factories has been outlawed. Prevailing wages to workers employed on Government contracts have been assured.

We pledge to continue to enforce fair labor standards; to maintain the principles of the National Labor Relations Act; to expand employment training and opportunity for our youth, older workers, and workers displaced by technological changes; to strengthen the orderly processes of collective bargaining and peaceful settlement of labor disputes; and to work always for a just distribution of our national income among those who labor.

We will continue our efforts to achieve equality of opportunity for men and women without impairing the social legislation which promotes true equality by safeguarding the health, safety and economic welfare of women workers. The right to work for compensation in both public and private employment is an inalienable privilege of women as well as men, without distinction as to marital status.

The production of coal is one of our most important basic industries. Stability of production, employment, distribution and price are indispensable to the public welfare. We pledge continuation of the Federal Bituminous Coal Stabilization Act, and sympathetic consideration of the application of similar legislation to the anthracite coal industry, in order to provide additional protection for the owners, miners and consumers of hard coal.

We shall continue to emphasize the human element in industry and strive toward increasingly wholehearted cooperation between labor and industrial management.

Capital and the Business Man

To make democracy strong, our system of business enterprise and individual initiative must be free to gear its tremendous productive capacity to serve the greatest good of the greatest number.

We have defended and will continue to defend all legitimate business.

We have attacked and will continue to attack unbridled concentration of economic power and the exploitation of the consumer and the investor.

We have attacked the kind of banking which treated America as a colonial empire to exploit; the kind of securities business which regarded the Stock Exchange as a private gambling club for wagering other people's money; the kind of public utility holding companies which used consumers' and investors' money to suborn a free press, bludgeon legislatures and political conventions, and control elections against the interest of their customers and their security holders.

We have attacked the kind of business which levied tribute on all the rest of American business by the extortionate methods of monopoly.

We did not stop with attack — we followed through with the remedy. The American people found in themselves, through the democratic process, ability to meet the economic problems of the average American business where concentrated power had failed.

We found a broken and prostrate banking and financial system. We restored it to health by strengthening banks, insurance companies and other financial institutions. We have insured 62 million bank accounts, and protected millions of small investors in the security and commodity markets. We have thus revived confidence, safeguarded thrift, and opened the road to all honorable business.

We have made credit at low interest rates available to small-business men, thus unfastening the oppressive yoke of a money monopoly, and giving the ordinary citizen a chance to go into business and stay in business.

We recognize the importance of small business concerns and new enterprises in our national economy, and favor the enactment of constructive legislation to safeguard the welfare of small business. Independent small-scale enterprise, no less than big business, should be adequately represented on appropriate governmental boards and commissions, and its interests should be examined and fostered by a continuous research program.

We have provided an important outlet for private capital by stimulating home building and low-rent housing projects. More new homes were built throughout the nation last year than in any year since 1929.

We have fostered a well-balanced American merchant marine and the world's finest system of civil aeronautics, to promote our commerce and our national defense.

We have steered a steady course between a bankruptcy-producing deflation and a thrift-destroying inflation, so that today the dollar is the most stable and sought-after currency in the world — a factor of immeasurable benefit in our foreign and domestic commerce.

We shall continue to oppose barriers which impede trade among the several states. We pledge our best efforts in strengthening our home markets, and to this end we favor the adjustment of freight rates so that no section or state will have undue advantage over any other.

To encourage investment in productive enterprise, the tax-exempt privileges of future Federal, state and local bonds should be removed.

We have enforced the anti-trust laws more vigorously than at any time in our history, thus affording the maximum protection to the competitive system.

We favor strict supervision of all forms of the insurance business by the several states for the protection of policyholders and the public.

The full force of our policies, by raising the national income by thirty billion dollars from the low of 1932, by encouraging vast reemployment, and by elevating the level of consumer demand, has quickened the flow of buying and selling through every artery of industry and trade.

With mass purchasing power restored and many abuses eliminated, American business stands at the threshold of a great new era, richer in promise than any we have witnessed — an era of pioneering and progress beyond the present frontiers of economic activity — in transportation, in housing, in industrial expansion, and in the new utilization of the products of the farm and the factory.

We shall aid business in redeeming America's promise.

Electric Power

During the past seven years the Democratic Party has won the first major victories for the people of the nation in their generation-old contest with the power monopoly.

These victories have resulted in the recognition of certain self-evident principles and the realization of vast benefits by the people. These principles, long opposed by the Republican Party, are:

That the power of falling water is a gift from God, and consequently belongs not to a privileged few, but to all the people, who are entitled to enjoy its benefits;

That the people have the right through their government to develop their own power sites and bring low-cost electricity to their homes, farms and factories;

That public utility holding companies must not be permitted to serve as the means by which a few men can pyramid stocks upon stocks for the sole purpose of controlling vast power empires.

We condemn the Republican policies which permitted the victimizing of investors in the securities of private power corporations, and the exploitation of the people by unnecessarily high utility costs.

We condemn the opposition of utility power interests which delayed for years the development of national defense projects in the Tennessee Valley, and which obstructed river basin improvements and other public projects bringing low-cost electric power to the people. The successful power developments in the Tennessee and Columbia River basins show the wisdom of the Democratic Party in establishing government-owned and operated hydroelectric plants in the interests of power and light consumers.

Through these Democratic victories, whole regions have been revived and restored to prosperous habitation. Production costs have been reduced.

Industries have been established which employ men and capital. Cheaper electricity has brought vast economic benefits to thousands of homes and communities.

These victories of the people must be safeguarded. They will be turned to defeat if the Republican Party should be returned to power. We pledge our Party militantly to oppose every effort to encroach upon the inherent right of our people to be provided with this primary essential of life at the lowest possible cost.

The nomination of a utility executive by the Republican Party as its presidential candidate raises squarely the issue, whether the nation's water power shall be used for all the people or for the selfish interests of a few. We accept that issue.

Developments of Western Resources

We take satisfaction in pointing out the incomparable development of the public land states under the wise and constructive legislation of this Administration. Mining has been revived, agriculture fostered, reclamation extended and natural resources developed as never before in a similar period. We pledge the continuance of such policies, based primarily on the expansion of opportunity for the people, as will encourage the full development, free from financial exploitation, of the great resources — mineral, agricultural, livestock, fishing and lumber — which the West affords.

Radio

Radio has become an integral part of the democratically accepted doctrine of freedom of speech, press, assembly and religion. We urge such legislative steps as may be required to afford the same protection from censorship that is now afforded the press under the Constitution of the United States.

WE MUST STRENGTHEN DEMOCRACY BY IMPROVING THE WELFARE OF THE PEOPLE

We place human resources first among the assets of a democratic society.

Unemployment

The Democratic Party wages war on unemployment, one of the gravest problems of our times, inherited at its worst from the last Republican administration. Since we assumed office, nine million additional persons have gained regular employment in normal private enterprise. All our policies — financial, industrial and agricultural — will continue to accelerate the rate of this progress.

By public action, where necessary to supplement private reemployment, we have rescued millions from idleness that breeds weakness, and given them a real stake in their country's well being. We shall continue to recognize the obligation of Government to provide work for deserving workers who cannot be absorbed by private industry.

We are opposed to vesting in the states and local authorities the control of Federally-financed work relief. We believe that this Republican proposal is a thinly disguised plan to put the unemployed back on the dole.

We will continue energetically to direct our efforts toward the employment in private industry of all those willing to work, as well as the fullest employment of money and machines. This we pledge as our primary objective. To further implement this objective, we favor calling, under the direction of the President, a national unemployment conference of leaders of government, industry, labor and farm groups.

There is work in our factories, mines, fields, forests and river basins, on our coasts, highways, railroads and inland waterways. There are houses to be built to shelter our people. Building a better America means work and a higher standard of living for every family, and a richer and more secure heritage for every American.

Social Security

The Democratic Party, which established social security for the nation, is dedicated to its extension. We pledge to make the Social Security Act increasingly effective, by covering millions of persons not now protected under its terms; by strengthening our unemployment insurance system and establishing more adequate and uniform benefits, through the Federal equalization fund principle; by progressively extending and increasing the benefits of the old-age and survivors insurance system, including protection of the permanently disabled; and by the early realization of a minimum pension for all who have reached the age of retirement and are not gainfully employed.

Health

Good health for all the people is a prime requisite of national preparedness in its broadest sense. We have advanced public health, industrial hygiene, and maternal and child care. We are coordinating the health functions of the Federal Government. We pledge to expand these efforts, and to provide more hospitals and health centers and better health protection wherever the need exists, in rural and urban areas, all through the cooperative efforts of the Federal, state and local governments, the medical, dental, nursing and other scientific professions, and the voluntary agencies.

Youth and Education

Today, when the youth of other lands is being sacrificed in war, this nation recognizes the full value of the sound youth program established by the Administration. The National Youth Administration and Civilian Conservation Corps have enabled our youth to complete their education, have maintained their health, trained them for useful citizenship, and aided them to secure employment.

Our public works have modernized and greatly expanded the nation's schools. We have increased Federal aid for vocational education and rehabilitation, and undertaken a comprehensive program of defense-industry training.

We shall continue to bring to millions of children, youths and adults, the educational and economic opportunities otherwise beyond their reach.

Slum Clearance and Low-Rent Housing

We have launched a soundly conceived plan of loans and contributions to rid America of overcrowded slum dwellings that breed disease and crime, and to replace them by low-cost housing projects within the means of low-income families. We will extend and accelerate this plan not only in the congested city districts, but also in the small towns and farm areas, and we will make it a powerful arm of national defense by supplying housing for the families of enlisted personnel and for workers in areas where industry is expanding to meet defense needs.

Consumers

We are taking effective steps to insure that, in this period of stress, the cost of living shall not be increased by speculation and unjustified price rises.

Negroes

Our Negro citizens have participated actively in the economic and social advances launched by this Administration, including fair labor standards, social security benefits, health protection, work relief projects, decent housing, aid to education, and the rehabilitation of low-income farm families. We have aided more than half a million Negro youths in vocational training, education and employment. We shall continue to strive for complete legislative safeguards against discrimination in government service and benefits, and in the national defense forces. We pledge to uphold due process and the equal protection of the laws for every citizen, regardless of race, creed or color.

Veterans

We pledge to continue our policy of fair treatment of America's war veterans and their dependents, in just tribute to their sacrifices and their devotion to the cause of liberty.

Indians

We favor and pledge the enactment of legislation creating an Indian Claims Commission for the special purpose of entertaining and investigating claims presented by Indian groups, bands and tribes, in order that our Indian citizens may have their claims against the Government considered, adjusted, and finally settled at the earliest possible date.

Civil Service

We pledge the immediate extension of a genuine system of merit to all positions in the executive branch of the Federal Government except actual bona fide policy-making positions. The competitive method of selecting employees shall be improved until experience and qualification shall be the sole test in determining fitness for employment in the Federal service. Promotion and tenure in Federal service shall likewise depend upon fitness, experience and qualification. Arbitrary and unreasonable rules as to academic training shall be abolished, all to the end that a genuine system of efficiency and merit shall prevail throughout the entire Federal service.

Territories and District of Columbia

We favor a larger measure of self-government leading to statehood, for Alaska, Hawaii and Puerto Rico. We favor the appointment of residents to office, and equal treatment of the citizens of each of these three territories. We favor the prompt determination and payment of any just claims by Indian and Eskimo citizens of Alaska against the United States.

We also favor the extension of the right of suffrage to the people of the District of Columbia.

TRUE FIRST LINE OF DEFENSE

We pledge to continue to stand guard on our true first line of defense — the security and welfare of the men, women, and children of America.

OUR DEMOCRATIC FAITH

Democracy is more than a political system for the government of a people. It is the expression of a people's faith in themselves as human beings. If this faith is permitted to die, human progress will die with it. We believe that a mechanized existence, lacking the spiritual quality of democracy, is intolerable to the free people of this country.

We therefore pledge ourselves to fight, as our fathers fought, for the right of every American to enjoy freedom of religion, speech, press, assembly, petition, and security in his home.

It is America's destiny, in these days of rampant despotism, to be the guardian of the world heritage of liberty and to hold aloft and aflame the torch of Western civilization.

The Democratic Party rededicates itself to this faith in democracy, to the defense of the American system of government, the only system under which men are masters of their own souls, the only system under which the American people, composed of many races and creeds, can live and work, play and worship in peace, security and freedom.

Firmly relying upon a continuation of the blessings of Divine Providence upon all our righteous endeavors to preserve forever the priceless heritage of American liberty and peace, we appeal to all the liberal-minded men and women of the nation to approve this platform and to go forward with us by wholeheartedly supporting the candidates who subscribe to the principles which it proclaims.

Republican Platform

INTRODUCTION

The Republican party, in representative Convention assembled, submits to the people of the United States the following declaration of its principles and purposes:

We state our general objectives in the simple and comprehensive words of the Preamble to the Constitution of the United States.

Those objectives as there stated are these:

"To form a more perfect Union; establish justice; insure domestic tranquility; provide for the common defense, promote the general welfare and secure the blessings of liberty to ourselves and our posterity."

Meeting within the shadow of Independence Hall where those words were written we solemnly reaffirm them as a perfect statement of the ends for which we as a party propose to plan and to labor.

The record of the Roosevelt Administration is a record of failure to attain any one of those essential objectives.

Instead of leading us into More Perfect Union the Administration has deliberately fanned the flames of class hatred.

Instead of the Establishment of Justice the Administration has sought the subjection of the Judiciary to Executive discipline and domination.

Instead of insuring Domestic Tranquility the Administration has made impossible the normal friendly relation between employers and employees and has even succeeded in alienating both the great divisions of Organized Labor.

Instead of Providing for the Common Defense the Administration, notwithstanding the expenditure of billions of our dollars, has left the Nation unprepared to resist foreign attack.

Instead of promoting the General Welfare the Administration has Domesticated the Deficit, Doubled the Debt, Imposed Taxes where they do the greatest economic harm, and used public money for partisan political advantage.

Instead of the Blessings of Liberty the Administration has imposed upon us a Regime of Regimentation which has deprived the individual of his freedom and has made of America a shackled giant.

Wholly ignoring these great objectives, as solemnly declared by the people of the United States, the New Deal Administration has for seven long years whirled in a turmoil of shifting, contradictory and overlapping administrations and policies. Confusion has reigned supreme. The only steady undeviating characteristic has been the relentless expansion of the power of the Federal government over the everyday life of the farmer, the industrial worker and the business man. The emergency demands organization — not confusion. It demands free and intelligent cooperation — not incompetent domination. It demands a change.

The New Deal Administration has failed America.

It has failed by seducing our people to become continuously dependent upon government, thus weakening their morale and quenching the traditional American spirit.

It has failed by viciously attacking our industrial system and sapping its strength and vigor.

It has failed by attempting to send our Congress home during the world's most tragic hour, so that we might be eased into the war by word of deed during the absence of our elected representatives from Washington.

It has failed by disclosing military details of our equipment to foreign powers over protests by the heads of our armed defense.

It has failed by ignoring the lessons of fact concerning modern, mechanized, armed defense.

In these and countless other ways the New Deal Administration has either deliberately deceived the American people or proved itself incompetent longer to handle the affairs of our government.

The zero hour is here. America must prepare at once to defend our shores, our homes, our lives and our most cherished ideals.

To establish a first line of defense we must place in official positions men of faith who put America first and who are determined that her governmental and economic system be kept unimpaired.

Our national defense must be so strong that no unfriendly power shall ever set foot on American soil. To assure this strength our national economy, the true basis of America's defense, must be free of unwarranted government interference.

Only a strong and sufficiently prepared America can speak words of reassurance and hope to the liberty-loving peoples of the world.

NATIONAL DEFENSE

The Republican Party is firmly opposed to involving this Nation in foreign war.

We are still suffering from the ill effects of the last World War: a war which cost us a twenty-four billion dollar increase in our national debt, billions of uncollectible foreign debts, and the complete upset of our economic system, in addition to the loss of human life and irreparable damage to the health of thousands of our boys.

The present National Administration has already spent for all purposes more than fifty-four billion dollars; — has boosted the national debt and current federal taxes to an all-time high; and yet by the President's own admission we are still wholly unprepared to defend our country, its institutions and our individual liberties in a war that threatens to engulf the whole world; and this in spite of the fact that foreign wars have been in progress for two years or more and that military information concerning these wars and the rearmament programs of the warring nations has been at all times available to the National Administration through its diplomatic and other channels.

The Republican Party stands for Americanism, preparedness and peace.

We accordingly fasten upon the New Deal full responsibility for our unpreparedness and for the consequent danger of involvement in war.

We declare for the prompt, orderly and realistic building of our national defense to the point at which we shall be able not only to defend the United States, its possessions, and essential outposts from foreign attack, but also efficiently to uphold in war the Monroe Doctrine. To this task the Republican party pledges itself when entrusted with national authority. In the meantime we shall support all necessary and proper defense measures proposed by the Administration in its belated effort to make up for lost time; but we deplore explosive utterances by the President directed at other governments which serve to imperil our peace; and we condemn all executive acts and proceedings which might lead to war without the authorization of the Congress of the United States.

Our sympathies have been profoundly stirred by invasion of unoffending countries and by disaster to nations whose ideals most closely resemble our own. We favor the extension to all peoples fighting for liberty, or whose liberty is threatened, of such aid as shall not be in violation of international law or inconsistent with the requirements of our own national defense.

We believe that the spirit which should animate our entire defensive policy is determination to preserve not our material interests merely, but those liberties which are the priceless heritage of America.

RE-EMPLOYMENT

The New Deal's failure to solve the problem of unemployment and revive opportunity for our youth presents a major challenge to representative government and free enterprise. We propose to recreate opportunity for the youth of America and put our idle millions back to work in private industry, business, and agriculture. We propose to eliminate needless administrative restrictions, thus restoring lost motion to the wheels of individual enterprise.

RELIEF

We shall remove waste, discrimination, and politics from relief — through administration by the States with federal grants-in-aid on a fair and nonpolitical basis, thus giving the man and woman on relief a larger share of the funds appropriated.

SOCIAL SECURITY

We favor the extension of necessary old age benefits on an ear-marked pay-as-you-go basis to the extent that the revenues raised for this purpose will permit. We favor the extension of the unemployment compensation provisions of the Social Security Act, wherever practicable, to those groups and classes not now included. For such groups as may thus be covered we favor a system of unemployment compensation with experience rating provisions, aimed at protecting the worker in the regularity of his employment and providing adequate compensation for reasonable periods when that regularity of employment is interrupted. The administration should be left with the States with a minimum of Federal control.

LABOR RELATIONS

The Republican party has always protected the American worker.

We shall maintain labor's right of free organization and collective bargaining.

We believe that peace and prosperity at home require harmony, teamwork, and understanding in all relations between worker and employer. When differences arise, they should be settled directly and voluntarily across the table.

Recent disclosures respecting the administration of the National Labor Relations Act require that this Act be amended in fairness to employers and all groups of employees so as to provide true freedom for, and orderliness in self-organization and collective bargaining.

AGRICULTURE

A prosperous and stable agriculture is the foundation of our economic structure. Its preservation is a national and non-political social problem not yet solved, despite many attempts. The farmer is entitled to a profit-price for his products. The Republican party will put into effect such governmental policies, temporary and permanent, as will establish and maintain an equitable balance between labor, industry, and agriculture by expanding industrial and business activity, eliminating unemployment, lowering production costs, thereby creating increased consumer buying power for agricultural products.

Until this balance has been attained, we propose to provide benefit payments, based upon a widely-applied, constructive soil conservation program free from government-dominated production control, but administered, as far as practicable, by farmers themselves; to restrict the major benefits of these payments to operators of family-type farms; to continue all present benefit payments until our program becomes operative; and to eliminate the present extensive and costly bureaucratic interference.

We shall provide incentive payments, when necessary, to encourage increased production of agricultural commodities, adaptable to our soil and climate, not now produced in sufficient quantities for our home markets, and will stimulate the use and processing of all farm products in industry as raw materials.

We shall promote a cooperative system of adequate farm credit, at lowest interest rates commensurate with the cost of money, supervised by an independent governmental agency, with ultimate farmer ownership and control; farm commodity loans to facilitate orderly marketing and stabilize farm income; the expansion of sound, farmer-owned and farmer-controlled cooperative associations; and the support of educational and extension programs to achieve more efficient production and marketing.

We shall foster Government refinancing, where necessary, of the heavy Federal farm debt load through an agency segregated from cooperative credit.

We shall promote a national land use program for Federal acquisition, without dislocation of local tax returns, of non-productive farm lands by voluntary sale or lease subject to approval of the States concerned; and the disposition of such lands to appropriate public uses including watershed protection and flood prevention, reforestation, recreation, erosion control, and the conservation of wild life.

We advocate a foreign trade policy which will end one-man tariff making, afford effective protection to farm products, regain our export markets, and assure an American price level for the domestically consumed portion of our export crops.

We favor effective quarantine against imported livestock, dairy, and other farm products from countries which do not impose health and sanitary standards equal to our own domestic standards.

We approve the orderly development of reclamation and irrigation, project by project and as conditions justify.

We promise adequate assistance to rural communities suffering disasters from flood, drought, and other natural causes.

We shall promote stabilization of agricultural income through intelligent management of accumulated surpluses, and through the development of outlets by supplying those in need at home and abroad.

TARIFF AND RECIPROCAL TRADE

We are threatened by unfair competition in world markets and by the invasion of our home markets, especially by the products of state-controlled foreign economies.

We believe in tariff protection for Agriculture, Labor, and Industry, as essential to our American standard of living. The measure of the protection shall be determined by scientific methods with due regard to the interest of the consumer.

We shall explore every possibility of reopening the channels of international trade through negotiations so conducted as to produce genuine reciprocity and expand our exports.

We condemn the manner in which the so-called reciprocal trade agreements of the New Deal have been put into effect without adequate hearings, with undue haste, without proper consideration of our domestic producers, and without Congressional approval. These defects we shall correct.

MONEY

The Congress should reclaim its constitutional powers over money, and withdraw the President's arbitrary authority to manipulate the currency, establish bimetallism, issue irredeemable paper money, and debase the gold and silver coinage. We shall repeal the Thomas Inflation Amendment of 1933 and the (foreign) Silver Purchase Act of 1934, and take all possible steps to preserve the value of the Government's huge holdings of gold and re-introduce gold into circulation.

JOBS AND IDLE MONEY

Believing it possible to keep the securities market clean without paralyzing it, we endorse the principle of truth in securities in the Securities Act. To get billions of idle dollars and a multitude of idle men back to work and to promote national defense, these acts should be revised and the policies of the Commission changed to encourage the flow of private capital into industry.

TAXATION

Public spending has trebled under the New Deal, while tax burdens have doubled. Huge taxes are necessary to pay for New Deal waste and for neglected national defense. We shall revise the tax system and remove those practices which impede recovery and shall apply policies which stimulate enterprise. We shall not use the taxing power as an instrument of punishment or to secure objectives not otherwise obtainable under existing law.

PUBLIC CREDIT

With urgent need for adequate defense, the people are burdened by a direct and contingent debt exceeding fifty billion dollars. Twenty-nine billion of this debt has been created by New Deal borrowings during the past seven years. We pledge ourselves to conserve the public credit for all essential purposes by levying taxation sufficient to cover necessary civil expenditure, a substantial part of the defense cost, and the interest and retirement of the national debt.

PUBLIC SPENDING

Millions of men and women still out of work after seven years of excessive spending refute the New Deal theory that "deficit spending" is the way to prosperity and jobs. Our American system of private enterprise, if permitted to go to work, can rapidly increase the wealth, income, and standard of living of all the people. We solemnly pledge that public expenditures, other than those required for full national defense and relief, shall be cut to levels necessary for the essential services of government.

EQUAL RIGHTS

We favor submission by Congress to the States of an amendment to the Constitution providing for equal rights for men and women.

NEGRO

We pledge that our American citizens of Negro descent shall be given a square deal in the economic and political life of this nation. Discrimination in the civil service, the army, navy, and all other branches of the Government must cease. To enjoy the full benefits of life, liberty and pursuit of happiness universal suffrage must be made effective for the Negro citizen. Mob violence shocks the conscience of the nation and legislation to curb this evil should be enacted.

UN-AMERICAN ACTIVITIES

We vigorously condemn the New Deal encouragement of various groups that seek to change the American form of government by means outside the Constitution. We condemn the appointment of members of such un-American groups to high positions of trust in the national Government. The development of the treacherous so-called Fifth Column, as it has operated in war-stricken countries, should be a solemn warning to America. We pledge the Republican Party to get rid of such borers from within.

IMMIGRATION

We favor the strict enforcement of all laws controlling the entry of aliens. The activities of undesirable aliens should be investigated and those who seek to change by force and violence the American form of government should be deported.

VETERANS

We pledge adequate compensation and care for veterans disabled in the service of our country, and for their widows, orphans, and dependents.

INDIANS

We pledge an immediate and final settlement of all Indian claims between the government and the Indian citizenship of the nation.

HAWAII

Hawaii, sharing the nation's obligations equally with the several States, is entitled to the fullest measure of home rule; and to equality with the several States in the rights of her citizens and in the application of our national laws.

PUERTO RICO

Statehood is a logical aspiration of the people of Puerto Rico who were made citizens of the United States by Congress in 1917; legislation affecting Puerto Rico, in so far as feasible, should be in harmony with the realization of that aspiration.

GOVERNMENT AND BUSINESS

We shall encourage a healthy, confident, and growing private enterprise, confine Government activity to essential public services, and regulate business only so as to protect consumer, employee, and investor and without restricting the production of more and better goods at lower prices.

MONOPOLY

Since the passage of the Sherman Anti-trust Act by the Republican party we have consistently fought to preserve free competition with regulation to prevent abuse.

New Deal policy fosters Government monopoly, restricts production, and fixes prices. We shall enforce anti-trust legislation without prejudice or discrimination. We condemn the use or threatened use of criminal indictments to obtain through consent decrees objectives not contemplated by law.

GOVERNMENT COMPETITION

We promise to reduce to the minimum Federal competition with business. We pledge ourselves to establish honest accounting and reporting by every agency of the Federal Government and to continue only those enterprises whose maintenance is clearly in the public interest.

FREE SPEECH

The principles of a free press and free speech, as established by the Constitution, should apply to the radio. Federal regulation of radio is necessary in view of the natural limitations of wave lengths, but this gives no excuse for censorship. We oppose the use of licensing to establish arbitrary controls. Licenses should be revocable only when, after public hearings, due cause for cancellation is shown.

SMALL BUSINESS

The New Deal policy of interference and arbitrary regulation has injured all business, but especially small business. We promise to encourage the small business man by removing unnecessary bureaucratic regulation and interference.

STOCK AND COMMODITY EXCHANGES

We favor regulation of stock and commodity exchanges. They should be accorded the fullest measure of self-control consistent with the discharge of their public trust and the prevention of abuse.

INSURANCE

We condemn the New Deal attempts to destroy the confidence of our people in private insurance institutions. We favor continuance of regulation of insurance by the several States.

GOVERNMENT REORGANIZATION

We shall reestablish in the Federal Civil Service a real merit system on a truly competitive basis and extend it to all non-policy-forming positions.

We pledge ourselves to enact legislation standardizing and simplifying quasi-judicial administrative agencies to insure adequate notice and hearing, impartiality, adherence to the rules of evidence and full judicial review of all questions of law and fact.

Our greatest protection against totalitarian government is the American system of checks and balances. The constitutional distribution of legislative, executive, and judicial functions is essential to the preservation of this system. We pledge ourselves to make it the basis of all our policies affecting the organization and operation of our Republican form of Government.

THIRD TERM

To insure against the overthrow of our American system of government we favor an amendment to the Constitution providing that no person shall be President of the United States for more than two terms.

A PLEDGE OF GOOD FAITH

The acceptance of the nominations made by this Convention carries with it, as a matter of private honor and public faith, an undertaking by each candidate to be true to the principles and program herein set forth.

We earnestly urge all patriotic men and women, regardless of former affiliations, to unite with us in the support of our declaration of principles to the end that "government of the people, by the people and for the people shall not perish from this earth."

Acceptance Speech by President Franklin D. Roosevelt
Washington, July 19, 1940

Roosevelt's acceptance speech to the Democratic national convention was delivered by radio commencing at 12:25 a.m. on July 19. In it he emphasized his willingness to continue to serve if drafted by the people and made clear the nature of the limited campaign he was willing to wage.

Members of the Convention — my friends:

It is very late; but I have felt that you would rather that I speak to you now than wait until tomorrow.

It is with a very full heart that I speak tonight. I must confess that I do so with mixed feelings — because I find myself, as almost everyone does sooner or later in his lifetime, in a conflict between deep personal desire for retirement on the one hand, and that quiet, invisible thing called "conscience" on the other.

Because there are self-appointed commentators and interpreters who will seek to misinterpret or question motives, I speak in a somewhat personal vein; and I must trust to the good faith and common sense of the American people to accept my own good faith — and to do their own interpreting.

When, in 1936, I was chosen by the voters for a second time as President, it was my firm intention to turn over the responsibilities of Government to other hands at the end of my term. That conviction remained with me. Eight years in the Presidency, following a period of bleak depression, and covering one world crisis after another, would normally entitle any man to the relaxation that comes from honorable retirement.

During the spring of 1939, world events made it clear to all but the blind or the partisan that a great war in Europe had become not merely a possibility but a probability, and that such a war would of necessity deeply affect the future of this nation.

When the conflict first broke out last September, it was still my intention to announce clearly and simply, at an early date, that under no conditions would I accept reelection. This fact was well known to my friends, and I think was understood by many citizens.

It soon became evident, however, that such a public statement on my part would be unwise from the point of view of sheer public duty. As President of the United States, it was my clear duty, with the aid of the Congress, to preserve our neutrality, to shape our program of defense, to meet rapid changes, to keep our domestic affairs adjusted to shifting world conditions, and to sustain the policy of the Good Neighbor.

It was also my obvious duty to maintain to the utmost the influence of this mighty nation in our effort to prevent the spread of war, and to sustain by all legal means those governments threatened by other governments which had rejected the principles of democracy.

Swiftly moving foreign events made necessary swift action at home and beyond the seas. Plans for national defense had to be expanded and adjusted to meet new forms of warfare. American citizens and their welfare had to be safeguarded in many foreign zones of danger. National unity in the United States became a crying essential in the face of the development of unbelievable types of espionage and international treachery.

Every day that passed called for the postponement of personal plans and partisan debate until the latest possible moment. The normal conditions under which I would have made public declaration of my personal desires were wholly gone.

And so, thinking solely of the national good and of the international scene, I came to the reluctant conclusion that such declaration should not be made before the national Convention. It was accordingly made to you within an hour after the permanent organization of this Convention.

Like any other man, I am complimented by the honor you have done me. But I know you will understand the spirit in which I say that no call of Party alone would prevail upon me to accept reelection to the Presidency.

The real decision to be made in these circumstances is not the acceptance of a nomination, but rather an ultimate willingness to serve if chosen by the electorate of the United States. Many considerations enter into this decision.

During the past few months, with due Congressional approval, we in the United States have been taking steps to implement the total defense of America. I cannot forget that in carrying out this program I have drafted into the service of the nation many men and women, taking them away from important private affairs, calling them suddenly from their homes and their businesses. I have asked them to leave their own work, and to contribute their skill and experience to the cause of their nation.

I, as the head of their Government, have asked them to do this. Regardless of party, regardless of personal convenience, they came — they answered the call. Every single one of them, with one exception, has come to the nation's Capital to serve the nation.

These people, who have placed patriotism above all else, represent those who have made their way to what might be called the top of their professions or industries through their proven skill and experience.

But they alone could not be enough to meet the needs of the times.

Just as a system of national defense based on man power alone, without the mechanized equipment of modern warfare, is totally insufficient for adequate national defense, so also planes and guns and tanks are wholly insufficient unless they are implemented by the power of men trained to use them.

Such man power consists not only of pilots and gunners and infantry and those who operate tanks. For every individual in actual combat service, it is necessary for adequate defense that we have ready at hand at least four or five other trained individuals organized for non-combat services.

Because of the millions of citizens involved in the conduct of defense, most right thinking persons are agreed that some form of selection by draft is as necessary and fair today as it was in 1917 and 1918.

Nearly every American is willing to do his share or her share to defend the United States. It is neither just nor efficient to permit that task to fall upon any one section or any one group. For every section and every group depend for their existence upon the survival of the nation as a whole.

Lying awake, as I have, on many nights, I have asked myself whether I have the right, as Commander-in-Chief of the Army and Navy, to call on men and women to serve their country or to train themselves to serve and, at the same time, decline to serve my country in my own personal capacity, if I am called upon to do so by the people of my country.

In times like these — in times of great tension, of great crisis — the compass of the world narrows to a single fact. The fact which dominates our world is the fact of armed aggression, the fact of successful armed aggression, aimed at the form of Government, the kind of society that we in the United States have chosen and established for ourselves. It is a fact which no one longer doubts — which no one is longer able to ignore.

It is not an ordinary war. It is a revolution imposed by force of arms, which threatens all men everywhere. It is a revolution which proposes not to set men free but to reduce them to slavery — to reduce them to slavery in the interest of a dictatorship which has already shown the nature and the extent of the advantage which it hopes to obtain.

That is the fact which dominates our world and which dominates the lives of all of us, each and every one of us. In the face of the danger which confronts our time, no individual retains or can hope to retain, the right of personal choice which free men enjoy in times of peace. He has a first obligation to serve in the defense of our institutions of freedom — a first obligation to serve his country in whatever capacity his country finds him useful.

Like most men of my age, I had made plans for myself, plans for a private life of my own choice and for my own satisfaction, a life of that kind to begin in January, 1941. These plans, like so many other plans, had been made in a world which now seems as distant as another planet. Today all private plans, all private lives, have been in a sense repealed by an overriding public danger. In the face of that public danger all those who can be of service to the Republic have no choice but to offer themselves for service in those capacities for which they may be fitted.

Those, my friends, are the reasons why I have had to admit to myself, and now to state to you, that my conscience will not let me turn my back upon a call to service.

The right to make that call rests with the people through the American method of a free election. Only the people themselves can draft a President. If such a draft should be made upon me, I say to you, in the utmost simplicity, I will, with God's help, continue to serve with the best of my ability and with the fullness of my strength.

To you, the delegates of this Convention, I express my gratitude for the selection of Henry Wallace for the high office of Vice President of the United States. His first-hand knowledge of the problems of Government in every sphere of life and in every single part of the nation — and indeed of the whole world — qualifies him without reservation. His practical idealism will be of great service to me individually and to the nation as a whole.

And to the Chairman of the National Committee, the Postmaster General of the United States — my old friend Jim Farley — I send, as I have often before and shall many times again, my most affectionate greetings. All of us are sure that he will continue to give all the leadership and support that he possibly can to the cause of American democracy.

In some respects, as I think my good wife suggested an hour or so ago — the next few months will be different from the usual national campaigns of recent years.

Most of you know how important it is that the President of the United States in these days remain close to the seat of Government. Since last Summer I have been compelled to abandon proposed journeys to inspect many of our great national projects from the Alleghenies to the Pacific Coast.

Events move so fast in other parts of the world that it has become my duty to remain either in the White House itself or at some near-by point where I can reach Washington and even Europe and Asia by direct telephone — where, if need be, I can be back at my desk in the space of a very few hours. And in addition, the splendid work of the new defense machinery will require me to spend vastly more time in conference with the responsible administration heads under me. Finally, the added task which the present crisis has imposed also upon the Congress, compelling them to forego their usual adjournment, calls for constant cooperation between the Executive and Legislative branches, to the efficiency of which I am glad indeed now to pay tribute.

I do expect, of course, during the coming months to make my usual periodic reports to the country through the medium of press conferences and radio talks. I shall not have the time or the inclination to engage in purely political debate. But I shall never be loath to call the attention of the nation to deliberate or unwitting falsifications of fact, which are sometimes made by political candidates.

I have spoken to you in a very informal and personal way. The exigencies of the day require, however, that I also talk with you about things which transcend any personality and go very deeply to the roots of American civilization.

Our lives have been based on those fundamental freedoms and liberties which we Americans have cherished for a century and a half. The establishment of them and the preservation of them in each succeeding generation have been accomplished through the processes of free elective Government — the democratic-republican form, based on the representative system and the coordination of the executive, the legislative and the judicial branches.

The task of safeguarding our institutions seems to me to be twofold. One must be accomplished, if it becomes necessary, by the armed defense forces of the nation. The other, by the united effort of the men and women of the country to make our

Federal and State and local Governments responsive to the growing requirements of modern democracy.

There have been occasions, as we remember, when reactions in the march of democracy have set in, and forward-looking progress has seemed to stop.

But such periods have been followed by liberal and progressive times which have enabled the nation to catch up with new developments in fulfilling new human needs. Such a time has been the past seven years. Because we had seemed to lag in previous years, we have had to develop, speedily and efficiently, the answers to aspirations which had come from every State and every family in the land.

We have sometimes called it social legislation; we have sometimes called it legislation to end the abuses of the past; we have sometimes called it legislation for human security; and we have sometimes called it legislation to better the condition of life of the many millions of our fellow citizens, who could not have the essentials of life or hope for an American standard of living.

Some of us have labeled it a wider and more equitable distribution of wealth in our land. It has included among its aims, to liberalize and broaden the control of vast industries — lodged today in the hands of a relatively small group of individuals of very great financial power.

But all of these definitions and labels are essentially the expression of one consistent thought. They represent a constantly growing sense of human decency, human decency throughout our nation.

This sense of human decency is happily confined to no group or class. You find it in the humblest home. You find it among those who toil, and among the shopkeepers and the farmers of the nation. You find it, to a growing degree, even among those who are listed in that top group which has so much control over the industrial and financial structure of the nation. Therefore, this urge of humanity can by no means be labeled a war of class against class. It is rather a war against poverty and suffering and ill-health and insecurity, a war in which all classes are joining in the interest of a sound and enduring democracy.

I do not believe for a moment, and I know that you do not believe either, that we have fully answered all the needs of human security. But we have covered much of the road. I need not catalogue the milestones of seven years. For every individual and every family in the whole land know that the average of their personal lives has been made safer and sounder and happier than it has ever been before. I do not think they want the gains in these directions to be repealed or even to be placed in the charge of those who would give them mere lip-service with no heart service.

Yes, very much more remains to be done, and I think the voters want the task entrusted to those who believe that the words "human betterment" apply to poor and rich alike.

And I have a sneaking suspicion too, that voters will smile at charges of inefficiency against a Government which has boldly met the enormous problems of banking, and finance and industry which the great efficient bankers and industrialists of the Republican Party left in such hopeless chaos in the famous year 1933.

But we all know that our progress at home and in the other American nations toward this realization of a better human decency — progress along free lines — is gravely endangered by what is happening on other continents. In

Europe, many nations, through dictatorships or invasions, have been compelled to abandon normal democratic processes. They have been compelled to adopt forms of government which some call "new and efficient."

They are not new, my friends, they are only a relapse — a relapse into ancient history. The omnipotent rulers of the greater part of modern Europe have guaranteed efficiency, and work, and a type of security.

But the slaves who built the pyramids for the glory of the dictator Pharaohs of Egypt had that kind of security, that kind of efficiency, that kind of corporative state.

So did the inhabitants of that world which extended from Britain to Persia under the undisputed rule of the proconsuls sent out from Rome.

So did the henchmen, the tradesmen, the mercenaries and the slaves of the feudal system which dominated Europe a thousand years ago.

So did the people of those nations of Europe who received their kings and their government at the whim of the conquering Napoleon.

Whatever its new trappings and new slogans, tyranny is the oldest and most discredited rule known to history. And whenever tyranny has replaced a more human form of Government it has been due more to internal causes than external. Democracy can thrive only when it enlists the devotion of those whom Lincoln called the common people. Democracy can hold that devotion only when it adequately respects their dignity by so ordering society as to assure to the masses of men and women reasonable security and hope for themselves and for their children.

We in our democracy, and those who live in still unconquered democracies, will never willingly descend to any form of this so-called security of efficiency which calls for the abandonment of other securities more vital to the dignity of man. It is our credo — unshakable to the end — that we must live under the liberties that were first heralded by Magna Carta and placed into glorious operation through the Declaration of Independence, the Constitution of the United States and the Bill of Rights.

The Government of the United States for the past seven years has had the courage openly to oppose by every peaceful means the spread of the dictator form of Government. If our Government should pass to other hands next January — untried hands, inexperienced hands — we can merely hope and pray that they will not substitute appeasement and compromise with those who seek to destroy all democracies everywhere, including here.

I would not undo, if I could, the efforts I made to prevent war from the moment it was threatened and to restrict the area of carnage, down to the last minute. I do not now soften the condemnation expressed by Secretary Hull and myself from time to time for the acts of aggression that have wiped out ancient liberty-loving, peace-pursuing countries which had scrupulously maintained neutrality. I do not recant the sentiments of sympathy with all free peoples resisting such aggression, or begrudge the material aid that we have given to them. I do not regret my consistent endeavor to awaken this country to the menace for us and for all we hold dear.

I have pursued these efforts in the face of appeaser fifth columnists who charged me with hysteria and war-mongering. But I felt it my duty, my simple, plain, inescapable duty, to arouse my countrymen to the danger of the new forces let loose in the world.

So long as I am President, I will do all I can to insure that that foreign policy remain our foreign policy.

All that I have done to maintain the peace of this country and to prepare it morally, as well as physically, for whatever contingencies may be in store, I submit to the judgment of my countrymen.

We face one of the great choices of history.

It is not alone a choice of Government by the people versus dictatorship.

It is not alone a choice of freedom versus slavery.

It is not alone a choice between moving forward or falling back.

It is all of these rolled into one.

It is the continuance of civilization as we know it versus the ultimate destruction of all that we have held dear — religion against godlessness; the ideal of justice against the practice of force; moral decency versus the firing squad; courage to speak out, and to act, versus the false lullaby of appeasement.

But it has been well said that a selfish and greedy people cannot be free.

The American people must decide whether these things are worth making sacrifices of money, of energy, and of self. They will not decide by listening to mere words or by reading mere pledges, interpretations and claims. They will decide on the record — the record as it has been made — the record of things as they are.

The American people will sustain the progress of a representative democracy, asking the Divine Blessing as they face the future with courage and with faith.

Address by Wendell L. Willkie
Seattle, September 23, 1940

Willkie's campaign address at Seattle contained some of his most pungent remarks on the failure of the New Deal to solve the problem of unemployment. In this speech Willkie argued that the New Deal had not done enough for either business or labor and expressed his own faith in an economy of abundance.

In 1932, Candidate Roosevelt said that our number one problem was jobs. He was right that time. In 1936, when Mr. Roosevelt was again a candidate, our number one problem was still jobs.

And now, in 1940, Mr. Roosevelt is still a candidate — and our number one domestic problem is still jobs.

The only difference is that today, Candidate Roosevelt is no longer talking about that subject. Some time back, the New Dealers gave up talking about jobs and just talked about unemployment.

According to no less an authority than Harry Hopkins, a large number of our people will always be out of work.

That proposition I totally reject. But I am not going to talk about unemployment tonight. I came here to talk about the cure for unemployment. I came here to talk about jobs.

Now, there are two ways for people to find work: one way is for them to work for themselves. Most farmers, many retail store operators, service station keepers and other small business men have that kind of job.

The other way to get work is to find an employer who will hire you. Most of us Americans would like ultimately to go in business for ourselves, to be our own employers. But we can't all do that. Even if we are ultimately able to work for ourselves, we have to start by working for somebody else. So, for most of us, getting a job means simply finding an employer. Now, there are two kinds of employer systems in the world, and only two.

Under one system, almost all of the people work for private employers. That is the system we have in democratic countries. Under the other system, almost all of the people work for one employer, namely the State. That is the case in Russia, and in effect, in Germany and the other dictator countries.

Under a dictatorship, there need never be any unemployment. The State tells you what you must do, where you must do it and how you must do it. You are sent away from home to work in the fields, or to build fortifications, or to dig in the mines, or to do anything else you are told. You have a job under those conditions, but for that job you have paid an intolerable price. You have bought that job with your freedom.

We in America have made our decision with regard to that issue. We want to work for and with private employers, to find new ways of creating jobs. And we believe in the freedom of the workers to take whatever jobs they want — whatever jobs provide them with the most worth-while life and the most hopeful opportunities.

That is the system I stand for. And if you elect me President that is the system you will get.

Now, let us look a little more closely at the problems facing those of us who work for employers in a free enterprise system.

I want to be very frank about these problems and very specific. To begin with, I think we must be careful not to dramatize these problems in a purely political way. By that I mean that we must not fall into the error — the fatal error — of believing that one political party is for labor and the other not. I think my speeches and writings put me on record as being willing to give credit wherever credit is due.

But if there is one kind of person more dangerous to our democracy than another, it is the smooth politician who claims everything for his side and grants nothing to the other side. For instance, take the National Labor Relations Act. When it was passed this act was long overdue.

America lagged behind every progressive nation in the world in protecting the fundamental rights of labor to organize and bargain collectively.

But the New Deal has issued tons of propaganda to claim exclusive credit for that act. Whereas in reality the National Labor Relations Act was modeled closely on the railway labor act of 1926, which was passed by a Republican Administration.

Now let me tell you straight from the shoulder. I stand for every one of the social gains that labor has made.

I stand for the National Labor Relations Act and the right of free collective bargaining. I stand for minimum wages and maximum hours, and for legislation to enforce them.

I stand for social security benefits and believe that they should be extended to other groups who do not yet enjoy them. I believe that we should be insured against unemployment and that our old age should be protected by adequate pensions.

These are minimum guarantees. They are minimum standards below which society dare not fall. No American can contemplate the future with an easy mind or an easy conscience unless he can see in that future a society willing and able to provide its workers with at least that much protection.

Now if the New Deal wants to claim credit for those minimum safeguards, I say let it have just as much as it deserves. I don't care how much credit the New Deal claims, because I know, and the record shows, that the New Deal has let labor down.

As indispensable as it may be, the Wages and Hours Act does not make jobs. And the right to collective bargaining, fundamental as it is, does not do any good to the man who has no job to bargain about.

An Administration that wants to do something for labor must go much further than minimum guarantees. Such an administration, while protecting labor's rights, must make jobs, and jobs, and jobs.

Now perhaps some of you who have jobs may say: "What has this got to do with me? I have a good job. I am all right. Let the other fellow who can't find a job go on relief. Let the government take care of him."

Now, in the first place, let me say yes, that is all right; we have relief, and we are going to keep relief. I give you that pledge. If I am President of the United States and you by some misfortune happen to lose your job, you will get relief.

But that is not enough. If you lost your job tomorrow you wouldn't want to go on relief if you could help it. You would go out looking for another job — a real American job, real work, earning real wages. But could you find that job today? Nine million six hundred thousand persons haven't been able to.

And the reason I am undertaking this campaign is because I want every man and woman in this country to find a job if he or she wants one. I want that just as much as you do, because I have given my pledge to labor, that I know what makes jobs and that I will get them for you.

And in the second place, with regard to this matter of relief, it would be short-sighted for those who have jobs to say that they are not interested in the unemployed. You are making the mistake of your lives if you think that just because you have a job you do not have to be concerned about the millions of your fellow-citizens who are looking for jobs.

There are three chief reasons why American workers should fear the continuation of unemployment.

First, there are 9,600,000 persons out of work today, which means that there are 9,600,000 persons looking for your job.

Secondly, ours is an expanding population. More than half a million new workers come to maturity each year. More than half a million young people are turned out of schools to look for new jobs that do not exist.

If these young people have no place to go, they will be out looking for your job, too. And the next year there will be another half a million of them.

But thirdly — and this is the most dangerous fact about unemployment — it is absolutely impossible for a government to go on supporting a growing number of unemployed. Somebody has to pay the bill. And don't kid yourselves that bill is being paid by those of you who have jobs.

The average income per individual in the United States last year was only $540; the average tax paid per individual was $110. One fifth of our national income goes for taxes. And the biggest single item on the tax bill, aside from defense, is relief for the unemployed.

Of course, the New Deal has found an easy method of paying for that big relief bill. Your taxes don't anywhere near cover it, so the New Deal borrows the money. In seven and a half years it has borrowed about twenty-two billion dollars. And you all know that this can't go on indefinitely.

If we go on living beyond our income, there is bound to be a collapse — a collapse that will drag down, not only the precious rights of labor and all the social gains that you have made, but also your jobs, your opportunities and your hopes for the future.

The one and only remedy for this increasing government debt, the one and only safeguard for your rights and your opportunities, is jobs and jobs and jobs.

Now what makes a job? That is a forthright question and it deserves a forthright answer.

Business makes jobs — little business, big business, corporations, partnerships and small companies. Under our system, if we are going to have jobs we must have employers.

It is not enough that the present employers should hire more men — although that is very important. There must be new employers — new employers every day. If we are to give our workers a chance, there ought to be about 200,000 new enterprises founded every year.

Now what has happened under the New Deal?

Between 1900 and 1929 the number of business enterprises per thousand of population increased about 17 per cent. We were growing and there were plenty of jobs.

Today, we have even fewer business enterprises per thousand of population than we had in 1929. Measured by the standard of our previous growth, we are short about 700,000 enterprises — that is, we are short about 700,000 employers.

Nowadays it is about as hard to start a new business as it is to rob a bank — and the risks of going to jail are about as great in both cases.

Now let us ask ourselves this question: Why are there fewer employers per thousand of population than there used to be?

Well, here's the answer to that one. If you want to become an employer you can't just go out and hire men. You have to have either money in the bank, or credit. And most important of all, you have to have a plant, a factory. Factories are really tools for the workers to use — tools that enormously increase their earning power.

But you will find your factory expensive to build. Taking an average across the country you will find that you have to invest about $4,000 for every man you employ.

In other words, it takes about $4,000 of investment to make one job.

Now there are two things about that $4,000 that you must understand.

In the first place, neither you nor anybody else will put up that $4,000 unless there is some chance of making a profit on it. That profit is what you earn from the factory that the workers are using.

Under the New Deal the employer who puts up money to make a profit has been in the doghouse. Government officials have encouraged the belief that he is a kind of conspirator against society — an exploiter of the workers.

Profits have come to be regarded, not as the legitimate reward of enterprise, but as a kind of tax laid upon society by privileged men.

Now if you really believe all that bunk, then you ought to change our system so that we can all go to work for the State. Because, so long as we keep our system of private enterprise, the employer will not put up $4,000 for your job unless he can make a profit on it.

I am not interested in profits as such. I am not interested in employers as such. But I am interested in both employers and profits as a means of making jobs for those who are now unemployed and as a means of making better jobs for those who are already employed.

I am pledged to get those jobs, and I intend to keep my pledge.

Now there is a second thing we must understand about that $4,000. The man who invests it must be given a clear chance by the government to make his factory work. But the New Deal has not done that. The New Deal has been hostile to employers. It has attacked them for almost everything they do or fail to do.

I am not going to give you the whole list of the things that the New Deal has done to make life difficult for the man who owns that factory.

You know, because I have said so many times, that I stand for the proper regulation of business — particularly big business. But it seems to me that it is in the interests of labor to make that regulation just as simple as possible and just as efficient as possible.

Too much red tape, too many reports to fill out, too much suspicion on the part of government representatives, takes the time of the business man away from his work and makes him inefficient. It also adds to his cost — and every item added to cost outside the shop simply decreases the earning power of the workers who make that product.

Also, as I have pointed out on many occasions, the New Deal tax structure is unscientific and inefficient. Businesses that make a profit should pay a tax. But we must be careful not to levy taxes that will discourage employers from starting new businesses, from hiring more workers.

And worst of all, the New Deal has constantly changed its laws, its taxes and its regulations. You understand that, in order to do business successfully, a man must be able to predict the future with some reasonable certainty.

It is the duty of government to stabilize our economic system as much as possible. When the system is kept in turmoil as it has been under the New Deal, a business man cannot predict the future, and, therefore, he won't risk his money in new enterprises to make new jobs.

Let me give you just one example of the kind of thing that has been going on all over the country during the past seven years. I have a report on a business concern in Ohio, founded in 1885. It is a small concern employing only fifty people; there are only twenty stockholders and the capitalization is only $200,000.

The highest salary paid in this business is $6,500, and dividends to the shareholders have never run over 4 or 5 per cent in good years. But recently there have been no good years. The president of that company is in despair and this is what he recently said;

"If the current tax burden, the weight of government demands for reports, and the snooping of government officials, continue, this business will be liquidated."

In that little example you have the whole story. Because of a generally hostile attitude on the part of the New Deal toward this small business, the owners of the plant are on the point of shutting down after fifty-five years. And that would mean fifty men added to the ranks of the unemployed.

Now the men who run that little business don't want to abandon it. They like it. They used to make a fair return out of it. They might even like to increase its size if they had a chance.

The mechanism of this system of ours, this system of private enterprise, is an exceedingly delicate mechanism. It's like a watch. And if you go after it with a crowbar and a pipe-wrench it won't keep time for you any more.

So here's my point: I am 100 per cent determined to keep the minimum safeguards that labor has won. I'd even be in favor of raising them whenever we can afford to do so. But I say those minimum safeguards are not enough. They cannot really protect you.

They cannot protect you from the threat of unemployment. They cannot protect you from the great load of debt and taxes that you are now carrying. And they cannot protect you from the collapse of our system, which will inevitably come if we continue as we are today.

The only thing that can really protect you, the only thing that can basically safeguard your rights and opportunities, is new employment — more jobs — more work — more growth — more expansion.

There are a lot of things that I would say to you if time permitted. We are living in bewildering times. Statesmen, business men, and working men are all confronted with problems that are difficult to solve.

I can understand your problems. I have worked with my hands on farms and in factories. I have been a business man too. I have seen the picture from both sides.

I know that if we are to preserve our system of private enterprise, of free enterprise, we cannot expect one side to get ahead at the expense of the other.

Believe me, if I am elected President of the United States, I shall protect your side of the industrial team. But this is the thought I want to leave with you tonight: The other side of the industrial team, the employer, must be given a chance.

We can lick the employer if we want to. We can beat him down, we can frighten him, we can even eliminate him. But if we do that — and that is what the New Deal is doing — you won't have any jobs. The only employer left under those circumstances would be the State.

The difference between me and my opponent for office is that I have faith in America. The New Deal candidate does not believe there are any more jobs, whereas I know there are. He does not believe that we can put the unemployed back to work, whereas I know that we can.

This is a critical issue. It is a terrible issue, when you stop to think about it. We know — all history provides us with proof — that this intolerable load of unemployment and debt must surely end with the destruction of our democratic way of life.

If we go on this way we shall surely lose those rights and liberties which are so precious to us. By his failure to revise our system Mr. Roosevelt is heading us toward a totalitarian State.

That is why I ask you to join me in this crusade; this crusade to make jobs; to put this country back to work; to build a new America with a higher standard of life than we have ever dreamed of before.

Democracy is rooted in prosperity. I have undertaken to restore prosperity, to open a greater opportunity for every one of us. And if you give me the chance to do that, I will not let you down.

"The Presidency" by Dorothy Thompson
in *The New York Herald Tribune*
October 9, 1940

Dorothy Thompson, long a severe critic of New Deal domestic policies, endorsed President Roosevelt for a third term because she felt his strong leadership was needed in the world crisis.

It is fair enough to ask a commentator and critic of public affairs what her stand is in the forthcoming election. I have been reluctant to state mine. I have wanted to be absolutely sure that it was mine — without any shadow of wavering. I think I reached a quick decision before this campaign began, back in May, in France, when I saw two thirds of the French Republic folding over the other third and knew that the great crisis was coming to a head. In that moment, I think, I knew that Roosevelt must stay in office and see this thing through. I indicated my feeling about this in a cable from Paris at that time.

But I waited, and watched the campaign, read the speeches and statements and watched the course of events and kept an open mind.

This column, in the five years in which it has appeared, has often criticized the Roosevelt administration, and sometimes very sharply. On the issue of the Supreme Court bill, the manner of the Spending Program, on the Silver policy and the Production versus Purchasing Power theory, and on some of the tax measures and the argument and means used for enforcing them this column has not seen eye to eye with the Administration. If I look back over those criticisms, there is not a great deal which I would rescind today, although I would modify some of my criticism. I know better now, than when I started to write, the difficulties of achieving perfection, the innumerable unsatisfactory compromises that have to be accepted in the adjustments between interests and ideas in a democracy.

And I have said before and I say again, the mistakes of the New Deal have been mistakes along a road in the right direction in pursuit of the right aim, the extension of the economic benefits of this society, with a larger degree of economic equality, to a larger section of the whole people, under a larger measure of popular control. The means used have sometimes been erroneous and the spirit too often punitive and bitter.

But here we are, and the year is 1940. We have behind us eight terrible years of a crisis we have shared with all countries. Here we are, and our basic institutions are still intact, our people relatively prosperous, and most important of all, our society relatively affectionate. No rift has made an unbridgable schism between us. The working classes are not clamoring for Mr. Browder and the industrialists are not demanding a Man on Horseback. No country in the world is so well off.

2981

The very election campaign — a campaign which this column dreaded, fearing that in the fight we would present a spectacle of disunity and division to hawk-eyed aggression — has demonstrated a deep, internal, spiritual health. The readers of this column may expect no virulent attack on Mr. Willkie. It has no acrimonious words for him. I have known him for several years. He is a very good human being. The things he loves and believes in are the things most of us love and believe in. He has courage and idealism and sincerity and spiritual grace.

Whatever the outcome, he has rendered his country a service which it should remember forever with gratitude. With a stubbornness reminiscent of the President himself, he has refused to throw into this campaign the issue of peace or war, knowing what a distortion such a campaign would make of the real issues in foreign policy, knowing how dangerous such a campaign would be to our world position. If now and then he has slipped a little, and seemed to carry water on both shoulders, the pressure has been almost overwhelming from those who know what political capital could be made of such distortions, and who would rather win with Willkie than save America. Mr. Willkie himself does not want, I think, to win that much.

They do this country no service whatsoever who try to make this campaign a fight between Roosevelt and Hitler or between Willkie and Stalin. Only in our quadrennial orgies of overheated partisanship could such preposterous ideas be rife. The truth is that if Franklin Roosevelt and Wendell Willkie were to sit down in the same room together and tell each other what they really think, there would be more agreement between them than difference — and the difference would be due to temperament and a variety of experience rather than philosophy. The President is a man whose life has been spent in affairs of state; the contender is a man whose experience is varied, but has been chiefly in the field of business. Both love this country more dearly than they love their lives, and for both "country" and "democracy" are synonyms. God must love America that this is so.

Both suffer more from their friends than from their enemies. And both are contending for a position that no man should envy them. Our hard times are ahead of us.

But I shall support the President because I think he has assets on his side that nobody can match — assets for this nation in this time.

The President *knows* the world. He knows it, in the most particular minutiae, better than any other living democratic head of a state or ex-head of a state. The range and precision of his knowledge — military, naval, political: his understanding of conflicting social forces; his grasp of programs — all these impress every person whose life has been spent in foreign affairs with whom he talks.

No new President could acquire this knowledge in weeks or in months or in four years. It antedates the Presidency. Mr. Roosevelt was Assistant Secretary of the Navy in 1917. His passionate interest in the Navy, and, through it, in world affairs, has never relaxed.

The President is a man of peace. No one who saw and talked with him, as I did, after the outbreak of the war, and in June, in the midst of the collapse of France, and saw how the war had stricken that naturally insouciant personality, marking his face with suffering, could ever dare to say that he is a warmonger.

The President tried to help world peace, tried to keep it by every possible means, and by the only possible means short of delivering all democracies over to the dictators — the use of the American weight for peace. It is not his fault that the custom and traditional behavior of America make it impossible for any administration to commit America for peace. Those who are loudest screaming warmonger are most responsible for that condition.

The President can be a very great man in times of emergency. He was a great man in 1933, and he has been a great man since the overwhelming crisis in June. He has met that crisis, that swift and dangerous disaster, with speed, timing, and immense courage.

He is the first President in our whole history to dare to call for conscription in the midst of an election campaign. In that he threw his political career into the scales. If some of Mr. Willkie's partisans — I will not call them his supporters — have their way, this issue of life and death importance to the nation will yet be exploited against the President and against our common safety.

While others talked of unity, the President moved swiftly to make unity real. He reorganized the Cabinet. He changed the most controversial figures in it. Mr. Hopkins gave place to Mr. Jesse Jones, about whom, in the circles hostile to Roosevelt, there is no controversy whatsoever. Miss Perkins plays a minor role today. The most important labor figure is Sidney Hillman, the representative of labor on the Defense Board, and no one who knows the labor bureaucracy is likely to challenge the statement that he is the most enlightened and statesmanlike labor leader in the country.

The President gave two of the most critical Cabinet posts — War and Navy — to two great patriots and two Republicans, one of them the man who, as Vice-Presidential candidate four years ago, made the sharpest attacks upon his policy. Not since that titanic conservative, Alexander Hamilton, handed the election of 1800 to his hated rival, the liberal Jefferson, to save and unite the nation in a time of crisis, has a political leader of America made a more magnanimous and wholehearted gesture. Those who say he did it for political considerations have dry hearts and limited imaginations. The President knows that more than his career or his party is at stake.

He unified the defense with Canada, making a military and political move of first-class statesmanship and importance.

He made a deal on air bases which is worth billions for the defense of these shores. In this he was conspicuously aided by Mr. Willkie, for the destroyer deal would perhaps have been too daring without the support of the contender. For this Mr. Willkie shares the orchids.

The President gathered to the defense counsel representatives of the great steel industry and of the great motor industry — neither of them his partisans — and in dealing with the industrialists in matters of defense production he has been generous in the extreme. Short of handing them Capitol Hill, he has complied with every reasonable demand.

The present Cabinet could hardly be improved from the viewpoint of national unity.

And every move he has made has been in the weeks preceding an election. If he did not consult Congress on the destroyers, he is submitting everything he has done to the crucial test of the polls. This is not the way dictators act. They do not have elections!

He possesses the greatest single asset that any leader of a democratic state can have in a crisis like this: the confidence of the rank and file of workers that he will not use conscription and defense to betray democracy itself and destroy their freedom.

Mr. Willkie might also in time come to have that confidence. I think he would. But he does not have it now. He would have to win it, and in winning it some of his supporters would be his greatest liability. Roosevelt has it, and time is of the essence.

Finally, the prestige of the President throughout the democratic world, what is left of it, free, and what still hopes and believes and struggles under tyranny, is immense. The blemishes on a personality are more visible the closer one is to it. From afar they diminish, and the figure is seen in relation to larger issues, and in the frame of the world and his times. In that frame the figure of the President looms above that of any statesman, except perhaps Churchill, whose stature grows under fire.

Among our friends in Latin America Roosevelt is the most popular President who ever sat in the White House.

These are assets that we have here and now; they are the result of accumulation; they are already on the ledger. Beside them, it seems to me, the question of a third term and a thousand other considerations become very minor indeed. Democracy is destroyed from within by the destruction of its content, not by its viability under new forms. The third term is a tradition. It is not a constitutional matter.

These are briefly the reasons why this column will support the President.

Speech by President Franklin D. Roosevelt
Philadelphia, October 23, 1940

Roosevelt did not openly participate in the campaign until October 23 in Philadelphia, where he delivered the first of five lengthy political speeches. This opening address attacked the record of the "Republican leaders" from 1932 onwards and pledged that his rearmament program was designed to preserve peace.

Mr. Chairman, my friends of Philadelphia:

Last July I stated a plain obvious fact, a fact which I told the national convention of my party that the pressure of national defense work and the conduct of national affairs would not allow me to conduct any campaign in the accepted definition of that term.

Since July, hardly a day or a night has passed when some crisis, or some possibility of crisis in world affairs, has not called for my personal conference with out great Secretary of State and with other officials of your Government.

With every passing day has come some urgent problem in connection with our swift production for defense, and our mustering of the resources of the nation.

Therefore, it is essential — I have found it very essential in the national interest — to adhere to the rule never to be more than twelve hours distant from our National Capital.

But last July I also said this to the Chicago Convention: "I shall never be loath to call the attention of the nation to deliberate or unwitting falsifications of fact," which are sometimes made by political candidates.

The time has come for me to do just that.

This night and four other nights, I am taking time to point out to the American people what the more fantastic misstatements of this campaign have been. I emphasize the words "more fantastic," because it would take three hundred and sixty-five nights to discuss all of them.

All these misstatements cannot possibly be what I called last July, "unwitting falsifications" of fact; many of them must be and are "deliberate falsifications" of fact.

The young people who are attending dinners in every State of the Union tonight know that they are already a part of the whole economic and social life of the nation. I am particularly glad to discuss with them — and with you — these misstatements and the facts which refute them.

Truthful campaign discussion of public issues is essential to the American form of Government; but wilful misrepresentation of fact has no place either during election time or at any other time. For example, there can be no objection to any party or

2985

any candidate urging that the undeveloped water power of this nation should be harnessed by private utility companies rather than by the Government itself; or that the social security law should be repealed, or that the truth-in-securities act should be abrogated.

But it is an entirely different thing for any party or any candidate to state, for example, that the President of the United States telephoned to Mussolini and Hitler to sell Czechoslovakia down the river; or to state that the unfortunate unemployed of the nation are going to be driven into concentration camps; or that the social security funds of the Government of the United States will not be in existence when the workers of today become old enough to apply for them; or that the election of the present Government means the end of American democracy within four years. I think they know, and I know we know that all those statements are false.

Certain techniques of propaganda, created and developed in dictator countries, have been imported into this campaign. It is the very simple technique of repeating and repeating and repeating falsehoods, with the idea that by constant repetition and reiteration, with no contradiction, the misstatements will finally come to be believed.

Dictators have had great success in using this technique; but only because they were able to control the press and the radio, and to stifle all opposition. That is why I cannot bring myself to believe that in a democracy like ours, where the radio and a *part* of the press — I repeat, where the radio and a *part* of the press — remain open to both sides, repetition of deliberate misstatements will ever prevail.

I make the charge now that those falsifications are being spread for the purpose of filling the minds and the hearts of the American people with fear. They are used to create fear by instilling in the minds of our people doubt of each other, doubt of their Government, and doubt of the purposes of their democracy.

This type of campaign has a familiar ring. It reminds us of the scarecrow of four years ago that the social security funds were going to be diverted from the pockets of the American working man.

It reminds us of the famous old scarecrow of 1932, "Grass will grow in the streets of a hundred cities; a thousand towns; the weeds will overrun the fields of millions of farms."

The American people will not be stampeded into panic. The effort failed before and it will fail again. The overwhelming majority of Americans will not be scared by this blitzkrieg of verbal incendiary bombs. They are now calmly aware that, once more, "The only thing we have to fear is fear itself."

I consider it a public duty to answer falsifications with facts. I will not pretend that I find this an unpleasant duty. I am an old campaigner, and I love a good fight.

My friends, the Presidency is not a prize to be won by mere glittering promises. It is not a commodity to be sold by high-pressure salesmanship and national advertising. The Presidency is a most sacred trust and it ought not to be dealt with on any level other than an appeal to reason and humanity.

The worst bombshell of fear which the Republican leaders have let loose on this people is the accusation that this Government of ours, a Government of Republicans and Democrats alike, without the knowledge of the Congress or of the people, has secretly entered into agreements with foreign nations. They even intimate that such commitments have endangered the security of the United States, or are about to endanger it, or have pledged in some way the participation of the United States in some foreign war. It seems almost unnecessary to deny such a charge. But so long as the fantastic misstatement has been made, I must brand it for what it is.

I give to you and to the people of this country this most solemn assurance: There is no secret treaty, no secret obligation, no secret commitment, no secret understanding in any shape or form, direct or indirect, with any other Government, or any other nation in any part of the world, to involve this nation in any war or for any other purpose.

The desperation of partisans who can invent secret treaties drives them to try to deceive our people in other ways. Consider, for example, the false charge they make that our whole industrial system is prostrate — that business is stifled and can make no profits.

The American people have not forgotten the condition of the United States in 1932. We all remember the failures of the banks, the bread line of starving men and women, the youth of the country riding around in freight cars, the farm foreclosures, the home foreclosures, the bankruptcy and the panic.

At the very hour of complete collapse, the American people called for new leadership. That leadership, this Administration and a Democratic Congress supplied.

Government, no longer callous to suffering, moved swiftly to end distress, to halt depression to secure more social and economic justice for all.

The very same men who must bear the responsibility for the inaction of those days are the ones who now dare falsely to state that we are all still in the depth of the depression into which they plunged us; that we have prevented the country from recovering, and that it is headed for the chaos of bankruptcy. They have even gone to the extent of stating that this Administration has not made one man a job.

I say that those statements are false. I say that the figures of employment, of production of earnings, of general business activity — all prove that they are false.

The tears, the crocodile tears for the laboring man and laboring woman now being shed in this campaign come from those same Republican leaders who had their chance to prove their love for labor in 1932 — and missed it.

Back in 1932, those leaders were willing to let the workers starve if they could not get a job.

Back in 1932, they were not willing to guarantee collective bargaining.

Back in 1932, they met the demands of unemployed veterans with troops and tanks.

Back in 1932, they raised their hands in horror at the thought of fixing a minimum wage or maximum hours for labor; they never gave one thought to such things as pensions for old age or insurance for the unemployed.

In 1940, eight years later, what a different tune is played by them! It is a tune played against a sounding board of election day. It is a tune with overtones which whisper: "Votes, votes, votes."

These same Republican leaders are all for the new progressive measures now; they believe in them. They believe in them so much that they will never be happy until they can clasp them to their own chests and put their own brand upon them. If they could only get control of them, they plead, they would take so much better care of them, honest-to-goodness they would.

This tune is, of course, only a rehash of the tune of 1936, but a little louder. In that election year the affection of these Republican leaders for the laboring man also rose to a high pitch. But after election day they and their friends did all they could in the Congress of the United States, before departments and administrative bodies, and in the courts, and in the press, to beat these measures down into the ground.

What are the plain facts about employment today?

There are nine million more men and women employed in private industry now than were employed in March of 1933.

In the month of August of this year over four hundred thousand were added to the payrolls. And last month, September, another five hundred thousand workers went to work in our industries.

The millions that have gone to work, and the other hundreds of thousands now going to work each month in private industry, are the unequivocal answer to the brazen statement made by the Republicans in this campaign, that this Administration has not added one private job since 1933. That statement of theirs can only be branded as a deliberate misstatement of fact. And I now so brand it.

Let us call the roll of some of the specific improvements in the lot of the working men and women that have come about during the past eight years.

More than forty-two million American employees are now members of the old-age pension system. An additional two million men and women, over sixty-five years of age, are now receiving cash grants each month.

Twenty-nine million American employees have been brought under the protection of unemployment insurance.

Collective bargaining has been guaranteed.

A minimum wage has been established.

A maximum work week of forty hours has been fixed, with provision for time-and-a-half for overtime.

Child labor has been outlawed.

The average hourly earnings of factory workers were fifty-six cents in the boom year of 1929. By February, 1933 — before I went to Washington — they had dropped to forty-five cents an hour. They are now sixty-seven cents an hour — not only higher than in 1933, but, mark you, nearly eleven cents an hour higher than in 1929 itself.

Factory pay envelopes — most of you get them — had fallen to five billion dollars a year by 1932. By 1940, factory payrolls are running at the rate of ten billion dollars.

And, something else, we must not forget that the cost of living today is twenty-two per cent lower than it was in 1929. That means something to the average American family.

An equally unpardonable falsification about our economy is made when Republican leaders talk about American business — how it cannot make a profit, how little confidence it has in this Administration, and how this Administration hates business.

We know, if we but look at the record, that American business, big and small business, is way up above the level of 1932, and on a much sounder footing than it was even in the twenties.

Do you need figures to prove it? Just a few:

Our national income has nearly doubled since 1932, from thirty-nine billions up to the rate of seventy-four billions in 1940. And if you properly consider the lower cost of living today than in 1929 the national income is even higher now than in that great boom year.

In the ten years before the crash of 1929, the years of the so-called prosperity boom, bank failures averaged over six hundred a year. The number of bank failures last year was only forty-two, and of those forty-two, thirty-two were not under Federal deposit insurance. Ten were. Those ten were under Federal deposit insurance set up by this Administration; in those ten banks, ninety-nine per cent of the depositors did not lose one dollar.

During this Administration the total number of bank failures for the entire seven years was less than the number of bank failures in any single year of the preceding ten years.

It is a funny world! You know, there are some banks now using money to advertise, or to send letters to their depositors, hinting that unless this Administration is defeated, the deposits of their banks will be in danger. That is sheer intimidation to blackjack the election, and to return the financial control of the Government to the very forces which had nearly wrecked the nation.

Now as to corporation profits. They were a minus quantity in 1932. Corporations as a whole showed losses of almost four billion dollars that year. By now, eight years later, that deficit has been not only wiped out, but corporations are reporting profits of four billion dollars a year.

And yet they say this Administration prevents profits and stifles business!

If it is true that the New Deal is the enemy of business, and that the Republican leaders, who brought business to the brink of ruin in 1932, are the friends of business — then I can only say that American business should continue to be saved from its friends.

The output of our factories and mines is now almost thirteen per cent greater than at the peak of 1929 — 1929, mind you, not 1932. It is at the highest level ever recorded.

We have passed the time when the prosperity of the nation is measured in terms of the stock ticker. We know that the well-being of a people is measured by the manner in which they live, by the security which they feel in their future.

For the American people as a whole — the great body of its citizens — the standard of living has increased well above that of 1929.

We do not advertise "a chicken in every pot" or even "two cars in every garage." We know that it is more important that the American people this year are building more homes, are buying more pairs of shoes, more washing machines, more electric refrigerators, more electric current, more textile products than in the boom year of 1929.

This year there is being placed on the tables of America more butter, more cheese, more meat, more canned goods — more food in general than in that luxurious year of 1929.

Last Sunday morning I had a good laugh, when I read the following in the financial section of the New York *Times* — a paper which is reputed not to love me too much. This is what a writer of the financial page of The New York *Times* said, I quote: "The Federal Reserve Board in the week added another point to its index of production for September, and the figure now stands at one hundred and twenty-five, or thirteen and a half per cent above the 1929 average" — mind you, not the 1932 average but the 1929 average. I quote further: "Dreams of business 'flat on its back' must come from smoking campaign cigars or else the speakers are talking about some other country."

Wouldn't it be nice if the editorial writers of The New York *Times* could get acquainted with their own business experts?

Every single man, woman and child has a vital interest in this recovery. But if it can be said to affect any single group more than any other, that group would be the young men and women of America.

It may be hard for some of you younger people to remember the dismal kind of world which the youth of America faced in 1932.

The tragedy of those days has passed. There is today in the youth of the nation a new spirit, a new energy, a new conviction that a sounder and more stable economy is being built for them.

In 1940, this generation of American youth can truly feel that they have a real stake in the United States.

Through many Government agencies these millions of youth have benefited by training, by education, and by jobs.

We propose in the interests of justice and in the interests of national defense, too, to broaden the work and extend the benefits of these agencies. For they are a part of the lines of defense-training men and women for essential defense industries and for other industries; educating them to self-reliance — to moral resistance against that way of life which ignores the individual.

The one thing which must be extended if we would help the young men and women of the nation, is to give them the opportunity to work.

We have recognized that to the right to vote, the right to learn, the right to speak, the right to worship, we, your Government, add the right to work.

We have that definite goal toward which we are aiming. We believe that if our boys or girls on reaching employment age have been unable to get a job in private industry, the Government owes them the duty of furnishing them with the necessary training to equip them for employment. We are determined during the next four years to make that our objective — to make work for every young man and woman in America a living fact.

Tonight there is one more false charge — one outrageously false charge — that has been made to strike terror into the hearts of our citizens. It is a charge that offends every political and religious conviction that I hold dear. It is the charge that this Administration wishes to lead this country into war.

That charge is contrary to every fact, every purpose of the past eight years. Throughout these years my every act and thought have been directed to the end of preserving the peace of the world, and more particularly, the peace of the United States — the peace of the Western Hemisphere.

As I saw the war coming, I used every ounce of the prestige of the office of the President of the United States to prevent its onset.

When war came, I used every ounce of the prestige of the office to prevent its spread to other nations. When the effort failed, I called upon the Congress, and I called upon the nation, to build the strong defenses that would be our best guarantee of peace and security in the American Hemisphere.

To Republicans and Democrats, to every man, woman and child in the nation I say this: Your President and your Secretary of State are following the road to peace.

We are arming ourselves not for any foreign war.

We are arming ourselves not for any purpose of conquest or intervention in foreign disputes. I repeat again that I stand on the Platform of our Party: "We will not participate in foreign wars and we will not send our army, naval or air forces to fight in foreign lands outside of the Americas except in case of attack."

It is for peace that I have labored; and it is for peace that I shall labor all the days of my life.

Speech by President Franklin D. Roosevelt
Cleveland, November 2, 1940

Roosevelt's last campaign address, delivered at Cleveland stressed the New Deal's accomplishments in strengthening the American people. Considered by many to be one of Roosevelt's most eloquent speeches, it was a reply to Willkie's charges of defeatism and mismanagement.

Mr. Chairman, ladies and gentlemen:

In making this, my final national address of the campaign, I express once more my deep regret that I could not carry out my wish to go to other States in the great Middle West, in the South and across the Mississippi River. It has been solely in the interest of peace and the maintenance of peace that your great Secretary of State and I have felt that we should both remain within easy distance of the National Capital in these trying days.

Tonight in Cleveland, I am happy, through this great audience of my old friends, to give this message to America.

For the past seven years I have had the high honor and the grave responsibility of leadership of the American people. In those seven years, the American people have marched forward, out of a wilderness of depression and despair.

They have marched forward right up to the very threshold of the future — a future which holds the fulfillment of our hopes for real freedom, real prosperity, real peace.

I want that march to continue for four more years. And for that purpose, I am asking your vote of confidence.

There are certain forces within our own national community, composed of men who call themselves American but who would destroy America. They are the forces of dictatorship in our land — on one hand, the Communists, and on the other, the Girdlers.

It is their constant purpose in this as in other lands to weaken democracy, to destroy the free man's faith in his own cause.

In this election all the representatives of those forces, without exception, are voting against the New Deal.

You and I are proud of that opposition. It is positive proof that what we have built and strengthened in the past seven years is democracy!

This generation of Americans is living in a tremendous moment of history.

The surge of events abroad has made some few doubters among us ask: Is this the end of a story that has been told? Is the book of democracy now to be closed and placed away upon the dusty shelves of time?

My answer is this: All we have known of the glories of democracy — its freedom, its efficiency as a mode of living, its ability to meet the aspirations of the common man — all these are merely an introduction to the greater story of a more glorious future.

We Americans of today — all of us — we are characters in this living book of democracy.

But we are also its author. It falls upon us now to say whether the chapters that are to come will tell a story of retreat or a story of continued advance.

I believe that the American people will say: "Forward!"

We look at the old world of Europe today. It is an ugly world, poisoned by hatred and greed and fear. We can see what has been the inevitable consequence of that poison — war.

We look at the country in which we live. It is a great country, built by generations of peaceable, friendly men and women who had in their hearts faith that the good life can be attained by those who will work for it.

We know that we are determined to defend our country — and with our neighbors to defend this Hemisphere. We are strong in our defense. Every hour and every day we grow stronger.

Our foreign policy is shaped to express the determination of our Government and the will of our people in our dealings with other nations. Those dealings, in the past few years, have been more difficult, more complex than ever before.

There is nothing secret about our foreign policy. It is not a secret from the American people — and it is not a secret from any Government anywhere in the world. I have stated it many times before, not only in words but in action. Let me restate it like this:

The first purpose of our foreign policy is to keep our country out of war. At the same time, we seek to keep foreign conceptions of Government out of the United States.

That is why we make ourselves strong; that is why we muster all the reserves of our national strength.

The second purpose of this policy is to keep war as far away as possible from the shores of the entire Western Hemisphere. Our policy is to promote such friendly relations with the Latin-American Republics and with Canada, that the great powers of Europe and Asia will know that they cannot divide the people of this hemisphere one from another. And if you go from the North Pole to the South Pole, you will know that it is a policy of practical success.

Finally, our policy is to give all possible material aid to the nations which still resist aggression, across the Atlantic and Pacific Oceans.

And let me make it perfectly clear that we intend to commit none of the fatal errors of appeasement.

We in this Nation of many States have found the way by which men of many racial origins may live together in peace.

If the human race as a whole is to survive, the world must find the way by which men and nations can live together in peace. We cannot accept the doctrine that war must be forever a part of man's destiny.

We do know what would be the foreign policy of those who are doubters about our democracy.

We do not know what would be the foreign policy of those who are obviously trying to sit on both sides of the fence at the same time. Ours is the foreign policy of an Administration which has undying faith in the strength of our democracy today, full confidence in the vitality of our democracy in the future, and a consistent record in the cause of peace.

Our strength is measured not only in terms of the might of our armaments. It is measured not only in terms of the horsepower of our machines.

The true measure of our strength lies deeply imbedded in the social and economic justice of the system in which we live.

For you can build ships and tanks and planes and guns galore; but they will not be enough. You must place behind them an invincible faith in the institutions which they have been built to defend.

The dictators have devised a new system — or, rather, a modern, streamlined version of a very ancient system.

But Americans will have none of that. They will never submit to domination or influence by Naziism or Communism. They will hesitate to support those of whom they are not absolutely sure.

For Americans are determined to retain for themselves the right of free speech, free religion, free assembly and the right which lies at the basis of all of them — the right to choose the officers of their own Government in free elections.

We intend to keep our freedom — to defend it from attacks from without and against corruption from within. We shall defend it against the forces of dictatorship, whatever disguises and false faces they may wear.

But we have learned that freedom in itself is not enough.

Freedom of speech is of no use to a man who has nothing to say.

Freedom of worship is of no use to a man who has lost his God.

Democracy, to be dynamic, must provide for its citizens opportunity as well as freedom.

We of this generation have seen a rebirth of dynamic democracy in America in these past few years.

The American people have faced with courage the most severe problems of all of our modern history.

The start toward a solution of these problems had to be made seven years ago by providing the bare necessities of life — food and shelter and clothing. The American people insisted that those obligations were a concern of Government; they denied that the only solution was the poorhouse.

Your Government assumed its proper function as the working representative of the average men and women of America. And the reforms in our social structure that we have achieved — these permanent reforms are your achievement.

The New Deal has been the creation of you, the American people.

You provided work for free men and women in America who could find no work.

Idle men were given the opportunity on roads to be built, homes to be erected, rivers to be harnessed, power to be made for farm and home and industry.

You used the powers of Government to stop the depletion of the top soil of America, to stop decline in farm prices, to stop foreclosures of homes and farms.

You wrote into the law the right of working men and women to bargain collectively, and you set up the machinery to enforce that right.

You turned to the problems of youth and age. You took your children out of the factory and shop and outlawed the right of anyone to exploit the labor of those children; and you gave to those children the chance to prepare in body and spirit the molding of an even fuller and brighter day for themselves. For the youth of the land you provided chances for jobs and for education. And for old age itself you provided security and rest.

You made safe the banks which held your savings. You stopped, once and for all, gambling with other people's money — money changing in the temple.

You advanced to other objectives. You gained them, you consolidated them and advanced again.

The task which this generation had to do has been begun. The forward march of democracy is under way. Its advance must not and will not stop.

During those years while our democracy moved forward, your Government has worked with you and for you. Your Government has at times been checked. But always, with the aid and the counsel of all the people, we have resumed our march.

Now we are asked to stop in our tracks. We are asked to turn about, to march back into the wilderness from which we came.

Of course we will not turn backward. We will not turn back because we are the inheritors of a tradition of pioneering, exploring, experimenting and adventuring. We will not be scared into retreating by threats from the doubters of democracy.

Neither will we be bribed by extravagant promises of fabulous wealth.

Those who offer such promises try to delude us with a mirage on the far horizon — a mirage of an island of dreams, with palaces and palms and plums.

And it is a curious fact of nature that a mirage is always upside down, above the horizon.

But then, the mirage — upside down or right-side up — isn't there at all.

Now you see it — and now you don't.

Of course we shall continue to strengthen all these dynamic reforms in our social and economic life; to keep the processes of democracy side by side with the necessities and possibilities of modern industrial production.

Of course we shall continue to make available the good things of life created by the genius of science and technology — to use them, however, not for the enjoyment of the few but for the welfare of all.

For there lies the road to democracy that is strong.

Of course we intend to preserve and build up the land of this country — its soil, its forests and its rivers — all the resources with which God has endowed the people of the United States.

Of course we intend to continue to build up the bodies and the minds of the men, women and children of the Nation — through democratic education and a democratic program for health.

For there lies the road to democracy that is strong.

Of course we intend to continue our efforts to protect our system of private enterprise and private property, but to protect it from monopoly of financial control on the one hand and from Communistic wrecking on the other.

Of course we shall continue our efforts to prevent economic dictatorship as well as political dictatorship.

Of course we intend to continue to build up the morale of this country, not as blind obedience to some leader, but as the expression of confidence in the deeply ethical principles upon which this Nation and its democracy were founded.

For there lies the road to democracy that is strong.

The progress of our country, as well as the defense of our country, requires national unity. We need the cooperation of every single American — our workers, the great organizers and technicians in our factories, our farmers, our professional men and women, our workers in industry, our mothers, our fathers, our youth — all the men and women who love America just a little bit more than they love themselves.

And if we can have the assistance of all these, we can promise that such a program can make this country prosperous and free and strong — to be a light of the world and a comfort to all people.

And all the forces of evil shall not prevail against it.

For so it is written in the Book, and so it is written in the moral law, and so it is written in the promise of a great era of world peace.

This Nation which is arming itself for defense has also the intelligence to save its human resources by giving them that confidence which comes from useful work.

This Nation which is creating a great navy has also found the strength to build houses and begin to clear the slums of its cities and its countryside,

This Nation which has become the industrial leader of the world has the humanity to know that the people of a free land need not suffer the disease of poverty and the dread of not being wanted.

It is the destiny of this American generation to point the road to the future for all the world to see. It is our prayer that all lovers of freedom may join us — the anguished common people of this earth for whom we seek to light the path.

I see an America where factory workers are not discarded after they reach their prime, where there is no endless chain of poverty from generation to generation, where impoverished farmers and farm hands do not become homeless wanderers, where monopoly does not make youth a beggar for a job.

I see an America whose rivers and valleys and lakes — hills and streams and plains — the mountains over our land and nature's wealth deep under the earth — are protected as the rightful heritage of all the people.

I see an America where small business really has a chance to flourish and grow.

I see an America of great cultural and educational opportunity for all its people.

I see an America where the income from the land shall be implemented and protected by a Government determined to guarantee to those who hoe it a fair share in the national income.

An America where the wheels of trade and private industry continue to turn to make the goods for America. Where no businessman can be stifled by the harsh hand of monopoly, and where the legitimate profits of legitimate business are the fair reward of every businessman — big and little — in all the Nation.

I see an America with peace in the ranks of labor.

An America where the workers are really free and — through their great unions undominated by any outside force, or by any dictator within — can take their proper place at the council table with the owners and managers of business. Where the dignity and security of the working man and woman are guaranteed by their own strength and fortified by the safeguards of law.

An America where those who have reached the evening of life shall live out their years in peace and security. Where pensions and insurance for these aged shall be given as a matter of right to those who through a long life of labor have served their families and their nation as well.

I see an America devoted to our freedom — unified by tolerance and by religious faith — a people consecrated to peace, a people confident in strength because their body and their spirit are secure and unafraid.

During these years while our democracy advanced on many fields of battle, I have had the great privilege of being your President. No personal ambition of any man could desire more than that.

It is a hard task. It is a task from which there is no escape day or night.

And through it all there have been two thoughts uppermost in my mind — to preserve peace in our land; and to make the forces of democracy work for the benefit of the common people of America.

Seven years ago I started with loyal helpers and with the trust and faith and support of millions of ordinary Americans.

The way was difficult — the path was dark, but we have moved steadily forward to the open fields and the glowing light that shines ahead.

The way of our lives seems clearer now, if we but follow the charts and the guides of our democratic faith.

There is a great storm raging now, a storm that makes things harder for the world. And that storm, which did not start in this land of ours, is the true reason that I would like to stick by these people of ours until we reach the clear, sure footing ahead.

We will make it — we will make it before the next term is over.

We will make it; and the world, we hope, will make it, too.

When that term is over there will be another President, and many more Presidents in the years to come, and I think that, in the years to come, that word "President" will be a word to cheer the hearts of common men and women everywhere.

Our future belongs to us Americans.

It is for us to design it; for us to build it.

In that building of it we shall prove that our faith is strong enough to survive the most fearsome storms that have every swept over the earth.

In the days and months and years to come, we shall be making history — hewing out a new shape for the future. And we shall make very sure that that future of ours bears the likeness of liberty.

Always the heart and the soul of our country will be the heart and the soul of the common man — the men and the women who never have ceased to believe in democracy, who never have ceased to love their families, their homes and their country.

The spirit of the common man is the spirit of peace and good will. It is the spirit of God. And in His faith is the strength of all America.

Speech by Wendell L. Willkie
New York, November 2, 1940

Willkie's wind-up speech at Madison Square Garden on November 2 is notable for the bitterness with which he attacked "the third-term candidate." Its tone was in striking contrast to that of his acceptance speech at Elwood, Indiana.

Mr. Simpson, people of America, citizens of New York:

This campaign is about to come to a close and I would not be true to myself if I did not at this time express my deep appreciation to Joe Martin for the able way in which he's handled the campaign.

And Ed Jaeckel, here in New York, has done a superb job as State chairman.

And I want to commend to you Bruce Barton, the candidate for United States Senator.

Well, I'm going to take you in on a little secret. I just listened over the radio from Cleveland, Ohio. And I tell you, I listened, you're all either Communists or Fascists. I have that on the highest authority.

I have been engaged in this campaign now for almost two months. And when I started I had not the slightest bitterness in my soul toward any one. The campaign is going to close Monday night and at that time I will have no bitterness in my soul toward any one.

Whether you be people who work on the farm, in the factory, in the office or in business, or in whatever occupation, you're all American citizens to me.

The American people have never risen up in any cause except the cause of freedom. And believe me, that is the cause today.

This is the Battle of America.

The drums of victory are rolling, rolling, rolling. The thunderous drums of an aroused electorate are beating in the nation tonight. Victory, victory, is on the march.

But it is not for me, alone. It is not for my party alone. Wendell Willkie, the man, has little meaning in this campaign.

This is the victory of the people.

We, the people, are defying political corruption. We are defying billions of public expenditures. We, the people, defy entrenched political power!

A free people now arise to write a single word across the vast American sky: Liberty. Liberty. Liberty.

Four years ago a candidate for President, the present third-term candidate, stood in this hall, upon this very platform, and spoke to the American people. And these were among his words, and I use them exactly:

"I should like to have it said of my first administration that in it the forces of selfishness and of lust for power met their match." I'm still quoting him. "I should like to have it said of my second administration that in it these forces met their master."

Tonight, people of America, I come before you with a different plea. I do not ask to be any man's master. People of America, I ask you to make me your servant.

* * *

The New Deal came to office with a solemn covenant to reduce government spending, to balance the budget — and to preserve at all hazards a sound currency.

But in nearly eight years it has spent more than sixty billion dollars — it has more than doubled the national debt — it has never in any single year balanced the budget.

In order to free itself from a career of spending, it abandoned the principle of a sound currency, it devalued the dollars. The ultimate answer of the third-term candidate to every domestic problem has been: "Spend more money. Give me more money to spend. I know how to spend it."

And, speaking on the volume basis of spending, I will agree with him that he's unusually able in that line.

His has been the greatest spending administration in our peacetime history.

So what is the principle that he stands for? Why, of course, he believes in an economy dominated by government spending.

That is the method of the New Deal. It is not the method of democracy.

Under the New Deal scores of government bureaus, boards and commissions have been created. The number of executive employees of the Federal Government has been increased to more than a million. That is the highest figure in our history — more government employees than we needed to fight the World War.

The third-term candidate has piled up a deadweight structure of bureaucracy on the back of American agriculture, business and labor. So he must believe in the principle of bureaucratic regulation.

That is the method of the New Deal. It is not the method of democracy.

* * *

The third-term candidate usurped the powers of the Legislature. Not content with that, he has sought to subjugate the courts.

When the Supreme Court stood between him and the unlimited exercise of his great powers, he tried to pack it. Our Congress prevented that; but he showed us then and there that he believed in the principle of a judiciary subservient to the Executive.

This is the method of the New Deal. But it is not the method of democracy.

Four years ago, when the third-term candidate sought office for the second time, more than nine million of our people were unemployed. Today more than nine million of our people are still unemployed.

And how has the third-term candidate met this problem?

Not once has he stimulated the expansion of enterprise, or of American industry. As a matter of fact, he has devoted most of his time to abusing it. Nor has he ever done anything for the creation of new industries that would give our people jobs.

Instead he has told us that our industrial plants are all built. His campaign manager recently declared that there can never be jobs in American private industry for all of the American people.

Surely, therefore, the third-term candidate does not believe that we can reemploy our people. I cannot conceive that he really believes in unemployment, but neither does he believe that jobs can be made.

He believes that millions of our citizens must always be held in hopeless misery, dependent on the government.

That is the belief of the New Deal. But that is not the belief of democracy.

*   *   *

I would stand in this matter where that simple, brooding figure, Abraham Lincoln, stood. He said, and I quote him, these were the words of Lincoln: "As I would not be a slave so I would not be a master." Lincoln also said: "That expresses my idea of democracy. Whatever differs from this, to the extent of the difference, is no democracy."

Why, of course there are forces of evil among us. And we must battle against them. But no one man, no single master, however well-intentioned, can determine, according to his own discretion, which one of us is good and which is evil.

These forces can be combated only by one who is your servant. They must be blotted out only in your name, not in his own name. Though he represents in person the greatest nation on earth — you, the people of America, are the sovereign of this land.

And believe me, you must be jealous of this power that you now hold.

People of America, it is not too late to save that great power. Almost no people on earth possess it today. I ask you, I beg you, think — think before you release it to those who prove a lust for power by seeking a third term.

For if you once release it, you hazard your chance of ever regaining your own power to rule yourselves. In this violent world, it's later than you think.

The issues with which you will be presented three days hence is the preservation of the free way of life in America.

Now the New Deal, of course, tells us that it also wants to preserve democracy. And it tries to confuse the issue by claiming exclusive possession of all the social advancement.

But whatever progress has been made we all accept. Having accepted it, let us go on from there to a greater America.

There can be no progress from 1940 on if we look only to the problems of 1932.

Today let us be grateful to God that there are certain principles that are accepted by substantially all of the American people. They cannot be treated as partisan principles. They are national policies.

For instance, the policy of providing the farmer with a fair share of the national income is a national policy, and Senator McNary and I stand firmly, shoulder to shoulder, on that problem.

We say to you workers that the right of collective bargaining by labor's own free choice is not a partisan right. It is a national right.

The principle of setting a floor under wages is likewise an established principle. That floor should be raised as rapidly as our increasing prosperity permits. And the only way it can be raised is by returning prosperity to this great land of ours. And this law should be enforced both in the North and in the South.

It is national policy to set a limit to the hours of labor. Whenever those hours are exceeded, overtime must be paid at the rate of time and a half.

Social security is a national policy. And so are old age pensions. Nobody has a patent on them.

It is national policy to care for the unemployed. We shall maintain Federal relief....

*   *   *

Furthermore, all of us — Republicans, Democrats and independents — believe in giving aid to the heroic British people. We must make available to them the products of our industry.

The people of Britain are fighting against tremendous odds for the freedom of individuals — the sacred right of free men to self-government — to tolerance — to freedom of speech, of press, and of religion. They stand in desperate battle to protect the ideal of society in which the government is the servant of the people.

Both parties talk about helping Britain. We really mean it, and know that the only way you can do it is by making America productive. We don't want to help her just on order. We will give her continuing production from expanding industries.

All of us believe in the need for a powerful national defense. But our Administration, understanding the forces of production, would have it so powerful that no aggressor would ever dare or seek to strike. Where, then, does the specific conflict lie in this campaign.

It is, and I say it solemnly and with full understanding of the terrible meaning of the word — it is that for nearly eight years our government has been carrying us step by step down a road that leads to the destruction of our free way of life in America. I do not pretend to know whether or not that road is paved with good intentions. I don't care much about that.

Now the third-term candidate has not told the people what principles he stands for, and he took four speeches not to tell them. Therefore, he must intend us to determine the real principles of the New Deal from the record of its actions.

By the declaration of sixty-seven emergencies the third-term candidate has gathered into his own hands powers that rightly belong to Congress.

By the device of "must" legislation his New Deal formulates important laws. These he forces through Congress, which sometimes does not even have the opportunity properly to consider them.

So the third-term candidate, judging by his actions, must believe in the principle of a Legislature subservient to the Executive.

That is the method of the New Deal, but it is not the method of democracy.

He has gathered into his own hands an enormous concentration of power. He has the power to close all stock exchanges, to shut down all radio broadcasting stations, to close all banks. By the full use of his power over money he could inflate the currency by twelve billion dollars tonight if he so chose. Through his boards and his commission he has power over labor and over agriculture.

He has secured from Congress $16,000,000,000 in blank-check appropriations. In his own words, The unlimited spending of borrowed money — the piling up of bureaucracy — the usurpation of powers reserved to Congress — the subjugation of the courts — the concentration of enormous authority in the hands of the executive — the discouragement of enterprise — and the continuance of economic dependence for millions of our citizens upon the government — these are the methods of the New Deal. But they are not the methods of democracy.

In his speech across the river in Brooklyn last night the third-term candidate said that this has been a "funny" campaign.

That was a flippant remark. I can tell you the American people are very, very serious about this crusade.

I have just seen you people who are listening in on the radio tonight. I've seen you in the cities and the towns and the villages, in shops and factories, on farms and in ranches in over thirty-four States of this country. I have talked to millions of you. I have seen ten million of you. I know, I know, I think, as well as anybody in these United States. You are in dead earnest, very dead earnest.

It may have looked funny to the cynics of the New Deal. But to any one who believes in the America of the people this is a sacred cause.

Also last night the third-term candidate said he found it ominous that men of diverse backgrounds, races, and creeds — men of different interests and hopes should be found supporting us.

It apparently has not occurred to him that patriotic Americans could be drawn into agreement upon principle and unite, unite, in their determination against self-perpetuating power. And also that people of all those diverse interests and beliefs could join together against being embroiled by a reckless attitude in some foreign war.

Since when has it been a crime in America for labor and industry to join hands? You would think from the recent speeches of the third-term candidate that the desirable condition in America is to keep industry and labor forever at war.

I want to unite all people in America. I have no prejudice against any. I want to unite labor, industry and agriculture. I want to unite Catholic and Protestant, Jew and Gentile, people of all races, creed and color.

People of America. If you listen to the kind of campaigning that attempts to throw group against group, I tell you, I pray with you, you will be betrayed. I have labored with my hands. I have worked in the factory, on the farm and on the range. And I have worked in the office. And I have been in business. And there are no such necessary antagonisms. There are no necessary groupings in America. There's room for peace and affection and loyalty among all of us.

I can look any man in the face, no matter what his occupation or his position in life, and feel at home with him and not despise any one of them.

Only desperate men would seek to persuade you that our great cause is the result of sinister forces. Why, the fact that men who lead labor, men who lead industry, men who lead agriculture, men who work in all those groups, have joined this great crusade, is one of the most wholesome things that has happened in America in your or my generations.

And let me say another thing to you. I know it's almost unnecessary to say it to you. I stand in the same position that I did the day after my nomination.

I welcome into this cause the support of any man who believes in the principles of our American freedom. I welcome them all. They are one with us. They make us strong.

Right at the beginning of this campaign I repudiated certain men and groups who tried to connect themselves with us. I still repudiate them. And I repudiate, now and forever, any and all men and women, individually or collectively, who practice or promote racial or religious intolerance or persecution.

I want ... I want ... I want specifically to denounce as malicious, reckless and harmful to all concerned the whispering campaign that is being conducted by the opposition to connect my name with any kind of intolerance.

That kind of a campaign is not a smear on Wendell Willkie, it's a smear on America.

I will defend and, may I proudly boast, I always have defended the rights and the civil liberties of all people, regardless of race, creed or color.

They are America to me, but there is no place in this crusade for Communists, Fascists or Nazis. And may I say that there will be no room or position in our administration for any fellow-travelers.

All of us represent different origins, different occupations, different interests, different hopes. I put it to you American people, who is the candidate that can bring all these elements into unity?

I will pledge to you, all of you, a unity that you have not had in the last eight years. I know the leaders of American labor, I know the leaders of American agriculture, I know the leaders of American industry, and they have confidence in me and I have confidence in them.

And out of unity will come a confidence of man in man, and in each other's motives and in each other's hopes. Out of that confidence will grow the new America — of which I have spoken so often during this campaign — will grow new industries, new business, new opportunity, new jobs.

We will bring to the solution of our economic and social problems the combined wisdom of labor, agriculture and industry. We will modify those laws, and particularly those practices which restrict and hamper the development of American agriculture and industry. We will see to it that taxes are levied not for the purpose of punishment but for the raising of revenue and in accordance with the ability to pay. And we shall levy them with certainty and in such a manner as to release the flow of money into productive enterprises which provide jobs for our people.

Confidence in one another, confidence in our government, confidence in our Constitution; that is the method of democracy. It is not the method of the New Deal.

People of America, a great decision lies in your hands. It lies with you to choose whether we shall continue on the course that leads us step by step to the destruction of our democratic life or whether we shall resume the interrupted forward march that made America the most productive and therefore the most powerful nation in this world.

People of America, this is your crusade. You carried it forward. And you will finish it next Tuesday.

The responsibility that faces us is a fearful and a fateful charge. During the next four years we shall be answerable to our children, and to those who come after them. We shall be answerable to civilization for the democracy that is now ours.

I want you to know that I realize that every, every moment of my life. And I want you to realize it, too.

When you go to vote next Tuesday you will hold in your hands the future of this great country of ours. You will hold in your hands, you will hold in your hands that precious, precious thing, our democratic way of life.

Within the hollow of your hands is shielded the last unquenched flame of democracy in all the world. All over the world that light has been going out. Here we must keep it burning — shield it, shield it — so that the imprisoned people of other lands may know that that light still burns, so that your sons and mine and the men that come after them may have that light to guide them, so that a strong America may once more see the path on which it shall go forward.

People of America, thus we will keep America strong.

Thus, we will keep America at peace.

Thus, with the help of Almighty God, we will keep America free.

THE VOTES IN THE 1940 ELECTION

States	Popular vote		Electoral vote	
	F. D. Roosevelt, Democrat	W. Willkie, Republican	Roosevelt and Wallace	Willkie and McNary
Alabama	250,726	42,184	11	–
Arizona	95,267	54,030	3	–
Arkansas	158,622	42,121	9	–
California	1,877,618	1,351,419	22	–
Colorado	265,554	279,576	–	6
Connecticut	417,621	361,819	8	–
Delaware	74,599	61,440	3	–
Florida	359,334	126,158	7	–
Georgia	265,194	23,934	12	–
Idaho	127,842	106,553	4	–
Illinois	2,149,934	2,047,240	29	–
Indiana	874,063	899,466	–	14
Iowa	578,800	632,370	–	11
Kansas	364,725	489,169	–	9
Kentucky	557,222	410,384	11	–
Louisiana	319,751	52,446	10	–
Maine	156,478	163,951	–	5
Maryland	384,546	269,534	8	–
Massachusetts	1,076,522	939,700	17	–
Michigan	1,032,991	1,039,917	–	19
Minnesota	644,196	596,274	11	–
Mississippi	168,267	2,814	9	–
Missouri	958,476	871,009	15	–
Montana	145,698	99,579	4	–
Nebraska	263,677	352,201	–	7
Nevada	31,945	21,229	3	–
New Hampshire	125,292	110,127	4	–
New Jersey	1,016,808	945,475	16	–
New Mexico	103,699	79,315	3	–
New York	3,251,918	3,027,478	47	–
North Carolina	609,015	213,633	13	–
North Dakota	124,036	154,590	–	4
Ohio	1,733,139	1,586,773	26	–
Oklahoma	474,313	348,872	11	–
Oregon	258,415	219,555	5	–
Pennsylvania	2,171,035	1,889,848	36	–
Rhode Island	182,182	138,653	4	–
South Carolina	95,470	1,727	8	–
South Dakota	131,362	177,065	–	4
Tennessee	351,601	169,153	11	–
Texas	840,151	199,152	23	–
Utah	154,277	93,151	4	–
Vermont	64,269	78,371	–	3
Virginia	235,961	109,363	11	–
Washington	462,145	322,123	8	–
West Virginia	495,662	372,414	8	–
Wisconsin	704,821	679,206	12	–
Wyoming	59,287	52,633	3	–
	27,243,466	22,304,755	449	82

Thomas, Socialist, 99,557; Browder, Communist, 46,251; Babson, Prohibitionist, 57,812; Aiken, Socialist-Labor, 14,861; other, 48,610. Total vote, 49,815,312.